Moving the Mountain

Moving
the
Mountain

THE WOMEN'S
MOVEMENT
IN AMERICA
SINCE 1960

Flora Davis

University of Illinois Press

Urbana and Chicago

Illini Books edition, 1999
© 1991, 1999 by Flora Davis
Reprinted by arrangement with the author.
Manufactured in the United States of America
P 5 4 3 2 1

♾ This book is printed on acid-free paper.

Library of Congress Cataloging-in-Publication Data
Davis, Flora.
Moving the mountain : the women's movement in America
since 1960 / Flora Davis.
p.   cm.
Originally published: New York : Simon & Schuster, c1991.
With new introd.
Includes bibliographical references (p.) and index.
ISBN 0-252-06782-7 (pbk. : alk. paper)
1. Feminism—United States—History. 2. Women—
United States—Social conditions.   I. Title.
II. Title: Women's movement in America since 1960.
HQ1421.D385   1999
305.42'0973—dc21   99-11521
                        CIP

In memory of my mother, Marion Ball,

who died before the second wave began.

This book is my end of a conversation

that we were never able to have.

Contents

PART 3: *Confronting the Political Realities*

Introduction: The View from the Kitchen Table

*T*his is an activists' history, short on feminist theory and long on accounts of political action. It is full of anecdotes—activists' "war stories"—and the nitty-gritty details of how women tackled the issues that confronted them. In writing it, the question that most interested me was: How did feminists achieve what they did? How did they "move the mountain" and in the process carry us from the staid and stifling 1950s, when most American women defined success as "finding Mr. Right," to the 1990s, which are (it seems to me) a better time for women but certainly not an easy one?

In short: How do people who are dissatisfied with the status quo achieve social change? In researching the women's movement, I found that, surprisingly often, change began with half a dozen women, sitting around a kitchen table, defining a problem and figuring out what they could do about it—that, in fact, it's thanks to the combined efforts of thousands of such women that we are where we are today. Though the media has often presented the movement as if it consisted of a handful of charismatic leaders and a few national organizations, in fact, it would take a book almost as long as this one to list the names of all the activists who have contributed in some way to the progress women have made. In the course of researching this book, I interviewed a fraction of them. Though the women I talked to included some famous feminists, I also sought out many activists who played vital roles but weren't well known outside the movement. By telling their stories, I hope to present a more balanced picture of what the movement has really been like.

I've tried to capture on these pages a sense of the excitement, the craziness, the sheer creative chaos of the women's movement at its peak. However, I want to emphasize that in most ways, feminism is typical of modern social movements. Excitement, creativity, and craziness are all par for the course.

Basically, a social movement is a messy, volatile conglomeration of groups and individuals, all inspired by similar ideas and bent on making changes. The various groups involved generally have somewhat different agendas; they may abhor one another's tactics, and they sometimes work at cross purposes. No one is really in charge. The leaders of major movement organizations can't be sure, if they call out the troops for a protest, that the troops will respond, and if their "followers" get ahead of them, the leaders may not be able to rein them in. Conflicts within the movement are normal—between leaders and among groups. Very few activists are paid for the time they invest; they're drawn in because they care about the cause. Predictably, they care enough to fight for their own priorities.

A dynamic social movement is hard even to keep track of. Its small groups wink in and out of existence, disappearing because they accomplish what they set out to do or because they burn out. During a crisis, a whole army of supporters may materialize and deluge movement organizations with phone calls, demanding to know what they can do—only to disappear again the minute the pressure is off. Chaotic as that may sound, social scientists believe that a movement that has jelled into a handful of well-defined organizations has lost its momentum and hardly deserves to be considered a movement any longer. In the early 1990s, that hasn't happened to the women's movement, nor does it seem likely to happen in the foreseeable future. Feminism's grass roots are alive and well, and new groups keep cropping up as particular issues become urgent.

Activists' achievements depend partly on their own skill and energy, but also on the political opportunities society offers them. American feminism, the strongest women's movement in the world, was never powerful enough to set priorities for the nation —if it had been, the ERA would have been ratified. Feminists have made progress by seizing chances where they found them —they have done what seemed doable.

The women's movement, as reincarnated in the 1960s, is often called the "second wave" of feminism, to distinguish it from the "first wave," which arose during the nineteenth century and won the vote for women in 1920. The wave analogy is helpful because it underscores the fact that the women's movement didn't die after 1920, though it did lose much of its momentum. The analogy also reminds us that major social changes tend to happen in waves. First, there's a lot of intense activity and some aspects of life are transformed; then, when the public has absorbed as much as it can stand, reaction sets in. Stability reigns for a while, and if there's a strong backlash, some of the changes may be undone. Eventually, if vital issues remain unresolved, another wave of activism arises.

When I decided to write this book back in 1982, I felt that feminism had reached a turning point. The ERA had been defeated despite broad public support. A right-wing administration was out to reverse many of the gains women had made. Progress had stalled and in some ways the movement was actually losing ground. I was afraid that the second wave was over. Instead, though feminists faced formidable opposition throughout the 1980s, the movement continued to grow and change. At times, it even seemed to thrive on opposition—which said something about how broadly based and deeply rooted it had become.

Nevertheless, the struggle continues. At every level in society, there are men—and women—who oppose further changes and want to roll back the progress that has been made. In the 1990s, two things are very clear: that in the past, changes only happened because thousands of women *made* them happen, and that in the future, women will gain more ground only if activists continue the effort.

That's why it seems important now to look back over the past thirty years of movement history and ask: How have we come this far? What have we accomplished and what remains to be done? With this book, I hope to provide not only a record of achievements but a grounding in facts—enough detail about how things were done and where the pitfalls lay to help activists work for a better future.

Thoughts on the 1999 Edition

*S*even years after *Moving the Mountain* was first published, I was given the opportunity to update the book for this University of Illinois Press edition. I revised and expanded the final chapter on the 1990s; I also added to the bibliography and the acknowledgments, but I did not change the index to include material from the new chapter 23.

While researching what had happened to the women's movement during the 1990s, I talked to the heads of national coalitions and major women's organizations and was struck by the way the media had largely ignored both women's issues and the movement. Many Americans were unaware of recent feminist gains and losses. It was a difficult decade as the struggle for women's rights continued against fierce opposition. Yet no one I talked to seemed discouraged. Rather, people spoke about how exciting it was to be part of a vigorous women's movement that was now worldwide.

In the 1980s, activists spoke of the graying of the women's movement. They were concerned because most young women not only took for granted the gains feminists had fought for but claimed that the battle was over, that women had achieved equality. In the 1990s, veteran feminists no longer worried about the need to pass the torch. Though many young women still denied that they were feminists (even as they supported women's issues), a significant number of them had become activists. They had joined feminist organizations or founded new groups of their own.

The older, larger women's organizations formed a kind of feminist establishment in Washington, D.C., and their offices buzzed with the voices of energetic student interns. Around the country, groups kept forming, dissolving, and coalescing, as always—the grass roots were still growing. Progress had been slow, but despite determined opposition there *had* been progress.

In short, as of late 1998 the women's movement is thriving, and there is every reason to believe it will continue to thrive for the foreseeable future.

PART ONE

The Second Wave Begins: Reinventing Feminism

chapter 1

The Opening Salvos

The turbulent, affluent, optimistic 1960s provided an unusually hospitable climate for feminism. The civil rights movement had broken new ground and a number of related social movements sprang up in its wake. One of them was the women's movement. Like a brush fire in a dry season, it ignited simultaneously in two different places: among older, liberal women and among the young radicals of the New Left.

Throughout the sixties, the women's movement grew steadily, but most Americans were barely aware of what was happening. Then in the early 1970s, feminism exploded across the national scene as groups of activists cropped up almost everywhere. Often, women coalesced around a single issue, pouring their efforts into a rape hotline, a battered women's shelter, or some other highly focused project.

At the same time, a broad-based right-wing backlash began to build, fueled by white male resentment at the challenges from feminists and from the civil rights movement. When conservatives won the White House in 1980, feminists were thrown on the defensive; for the next decade, they had to fight to hang onto the ground they'd already gained. They lost some battles and won others, and overall, progress for women stalled. Nevertheless, new feminist groups kept emerging, many of them now being formed by women of color. Going into the 1990s, the women's movement was bigger, stronger, and more diverse than ever.

Between 1960 and 1990, feminists achieved half a revolution. Laws were passed, court decisions were handed down, and sex discrimination was officially prohibited; women were elected to office, grudgingly accepted into male occupations, and promoted to positions that women had never held before. New terms entered the nation's vocabulary: People spoke of "sexism" and "male chauvinism." Probably, the movement's single greatest achievement was that it transformed most people's assumptions about what women were capable of and had a right to expect from life.

THE BATTLE WITH THE AIRLINES

The story of how airline stewardesses forced American airlines to change unfair work rules is the perfect introduction to the second wave. By throwing into sharp relief the old attitudes to women and the impact those attitudes had on people's lives, it shows just how far women have come. The activists involved were few in number, and they challenged just one aspect of the pervasive problem of sex discrimination. That was typical of the second wave and illustrates the point that social transformations, like jigsaw puzzles, are put together one piece at a time.

The battle with the airlines spanned a crucial period in the history of the women's movement. Stewardesses fought to be treated as workers, rather than as sex objects, at a time when the term "sex object" hadn't yet been invented. The work rules they challenged decreed that to keep their jobs they must remain single, and they were fired the minute they married. Many airlines fired them, in any case, as soon as they turned thirty-two, while others set the limit at thirty-five. Women much over the age of thirty were no longer considered attractive enough to fly for an airline. It hadn't even occurred to most Americans that the system was unfair, and that made changing the rules an uphill fight in a way it wouldn't have been a few years later.

The stewardess unions actually began their campaign before the second wave, at a time when few people had any interest in women's rights. When the women's movement caught up with them, union leaders used its impetus, and as they did, they quickly came to identify themselves as feminists fighting sex discrimination, not just as unionists confronting management.

At one time or another, stewardess unions at most of the major airlines joined the struggle to change the work rules. There was some communication between union leaders, but they never really made a coordinated effort. Instead, the battle was fought simultaneously on many different fronts by different groups. The women who worked for American Airlines belonged to a union called ALSSA—the Air Line Stewards and Stewardesses Association—and their campaign was typical.

The Age and Marriage Issues

In the hierarchy of "glamour" jobs open to white women in the early sixties, stewardesses ranked right after movie stars and models.* In fact, for every woman hired as a stewardess, more than a hundred applicants were turned away. Those who were chosen embodied the American image of the wholesome girl-next-door.

As the airlines saw it, these "girls" would fly for a few years, then leave the job to marry and settle down. In the midsixties, stewardesses lasted 32.4 months, on the average, less than three years. "If that figure ever got up to thirty-five months, I'd know we're getting the wrong kind of girl. She's not getting married," a personnel manager for United Airlines said solemnly in 1965.

In the early 1960s, the social pressure to marry was relentless. The average woman became a wife at age twenty, younger than in any generation since the turn of the century. Seventy percent of American women made it safely to the altar before they were twenty-four, and a woman still unmarried at the advanced age of twenty-five was considered an "old maid." She was pitied, and people wondered what was wrong with her that no man had asked her to be his wife. Most stewardesses themselves assumed when they were hired that they'd marry within a few years. In fact, at American Airlines the gold wings presented to a woman after five years of flying were known as "your failure pin," because they signified that she had so far failed to marry.

By becoming a stewardess, an adventurous young woman had a chance to travel and meet interesting people in the time warp

* Stewardesses (also called air hostesses) became known as "flight attendants" during the 1970s, as men began to be hired for the job.

between the end of her schooling and the beginning of marriage. And the job was said to be good experience for marriage. At the airline training schools the women learned safety procedures, but also took classes in make-up, grooming, and social skills, "the perfect course for being a perfect hostess at home," according to one stewardess. (At American, the school was known irreverently as "the charm farm.")

Although most stewardesses seemed to love their jobs, they lived with more restrictions than the most overprotected teenager. They were told how long to wear their skirts and their hair and how high their heels could be. They could be fired for gaining too much weight. Girdles were generally required and supervisors did "touch checks" to make sure employees were wearing them. In addition, the women were paid so little that home was often a small apartment shared with as many as half a dozen other stewardesses.

Almost from the beginning, most airlines expected their stewardesses to resign when they married. Age didn't become an issue until the early 1950s, when American Airlines became the first company to retire the women as soon as they reached their midthirties. To get the union to agree to the age limit, management negotiators exempted those already working for the company. They stipulated that only women hired after November 1, 1953, would be forced to retire at thirty-two.

Dusty Roads got in under the wire. So did Nancy Collins, who would become the union's master executive chairman (equivalent to being its president) in the early sixties. They led the long struggle to get the airline to lift the age restriction, because both felt a moral issue was involved.

As the 1950s wore on, more and more airlines routinely dismissed stewardesses for growing too old. By 1965, fifteen of the thirty-eight U.S. airlines were doing it. "I was twenty-eight when we fought the age issue, and I was absolutely hysterical," said Lynda Oswald, who was with American Airlines. "I was trying to prepare myself for another job, but when I tried to get into a university, they wouldn't accept me as a part-time student. The whole climate was catch-22."

Yet many stewardesses saw nothing wrong with the airlines' regulations, and union leaders found it hard to marshall support. Roads recalled that "some of our own flight attendants would say, 'I don't think you should fly when you're fat or old.'" Younger women weren't interested in the age issue. "When you're twenty, you don't believe you're ever going to be thirty-two," Roads observed drily. Older women, as their thirty-second birthday approached, often cast about desperately for a ground job with the company. Reluctant to antagonize management, most "retired" from flying without a protest. As for the marriage regulation, many women did marry and kept their marriage a secret. At one point, airline officials estimated that 30 to 40 percent of stewardesses were secretly married.

In short, the battle with the airlines was fought by a minority of activists who were willing to take risks. Most of the women who ultimately benefited from their efforts were initially too timid or indifferent to take part, or actually opposed any change in the status quo. That was the case with the first challenges to sex discrimination in many occupations.

In defending their regulations, the airlines talked a lot about the image of a stewardess as a young, single woman, and the importance of maintaining that image. However, the union's leaders were well aware that, as Collins put it, "Ninety percent of this had to do with economics." Money was usually the bottom line when employers discriminated against women. In their stewardesses, the airlines had the ideal work force. Few stayed long enough to earn more than beginners' wages, and the savings on fringe benefits must have been considerable. What other company could guarantee health insurers a group of insurees who would never be older than thirty-two?

In the beginning, ALSSA's leaders believed their problem was unique; they didn't see it as part of a pattern of discrimination against women. Dusty Roads's eyes were opened in the late fifties. She had a good friend, Ann Cooper Penning, who was administrative assistant to Congresswoman Martha Griffiths, a Michigan Democrat. Roads recalled that "I was telling Annie about things the airlines did, and she said, 'You've got to be kidding me. I can't wait to tell this to Martha.' Eventually, I met Martha." Before that, Roads had more or less accepted the way stewardesses were treated. "But Martha was so upset about it," she said. From conversations with Griffiths, Roads came to realize that sex discrimination was widespread.

''The Old Broads' Bill''

At that point, there seemed to be two possible strategies open to the stewardesses. They could try to persuade the airlines at the bargaining table to drop the age and marriage regulations, or they could push for legislation.

Stewardess leaders tried bargaining first. However, they got minimal support from male union colleagues. All the stewardess unions were actually subunits of huge, male-dominated unions, and the union men were mostly blue-collar males who had come up the hard way. In dealing with the stewardesses, they were protective but autocratic. They had traditional ideas about a woman's role and little sympathy for women's issues.

Without the support of male unionists, the stewardesses were unable to get rid of the age and marriage restrictions. It was also clear that no airline was likely to give up these money-saving measures as long as other airlines were still taking advantage of them. Thus, in the early sixties, Collins and Roads tried to solve the problem by getting Congress to pass a law.

By that time, Roads was ALSSA's official, if unpaid, lobbyist. She was chosen for the job in 1958 because she was flying in and out of Washington, D.C., regularly, was dating a congressman, and could count Congresswoman Griffiths as a friend. Roads did her lobbying on her own time between flights. She had no trouble getting appointments with male members of Congress; she was a stewardess, and the men simply assumed that she would be young and attractive. Once through the door, she could often interest them in her union's case against the airlines.

Roads's efforts resulted in one early attempt to pass a law against the airlines' restrictions, but it was a piece of legislation few were comfortable with. Was it fair for Congress to target one industry and forbid one or two specific practices? "They didn't know how to go about this," said Roads. "To introduce a bill that would keep a company from firing anybody at the age of thirty-two was kind of preposterous. It was a very narrow attack on a very broad issue, which was age discrimination or discrimination against women. Eventually, the bill became a joke—they called it 'the old broads' bill.' "

In 1963, Collins and Roads decided to go public with their problem. They held a press conference at the Commodore Hotel in New York City. Collins wanted stewardesses there in significant numbers, to prove a lot of them cared about the age issue, but it wasn't easy to find women who were willing to take a public stand and risk their jobs.

Once again, the aura of glamour that came with the stewardess job paid off. Many newspapers sent reporters and photographers, and after Roads pointed out that four of the stewardesses in the room were actually over thirty-two—hired before November 1953, they couldn't be fired—one photographer seized the chance to set up a picture that ultimately appeared in papers across the country. It showed nearly a dozen uniformed women, shoulder to shoulder and displaying quite a lot of leg, over a caption that in many cases invited readers to guess which of the women were over thirty-two. Columnist Art Buchwald maintained that older stewardesses were better cooks and were just as attractive—missing the point, that the women had a right not to be fired arbitrarily. Collins and Roads were willing to be patronized as long as they got the story out. The press conference produced sheaves of clippings, but there was still no progress on the age issue.

In 1964, stewardess unions filed a complaint against American and TWA with the New York State Commission for Human Rights. New York and some other states had laws against discrimination because of age, but had nothing on the books as yet about sex discrimination.

Congress, too, was concerned about just treatment for older workers. On September 2, 1965, women from several airlines appeared before a House Labor subcommittee to talk about the age issue; other stewardesses, many in uniform, were in the audience to show support. One of the congressmen on the committee seemed to think it funny that attractive women in their thirties were talking of discrimination because of age. Representative James H. Scheuer, a Democrat from New York, turned to the stewardesses and asked them to "stand up, so we can see the dimensions of the problem."

Colleen Boland, then head of ALSSA, testified that an airlines executive had explained the age regulation this way: "It's the sex thing. Put a dog on an airplane and twenty businessmen are sore for a month." Representative Scheuer gallantly replied, "I would oppose with my dying breath the notion that a woman is less beautiful, less appealing, less sensitive after thirty. . . ." Nancy Collins said, "In those days, we felt we were being patted on our little heads about 90 percent of the time."

The congressional hearing brought no visible progress, and in New York the age discrimination case dragged on through hearings and appeals. It wasn't until early 1968 that the state's five-man Appellate Court ruled unanimously against the stewardesses on the grounds that the age law was intended to apply only to those between forty and sixty-five.

Though the stewardesses' glamour image gave them advantages in pressing their case, they were very much aware of the way society devalued older women. Once a woman was no longer young and sexually appealing to men, she had lost whatever leverage she originally had.

The EEOC: Reluctant Enforcer

In 1964, as part of a landmark civil rights bill, Congress banned sex discrimination by employers and created a new federal agency, the Equal Employment Opportunity Commission (EEOC), to enforce the law. The stewardess unions were quick to seize the chance it offered them, and when the EEOC officially opened its doors in the summer of 1965, two American Airlines stewardesses were among the first people through them.

"We got there so early, we had to help unpack the typewriters; they were still in boxes," said Dusty Roads.

With Roads that day, ready to sign a sex discrimination complaint, was Jean Montague, who was due to be fired by American because she would soon turn thirty-two. The women assumed that, thanks to the section of the new civil rights law known as Title VII, the airlines would have to mend their ways. "We were naive," Roads admitted later.

The EEOC staffer who handled their complaint that day was an African-American woman. At first she couldn't see how young, educated, white women could possibly be victims of discrimination, but she soon got into the spirit of the thing. "Do they fire pilots at thirty-two?" she asked Roads. "Do they fire flight engineers?" When Roads assured her the airlines didn't, she said with relish, "Go get 'em." That's just what Roads and her union did.

However, it took almost a year before the EEOC finally held a hearing on the women's charges in May 1966. Afterward, Roads couldn't be certain how the session had gone, but it was clear that at least one of the five commissioners, Aileen Hernandez, was sympathetic. In an unexpected way, Hernandez played a key role in the stewardess story. She resigned from the EEOC in October that year, disillusioned because the Commission was so reluctant to act on women's issues. Later, she recalled that "Commission meetings produced a sea of male faces, nearly all of which reflected attitudes that ranged from boredom to virulent hostility whenever the issue of sex discrimination was raised." Hernandez noted that the EEOC's priority was race discrimination—but apparently only as it affected black *men*. She was particularly frustrated by the long delay in ruling on complaints brought by stewardesses. At the time she resigned, there were ninety-two such cases pending, and some were more than a year old.

Hernandez resigned on October 10, giving a month's notice. On the last weekend in October, a brand-new feminist organization, NOW (the National Organization for Women), held its founding conference. Afterward, the women issued a press release. Among other things, it backed the stewardesses; it also announced that Hernandez had been elected executive vice-president of NOW, subject to her consent. According to Hernandez, her election was "a charitable, but unauthorized gesture," apparently intended to express support for her decision to resign from the EEOC.*

On November 9, the day before Hernandez's resignation was to take effect, the Commission finally ruled that company policies setting age limits for stewardesses amounted to sex discrimination. Just two weeks later, the airlines won a temporary court order which blocked the ruling on the grounds that Hernandez had a conflict of interests, because presumably she was a member of NOW. In an effort to prove she was, they had a federal court subpoena Betty Friedan, NOW's newly elected president, and Muriel Fox, who was in charge of public relations, and dragged them into court in New York City on Christmas Eve, while on the West Coast Hernandez was subpoenaed in the same way. A lawyer for the airlines demanded that Friedan produce a list of NOW's members; she declined. "We had all agreed to keep the membership list of NOW secret," Friedan wrote later, "for in those early days no one was sure she wouldn't be fired or otherwise excommunicated for belonging to an organization to overthrow sex discrimination."

In February 1967, a federal district court judge issued an injunction that, in effect, erased the EEOC decision on the age question because of Hernandez's supposed conflict of interests. The Commission and the stewardesses had to begin all over again with hearings.†

Meanwhile, the unions were trying to end the marriage restriction, working on it as a separate issue from the age limit. The airlines resisted, maintaining that married women would miss work too often and would gain weight. (Some supervisors apparently believed that with marriage a woman inevitably became plump and docile.) Eventually, the unions brought marriage-

---

* In 1970, Hernandez succeeded Betty Friedan as president of NOW.
† NOW ultimately did help the stewardess unions a great deal by persistently lobbying the EEOC on their behalf.

regulation complaints, too, to the EEOC. In June 1968, the agency finally announced in a case involving an American Airlines stewardess that the marriage restriction violated Title VII. In the meantime, unions at other airlines had been able to resolve the marriage issue at the bargaining table.

There was still no word from the EEOC about the age restriction, and ALSSA was soon deep in contract negotiations with American with the age limit a key issue. "We were ready to roll on a strike then," said Roads. "I called Martha and said, 'If you know anyone on the Commission, call them and tell them that if they would just make a decision, there wouldn't have to be a strike.' "

Griffiths made the phone call, and on August 10, 1968, the EEOC finally released new guidelines that barred the airlines from dismissing stewardesses for being overage. The following day, ALSSA reached agreement with American on a new contract, and, as Nancy Collins put it, "The age and marriage issues just faded into the woodwork."

From the time the women filed their complaint with the EEOC in July 1965, more than three years had passed; it had been five years since Roads and Collins staged their press conference. However, the struggle wasn't over yet. Some stewardesses took the airlines to court, because they not only wanted to return to their jobs but they wanted back pay and accumulated seniority. There were many individual suits as well as class-action suits. The stewardess unions also challenged the airlines successfully on the question of whether a woman should be allowed to return to her job after having a baby.

Throughout the sixties, class and race were invisible elements in the struggle between women and the airlines, for the unions never addressed the fact that women of color and white women from working-class backgrounds were seldom hired as stewardesses. At the time, most white feminists saw "women's issues" solely in terms of white women's issues—and were unaware that that was what they were doing. The second wave's size and scope were limited as a result.

THE AFTEREFFECTS

In tackling the age and marriage restrictions, stewardesses assaulted some of society's ingrained assumptions: that marriage was all women really wanted; that it was perfectly natural to judge a woman solely on her looks; and that men somehow had a right to the services of women—and if it could be arranged that the women doing the serving were young, single, and attractive, so much the better.

Lynda Oswald said, "I think many of us who were stewardesses during the 1960s suffered deep psychological scars. We still have a terror of age and of being discarded because our skin isn't quite smooth enough any more."

Roads, Collins, and other activists improved the lot of most women and men who were subsequently hired as (gender-neutral) "cabin crew." In 1985, flight attendants kept their job, on the average, for ten years; they were now required to retire at age seventy; and some long-term employees were making more than $40,000 a year.

There were other, less tangible gains as well. As they stood up for their rights, the stewardesses found that their image of women and of themselves changed profoundly. A story Roads liked to tell summed up the difference. A male passenger once complained to her, "I don't know why you girls should object to being called 'girls.' "

"That's because you don't know the difference between a girl and a woman," she told him. "A 'girl' is somebody who rents an apartment. A 'woman' owns a house."

In 1991, Dusty Roads and Nancy Collins were still flying. Their names weren't likely to be the first to pop into anyone's mind during a discussion of the women's movement, but their victory was typical of the second wave. American women owed the progress they made largely to thousands of unknown activists like Roads and Collins, who tackled a small piece of the overall problem of sex discrimination. Social change advanced like an incoming tide at many different points simultaneously.

chapter 2

The Resurgence of Liberal Feminism

⁓

Most Americans were taken by surprise when the second wave of feminism swept the nation in the 1960s. Women's rights had been considered a dead issue—in the words of *Life* magazine, feminism seemed "as quaint as linen dusters and high-button shoes." Supposedly, it lost its relevance once women won the vote.

In fact, though the first wave receded after 1920, the women's movement survived on a smaller scale as suffragists founded new organizations. More than forty years later, those groups played a vital role in the resurgence of feminism. Social movements aren't formed by isolated individuals who somehow find one another and band together; they almost always develop out of networks already in place. The existing women's rights movement, limited though it was, served as the launching pad for the liberal wing of feminism in the midsixties.

However, the women's rights veterans did more than that. In the early 1960s, a decades-old struggle between factions within the movement came to a head—and unexpectedly set off a chain reaction that electrified a new generation of activists. The struggle began in 1920 when the women's movement divided into two camps: those in favor of an equal rights amendment and those who opposed it. In the early 1960s, both sides—each bent on its own ends and intent on defeating the other—made significant gains, and those gains raised women's expectations and made it respectable once again to talk of women's rights.

1920–1960:
THE MOVEMENT BETWEEN THE WAVES

Historians today speak of the first and second waves of feminism to underline the fact that there has been one long, continuous women's movement rather than two, separated by a forty-year hiatus. A movement that's already over a hundred years old and that has crested several times is something to be reckoned with. Yet for years, many Americans assumed that feminism had died in 1920 when women won the vote and suffragists supposedly retired to private life. History was distorted because contemporary journalists and other observers eagerly seized on every sign of fading feminist vitality. (During the second wave, too, the media kept reporting the death of feminism.)

The truth was, women had demonstrated impressive political muscle during the suffrage campaign, and some men—nervous about a possible women's voting bloc—were hoping that activists would disband. Women's organizations were under heavy pressure during the 1920s not to try to organize voters. Conservatives argued that if women voted as a bloc, they would threaten America's free institutions. Right-wingers accused activists not only of "sex antagonism"—the 1920s equivalent of man-hating—but also of lesbianism and Communism.* In 1924, a group within the War Department circulated a chart that depicted an interlocking network of fifteen women's organizations and twenty-nine leaders, all supposedly Communist sympathizers. Among the organizations pilloried by the so-called Spider-Web Chart were the PTA, the YWCA, and the League of Women Voters.

These strategies succeeded in deepening existing divisions within the movement and made most women's groups more cautious. However, a bigger blow was the fact that women didn't flock to the polls during the 1920s. Neither did men, but no one paid much attention to that. Instead, the newspapers featured

---

* During the 1970s and 80s, conservatives resorted to similar red-baiting.

interviews with housewives who said that they just weren't interested in politics. Politicians and the press concluded—on the basis of skimpy evidence and with barely disguised relief—that suffrage was a failure and that feminism was dead.* Many Americans believed them.

Yet women's groups actually proliferated in the early 1920s. For every suffrage organization that died, several new, smaller groups were founded as activists took on fresh causes. Of the major, predominantly white organizations, the militant National Woman's Party (NWP) lost its mass membership but continued as a small, elite group. NAWSA (the National American Woman Suffrage Association) disbanded, but its leaders promptly founded the National League of Women Voters (LWV). Some NAWSA members joined the League, while others became involved in one of the political parties. Meanwhile, activists were also turning their attention to the battle for birth control and the women's peace movement. In its heyday, the peace movement brought together into a single coalition eleven different organizations with over five million members.

For the most part, women of color organized separately and focused on the needs of their communities and on combating racism. Few joined the predominantly white groups because they didn't feel welcome. African-American women, in particular, couldn't forget that while their organizations were campaigning for women's suffrage, some white women were arguing that one way to ensure white political supremacy in the South was to give women the vote. In the 1920s, when black voters of both sexes were being terrorized by southern racists and prevented from voting, black women appealed to the National Woman's Party for support. The NWP refused on the grounds that racial, not sexual, injustices were involved.

In short, the women's rights movement between the waves was vigorous but limited in size and almost entirely white. Its goals were often modest because the social climate was hostile. The media ridiculed feminists, portraying them as shrill, hysterical misfits. Consequently, those who belonged to the various women's organizations seldom referred to themselves as feminists; in fact, many emphatically denied it.

---

* The gender gap was temporarily discredited in a similar way in 1984 (see chapters 19 and 22).

THE ERA VERSUS
THE PROTECTIVE LABOR LAWS

In 1923, the National Woman's Party saw to it that a constitutional amendment was introduced in Congress which said simply:

> Men and women shall have equal rights throughout the United States and every place subject to its jurisdiction.*

To the women of the NWP, the Equal Rights Amendment was the next logical step after the vote. With one stroke, it would overturn scores of laws that discriminated against women. However, most other predominantly white women's groups initially opposed it, including the League of Women Voters and the influential Women's Bureau, an agency within the U.S. Department of Labor. Black women's organizations also split over the ERA: The National Association of Colored Women was pro-amendment and the National Council of Negro Women was against it.

The controversy continued for more than forty years. The labor movement and the women's organizations opposed to the ERA raised objections that were entirely different from those the right wing would raise during the 1970s, and most of the original opponents eventually became converts to the cause. However, one thing didn't change from the 1920s through the 1980s: The controversy centered on what "equality" meant. Pro-ERA activists believed that women should be treated exactly the same as men—no worse and no better—while the opposition was convinced that because women were wives and mothers, they must have certain laws to protect them.

At the root of the dispute was a fundamental disagreement about the nature of women. Throughout the first wave of feminism and much of the second, there was an ongoing debate between those who believed that women and men were very similar and that therefore women deserved equal treatment, and those who believed that the sexes were very different, that women were in some ways superior, and that therefore women and men should be on an equal footing. The two sides are sometimes referred to as *equality feminists* and *difference feminists*. This contro-

---

* In 1943, the wording of the ERA was revised to read: "Equality of rights under the law shall not be denied or abridged by the United States or by any State on account of sex." The wording was changed to bring it into line with the suffrage amendment.

versy plagued campaigns for women's rights for at least a century. In fact, feminism could be described partly as an ongoing struggle over how to define the word *woman*.

The men in power were always sure that the sexes were very different. Some seemed to consider females almost a separate species. In any case, sex differences were the usual excuse for keeping women out of public life. White, middle and upper class women, at least, were considered too sensitive, too emotional—and too necessary in the home—to lead much of a life outside of it.

Again and again, feminists themselves disagreed over the issue of gender differences. This was "the feminist divide," according to scholar Ann Snitow, a fissure that kept opening up, splitting the ground under women in different ways.

During the nineteenth century, those who fought for women's rights both denied and affirmed gender differences. Some insisted that women and men were equal (and presumably, similar). Others based their arguments on traditional feminine virtues: Women must have their rights because they were, by nature, maternal, devout, respectable. Activists sometimes swung from one point of view to the other as their own internal compasses gyrated—or simply in the interests of strategy. When attacked for "unsexing women," they replied by stressing female virtues; when facing opponents who insisted that women were different and inferior, they stressed the common humanity of male and female.

After the turn of the century, the terms of the prevailing argument changed. Many Americans now lived in cities and worked in factories, and laissez-faire capitalism had produced slums and sweatshops. Reform was in the air. For years, women's groups had been pressing the government to regulate factory working conditions, housing, and community health. Now, suffragists began to argue that women must have the vote to protect their families. They would use it to perform a kind of "social housekeeping," to force the government to address the issues they were concerned about. They maintained that voting would be merely an extension of their traditional role within the home. To many, the vote still represented equal rights, but now it was also presented as a way a woman could make a special contribution *as* a woman.

During the last years of the suffrage campaign, conflicts divided the women's movement. The animosities generated at that time would eventually deepen the split that developed after 1920 over the ERA. Beginning in 1917, the National Woman's Party resorted to militant tactics: Members picketed the White House, were arrested, and staged hunger strikes in prison. Many NAWSA members disapproved, convinced that the NWP was damaging the cause. When women finally won the vote, both the NWP and NAWSA claimed the credit. Both had contributed in different ways, the Woman's Party by heating up public interest in the issue until politicians could no longer avoid it, NAWSA by keeping the lines of political communication open. That kind of bad-cop/good-cop strategy often works well for social movements, yet typically the various factions don't set out to use it as a strategy—they're genuinely outraged at one another's behavior.

After 1920, conflicts within the movement continued, but now the main problem was the feminist divide. On one side were the National Woman's Party and a few other groups, pressing for an equal rights amendment. On the other side were most other women's organizations, determined to forestall an ERA because it would invalidate labor laws designed to protect women—by limiting the number of hours they could be required to work, for example. The Supreme Court had thrown out similar laws regulating working conditions for men, but in a famous case decided in 1908, *Muller* v. *Oregon*, the justices had concluded that even a single woman should not work long hours because it might endanger her ability to have babies in the future. They reasoned that healthy mothers were essential to vigorous offspring, and that "the physical well-being of women becomes an object of public interest in order to preserve the strength and vigor of the race."

In 1925, almost all states limited the number of hours women could work; eighteen required that they be allowed rest periods and time off for meals; sixteen forbade night work in certain occupations; thirteen set a minimum wage for females. Labor leaders clung to the laws regulating working conditions for women partly because they hoped that someday the courts would allow them to be extended to cover men.

Alice Paul, head of the NWP, believed that the protective laws were bad for women and prevented them from competing with men for the better jobs. She argued that the ERA must ban all statutes that treated the sexes differently, with no exceptions for dubious protective benefits. A 1923 Wisconsin ruling illustrated what could happen when exceptions were allowed. Wisconsin had an equal rights law that guaranteed women the same rights and privileges as men—except for special protections and privileges already legally granted them. Despite that statute, the state's attorney general upheld an older law that said the state legislature couldn't employ women. The ban on hiring women was justified, according to his ruling, because it was similar to protective labor laws that limited the number of hours women could work; supposedly, those who worked for the legislature were required to put in unreasonably long hours.

On the difference side of the divide, feminists were convinced that working women needed some protections. They argued that the ERA was a blunt instrument that would do away with good laws and bad, and that it was better to tackle bad laws one at a time. Mary Anderson, the first head of the Women's Bureau, insisted that equality was a myth in any case. Obviously, there was no real equality among men, and achieving equal legal status for women would "mean little in our everyday life." ERA opponents also accused the amendment's supporters of being elitists, indifferent to the needs of working-class women. Certainly, equality and difference feminists saw women very differently. ERA supporters assumed that, given a fair chance, females could take care of themselves, while to ERA opponents working women seemed vulnerable, doubly burdened as they often were by job and motherhood.

Probably, the protective laws initially helped more women than they hurt. However, they didn't cover either farm work or domestic service—the two most common female occupations; they also limited women's job opportunities because many employers, forced to make special concessions for women, refused to hire them. In the end, the laws helped to shape a labor market in which some occupations were reserved for men and others, less desirable, were relegated to women.

In 1938, Congress undercut the arguments for the protective laws by passing the Fair Labor Standards Act (FLSA). Affirmed by the Supreme Court in 1941, it extended a minimum wage and other types of protection to men. Yet afterward, organized labor and most women's organizations continued to oppose the ERA. Clearly, the equality-difference issue ran deeper than a purely rational defense of the protective laws. In part, the conflict was fueled by the animosities that took root during the suffrage campaign.

After World War II, the conflict over the ERA actually escalated. For a short time, there was a window of opportunity for feminists because Congress seemed inclined to reward women for the war work they'd done. Both sides tried to seize the chance. In 1946, the Senate actually approved the ERA, though not by the two-thirds majority necessary for a constitutional amendment. That same year, difference feminists lobbied hard for a law requiring equal pay for women. Some pro-ERA groups backed the bill, but the NWP remained officially neutral, deducing (correctly) that the equal pay initiative was intended partly as a diversion from the ERA. Strongly opposed by business, the bill was dropped.

A year later, the coalition of women's groups opposed to the amendment proposed the so-called Status Bill as an alternative to the ERA. It would have established a commission to review the legal status of women; it also contained a policy statement, a rewording of the ERA's basic principle, which declared that "no distinctions on the basis of sex shall be made except such as are reasonably justified by differences in physical structure, biological or social function." Equality feminists pointed out that differences in "social function" (meaning, in traditional sex roles) could be used to justify almost any type of sex discrimination. The bill failed to pass.

In 1950, the Senate found a way to put the amendment on hold while acknowledging the demands of both feminist factions and satisfying neither. Democrat Carl Hayden of Arizona added a rider to the ERA, which read: "The provisions of this article shall not be construed to impair any rights, benefits, or exemptions . . . conferred by law upon persons of the female sex." Presumably, the protective labor laws were a benefit, and many other discriminatory laws could be justified by claiming that they conferred exemptions or special rights. The Senate passed the ERA with the Hayden rider attached, but it died in the House. From that time on, the ERA was stymied because the Senate refused to pass it without the Hayden rider, which rendered the amendment useless, according to its backers. The House wasn't allowed to vote on the ERA because Representative Emanuel Celler, the New York Democrat who chaired the powerful Judiciary Committee, saw to it that it was never released by his committee.

By 1961, equality feminists had been demanding an ERA and difference feminists had been opposing them for almost forty years. The majority of women's organizations were still lined up on the difference side of the divide.

The NWP led the pro-ERA groups. By the 1960s, it was down to a few hundred active members; the ERA was their primary concern. As lobbyists, they operated out of the Alva Belmont

House, the NWP headquarters in Washington, which also served as a kind of hotel for visiting feminists. Members were conservative on most social issues and some were racist. Women who had fought for suffrage had special status in the NWP, especially if they had ever been jailed, gone on a hunger strike, and been force-fed. In addition to NWP, two huge national organizations, the National Federation of Business and Professional Women's Clubs (BPW) and the General Federation of Women's Clubs, now supported the ERA. In 1960, BPW had clubs in virtually every congressional district and experience in lobbying. It would play a major role in the second wave.

Most activists on both sides of the issue were white, middle to upper class, and well educated. Many were businesswomen or professionals, and most were past middle age. They were aware that their organizations needed younger members, but recruiting them was difficult. The older feminists complained, as movement veterans often would in the 1980s, that young women took their hard-won rights for granted.

THE KENNEDY COMMISSION

The window of opportunity opened up for feminists once again in 1960 when John F. Kennedy was elected President, reviving the hopes of most liberals. Equality feminists put pressure on the new President to act on the ERA. Because other women's groups adamantly opposed it, whatever Kennedy did, he was bound to alienate someone. Personally, he was anti-ERA, according to Esther Peterson, one of the few women he appointed to high office. He owed his election partly to organized labor, which was against the amendment.

Peterson herself had been a labor movement lobbyist before Kennedy made her Assistant Secretary of Labor and Director of the Women's Bureau, and she believed in the protective labor laws. Looking back, many years later, she wrote that "given the climate of the time, there was a legitimate fear that the all-male and very conservative Supreme Court would interpret 'equality' in a way that could hurt working women."

In June 1961, Peterson suggested in a memo that if the President appointed a commission to study the status of women, that might "substitute constructive recommendations for the present troublesome and futile agitation about the 'equal rights amendment.' " The commission seems to have been primarily a Trojan horse, like the one proposed in the 1940s—an attempt to undermine the ERA. However, it unexpectedly produced a compromise that partly mended the rift in the women's movement. In the process, it set into motion forces that soon acquired their own momentum.

In December 1961, Kennedy issued an executive order creating the President's Commission on the Status of Women (PCSW), which was also known as the Kennedy Commission. It had twenty-six members, fifteen women and eleven men, all handpicked by Peterson and almost all known to be opposed to the Equal Rights Amendment. Eleanor Roosevelt chaired PCSW until her death in November 1962. The other members included Cabinet officers, members of Congress, two college presidents, a magazine editor, labor leaders, the national presidents of several major women's organizations, and Washington attorney Marguerite Rawalt, the lone voice strongly in favor of the ERA. Because the dispute over the amendment could ruin the Commission, Peterson felt that someone like Rawalt had to be included. The executive order establishing the Commission also promised to analyze the ERA issue objectively, and as a result, a number of pro-ERA organizations supported PCSW.

In the coming years, Marguerite Rawalt would play a major role in the second wave of feminism. Tall, distinguished, dignified—and already approaching the age at which most people retire—she became the link between new, grass-roots activists and established women's organizations. She was a past president of both BPW and NAWL (the National Association of Women Lawyers), a member of the NWP, and had been the first woman ever elected president of the Federal Bar Association.

During the two years the Kennedy Commission was given to complete its task, it met only eight times. The brunt of the workload was borne by seven committees, each chaired by a member of the parent body but made up largely of outside experts. The issue of the ERA was assigned to the Committee on Civil and Political Rights. Rawalt was its cochair, together with Congresswoman Edith Green of Oregon, and the members included two women who headed pro-ERA organizations, a number of people known to oppose the amendment, and some who were neutral.

It was one of the neutrals who unexpectedly proposed a new strategy as an alternative to an equal rights amendment. Pauli Murray, a brilliant civil rights lawyer, argued that laws that discriminated on the basis of sex violated the fourteenth amendment of the Constitution, just as racially discriminatory laws did, and she suggested bringing a test case before the Supreme Court. Murray hoped to persuade the Justices to distinguish between women who had family responsibilities and those who didn't. She felt that some protective laws, including the controversial state labor laws, should be preserved for the sake of mothers and families, but she argued that applying such statutes to childless women as well violated *their* right to equal protection under the Constitution. Others liked the idea that the Supreme Court might be flexible, upholding some laws that treated the sexes differently while striking down others.

In the end, the committee drafted a carefully neutral statement on the ERA and the full Commission rejected it, replacing it with a recommendation that stated that a constitutional amendment shouldn't be pursued unless future court decisions proved that it was necessary. At the final meeting of the full Commission, Rawalt was able to wring just one concession from the group: They agreed to add the single word *now* to the recommendation, so that the final version said, "a constitutional amendment need not *now* be sought."

Though most pro-ERA feminists doubted that the Supreme Court would respond positively to a test case, the Murray proposal was the nearest thing to a compromise that either side had been able to produce in forty long years. Peterson had succeeded in finding an alternative that made the ERA seem less appealing, but the Commission's report did acknowledge that if the fourteenth amendment strategy failed, a constitutional amendment might be necessary.

Rawalt recalled her years on the Kennedy Commission as "a lonely time." Catherine East, a civil service professional who did staff work for the Commission, remembered that its headquarters were across the street from the handsome old Belmont House, headquarters of the NWP. Alice Paul lived there with several other elderly members. "We used to see them leaving the house at times," said East, "and some of the women on the Commission would laugh at them. They saw them as little old women in tennis shoes."

Unexpected Gains

PCSW formally presented its report to Kennedy in October 1963. Esther Peterson noted that it "made few avant-garde recommendations; we did not propose to restructure society. Rather, we strove to fit new opportunities into women's lives *as* *they were*. We were practicing the art of the possible." Nevertheless, the report accomplished a great deal. It documented discrimination against women, including the fact that men earned considerably more than women and that since 1945 the pay gap had grown.* Suddenly it was respectable to talk about women's rights again. And people *did* talk: 64,000 copies of the report were sold in less than a year.

The report made twenty-four specific recommendations, and though it simply assumed that motherhood must come first for women, some of its suggestions were surprisingly far-sighted. Among them was the then-revolutionary proposal that marriage should be considered an economic partnership and that any property acquired during the marriage should belong to both spouses. At the time, Rawalt said, many people didn't see why a wife should be entitled to a half share when "she doesn't do anything but wash the dishes and cook the meals." In addition, the report stated that child care services should be available to families at all income levels. It championed paid maternity leave and equal pay for comparable work. It asked the President to require every company with a federal government contract to hire, train, and promote women on an equal basis with men—something the administration could do just by issuing an executive order.

The experience of working for the Commission opened the eyes of several women who later became leaders of the revitalized women's movement, including Catherine East, a young attorney named Mary Eastwood, and Pauli Murray, the civil rights lawyer. Years later, Murray described the experience as "intensive consciousness-raising." Afterward, all three women became part of an informal network of feminists brought together because of the Commission.

Even as the Kennedy Commission was meeting, there was some progress for women. In July 1962, Kennedy issued a directive to all federal agencies, saying that they must now hire, train, and promote employees regardless of sex. This led to a metamorphosis of the civil service. A year later, Congress passed the Equal Pay Act, eighteen years after it was first proposed. It was a breakthrough—the first federal law forbidding sex discrimination by private businesses. However, in order to get the bill out of the subcommittee charged with considering it, Congresswoman

---

* In 1960, women with full-time, year-round jobs earned 60.6 percent of what men earned; black women earned just 42 percent. On the average, women college graduates earned less than men with only high school diplomas.

Edith Green had to agree that it would not cover women who held professional, executive, or administrative jobs.

On the national level, the Kennedy Commission asked the President to set up an ongoing organization to continue its work. Within a month, just days before his assassination, Kennedy established the Citizens' Advisory Council on the Status of Women (CACSW). He invited members of the old Commission to serve on it. At the same time, he created a Cabinet-level Interdepartmental Committee on the Status of Women (ICSW), made up of government officials. The Citizens' Advisory Council survived until 1977, through the Johnson, Nixon, and Ford administrations. Carter appointed a similar advisory council, but Reagan and Bush dispensed with it altogether. Most of the women on the first Advisory Council—appointed by Johnson after Kennedy's death—were anti-ERA, once again with the exception of Marguerite Rawalt. Nevertheless, they were a strong voice for women's rights and an influence on Congress.

Even before the Kennedy Commission's report was issued, local women's organizations, led by BPW, began to urge state legislatures and governors to set up status-of-women commissions of their own, to study state laws as they applied to women. According to Catherine East, the network of commissions that developed as a result was one of the PCSW's most important legacies. By 1967, all fifty states had commissions in operation,* which did research, held conferences, and often published a newsletter. Some groups were more effective than others, but at the very least they started women thinking about the issues and brought new leaders into the field. Beginning in 1964, the ICSW sponsored annual meetings of the state commissions. This gave the women a chance to compare strategies and established a rudimentary communications network for budding feminists.

TITLE VII: "THE SEX AMENDMENT"

In the liberal atmosphere created by the Kennedy administration, equality feminists, too, were alert for opportunities. In 1964, as Congress prepared to pass landmark civil rights legislation, they saw their chance and insisted that women be included in the section of the new law called Title VII. As a result, Congress

---

* Many states, counties, and cities still have a status-of-women commission today.

banned sex discrimination in the workplace, along with racial discrimination. In effect, feminists had piggybacked a major gain for women on an African-American victory—a tactic they would use more than once.

It's impossible to overemphasize the significance Title VII had for women. Much broader than the Equal Pay Act, it applied to jobs at all levels and to most American businesses. It led to the downfall of the protective labor laws, and that, in turn, undercut much of the opposition to the ERA. Yet to this day, even feminists sometimes say that the sex amendment was originally passed as a joke. It was probably *proposed* as a joke, but that simply gave feminists the chance they'd been waiting for.

In the late 1950s, Alice Paul had tried unsuccessfully to have women's rights included in civil rights legislation that was being considered by Congress. When the Kennedy administration proposed a sweeping new law in June 1963, NWP again saw the possibilities. In December 1963, a few weeks after Kennedy's assassination, Paul had two NWP members write to Congressman Howard W. Smith of Virginia—both knew him personally—suggesting that he amend the civil rights bill so that it would prohibit sex discrimination. As a southern conservative, Smith might seem an unlikely backer for women's rights. A member of the House for thirty-three years, he was eighty years old in 1964, one of the most intimidating men on Capitol Hill. "Tall, slightly stooped, rumpled, spry and alert as a cat, Judge Smith ambles along with an artless courtesy that masks a will of steel," said *Newsweek* magazine. A *New York Times* writer noted that he had "killed, watered down or postponed more progressive legislation than any other Congressman in modern times." However, in the past Smith had also been one of the House sponsors of the ERA —though that may have been primarily because he was anti-union (and the unions were anti-ERA) and in any case didn't expect it to pass.

Both of the NWP women pointed out in their letters to Smith that a sex amendment might divert some of the pressure for a civil rights bill—in other words, with sex added, the legislation might be too controversial to pass. In any case, Smith probably felt that just by suggesting a sex amendment, he could hold the whole bill up to ridicule. According to one of her lieutenants, Alice Paul expected him to see things that way, but apparently believed it would be worth it to get a ban on sex discrimination considered. Smith's reply to the NWP women was polite but noncommittal. Then on January 26, 1964, he was interviewed on television by a panel of journalists including May Craig, a member of the NWP. When she asked him whether he would offer a sex amendment, he said he might.

Congresswoman Martha Griffiths, the Michigan Democrat who was Dusty Roads's mentor in the American Airlines case, was watching the program. She had considered making a case for a sex amendment herself during hearings on the bill, but bided her time because she knew that as soon as she raised the possibility, every industry that employed women would rush to lobby against a sex discrimination ban. Now, it seemed that Smith might offer the amendment. Griffiths estimated that 118 southern and conservative legislators would vote for it just because it was Smith who proposed it. She hoped that during the floor debate she could marshall the other 100 votes needed for passage. She recalled thinking that "if I can't argue enough to get that other hundred, I ought to leave Congress." Determined to use the element of surprise, she discussed her strategy with only a few close friends.

An attorney, a former judge, and a former Michigan legislator, Martha Griffiths was a vigorous, no-nonsense individual in her fifties, who was respected by her colleagues in Congress because she had played the game by the rules. Congressional careers were built on committee work, and members achieved a reputation on Capitol Hill by developing expertise in the areas with which their committees were concerned; by asking good questions at hearings and introducing useful amendments; and by respecting seniority. Griffiths was the first woman to be a member of the powerful House Ways and Means Committee, and she probably knew more about tax law than anyone else in the House except Wilbur Mills, chairman of the committee. As a lawyer and a legislator she also knew, better than most, how many laws there were at both state and federal levels that were unfair to women.

In the House, the floor debate on the civil rights bill began on Friday, January 31. Though southerners and conservatives immediately began to introduce amendments intended to weaken the bill, liberals were in the majority, and it was expected to pass. On Wednesday and Thursday, Congressman John V. Dowdy tried repeatedly to add the word "sex" to different sections of the bill that prohibited discrimination, but no one took him seriously. He was a Texas Democrat opposed to civil rights and was obviously one of those trying to amend the bill to death. He didn't have Smith's following.

On Saturday, February 8, the House met to take up Title VII. It was the most controversial section of the bill because it prohibited discrimination in employment and would establish a government agency to investigate complaints. Many conservative Americans believed the government had no right to tell a businessman whom to hire. So far, the liberals had held their ground, and despite all attempts to amend it, the bill was virtually without major changes. Then Congressman Smith weighed in with an amendment that would add the word "sex" wherever Title VII prohibited discrimination in employment on the basis of race, color, religion, or national origin.

With his tongue tucked firmly into his cheek, Smith drawled, "Mr. Chairman, this amendment is offered . . . to prevent discrimination against another minority group, the women, but a very essential minority group, in the absence of which the majority group would not be here today. Now I am very serious about this amendment. . . . I do not think it can do any harm to this legislation; maybe it can do some good. . . . I think we all recognize and it is indisputable fact that all throughout industry women are discriminated against in that just generally speaking they do not get as high compensation for their work as do the majority sex."

Then, supposedly to show his colleagues how "some of the ladies" feel about discrimination, Smith read from a letter he said he'd received from a lady with "a real grievance on behalf of the minority sex." The letter read:

> I suggest that you might also favor an amendment or a bill to correct the present "imbalance" which exists between males and females in the United States.
>
> The census of 1960 shows that we had 88,331,000 males living in this country, and 90,992,000 females, which leaves the country with an "imbalance" of 2,661,000 females.
>
> Just why the Creator would set up such an imbalance of spinsters, shutting off the "right" of every female to have a husband of her own, is, of course, known only to nature.
>
> But I am sure you will agree that this is a grave injustice to womankind and something the Congress and President Johnson should take immediate steps to correct, especially in this election year.

Smith had to pause several times in his reading as the legislators roared with laughter.

When he finished, Congressman Emanuel Celler took the floor to reply. Celler, a seventy-five-year-old New Yorker, was a veteran of forty-one years in the House. He was also one of the most prominent supporters of the bill among the Democrats (as he was one of the most influential opponents of the ERA). He began:

> Mr. Chairman, I heard with a great deal of interest the statement of the gentleman from Virginia that women are in the minority. Not in my house. I can say as a result of 49 years of experience—and I celebrate my 50th wedding anniversary next year—that women, indeed, are not in the minority in my house. As a matter of fact, the reason I would suggest that we have been living in such harmony . . . is that I usually have the last two words, and those words are, "Yes, dear."

Today, few politicians in their right mind would make remarks in public such as those Smith and Celler made; that's one measure of how far women have come.

Marguerite Rawalt was in the gallery of the House that day, as were others who were expecting Smith to offer a sex amendment. She recalled that as the debate continued, most of the legislators were milling around in the aisles, making jokes and laughing at the very idea of banning discrimination against women. Congresswoman Leonor K. Sullivan of Missouri, a friend of Martha Griffiths who knew what she proposed to do, turned to her and said, "Martha, if you can't stop that laughter, you're lost." Finally, the chair recognized Griffiths. She stood and said firmly:

"Mr. Chairman, I presume that if there had been any necessity to have pointed out that women were a second-class sex, the laughter would have proved it." That put an end to the hilarity. Rawalt recalled that the men responded like scolded children. ". . . they quieted right down and got back into their seats, most of them, and listened."

Griffiths began by asking Celler whether, in his opinion, the civil rights bill would protect black men and women equally. He tried to evade the question by saying that it would apply to every American. She persisted. If a black woman applied for a job as a dishwasher, she asked him, at a restaurant that employed only white males as dishwashers, and was turned away, would the Civil Rights Act protect her, even if the restaurant owner insisted that he was refusing to hire her not because she was black, but because she was a woman? Celler said it would be necessary to get the facts (presumably, to find out the owner's real reason). What about a white woman applying to the same restaurant for the same job, Griffiths asked him. Was she protected under the new law? Again, Celler was evasive. For a few moments longer, they sparred, and then Griffiths went on to hammer home her point: that without a sex amendment, white women would be last hired and first fired.

". . . if you do not add sex to this bill . . . you are going to have white men in one bracket, you are going to try to take colored men and colored women and give them equal employment rights, and down at the bottom of the list is going to be a white woman with no rights at all."

Years later, Martha Griffiths still marveled that no one in Congress seemed to have seriously considered what would happen if the bill were passed *without* a prohibition against sex discrimination. To many whites, "blacks" meant black men, and black women might as well have been invisible.

Griffiths was convinced that the men who wrote the Act never even thought about whether black women would receive any rights, or about the fact that white women didn't have any. The legislators believed they would give black men some rights and that black women would be treated about like white women. She was sure it hadn't occurred to most of the black organizations supporting the bill that there was any discrimination against white women. They would have been very surprised, she said, at the way things would have turned out without the sex amendment. Either women of color would have had no help from the law, or enforcement would have bogged down completely in suits brought by black women, struggling to prove they were victims of racial, rather than sexual, discrimination.

When Griffiths had finished, other congresswomen spoke in support of the amendment. Only Edith Green was against it. She argued that "for every discrimination that has been made against a woman in this country there has been ten times as much discrimination against the Negro." The amendment would "clutter up" the bill, she warned, and might be used later "to help destroy this section of the bill by some of the very people who today support it." That was clearly a reference to Smith.

Late in the afternoon, the sex amendment passed the house. Many Republicans as well as some northern Democrats joined the southerners in voting for the amendment.

Private Pressures, Public Silence

On February 10, the House approved the entire civil rights bill and the action shifted to the Senate, where southern senators immediately began a filibuster that brought all other Senate activity to a halt for fifty-seven days. During all that time, sex discrimination was rarely mentioned. However, there was much activity behind the scenes.

Soon after the bill passed the House, Senate Minority Leader Everett McKinley Dirksen announced that he would amend Title VII to strike the word "sex." Dirksen was the leader of a small group of Republicans whose support was critical if the bill was to pass the Senate. When Martha Griffiths learned of his threat, she immediately called the White House and left a message for President Johnson: "I told him that if that amendment came out of there, I would, at my own expense, have my speech reprinted and I would send it into every home in the districts of those who had voted against [the amendment]," she recalled.

Meanwhile, Rawalt and other Washington women contacted every pro-ERA women's organization in Illinois, Dirksen's home state. Their members bombarded the senator with telegrams. When Dirksen tried to persuade others in the Republican Conference, the party caucus in the Senate, that the sex amendment had to go, Senator Margaret Chase Smith repeatedly opposed him. He was never able to persuade a majority of conference members to vote with him, and eventually, he dropped the effort. NWP members persistently lobbied the Senate on behalf of the amendment, as did Esther Peterson and others. Peterson had originally opposed the sex amendment, thinking it might jeopardize the civil rights bill, but afterward changed her mind.

President Johnson finally threw his support behind the sex amendment in April. In the end, the bill's Senate backers decided to let the amendment stand because they knew the bill would pass by a small majority, and they couldn't risk losing the votes of those who supported the sex provision. Probably, they hoped it would never be enforced. Johnson signed the 1964 Civil Rights Act in July; it was to take effect a year later.

Rawalt believed that the sex amendment should really be known as "the Griffiths amendment." According to the custom of Congress, it couldn't be, because Howard Smith first proposed it, but the congresswoman was the prime mover behind it. Individual women and women's organizations supported her with a substantial if somewhat uncoordinated effort. There was no formal women's coalition and, in fact, little communication among feminists—for instance, Griffiths was never approached by the NWP and she didn't know until afterward that they'd been lobbying Smith.

Harvard historian Carl M. Brauer suggested that Smith might have been motivated partly by old-fashioned chivalry: He may have felt that if black women and men were going to be protected against discrimination, white women should be, too. However, Martha Griffiths recalled that once, years after Smith had retired, he returned to Capitol Hill for a visit. "I hugged him and said, 'You know, our amendment is doing more than all the rest of the Civil Rights Act.' And he said, 'Martha, I'll tell you the truth. I offered it as a joke.' "

It wasn't passed as a joke, and in the end if there was a joke, it seems to have been on Smith.

THE EEOC AND THE "BUNNY LAW"

Feminists soon learned that getting a law passed was only the first step. After that, there was the problem of getting it enforced. In the end, the federal government's reluctance to do anything about sex discrimination became the catalyst for the second wave.

At first, opponents tried to ridicule the sex amendment out of existence. Griffiths recalled their effort as "one of the most amazing campaigns in American history. Otherwise perfectly intelligent men began saying that the addition of 'sex' was really a joke and had no real standing at all. Otherwise perfectly intelligent women believed these silly statements and repeated them." Griffiths couldn't understand how smart people could for a moment think that Congress would add *any* word to a law as a joke.

Responsibility for enforcing Title VII of the Civil Rights Act fell to a new agency created by the law to handle complaints of discrimination, the Equal Employment Opportunity Commission (EEOC). Its five permanent commissioners, appointed by President Johnson, included just one woman, Aileen Hernandez. In the first two years after Title VII went into effect, women filed more than 4000 complaints with the EEOC, or about one quarter of the total.

Sex discrimination was ultimately defined not by the statute itself, but by guidelines drawn up by the EEOC. For women, the most important ones had to do with bona-fide occupational qualifications (called bfoq's). The law stipulated that an employer couldn't be required to give both sexes equal consideration if a job genuinely needed to be filled by one sex rather than the other —a movie director couldn't be required to hire a woman to play a man's role, for example. The big question was: In what other occupations was sex a bfoq? The EEOC was in a quandary. When federal agencies and the courts interpreted laws, they must consider what Congress's original intentions were, as reflected in committee reports on the bill and in statements made by the bill's supporters during floor debate. Because the sex amendment was sprung on the House and never really debated in the Senate, there was almost nothing in the record about what jobs Congress had in mind when it allowed exceptions for bfoq's.

In the beginning, EEOC representatives treated the problem frivolously, fastening on the fact that Congressman Smith didn't sound serious when he introduced the bill. Thus, at one point, EEOC director Herman Edelsberg called the sex amendment "a fluke . . . conceived out of wedlock." At another point, he told reporters that he thought men were entitled to have female secretaries.

In August 1965, the White House sponsored a conference for employers to explain what the new law required of them. At the panel on women's rights, men in the audience wanted to know whether an executive looking for a secretary could legally choose a pretty blonde over a male applicant. They also asked: What if a woman applied for a job as a locomotive engineer? Could the railroad safely turn her down? No one seemed very sure of the answer, and someone joked that the law might even require Playboy Clubs to hire male "bunnies." The press immediately dubbed the sex amendment the "bunny law."*

Nevertheless, when the agency finally issued its guidelines, they defined sex discrimination quite broadly and incorporated many suggestions made by the Citizens' Advisory Council. For instance:

- Employers were told they couldn't choose one sex or the other simply because customers preferred it, nor could they justify discrimination by citing sex stereotypes—that men made more aggressive sales representatives, for example.
- Factories must lay off men and women strictly on the basis of seniority without regard to sex.
- Companies could refuse to hire married women, as a matter of policy, only if they also refused to hire married men. They couldn't fire women after they married unless they fired men in the same circumstances, nor could they refuse to hire mothers of small children.

* In October 1985, the Playboy Clubs—responding to a slump in membership—did begin to hire male "rabbits."

- If a business paid for medical insurance for families of male employees, it must provide the same benefits to families of female employees; it could not provide medical coverage only for men or give them larger death benefits under a life insurance program.

All these things that had now become discrimination were common business practices at the time. They continued to be common, because many companies ignored the EEOC. Unfortunately, the agency had been given no real power to enforce the law. It could investigate complaints and attempt conciliation. If that failed and a broad pattern of discrimination appeared to exist, it could ask the Attorney General to sue on behalf of the complainant, but he could choose not to do so. As a last resort, the person who lodged the complaint could sue as an individual under Title VII.

Despite the generally favorable guidelines, the EEOC remained basically unsympathetic to women's rights. The spring 1966 issue of the agency's newsletter answered questions about sex discrimination by concentrating on odd or hypothetical cases—on whether Title VII required a college sorority to hire a man as "house mother," for example. This was too much for Martha Griffiths and on June 20, she denounced the EEOC in scathing terms on the floor of the House:

"I charge that the officials of the Equal Employment Opportunity Commission have displayed a wholly negative attitude toward the sex provisions of Title VII. . . . What is this sickness that causes an official to ridicule the law he swore to uphold and enforce? . . . What kind of mentality is it that can ignore the fact that women's wages are much less than men's, and that Negro women's wages are least of all?"

Griffiths got so many requests for copies of the speech that she had copies printed at her own expense. Because it pointed out so clearly the problems with the EEOC, Catherine East used it just days later to convince other women that it was time to organize.

THE SECOND WAVE GATHERS

Surprisingly, both the establishment of the Kennedy Commission and the passage of Title VII happened before the second wave got under way. They were, in fact, part of what made it possible. Together, they legitimated sex discrimination as an issue.

In June 1966, various strands of the growing movement would converge—the next chapter tells that story. At the annual meeting of the state status-of-women commissions, frustration over the government's failure to enforce Title VII would come to a head, and some veterans of the movement between the waves would join forces with activists inspired by the mother of grassroots liberal feminism, Betty Friedan.

During the late 1960s, the feminist divide would disappear for a while, and most activists would take the equality point of view for granted. By midcentury, many women felt that the similarities between the sexes were more significant than the differences. Some feminists rediscovered gender differences and female values in the 1970s and by 1980 the debate was on again.

chapter 3

The Founding of NOW

In the early 1960s, as status-of-women commissions were set up around the country, feminism began to attract new recruits. With the founding of NOW in 1966—the movement's first new mass-membership organization—the second wave was solidly under way.

In the beginning, NOW focused mostly on sex discrimination in the work place. Finding a decent job was the primary problem for many women in the 1960s, and the determination to crack the job market drew many activists into the movement. Once in, they became caught up in a multitude of other issues.

NOW was barely a year old when the membership voted to campaign for the ERA and for repeal of anti-abortion laws—decisions that splintered the organization. Afterward, disgruntled midwesterners departed to found the more conservative WEAL, the Women's Equity Action League; the second wave gained as a result.

THE BOOK THAT CHANGED LIVES

Betty Friedan's feminist classic, *The Feminine Mystique*, laid the groundwork for the new mass movement and provided the first inkling that women's rights might attract broad support once again. The book was published in 1963, eight months before the Kennedy Commission issued its report. At the time, Friedan was a free-lance writer, a graduate fellow in psychology, and a suburban mother of three.

Some years earlier, Smith College, her alma mater, had asked Friedan to conduct a survey of the women who graduated with her in 1942. She expected it to disprove a theory popular at the time: that higher education somehow masculinized women and prevented them from finding happiness as housewives and mothers. To her surprise, she found that the theory was half right. Two hundred women answered her questionnaire, 89 percent of them housewives. Many said that they regretted just one thing: that they had not put their education to serious use. Though she might have concluded from this that higher learning had made them dissatisfied, Friedan reasoned instead that something important was missing from the lives of housewives—she dubbed this "the problem that has no name."

Most women were only dimly aware that they had a problem, because they'd bought into the belief system Friedan called "the feminine mystique." Almost every girl growing up in the 1950s absorbed this mystique. She learned that men and women were profoundly different and had different needs and ambitions; that a woman could find happiness only by marrying a male who was man enough to dominate her and by having his children; that women who wanted more out of life were unnatural and unfeminine. Of course, the notion that the sexes were very different simply papered over the conviction that women were, in fact, inferior. Friedan denied that the sexes were as different as the mystique made them out to be.*

Adlai Stevenson described the middle class housewife's dilemma as well as anyone ever did. Stevenson, a Democrat who ran for President twice during the 1950s, was the darling of the liberals in his day, a witty, high-principled intellectual. Speaking at Smith College in 1955, he noted that

* The mystique was actually the latest version of the nineteenth century's "cult of true womanhood," which assumed that a woman's nature and needs were dictated by her biology.

[M]any women feel frustrated and far apart from the great issues . . . for which their education has given them understanding and relish. Once they wrote poetry. Now it's the laundry list. Once they discussed art and philosophy until late in the night. Now they are so tired they fall asleep as soon as the dishes are finished. There is, often, a sense of contraction, of closing horizons and lost opportunities. They had hoped to play their part in the crises of the age. But what they do is wash the diapers.

Stevenson had a solution for the problem. A woman could best tackle "the crises of the age," he told his audience, by helping her husband find values that would give purpose to *his* daily chores. "Women, especially educated women, have a unique opportunity to influence us, man and boy," he asserted. He added that a woman could also teach her children about the uniqueness of each individual, and that these were assignments she could fulfill with a baby in her lap or a can opener in her hand. No one rose to protest his remarks; in fact, it's likely that there were very few young women in the audience who felt there was anything wrong with what he'd said, so powerful was the mystique.

During the 1950s, men, too, were under pressure to conform to a gender stereotype. "Normal" males were expected to marry and support their wives; those who didn't were said to be immature—or possibly homosexual. However, the breadwinner ethic began to collapse in the 1950s, long before feminists challenged it. The collapse was instigated by male writers who lashed out at middle class conformity, often presenting it as a kind of emasculation. They wrote of despondent men trapped in dull jobs because they had families to support, and of status-hungry housewives with nothing better to do all day than spend money. Author Barbara Ehrenreich observed that "most women were numbed by the mixed message: If you didn't grow up to be a full-time housewife, you were a failure; if you did, you were a parasite. . . ."

The Feminine Mystique was published with little fanfare in February of 1963. Soon, Friedan was getting calls from television talk shows. *Life* magazine interviewed her—and photographed her dusting a bust of Lincoln. Another photo (the caption described her snidely as "Nonhousewife Betty") caught her making milk shakes for her sons. As her fame spread, she became something of an outcast in the suburb where she lived. She and her husband were no longer invited to dinner parties, and they were dropped from a car pool after she hired a taxi to deliver the children because she herself had other commitments.

Friedan's book was so controversial that those who read it couldn't stop discussing it, for it challenged the very basis of many middle class women's lives. It angered some and came as an enormous relief to others, especially to women with jobs who felt guilty about working, and to housewives who felt like freaks, unhappy in a situation that was supposed to be the answer to every normal woman's prayers. The book explained away their guilt and justified their ambitions.

In retrospect, one of the more fascinating things about *The Feminine Mystique* is that it didn't stress sex discrimination. Friedan, politically inexperienced, apparently assumed that all women had to do was take their abilities seriously and demand benefits like maternity leave and professionally run nurseries. She wasn't alone in her naiveté. Many middle class women were misled by the fact that government and business leaders seemed to want women to play a larger role in the labor force and often spoke of them as an untapped resource. That didn't sound like discrimination. However, women who joined the work force quickly discovered that they were only welcome in lower-level jobs. Many undoubtedly concluded that they simply weren't good enough to be promoted.

The Feminine Mystique created a small army of converts to feminism, who assumed that the women's movement was reborn when the book was published. The movement's origins were more complex than that, but it's significant that a best-seller played such a vital role. The second wave's greatest triumph was a transformation of consciousness: It changed the way most American women saw themselves and the world around them. That remarkable re-envisioning of reality was brought about via the media—by books, articles, films, and television shows that spread feminist ideas.

THE FOUNDING OF NOW

As Betty Friedan's fame spread, she was invited to speak before women's groups all over the country. She had begun work on a second book, never finished, about life patterns that would help women move beyond the feminine mystique. For several years, everywhere she went, she interviewed local women, looking for such patterns, but all she found were "the same old apologetic, makeshift, hassles." She began to realize that unless society changed, women would remain trapped in the home.

As part of her research, Friedan was now spending time in Washington, where Catherine East and Mary Eastwood introduced her to a growing network of feminists and kept urging her to organize a new pressure group for women. East was—in Friedan's words—the "midwife" to the birth of the women's movement. She had worked for the federal government for twenty-three years before she was assigned to the Kennedy Commission to do staff work. When the Commission dissolved, she became executive secretary of the new Citizens' Advisory Council. For the next fifteen years, she was the staff director or deputy staff director of each of the government bodies concerned with women's rights that succeeded the Council. She was also the chief source of information for feminists who wanted statistics or position papers, to prove that discrimination existed and to demonstrate the need for change, or who simply needed a Washington insider's view of what was happening in Congress. East suggested strategies for lobbying and supplied names of government officials to contact. Feminists visiting Washington often stayed at her house.

Richard Graham, one of the five EEOC commissioners, had convinced East that to get action on sex discrimination, women needed a feminist equivalent of the NAACP (the National Association for the Advancement of Colored People). None of the existing women's organizations seemed adequate to the job. The NWP was tiny and relatively conservative. BPW had almost 180,000 members, but in 1966 they actually rejected suggestions that BPW become an NAACP for women.

East felt that Betty Friedan was the only woman well enough known to pull other women into a new organization. Friedan was initially reluctant. "I've never been an organization woman . . ." she wrote later. "I was a writer, a loner. Still, as a result of my book . . . I did know various people in different fields who were at the same point of impatience." After Friedan had spent a day in Washington doing research, Catherine East would often come to her hotel room after dinner, together with Mary Eastwood, the young Justice Department attorney who had worked for the Kennedy Commission. Friedan recalled that they would "somehow start me making hypothetical lists of women I had met," women of influence who might want to join an activist organization. Ultimately, as the EEOC dragged its feet and government promises began to look like lip service, Friedan became convinced that women must organize.

In June 1966, Catherine East saw to it that Friedan was invited to the annual conference of state status-of-women commissions. She also arranged to have Congresswoman Martha Griffiths's speech castigating the EEOC distributed to all who attended the meeting. Nevertheless, when approximately fifteen women got together in Friedan's hotel room on the first evening of the conference, they decided after hours of discussion that it wasn't necessary to form an organization. Instead, they would simply pass a resolution demanding the enforcement of Title VII and calling for Richard Graham's reappointment. Graham was the only one of the four male EEOC commissioners who was sympathetic to women's claims and his term was nearly up. However, the next morning when the women informed Esther Peterson that they wanted to propose a resolution, she told them the purpose of the conference was to share information, not to take action, and that no resolutions would be allowed; they were outraged.* Marguerite Rawalt, who was attending the conference, observed drily, "If you really want to start something up, all you have to do is shut off debate."

During lunch that day, Rawalt watched from the head table while Friedan and other women, sitting together at two tables, whispered and passed notes scrawled on napkins. NOW, the National Organization for Women, was formed on the spot, "to take the actions needed to bring women into the mainstream of American society," as Friedan wrote on one of those napkins. Before lunch was over, twenty-seven women had joined NOW; each contributed five dollars. Rawalt herself joined later.

Sometimes it takes a crisis to launch an organization or a movement. If conditions are right, even a small crisis will do, provided those who experience it see it as something that embodies their grievances. NOW was formed in just that way: Feminists were already angry because of the EEOC's intransigence, and what happened at the conference was the last straw.

If frustration with the EEOC sparked the formation of NOW, continued frustration with the agency kept the new organization growing in its early years. Writing in 1975, former EEOC commissioner Aileen Hernandez suggested that an analysis of the Com-

---

* Catherine East believed that Peterson welcomed a feminist revival but wanted to control it, to make sure activists moved slowly enough to avoid stirring up real opposition. However, once the action started, no one could control it—it went off like a bomb.

mission's handling of the major women's issues "could easily support the conclusion that the Equal Employment Opportunity Commission was a major force in the development and growth of the National Organization for Women. Reluctantly pregnant with sex discrimination responsibility . . . the EEOC went into hard labor and became the disinterested parent of NOW and many other feminist groups which sprang up in the decade between 1965 and 1975."

THE TIMING OF THE WAVE

With the founding of NOW, the second wave—which had been gathering energy for several years—achieved lift-off. Why was feminism virtually reinvented in the 1960s, rather than earlier or later? A number of explanations have been suggested; all contain elements of the truth.

During the first half of the twentieth century, women's lives changed enormously. By 1960, there were many women who were well educated and many more white middle class women were part of the work force.* Some were in a position to help the cause. Because Americans now lived longer, mothering no longer consumed most of a woman's adult life. In addition, as the divorce rate climbed, housewifery no longer seemed such a safe choice. All over the Western world, feminism revived during the 1960s and early 70s, partly because women in other countries were inspired by the American women's movement, but also because their lives and their needs had changed in similar ways.

Though the ground was prepared by life changes, a mass movement couldn't begin without a change in consciousness as well. Enough women had to question the feminine mystique, realize that sex discrimination existed, feel that it was legitimate to fight it—and believe they could do something about it. Thanks to the Kennedy Commission, Title VII, and Friedan's best-seller, by the midsixties it was once again acceptable to talk of women's rights. Title VII provided activists with a weapon, and the civil rights movement set an example for them and gave them hope.

In fact, the civil rights movement supplied a model and inspiration for all the social movements that sprang up in the 1960s and 70s, from the disability rights movement to the New Right. In addition, the 1960s provided exceptional political opportuni-

---

* Women of color and working-class white women had always had jobs.

ties. In Washington, liberals were in the driver's seat, and the nation was conscience-struck by the evidence of racial injustice in the South and relatively responsive to demands for change. Historically, American feminism has flourished during periods of social reform; in fact, demands for women's rights have twice followed on the heels of African-Americans' demands for justice. In the nineteenth century, many women were abolitionists before they became concerned about women's rights. Something similar happened during the 1960s: Young women who went south to work in the civil rights movement turned to feminism afterward.

The fact that a women's movement already existed in 1960 was also important. It provided much of the wherewithal for the second wave: whole organizations that could be recruited to the cause, and communications networks that linked like-minded women all over the country. The old organizations also had leaders with experience in lobbying and contacts in government. In fact, it was an enormous help that some women had already achieved positions of influence. In the coming years, congresswomen, lawyers, civil servants, reporters, historians, political scientists, and many, many others would use their skills and connections in the interests of feminism.

SMOKE AND MIRRORS—AND HARD WORK

Thirty women attended NOW's founding conference, held in Washington, D.C., on October 29 and 30, 1966. They elected officers, adopted a statement of purpose, and appointed Marguerite Rawalt head of a legal committee that was instructed to offer assistance to women who were suing to overturn protective labor laws. The founders decided that the members themselves would set policy during national conventions, and between conventions those policies would be carried out by the national officers and a board of directors. Local chapters were to be formed and would have a great deal of autonomy.

Though NOW ultimately became one of the largest feminist organizations in the world, that was not what its founders originally had in mind. They wanted to bring together a select group of women who could move quickly on problems like the enforcement of Title VII. The new organization got a number of its earliest recruits from the state status commissions. Kay Clarenbach, who chaired the national board, had been head of the highly active Wisconsin commission—in fact, of the roughly 300 women and men who became charter members of NOW, 126 lived in Wisconsin.*

In those early months, women from the NOW board of directors were highly visible in Washington. They met with the Attorney General, the Secretary of Labor, the director of the EEOC, and the chairman of the Civil Service Commission, John Macy, who was close to President Johnson. They reminded Macy that Johnson hadn't fulfilled his promise to appoint fifty women to top-level government jobs. They also asked for an Executive Order that would prohibit companies that did business with the federal government from practicing sex discrimination. There was already an order forbidding discrimination on the basis of race, color, religion, or national origin.

In May 1967, responding to pressure from NOW, the EEOC finally held public hearings on the sex provision of Title VII. In October, President Johnson signed Executive Order 11375, forbidding sex discrimination by federal contractors and subcontractors. For some women, this would prove to be an even more effective weapon than Title VII. Meanwhile, the Civil Service Commission invited women's organizations and individuals to submit the names of women who might qualify for top posts.

How did NOW achieve these early gains so quickly? The names listed as members of the board of directors read like entries from a "Who's Who" of American professional women, and Catherine East suggested that the administration responded to their prestige. NOW's president, Betty Friedan, was a best-selling author; the board was chaired by Kathryn (Kay) Clarenbach, the distinguished academic who headed the Wisconsin Status-of-Women Commission. Other board members included Muriel Fox, a vice-president of one of the top public relations agencies in the country; Caroline Davis, director of the Women's Department of the United Auto Workers (UAW); and Richard Graham, the former EEOC commissioner. Congresswoman Martha Griffiths publicly supported NOW.

However, East also noted that the NOW leaders "were perceived to have more power than they actually had." In fact, NOW succeeded partly through the use of smoke and mirrors—by encouraging the illusion that it was bigger and more powerful than it was. In its early years, the organization was strikingly makeshift. The treasury never had more than a few hundred dollars in it, and board members traveled to meetings at their own expense.

* NOW always had a handful of male members.

Membership records, printing, and mailing were handled by Caroline Davis, using the UAW's facilities in Detroit. It was three years before NOW actually had a central office, and its first employee, a secretary, worked on a borrowed typewriter in Muriel Fox's office at a New York public relations agency "until one of the top executives said he didn't think it was a very good idea," Fox said. After that the secretary worked in Betty Friedan's New York apartment.

Even the membership wasn't quite what it appeared to be. Fox, who handled all publicity for the fledgling organization, recalled that at the time of the founding conference she wrote in her first press release that NOW had 300 members nationwide. "I'm sure it was much less than 300 members if anyone had really counted correctly," she said. In its early days, NOW often exaggerated the size of its membership and thus its power-base* (the women sometimes joked about "the mythical marching millions"). After 1970, the membership mushroomed and there was no longer any need to exaggerate.

Many of NOW's achievements in its early years were due to the efforts of its local chapters. New recruits joining almost any NOW chapter were immediately invited to sign up for a task force and go to work in some area that interested them: They could tackle sex discrimination in employment or education, for example, or join a group that was analyzing the state's marriage and divorce laws or the media's image of women. Task forces had also been established on the national level to try to coordinate local efforts, and a national newsletter eventually kept members in touch with one another. Most chapters mounted frequent demonstrations—for instance, they staged sit-ins at bars and restaurants that refused to admit women and picketed local supermarkets to urge shoppers to boycott Colgate-Palmolive products (the company was being sued by women workers).

NOW's leaders expected much of the action to take place at the local level. Friedan wrote that "we wanted [members] to move in their own style, according to their own priorities. . . ." Thus, women concerned about a particular issue—the blatant bias against females in high school textbooks, for example—were encouraged to work on it. Jennifer Macleod, first president of the Central New Jersey chapter of NOW, recalled that "I used to assure new members that they weren't buying into a whole package. They could devote their efforts to something they believed

---

* This is a tactic typical of social movement organizations.

in." In any case, most soon developed broader interests. For Macleod and others, feminism was eye-opening—they experienced a cascade of insights as they realized just how widespread sex discrimination was.

THE CONFLICT OVER WANT ADS

Employment was the top issue for many NOW activists. By 1960, 40 percent of all American women over age sixteen were employed, and most were locked into the low-paying occupations considered appropriate for a woman—they were secretaries, sales clerks, nurses. Official and unofficial quotas kept all but a few out of graduate schools, medical and law schools; women executives were rare; and the protective laws that limited the number of hours women could work prevented those with jobs in industry from earning overtime or holding supervisory positions. Married women were often denied promotions on the grounds that they were bound to become pregnant and quit; they were often denied credit for the same reason. Pregnant women who didn't quit were likely to be fired anyway. In spite of all this, most people believed that American women were privileged— believed, too, that because men had families to support, they had a right to the better jobs and higher pay.*

When NOW demanded an end to sex discrimination in the work place, men in positions of power resisted. They often cited the old stereotypes about a woman's nature, abilities, and proper role in life. NOW's stubborn, nine-year campaign to change the way jobs were advertised revealed the strength of such prejudices.

In the early 1960s, most American newspapers ran help-wanted ads in columns labeled either "Male Help Wanted" or "Female Help Wanted." Many also listed jobs reserved for whites and jobs for blacks in separate columns. In 1965, the EEOC ruled that newspaper advertising could no longer discriminate on the basis of race, religion, or national origin; it refused to apply the same standards to sex discrimination.

There was no question that sex-segregated job ads discouraged

---

* Women of color generally had even more limited choices and were paid less—for example, in 1961 black women with full-time jobs earned just 57 percent of white women's wages. Though NOW's leadership included a number of distinguished African-Americans, its rank-and-file members were almost all white, and their indignation about the job situation failed to impress most women of color.

women from competing with men. In the late 1960s, a woman with a degree in mathematics who checked the "Female Help Wanted" columns in the Pittsburgh newspapers would find jobs for key punch operators between the ads for "Invoice Clerk" and those for "Kitchen Help" but she would almost certainly find nothing listed for systems analysts or programmers. Most women wouldn't dream of applying for positions listed under "Male Help Wanted." The few with nerve enough to test the ad barrier were apt to be treated rudely.

Late in 1967, the NOW board of directors called for action around the country to protest the EEOC's position on sex-segregated want ads. Every NOW chapter was asked to take part, and on December 14 there were demonstrations in half a dozen different cities. In New York, NOW members invaded the regional office of the EEOC carrying huge bundles of newspaper—classified sections bound with red tape to symbolize the bureaucratic barriers women faced. Then Betty Friedan announced to the press that NOW was going to sue the EEOC for not enforcing Title VII. The lawsuit was duly filed but was dismissed a few months later when the EEOC promised to do a better job. The following August, the Commission finally issued revised guidelines, stating that sex-segregated want ads were indeed sex discrimination. The major New York City newspapers capitulated— they'd been under heavy pressure from NOW's New York chapter—and integrated their classified ads. However, many publishers simply ignored the EEOC guidelines, and the Commission had no enforcement powers.

Local NOW chapters, heartened by the precedent-setting victory in New York, kept hammering away with letters, demonstrations, and sometimes lawsuits against local newspapers. In the end, the definitive case developed in Pittsburgh, where Wilma Scott Heide, a future president of NOW, had persuaded the City Council to include in a city ordinance a ban on sex discrimination. In October 1969, Pittsburgh NOW filed a formal complaint against the *Pittsburgh Press* under the ordinance. The case eventually reached the U.S. Supreme Court, which ruled against the *Press*—and settled the issue once and for all—in 1973.

It took almost a decade to force newspapers to change their want-ad policies. In retrospect, it seems amazing that they put so much energy into resisting such a small change. When they were challenged, newspaper executives explained that they segregated the ads by sex for the convenience of their readers and argued that they would lose money if they stopped doing it. It was true that advertisers willing to interview both sexes to fill a position sometimes bought two ads, one to run in the female section and one for the male section, but once the New York papers integrated their want ads, their experience proved that the anticipated financial hardship didn't amount to much.

Sex-segregated want ads symbolized male dominance in the job market. Many men didn't want to have to compete with women for jobs and objected strenuously to working under a female boss. At an EEOC hearing in early 1968, a man representing the American Jewish Committee stated that because most men were subjected to the tyranny of women as children, they refused to submit to it again with women supervisors. Perhaps males raised to believe they weren't quite masculine if they couldn't keep women in their place were uneasy about changes that would put them to the test more often.

Some men, aware that gender-neutral want ads were the opening wedge, predicted dire consequences, such as unisex public bathrooms. Cartoonists sketched militant women marching on men's restrooms, and newspapers were filled with half-serious complaints that it was becoming much too difficult to tell the girls from the boys, what with unisex clothing and integrated classifieds. Baffled feminists wondered aloud what men were afraid of. In the coming years, a small cottage industry would develop as theorists set to work analyzing male fears.

LANDMARK LEGAL DECISIONS: INVALIDATING PROTECTIVE LABOR LAWS

In the late 1960s and early 70s, NOW's legal committee won a number of landmark decisions in court cases that challenged the protective labor laws. These victories eventually convinced labor leaders that the protective laws were dead and that, therefore, it was a waste of energy to continue to oppose the ERA.

Earlier in the century, when sweatshops were common, the state laws prescribing working conditions for women were probably of some benefit. However, by the 1960s they had become primarily an excuse for barring females from many better-paying jobs. Some protective statutes stipulated that a woman couldn't be required to lift more than a certain weight—the range was from twenty-five to fifty pounds—even if she only had to do the lifting occasionally (toddlers often weigh thirty pounds or more). Others said that employers couldn't require women to work more than eight hours a day or forty-eight hours a week; that often ruled out any chance of promotion, along with extra pay for over-time. Some states forbade hiring women at all for certain physi-cally hazardous occupations, and in ten states women weren't allowed to hold the morally hazardous job of bartender.

NOW's legal committee consisted of four high-powered Wash-ington lawyers, all volunteers. Like the rest of the organization, the committee operated on a shoestring. The attorneys shared a one-room office and sometimes typed their own legal briefs on a typewriter donated by feminist judge June Green. They usually paid for their own office supplies and sometimes advanced the money to cover other costs as well. Friedan, traveling the coun-try, constantly appealed for funds to support the legal work and the money dribbled in—contributions of $1, $5, $25.

Three of the lawyers could give their time only on evenings and weekends. By day, Mary Eastwood worked for the Justice Department, Caruthers Berger for the Department of Labor, and Phineas Indritz for a congressional committee. However, Mar-guerite Rawalt was full-time. She had retired in 1965 and in 1966 she plunged into demanding, unpaid work for NOW "as a way of forgetting that Harry [her husband, who had died in 1963] wasn't there any more." The work developed into a totally ab-sorbing new career as a feminist lawyer.

Almost from the beginning, letters poured in from women who wanted legal help to fight discrimination on the job. NOW's goal was clear: to use Title VII to invalidate the protective laws. That meant the lawyers had to put their efforts into suits where the facts might support a precedent-setting decision. There was no dearth of cases to choose from—the legal committee was inun-dated with letters imploring help.

Most of the cases the lawyers ultimately chose to pursue were at the appeals level: The women involved had already lost the first round in a lower court. *Weeks* v. *Southern Bell* was fairly typical. It began for NOW in 1967 when Rawalt spotted a news item reporting that a Georgia woman, Lorena Weeks, had lost a case she'd brought against Southern Bell Telephone under Title VII. Weeks had put in a bid for the position of switchman, a job that involved testing and maintaining switching equipment and that paid almost twice as much as she was earning at the time. She'd already proved she could do the work: While the man who had the position was on vacation, she was always his substitute. However, Southern Bell gave the job instead to a man with less seniority and told Weeks that it had closed such jobs to women, largely because of a state law that said a woman employee couldn't be required to lift more than thirty pounds.

When Rawalt and her committee read that Weeks had lost the case, they decided that the decision couldn't be allowed to stand as a precedent. Rawalt called Weeks and asked if she planned to appeal the decision. She said she couldn't afford to—so far, she'd had a court-appointed lawyer. Rawalt told her that NOW might take the case without charging her a fee, but only if she'd agree to stay in her job, because if she quit, that would end the suit. Rawalt also warned her, "If you appeal this case, Mrs. Weeks, you will probably be harassed." Weeks was a determined woman. She'd already been made fun of, her supervisor had let her know he was displeased, her lawyer had warned her that she might lose her job, her husband couldn't understand why she wanted to cause trouble, and her children were embarrassed. Nevertheless, she assured Rawalt that she'd stick it out through an appeal.

Sylvia Roberts of Baton Rouge, Louisiana, agreed to act as NOW's local attorney for the Weeks case, and she and Rawalt worked on the brief together. They felt, Rawalt said, "like Davids against the Goliaths of the big law firms," for Southern Bell was represented by attorneys from major law firms in both Atlanta and New York City.

Before the Weeks appeal was heard, the Georgia legislature repealed the weight-limitations law. As a result, Southern Bell could only argue that the company rule on weights was acceptable under Title VII as a bfoq—a bona-fide occupational qualification. Arguing the case for NOW, Sylvia Roberts, who was five feet tall and weighed about 100 pounds, casually picked up all the equipment the job required and carried it around with her with one hand.

In March 1969, the appeals court ruled that Southern Bell *had* violated Title VII and that the weight-lifting restriction was based on a stereotype about women that didn't apply to all women. The burden of proof was on the employer, said the court, to show that all or "substantially all" women would be unable to do what the job required. In addition, the court noted that men had always had the right to decide whether it was worth taking a strenuous, dangerous, or obnoxious job for extra money. "The promise of Title VII is that women are now to be on equal footing," the court opinion stated.

Southern Bell was ordered to give Weeks the job, plus almost $31,000 in back pay. However, the company delayed, and it wasn't until April 1971, after NOW chapters had staged protest demonstrations in cities around the country, that Lorena Weeks finally got the position and the money.

The legal committee won a number of other victories as well. As in the Weeks case, the employer typically used delaying tactics to try to wear the plaintiffs down; the women were often harassed or even threatened by male co-workers and supervisors; and sometimes after winning an appeal they had to go back to court again to have the decision enforced. Some of the suits were handled by lawyers who belonged to local chapters of NOW. Rawalt noted that after feminists won the first few precedent-setting decisions under Title VII, male lawyers, too, began to take on sex discrimination cases.

At least three of the early, landmark cases began as complaints filed with the EEOC. However, the Commission was divided on the merits of the state protective laws and deliberately left it to the courts to settle the controversy. In any case, the EEOC wasn't authorized to file lawsuits; as Aileen Hernandez pointed out, that meant that the battle against the protective laws "was left largely to individuals who were morally, legally and financially supported by the fledgling women's civil rights groups. . . ." Thousands of jobs eventually opened up to women as the laws were overturned by the courts or repealed by state legislatures.

Of course, feminists didn't always win. Betty Lehan Harragan, who sued an advertising agency for sex discrimination, not only lost her job but couldn't get another one in advertising. To justify firing her, the agency claimed she was "abrasive." Suing as an individual was risky, said Muriel Fox, because an employer could always argue that a woman was unpromotable because of some character flaw. Class-action suits, based on a pattern of discrimination, were safer and more apt to succeed. "All the same, a lot of women in advertising benefited because of Betty Harragan," said Fox.

SEX BIAS IN CRIMINAL LAW

The NOW legal team also won another significant victory in a case that didn't involve the protective statutes. In the late sixties, several states had laws requiring that a woman convicted of a crime be given a longer sentence than a man convicted of the same crime. To a Pennsylvania woman named Jane Daniel, that meant, in effect, that she was sentenced to four years in prison for committing a robbery—and six more for being female.

In May 1966, Daniel was sent to prison for robbery—she and a male companion had held up a bartender. Given a one- to four-year sentence, she would be eligible for parole in a year and would be imprisoned for four years at most. However, a month later the judge resentenced her to an "indeterminate" term of up to ten years. That was a longer sentence than her male partner in crime received, though he had a record and she had none.

The judge lengthened Daniel's sentence after the district attorney reminded him that the case fell within the purview of the state's Muncy Act. Passed in 1913, Muncy stipulated that if a woman was convicted of a crime that, by law, required imprisonment for more than a year, she had to be sentenced for an indeterminate period. What's more, if the law prescribed a maximum sentence for that crime that was longer than three years, she had to be given the maximum. In Daniel's case, the Muncy Act added six years to her original maximum sentence. Though theoretically, with an indeterminate sentence, she could be paroled within days or weeks, in reality the parole board wouldn't even consider a female prisoner's case until she had served a substantial proportion of her maximum sentence. Pennsylvania women sentenced under the Muncy Act spent over 50 percent longer in prison than did men convicted of similar crimes.

Why was such a law ever passed? One possible explanation is suggested by an article published in the *Journal of Criminal Law and Criminology* in 1913, at about the time the Act went into effect. Arguing in favor of Muncy, the author, Katherine Bement Davis, wrote that:

> There is little doubt in the minds of those who have had much experience in dealing with women delinquents, that the fundamental fact is that they belong to the class of women who lead sexually immoral lives.
>
> [The Muncy Act] would do more to rid the streets . . . of soliciting, loitering, and public vice than anything that could be devised. There is nothing the common prostitute fears so greatly as to know that if she offends and is caught she will be subject to the possibility of prolonged confinement.

To Phineas Indritz, who worked with Rawalt in drafting NOW's legal brief in the Daniel case, Muncy was "symptomatic of legislation that in many societies has punished women more severely than men."

Though the Pennsylvania Superior Court affirmed Jane Daniel's sentence in 1967, in July 1968 the Pennsylvania Supreme Court not only reversed both lower courts but ruled that the Muncy Act was invalid. (A few months earlier, a federal court had struck down a similar Connecticut law.) After the decision, Pennsylvania authorities reviewed the cases of 200 women originally sentenced under the Muncy Act. Rawalt noted that "most of them were released from prison, having already served longer than a man convicted of the same offense. . . ."

THE MOVEMENT SPLINTERS—AND GROWS

NOW's second annual conference, held in Washington in November 1967, was very different from the first. Over 300 women and men attended, and this time they were asked to set policy on some highly controversial issues. Even by NOW's feisty standards, it was a "very stormy" meeting, according to Muriel Fox, who added, "People thought the organization would break apart." The big debates that year were over the ERA and abortion. Jean Faust recalled that some members were utterly confident not only that it was right for NOW to support both, but that those two issues were vital if the organization was to grow. In fact, NOW emerged from the conflict stronger than before.

Though Betty Friedan was originally not enthusiastic about the Equal Rights Amendment—she told Fox at one point that it was "old hat" because it had been around for so long—by 1967 she had changed her mind. She now proposed including it in a Bill of Rights for Women that would demand abortion repeal, day-care centers, and other essentials as well. Though to some NOW members the ERA was about as controversial "as God and motherhood," to quote Muriel Fox (motherhood was not considered controversial at the time), there were women within NOW who opposed it because they felt the protective labor laws must be preserved. Others, like Marguerite Rawalt, believed it was simply not the right time to push for the ERA. She pointed out to Friedan that women who worked for the UAW had been very active in NOW—in fact, the UAW handled all printing and mailing for the organization. These union women were trying hard to sell UAW's leadership on the ERA but hadn't yet succeeded. If NOW publicly supported the amendment, they would be forced to resign from it. Other members might be alienated if abortion were included in the Bill of Rights. However, Friedan felt that both issues were too important to sidestep.

When the National Woman's Party learned that NOW would be considering the ERA, six or seven former suffragists promptly joined the organization so that they could cast votes in favor of the amendment. Rawalt was on the platform when the meeting began and she recalled that ". . . at my left, as I looked down upon their faces, were two rows of elderly dignified women. They were headed by Alice Paul . . . dear members of the National Woman's Party, whose sole purpose in life was the Equal Rights Amendment. . . . They were tense. . . . a few rows back of them sat the United Automobile Workers."

It seemed to Friedan that when the NWP women got up to speak on the Equal Rights Amendment, very young women who had never heard of the ERA before were excited by the idea "as they had not been by narrow job issues." At any rate, after prolonged debate the members passed that section of the Bill of Rights. Caroline Davis of the UAW subsequently resigned as NOW's secretary-treasurer and the organization had to make other arrangements for its printing and mailing. However, within a year the UAW women had persuaded their union to endorse the ERA—it was the first union to do so.

Abortion was an even stickier issue for some, but the NOW membership passed that plank too. Muriel Fox recalled that "I spoke out very strongly against NOW getting involved with abortion that early. I thought we were too young an organization and it would make us too many enemies. I was wrong. It turned out actually that we got a lot more new members as a result of taking that very courageous stand. . . ."

However, NOW also lost some old members. Attorney Elizabeth Boyer of Novelty, Ohio, an old friend of Rawalt's, had come to the meeting with about a dozen other women from Ohio. Though Boyer supported the ERA, the abortion plank seemed much too controversial to her. After the conference, she decided that women needed a new organization that those in middle America could identify with, one "which would proceed along more accustomed lines, which would adopt a well-thought-out purpose clause and abide by it, so that the women joining it would know what they were getting into, and that it would be in accord with their views and actions." Such an organization would work within the system and would be "patient, determined and diplomatic."

And so, in the spring of 1968, the Women's Equity Action League (WEAL) was founded in Cleveland. As its first activity, it sponsored a talk by Congresswoman Martha Griffiths, who spoke on sex discrimination in jobs and education. The women of WEAL would devote most of their energy and abilities to ending discrimination in those two areas.

Though Boyer's departure from NOW caused some hard feelings, they dissipated rather quickly. Boyer wrote to Friedan and other NOW members to explain that she wasn't trying to set up an organization that would compete with NOW. She wouldn't ask NOW members to join WEAL; if they wanted to join, they would have to approach her. She knew WEAL could pick up members elsewhere.

Summing up the impact of the 1967 conference a year later, Friedan wrote that ". . . the Equal Rights Amendment and abortion were and are the two gut issues of the women's movement essential to real security—and equality and human dignity—for all women. . . ." The ERA and abortion would, in fact, become the focal issues in the struggle between feminists and antifeminists.

NOW's victories during the 1960s jolted the old stereotypes about women. They opened doors so that eventually many women would be able to work as police officers and mail carriers, as astronauts, engineers, and surgeons. However, the liberal feminists were basically reformist: They focused on opening up the male world to women at all levels. By 1968, a much more radical form of feminism was taking root in the United States as women's liberation groups began to spring up around the country.

chapter 4

The Birth of
Women's Liberation

———

The women's liberation movement developed independently from liberal feminism. It was sometimes referred to as the younger branch of the movement because most of the women who founded its early groups were in their twenties. Rooted in a different political tradition than the liberals, many had worked in the civil rights movement or had been campus radicals, vehemently opposed to the war in Vietnam. When it came to tactics, they thought in terms of civil disobedience—revolutionary tactics designed to force revolutionary changes.

The women's liberation movement got under way in 1967, and reached a peak of intensity in the early 1970s, but most of its original groups had disappeared almost entirely by 1975.* Those eight short years from 1967 to 1975 were a unique period in the history of feminism. The joy, the yeastiness—the sheer, creative chaos of those years—were extraordinary and had a permanent impact. Women's lives, and men's, would never be quite the same.

* This chapter describes the movement's growth; chapter 8 traces its decline.

It was a time of fierce passions and endless debates. Women's liberation was still in its infancy when disputes erupted between women (sometimes called politicos) who believed that the nation's political and economic system was responsible for women's problems, and radical feminists, who argued that the main problem was male supremacy, and that even a government based on socialist principles wasn't likely to make much difference as long as it was dominated by men.

Radical feminists were a minority in most women's liberation groups at first, but they soon became the movement's major theorists and cutting edge. Their insights first shocked the public (and other feminists), then gradually began to change people's thinking. They were outrageous, articulate, and angry, and they got the attention of the press. Virtually ignoring many legal inequities, they turned their attention to people's private lives and condemned the patriarchal system that gave men the right to dominate women. Their ideas brought thousands of new recruits into the movement, swelling the ranks of NOW chapters as well as women's liberation groups. Ultimately, many liberals and politicos began to think more like radical feminists.

One could argue that for a few years during the late 1960s and early 70s, there were two competing feminist movements—liberal feminism and women's liberation.* It's true that the two developed independently and had somewhat different goals. However, the goals overlapped and women of different persuasions often worked together. At least in retrospect, the second wave appears to have been just one, highly complex movement from the beginning. The competing factions were like tributaries of the same river: Though they arose under different circumstances, from the first they were fated to mingle.

THE ROOTS OF WOMEN'S LIBERATION

During the sixties, tens of thousands of young Americans came to think of themselves as radicals who were part of "the Movement." By that, they sometimes meant the civil rights movement, sometimes the New Left, and sometimes both.†

Because many early women's liberationists were Movement

---

* In Western Europe, the same factions developed in many countries.
† The term "New Left" was coined by the SDS to distinguish student political groups which were loosely socialist from old-line Marxist organizations such as the Communist party.

veterans, to understand women's liberation, one must know something about its roots in the broader Movement. The experiences young women had there explain how they came to be gripped by a vision of radical equality; why many distrusted both the government and liberal feminists; why white and black women who had been in the Movement had different attitudes toward feminism—and, at times, an uneasy relationship with one another; and why some radical feminists turned against the sexual revolution.

SNCC: The Vision of Radical Equality

The gains that blacks made in the 1960s—and the justice of their struggle—kindled the idealism of the young. Because Western nations were experiencing great affluence, for a time almost anything seemed possible. Young people came to believe that society could be changed fundamentally for the better and that, given the abundance they saw all around them, a decent life should be within the reach of all.

For the young, the Student Nonviolent Coordinating Committee (SNCC) was the key civil rights organization. It was founded in 1960 by black college students, who had begun to stage sit-ins at southern lunch counters that refused to serve African-Americans.

In its early days, SNCC was profoundly influenced by Ella Baker, an older woman who helped the students organize. Baker had held key positions in two other major civil rights organizations and she had strong ideas about how a grass-roots movement should operate. Those ideas subsequently influenced both the New Left and feminists and are alive in the women's movement today.

As Baker saw it, the major barrier to grass-roots organizing was the fact that most people submitted passively to authority. She believed that virtually everyone—no matter how humble—had some potential for leadership, and she convinced SNCC's student leaders that their task was to go out into rural communities and help them develop their own leaders; they must teach the people to make decisions, to take responsibility for themselves and be ready to accept the consequences, so that before long they would no longer need outside help. Though most SNCC field workers were black, city-bred college students, inspired by Baker's vision of radical equality, they tried to approach uneducated rural people with open minds and learn from them.

SNCC itself was also run according to principles of radical equality.* At meetings, everyone's opinion counted, and in making decisions the staff generally struggled to reach a consensus. This sometimes led to long, exhausting debates—or to sheer chaos. However, Mary King, a SNCC staffer, felt that "SNCC was grounded in the purest vision of democracy that I have ever encountered." Close-knit, utopian, predominantly (but not entirely) black, the organization was known to members as "the beloved community," and those who belonged to it shared an intense experience. Rage, fear, and idealism were all part of it, because SNCC was forged in fire. During the early sixties, violence erupted across the South as whites lashed out at African-Americans. Black activists were jailed and beaten, and some were murdered. The federal government failed to act and the press paid little attention.

In 1964, SNCC's leaders took the step that brought hundreds of young women south: They set out to recruit white college students to help with "Freedom Summer," a voter registration drive. They hoped that if SNCC's field workers included white students, the government would provide some protection and the media would cover events. More than 800 college volunteers, male and female, went to Mississippi to work for SNCC in 1964. They lived in the black community and were often harassed by local whites.

Historian Sara Evans wrote that most of the women came home "seared by an experience that marked a turning point in their lives." Many learned to distrust the authorities. Three civil rights workers disappeared that summer, among them one of the student volunteers. Six months later, the sheriff and deputy sheriff of Neshoba County were among those arrested for the crime. Though the FBI had worked hard to find the killers (two of the victims were white), a number of black activists were also murdered that year, and the agency apparently had no interest in those cases or in other violent incidents at SNCC projects.† Some

---

* In the 1960s and 70s, radicals were more likely to speak of *participatory democracy* than of radical equality. The term referred primarily to the way groups made decisions: not by majority rule but by consensus, and not by elected representatives but by all members, meeting face to face. According to the group ethic, all should feel like equals. I prefer to write of radical equality because *participatory democracy* seems dated, and in the 1990s many feminist groups still believe in radical equality, though usually in some modified form.

† That summer, 1000 civil rights workers were arrested, 80 were beaten, 4 were critically wounded, and 4 were killed; 37 African-American churches and 30 black homes or businesses were bombed or burned.

women also became leery of liberals because many seemed faint-hearted in their support for civil rights and were slow to oppose the Vietnam War, and because their goal was to reform the system, rather than to replace it.

Freedom Summer also opened many women's eyes to sex discrimination, but black women reacted differently than whites. To the African-Americans, gender bias seemed trivial compared with racial prejudice. Most had grown up in communities where older women were greatly respected: Always the backbone of the black churches, they were now the mainstay of the civil rights movement as well. Though its formal leadership was almost entirely male, women often predominated in boycotts, demonstrations, and voter registration drives. A few had become famous—Rosa Parks, for example, whose refusal to sit at the back of the bus sparked the Montgomery bus boycott, and Fannie Lou Hamer, a SNCC field secretary who was jailed, beaten, and permanently disabled in 1963 but went on to become one of the founders of the Mississippi Freedom Democratic Party.

Though most of SNCC's leaders, too, were men, compared to other civil rights groups it was relatively free of sex bias, at least where black women were concerned. A few of them—such as Ruby Doris Smith, Diane Nash, Cynthia Washington, and Donna Richards Moses—were part of the inner circle or were project directors. They seemed to assume that they could do anything the men could do, even if it meant facing physical danger.

Most of the white female summer volunteers were given little responsibility and were assigned to do office work or to teach in one of the "freedom schools." That may have been partly because it seemed safer to give them less visible jobs. Their presence in the black community stirred up southern whites, who were enraged at the very idea that the women might be having sex with black men. However, sexism was undoubtedly involved as well. Notes taken by those who interviewed prospective volunteers before the summer suggest that the women were often judged on their looks—and some were rejected for being too outspoken.

Some of the black women in SNCC objected to the fact that men held most of the leadership positions, but to others that seemed irrelevant. Some weren't even aware that the white female volunteers were being given the least responsible jobs. Many of the black women resented the white women anyway, because SNCC's black males seemed to prefer them as sex partners. Cynthia Washington, a black project director, recalled that "We did the same work as men . . . usually *with* men. But when we finally got back to some town where we could relax and go out, the men went out with other women. Our skills and abilities were recognized and respected, but that seemed to place us in some category other than female."

For many white women, sex was part of the experience of Freedom Summer. SNCC, the beloved community, was seen as a model of what the world could become, and in that context a sexual connection between a black man and a white woman seemed the ultimate expression of love and equality. However, there were also white women who were harassed because they said no, and a few who said yes found that their morals were questioned and they were asked to leave. The sexual double standard was strong and was complicated by racial tensions—for example, when a black woman dated a white man, the other men berated her. In retrospect, the whole experience taught some women of both races that in too many cases, the sexual revolution simply freed men so that they could use women. That conclusion would ultimately find expression in feminist theory.

At the end of the summer, eighty white volunteers stayed on. SNCC had rarely had more than a hundred members before, most of them black. Because many of the whites who stayed were women, racial and sexual tensions continued to build—they would ultimately contribute to the decision to expel whites from the group. However, SNCC was experiencing many other problems, as well. As it nearly doubled in size, factions developed, and its informal, almost leaderless structure and practice of making decisions by consensus no longer worked well. In addition, after years of being subjected to white violence, many members were bitter and ready to reject nonviolent social protest as a tactic.

THE KING-HAYDEN PAPER

In November 1964, SNCC held a staff retreat in Waveland, Mississippi, that became a milestone in feminist histories. Mary King and Casey Hayden, two white staffers, had drafted a paper protesting the position of women in SNCC and they had it distributed anonymously—they were afraid of being ridiculed. In it, they described a number of incidents in which women had been passed over in favor of men,* and went on to note that "the average SNCC worker finds it difficult to discuss the woman

---

* For instance: "Two organizers were working together to form a farmers' league. Without asking any questions, the male organizer immediately assigned the clerical work to the female organizer although both had had equal experience. . . ."

problem because of the assumption of male superiority. Assumptions of male superiority are as widespread and deep-rooted and every [bit as] . . . crippling to the woman as the assumptions of white supremacy are to the Negro." Though some staffers made fun of these statements, others were supportive.

The King-Hayden paper is sometimes described as the first blow struck for women's liberation. Surprisingly, in 1987, Mary King more or less repudiated that idea, arguing that to emphasize sex discrimination in SNCC "overlooks the truly significant roles women played, the responsiveness of SNCC to women leaders . . . and the fact that, by and large, the movement was peopled by women. . . ."

King insisted that she and Hayden never meant to make a major issue of their status in the movement. Rather, they were primarily concerned—as most SNCC staffers were then—about the future direction of the organization. There was much debate at the time between those who wanted strong, centralized leadership and those (including King and Hayden) who wanted to retain SNCC's loose, highly democratic structure. King anticipated that if SNCC's local groups were more or less autonomous, some might take up women's issues. However, she was swimming against the tide, because SNCC was about to opt for a centralized, hierarchical structure. As women's liberation groups would eventually discover, it was difficult to undertake organized political action while maintaining radical equality within a large group. James Forman, executive director of SNCC, suggested that the organization had confused fighting for a better society with "SNCC as that better society itself."

THE DREAM OF THE BELOVED COMMUNITY

The dream of the beloved community would haunt other social movements for years. Long after Freedom Summer, many SNCC staffers and volunteers still hungered for the feeling that they were part of something bigger—a close and supportive group and a meaningful struggle for change. The United States was probably the most individualistic nation in the world, and that hunger for community was a motivating factor, seldom recognized, in many of the conflicts of the seventies and eighties. Again and again, young people set up leftist or feminist groups, collectives or communes, with the idea that they could create a model of a better society and then use it to transform the world around them.

Women of the New Left

In 1965, two things happened that led many young whites to shift their attention from black civil rights to other issues. SNCC's leaders began to talk of black power, and whites were less and less welcome in the organization. At about the same time, the Vietnam War began to override all other problems for college students, as President Johnson stepped up the draft. As a result, the college-based "New Left" expanded vigorously. It was a loosely connected network of campus groups that were intent on reforming everything from the universities themselves to the nation's political and economic systems. In general, the student radicals were against racism at home and American imperialism abroad. They were basically anticapitalist and wanted to see society's resources distributed more fairly. Once again, feminists-to-be were involved, and once again they learned lessons about sexism.

For the young, the Students for a Democratic Society (SDS) was the key New Left organization. It had been trying to organize poor urban blacks in the North while hammering out a critique of American society. Now, with feeling against the draft running high, SDS entered a period of explosive growth. Eventually, it would have over 10,000 members at colleges around the country. Students who had been to the South often provided the leadership and suggested tactics and ideology.

Though women had had their problems in SNCC, by all accounts the SDS was much worse. Typically, the men made the decisions while the women made coffee and did office work. Nevertheless, some SDS women played important roles in the effort to mobilize the poor. In several cities, they successfully organized welfare mothers into stable pressure groups, and because they *were* successful, they gained in self-respect. That, in turn, increased their resentment when radical men treated them like clerical help—or sex objects. By 1965, women in the community-organizing groups had begun to talk among themselves about "the woman question."

There were some intriguing parallels between the events that led women's liberationists to organize and those that triggered the resurgence of liberal feminism. In 1965, Mary King and Casey Hayden (the authors of the anonymous paper protesting the position of women in SNCC) mailed a long memo to forty women activists, eloquently describing the gap that existed in the Movement between the ideal of equality and the sex caste system that kept women in subordinate positions. The memo was published in *Liberation* magazine in the spring of 1966, and it may have done as much to ignite the women's liberation branch of the movement as Betty Friedan's book did to spark liberal feminism. Yet Mary King recalled years later that, though she and Hayden thought it might be possible to develop a women's network within the Movement, "Even in our fantasies, we had no hope that a [women's] movement would develop."

King acknowledged that they were mistaken about several things. In the memo, they wrote that "The [sex] caste system is not institutionalized by law." At the time, they didn't realize how many laws discriminated against women. They also believed that the sex-caste system was "volitional," and that men and women could do away with it in their personal relationships simply by agreeing that it was unjust. Like Betty Friedan, they underestimated the social forces at work and male resistance to change.

Though occasional workshops on "the woman question" were held during SDS meetings in 1966, organizing didn't actually begin until the summer of 1967, when a small group of Chicago women got together to draft a list of demands to present at a convention of the National Conference for a New Politics (NCPC). The NCPC was a fledgling political organization, and the convention was its attempt to unify various groups, including SNCC, the Black Panthers, and the SDS, behind a single coherent program.

Unfortunately for the goal of unity, tensions between blacks and whites dominated the convention. African-Americans demanded half the votes and half the committee slots, although only about one sixth of those attending the meeting were black, and in the end, the white majority gave them what they wanted. However, when a women's caucus demanded 51 percent of the committee seats, on the grounds that women were 51 percent of the U.S. population, and also tried to raise other women's issues, they weren't even permitted a hearing.

In Washington a little over a year earlier, women had founded NOW out of frustration when they weren't allowed to present resolutions at a conference. The young radical women, faced with a somewhat similar situation, also began to organize as a result. The Chicago group grew rapidly and within six months had spun off four others. Women's liberation groups also cropped up independently in four other cities in 1967 and 1968.

HOW TO ORGANIZE A MOVEMENT

To become more than a local phenomenon, social movements need some way to communicate with potential supporters. Just as the liberal feminists built on the existing network of women's rights organizations, women's liberationists used the Movement. For instance, in 1967, when Shulamith Firestone and Pam Allen set out to form New York Radical Women (NYRW), they recruited members from a local SDS women's caucus and at a regional SDS meeting. Meanwhile, Chicago women, traveling widely to New Left conferences and demonstrations, were helping to spread the word. New Left publications carried reports— sometimes derogatory—of the women's demands at the NCPC convention and of the new groups that were forming. During 1968, as young women learned by one means or another that in other places radical women were meeting to discuss their issues, they began to form their own groups in virtually every major city in the country.

The women's liberationists also used a national antiwar meeting to make contact with one another. In January 1968, a coalition of women's peace groups called the Jeannette Rankin Brigade staged a protest in Washington, a combined demonstration and convention that drew 5000 women. Radical groups from Chicago, New York, and Washington, D.C., decided to hold their own demonstration during the convention. They objected to the fact that the Brigade was presenting women primarily as wives and mothers of fighting men, "tearful and passive," as Shulamith Firestone put it, and basically powerless. To dramatize their point, they staged a funeral procession at Arlington Cemetery carrying a dummy of "Traditional Womanhood," laid out as if for burial. Kathie Sarachild gave an impassioned speech on behalf of the NYRW contingent, attacking the old ideas about women, and calling for a grass-roots movement "so that we can have independent lives." A pamphlet written by Sarachild proclaimed that "sisterhood is powerful."

The demonstration succeeded beyond the New Yorkers' most ambitious dreams. Five hundred radical women soon left the main convention to meet as a counter congress. No one was prepared for such a massive response and there was chaos. The NYRW women had no coherent program or action to suggest, nor did anyone else. Nevertheless, new women's liberation groups soon formed in several cities. The demonstration in Washington deepened a split that was already developing among radical women between radical feminists and politicos. Many of the New York City politicos felt that the mock funeral was irrelevant to the antiwar effort, which was their first priority, and in the months that followed they began to meet separately as a subgroup. Similar factions also developed in Chicago and in other places.

Women's liberation activists launched several publications in 1968 that helped build the movement. In March, Chicago women published the first issue of *Voice of the Women's Liberation Movement*, a newsletter that reached radical women all over the country and that generally presented the politico point of view. In June, the radical feminists of NYRW brought out *Notes from the First Year*. At about the same time, two women from Gainesville produced a document that came to be known as "the Florida paper." Though they had had no contact with the New York group, it was obvious that they'd been thinking along similar lines. They questioned the traditional goals of women's lives— love, marriage, children. Declaring that men were the enemy, they recommended that their female readers try karate, periodic celibacy, and living in women's communes. Both the Florida paper and *Notes from the First Year* were widely read, though in the beginning politicos tended to scoff at them, pointing out that they were about personal issues rather than the serious stuff of politics.

In August 1968, twenty women from various cities met in Sandy Springs, Maryland, to discuss their issues. Arguments between politicos and radical feminists erupted again and again. Then, as the women set about planning a much bigger conference in November, there was a debate over whether to invite some of the radical black women who were involved in civil rights or welfare rights groups but not in women's liberation. Some white activists said that they must be included if feminists wanted to understand how all women were oppressed, but others pointed out that many black women scoffed at the whole idea of women's liberation. The white feminists were afraid that if they talked in front of black women about the oppression of white middle class housewives, there would be "snickers and sneers." They were feeling defensive because New Left males so often insisted that women's issues were trivial compared to racism and the Vietnam War. Some of the women argued, too, that they needed time to analyze their own oppression. Afterward, they could have a conference that would include the black women. That was more or less the way it was left, and when more than 200 women from thirty-seven states and Canada met in Chicago over the Thanksgiving weekend that year, black women's groups weren't represented.

In retrospect that seems like an important missed opportunity. However, radical black women probably wouldn't have come to the conference if they'd been invited, according to Charlotte Bunch, because of the impression they had of the women's liberation movement—many saw it as bourgeois or felt that fighting racism had to be their priority. Bunch was a member of the Washington group that organized both the Sandy Springs meeting and the Thanksgiving conference. Over the next two years, her group, the D.C. Women's Liberation Movement, tried unsuccessfully a number of times to draw groups like the Black Panther women into women's caucuses. For a while, the feminists did work closely with the National Welfare Rights Organization (NWRO) on the issue of health care at D.C. General Hospital, but the NWRO women—who were predominantly black—weren't interested in becoming involved in other issues as well.

"I had lots of conversations with black friends . . . about feminism," said Bunch, "and they were not unsupportive of my doing it, but they weren't interested themselves. In the black movement, women were simply not at a point where it made any sense to them to join us. . . . They often didn't like the way they were treated by the black men, but they didn't feel alienated from their own movement the way some of us did from the white antiwar movement."

Bunch also suggested that when activists first begin to explore their issues, a period of separation may be inevitable. White feminists needed time to define their own problems. "In terms of racism," Bunch said, "I think the worst mistakes came later." Over the years, white women made too few efforts to build coalitions with women of color and to understand and address their issues. Thus, the second wave remained largely a white women's movement until the 1980s, when women of color, who had organized their own groups, demanded that white feminists give more than lip service to their issues.

WOMEN'S LIBERATION IN ALL ITS VARIETY

It's difficult to generalize about the women's liberation movement because it developed so differently in different cities. Charlotte Bunch suggested that to some extent, feminists' priorities reflected regional interests.

In New York, women's liberation groups were creative, volatile, combative—perhaps hyperstimulated because the city was the media capital of the nation. Believing passionately in their own brands of feminism, women fought for the chance to define the issues for the press. In the process, many were "trashed" because their groups were committed to the SNCC ideal of radical equality, and those who strove to be leaders or to stand out in any way were distrusted.

The New York movement grew largely through fission. Feminists organized, debated the issues passionately, and arrived at a point where they disagreed over goals or tactics; then the group split into two or more grouplets, and these offshoots typically continued to grow until they, too, splintered. Thus, by mid-1969, NYRW had disappeared but had spun off Witches (politicos) and Redstockings (radical feminists). Meanwhile, Ti-Grace Atkinson had emerged from a major confrontation within the New York chapter of NOW to found The Feminists. In 1969, disaffected members of that group joined with Redstockings dropouts to form New York Radical Feminists (NYRF). Virtually all the groups were wonderfully innovative in developing both theories and tactics (more about that later).

There was more conflict in New York than anywhere else in the country, partly because in smaller cities there weren't enough activists that groups could afford to split. Where factions developed, they generally pursued their own projects within the group or if the group split, the offshoots often worked together.

In Washington, D.C., women's liberationists—highly conscious of what Congress was up to—were policy-oriented and tended to see issues in terms of the whole nation. According to Charlotte Bunch, the movement in the capital wasn't as defined by ideology because Washington itself was a city more interested in pragmatic politics than in systems of belief. Boston and San Francisco, on the other hand, had major academic communities, so movement theory and ideology loomed large there. Chicago's liberationists, with midwestern practicality, tended to focus on bread-and-butter issues such as day care.

In many cities during those early years, there were divisions of one sort or another between politicos and radical feminists. However, the factions—and the issues—were far from clear-cut. In the broadest sense, activists disagreed about whether women were oppressed by the nation's political system or by male supremacy. Politicos were generally more closely tied to the New Left, and many favored some form of socialism. Yet the groups usually identified as politico also had nonsocialist members and members who had never been particularly interested in any kind of politics. Furthermore, some radical feminists were strong socialists—they believed women were oppressed both by men *and* by capitalism, but they felt that male supremacy was the first and most fundamental problem.

On one level, the debate between the factions was over priorities, about where feminists should invest their energy. On another level, many politicos dismissed the radical feminists as hopelessly antimale, while the feminists insisted that the politicos too often played to an "invisible audience" of New Left men.

The history of the women's liberation movement in Boston provides some of the clearest examples of the issues (and gut feelings) that divided politicos and radical feminists. Boston women eventually formed two of the better known and more creative women's liberation groups, Bread and Roses, which was politico in its orientation, and radical-feminist Cell 16. Their story also captures the sense of limitless possibilities that lit up those early years.

BOSTON POLITICOS

It was a radical feminist who first broached the possibility of a liberation movement to a key Boston New Left activist. In the fall of 1967, Kathie Sarachild came to Boston to visit Nancy Hawley, an old friend who had been one of the founders of the first chapter of the SDS. Hawley was married and had a small child, and she recalled that when Sarachild began to talk to her about her own evolution as a feminist, "I couldn't understand what she was saying and how it was relevant to me. . . . I kept thinking to myself that she was just talking about women because she didn't have a man and *I* was happily married and didn't have to worry about *that*!" However, Hawley did think about it, she explained, "as I always thought about stuff that Kathie raised for me."

A few months later, Hawley got into a conversation with a couple of other politically minded women "about us, as women." They found the subject as gripping as she did, so in April 1968, she invited a handful of friends to meet at her house on an evening when her husband was out. "We talked about our families, our mothers, our fathers, our siblings; we talked about our men.

. . . For hours we talked . . . and left feeling high." The group met every week through the spring and summer of 1968 and eventually grew to include about twenty women. In June, during a local antiwar conference, Hawley presented a paper on women's oppression.

Hawley, like many other young radicals, had parents who were very concerned about politics. Growing up, she assumed that getting involved in a political group was "just something you did." All through college, when she was heavily committed to the New Left, she felt "that I was working for other people and that my needs were put aside. It really was when Kathie first started talking to me about women's issues that . . . I felt I had reached home."

The Birth of Cell 16

In the summer of 1968, even as Hawley's group was meeting, so was another small band of feminists. Roxanne Dunbar launched the group by placing an ad in an underground newspaper. It announced the formation of "a Female Liberation Front . . . To question: all phallic social structures . . . To Demand: free abortion and birth control on demand—communal raising of children by both sexes and by people of all ages . . ." Though Dunbar, like Hawley, had a New Left background, her ideas on women's issues were much more radical. The group she created, originally called the Female Liberation Front, eventually took the name Cell 16.

Betsy Warrior was a welfare mother when she attended that first meeting of Female Liberation. Warrior had dropped out of high school in tenth grade to work in a factory. A battered wife for seven years, she applied for welfare after her divorce because she had no one to leave her child with while she went out to work. She came to the first meeting of Female Liberation Front "just to see what it was like." There were about eight women present, and Warrior listened with a startled sense of recognition as they put into words many of the ideas about women and men that she herself had had.

The women of the Female Liberation Front got off to a fast start with the two projects they were to become known for. They began to take classes in karate—a decision that grew out of discussions of rape and women's vulnerability—and they started to publish *No More Fun and Games: A Journal of Female Liberation.*

Warrior recalled that she and a friend hawked the early issues of the journal on Harvard Square with three small children in tow. "It was like a circus," she said. The Black Panthers were there and people from New Left groups and local communes, all selling their literature. It was a time and a place open to new ideas; still, many people found those advanced by Female Liberation too extreme to take seriously. Nancy Hawley remembered thinking that "it was one thing to be for women's liberation but another to be against men. . . . So I laughed. . . . But it made an impression." A blunt editorial in the second issue advised women to learn karate for self-defense, to remain single and avoid having children, to give up traditional surnames because they were men's names (a father's, a husband's), and to foreswear make-up and dressing to attract men.

Though the split between politicos and radical feminists was partly over priorities—over whether women should spend their energy attacking the political system or attacking male power—there sometimes seemed to be an undercurrent of fear in the reactions of the politicos. According to Betsy Warrior, the political women "considered us man-haters and weirdos. . . . I think they probably despised and feared us because we were articulating their own doubts." Hawley acknowledged that "it was very personal for many people who were for the first time struggling with issues in their relationships [with men] that hadn't surfaced before."

Exponential Growth

The handful of Boston women who attended the 1968 Thanksgiving conference in Chicago included Hawley, Roxanne Dunbar, and others, and there was friction between Dunbar and some of the others. Hawley also remembered feeling acutely uncomfortable when some participants declared that the nuclear family was a trap for women. She was pregnant and very much aware that this was the first time since her oldest child was born that she'd been away from her family.

Back in Boston, the women (most were politicos) held an open meeting at MIT (the Massachusetts Institute of Technology) to report on what had happened in Chicago. Forty women came and before the evening ended, they decided to meet again a month later. One hundred women turned up the next time; 150 the time after that; and then 200. It was exciting, said Hawley, but also overwhelming, and large meetings didn't satisfy the need most of the women felt to come together in small numbers for intense discussions. Meanwhile, the women who had begun meeting at Hawley's home the previous spring had split into two groups, because two factions had developed—politicos and radical feminists.

In the spring of 1969, some of the women who had been meeting at MIT got together with the Female Liberation Front to hold a conference at Emmanuel College. Unexpectedly, more than 600 people came. Kris Rosenthal, one of the MIT organizers, recalled that the Female Liberation group seemed so militant that some of the other women were afraid they would alienate newcomers. However, the group's karate demonstrations apparently made a deep impression.

A generally snide article in *New York* magazine described the opening karate session this way:

> Abby [Rockefeller] and two fellow Movement women, Jayne West and Dana Densmore, like three pajamaed Statues of Liberty, stomp and punch their way across the Emmanuel College gym in Boston. Zapping the air, they move in unison: a perfect chorus line except for their prison-matron eyes, gritted teeth, clenched fists, and war cries. The unbleached canvas of their Korean peasants' uniforms snaps smartly with each blow. They even bow after the movements.

Later, Rockefeller split a board with her head on the second try. Even the politicos were impressed. According to the radical feminists, karate offered fringe benefits such as physical fitness and self-confidence, but the main point of it was self-defense.

After the conference, many women were eager to join Female Liberation, which had been renamed Cell 16. However, its members were reluctant to expand the group. Because they'd already spent months analyzing women's issues, they were afraid that newcomers might treat them as leaders and that a hierarchy might develop. They believed in radical equality.

The MIT group was also beset with new recruits. Their next meeting drew several hundred women. The enthusiasm was contagious but the numbers, almost unmanageable. There was some danger that the strategic moment would get away from them. That summer, some of the women began to talk about how to organize Boston's growing population of feminists. The discussions dragged on for months. Some, who wanted to build a mass movement, argued that even women who were totally naive about politics might come to see the need for a socialist revolution once they were part of the organization. However, others vehemently rejected the notion of a small, elite, political cadre steering the politics of the masses. They not only disliked hierarchies but were unwilling to create a structure that might one day put power into the hands of some individual or of a small, militant group. (They may have had Cell 16 in mind.)

Nevertheless, it seemed clear that even minimal organization would give feminists more clout. If small groups of women, tackling projects on their own, all said they were from the same organization, that organization would become a power base for everyone, and when any group succeeded, all could share the sense of accomplishment.

Bread and Roses

Bread and Roses was finally founded in September 1969. It was named for a famous strike: In 1912 the women of Lawrence, Massachusetts, struck a textile plant for "bread" (money) and "roses" (a good life). Though the new organization's charter used the phrase "socialist revolutionary," no one made any attempt to define either word. Kris Rosenthal speculated that the group's organizers may have been afraid that if there was a discussion of exactly what "socialist" and "revolutionary" meant, vast differences of opinion would surface.

Bread and Roses was basically a loose network of small collectives. That was the form feminism took in many major cities in the United States and Europe. Nancy Hawley estimated that at one point Boston had more than thirty groups "and new women kept coming and coming." Most of the collectives held weekly meetings, and there was also a weekly mass meeting for everyone. All groups were encouraged to develop their own projects. Thus, over the next few years, women from Bread and Roses took part in antiwar demonstrations and taught courses on auto mechanics; some wrote and produced feminist plays, while others met with suburban housewives who called the Bread and Roses office to ask if someone would come and tell them about women's liberation. Periodically, there were zap actions—for instance, when a local radio station, in asking for volunteers, mentioned that it could use some "chicks" to do typing, feminists called on the manager and dumped live baby chicks on his desk in the name of Bread and Roses.

Most new members were recruited at orientation sessions, which were held one evening a week at a coffeehouse. By that time, consciousness-raising had been invented in New York (more about that later), so C-R groups were formed on the spot for those who were interested. Eventually, these groups were expected to vote on whether to join Bread and Roses. "Some of them decided to, in which case they got on the telephone tree," said Jane Mansbridge, one of the organizers, "and some of them decided not to. In that case, the individual members of the group could still attend meetings." Mansbridge remembered the telephone tree as "some pieces of paper"—phone numbers used to make contact with the various groups. It wasn't the most efficient system in the world. Mansbridge noted that "none of the organization really worked. . . . But for all of us, there was this sense of creating brand-new things."

During the early 1970s, many of the politicos came to agree with the radical feminists' basic analysis of patriarchal power, and the conflicts between socialist and radical feminists petered out. However, the factions still had different priorities. Many politicos became involved in the campaigns for day care and for abortion rights. They also tackled the labor movement and founded women's unions around the country. For a few years, the unions flourished, but in the midseventies, leftist sects attacked more than twenty of them. Determined to pull women back into the class struggle, the leftists joined some unions and then almost literally talked them to death with endless arguments about the correct political line. The sects also destroyed some women's liberation groups and women's centers (chapter 8).

Probably, the politicos' most significant achievement was their contribution to nonsexist education. In some cities, they taught classes and organized whole schools for adults that offered courses in everything from karate to women's history; many activists eventually became academics and pioneered women's studies on college campuses.

THE INVENTION OF CONSCIOUSNESS-RAISING

Radical feminists owed many of the insights that were their hallmark to consciousness-raising sessions. C-R, as it came to be called, was developed in 1968 by New York Radical Women. An organizing tactic that would shape the movement for years to come, it was at first scorned by many politicos and the women of NOW.

Kathie Sarachild recalled that Ann Forer, a member of NYRW, first spoke of the need to raise consciousness during a meeting shortly after the group was founded. To explain what she meant, she began to talk about how her own thinking had changed—and her consciousness had been raised—as she considered the pressure on women to be attractive to men. Sarachild recalled:

> . . . I just sat there listening to her describe all the false ways women have to act: playing dumb, always being agreeable, always being nice, not to mention what we had to do to our bodies with the clothes and shoes we wore, the diets we had to go through, going blind not wearing glasses, all because men didn't find our real selves, our human freedom, our basic humanity "attractive." And I realized I still could learn a lot about how to understand and describe the particular oppression of women in ways that could reach other women in the way this had just reached me. The whole group was moved as I was, and we decided on the spot that what we needed—in the words Ann used—was to "raise our consciousness some more."

Sarachild saw C-R as a way to start a mass movement for women's liberation. She recalled that politicos initially worried that it would turn women against men, while NOW members felt that it substituted talk for action. In fact, C-R led directly to two of the most effective actions feminists ever staged: The discussions on attractiveness inspired the famous Miss America protest, and an emotional session on abortion prompted the first speakout, where women testified in public about their own experiences.

In the late 1960s and early 70s, thousands of C-R groups formed around the country. The women who joined them found that consciousness-raising challenged many of their basic assumptions about themselves and their relations to men. The gurus of the New Left, especially Frantz Fanon, had described the way people internalized their own oppression by buying into the stereotypes created by the larger society. Because they believed in their own inferiority, it didn't occur to them to challenge the system. For example, women who believed that females really were less capable than males were unlikely to become feminists. Consciousness-raising was a powerful way to change such beliefs. As women talked in small, homogeneous groups about various issues, they discovered that problems they'd thought were theirs alone were shared by all—and created by the male-dominated culture.* However, Sarachild and others in NYRW had

---

* C-R groups discussed such topics as the lessons girls learned from their parents about a woman's proper role, what various religions had to say about women, and so on.

believed that C-R should do much more. Their idea was that, as women came to understand that their problems had political and social origins and couldn't be solved by individual action, they would move on to consider what kind of collective, political action to take. If C-R didn't lead to collective action, it was simply a form of therapy, aimed at changing women themselves rather than at changing society.

In the end, consciousness-raising drew thousands of women into the movement. Within a very few years, most of its critics had embraced it enthusiastically.

THE FIRST SPEAKOUT

The idea of holding "speakouts" also grew out of consciousness-raising. In 1968, during a C-R session, several NYRW women talked about their abortions. Most had never told their stories to anyone before, except perhaps to a few close friends, because abortion was a crime almost everywhere (except in certain circumstances, such as when the woman's life was in danger). The open discussion had a tremendous impact on everyone present and suggested to some that public testimonials might be an effective way to arouse support for the repeal of restrictive abortion laws.

Early in 1969, some women, including Kathie Sarachild, founded Redstockings.* They intended it to be a radical feminist action group under the umbrella of NYRW, and for their first major action, they targeted a legislative hearing on abortion reform. An all-male committee of the New York legislature had invited fifteen "expert" witnesses to testify—fourteen men and a nun. A few minutes after the hearing began, Sarachild stood up and demanded a chance to speak, on the grounds that women who had had illegal abortions were the only true experts on the subject. Predictably, the committee refused to listen.

Balked only temporarily, Redstockings organized the first speakout a month later. At a public meeting held in a church, twelve women described their own abortions to an audience of over 300. One told of paying $900 for an illegal operation. Another recalled that she applied to ten hospitals before she found one willing to give her an abortion—provided she'd agree to be

---

* The name Redstockings was a synthesis: It mixed "the red of revolution" with *Bluestockings,* a derogatory name given to some first-wave feminists.

sterilized at the same time; she was then twenty years old. Afterward, women in the audience stood up and told their own stories. The abortion speakout became the model for speakouts on other sensitive subjects, such as rape, sexual harassment, and incest. Each exposed unfair laws and misogynist attitudes.

RADICAL FEMINISM, IN THEORY

During the late 1960s, radical feminists plunged into print to challenge many basic assumptions about women. They focused on the family, the division of labor within the home, and sexual relations between women and men, pointing out that all of these areas were organized so that males could dominate females. Some of the earliest expressions of radical feminism were collected in *Notes From the First Year*, published by NYWR in 1968. Together with *No More Fun and Games* and the Florida paper, *Notes* broke new ground.

Critics, including politicos, said the issues radical feminists raised were trivial and personal; the radical feminists replied that the personal *was* political, because it helped to maintain a power structure based on gender, and because to do anything about it, women must organize. The insights of radical feminism ultimately brought thousands of new recruits into the movement. However, their major theories were hotly disputed at first by other feminists.

Radical feminists took on the institution of marriage, both in what they wrote and with public protests. Ti-Grace Atkinson concluded that love was "the psychological pivot in the persecution of women" and that marriage must be destroyed. On September 23, 1969, her group, The Feminists, made headlines by invading the New York City marriage license bureau armed with leaflets and accompanied by the press. They recommended eliminating marriage and raising children communally. Meanwhile, some activists took new surnames, rejecting the patriarchal tradition by which a woman bore her father's name until she married and her husband's after that.* However, not all radical feminists were antimarriage. The "pro-woman" faction within Redstockings maintained that the real problem was male supremacy within the family—that was what had to be changed.

* Kathie Sarachild, who was originally Kathie Amatniek, invented her own matrilineal surname during the 1968 Thanksgiving meeting. Because her mother's name was Sara, she hitched "child" onto that to become Kathie Sarachild—child of Sara.

Radical feminists also challenged people's assumptions about sex itself. Anne Koedt's radical feminist classic, "The Myth of the Vaginal Orgasm," created a furor. In it, Koedt disputed the common belief that all normal, mature women had vaginal orgasms and that a woman who needed clitoral stimulation to have an orgasm was frigid. "There is only one area for sexual climax . . . the clitoris," Koedt wrote. "All orgasms are extensions of sensations from this area. . . . this leads to some interesting questions about conventional sex and our role in it. Men have orgasms essentially by friction with the vagina, not the clitoral area. . . . Women have thus been defined sexually in terms of what pleases men. . . ." Liberal feminists and many of the socialists were embarrassed, even appalled, by this emphasis on sex. Betty Friedan insisted that "the point is not to focus on the kinds of sexual orgasm, but on the basic human relations that need to be changed." However, for some women, Koedt's insights were a revelation.

One of the most basic issues radical feminists addressed was the question: If women are oppressed, who or what is oppressing them? As noted earlier, some blamed men—for instance, Beverly Jones and Judith Brown argued in the Florida paper that all men benefit from "the male mystique" and that each man "rests his ego in some measure on the basic common denominator, being a man." However, other radical feminists, including Kate Millett, author of *Sexual Politics*, blamed sex roles instead. According to the sex-roles theory, which surfaced in Sweden in the early 1960s, both women and men were trained from birth to behave in particular sex-stereotyped ways, and men were as damaged by this training as women were. Many liberal feminists and politicos adopted this explanation.

In naming the oppressor, feminist groups often defined the kind of action they were likely to take. Thus, during the 1970s liberal NOW sponsored men's consciousness-raising groups in the hope of re-educating men. Many of the radical feminists felt it was a lost cause, because males weren't likely to give up their power and status willingly. Reforming men was "a little too much like the chickens trying to educate the chicken farmer," as novelist Marge Piercy put it.

Many radical feminists believed that male supremacy was the earliest form of oppression and the root of all other forms, including racism; thus, sexism must be tackled first. This theory thoroughly alienated many women of color.

How did men come to be the dominant sex? According to Ti-

Grace Atkinson, they got the upper hand because women had the burden of reproduction and men "had the wit to take advantage of that. . . ." In her 1970 book, *The Dialectic of Sex*, Shulamith Firestone said much the same thing: "The heart of woman's oppression is her childbearing and child-rearing roles." Pursuing the argument to its logical conclusion, Firestone insisted that women must be freed from "the tyranny of their reproductive biology by every means available. . . ."* However, biological explanations for male dominance were almost a form of heresy to most activists, including many radical feminists. During the early years of the second wave, both branches of the movement were committed to equality feminism. Intent on undermining sex stereotypes, feminists denied that there were any truly significant differences between women and men.

If women were oppressed, why didn't more of them *feel* oppressed? Some radical feminists argued that females were brainwashed into believing that women were inferior and that men were meant to dominate. Parents, the media, the whole culture, conspired to deliver the message. However, the socialization theory didn't convince everyone, and Redstockings were divided on the issue. Some members believed in the importance of brainwashing, but others (the "pro-woman" faction) argued that most women tolerated their subordinate role because of "continual, daily pressure from men. We do not need to change ourselves, but to change men." The pro-woman group was determined to focus on what men did to keep women down and on organizing to fight that, rather than on what women must do to change their thinking, which they saw as a form of "blame the victim." They were also afraid the brainwashing argument would be used against women, who might be refused jobs, for example, on the grounds that they weren't aggressive enough, because they'd been brainwashed to fit the traditional feminine role.

From the outset, women's liberation groups were often torn by conflict. The battles over theory and tactics were painful for the women involved and sometimes damaging to the movement. Even activists who believed that feminism must include many different points of view often lost sight of that fact in the heat of the moment, as they struggled to reach agreement on a theory or a course of action.

---

* In the 1980s, when medical researchers began to move reproduction out of the body into the lab, many feminists called it a new form of tyranny.

In retrospect, it's clear that the second wave needed all of its various factions, from the radical to the relatively conservative, for feminists tackled an incredible spectrum of issues. A social movement that's too cautious, afraid to work outside established channels, has a very limited impact; one that's too radical—that uses revolutionary tactics to pursue revolutionary goals—unites the opposition and is almost certain to be crushed. A movement that includes both extremes and many groups in between has the best chance. From the late sixties on, the second wave was highly diversified, and that was one of its strengths.

chapter 5

Experiments in Radical Equality

$\diagup\!\!\!\diagup$

Many things separated women's liberationists from liberal feminists. The women generally came from different generations, had cut their teeth politically under different circumstances, and their priorities were seldom the same. Nevertheless, it may have been as much style as substance that made them incompatible. Liberal groups were organized along traditional, hierarchical lines: Members elected officers, voted on major decisions, and large meetings always had a chairperson. Most women's liberation groups, on the other hand, were determined to operate without leaders and to arrive at decisions by consensus.

The commitment to radical equality that was characteristic of women's liberation was carried to harmful extremes in some groups. However, when it worked, it generated such a powerful experience that eventually it influenced liberal feminists as well. Ideas that had originated with Ella Baker in SNCC, although much modified, were still part of the *zeitgeist* of the movement in 1990. It is important, therefore, to understand why women's liberation groups insisted on radical equality in the first place, how it went wrong, and why the basic principles survived in spite of that.

WHY RADICAL EQUALITY?

In the 1960s, young people all over the United States and Western Europe got together to form left-wing collectives run in a highly egalitarian fashion. They established free schools, health clinics, law communes, underground newspapers, food co-ops, and women's centers, as well as activist political groups.

In the United States, SNCC was the model for radical equality for many Movement people, but the SDS also made "participatory democracy" a central tenet. The founders of the SDS believed that people must have a direct say in the decisions that affected their lives—must be allowed to cast their own votes rather than merely choosing representatives to decide things for them, because even democratically elected hierarchies couldn't be trusted.

Most middle-aged Americans couldn't understand what made radical equality so appealing. Political scientist Jane Mansbridge suggested that the idea gripped the young because many of them felt powerless to affect the course of their own lives. The institutions that controlled society hadn't responded to their demands, and they believed that liberal democracy had failed them. Actually, some people have experimented with participatory democracy in almost every era, according to Mansbridge. Probably the oldest form of human organization, it's a fundamental element in everyone's experience because friendships operate on the same general principles. Friends treat each other as equals, establish no hierarchies, and seldom vote on decisions because a formal vote would only call attention to divisions within the group and might deepen them.

For feminists and others, group experiments with radical equality served several purposes. They were convinced that meaningful change had to begin on the personal level. In addition, when it worked well, radical equality created a close-knit, supportive group; alienated as they were from the mainstream, many activists needed that sense of support.

EARLY EXPERIMENTS

Women's liberationists invented their own versions of radical equality in the late sixties and early seventies. Once again, some of the most creative thinking and some of the hottest conflicts occurred in women's liberation groups in New York City. Their history illustrates the promise and the problems of attempting to create, in microcosm, an utterly just society.

The problems first surfaced irrepressibly late in 1968 in—of all places—the New York chapter of NOW, a bastion of liberal feminism. NOW-New York, the organization's largest and most vigorous chapter, had more than 300 members, who governed themselves according to a traditional hierarchical structure. Day-to-day decisions were made by an executive board that consisted of elected officers and committee heads; it met once a week. The general membership gathered once a month for meetings that sometimes drew 200 women.

Beginning in about August 1968, there were heated conflicts within the chapter. Muriel Fox, a board member, recalled that "for a while there, nobody dared miss the weekly board meeting because there might be a vote to do something that they didn't believe in." At the center of the most significant controversy was Ti-Grace Atkinson, who had been elected president of NOW-New York in December 1967. At the time, Atkinson was a graduate student at Columbia University. A contemporary news report spoke of her "dreamy, softly sexy style," and Betty Friedan later recalled her own first impression: "[Ti-Grace's] Main Line accent and ladylike blond good looks would be perfect, I thought, for raising money from those mythical rich old widows we never did unearth." Instead, Atkinson was to become famous as one of the most militant of the new American feminists—but before that, she tried hard to push NOW into a more radical stance.

As a graduate student on a campus with a high-profile SDS chapter, Atkinson had become a convert to participatory democracy. Convinced it would be good for NOW, she proposed to the national board that instead of electing officers, NOW chapters should hold lotteries at frequent intervals and allow members to draw lots for the leadership positions. To no one's surprise, the board turned down the proposal. Betty Friedan pointed out that if leaders were selected by lot, members would have no way to hold them accountable. They could do exactly as they pleased, knowing that their post would pass to someone else anyway in a very short time.

Atkinson admitted defeat at the national level but pressed for a restructuring of the New York chapter. Matters came to a head at a general membership meeting on October 17, 1968, when the faction led by Atkinson attempted to revise the chapter's bylaws so that its offices would be filled on a rotation basis. Jean Faust, the first president of the chapter, recalled that during the debate on the proposal, "the dissident group claimed that all women were equally talented and should have equal opportunities to hold leadership positions." What they didn't understand, said Faust, was that the chapter needed to have some people who would assume daily, continuing responsibility for the work of the organization.

The proposal was defeated, and Atkinson resigned from NOW and went on to found The Feminists, a new, radical feminist group. Over the next few years, they became famous for their stand on issues such as marriage and for a lottery system that resembled the one NOW had spurned. On a regular basis, The Feminists rotated positions that were part of a formal hierarchy in most organizations—for example, at each meeting they drew lots for the job of chairing the meeting. In addition, tasks were assigned by lot, and members who already had desirable skills— they'd done speechwriting, for example—were actually requested not to put their names in the pool for those assignments but to be ready to help when asked. Obviously, this system sacrificed efficiency, but it did help some members develop new abilities. Many women had never before had a chance to chair a meeting, write a speech or press release, or in general find out what they might be capable of.

At the heart of the lottery system was a deep suspicion of leadership itself and of anyone who had power over others. As Atkinson put it in her letter of resignation from NOW, "We want to get rid of the positions of power, not get up into those positions . . . the power relationships we have among ourselves are a good indication of what we *really* want in the world at large."

As the women's liberation movement evolved, many feminists became convinced that it was simply natural for women to operate without hierarchies—without "power trips." They pointed out that females were brought up to handle relationships very differently than males, with more emphasis on cooperation and much less on competing and oneupmanship.* Even liberal feminists liked that idea, and it became widely accepted within the movement that feminists should play down hierarchies.

TRASHING: THE MOVEMENT'S "McCARTHY ERA"

Radical equality turned out to be a mixed blessing for women's liberation. Groups that functioned without a hierarchy often generated an intense feeling of community, an almost ecstatic closeness. The leaderless format was especially good for consciousness-raising groups, and the intensity of the experience was partly responsible for the enormous impact they had on their members. However, some women's liberation groups became preoccupied with internal issues of power and carried their aversion to hierarchies to extremes. Women who stood out from the rest for any reason were accused of elitism and "trashed." Within the movement, the period from 1969 to 1971 became known as feminism's "McCarthy era" because of the dogmatism of some groups.

Trashing was a form of character assassination, an attack on a woman's personality, motives, or commitment to the cause. Sometimes those trashed were activists with strong personalities, who were charged with behaving like "male heavies"—in other words, with trying to dominate a meeting or a group. In other cases, so-called "media stars" were trashed for elitism. Women who wrote articles on the movement and had them published or had feminist plays produced were apt to be attacked as opportunists who had risen to prominence on the backs of their sisters.

Because many women's liberation groups refused to identify any of their members as leaders, that left reporters free to make their own selection, and—especially in New York—the media zeroed in on a few charismatic personalities. These women appeared on television talk shows, were interviewed by the press—and were often fiercely resented by other feminists. Author Kate Millett noted that the movement sent "double signals: you absolutely must preach at our panel, star at our conference—implying, fink if you don't . . . and at the same time laying down a wonderfully uptight line about elitism."

* In the 1980s, the idea that women had a different, more egalitarian management style turned up in books written for the business community.

Though resentment of the media stars was partly motivated by envy, there was also a group ethic involved. Well aware that some people had had more advantages than others, many women's liberationists assumed that if all women just had equal opportunities, all would be equal in ability. Sometimes it worked that way, and women who had never had much self-confidence were transformed. A member of Jane, a Chicago abortion collective, talking about the impact the experience had on her, explained that "I can do things that I never felt I could do. . . . All that crap about how you have to be an expert . . . it's just a ruse to make you feel incompetent in your own life." Many young people saw expertise as one more way of maintaining the old hierarchies. This resulted, at times, in narrow-minded anti-intellectualism (in China, it resulted in the Cultural Revolution).

Many groups, determined to ensure absolute equality, used the methods pioneered by The Feminists in allotting menial tasks and more important responsibilities. They assumed that everyone could, and should, do a little of everything. Though this sometimes worked nicely, at times the principle was carried to extremes. Robin Morgan worked on the New Left newspaper *Rat* during a period when it was being produced by a women's collective. A published poet, she readily agreed when the collective decided it would be elitist for any member to sign her name to what she'd written. Later, accused of writing in a style that was still identifiably hers, Morgan actually tried to "worsen" her writing. She even acquiesced when asked not to write at all but to stick to proofreading and other, more mundane tasks to give others a chance. However, after about a month of that, she quit the paper because, as she put it, "something cracked open inside me. . . ."

Why Trashing Occurred

Few feminists understood that in trying to function without a hierarchy, they were tackling something very difficult. As political scientist Jo Freeman pointed out, despite the best intentions, virtually every group eventually developed its own *informal*, invisible power structure. Many were dominated by a handful of close friends. At meetings they listened to one another more attentively, interrupted less often, and backed up one another's arguments. Between meetings, they got together to discuss issues and activities and share information. Other members who found themselves locked out of the inner circle were baffled and frustrated. When, as sometimes happened, it was the working-class women who wound up on the outside, class differences became another divisive issue.

Some women undoubtedly expected too much. They were drawn into the movement by the talk of "sisterhood" and the promise that here, at least, there would be no hierarchies. Author Susan Brownmiller, a key figure in women's liberation circles in New York, explained that "they were horrified and hurt to discover that even within the women's movement we weren't all equal, that some people suddenly were on television . . . that some had articles printed." It seemed that they had landed at the bottom of yet another heap, but this time their anger was fueled (and legitimated) by the belief that in a women's group there should be no elite.

Why was there so much free-floating hostility in the movement? Some of the anger was misdirected frustration. As Jo Freeman said, "Trying to change an entire society is a very slow . . . process in which gains are incremental, rewards diffuse, and setbacks frequent." The outrage that many activists felt needed an outlet, and other women were more available as targets than men were. Feminist attorney Flo Kennedy described the result as "horizontal hostilities."

In the early 1970s, according to Brownmiller, "The antileadership thing . . . took up more energy than anything." Some women's liberation groups were undermined by their own authoritarianism and the practice of trashing.

THE "OUR BODIES, OURSELVES" COLLECTIVE

Radical equality was definitely not an unmitigated disaster, however. Long after most women's liberation groups had faded from the scene, feminist collectives kept forming. Many found ways to apply the principles of equality less rigidly and thrived as a result. The Boston Women's Health Book Collective is perhaps the best example. It was twenty years old in 1990, and continues to be one of the most influential advocates for women's health in the country. Especially in the early years, members were often invited to talk to other feminists about how to work effectively as a collective.

The Boston group grew out of a workshop that Nancy Hawley presented during the women's liberation conference at Emmanuel College in the spring of 1969. Her subject, women's health, aroused so much interest that some participants began to meet regularly to discuss it. Ultimately, they decided to do research on health issues and pass the information on to other women. In 1970, at the collective's expense, the New England Free Press published the newsprint booklet that would ultimately become the best-selling *Our Bodies, Ourselves*. In a fresh, unpretentious way, it combined medical information with vignettes of women's personal experiences. The subjects it covered ran the gamut from sexuality, venereal disease, and pregnancy to "Women, Medicine, and Capitalism." Though the book was never advertised, it sold more than 200,000 copies over the next few years. As the money began to come in, the New England Free Press reduced the price of the first printing from 75 cents to 30 cents so that it could reach more women.

During the summer and fall of 1971, New York publishing houses began courting the group, and that initiated a difficult decision-making process. The book would reach many more women if it were published commercially, but the price would inevitably go up so that poor women could no longer afford it. In the end, the collective decided to accept the publisher's offer but with several stipulations. They agreed among themselves that all the money earned as royalties would be used to support health education projects for women; and they had clauses written into their book contract that set a ceiling on the book's price and allowed a 70 percent discount for clinics or other nonprofit organizations involved in women's health counseling. In 1972, the collective incorporated—it had to, in order to sign the contract. At the same time, it closed its ranks to outsiders, freezing its size for almost a decade at twelve members.

Our Bodies, Ourselves was published by Simon and Schuster in 1973, and over the next seventeen years sold more than three million copies in English and eleven other languages. To the women of the collective, the money was a responsibility. Judy Norsigian, a member of the group, recalled that "we started giving money to other women's health projects—we saw ourselves as a mini-foundation."

Over the years, the women of the collective remained committed to the principles of radical equality. Though small decisions were left to subgroups responsible for particular tasks, the big ones were still made by consensus at the weekly meeting of the whole collective. Vilunya Diskin, a member, explained:

"On any issue that we have to decide, we've always gone around the circle, with everyone saying their feelings and ideas.

You get in the habit of listening. Many, many times, I've been in the group and had my opinion, and couldn't wait to tell it to everyone—and then changed my mind three times as I waited for it to be my turn. It makes you understand how you can look at the same issue in many different ways."

Sometimes, if several people were against something everyone else favored, the discussion continued until all felt they could "live with" the majority decision. Sometimes, if those in the minority felt very strongly, the rest agreed to go along with them. Sometimes, the matter was shelved for a week or so, to give everyone a chance to mull it over. And once in a long while, when the decision-making process dragged on for too long, the group agreed—by consensus—to put the matter to a vote. In the aftermath of a particularly difficult decision, the members occasionally felt burned-out for a while. According to Norsigian, decision by consensus took longer, "but when you're done, you have much more support in the group for the decision that was made." Consensus also tended to wring all pertinent information from the group. Diskin added that "with practice, you get adept at it."

Hawley recalled that it was hard in the beginning to believe that conflict over issues would lead to something good, that it wasn't going to become trashing. She said, "At different points in our history, we pushed things under the rug because we didn't know how to handle them. There have been a couple of striking times when that didn't happen and I think we grew enormously from those times."

Leadership was the issue on one of those occasions. In the early years, Hawley did more work than anyone else, and for a time she more or less led the group—for instance, at meetings she was the one most likely to win others over to her point of view. Finally, someone challenged her. In the ensuing discussion, Hawley realized that she was ready to pull back and let others take the lead, and the others came to understand that if they wanted more influence in the group, there was a way to get it. Diskin said, "In a structureless group, the way you get power is to do work. The more you do, the more powerful you become. . . . Power isn't finite, either. There's plenty to go around. You want more power, you think of another project."

In the beginning the women assumed, as other feminists did, that everyone should do all jobs and that—given the chance—all could probably do them equally well. Hawley said, "We weren't acknowledging the fact that some people preferred certain jobs, or that some people were better able to exert leadership and more interested in doing that. . . . Over time we recognized all that."

At first, the members weren't paid for work they did, but eventually they rejected "volunteerism," as other feminists were doing. From that point on, some worked for the collective and others had outside jobs, and everyone was paid by the hour when they worked on group projects. Because there was no hierarchy and all were paid at the same rate, there was little incentive to compete and every reason to help one another out. Though there was no way to fire someone who wasn't doing her share (a major stumbling block for some other feminist collectives), that became a problem only on a few occasions.

Looking back, members of the collective identified three major factors that kept the group together over the years. Hawley mentioned "the richness of the connection between us. We've not only worked together but held one another's hands through divorces, new marriages, babies, operations." Norsigian cited the fact that "we produced something that generated money, which we therefore had a responsibility for." The third factor was that the group was unusually homogeneous. All the members were white and college-educated and most came from a strong ethnic background where families were important. The collective became a kind of extended family for them.

In addition, the collective stayed flexible—the women didn't insist that every single decision had to be made by consensus, for example—and it stayed small. In a large group, decision by consensus can become unbearably time-consuming.

FEMINIST UTOPIAS

The ideal of radical equality took root in the women's movement to a degree that it never had in the New Left. As Jane Mansbridge said, women were good at relationships—usually, better than men. Many women's liberationists believed that if they could learn to work together effectively in their own group without a hierarchy, they could use what they'd learned to change the outside world.

"Unfortunately, the experience wasn't transferable," said Charlotte Bunch. In 1973, she was one of a group of Washington feminists who founded a journal called *Quest: A Feminist Quarterly*. Over a period of years, the women experimented with group structure. They were determined to be nonauthoritarian, yet, unlike many collectives, they wanted to encourage individual leadership and believed that some responsibilities couldn't be shared. Thus, they practiced "horizontal leadership." Tasks and responsibilities were clearly defined, but every staffer handled both creative and mundane tasks in her own area, so that no one got only the best or worst jobs. Unusual financial arrangements increased the sense of sharing. Members with well-paid jobs in the outside world tithed—they made monthly contributions to support the journal, each deciding for herself how much she would give. Some others with less earning ability actually worked for *Quest* and were paid salaries. As the women saw it, some people gave more money, while others gave more time, and they were all partners in the venture.

Quest's core group stayed together for almost five years. They began to disperse in 1978, not because of conflicts within the group, but because some members wanted to move on to other projects. The publication survived until 1982. The big disappointment for the founders was that "we didn't know how to transfer what we had to other people," said Bunch. The group originally intended to form a national organization based on the egalitarian principles they developed. That never happened. Other feminists, too, found that there was no way to translate the models they'd created in microcosm to the outside world. "All the same," said Bunch, "I think the collectives were enormously important in the lives of the people involved . . . because they carried into the world the principles and values they developed there." As individuals, working in universities or corporations, many feminists tried to share perks and power more evenly and made a point of acknowledging that other people's work was important, no matter what their position.

The second wave of feminism was about power: not only about how it was distributed in society, but how it might be used differently. Traditionally, those high on the ladder of hierarchy used their power to control what others did and were admired for it. In the women's movement, what many activists valued was the ability to *empower* others—to find out what their needs and hopes were and work together toward mutual goals. That became the feminist ethic for women's liberationists and liberal feminists alike. As with any ethic, it sometimes received only lip service.

Throughout the 1980s, small feminist groups still operated—almost automatically now—in a roughly egalitarian fashion. Women who achieved positions of authority often chose to orga-

nize their staff in a kind of flattened hierarchy that spread responsibility around. Meanwhile, under pressure from feminists of
color, many activists were beginning to look at power from a
different angle. Instead of focusing on relationships that set one
individual above another, they were looking at systems of domination that put one group above another—men over women,
whites over people of color, heterosexuals over gays, and so on.
The basic problem, they now argued, was the ideology of domination, which assumed that such hierarchies were natural and
inevitable.

chapter 6

The Media and the Movement

Social movements need press coverage. That's how they get their message out to the general public. Though the mass media were, for the most part, hostile to feminism, they made its boom years possible. Starting in 1969, they lavished attention on women's liberation groups until there was hardly an American who hadn't heard of the movement. As a result, thousands of women joined feminist groups, tried consciousness-raising, and turned out for rallies and demonstrations.

However, the media had other, more ambiguous effects as well. When they discovered the movement in 1969, they initially spotlighted the most colorful of the radical feminists because they were "good copy." As those women became old news, and as some feminist ideas were accepted by the public, the press reduced its coverage of the women's movement and in addition reporters began to seek out liberal feminists when they needed someone to speak for the movement. In the process, they "de-radicalized" the second wave, at least as far as the public was concerned.

Meanwhile, feminists had begun a long struggle to reform the media: to improve the way the press covered the movement, to undercut the sex stereotypes it perpetuated, and to end the sex discrimination that trapped women employed by the media in dead-end jobs. To a degree, these efforts were successful.

HOW THE MEDIA AFFECTED THE MOVEMENT

From the beginning, feminists found allies in the media—generally, other women. However, the decision-making power was almost always in the hands of white males, and they reacted to the women's movement much as they responded to any protest movement that seemed to threaten the status quo: with hostility that gradually gave way to a grudging, partial acceptance when it became obvious that many feminist goals had significant public support.

The women of NOW were media experts, and between 1966 and 1969 they were able to generate press coverage despite the fact that at the time NOW was a very small organization. However, the coverage was modest and sporadic—for instance, as early legal victories chipped away at the protective labor laws, the New York Times generally reported landmark cases in a paragraph or two, buried on an inside page.

With the Miss America protest in September 1968, feminism suddenly burst into the headlines. The demonstration against the annual beauty pageant was spearheaded by New York Radical Women. It brought out almost 200 activists, who assembled on the boardwalk in Atlantic City to protest the fact that "women in our society [are] forced daily to compete for male approval, enslaved by ludicrous 'beauty' standards. . . ." The protestors crowned a live sheep Miss America, to make the point that contestants were being judged like animals at a county fair. They also tossed curlers, girdles, high-heeled shoes, women's magazines, and the odd brassiere into a "freedom trash can," thus symbolically rejecting woman's status as a sex object. Though the press reported that the demonstrators had burned their bras, in fact, no one lit a match to the trash can—America's most famous bonfire was strictly a media invention.

The result was a mixed blessing: feminists were derided as "bra burners" from that time on, but on the other hand, newspapers around the country did cover the protest, and many women began to think about what it meant to be a sex object. By 1968, the media and the public had both become blasé about demonstrations. Earlier that year, when the Jeannette Rankin Brigade descended on Washington for an antiwar protest, the press paid scant attention because—as a *New York Times* editor explained it —no one expected violence. Apparently, it took violence—or an approach that seemed both fresh and funny—to get into the newspapers.

In 1969, women's liberationists made the headlines regularly. Their tactics were often outrageous, their ideas, startling. The real "press blitz" began in the fall. Over the next six months or so, virtually every major magazine, from *Life* to *Playboy*, ran a cover story on the new feminism, and the television networks offered "specials" as well. Some of the magazine pieces were personal conversion stories, written by women who started out hostile to the movement and became converts to the cause in the course of researching their article. Under the impact of all the media attention, over the next few years feminist groups grew exponentially. In NOW alone, membership rocketed from 3000 in 1970 to over 50,000 in 1974.

There are circumstances in which any publicity is good publicity, and going strictly by the numbers, that seemed to be true for the women's movement. However, some liberal activists were appalled because the media often portrayed feminists as a kind of lunatic fringe; the liberals blamed the women's liberationists.

It was true that many reporters, alert for excuses to ridicule feminism, focused on radical activists. When covering a demonstration, they homed in on the revolutionaries in the group, eager to quote their most extreme statements. Television talk shows also featured militants. Journalist Gloria Steinem once noted that "I personally have seen memos directing talent bookers for the Johnny Carson and David Frost shows to 'get the nuts.'" In most cases the "nuts" were radical feminists, with their controversial focus on personal issues, including sex.

Press coverage was also condescending. Print reporters, interviewing activists, seldom failed to note what they were wearing and how "feminine" or "unfeminine" they were. In writing about *any* woman, journalists routinely defined her in terms of traditional female roles, noting whether she was a wife, mother, or grandmother.* Reporters also provided physical descriptions of women, though they seldom did of men. In 1971, a New York newspaper wrote of Judge Mildred Loree Lillie, "In her mid-50s,

* The press often thought it worth mentioning that Golda Meir, the Israeli prime minister, was a grandmother, but it never seemed to occur to them to describe Georges Pompidou, the French premier, as a grandfather.

she still has a bathing beauty figure." Judge Lillie made the news as a possible nominee for the Supreme Court.

Many editors were openly hostile to the movement. One reporter was told to "find an authority who'll say this is all a crock of shit." Such attitudes reflected more than just male chauvinism. The media played a stabilizing role in American society and they were usually leery of social movements. Civil rights and New Left activists also went through periods when they were virtually ignored by the press, and at other times had to watch while reporters singled out radicals and turned their most extreme statements into headlines.

Most activists were aware that the mass media offered the best chance to reach women outside the movement. However, some women's liberation groups wanted nothing to do with the press because they'd seen the kind of hostile coverage New Left groups often got. They barred the press from meetings and refused to be interviewed. Reporters had their notes snatched, their microphones smashed, their film stolen. On occasion, male reporters were thrown out of meetings by squads of women eager to use their karate training. At the beginning of 1970, feminist sympathizers among the press complained that some militants were making it impossible for them to cover movement news.

Nevertheless, they kept trying. Political scientist Jo Freeman noted that, for journalists, "There was something intriguing about the very difficulty of covering the new movement. Further, the idea that *men* were being excluded from something . . . generated much more interest than women normally get." In addition, because many women's liberation groups refused to talk to male reporters, editors were forced to assign women to cover the movement. As a result, some women finally escaped the ghetto of the women's page.

Many American women were undoubtedly turned off by news stories and articles about "militant man-haters." However, others apparently read between the lines, because the movement kept on growing.

HOW THE MOVEMENT AFFECTED THE MEDIA

Even as the second wave exploded into the public consciousness, thanks to the press, feminists were beginning to challenge the media, for in the interplay between movement and media, women were partners in the dance. Beginning early in 1970, groups and coalitions all over the country began to take on local newspapers, magazines, television and radio stations, determined both to end sex stereotyping and to improve the way they treated women employees.

Many activists saw stereotyping as a major problem. They were convinced that the images of women purveyed by the media not only lowered the self-esteem of every woman who believed in them, but restricted the opportunities of all women because most Americans evidently accepted them without a second thought. In the late 1960s, at a time when 42 percent of all women had jobs, the women's page in most newspapers was devoted to society news and household hints. Magazine fiction, TV dramas, and commercials virtually always presented women as full-time housewives. In fact, on television, women were nearly invisible.* They were rarely seen on newscasts—as reporters or as newsmakers—and on evening dramas and comedies, the leading characters were male almost three quarters of the time.

Sometimes feminists used civil rights laws to go after what they wanted; sometimes they resorted to civil disobedience. A single week in March 1970 saw major actions of both types. On March 16, *Newsweek* magazine appeared on the newsstands with a cover story on feminism; the same day, forty-six women who worked for *Newsweek*—practically every woman on the professional staff —held a press conference to announce that they had filed sex-discrimination charges against the magazine. Three days later, on March 19, over a hundred women invaded the *Ladies' Home Journal* and staged an eleven-hour sit-in. In different ways, each action kicked off major changes.

The Newsweek Confrontation

The women of *Newsweek* had long been indignant over the fact that the magazine hired women as researchers but rarely promoted them to jobs as reporters, writers, or editors. The cover story on the women's movement brought matters to a head. Assistant editor Lynn Young, one of the privileged few not trapped in the researcher slot, was originally assigned to write it, but her piece was rejected by male editors, who claimed it wasn't objective enough. Over a period of several months, the story was rewritten a number of times, at one point by a male staffer at the urging of a male editor, who insisted that only a man could por-

---

* Women and men of color were even less visible on TV than white women.

tray "the ludicrous soul of this story." Finally, the assignment was given to a free-lance writer, Helen Dudar, who was the wife of a *Newsweek* senior editor. To hire an outside writer to do a cover story was almost unprecedented.

Meanwhile, some of the women had contacted the EEOC to find out how to file a sex discrimination complaint. To ensure maximum publicity (and maximum pressure on management), the group decided to hold a press conference the day the *Newsweek* story on feminism hit the newsstands. At the conference, the women laid out the vital statistics: Of the magazine's thirty-five researchers, one was a male; of its fifty-two writers, one was female. Later, the magazine's editor-in-chief insisted that if most researchers were women, it was because of a "news magazine tradition going back almost 50 years." However, he was clearly on the defensive, and over the next five months *Newsweek* worked out a settlement with its women staffers. The *Newsweek* case inspired others, and media giants such as *Time* and NBC soon faced charges of sex discrimination as well.

The Ladies' Home Journal *Sit-In*

The *Ladies' Home Journal* demonstration was staged by a feminist coalition that included members of NOW, Redstockings, NYRF, OWL (the Older Women's League), and other New York City groups. Susan Brownmiller, then in an organization called Media Women, headed the coalition, which spent months planning the action. The women picked the *Journal* as a target because it had 14 million readers, and—apparently untouched by the movement—it was geared entirely to housewives.

At 8:45 on the morning of March 19, John Mack Carter, editor-in-chief and publisher of the *Ladies' Home Journal*, was in his office conferring with executive editor Lenore Hershey when suddenly women began streaming into the room. According to Hershey, "In an office which normally had seating room for a dozen, there suddenly were women everywhere, standing, sitting on the floor, draped over the table and the windowsills, and spilling out into the halls. For the first few moments, they all seemed to shout at once." She also noted that "they were . . . of all ages, without makeup, in fashions more *lumpen* than Halston, costumed for revolt."*

---

* One of the demonstrators, taking note of apparel in her turn, wrote in an article on the sit-in that Hershey herself was "crowned by a Schrafft's-Lady hat." Schrafft's was a Manhattan restaurant popular with suburban women.

Soon after that, reporters and television crews arrived, and the women distributed a press release. It stated that " 'the Magazine Women Believe In' [the *Journal*] deals superficially, unrealistically, or not at all with the real problems of today's women: job opportunity, day care, abortion. Though one out of every three adult women in America is single, divorced, or widowed, the *Journal* depicts no life style alternative for the American woman, aside from marriage and family." The release protested both the kind of ads the magazine ran and the image of women it promoted, particularly its unrelenting emphasis on looking young.

In a carefully prepared presentation, the women took turns stating and explaining their demands. Among other things, they wanted Carter replaced with a woman; they also wanted a day-care center for the children of employees and a training program to help secretaries escape their dead-end jobs. However, their primary demand was for the chance to put out an issue of the magazine, to be called *The Women's Liberated Journal*. They had come prepared with a dummy cover for that issue, which showed a pregnant picketer, carrying a sign that read, "Unpaid Labor." The group also presented Carter with a list of the articles they proposed for the issue. The subjects ran the gamut, from women and aging, to prostitution and the law.

At first, Carter refused to negotiate, and there was a long, tense confrontation. Vivien Leone, one of the many writers present, reported later that "a small faction of separatists, led by the famous . . . Ti-Grace Atkinson, had phoned Media Women the previous night to ask if they might participate. Their tether was short. When one of them said she had not come there to talk, but to Destroy, it took an hour of honey-coated filibustering to get things back into focus, during which Destroyer leapt on the desk, intent on Carter's forcible eviction. 'We can do it,' she urged, 'he's small.' . . . I lent my own hands to the several pair that evicted the potential evictress from the table-top. It was then that Ti-Grace . . . added it up very neatly for Carter. 'If you don't deal with them,' she reminded him [referring to the less militant demonstrators], 'you get us.' "

The sit-in lasted all day and into the evening, and eventually Carter did negotiate. In the end, he agreed to include an eight-page feminist supplement in the magazine's August issue, to be written by a collective; the group would be paid $10,000. By the time the sit-in ended, Hershey wrote, the women "had smoked the cigars on John's desk, taken over the men's room, and left the editorial offices in a mess. . . . Wearily, we closed up shop and everyone on both sides rushed to watch the TV news and wait for tomorrow's newspapers, all of which were generous in their coverage."

The women had begun by demanding the right to put out an entire issue, but they were prepared to bargain and planned to retreat to a demand for a regular feminist column (considered possible but unlikely) and then to a demand for one article on why they'd staged a sit-in (they were determined to hold out for the article). Instead, they were offered an eight-page supplement, "a lot more victory than was strictly needed to get rid of us," said Vivien Leone (though some radical women considered it a sell-out). The supplement came out in August, produced by a collective of thirty women. The articles in it—all unsigned, in the collective spirit—included: "Should This Marriage Be Saved?" "Women and Work," "Housewives' Bill of Rights," and "How to Start Your Own Consciousness-Raising Group." There was also a list of feminist groups for readers to contact.*

What did the sit-in accomplish? For the first time, articles by feminists explaining what the new feminism was all about reached nonmovement women across the country. Furthermore, according to NOW's Muriel Fox, "I think it scared the whole women's magazine industry. . . ."

The action also had a considerable impact on John Mack Carter. Years later, Carter recalled that on the day of the sit-in, he reacted by closing his mind to what the demonstrators were saying. "It's a natural human response," he explained. "You say, 'Obviously, I can't accept any of that, because it means that what I'm doing is all wrong.' " However, it took about three months to produce the eight-page supplement, and during that time he had to review the women's articles more than once, "and I had to conclude . . . that there was a lot of injustice out there."

He continued wryly, "Confrontation is certainly effective on the confrontee. . . . it focuses the mind mightily on the issues. And it changed the magazine, though not in a dramatic way." The *Journal* began to carry a column for working women, written by a feminist, and the regular feature "Can This Marriage Be Saved?" occasionally described marriages that could not and should not be saved—something it had never done before. If the

---

* This was to prove a great service. By the end of 1970, the White House was getting three letters a week from women asking where they could find a women's liberation group to join; the White House staff routinely referred such letters to the Women's Bureau, which answered them using—among other resources—the list printed in the August 1970 *Ladies' Home Journal.*

changes weren't revolutionary, according to Carter, it was partly because magazine editors try to give readers what they want, and readers' responses to the feminist supplement were more negative than positive: 34 percent were favorable, 46 percent against, and 20 percent "mixed." Carter noted that most people were wary of new ideas, and suggested that many women were afraid to step out of their traditional role and even more afraid to face the question, "Have I wasted part of the only life I'm going to have?" Some of the magazines geared for younger women were quicker to take up feminist issues.

Other Actions Across the Country

The events of March were soon followed by other actions against the media in cities across the country. In San Francisco, nine women from the Women's Liberation Front disrupted the annual meeting of CBS stockholders, shouting that the network was presenting "derogatory images of women in programming and commercials." Fifty feminists invaded the *San Francisco Chronicle* and presented the publisher with a list of demands. In Washington, an ad hoc committee of women journalists demanded that the city's dailies stop discriminating against women employees and end sexist references in news stories. In some cases, the women won concessions that weren't immediately obvious—for example, in August 1970 an internal CBS memo was leaked to the press. It began, "Television must show a new image of a woman as a doer, as an educated, serious-minded individual person." Obviously, someone at the stockholders' meeting was listening.

WOMEN'S STRIKE DAY

During the summer of 1970, the women's movement came of age and proved to the media and the nation that Americans were going to have to take feminism seriously. First, the *Ladies' Home Journal* appeared on the newsstands with its liberated supplement. Then, on August 10, the House passed the ERA for the first time. Finally, on August 26, tens of thousands of women in cities all over the country took to the streets to demand equality —and shocked the nation by their sheer numbers. This massive demonstration, known as Women's Strike for Equality, was such a publicity coup that it triggered a further growth spurt in the movement.

Women's Strike Day was the brainchild of Betty Friedan. Believing that women around the country "were ready to move in far greater numbers than even we realized," she envisioned a nationwide demonstration, something women could do in their own communities that could be coordinated by local coalitions of feminist groups without much central organization. In March of 1970, Friedan was about to step down as president of NOW; in an address to the organization's convention that lasted almost two hours, she proposed "a twenty-four-hour general strike . . . of all women in America against the concrete conditions of their oppression," to be held on August 26, 1970, the fiftieth anniversary of the suffrage victory. Some officers of NOW were dubious, because a strike that failed would embarrass the organization, but the membership voted in favor.

Soon, feminist groups in cities around the country were busy organizing. The majority agreed that the word "strike" mustn't be taken too literally. Most women were in no position to walk off their jobs for the day—they couldn't risk being fired. The various coalitions found their own solutions and organized sit-ins, lunch-hour rallies, and—in New York—a march down Fifth Avenue that began late in the afternoon. Of course, marches, too, had their risks. They were really a type of petition in which demonstrators put their bodies on the line, rather than their signatures. The object was to get media coverage, and success was measured in terms of a head-count. If too few marchers turned up, the media might write off the movement. What's more, according to most activists, the authorities always undercounted demonstrators.

In the end, even undercounting couldn't detract from the success of Women's Strike Day, especially in New York. The city had refused to close off Fifth Avenue to traffic, but feminists were determined to march down the avenue anyway, if necessary keeping to the sidewalks. However, as Friedan wrote later, "We came out of the park onto Fifth Avenue, and sure enough there were the police on horses, trying to shunt us off to the sidewalk. But there were so many women. I was walking between Judge Dorothy Kenyon, who in her eighties refused to ride in the car we'd provided for the suffragette veterans, and one of the young radicals in blue jeans. I took their hands and said to the women on each side, *take hands and stretch across the whole street.* And so we marched, in great swinging long lines, from sidewalk to sidewalk, and the police on their horses got out of our way." Officials announced later that there were approximately 10,000 marchers; feminists estimated that there were anywhere from 35,000 to 50,000.

Women demonstrated that day in practically every major city in the country, and in some smaller ones as well. There was even some action overseas. Dutch women marched on the U.S. Embassy in Amsterdam to demonstrate their support, while in France nine feminists bore down on the Arc de Triomphe, carrying a banner that read, "More Unknown Than the Unknown Soldier: His Wife." The French feminists made headlines in every major Paris daily and their action marked a revival of the women's movement in France.

Strike Day was a high for virtually everyone involved. Nevertheless, the press response was mixed. The *Chicago Tribune* dubbed the effort a "flop," though a rally in Chicago brought out 5000 supporters. The *New York Times* concluded that Strike Day's impact was minimal because in New York and other large cities businesses reported no unusual absenteeism that day. However, the *Times* did carry the story on its front page.

MAINSTREAMING FEMINIST IDEAS

The public also learned about feminism through a handful of best-selling books and a new national magazine. In the publishing world, 1970 was a banner year for the women's movement. Kate Millett was featured on the cover of *Time* magazine in August. Amazingly, her book, *Sexual Politics*, a radical feminist treatise, had become an overnight best-seller, and it was just the first of a number of important feminist books to appear. In *Sexual Politics*, Millett argued that all societies were patriarchies and that the relationship between the sexes was as political as the relationship between blacks and whites. She illustrated her argument with passages drawn from the works of Norman Mailer, Henry Miller, D. H. Lawrence, and other male authors who had glorified the sexual abuse of women. *Time* described Millett as a "brilliant misfit in a man's world," while the *New York Times* referred to her as the "principal theoretician of the movement."

October 1970 saw the publication of *The Dialectic of Sex* by Shulamith Firestone and Robin Morgan's anthology of feminist writing, *Sisterhood Is Powerful*. Early in 1971, Germaine Greer's *The Female Eunuch* appeared. All became feminist classics.

Meanwhile, a group of New York women who were writers or editors had begun meeting to discuss a joint project. Though press coverage was gradually becoming less hostile, the improvement was spotty, and they longed for a medium, such as a magazine, that they could control that would also have national circulation. The women's movement already had its own communication network: By 1971, there were over 100 feminist journals and newspapers, and there were also a few women's publishing houses. They were the glue that held the movement together, but for the most part they preached to the converted. The New York group, which included journalist Gloria Steinem and Pat Carbine, a former editor of *McCall's*, believed that a glossy magazine that appeared every month on newsstands around the country might make feminists of thousands of women.

Launching a magazine was not only expensive and risky, but for feminists the process was full of traps. They would have to find investors, and those who put their money into magazines generally insisted on having editorial control. They would eventually need advertisers as well. Would that mean the magazine had to carry ads that were insulting to women? The group spent months looking for backers. In the end, *New York* magazine offered to produce a preview issue of the new magazine, which was to be called *Ms.* The women were to have complete editorial control, but no say about which ads were accepted.

No one had any idea whether there was a market for such a magazine. Some of the financiers who had turned the *Ms* group down had estimated that there weren't more than 10,000 or at most 20,000 American women who would be interested in reading a feminist magazine—not enough to support it. However, when the preview issue appeared on the stands in January 1972, all 300,000 copies sold out in just eight days. Afterward, 20,000 letters poured in from women all over the country, and there were 50,000 subscription orders.

Unfortunately, there still wasn't nearly enough money to bring out another issue, so the group set out once more to look for financial backing. Three months later, Warner Communications agreed to invest up to a million dollars in return for just 25 percent of the stock, which meant the women had editorial control. The first regular issue of *Ms* appeared in July 1972.

A MEASURE OF SUCCESS

Thanks to the books, the magazine articles, the newspaper and television coverage, and *Ms*, the feminist message reached every corner of the country in the early 1970s—and the movement not only grew, but changed. As the publicity brought more and more women into feminist groups, the old, conflict-ridden distinctions between the branches of the movement blurred somewhat.

Women journalists were gaining ground within the media, but progress was slow—in many areas, glacially slow. For instance, in May of 1972 *Newsweek*'s female staffers filed a second complaint; it had been nearly two years since the settlement, and the magazine still had only four women in writing positions. The situation was no better on big-city newspapers. That year there were 557 professionals working on the news staff of the *New York Times*, and only 64 of them were women.

As for television, most of the women employed by commercial TV stations had clerical jobs. However, on the up side, the handful who *had* succeeded in landing better jobs were beginning to make a difference. At a Seattle TV station, women saw to it that a segment on breast cancer was aired despite male arguments that it was the wrong subject to present during the dinner hour; in Detroit, women staffers pioneered a special on rape; in Chicago, they fought for a story on the dangers of some IUDs, after male colleagues claimed the subject was unimportant. As more women became on-camera reporters, there was no drop in ratings, disproving the common contention that viewers wouldn't accept women because they didn't sound "authoritative" enough.

THE "DERADICALIZATION" OF FEMINISM

Under pressure from feminists and from a general public that was beginning to include many feminist sympathizers, media decision-makers finally had to acknowledge that women had some legitimate complaints. As they began to treat the movement with more respect, they abandoned the more militant radical feminists. Now when they needed a comment on a feminist issue, they contacted Gloria Steinem of *Ms*, the articulate leaders of NOW, or women in politics or academia. By the midseventies, most of the radical feminists who had written the books and lit up the talk shows were no longer heard from.

Though some women dropped quietly into obscurity, a handful of Redstockings protested vigorously. They understood the role the mass media had played, and they were particularly angry at Steinem, who was often quoted or invited to appear on talk shows. They insisted that feminist publications were part of the problem as well—even within the movement, they felt as if they had suddenly become invisible. Carol Hanisch reported that "we are not asked to speak or write for movement programs and journals and newspapers. . . . We are not listed in most bibliographies of movement papers and publications and speakers bureaus."

In 1972, Kathie Sarachild, Hanisch, and a few others revived Redstockings on a smaller scale and set to work writing a book. *Feminist Revolution,* published in 1975, stated their case against the rest of the movement. In it, they accused liberal feminists of taking over, and "cultural" feminists of retreating from the fray into a feminist counterculture. They also noted bitterly that other groups were taking credit for radical feminist inventions such as consciousness-raising and for concepts such as male supremacy and "Sisterhood is powerful." Furthermore, the original ideas were being watered down. Consciousness-raising, originally intended to lead to political action, had become therapy, a way for women to overcome childhood conditioning. "Sisterhood," first proposed as the route to power, now most often referred to a sense of community.

As the radical feminists were crowded off the national stage, some movement women breathed a sigh of relief. Betty Friedan, writing in August 1972, suggested that ". . . the women's liberation movement has had enough of sexual politics." She continued, "I have always objected to rhetoric that treats the women's movement as class warfare against men—women oppressed, as a class, by men, the oppressors. . . . Men are *not* a class." Though some males might be the enemy, others were potential allies, Friedan said, and she warned feminists that "if we *make* men the enemy, they will surely lash back at us."

Naturally, there were others who disagreed. Sociologist David Bouchier argued that, in fact, ". . . radical idealism was the *right choice* for feminists. . . . because it produced a movement which was able to involve people on the basis of their *own* experiences of oppression . . . perhaps the *only* way in which large numbers of people can be engaged in a radical cause. . . ." in the face of a powerful opposition.

Though the media were clearly implicated in the eclipse of radical feminism, other factors were involved as well. Virtually all social movements go through a fairly predictable process of growth and institutionalization, and in the process some radical ideas are adopted and watered down, and radical voices are apt to be silenced. The American social and political systems survived for more than 200 years because, confronted with radical movements, they were able to adjust, changing just enough to deflect the push for more drastic measures.

In addition, the movement's explosive growth ultimately helped to dull its radical edge, as it absorbed a huge influx of women with no background in radical politics. Though they were drawn by the issues radical feminists raised, they hadn't the same commitment to social revolution. Finally, radical feminists themselves were partly responsible for what happened. Though they set out to transform society, they never developed a coherent, long-range plan of action. One-time Redstocking Ellen Willis suggested that they put too much of a premium on unity among women and should probably have been more skeptical of the idea that ". . . if there were no women willing to 'scab'—then men would have no choice but to accept the new order. . . . I don't see universal sisterhood as a practical possibility." Transforming an entire social order was such a gargantuan task that it was difficult even to decide where to begin.

Throughout the seventies and eighties, the media continued to be a mixed blessing for feminists. On one hand, they educated the American public about a multitude of issues, from wife-beating to the gender gap. On the other hand, they failed to cover much of what happened in the movement and often distorted what they did cover. A feminist conference wasn't considered news, for example, unless the women were at one another's throats, fighting for power. Conflict was news, people with famous names were often news, but ongoing struggles with stubborn problems—and gradual progress—were not.

However, as journalism schools began to graduate more women than men, some feminists came to believe that the handwriting was on the wall: Sooner or later, there would be enough savvy women in top media jobs that fair coverage could be taken for granted.

chapter 7

Congress Passes the ERA

*E*arly in 1972, Congress passed the ERA—almost fifty years after it was first proposed. The vote was the result of massive and unprecedented lobbying by women's organizations. In fact, the intense two-year struggle to get the ERA through Congress was the fire that forged liberal feminists into a coherent political force.

In the months that followed, as state after state voted for ratification, it seemed that the battle was over. For a time, the amendment appeared to be barely controversial—an idea whose time had come. However, the struggle was just beginning. With the passage of the ERA, traditionalists were finally forced to take the women's movement seriously, and in short order, the right wing organized to block ratification.

WOMEN: BYPASSED BY THE CONSTITUTION

To liberal feminists, the need for the ERA was obvious: Women were simply not covered by the U.S. Constitution. Though many

Americans, including lawyers, found this hard to believe, in fact, the founding fathers simply ignored females, apparently assuming that women were the property of their husbands, or that the family unit should be represented solely by the male head of household. The Constitution didn't mention either sex, but whenever a singular pronoun was called for, it used *he*.

The word *male* was first added to the Constitution in 1868 in the fourteenth amendment, which prescribed penalties for any state that denied the right to vote to *male* citizens. Feminists like Elizabeth Cady Stanton and Susan B. Anthony understood immediately that this wording meant that it would take another constitutional amendment to give women the vote in federal elections.* Though females had never been written into the Constitution, in effect they had now been written out of it. Fifty years later, when they finally attained suffrage via the nineteenth amendment, which said that citizens couldn't be denied the right to vote "on account of sex," many people assumed that all of the Constitution's guarantees now applied to females. However, women had won the vote and nothing more—in 1947 the Supreme Court confirmed that in so many words. Upholding a law that exempted women from jury service, the Court noted that changing views of the rights and responsibilities of women had achieved "constitutional compulsion . . . in only one particular —the grant of the franchise by the nineteenth amendment."

Some second-wave activists argued that the Court might be persuaded to change its mind, and with that hope feminist attorneys brought a series of cases, challenging laws and practices that treated women and men differently. By 1976, they had won a partial victory. However, in 1970, most liberal feminists were convinced that the only way to ensure equal rights for women was to amend the Constitution. For almost fifty years, the ERA had been introduced in each session of Congress, but it seldom even came to a vote. Now many feminists felt that for the first time there was a real chance of success. According to NOW's analysis, more than eighty senators had spoken in favor of the amendment at one time or another. In addition, because feminists had gone to court and had already succeeded in overturning some of the protective labor laws, opposition to the ERA was fading.

The second wave's campaign to pry the amendment out of

* Before the fourteenth amendment was adopted, individual states' constitutions determined whether or not women could vote. Most states limited the right to vote to white males, but in New Jersey, which initially failed to exclude females, some women voted until 1808, when the state legislature formally disenfranchised them.

Congress began with civil disobedience. On February 17, 1970, a number of activists had come to Washington for a pro-ERA demonstration. Wilma Scott Heide, who would become national president of NOW in 1971, persuaded about twenty women from her own Pittsburgh chapter to disrupt a Senate hearing. The subcommittee responsible for considering constitutional amendments was taking testimony on a proposal to allow eighteen-year-olds to vote. The Pittsburgh women—all well-dressed and mostly middle-aged—quietly took seats in the audience. Then, during a brief lull in the proceedings, they suddenly rose to their feet and hoisted hand-made signs above their heads. As television cameras focused on them, Heide began to speak, demanding immediate action on the ERA.

Interrupting a congressional hearing was an offense for which they could have been arrested, and Wilma Heide recalled later that ". . . we were all scared to death. Security guards started to move forward, but at a signal from one of the senators, did not do anything. At that moment I knew we could do almost anything and get away with it . . . they didn't want to make martyrs out of us." Senator Birch Bayh, who chaired the committee, met with the women privately later in the day and assured them that his committee would hold hearings on the ERA in the spring. Bayh later acknowledged that by disrupting the hearings, they'd convinced him that it was time the committee acted.

In April, the United Auto Workers voted to endorse the ERA, after a long campaign by two UAW women who were among the founders of NOW. That was the first clear sign that labor's opposition to the amendment was eroding.

IN 1970, A NEAR VICTORY

On May 5, Senator Bayh's subcommittee opened its hearings on the amendment in a room jammed with spectators. Marguerite Rawalt was one of those asked to testify. She had spent two months researching Supreme Court decisions in which gender was an issue, and her testimony demonstrated conclusively that women had never been legally endowed with the rights that men had under the Constitution. After three days of testimony, most of it pro-ERA, Bayh's subcommittee reported favorably on the amendment to the full Judiciary Committee. Rawalt and other feminists were elated, convinced now that the House would be the real bottleneck. However, there were ominous signs in the

Senate even then. Few senators bothered to attend the subcommittee hearings—of the nine members, only Bayh and Senator Marlowe Cook turned up regularly.

With the amendment likely to reach the floor of the Senate within a few months, the women turned their attention to the House Judiciary Committee, where the ERA had been bottled up for years, thanks to committee chairman Emanuel Celler. Marguerite Rawalt and Catherine East went to Congresswoman Martha Griffiths and persuaded her to try to bypass Celler by filing a discharge petition in the House. If two thirds of the members signed it, the ERA would come up for a vote on the floor of the House even though it hadn't been released by the Judiciary Committee. The strategy was a longshot. Over the past sixty years, 825 discharge petitions had been filed, and only 34 had been successful. The men who chaired committees tended to support one another when it was a matter of committee prerogatives and to lean on their members to do the same. Petitions generally got no more than about thirty signatures, according to Griffiths, who didn't really believe the plan would work.

There was probably no other congresswoman who could have brought it off. Griffiths had some unusual advantages. She was a member of both the Ways and Means Committee and the Democratic Committee on Committees, which handed out committee assignments. Over the years, any number of people had come to her and asked to be placed on particular committees or had asked her to support bills they were sponsoring, and they now owed her something. Ordinarily, she might have used up much of this "credit," trading it for support for bills coming out of Ways and Means. However, Wilbur Mills, who chaired Ways and Means, liked to handle all such negotiations himself. That meant Griffiths was now in a position to call in her debts: to approach members who owed her something and ask them to return the favor by signing her petition.

Griffiths herself was not pro-ERA when she first came to Congress. Well aware of just how pervasive sex discrimination was, she nevertheless had felt that women should tackle the issues on a case-by-case basis. Eventually, she realized "that every suit that had ever been brought we had lost," that on the subject of women the Supreme Court was "apparently unteachable." Once committed to the effort to pass the amendment, she threw all her energy and her considerable influence into the struggle.

On June 11, 1970, Griffiths filed the discharge petition. According to the custom, it was placed on the clerk's desk at the front of the chamber. It would take exactly 218 signatures to wrest the ERA from the Judiciary Committee, and Griffiths knew she had to accumulate those names quickly. Many members would sign if they believed the petition was likely to succeed, but otherwise they would hang back, reluctant to risk reprisals from powerful committee heads. She needed to establish some convincing momentum early on.

Every morning, Griffiths would go up and look at the petition to see who still hadn't signed it. Then, during roll calls as members poured back into the chamber to vote, she'd accost some, take them by the arm and actually walk them up to the table where the petition was waiting. She recalled that majority leader Hale Boggs of Louisiana was one of the first people she approached. "Hale said, 'Now Martha, I want to be number 200.' Usually, you got about 30 signatures, so I knew what he was saying. . . ."

Within the first few days, seventy-five representatives signed the petition. They were responding either to Griffiths or to mail from their constituents, for Rawalt, who belonged to half a dozen major national women's organizations, was using her contacts for all they were worth, and at her urging women from all over the country were writing to their members of Congress on behalf of the ERA.

Griffiths had help from other feminists as well. On June 10, the day before she filed the discharge petition, she had addressed a local NOW chapter and explained her strategy. On the spot, some of the members formed the National Ad Hoc Committee for the Equal Rights Amendment. They immediately began lobbying House members in person, urging them to sign the petition. The Committee also developed a mailing list and was soon getting out memos regularly to a list of 500 activist women and pro-ERA organizations to let them know what was going on and which House members still hadn't signed.

Gradually, the list of names on the petition grew longer. Griffiths recalled, "When I got to 150, I went to Jerry Ford [the minority leader], and I said, 'Jerry, I have 150 . . . but when I look over [the petition], there's not a Republican signature, and Republican women espoused the ERA first. . . . You look like a bunch of jerks, not signing.' Well, he didn't say anything."

In mid-July, Rawalt had to leave town for the BPW annual convention, which was being held that year in Honolulu. Soon after she arrived, she got a phone call from Griffiths, who wanted the BPW women to bombard their members of Congress with telegrams. Because approximately 3000 women from all over the United States were attending the convention, it was a major project. Every night, Griffiths would call Rawalt or Virginia Allan in Honolulu and give them a list of representatives who hadn't yet signed. Rawalt and Allan would read off the names to the assembled convention. To handle the huge volume of telegrams this generated, Western Union sent several clerks to sit at tables just outside the convention hall. Back in Washington, "the signing business picked up immensely," according to Griffiths. In fact, congressmen were soon begging her to call off these women who were flooding their offices with telegrams.

On July 20, when Griffiths checked the petition, there were 199 names on the list. She rushed over to Hale Boggs, and he made good on his promise to provide the 200th signature. Then she was called off the floor by a reporter. "When I came back I could hardly get in the door. Here was a whole line of people in front of the Speaker's desk, and I asked someone what it was, and they said, 'This is the group that's signing the discharge petition on equal rights.' " After Boggs—the leader of the Democratic majority—signed, minority leader Jerry Ford apparently realized that the petition was going to succeed and quickly rounded up more than a dozen Republicans, enough to bring the list to 218 signatures.

Debate in the House

After nearly fifty years in limbo, the ERA would be debated on the floor of the House for exactly one hour, because House rules set a time limit for bills brought up through a discharge petition. The debate was scheduled for August 10, and Rawalt rushed home from Hawaii to help Griffiths prepare for it. Using the Congresswoman's office as headquarters, a team of feminists got to work contacting women all over the country by phone or by mail; thousands responded by putting pressure on their own members of Congress to be present for the debate and to vote for the ERA. Members of the Ad Hoc Committee also had a telephone team calling House members.

Griffiths had the job of scheduling those who were going to speak in favor of the amendment and of coordinating what they said. If the ERA passed, their statements would form the amendment's legislative history. In the future, when the Supreme Court was asked to decide whether a law violated the ERA, the justices would refer to that history to learn how Congress had intended it to be interpreted. In her own presentation, Griffiths touched on subjects ranging from the protective labor laws (the ERA would invalidate them) to married women's property rights (it would wipe out state laws that gave husbands control of a couple's property).

Opponents raised many objections. Emanuel Celler, for example, argued that men and women should be treated differently because there was "as much difference between a male and a female as between a horse chestnut and a chestnut horse." However, in the end they failed to send the bill back to the Judiciary Committee and it passed the House by a huge margin, 350 to 15, with 64 members not voting. Griffiths noted that for a Monday in an election year that was a big head count. Many members normally went home on the weekends to campaign. All that intensive lobbying had obviously paid off.

Afterward, the reaction in the press was largely negative. An editorial in the *New York Times*, entitled "The Henpecked House," supported equal rights for women but spoke favorably of the protective labor laws and criticized the House for approving, "without committee hearings and after only an hour's debate, a constitutional change of almost mischievous ambiguity." Syndicated columnist James J. Kilpatrick went further. To him, the ERA was "the contrivance of a gang of professional harpies, descendants in zealotry of the late Carrie [sic] Nation. . . . The . . . men who voted for this resolution had but one purpose in mind, to get these furies off their backs."

Because the ERA hadn't followed the usual slow route from committee hearings to floor vote, some claimed that it had been steamrollered through. Griffiths said, "The real truth was that most of those men were very decent men and in their hearts, they knew . . . they should help. The Constitution should apply to women."

Defeat in the Senate

The House bill immediately went to the Senate, where its chief opponent, Sam Ervin, insisted that his Judiciary Committee must schedule more hearings on it—despite the fact that he hadn't bothered to attend those held in May. Meanwhile, a poll showed that the ERA had lost many of its supporters in the Senate now that it was no longer conveniently bottlenecked in the House and passage was a real possibility.

With Ervin presiding, the new hearings began on September 9.

For three days the senator called on known opponents only; then he announced that he didn't have time to take any more testimony. In the end, Senator Cook presided over a final day of testimony by the pro-ERA forces.

By October, the ERA had reached the Senate floor. There, its opponents proceeded to amend it to death. The Senate voted, 36 to 33, to add language exempting women from the draft, and then on top of that agreed to a rider to permit prayer in public schools. On the key vote on the draft, the pro-ERA side lost by just 3 votes; many senators were absent. Time was running out. When the 91st Congress came to an end in December, the ERA would die with it; it would have to be reintroduced in the House and the whole process begun again.

With that in mind, just before Congress adjourned for the election recess, Senator Bayh introduced a substitute for the ERA, evidently hoping it would be less controversial, that would simply extend the protection of the crucial fourteenth amendment to women. Over the recess, the leaders of various pro-ERA organizations conferred, getting together for the first time to coordinate policies. Some were reluctant to oppose Bayh's substitute amendment for fear of alienating one of their few powerful allies in Congress. However, most were convinced the substitute wouldn't be as comprehensive as the ERA and feared it might permit women to be excluded from the draft—might even legitimize the protective labor laws.

On the issue of the draft, many feminists felt strongly that equality for women must mean equal responsibilities as well as equal rights. That was an uncomfortable stand to take at a time when American casualties in Vietnam were almost 35,000 a year. Like most Americans, liberal feminists were sick of the war, but they were unwilling to compromise on full equality. They were afraid an amendment that shielded young women from the draft would leave the door open for judges and legislators to continue to "protect" women in other ways as well. After a number of emergency meetings, all of the organizations except BPW ultimately decided against the substitute. Having achieved near-consensus, they met with Bayh on November 18 and told him they couldn't support his ERA alternative. According to Rawalt, he took it well.

In December, a handful of feminists, including Rawalt and Griffiths, got together to discuss future strategy and the need to organize support for the ERA among women's groups. They agreed that a formal, coordinating council made up of representatives from national women's organizations would be too slow to act, because the representatives would have had to check back continually with their own executive boards for authorization. As an alternative, they decided to enlist a small number of Washington activists who belonged to national women's organizations but wouldn't officially represent them. They could serve as a central clearinghouse for information and could mobilize support around the country when it was necessary. They decided to call the group simply Women United. Marguerite Rawalt was to be a key figure in this venture, because she was a member of many of the pro-ERA organizations and knew their leaders personally. She had served on the board of directors of BPW, NOW, WEAL, NAWL (the National Association of Women Lawyers), the General Federation of Women's Clubs, and Zonta International (a federation of service clubs for businesswomen).

At about that time, the Ad Hoc Committee "faded away," in the words of Flora Crater, who had chaired it. However, Crater and a few others who had been on the Committee formed the core of a small group of determined lobbyists, working independently for the ERA, that came to be known on Capitol Hill as "Crater's Raiders." Through a newsletter that Crater published, they were in contact with many organizations around the country that Women United didn't reach.

THE ERA CAMPAIGN, 1971

In January 1971, when Congress reconvened, Senators Bayh and Cook announced that they would reintroduce the Equal Rights Amendment. However, they wanted to make a few changes in the wording to answer some objections that had been raised, the most significant difference being a provision that said the amendment must be ratified within seven years. By mid-January, with Women United acting as liaison, most of the major pro-ERA organizations had approved these changes, much to the indignation of Alice Paul and the National Woman's Party. Paul insisted—prophetically, as it turned out—that it might take longer than seven years to get the ERA ratified.

In the House, the Amendment had acquired a strong new ally in Representative Don Edwards of California, who chaired a subcommittee of Celler's Judiciary Committee. Edwards held hearings on the ERA in late March. On the last day of the hearings, approximately fifty young women from a George Washington University women's liberation group attended, some with babies stowed in baby-carriers on their backs. Because they were draft age, the Ad Hoc Committee had asked them to work out a position on whether women should be drafted. Stating that position now, a representative of the group said what some other young women's groups were also saying at the time: that none of them were for the draft, and none wanted to go to war, but if there had to be a draft, they were as ready as men were to do their part.

Edwards's subcommittee reported favorably on the ERA and sent it on to the full Judiciary Committee. There, Representative Charles Wiggins succeeded in adding to it the so-called Wiggins amendment, which not only exempted women from the draft, but also stated that the ERA wouldn't invalidate any law that "reasonably promotes the health and safety of the people." That left ample room for the courts to uphold statutes, such as the protective labor laws, that were supposedly in women's best interests. Knowing that this would be unacceptable to feminists, Congressman Celler crowed that it was "the kiss of death." Martha Griffiths said grimly, "If we can't take it out on the [House] floor, I'll vote against the bill myself."

It took months of intensive lobbying to get the ERA, even as amended, out of the Judiciary Committee. Finally, on October 6, 1971, the debate in the House began. Once again, those who were pro-ERA concentrated on building a solid legislative history. Meanwhile, the opponents pulled out all stops. Emanuel Celler embellished his arguments with a new simile: "There is as much diversity between a man and a woman as there is between lightning and a lightning bug." Others claimed that if the ERA were ratified, husbands would no longer have to support wives, men and women would have to share public bathrooms, and women who were drafted would be assigned to fight alongside men in the front lines. The idea of weapons in the hands of women was intolerable to some. Mississippi Democrat Thomas G. Abernethy stated solemnly that he wouldn't want to be responsible for putting women at the "triggers of cannons." The House finally voted on October 12. By a resounding 354 to 23, it passed the ERA without the Wiggins amendment.

THE CAMPAIGN IN THE SENATE, 1972

Meanwhile, the Senate had been biding its time. Ervin had promised action, but by February 1972, the amendment still hadn't been reported out by the Judiciary Committee.

The women's lobby stepped up the pressure. Crater's Raiders had developed a system. During 1971 and early 1972, fifteen or twenty of them would gather every Wednesday, whenever Congress was in session, in either the House or Senate cafeteria to discuss which legislators to visit. Once decisions were made, they'd fan out, carrying bright pink tally sheets, developed by Crater, who had had twenty years' experience in Democratic politics in Virginia. Each sheet had space to record a senator's name and record on the ERA and any new information the lobbyist gleaned.

Whenever it was possible, the Raiders spoke to senators themselves, but otherwise they talked to staffers. They had, in fact, developed their own intelligence network, a kind of feminist underground of legislative assistants and office workers. Martha Griffiths later remarked that "if the Senate had ever realized what we knew about what was going on in those offices, I will swear that they would have fired every employee . . . we knew exactly where to apply the pressure."

Once the Raiders had gathered their information, the next step was getting the word out. That was generally done through Crater's newsletter, *The Woman Activist*, which was mailed to women around the country, including many who were officers of women's organizations at the state or local level. Those officers, in turn, passed the latest ERA information along to their members. Thus, the news quickly reached thousands of ERA supporters.

Women United, BPW, and Common Cause, the liberal lobbying organization, were involved in similar efforts to stimulate grass-roots lobbying. When a really fast response was needed, Washington feminists used the telephone instead of the postal service. All over the country, women responded enthusiastically when approached, even those who had been turned off by slanted media coverage of "women's lib." To many, the ERA was a matter of simple justice. For months, they deluged Congress with letters. The whole system was so efficient that, according to Val Fleishhacker, a member of Crater's group, "Toward the end, it got so you could make twelve phone calls and [generate] five to ten thousand letters."

Ultimately, the Senate responded. On February 28, the Judiciary Committee approved the ERA without crippling amendments by a vote of 15 to 1, with only Sam Ervin in opposition. Debate on the Senate floor began on Friday, March 17. The following Tuesday, Ervin weighed in with a fistful of protective amendments. Beginning with a provision to exempt women from the draft, he spoke of young women ". . . sent into combat, where they will be slaughtered or maimed by the bayonets, the bombs, the bullets, the grenades, the mines, the napalm, the poison gas, or the shells of the enemy."* The senator had other issues on his mind as well, and he continued, ". . . the equal rights amendment will prohibit the discharge from the armed services of any single woman for pregnancy or childbearing no matter how often she becomes pregnant or how many bastards she bears."

Senator Bayh acknowledged that for the ERA's supporters, the draft was the single most difficult issue to deal with. Everyone agreed that if the amendment passed without a provision specifically exempting women from military service, they would, indeed, be subject to the draft along with men. However, some proponents had pointed out that Congress already had the power to draft women. The issue of whether women would serve in the front lines was even stickier. According to political scientist Jane Mansbridge, if the ERA *had* been ratified and the Supreme Court had gone back over its legislative history one day to determine whether Congress actually wanted to send women into combat, the justices would have found the record ambiguous.

The amendment's backers could easily have argued that in the past the Supreme Court had allowed the military wide latitude, basing its decisions on the "war powers" clauses of the Constitution. It was clear that soldiers didn't have all the constitutional rights of ordinary citizens, and it was hard to imagine that the Court would ever order the Pentagon to put women in the front lines if the top brass didn't want them there. Some of the ERA's sponsors hinted at some such interpretation, but Bayh, in particular, sent mixed signals. At one point, he quoted Martha Griffiths, who had told the House, "The draft is equal. That is the thing that is equal. But once you are in the Army you are put where the Army tells you to go." This suggested that women would not necessarily be sent into combat, and sure enough, Bayh also referred to the fact that the Israeli army drafted women but used them in noncombat positions.

However, in another context, Bayh seemed to be saying that at least a few women might end up fighting beside the men. He reported that of the men currently being called up, only 15 percent actually saw action. Because women in the military would

* Years later, Jane Mansbridge noted that when speaking on the ERA, Ervin often recited this list of weapons, always in alphabetical order.

have to meet the same physical standards as men, he said, fewer women than men would be drafted in the first place, and of those who *were* drafted, presumably a much smaller proportion would wind up in combat. Thus, he didn't really state unequivocally that the ERA would never require any American woman to serve in the front lines. Bayh may have been influenced by feminists who had made an ideological commitment to total equality. In addition, he probably took into account an analysis published in 1971 in the *Yale Law Journal* which stated that "[The] principle of the Amendment must be applied comprehensively and without exceptions. . . . Only an unequivocal ban against taking sex into account supplies a rule adequate to achieve the objectives of the Amendment."*

The women-in-combat issue would haunt the debate over the ERA for the next ten years, as would some of the other objections Ervin raised. He insisted that the ERA would deprive divorced women of alimony and child support and would wipe rape laws from the books. He brought up unisex bathrooms, and asserted that the ERA would also require unisex cells for male and female convicts. ERA backers, who found these arguments absurd, retorted that sex-neutral divorce laws could easily be written so that alimony was possible for either husband or wife, as circumstances warranted, and that sex-neutral rape laws could be written as well. They pointed out that the right to privacy, implied in the Constitution, would preserve separate restrooms and cells.

Above all, Ervin seemed convinced that the ERA would destroy the family. He predicted social disruption, more divorces, more men deserting their families, a weakening of family ties that would in turn lead to "increased rates of alcoholism, suicide, and possible sexual deviation."

For two days, Senator Ervin kept offering amendments to the ERA. Its backers couldn't afford to accept any amendment, because if the Senate passed a version that was at all different from the House version, the ERA would have to go to a House-Senate conference committee, where hostile members of the House would probably succeed in killing it. The atmosphere was tense, but Rawalt recalled that there was "such a sense of possibility." Each time Ervin proposed an amendment, a groan went up from the Senate gallery, which was packed with women. As his pro-

---

* Actually, the authors of the analysis felt that the ERA allowed two exceptions: It would not invalidate laws that guaranteed the right to privacy of each sex—so "Men's Rooms" were in no danger—nor would it strike down laws related to an actual physical characteristic that only one sex had—for example, laws concerning wet nurses.

posals were voted down by wider and wider margins, the audience applauded, cheered, and sometimes let out whoops of joy —behavior unheard of in the sedate Senate.

Late on the afternoon of March 22, the Senate finally passed the ERA. The vote was 84 to 8, a much wider margin than the two-thirds majority required in each house for constitutional amendments. Half an hour later, Hawaii became the first state to ratify. Within the week, five more states followed suit. Senator Bayh predicted that in two years the ERA would become the law of the land.

The passage of the ERA was a coup for the fledgling feminist lobby. Women United ultimately tapped the resources of ninety-two national organizations, ranging from NOW to the Teamsters Union. Members of those organizations deluged Congress with letters and telegrams. New York Senator Jacob Javits alone reported receiving 10,000 letters; some sources estimated that, overall, congressional mail on the ERA topped five million letters.

Beyond the mail campaign, there was the lobbying women did in person. In fact, writing in the *Washington Star*, reporter Isabelle Shelton gave the lion's share of the credit for passing the ERA to Crater's Raiders, calling them "one of the most powerful and unlikely pressure groups that Congress has ever seen in operation." Of the overall feminist effort, Shelton reported that "Capitol Hill veterans were gasping. 'I've never seen anything like it in all my years here,' said one long-time senator. 'In their hearts, many of those guys out there don't really believe in this amendment. But they were getting so much heat from the women, they didn't have any choice.' . . . female constituents have hounded the legislators back home to the point where some of them dreaded going home during recess."

ERA: EFFECTS AND SIDE EFFECTS

This is the text of the Equal Rights Amendment, as it was passed by Congress in 1972:

1. Equality of rights under the law shall not be denied or abridged by the United States or by any state on account of sex.
2. The Congress shall have the power to enforce, by appropriate legislation, the provisions of this article.

3. This amendment shall take effect two years after the date of ratification.

Summing up the changes expected to occur if the ERA were to be ratified, the *New York Times* made the following points. In a post-ERA America:

- If men were drafted, women would have to be drafted too.
- Men and women volunteering to serve in the military must be judged by the same standards.
- Laws that restricted a woman's right to buy or sell property or conduct a business would be struck down.
- Boys and girls applying for admission to public schools and other tax-supported educational institutions would have to be judged by the same standards (some schools had stiffer requirements for girls). Once admitted, both sexes would have to be provided with the same facilities and allowed to take the same classes—girls could no longer be automatically consigned to home economics and boys to shop.
- Laws that prescribed different jail terms for men and women would be invalidated.
- So would those that automatically gave mothers custody of their children in a divorce. As for alimony, it would no longer be available only to women. In awarding it, judges would be legally required to consider the financial situation of both parties.
- Pregnant women who were able and willing to work would be allowed to collect unemployment if they were fired or laid off. Legally, pregnancy must be treated like any other temporary physical disability.
- The law could no longer distinguish between males and females in establishing an age at which young people legally came of age, or were allowed to marry without their parents' consent, or—in later life—an age at which men and women became eligible to begin collecting on tax-supported retirement plans.

The ERA was never ratified. In the end, it fell three states short of the thirty-eight needed to pass a constitutional amendment. Yet during the 1970s and 1980s, feminists won most of the changes the ERA would have mandated. Though that suggests that they could have challenged discriminatory laws one at a time, in fact, American women would have made much less progress without the struggle for the ERA. The Amendment attracted massive support, educated the public on women's issues, and mobilized women who wouldn't have been drawn from the sidelines by anything else. It connected with traditional American values—it harked back to the idea, embodied in the Declaration of Independence, that "all men are created equal." As Martha Griffiths put it, "The ERA created a moral climate for reform."

In 1972, feminists expected a battle with labor over ratification. However, the real opposition hadn't even been organized yet, and trouble would come from a different direction. Title VII, which mandated equal treatment for women in the job market, had killed the protective labor laws, which promised women special treatment (supposedly, better than equal). With those laws out of the picture and labor's opposition defused, it was possible to get the ERA through Congress. If it had been ratified, it would have required equal treatment for women across the board. However, in the coming years, the Amendment would be opposed by antifeminists, indifferent to the protective labor laws, who still felt women needed special treatment.

There were clues to the form the opposition would take in Sam Ervin's diatribes about the danger to the American family. As a lawyer and a long-time legislator, he must have known that he was raising false issues when he focused on unisex bathrooms, for example, and when he argued that the ERA would require women to provide half the family's support. In a sense, these exaggerated claims seemed to symbolize deeper fears about changes within the family, changes in women's status, and a possible blurring of gender identity—to say nothing of the threat to traditional male privileges and power.

Just as the ERA became a symbol for feminists of all the changes they wanted made—including many that were beyond the reach of a constitutional amendment—it would become a symbol to the opposition as well. If some liberal feminists had the illusion that a ratified ERA would solve most of their problems, the opposition's illusions were the mirror image: They seemed convinced that if they could just defeat the amendment, Americans would return to the traditional family and the traditional way of life.

chapter 8

Turning Points

I f a social movement is to survive, from time to time it must virtually reinvent itself to cope with new needs and circumstances. Between about 1972 and 1975, the women's movement went through that sort of metamorphosis.

It changed in four major ways.

- First, most of the original women's liberation groups died. Almost by default, liberal feminism became the mainstream of the second wave.
- Second, as the women's movement continued to expand and new groups kept forming, most of them coalesced around some single specific problem, such as rape, in contrast to the early feminist groups, which tackled a broad spectrum of issues. As a result, the second wave began to spin off a barrage of other movements: there was a battered women's movement, a women's health movement, and so on. Often the new movements' actions were coordinated by a formal coalition that linked groups and could mobilize individual supporters as well. Each of these alliances drew on a specific

population of activists and had its own objectives and its own communication network. The activists generally thought of themselves as part of that specialized alliance—they would say they were involved in the women's health movement, for example. However, most also identified themselves as feminists and assumed that their group was one component in a broader, nationwide women's movement. The remaining general-interest groups, such as NOW, worked with the coalitions at times on particular issues.

- Third, a women's counterculture took root as feminists around the country opened women's bookstores, founded small presses and record companies, and so on.
- Fourth, a small but influential feminist "establishment" developed in Washington, where women's organizations were increasingly skillful at lobbying and dealing with the federal government.

As a result of these changes, the second wave looked very different in 1980 from what it was in the early 1970s. It had become a network of interlocking movements.

The next ten chapters—Part 2 of the book—describe the way the movement multiplied during the 1970s and 80s, branching out in new directions. This chapter will focus on the turning points: on what changed and why in the early-to-mid-70s as the second wave began to assume new forms.

THE DECLINE OF WOMEN'S LIBERATION

By 1975, most of the early women's liberation groups had vanished. How could they achieve so much and then just disappear? A number of explanations have been suggested.

One theory is that the groups self-destructed, done in by dissension. Certainly, internal conflicts blew some groups apart, especially in New York City. Usually, several thorny issues were involved. One of them was apt to be the gay-straight split, which pitted lesbians against heterosexual feminists. Trashing was another common problem, and class differences frequently generated painful tensions. At times, dissension was aggravated by outsiders, primarily by the Socialist Workers' Party (SWP), an old left organization that infiltrated a number of women's liberation groups. Other groups were spied on by FBI informers, who may have deliberately fanned the flames of conflict.

However, dissension was certainly not the whole story. According to some feminists, burnout played a role. Others argued that many groups dissolved because they'd fulfilled their purpose: Members had wrung out of them all the insights and support they needed and moved on to other projects.

There's some truth in all of these explanations. Any group, examined individually, succumbed for a variety of reasons—including some of the above.

Attacks from the Left

Between 1970 and 1972, the Socialist Workers' Party made a number of attempts to take over women's centers, women's unions, and feminist groups. In the fall of 1970, the SWP succeeded with Boston's Cell 16. The story illustrates how the leftists undermined some groups and why many feminists were leery of political manipulation—and unwilling to urge their own beliefs on others.

The SWP was founded in 1925 by Trotskyite defectors from the Communist Party. During the 1960s, the "Trots," as they were called, actively recruited students, and their youth arm, the Young Socialist Alliance (YSA), grew. Compared to feminist groups, the Trots were highly disciplined. Organizing the masses had always been their primary goal, and in the women's liberation movement they saw an opportunity to recruit thousands of young, already radicalized women. Their methods were bitterly resented by many radical feminists and politicos.

At the national YSA convention in December 1969, plans for "intervening" in feminist groups and "helping to broaden" them were openly discussed. In 1970, at an SWP meeting in Boston, several individuals reported that they were working within the local women's liberation movement, and had even taken leadership in some areas. One of their goals was "pushing the demands and basic policy . . . as far to the left as possible." Later, Cell 16 was specifically targeted.

According to Betsy Warrior, YSA women first made contact with Cell 16 by attending the group's karate classes. Then, during the summer of 1970, they persuaded some members to join them in working up a lecture series and thus gained access to Cell 16's office. At the time, Warrior and others were feeling overwhelmed by the amount of work they'd taken on. There were articles to write or edit for *No More Fun and Games*, copies of the journal to be mailed out, and the letters that flooded in had to be answered.

When the woman who had been paid to handle the office work left, one of the Trots offered her services. Then when the office had to be moved to a new location, some of the YSA members stored back issues of the journal and copies of a Cell 16 poster in their homes temporarily. Sales of these items were the group's sole source of income.

Matters came to a head in the fall of 1970. Betsy Warrior recalled that "one day I found a piece of paper on the [office] floor. It was a plan for infiltrating NARAL [the National Association for the Repeal of Abortion Laws], and it showed . . . what Trotskyites would be planted on which committees and how they would bring up suggestions and eventually take over and direct policy." Warrior showed the plan to other members of Cell 16 and told them, "Maybe we consider NARAL liberal in comparison to us, but they're decent people, they don't deserve this."

There was a major confrontation. At first the YSA women denied everything. Finally, said Warrior, "They laughed and said that these people [NARAL] are so liberal and so stupid, you have to do something to get them going in the right direction." The radical feminists were not reassured, and the two factions agreed to part company. However, the Cell 16 women soon realized that they'd lost control. The Trots had their mailing list; they had the signature on the bank account, which meant they had access to the group's savings; and they had most of the back issues of the journal and the posters.

Cell 16 survived for a time, but the conflict with the Trots had left the women demoralized, and eventually they all went their own ways—though before that happened Warrior sent a letter of warning to other feminist groups, describing their experience. Meanwhile, the Trots, calling themselves Female Liberation, set up a new office and were soon thriving because they now filled a partial vacuum. Boston's other major feminist organization, Bread and Roses, was having problems—many members had apparently burned out. For a time, the only easy way for newcomers to connect with a feminist group was to go to a Female Liberation meeting.

In Boston and elsewhere, the Trots had a lot of appeal for those who couldn't deal with the confusion of a leaderless women's liberation group. In addition, as women's liberationists began to explore the class issue, the SWP made converts because of its Marxist philosophy. There was no obvious way to avoid takeover attempts by the Trots, because most feminist groups felt they should be open to all comers. Jane Mansbridge of Bread and

Roses recalled that for a while there was a lot of discussion about "how to anti-Trot yourself without making people too paranoid and while keeping the doors open."

The Trots left their tracks in the histories of a number of women's groups during the early 1970s. Even when they seemed to be working hard for the right issues, they were resented. Feminists complained that the YSA women were simply following party orders; that they saw themselves as a political elite, destined to lead the masses in a socialist revolution; and that they were interested in women's issues only as a means of recruiting women to their own cause.

FBI Surveillance

During the sixties, American intelligence agencies infiltrated the civil rights movement and the New Left. Many feminists never doubted that the women's movement was a target as well. In fact, the FBI was apparently happy to have it known that it had a network of agents keeping tabs on protest groups—that was one way to intimidate the protestors. It wasn't unusual at a demonstration or rally to see bystanders ostentatiously snapping pictures of the demonstrators and taking down car license numbers. Women who had been student activists almost took such things for granted. Suspecting that there were informers in their midst, feminists addressing a meeting sometimes cleared their throats and began, "Sisters and special agents . . ."

Senate hearings in the mid-1970s revealed that from 1969 to 1973 the FBI did indeed have informers in feminist groups. Subsequently, *Ms* magazine and the *Los Angeles Times* independently requested the FBI's file on the women's liberation movement under the Freedom of Information Act. They received a document that was almost 1400 pages long, with many names and certain details carefully deleted to protect the identities of informers.

The document revealed that when FBI Director J. Edgar Hoover originally ordered surveillance of the WLM, as he called the Women's Liberation Movement, some FBI field offices were unenthusiastic. One bewildered agent wrote that his informers "had no information concerning a group or organization called the 'Women's Liberation Movement.' . . . It would seem an abortive attempt may have been made to organize or affiliate all women into an organization but it never materialized." However, Hoover would brook no opposition. In one ponderous memo, he noted disapprovingly that ". . . it is absolutely essential that we conduct sufficient investigation . . . to determine the potential for violence presented by the various groups connected with this movement as well as any possible threat they may represent to the internal security of the United States."

Spying on the women's movement must have posed a challenge to the Bureau. Most women's liberation groups had no male members and wouldn't allow men to attend meetings, and the FBI didn't employ women as agents until July 1972. Before that, presumably, it was forced to use part-time female operatives, either antifeminist volunteers or paid free-lancers.

From the FBI file that *Ms* acquired, it was clear that when feminists attended Women's Strike Day rallies, demonstrated against the Miss America Pageant, and on many other occasions, the FBI was there. Informers even reported on women's studies courses and meetings of consciousness-raising groups. They repeated gossip about which women were lesbians. Most of the information collected was mundane, but the conclusions the FBI's spies drew were sometimes jarringly inaccurate. A summary of the situation in New York City, dated April 1969, concluded that ". . . WLM is a larger movement probably with headquarters, or at least a publication in Chicago . . ." Later, a Boston informant notified Washington that Bread and Roses was essentially Communist.

Were feminists manipulated even as they were spied on? Did FBI plants push some groups into extreme positions and fan the flames of dissension in others? Feminists may never know. There was no evidence of it in the WLM file, but some activists were convinced the FBI wouldn't release that kind of information anyway. Certainly, the fear that agents might be trying to destroy the movement from within contributed at times to an atmosphere of distrust. However, many activists would agree with radical feminist Susan Brownmiller, who said, referring to the conflicts that roiled some groups, "We didn't *need* FBI agents to do us in. I have always said that one crazy movement person could do the work of ten *agents provocateurs.*"

Groups Died Because They'd Served Their Purpose

For many feminists, the early seventies were the best and worst of times. For a few months or years, women's liberation *was* their life. Consciousness-raising had turned their world on its head.

Marriages shattered under the impact, and women emerged confused, shaken, enraged—but often, through it all, exhilarated, for they had a sense that they were making history. Diane Balser of Bread and Roses said, "It was as if this thing took over that was larger than any of us." The experience was so intense that it couldn't have continued indefinitely.

For a time, feminists were wide open to new ideas. They were busy redefining themselves and all their relationships, and there were no questions so outlandish that they couldn't be raised. For example, on a college campus, if a drunken male student barged into a meeting that was closed to men and refused to leave, should the women eject him themselves, rather than sending for campus security (other males)? If a man asked to attend meetings of a women's group on the grounds that his anatomy was a mistake and he felt like a woman, should he be allowed to?

In the beginning, Jane Mansbridge said, "We had the feeling that we were, like Columbus, sailing at the edge of the world. Everything was new and intense. But after a while we'd had all the breakthrough experiences." Consciousness-raising, in particular, no longer had the same impact, because by the mid-1970s many books and articles had been written, insights had been shared, and there wasn't the same sense of discovery. In addition, more feminists now felt the need for action.

Thus, many of the early women's liberation groups died because they'd done their job. Members used the support of the group to make changes in themselves and their circumstances. They then moved on to new challenges, for though the groups were gone, often the women were simply recycled. Over the years, they continued to work for the movement in other ways.

Jane Mansbridge observed that in any case, for some radicals of that era preserving a particular group or organization wasn't a priority. If the group's energy flagged and members dropped out, they assumed that some sort of natural process was at work. As people's needs changed, new and more appropriate organizations would spring up. In the women's movement, that was, in fact, what happened.

THE RISE OF SPECIALIZED GROUPS AND MOVEMENTS

In purely practical terms, what the second wave needed in the mid-1970s—and what it got—were specialized groups that could focus on a particular problem and devote all their energy to it until they'd made some progress. The movement needed such groups partly because there was work to be done in so many different areas. Feminists had accomplished a great deal, but the easy victories were behind them.

Resistance was also increasing, and the political atmosphere had changed. The Vietnam War was over, the New Left had disintegrated, and many young people had resumed a more conventional lifestyle. With unemployment growing, the driving idealism of the late sixties was a memory, and most activists no longer believed that they could accomplish a social revolution overnight. However, a group that maintained a rape crisis center or that set out to change state rape laws could expect to see results. That appealed to a lot of women.

Of course, some groups, such as NOW, continued to be concerned with many different issues. However, NOW chapters had always had task forces so that members could choose a problem and pursue solutions. As the seventies rolled on, many of the general-interest organizations other than NOW carved out particular areas of expertise for themselves. For instance, WEAL focused strongly on educational equity, though it also worked with other women's organizations on issues ranging from discrimination against pregnant workers to the need for pension reform.

The new specialized groups absorbed many women newly interested in feminism and mobilized others who might not have been drawn into the movement if they hadn't felt strongly about one particular issue, such as wife-beating. Nevertheless, as some feminists developed new priorities and narrower goals, that did create tensions at times within groups or in the feminist community. Events that occurred in Boston illustrate the complexity of the issues involved. They're also a snapshot of the women's movement at a moment of transition.

In the early 1970s, a number of Boston's feminist groups jointly raised the money to buy a building. They believed that if feminists had their own shared space, communication between groups would be improved and the local movement strengthened. The Cambridge Women's Center opened its doors in 1972. By the spring of 1973, battered wives and women who had been raped were beginning to turn up on the doorstep, pleading for help. Their plight split the feminists into opposing factions. According to Libby Bouvier, the Center's archivist, on one side of the rift were those who wanted to set up a rape crisis center and a battered woman's shelter as quickly as possible. On the other side were politicos who felt that, rather than trying to help individuals, feminists should put their energy into fighting the system that was the basic cause of problems like rape. Most of the politicos were involved in the Women's School that held classes at the Center.

Beyond the basic issues of how the Center's space and the movement's energy should be used, there were other tensions. The politicos were a rather homogeneous group: middle class, college-educated, with experience in the New Left. Though there were both gay and straight women among them, they were mostly straight. The women who were for providing services were more diverse, and, as Bouvier pointed out, "Some had themselves been in life-threatening situations—they knew what it was like to be battered or raped." More of them came from poor or working-class backgrounds and more were lesbians, and these differences added to the problem. In confrontations with the politicos, some working-class women felt patronized. "They felt not listened to because they weren't experienced enough or hadn't been involved in the antiwar movement," said Bouvier. "They were very sensitive to all kinds of nuances. They had just discovered sisterhood and now they felt other women were treating them as men had." In the end, the Women's School moved out of the Center. "I thought at the time that it was a terrific tragedy," said Jane Mansbridge.

The rift in Boston's feminist community was eventually mended and the School moved back to the Center. Activists on both sides accepted the fact that feminists whose priorities differed had something important to contribute.

GROWTH OF THE FEMINIST COUNTERCULTURE

At the same time that some activists were being drawn into specialized groups, others were becoming involved in feminist communities that developed in some cities as a women's counterculture began to flourish. There were feminist restaurants, bookstores, publishing houses, record companies, cooperative art galleries, health centers, abortion counseling services, credit unions, day-care centers, furniture-moving companies—the list goes on and on. Operating the way American immigrants always had, the women tried to do business with one another whenever possible. Some went further: They not only refused to hire men, they didn't even want them as customers or clients.

Especially on the West Coast, lesbians played an important role in the feminist counterculture. Most groups were collectives;

most had to struggle to stay alive commercially. Many eventually died, though some survived into the 1990s. The women involved generally felt that their work expressed women's values, which were different from men's, and the emphasis on female values was often unifying. It gave gay and straight women, in particular, something they could agree un. In addition, feminist ventures provided some women with a way to support themselves by doing movement work. Many, moved by a strong separatist impulse, hoped that the counterculture would ultimately provide ways for most women to be independent of men.*

The New ''Radical Feminists'': Difference Feminism Reemerges

The women who created the new ventures often thought of themselves as radical feminists. However, some of the original radical feminists insisted that they were really "cultural feminists" and accused them of retreating from the struggle against male supremacy—of giving up hope that change was possible. Thus, writing for Redstockings, Brooke defined cultural feminism as "the belief that women will be freed via an alternate women's culture. . . ." It was a belief, she said, that led women to focus on lifestyle and their own personal liberation, rather than on the need to create a mass movement to overthrow male supremacy —the goal of radical feminists such as Redstockings. Other activists welcomed the women's subculture as a temporary haven from the struggle. They insisted that it was good for the movement as long as most feminists continued to work for change.

With the advent of the counterculture, the old rift between equality and difference feminists opened up once again. Originally, most liberal feminists and women's liberationists agreed that women and men were similar and that women simply needed equal treatment. Because they were intent on discrediting damaging sex stereotypes, activists of both persuasions tended to downplay gender differences and dream of an androgynous future. However, as the stereotypes became less compelling and some feminists began to fear that women would simply become male clones, some theorists reevaluated gender differences and rediscovered women's values. By the 1980s, the women usually

---

* Many social movements develop a separatist strand—it's generally born out of frustration. For the civil rights movement it was black power; for the New Left, the hippie counterculture of the early seventies.

thought of as "radical feminists" were those who argued most strongly that the sexes were different and that women's values were superior. Though some of the original radical feminists, such as Redstockings, were still active, over their protests the term was also now applied to others with whom they had little in common.*

THE LIBERAL MAINSTREAM

As women's liberation groups declined between 1972 and 1975, many liberal feminist groups kept growing. Mass-membership organizations such as NOW had traditional structures with elected officers, dues-paying members, and so on. They were designed to survive, unlike the small, intense, localized liberation groups. If a NOW chapter lost members and became semi-dormant for a time or folded altogether, the national organization still survived and the chapter could easily be revived at some later date.

By the mid-1970s, liberal feminist groups were becoming an accepted part of the political scene in Washington. Organizations such as NOW, WEAL, BPW, the League of Women Voters, and the American Association of University Women (AAUW) joined forces with newer groups and formed shifting coalitions to work for particular pieces of legislation. Always pragmatic, the liberal women walked in the footsteps of generations of liberal men who believed in individualism and equal rights (for men). The women demanded social and political changes that would give females all the things males took for granted: economic independence, equal access to education and jobs, and so on.

For liberal feminists, living in Washington and concerned with national issues, the early to middle seventies were "the golden years," according to some. Astounded by the upwelling of support for the ERA, Congress was in a receptive mood. Feminists themselves were rapidly learning their way around, and they achieved some major gains.

One of those gains was the Equal Credit Opportunity Act (ECOA), passed in 1974 after a sustained effort by a coalition of feminists. Their campaign offers a glimpse of liberal feminism at

---

* One of the meanings of *radical* is "extreme." Ironically, as ideas advanced by the original radical feminists were accepted, other factions emerged to push theory and action toward new ("extreme") frontiers.

a turning point. Lobbying was still a seat-of-the-pants operation for women at the time, yet activists were already beginning to specialize—and to turn professional.

Before the campaign began, most Americans weren't even aware that women had difficulty getting credit. Those who were turned down often assumed it was their own personal problem. The facts began to surface after the National Commission on Consumer Finance held hearings on the subject in the spring of 1972. Afterward, women from all over the country contacted NOW to describe their own experiences; NOW had already established a Task Force on Consumer Credit, headed by Washington attorney Sharyn Campbell. Before long, WEAL, Parents Without Partners, and the ACLU, among others, also began to investigate complaints *they* were receiving. As the evidence piled up, a broad pattern of discrimination became clear.

- Single women were much more likely to be refused a loan than single men.
- When a woman married, she was usually required to reapply for credit. All the couple's accounts were then automatically put into the husband's name, even if the wife was their sole support. For credit purposes, she ceased to exist.
- If she was subsequently divorced, she lost the right to use all those accounts and might find it impossible to open new ones or to negotiate a loan. Because everything was in her husband's name, she no longer had any credit record herself. Furthermore, in considering applications from divorced women, many lenders refused to count alimony and child support as real income.
- When married couples applied for a mortgage, the wife's income was often ignored. However, sometimes they were told they could have the mortgage if they could produce a note from a doctor certifying that the wife was taking birth control pills or had been sterilized.

Single women were said to be poor risks because they might marry and stop working, and married women were poor risks because they might have a baby and stop working. In the early 1970s, 42 percent of all wives were employed, as were one third of all mothers with children under six, while mothers of older children were even more likely to have jobs. These facts had apparently made little impression on the credit industry, which continued to treat all women as if they were walking wombs, perpetually pregnant or on the brink of pregnancy.

In January 1973, several credit discrimination bills were introduced in Congress. Senator William Brock of Tennessee sponsored one of them. As a relatively conservative Republican, Brock was probably the ideal backer for the legislation, because he won the support of Republicans who might otherwise have opposed it. The bill was actually drafted by one of Brock's aides, a feminist political scientist named Emily Card. In the months that followed, Card provided women's organizations with a useful link to the senator.

Two other feminists also played key roles in the campaign for ECOA. Economist Jane Roberts Chapman and attorney Margaret Gates met one evening at their local NOW chapter. "We started talking," Chapman said. "We left the meeting, and just never went back."

Like the women who were beginning to establish feminist bookstores and record companies, Gates and Chapman were eager to turn their activism somehow into full-time paid jobs so that they could devote all their energy to the movement. They decided to apply for foundation grants to do research on legal and economic issues affecting women, and they were mulling over ways and means when "out of the blue, we discovered that Ralph Nader's organization had given us a $10,000 seed grant," Chapman said. Nader knew Gates from other projects she'd been involved in.

In March 1972, the two women used the money to found the Center for Women Policy Studies (CWPS). A few months later, they were beginning to home in on the credit issue when they heard that the Ford Foundation was interested in it as well. In December 1972, the Foundation gave CWPS $40,000—its first grant to any feminist group—to study sex discrimination in credit.

Through their research, Chapman and Gates became experts on the subject. They testified at hearings and were consulted by congressional committees and the staffs of various members of Congress. They also held briefings for women's organizations, to pass on what they had learned and suggest positions the groups might take as the legislation developed. As a result, women presented a united front most of the time, and their organizations stirred up enough grass-roots activity to convince Congress that voters were concerned about the issue.

The credit industry hesitated to openly oppose a law banning credit discrimination. After all, women were only asking to be granted as much credit as they deserved, according to the standards routinely applied to men. Credit was "a nice clean issue, not like abortion," as one feminist put it. Already in some cities, lenders were easing the restrictions on women—some, because they were being pressured by local chapters of NOW.

In the end, Brock's bill passed the Senate unanimously and the vote in the House was 355 to 1. President Ford signed ECOA in October 1974. It prohibited discrimination on the basis of sex or marital status during credit transactions, and it applied to retail stores, credit card companies, banks, and home finance and home mortgage lenders. Stiff penalties were prescribed.

"Some of the women's groups just dropped off the vine after the law was passed," said Jane Chapman. She and Gates knew that passing the legislation was only the first step. There were still the regulations to come and the problem of enforcement. CWPS was able to stay with the issue, thanks to a small additional grant from the Ford Foundation.

The regulations for ECOA were to be drawn up by the Federal Reserve Board, which was supposedly partial to business interests. In fact, many political analysts believed that administrative agencies such as the FRB were even more likely than Congress to be overly influenced by organizations that had money and technical expertise. It was a surprise, then, when the Board invited CWPS to work with its staff in drafting the regulations. By that time, Chapman and Gates knew more about credit discrimination than almost anyone else in Washington. In addition, Chapman said, "I believe they thought this would pacify the women's organizations."

The first draft of the regulations delighted feminists, but the credit industry complained that the cost would be prohibitive and the rules required too much paperwork. The FRB responded by rewriting the "regs," this time without any input from CWPS, weakening them in the process. When the revised version was published, CWPS hastily contacted the major women's groups, and their members began to pressure the FRB and Congress. Meanwhile, Congresswoman Bella Abzug of New York, an outspoken feminist, descended on the Chairman of the FRB, leading a deputation of twelve other congresswomen, all of them upset about the revised rules.

In the end, the agency went back to the drawing board to make further changes. The final regs, issued in October 1975, were a compromise, better for women than the second draft but not as good as the first. Not entirely satisfied, women's groups kept up the pressure until the rules were amended in 1976. The most significant change was a regulation that said that those who were refused credit must be given a written explanation or must at least be told they had a right to ask for one. To prove sex discrimination, women needed to have something in writing.

Once the regulations were amended, most women's groups apparently lost interest. For a few years, Emily Card, Senator Brock's aide, ran a hotline to take credit complaints, but very little else was done to monitor the law's effects. Chapman and Gates wanted to do research on how well the credit industry was complying with ECOA, but they were unable to get funding. Over the years, relatively few complaints were filed under the law, and it wasn't clear whether that was because discrimination had disappeared or because few chose to challenge it. However, in the 1980s, Card reported that everywhere she went, she still met women who told her they had trouble getting credit.

Certainly, ECOA achieved major improvements. After it went into effect, many women who were refused credit found that when they asked for a written explanation, the credit was granted after all, either because they were able to furnish additional evidence that they were credit-worthy or because the company involved preferred not to risk a sex discrimination complaint. The mortgage situation, in particular, changed drastically. In 1980, single women bought one third of the condominiums sold in the United States, and one tenth of the homes—something that couldn't have happened before ECOA.

As women's issues go, credit discrimination was a relatively easy one. After the vigorous campaign for the ERA, members of Congress apparently expected that support for women's rights would translate into votes at the polls. ECOA gave them a chance to show that they cared. Furthermore, they could pass it without spending the taxpayers' money, and there was little opposition, even from the industry. Most credit executives were undoubtedly aware that if women who deserved credit anyway were now given what they deserved, that could only be good for business.

Political scientists Joyce Gelb and Marian Lief Palley suggested that in addition there was less resistance because ECOA involved "role equity" rather than "role change." It simply extended to women the rights that men already had; it didn't appear to threaten their traditional dependent role. Actually, the credit bill was bound to have far-reaching effects. Anything that improved women's economic status increased their independence and ultimately had an impact on traditional sex roles.

Feminism: The Profession

In the late 1980s, Jane Chapman recalled with nostalgia the excitement of seat-of-the-pants lobbying in the early 1970s. "There were relatively few women who were active on the issues," she said, "so they didn't really specialize. . . . it was a lot of fun. People used to say that it was all done with smoke and mirrors because we had no resources, no staff, but somehow or other we were coming up with what was needed. . . . I always thought it was like the Wizard of Oz: We gave the impression that we had power and influence, as long as nobody could see . . . behind the curtain."

By 1972, all of that was already changing, and Chapman and Gates were part of the transformation. Just as specialized feminist groups were beginning to form around the country, women in Washington were starting to specialize in particular issues. It was important for feminists to develop expertise. Especially in drafting regulations, said Chapman, women had to be able to come up with sophisticated, highly technical language to put teeth in a bill. It might be more fun to be a generalist, but knowledge was power, especially in Washington.

Another new development was the fact that Chapman and Gates and some other Washington women were finding ways to make a career of feminism, just as women in the feminist counterculture were doing. Though some activists were suspicious of women who seemed to be profiting from the movement, the advent of professional feminists was a significant step, especially in the nation's capital. Women's organizations were at a disadvantage as long as they had to rely on volunteers to fight their battles in a city where most groups had paid lobbyists and house experts.

THE INFLUENCE OF GRANT MONEY

Another important change was the fact that foundations began to support some feminist projects. The Ford Foundation made a major contribution to ECOA by enabling Chapman and Gates to work on credit discrimination full-time for almost two years. Though Ford was the first and biggest contributor, nearly a dozen other foundations also gave grants to feminist groups during the

1970s, and many of those groups received grants from government agencies as well. For instance, when Chapman and Gates wanted to do research on the treatment of rape victims, they received funding from the U.S. Department of Justice.

Though grant money allowed a number of women's organizations to thrive, it had at least one drawback: It was almost always earmarked for specific purposes. Feminists' priorities therefore were temporarily determined by the particular projects that foundations and government agencies chose to anoint. However, according to Eileen Thornton, who was president of WEAL from 1976 to 1978, so much needed to be done that few important compromises were made because of the realities of funding; the projects blessed with grants were always worthwhile. Jane Chapman noted that the need for grants tended to eliminate particular tactics rather than eliminate issues. "It turns you toward research or delivering services," she said, "because [foundations] don't want to fund troublemakers. You can't get money to go out and bug federal agencies or bring lawsuits."

Though grants helped feminists make progress, they were mere crumbs from the overall banquet of funding. Only a tiny fraction of the money available went to projects to improve the status of women, and all the women's organizations active in Washington were chronically short of money. After Ronald Reagan was elected President in 1980, government grants dried up almost completely, and private foundations revised their priorities in an effort to help low-income Americans, who were hard-hit by cuts in social services. Many feminist organizations lost out.

However, by that time, feminists were entrenched in Washington. The major women's organizations now had professional lobbyists on staff. There were also public interest law firms and legal defense funds that focused entirely on women's issues. There were feminist PACs (political action committees, which raise money for candidates), a host of specialized groups such as NARAL (the National Abortion Rights Action League),* and a growing number of women-of-color groups. All of the women's organizations joined forces at times and formed shifting coalitions with civil rights, environmentalist, and consumer groups.

In the United States, power lives in many different places. Political scientist Joyce Gelb suggested that the dispersal of power

---

* After abortion was legalized in 1973, NARAL changed its name but not its initials.

gave American feminists many points at which they could apply pressure to the system: They could mount protests, but they could also lobby Congress and state legislatures, pressure government agencies, become policy experts, bring court cases—and more. When progress bogged down in one area, activists changed strategies and applied pressure somewhere else.

During the 1970s, the federal government was relatively receptive, and so liberal feminists in Washington often carried the ball for the movement. At the same time, all over the country, other activists were setting up rape hotlines, women's studies programs, welfare rights groups, and so on. Thus, semicoordinated, constantly retracting and expanding, the second wave rolled into the future.

PART TWO

The Movement Divides and Multiplies

chapter 9

The Relegalization of Abortion

———

During the 1960s, according to some estimates, more than one million illegal abortions were done every year in the United States.* They were performed by moonlighting clerks, salesmen and barbers, and—less often—by doctors willing to risk imprisonment. Every year, more than 350,000 women who had had an illegal abortion suffered complications serious enough to be hospitalized; 500 to 1000 of them died.

From the beginning of the twentieth century until the late 1960s, abortion was a crime in every state in the union except when it was done to save the life of the woman or for other reasons that fell into the category the law defined as "therapeutic." As the second wave got under way, changing state laws became a priority both for liberal feminists and women's liberationists. They soon found that there was already a modest-sized prochoice movement that had been launched a few years ear-

---

* For comparison purposes: In the 1980s, approximately a million and a half legal abortions were done annually.

lier primarily by professional *men*, especially clergymen, who were appalled at the harm done by anti-abortion laws.

As feminists got involved, they transformed the debate. Many of the original activists had assumed that reform was the best they could hope for, and they were working to legalize abortion for women who had been raped or were victims of incest, for example, or whose health was threatened by pregnancy. Feminists insisted that the laws banning abortion must be repealed, rather than simply reformed. They maintained that the government had no right to tell a woman whether or not she could have an abortion, just as it had no right to deny her any other medical procedure. As it evolved, the reproductive rights movement brought together second-wave feminist groups like NOW, new specialized groups that coalesced around the abortion issue, and older organizations, such as Planned Parenthood, which had long been concerned about birth control. When action was necessary, they joined forces in loose coalitions at the state and national levels.

The U.S. Supreme Court's 1973 decision legalizing abortion was the second wave's biggest, most significant victory, but that victory spurred a major backlash. The New Right, an ultraconservative movement that was just a cloud on the horizon in 1973, used the abortion issue to recruit thousands of individuals and groups to the conservative cause. Ultimately, those groups helped the right wing win the presidency in the next decade.

HOW ABORTION BECAME A CRIME

Many Americans assume that in the past abortion was universally regarded as sinful and that it was legalized for the first time in 1973. In fact, neither assumption is true. Throughout recorded history, scholars and theologians have argued about when in a pregnancy the fetus came "alive" or had a soul and therefore could be said to have a right to live. Christian theologians split on the subject. In the Catholic Church, for example, though some were convinced that ensoulment took place at the moment of conception, many others believed it happened at the time of quickening, when the woman first felt the fetus move in the womb during the fourth or fifth month of pregnancy.* That was

---

* In several different cultures in different eras, philosophers suggested that male fetuses acquired souls considerably earlier than females.

the view that generally prevailed from the twelfth century until 1869, when Pope Pius IX declared all abortions a mortal sin.

In the United States, it wasn't until the last half of the nineteenth century that most states passed laws making abortion a crime throughout pregnancy. When the U.S. Constitution was signed, none of the colonies had laws regulating abortion. British common law prevailed, and it made abortion a crime only after quickening and only for the abortionist. Most people apparently believed that the pregnant woman was to be pitied and shouldn't be punished. At any rate, the penalty for performing an abortion was much less harsh than the penalty for infanticide; clearly, it wasn't regarded as the same thing.

Eventually, most states began to adopt stronger measures. There were several reasons. For one thing, after 1840, abortion suddenly became much more visible. Publications were full of ads for "female pills" and for practitioners who specialized in "female complaints"—euphemisms for abortifacients and abortionists. Apparently, many more women were now resorting to abortion, including not only young, single women but also middle- and upper-class wives. In addition, antifeminist backlash undoubtedly motivated some state legislators, for at the time women were demanding the vote and other legal rights.

However, according to scholars, the *main* reason abortion was criminalized was that doctors campaigned for the new laws. The American Medical Association (AMA) was founded in 1847, and in 1859 it launched an aggressive drive against abortion. Physicians lobbied legislatures and wrote books denouncing it. Many were undoubtedly troubled on moral grounds, but a number of historians have suggested that some had other, less noble motives as well: They saw a chance to suppress the competition. At the time, the United States had no licensing laws and anyone could practice medicine. From about 1800 on, so many people preferred healers, midwives, and homeopaths to physicians that some doctors were actually driven out of business. As historian James Mohr put it, ". . . by raising the abortion question and by highlighting the abuses and dangers associated with it, regular physicians could encourage the state to deploy its sanctions against their competitors." The doctors lobbied successfully for laws that would put them in control—that would allow abortion only in cases where a physician felt the woman's life would otherwise be in danger. Thus, they became inextricably involved in the abortion controversy.

There were probably other factors behind the medical anti-abortion campaign as well. In what they wrote, doctors often complained about American wives who were unwilling to remain in their place, bearing and raising children. What better way to subdue them than to make it more difficult for them to control their own fertility? The doctors may also have been concerned— as some people were at the time—because white, Protestant, native-born, middle- and upper-class families were producing fewer children than were immigrants, the poor, and people of color. Many upper-crust Americans feared that the "better" classes were being outbred.

The doctors' anti-abortion campaign didn't have an easy time. At first, the courts were reluctant to enforce the new anti-abortion laws, and physicians got very little support from the clergy or the public. Nevertheless, by 1900 almost every state had prohibited abortion at any point in a pregnancy, except to save the life of the woman.

THE FEMINIST CASE AGAINST ABORTION

Many nineteenth-century feminists were against abortion and opposed birth control as well. Their reasons—as reconstructed by historians—foreshadowed the motivations of many women who became anti-abortion activists in the 1970s and 80s.

Though most of the women involved in the first wave of feminism believed that no woman should be forced to have children she didn't want, they proposed that women achieve control over childbearing not by birth control, but by avoiding sex, periodically or permanently. To some extent, their attitude reflected Victorian prudery. Many nineteenth-century wives, including feminists, were undoubtedly less than enthusiastic about sex— and with good reason. As feminist historian Linda Gordon has pointed out, at the time, pregnancy, childbirth, and abortion were all risky and painful, and venereal disease was common. Husbands, brought up to believe that good women disliked intercourse, were undoubtedly quick and clumsy in their lovemaking.

However, Gordon suggests that, in addition, the feminists distrusted birth control because it didn't seem to be in women's best interests.* Many people were convinced that fear of pregnancy

---

* Gordon argued that women were never just victims of male supremacy, that the conditions of their lives were created by both sexes: Within the limits set by patriarchal societies, women bent to the system where they had to and resisted where they could, and in so doing, helped to define the conditions in which they lived.

was all that kept most women virtuous. If birth control were to remove that fear, more women might become sexually available, and husbands would be tempted into extramarital affairs. Respectable wives would be deserted; families would suffer. Most women were completely dependent on their husbands and had no other realistic options. Furthermore, most nineteenth-century women, including feminists, had no wish to break the connection between sex and procreation because they felt that children were what held families together. As Linda Gordon puts it, "Pregnancy is woman's burden and her revenge."

"THERAPEUTIC" AND BACK-ALLEY ABORTIONS

During the first half of the twentieth century, women's opportunities broadened until they weren't quite so dependent on men. However, there was still no real outcry against the abortion laws. The whole subject smacked of illicit sex, and people weren't comfortable talking about it. Many Catholics probably felt that abortion was taking a human life, and many non-Catholics assumed that a fetus was only a potential person. Because the issue was seldom discussed, it remained only a potential controversy.

The laws that had criminalized abortion made one exception: "Therapeutic" abortions were permissible to save the life of the mother. During the 1960s, only 8000 therapeutic procedures were done in the United States every year, in contrast to the estimated million illegal abortions. There were very few medical conditions left that were life-threatening for pregnant women, and it was difficult for a sympathetic doctor to pretend such a problem existed because most legal abortions were performed in hospitals and had to be approved by a board, a special committee of physicians. The boards refused most requests. Often, the doctors on the committee seemed to feel that pregnancy and childbirth were suitable punishment for a woman's sexual sins. As one board member put it, "Now that she has had her fun, she wants us to launder her dirty underwear." In general, poor women, especially women of color, were more likely to be turned away by hospital boards.

Many women with no hope of getting a therapeutic abortion attempted to self-abort. One nineteen-year-old tried "massive doses of gin, nutmeg, mustard baths, moving heavy furniture." When these failed, she took an overdose of "large blue pills usually used for migraine headaches. . . ." She went deaf for twelve hours as a result, but still didn't miscarry. In the end, her hearing returned, and she went looking for an abortionist.

Finding a competent illegal abortionist was difficult, frightening, and dangerous—much more so for poor women than for those with money. In many (but not all) states, a woman risked criminal prosecution.* In actual fact, few women were ever prosecuted, but most didn't know that. What they did know was that by having an illegal abortion, they were taking their lives in their hands. Susan Brownmiller was young and unmarried in 1963 when she discovered that she was pregnant. She begged her gynecologist to help her find a doctor to do an abortion. Apparently frightened by her request, he refused. His fear was understandable, because under the law anyone who helped a woman obtain an abortion by giving her the name of an abortionist was legally an accomplice to a crime and could be arrested.

Desperate to find help, Brownmiller recalled that she'd heard of a Dr. Robert Spencer in Ashland, Pennsylvania, who did abortions. Spencer—known in the abortion underground for his skill and compassion—had been operating fairly openly for generations, and though the authorities had closed down his clinic a few times, he had somehow avoided prison. Unfortunately, Brownmiller called him during one of the periods when he was closed down. Nevertheless, he gave her the name of a doctor in Baltimore, though he cautioned her that he didn't know much about the man. The Baltimore doctor agreed to do the abortion, but insisted on using a new method that involved injecting a substance through the abdominal wall. Brownmiller knew that wasn't the way abortions were usually done, and at the last minute was too frightened to go through with it. Later, she realized that he was probably experimenting with the saline method used to bring on contractions in the later stages of pregnancy and not recommended for women less than five months pregnant (at the time, she was barely three months along).

Many desperate phone calls later, Brownmiller wound up in San Juan, Puerto Rico, in the office of a doctor who immediately wanted to know how much money she had brought with her. All she had was $300; he insisted that his price was $700 and tried to send her away. She burst into tears, but she also told him, "I am not going to leave your office until I have an abortion." Apparently realizing that she meant what she said, and that

* In some states, abortion was a crime for the abortionist but not for the woman involved.

he couldn't afford to have her make a fuss, the doctor finally did the abortion.

Brownmiller was middle class and resourceful, had friends she could turn to for information, and was able to raise a substantial amount of money—she figured the whole episode cost her at least $700, including travel expenses. Other women, especially poor women, often didn't fare as well.

BIRTH OF THE ABORTION-RIGHTS MOVEMENT

In 1962, abortion finally became a national issue when the Sherri Finkbine case brought it out into the open. Finkbine, who already had four children, was pregnant with the fifth when she learned that a sleeping pill she'd been using had caused birth defects in thousands of babies whose mothers had taken it during pregnancy. The drug was called Thalidomide, and infants exposed to it in utero were often born with flipper-like arms and legs. Finkbine's obstetrician scheduled an immediate abortion. She herself was concerned about other women who might be taking Thalidomide, unaware of the danger, so the day before the abortion was supposed to take place, she told her story to a friend who worked for a local newspaper.

The story appeared the next day, and the hospital immediately canceled Finkbine's abortion. A few days later, her doctor applied for a court order to force the hospital to cooperate. The wire services picked up the story, and Sherri Finkbine suddenly became a public figure. Letters and phone calls poured in, including several death threats, and the FBI had to be brought in to protect her. Ultimately, she had the abortion in Sweden, but in the meantime she lost her job.

During the public debate over the Finkbine case, the controversy over whether a fetus was a person or only a potential person was forced into the open, and both sides began to mobilize. The abortion controversy made news again in 1963 and 1964, when a rubella epidemic resulted in the birth of 30,000 American children with birth defects.

As a result of all this, some doctors began to press for new, liberalized state abortion laws. In 1959, the American Law Institute (ALI) had drafted a Model Penal Code that recommended allowing abortion not only when the woman's life was in danger, but also when pregnancy or childbirth might damage her physical or mental health, when birth defects were very likely, or in cases of rape or incest—a now-familiar cluster of reasons. Many doctors undoubtedly favored an ALI-type law because it would legalize what they were inclined to do anyway.

The demand for abortion kept growing during the 1960s, for women's lives had changed. More of them were part of the work force and were determined to control their own fertility. Yet contraceptives were often unreliable or else had unpleasant or possibly dangerous side effects. One national study of married women found that during a five-year period, over one third became pregnant in spite of using birth control.

As noted earlier, professional men were the first to attack restrictive abortion laws. The early activists included lawyers, doctors, members of the clergy, public health officials, and a few lawmakers. They pressured state legislatures to change the laws, and in 1967 their efforts paid off for the first time when three states—Colorado, North Carolina, and California—passed new, ALI-type laws. The activists also pursued test cases in the courts and, in addition, set up abortion referral services—a risky form of civil disobedience, since anyone who did referrals became an accessory to a crime.

ABORTION REFERRAL SERVICES

Author Larry Lader was virtually the father of the reproductive rights movement on the East Coast. His book, *Abortion*, demanded repeal of the laws that made abortion a crime. When the book came out in 1966, Lader was immediately deluged with appeals from women desperate to find doctors willing to do abortions in their offices. "I was engulfed in misery," he recalled. From his research, he knew there were doctors who would do abortions in secret for a reasonable fee, and one day at a press conference he announced that he was willing to "try to help women." He didn't say in so many words that he would provide the names of abortionists, "but that was obviously what I meant," he admitted. A radical who had been deeply involved in politics, he was also a feminist. Between 1966 and 1970, he referred about 2000 women to doctors willing to perform abortions despite state laws.

A woman in California also began doing referrals in 1966. Five years earlier, Patricia Maginnis had founded an organization to lobby for the repeal of California's anti-abortion law. When her efforts were unsuccessful, she turned to civil disobedience. She went to Mexico and personally inspected a dozen small abortion clinics (though abortion was illegal in Mexico, it was tolerated). Returning home, she mimeographed a list of the best clinics and began distributing it to women on San Francisco street corners. At about the same time, she started to give free public lectures around the state to explain to women how to do self-abortions. She admitted that the technique she described was risky; her real purpose in presenting it was to dramatize the injustice of the law.

In July 1966, Maginnis was arrested in San Francisco for her street-corner activities—she was charged with distributing lewd and obscene literature—and the following February she was arrested in San Mateo County for her lectures. Both cases went to trial; in the first, she was released on a technicality, and in the second, she was acquitted on the grounds that her arrest had interfered with her right to free speech.

In 1967, the anti-abortion cause got an enormous boost when a New York City minister, the Reverend Howard Moody, founded the Clergy Consultation Service on Abortion. At a press conference that got front-page coverage in the *New York Times*, Moody announced that twenty-two ministers and rabbis had volunteered their time to counsel women with "problem pregnancies" and help them arrange an abortion, if that was what they wanted to do. Over the next few years, Moody developed a national network of clergy referral services, covering about twenty-four states and involving more than 1000 counselors. All risked arrest, and a few were actually brought up on charges. The Clergy Consultation Service was very important, according to Lader, because "it brought the moral weight of prominent and outspoken clergymen behind the principle of referral. . . ." Other referral services soon sprang up as well.

FEMINISTS TAKE UP THE ISSUE

Once the second wave began, feminists soon focused on the abortion problem. NOW took a stand on it in 1967. Radical feminists caught the attention of the press in 1969 when they disrupted a New York State hearing on a reform bill and afterward held a speakout on abortion.

According to abortion historian Rosalind Petchesky, feminist activists were the "shock troops" of the abortion rights movement. They did underground referrals and counseling and held speakouts, sit-ins, and other demonstrations. By making abortion a highly visible issue, they helped create the climate of opinion that made repeal more likely. By insisting that abortion was a woman's right, they made it more difficult to pass it off as a controversy for professional men—doctors, judges, legislators—to resolve through reforms that still left professional men in charge.

Even feminists who were focused primarily on employment saw abortion as a key issue. If women wanted an equal chance to earn a living, they must be able to control their fertility. However, for many feminists, the true heart of the issue was bodily integrity. As one California woman put it, ". . . we can get all the rights in the world . . . and none of them means a doggone thing if we don't own the flesh we stand in . . . if the whole course of our lives can be changed by somebody else that can get us pregnant by accident, or by deceit, or by force." Writer Ellen Willis went further: "There is no way a pregnant woman can passively let the fetus live; she must create and nurture it with her own body. . . . However gratifying pregnancy may be to a woman who desires it, for the unwilling it is literally an invasion—the closest analogy is to the difference between lovemaking and rape."

Feminists insisted, almost unanimously, that there should be no limits of any kind on abortion: They were for "abortion on request." New York activist Lucinda Cisler noted that "proposals for 'reform' are based on the notion that abortions must be regulated, meted out to deserving women under an elaborate set of rules designed to provide 'safeguards against abuse.' "

The reform laws, Cisler explained, generally contained several unacceptable restrictions. Among other things, they said that abortions could only be done in hospitals, which raised the cost of the procedure. They also sometimes required the consent of the woman's husband or of her parents if she was a minor—again, decreeing that her body was not her own.* Furthermore, some feminists were convinced that abortions could be performed safely by nonphysicians in the right circumstances.

---

* In the 1980s, as the Supreme Court began to back away from its 1973 decision, a number of states passed laws with similar restrictions; as they took back abortion access, it was like a film of the late 1960s, run in reverse.

THE ABORTION COLLECTIVE CALLED JANE

During the early 1970s, the activities of a feminist collective provided stunning evidence that abortions had become potentially simple and safe to do for those with minimal training. Between 1969 and 1973, the women of the collective performed about 11,000 illegal abortions. Their safety record for first-trimester procedures was as good as that of clinics in New York State, after New York legalized abortions.

"Jane" was originally a pseudonym used by a University of Chicago student who did abortion referrals from her dorm. Feminists from the Chicago Women's Liberation Union took over the project in 1969 and called their collective Jane. At first, the women simply did counseling and referrals. Eventually, they realized that although the abortionists they were using were *not* doctors, they *were* competent. One of these men taught a member of the collective how to do abortions and she taught others. During the winter of 1971, the Jane women began to perform abortions themselves.

The history of Jane provides a fascinating look at a model radical-feminist collective in action. The women were highly organized. Theoretically, in typical collective fashion, all members were expected to do all jobs. Understandably, not everyone wanted to be an abortionist or to assist during procedures, so exceptions were made for those tasks. However, all members were required to work sometimes as counselors, so that they would never lose touch with the needs of the women they were serving.

A woman who needed an abortion would get Jane's phone number from friends or from the Chicago Women's Liberation Union. She would call and leave her own name and phone number on an answering machine. Every two hours, a Jane member —known as Call-back Jane—collected the messages and returned calls. Over the phone, she took a medical history, and then told the woman that a counselor would contact her.

The counselor was given the medical information and saw the woman either alone or in a group for a counseling session. During the session, the counselor explained exactly what the woman could expect, purposely demystifying the procedure. Members of the collective wanted every woman to feel that she was in charge of her own health and her own body—they insisted that they did abortions *with* women, rather than to women or for them.

Then the woman was given an appointment and the address of "the Front," a kind of staging place used so that nonmembers wouldn't know where the abortions actually took place. From the Front, women were taken by a Jane driver to the apartment where the procedures were done. The collective had a fully equipped operating room and an ample supply of the necessary drugs on hand; they even did a Pap smear as part of their routine. Afterward, the women were returned by car to the Front and were told to phone their counselor the following week, so she could be sure there were no complications; if a woman failed to call, the counselor would call her. The average fee was $50 but no one was ever turned away for lack of money.

In 1973, police raided the apartment where Jane women were performing abortions and arrested seven members of the collective. Four were students; the other three were mothers of small children. All spent the night in jail. The police had been tipped off by the sister-in-law of a woman who was getting an abortion. All charges were eventually dropped, perhaps because of the Supreme Court's abortion decision that year.

THE FOUNDING OF NARAL

By 1968, there were organizations all over the country committed to changing state abortion laws either by reform or repeal. Dr. Lonny Myers, leader of a Chicago group, proposed a conference to bring them all together. She saw it as a chance to convert the reformers to the repeal position. Larry Lader suggested that they also use the conference to found a national organization.

In February 1969, 350 abortion activists met in Chicago. Twenty-one organizations had sent representatives, and YWCA women mingled with radical feminists, law professors, sociologists, doctors, and legislators. The debate between the reformers and the repealers was heated, but in the end they agreed to form a coalition that would be called NARAL: the National Association for the *Repeal* of Abortion Laws. Larry Lader served as its first chair.

Practical experience with reform laws had finally convinced many waverers that reform just didn't make enough of a difference. In Colorado, for example, hospital boards were rejecting nineteen out of every twenty requests for abortion. They made it so difficult to get approval that most women gave up after a few weeks. If a woman said she needed an abortion to preserve her own mental health (one of the grounds allowed under the reform law), some boards demanded proof that she'd had psychiatric treatment in the past; others wanted two letters from psychiatrists, though the law itself required only one. Local psychiatrists, who knew a good thing when they saw one, charged $50 or more per letter; hospital abortions themselves cost a minimum of $500. By 1969, Representative Richard Lamm, who had sponsored the reform law, announced that "we're going to try to repeal it or overturn it. . . . We tried to change a cruel, outmoded, inhuman law . . . what we got was a cruel, outmoded, inhuman law." In North Carolina, a reform law had produced similar situations.

Over the next few years, it became obvious that even repeal wasn't the whole answer. In the fall of 1969, in a case called *United States* v. *Vuitch*, a Washington, D.C., court threw out the District's abortion law, in effect repealing it and leaving D.C. with no abortion law at all. Soon afterward, D.C. General, the major public hospital serving the poor, clamped down on abortions almost completely—in the first two months of 1970 it performed only ten. Private hospitals were also restrictive, and were expensive as well. NARAL ultimately sued D.C. General, with help from the ACLU, but it took two lawsuits and two court orders before the hospital finally agreed to handle 1000 abortion patients a year.

Meanwhile, thanks to a legal decision, California's *reform* law was working so well that the state became one of the best in the nation for abortion. In September 1969, the California Supreme Court invalidated its old abortion law (not the new, reform law) in a case called *People* v. *Belous*, citing the right to privacy in matters related to marriage, family, and sex. The *Belous* decision cut the ground out from under those who wanted the new law interpreted as narrowly as possible, because it strongly suggested that if the new law were challenged, the court would probably invalidate it as well. In addition, the justices had held that in deciding whether to do an abortion for a woman, a physician could weigh the statistical risk she ran in having the abortion against the statistical risks of childbirth. Because early abortion was less risky than childbirth, in effect the Court had provided a rationale for virtually all early abortions.

In the wake of *Belous*, pro-abortion activists pressured hospitals to perform more abortions, and the Clergy Consultation Service made it clear that it would channel referrals to those that handled abortion best. The net result, according to Lader, was a "soaring approval rate, low costs, and high-quality care. . . . California thus became a unique example of an unworkable law that was made to work through the inferences of a court decision and hard-fisted medical politics."

All the same, watered-down repeal seemed to be the wave of the future. In 1970, new laws went into effect in both Hawaii and Alaska that permitted abortion for any reason whatsoever during the first six months of pregnancy. In both cases, however, the new law required that the procedure be done in a hospital and it stipulated that the woman must have lived in the state for a month or more. No other medical procedure was limited to state residents. That same year, the state of Washington also passed a modified repeal bill.

NEW YORK: WIN AND NEAR-LOSS

The New York State legislature passed a repeal bill in 1970. Two years later, the legislators changed their minds and only the Governor's veto saved abortion rights. The whole episode foreshadowed the bitter controversy that would develop after the Supreme Court's 1973 decision and some of the tactics anti-abortion organizations would use. It also demonstrated that to preserve reproductive rights, feminists would need to be vigilant.

In 1970, NARAL and approximately fifty other organizations decided to back a repeal bill in New York. Because Catholics made up 40 percent of the state's population and were a powerful lobby, few people thought the bill stood any chance. However, abortion-rights activists worked hard and public support kept growing. On March 18, 1970, to almost everyone's surprise, the State Senate passed the bill, 31 to 26. As the action shifted to the Assembly, the Catholic hierarchy, galvanized into action, had a pastoral letter read in all Catholic churches urging parishioners to pressure their legislators.

When the bill reached the floor of the Assembly on April 9, the galleries were full. The voting began late in the afternoon, and it became obvious as the roll call progressed that the bill was about to be killed by a tie vote. However, before the clerk could announce the final tally, Democratic Assemblyman George Michaels got to his feet and—his face white, his voice shaking—began to speak. Michaels, who had already cast his vote against the bill, represented a conservative, largely Catholic district. He was a liberal by inclination, but in the past he had tried to vote as his district seemed to want him to—supporting welfare cuts, for example—and had felt like a hypocrite. Though his family and friends had urged him to vote for the abortion bill, he had voted against it, hoping that it would pass anyway. Now, he announced to a stunned Assembly that he was changing his vote from No to Yes. His eyes filled with tears, he asked, "What's the use of getting elected if you don't stand for something? I realize . . . that I am terminating my political career, but I cannot in good conscience sit here and allow my vote to be the one that defeats this bill. . . ."

Thanks to Michaels, the repeal bill became law, and New York suddenly had the most liberal abortion law in the country. In the first year, almost 165,000 abortions were performed in the state, over half of them for women who were not New Yorkers (the law had no residency requirement). During that time, deaths in New York City related to pregnancy, which had always been caused primarily by back-alley abortions, dropped by two thirds.

However, the battle over abortion had just begun. In April 1971, New York's Commissioner of Social Services announced that Medicaid wouldn't cover "elective" abortions. A little over a year later, a court decision overruled this directive, but the basic tactic—denying Medicaid payments—was used successfully in the late 1970s when Congress passed the Hyde Amendment.

By 1972, many of the legislators who had voted for the law were being challenged by anti-abortion opponents. Michaels himself *was* defeated in the next election, just as he'd predicted. The election results convinced many politicians that it was extremely risky to support abortion, a view that wasn't seriously challenged until the late 1980s.

Efforts to persuade the legislature to revoke the new abortion law began in earnest early in 1972. Three days a week, from January on, buses rolled into Albany from every parish in Nassau and Suffolk counties, bringing high school students and housewives, shepherded by teachers and priests, to demonstrate against abortion and to lobby. Lader recalled that they were "always armed with their brochures and grotesque, colored fetus pictures." The campaign was well financed and well organized.

NARAL tried to mobilize the abortion rights forces to defend what they'd won, but got little response. Governor Nelson Rockefeller had promised to veto any bill designed to undo the 1970 abortion law, and evidently most people were relying on that. Public complacency became a chronic problem for the reproductive rights movement after 1973.

The campaign to save legalized abortion in the state didn't

really get under way until mid-April, and even after that a New York City march brought out only 1500 demonstrators. In May, the state legislature voted to rescind the new abortion law, and the prochoice side, energized at last, deluged Rockefeller with letters and telegrams. As promised, he vetoed the bill. Chastened, the prochoice activists understood that their law was still in danger—the governor might not be there to save it the next time. Thus, in the end, the near loss of the abortion law led to the development of an enduring feminist lobby in Albany. In addition, according to Larry Lader, the experience with safe, widespread, legalized abortion in New York State almost certainly influenced the Supreme Court's decision.

THE ROE AND DOE CASES

By the early 1970s, when the Supreme Court agreed to hear two abortion cases, the situation in the United States was chaotic. About one third of the states had liberalized abortion restrictions to some extent, and four had virtually repealed them. As a result, women with money who were determined enough could usually get an abortion by traveling out of state if they had to. Low-income women were out of luck unless they happened to live in the right state. By the end of 1972, further efforts to change state laws had apparently been stalled by a determined opposition, led by the Catholic Church. However, in eight states the lower courts had thrown out abortion laws on constitutional grounds, and a number of cases were making their way up through the appeals systems. Most were litigated by the ACLU Reproductive Freedom Project.

Meanwhile, public support for abortion had been growing. In 1965, 91 percent of those polled were opposed to changing the abortion laws. Just seven years later, in 1972, a Gallup poll reported that 64 percent of the general public (including 56 percent of Catholics) felt the abortion decision should be left to the woman and her doctor. A number of powerful national organizations, such as the American Bar Association, were now backing repeal, and groups such as Zero Population Growth had become involved because they were concerned about overpopulation.

When the Supreme Court handed down its historic 1973 decision legalizing most abortions, two cases were involved, *Roe* v. *Wade* and *Doe* v. *Bolton*. They're sometimes referred to collectively as *Roe* v. *Wade*, but of the two, *Doe* was more difficult to argue and perhaps more significant, because it involved a liberalized, ALI-type law.

The woman who made legal history as Mary Doe was a twenty-two-year-old mother of three who was pregnant for the fourth time. She was married to a man who did odd jobs when he could get them, and didn't earn enough to support a family. A state agency had placed Doe's first two children in foster homes, apparently because the couple couldn't provide for them. Doe herself placed her third baby with a relative for adoption when her husband threatened to divorce her if she didn't give the baby away. Pregnant again, she was afraid that if she had the baby, he would leave her and she'd lose the child as well. She had been a patient in a mental hospital and had been advised not to have another baby.

Doe lived in Atlanta, Georgia, where state law permitted abortion for birth defects, in rape cases, and to preserve the health of the mother as well as her life. However, the procedure for getting a Georgia abortion was designed to be complex and forbidding. A woman who wanted an abortion for medical reasons had to have the approval of three doctors plus a hospital board, and she was given no opportunity to appear before the board and plead her case. When Mary Doe was turned down by a local public hospital, she went to the Legal Aid Society, hoping that something could be done.

That's how she came to the attention of a group of four women lawyers, who had decided to mount a class-action suit to challenge Georgia's abortion law. Doe agreed to become part of the suit, which would be brought on behalf of herself "and others similarly situated." Though the lawyers promised to try to keep her identity secret, they warned her that it was possible she'd have to testify in court and that even a decision in her favor would probably come too late for her to have an abortion. On the other hand, there was little they could do for her legally other than to challenge the Georgia law.

As the weeks passed, the attorneys became concerned about Doe and decided to try to get her an abortion before the trial. Between them, they raised enough money to pay for it and found a doctor who was able to get approval from a private hospital—"which demonstrated that if you had money, you could get it done," said Margie Pitts Hames, the lawyer who eventually argued the case before the Supreme Court. It was possible that if

Doe had the abortion, her case would become moot. "We didn't know," said Hames, "so we were prepared to amend and add additional plaintiffs."

However, before the abortion could be performed, and with the trial less than a month away, Doe's husband took her on a trip out of town; for several weeks she simply dropped out of sight. Finally, she telephoned to explain that her husband had taken her to Oklahoma and had abandoned her there. She said she had felt the baby move and no longer wanted to end the pregnancy. The lawyers agreed to spend the money they'd raised for the abortion to fly her back to Atlanta in time for the trial.

When Doe appeared in court on the morning of the trial, so did nearly a dozen other pregnant women, recruited by her lawyers as decoys to prevent the press from identifying her as the plaintiff. That way, if she wasn't called to testify, her identity would remain a secret. To Hames's relief, the court announced that it wouldn't hear any witnesses at all but would take oral arguments on the constitutional issues only.

On July 31, 1970, the court declared Georgia's abortion law unconstitutional on privacy grounds, because it interfered with a personal medical decision that a woman had a right to make in conjunction with her doctor. The state decided to appeal, and the case was on its way to the U.S. Supreme Court.

The more famous *Roe* v. *Wade* case challenged a Texas law that permitted an abortion only when it was necessary to save the woman's life. Attorneys Linda Coffee and Sarah Weddington had decided to bring a test case, and the plaintiff they chose was a twenty-one-year-old single woman who worked as a waitress in a Dallas bar and was so poor she couldn't even afford a local illegal abortionist. Her name was Norma McCorvey, but to protect her identity she was referred to throughout the legal proceedings as Jane Roe. McCorvey claimed to have been gang-raped. However, many years later she confessed that she had become pregnant "through what I thought was love." According to Margie Hames, in those days single women often said they'd been raped because they hoped to persuade a sympathetic doctor to perform an abortion for them. At any rate, rape played no part in the legal argument used in the *Roe* case, because the Texas statute didn't include an exception for rape.

In June 1970, a panel of three judges declared the Texas law unconstitutional. By that time, it was too late for McCorvey to have an abortion. Both she and Mary Doe had their babies and put them up for adoption.

Abortion and the Right to Privacy

In the *Roe* and *Doe* cases, there were many possible ways to argue for a woman's right to abortion. The lawyers could maintain that anti-abortion laws interfered with the right to bodily integrity, that they amounted to sex discrimination, or that they invaded a woman's privacy. The Supreme Court eventually based its decision on the privacy argument. Afterward, a cottage industry sprang up as scholars criticized the decision, citing other approaches that might have provided a stronger basis for abortion rights.

To most feminists, bodily integrity was the fundamental issue. They believed in a woman's right to determine what would happen to her own body—what Margie Hames called "the absolutist argument." Hames didn't think the Court would go along with it because the justices had heard it before, in the *Vuitch* case, and hadn't responded.

Legal decisions are based on precedents, and the precedents for the privacy argument were the most promising. None were abortion cases, but lawyers often argue by analogy, citing decisions that involve similar issues or principles of law, even though otherwise the cases are very different. In the past, in a handful of key decisions, the High Court had addressed the question: To what extent may the government legitimately interfere in an individual's private life? The justices had concluded that it couldn't interfere, for example, with a family's decision to send its children to private school, rather than public, or with a man's right to reproduce, even if he was a habitual criminal (the law that was struck down had prescribed sterilization for those found guilty of "felonies involving moral turpitude").

For abortion-rights advocates, the most promising precedent was *Griswold* v. *Connecticut*. In 1965, in *Griswold*, the Supreme Court struck down a Connecticut law that made it a crime for a couple to use contraceptives to prevent conception, though they could use them legally to prevent venereal disease. No one had ever been prosecuted under the law and practically every drugstore in Connecticut sold condoms openly—supposedly, to prevent disease. The law would have been a total anachronism, except that it made anyone who provided birth control information an accessory to the crime of using birth control. Thus, the executive director of Connecticut's Planned Parenthood League deliberately invited arrest in order to test the law.

In striking down the Connecticut statute, the Supreme Court cited the right to marital privacy. The majority opinion, written by Justice Douglas, asked:

> Would we allow the police to search the sacred precincts of marital bedrooms for telltale signs of the use of contraceptives? The very idea is repulsive to the notions of privacy surrounding the marriage relationship.
>
> We deal with a right of privacy older than the Bill of Rights. . . .

Even as the Supreme Court took *Roe* and *Doe* under consideration, Justice William Brennan was drafting the majority opinion in another privacy case that would add to the legal precedents on which the 1973 decision would eventually be based. In *Eisenstadt v. Baird* the issue, again, was contraception. Bill Baird, a birth-control activist, had deliberately challenged a statute that made it a crime to distribute contraceptives to the unmarried in Massachusetts (it was known as the "Crimes Against Chastity" law). Married couples could buy them, but only from doctors or with a doctor's prescription.

During a lecture at Boston University, Baird gave contraceptive foam to twelve students, all single women, while several police officers watched from the wings and his ACLU lawyer waited in the audience. Baird was arrested, convicted, and spent over a month in a Boston jail. In 1972, the Supreme Court overturned his conviction on the grounds that the Massachusetts law treated the unmarried differently than the married and thus violated the equal protection clause of the fourteenth amendment. In writing the opinion on *Eisenstadt*, Justice Brennan noted that "if the right of privacy means anything, it is the right of the *individual*, married or single, to be free from unwarranted governmental intrusion into matters so fundamentally affecting a person as the decision whether to bear or beget a child." Court observers believe he inserted the word "bear" with the thought that it might prove a useful reference for the abortion cases the justices were even then considering.

The right of privacy wasn't spelled out in so many words anywhere in the Constitution, and for that reason the birth control decisions (and later the abortion decision) were vulnerable. At various times, the High Court held that a guarantee of privacy was *implied* in five different amendments to the Constitution (the first, fourth, fifth, ninth, and fourteenth), and in the *Griswold* opinion Justice Douglas took yet another tack: He wrote that the privacy right was actually to be found in the penumbras* of the guarantees in the Bill of Rights, and that it gave those vital amendments "life and substance." In other words, the amendments that promised freedom of religion, prohibited unreasonable searches and seizures, and so on, were based on a fundamental respect for privacy; therefore, a citizen's privacy was also protected.

Ultimately, Hames and Weddington focused on the ninth and fourteenth amendments.† The ninth asserted that the American people had rights other than those mentioned in the Constitution. It was added to the Bill of Rights because there was no way to draft a Bill so comprehensive that it covered all essential rights. Congress wanted to guarantee that, in the future, citizens couldn't be denied some fundamental right on the grounds that they weren't intended to have it because it wasn't mentioned in the Bill of Rights. In the *Roe* case, the lower court cited the ninth amendment, among others, in overturning the Texas abortion law.

However, no Supreme Court majority had ever struck down a law because it violated the ninth amendment. Margie Hames believed that the fourteenth amendment was a more likely prospect. The fourteenth says that a state may not make laws that "deprive any person of life, liberty, or property without due process of law. . . ." Essentially, this meant that before citizens could be convicted of a crime or deprived of any of their rights, they must be given a hearing ("due process") and a chance to defend themselves. Thus, Hames decided to argue that the Georgia law denied women the right to seek medical care and denied physicians and nurses the right to administer such care. Therefore, it deprived them all of liberty, as guaranteed by the fourteenth amendment. Doctors, nurses, social workers, and ministers were all plaintiffs in the Georgia case, along with Mary Doe.

The abortion laws unquestionably *did* interfere with medical decisions, and it was on that basis that Hames and her colleagues had won their case in the lower court. Moreover, Hames had consulted Fred Graham, a law school friend who was covering the High Court as a reporter. He had convinced her that the fourteenth amendment was a better way to go, because Justices

---

* Penumbras are vague, borderline areas—like the partly lighted halo around the moon during an eclipse.
† Margie Hames argued the *Doe* case, while Sarah Weddington argued *Roe*.

Potter Stewart and Harry Blackmun took the responsibilities of professional men very seriously, and Blackmun had actually been legal counsel for the Mayo Clinic at one time. Graham believed that the legal reasoning in the Georgia court decision would sit well with Stewart and Blackmun, especially the argument that medical personnel had a right to treat patients without interference from the state.

"Ladies' Day" in the Supreme Court

On December 13, 1971, when Margie Hames and Sarah Weddington came to Washington to argue their cases before the Supreme Court, there were only seven justices on the bench. President Nixon's appointees, William Rehnquist and Lewis Powell, had not yet been sworn in. Many people assumed that the justices would be reluctant to take on a controversial issue such as abortion without a full Court, and therefore expected them to dispose of *Roe* and *Doe* rather quickly on procedural grounds. However, Hames recalled that "when Fred Graham met me outside the Court that day, he told me, 'They're saying that this is ladies' day in court.' Five of the seven justices' wives were in the courtroom. So I knew we were going to be talking about abortion, not jurisdiction."

Weddington, who argued first, spoke at length about the terrible dilemma women faced in states like Texas, where abortion was virtually outlawed. She cited both the right to privacy, derived from the ninth amendment, and a woman's basic rights. When Hames's turn came, she stressed the fourteenth amendment liberty interest and the medical angle. Meanwhile, the opposition not only argued that the states had the right to regulate abortion, but maintained that since Roe and Doe had already had their babies, their cases were moot; and that, furthermore, no pregnant woman could ever win an abortion decision, because the appeals process took so long that she would inevitably have had her baby before the case reached the Supreme Court.

It took over a year for the High Court to announce its abortion decision. As reporters eventually reconstructed events within the Court, the initial vote was 5 to 2 in favor of striking down the abortion laws of both Texas and Georgia. Justice Blackmun was assigned to write the majority opinion, to the chagrin of the more liberal justices, who were afraid his opinion wouldn't go far enough. A slow and meticulous worker, Blackmun wrote one draft of the opinion and then withdrew it. During the summer, he did research on abortion in the medical library at the Mayo Clinic. The case was reargued in the fall, because by that time Justices Lewis Powell and William Rehnquist had joined the Court. From the questioning during the second hearing, it was obvious to Margie Hames that the justices were trying to decide whether abortion should be legalized throughout pregnancy or only up to some particular stage of it. "We felt pretty good about the potential for victory," she said.

The *Roe* v. *Wade* Decision

On Tuesday, January 22, 1973, headlines in most newspapers reported that former President Lyndon Johnson had died of a heart attack the day before; that, thanks to the peace negotiations in Paris, the end of the Vietnam War might be in sight; and that the Supreme Court had struck down almost every state abortion law in the land by a vote of 7 to 2, with only Justices William Rehnquist and Byron White dissenting. Elated feminists believed the battle was over.

The *Roe* decision declared that laws of the Texas type violated the due process clause of the fourteenth amendment. However, in his opinion, Blackmun explicitly rejected the argument that a woman's right to abortion was absolute. He explained that the government could limit an individual's rights when it had a compelling interest at stake, and that in abortion cases, the State had an interest in safeguarding women's health and in protecting potential life.

Blackmun then laid down a formula for balancing the conflicting interests of the woman and the State. Until approximately the end of the first trimester of pregnancy, he wrote, the abortion decision "must be left to the medical judgment of the pregnant woman's attending physician." After the first trimester, the State could regulate abortion procedures in order to protect women's health. In the third trimester, once the fetus reached the point where it was viable—that is, capable of surviving outside the womb—the government could regulate and even prohibit abortion in the interests of preserving potential life. However, even in the third trimester, the State must allow abortion if the woman's life or health were at stake.

Blackmun noted that "the abortion decision in all its aspects is inherently, and primarily, a medical decision, and basic responsibility for it must rest with the physician." Turning to the argument that the fetus was a person, he wrote:

. . . our observation that throughout the major portion of the 19th century prevailing legal abortion practices were far freer than they are today, persuades us that the word "person," as used in the Fourteenth Amendment, does not include the unborn. . . . We need not resolve the difficult question of when life begins. When those trained in the respective disciplines of medicine, philosophy, and theology are unable to arrive at any consensus, the judiciary, at this point in the development of man's knowledge, is not in a position to speculate as to the answer.

In the Georgia case, the Court again emphasized the doctor's right to make medical judgments (as opposed to citing women's rights). The *Doe* decision struck down all ALI-type laws, with their bureaucratic restrictions. It said that states couldn't require abortions to be done in hospitals during the first trimester, nor could they require a woman to get the approval of a hospital committee or of independent physicians. In addition, states could no longer limit abortions to state residents.

In effect, the Supreme Court had relegalized abortion and reinstated something like the situation that had prevailed until the late nineteenth century. Early abortions were once again perfectly legal, while later ones (past the point of viability now, rather than past the point of quickening) could be prohibited. The decision carefully made no concessions to feminist demands for absolute reproductive freedom.

Roe v. *Wade* was immediately criticized, not only by anti-abortionists, but by some legal scholars, who maintained that its trimester formula was so specific that it was more like legislation than like a court decision defining constitutional principles. However, to Margie Hames the opinion was, in fact, "very practical. Without it, the states would have attempted many different kinds of abortion limitation." On the other hand, some abortion rights activists, including Larry Lader, believe that the decision was more vulnerable to right-wing pressures because it emphasized the physician's rights rather than those of the woman. "In philosophic terms, there is a void," Lader said. Be that as it may, *Roe* v. *Wade* gave feminists what they wanted. For a time, any woman who needed an abortion could get one, even if she was penniless, for until Congress passed the Hyde Amendment a few years later, Medicaid paid for abortions for the poor.

THE ROE DECISION INFLAMES THE RIGHT-TO-LIFE MOVEMENT

In 1983, a Planned Parenthood executive, speaking of the abortion decision ten years earlier, recalled ruefully that at the time "[m]ost of us really believed that was the end of the controversy. The Supreme Court had spoken, and while some disagreement would remain, the issue had been tried, tested and laid to rest." In fact, the struggle over abortion was about to escalate dramatically.

Immediately after the decision, new Right-to-Life groups began forming all over the country.* Their letters poured into the Supreme Court. Many were addressed to Blackmun and used words like "murderer." Years later, Blackmun told a reporter, "People misunderstand. I am not for abortion. I hope my family never has to face such a decision." He added, "I still think it was a correct decision. We were deciding a constitutional issue, not a moral one."

Within a matter of hours after the *Roe* decision was announced, hospitals began to get phone calls from women who needed an abortion. However, hospitals and physicians were very slow to respond, just as they had been in states that had passed reform laws. The decision was handed down in January 1973; by July, NARAL and the ACLU had filed lawsuits in nine states to compel public hospitals to perform abortions. Many states were also slow to change their anti-abortion laws; Right-to-Lifers were exerting a lot of pressure on legislators. At the end of the year, it was still hard for a woman to get an abortion in many parts of the country. Meanwhile, the Right-to-Life Coalition had launched a full-scale campaign in Congress for an amendment to the Constitution that would undo the Supreme Court's decision.

The activists who opposed abortion called themselves *prolife* because they believed that the fetus was an unborn child and had a right to live. Abortion rights groups, on the other hand, often called themselves *prochoice,* rather than *proabortion,* to underline the fact that they would never urge anyone to have an abortion; they believed, however, that every woman had the right to make that choice for herself.

* The Catholic church began organizing Right-to-Life groups in 1970 to protest changes or proposed changes in state anti-abortion laws.

WHAT MADE ABORTION A PIVOTAL ISSUE?

The anti-abortion movement was the leading edge of the conservative backlash against women's gains, but it was also more
than that. By 1974, many activists on both sides of the controversy were women, and research suggested that for many of
them abortion had become a powerful symbol. California sociologist Kristin Luker observed, "While on the surface it is the embryo's fate that seems to be at stake, the abortion debate is
actually about the meanings of *women's* lives." During the late
1970s and early 1980s, Luker interviewed more than 200 California women who were active either in the Right-to-Life or the
prochoice movement, and she found that they differed not just
over abortion but globally, in the way they saw the world.

To begin with, the prolife women were convinced that raising
children was the most fulfilling thing a woman could do, and
they believed strongly in the traditional family. In fact, Luker
suggested that abortion seemed wrong to them not only because
it was murder but because it threatened "an intricate set of social
relationships between men and women that has traditionally surrounded (and in the ideal case protected) women and children."
For example, if women had complete control over their own fertility thanks to birth control and abortion, then men could no
longer be held responsible for the consequences of the sex act.
According to some prolifers, abortion actually encouraged men
to exploit women sexually.

Virtually all of the prolife women in Luker's study believed that
the pill and the IUD were abortifacients. In fact, they disapproved
of every form of birth control except natural family planning,
which required abstaining from intercourse for eight or nine days
each month at around the time when the woman was ovulating.
What made sex sacred, they felt, was the very fact that it created
life.

In contrast, prochoice activists were convinced that women and
men were substantially similar and that women had a right to a
life outside the home. They saw motherhood and women's traditional role in the family as potential barriers to full equality.
After all, when employers denied women jobs or promotions,
they had always justified it by claiming that there was no point
in giving females responsible jobs because they would just get
pregnant and quit.

The prochoice women valued sex as a way to achieve intimacy

as well as pleasure. They not only believed in birth control but felt that it was irresponsible to have a baby unless one had the resources to raise a child. To them, an embryo wasn't an unborn baby but only a potential person, not much different in the early stages from an unfertilized ovum. However, most opposed abortion as a routine method of birth control and disapproved of multiple abortions.

Luker concluded that abortion was the tip of the iceberg for both sides. The rest of the iceberg consisted of the women's most cherished beliefs, values that usually went so deep that they'd like to think everyone else shared them. Because pregnancy and motherhood were so central to the lives of anti-abortion activists, they were apt to feel that the *Roe* decision, by implication, called into question not only the value of motherhood but their own personal worth. Prochoice activists, on the other hand, felt that a woman who couldn't control her own fertility could never achieve her true potential.

Luker's study focused on activists, women with strong views. For many Americans, the issue was less clear-cut—they approved of abortion in some circumstances (in cases of rape or incest, for example) but not in others. Furthermore, there were women who were feminists in practically every way except that they believed abortion should be illegal. Others would never consider having an abortion themselves but felt strongly that other women had a right to decide for themselves what to do about an unwanted pregnancy.

Because the abortion issue had so much resonance for so many people, the battle over reproductive rights actually intensified after the *Roe* decision. During the seventies and eighties, anti-abortion forces succeeded in passing laws and winning court decisions that made it progressively harder for American women—especially poor women—to get an abortion. By the early 1990s, some prolife activists were predicting that the Supreme Court would soon overturn *Roe* itself.

chapter 10

Women in Politics

In 1972, Elizabeth Holtzman, a thirty-year-old lawyer with limited experience in public life, challenged the redoubtable Emanuel Celler for his seat in the U.S. House of Representatives. Celler, archfoe of the ERA, was eighty-four years old at the time, had been in Congress for almost fifty years, and as chairman of the House Judiciary Committee was one of the most powerful men in Washington.

The story of Holtzman's triumph over Celler captures the optimism of the early 1970s, when it seemed there was almost nothing feminists couldn't do. It also serves as a baseline, illustrating what it was like to run for office when women first began to move into politics in significant numbers. It's still possible for a woman to mount a Holtzman-style, grass-roots campaign, but only for local and state offices. Running for Congress today is much more difficult.

Over the years since 1972, political women made great progress in some ways and were stymied in others. Meanwhile, the major feminist organizations focused increasingly on politics. This chapter and chapter 19 tell the story of the progress women made and the obstacles that blocked them.

TOPPLING THE WASHINGTON MONUMENT

In 1972, when Liz Holtzman fought Emanuel Celler for the Democratic nomination for Congress, she was virtually unknown. Celler declared that trying to defeat him would be like trying to topple the Washington Monument with a toothpick. Many people assumed this was only a slight exaggeration.

However, Holtzman believed she could win. She had run successfully for party office in 1970 as a reform Democrat, bucking the political machine in Brooklyn. As she became more involved in party activities, she realized that Celler was taking the voters for granted to a dangerous degree. He never held meetings in the Brooklyn district he represented; he never even sent mailings to voters. He opposed the ERA and supported the Vietnam War. Holtzman suspected that these were unpopular positions in his mostly middle class, heavily Jewish district.

A public opinion poll might have proved it, but Holtzman, badly underfinanced, couldn't afford to have a poll done. She'd been told she'd need $100,000 to pay for the primary campaign, but $32,000 was all she could raise; she borrowed another $4000. Running a shoestring campaign, she hit the streets for long hours every day with a group of volunteers, shaking hands, talking to voters.

Feminist groups gave Holtzman little help. The National Women's Political Caucus (NWPC) had been founded the year before, but its resources were stretched thin, and in any case, no one thought she could win. The volunteers who worked for her were primarily women from the district. Some were angry at Celler's support for the war; others liked the idea of sending a woman to Congress; all wanted "a different kind of representation," said Holtzman. In street-corner encounters, the people of the district seemed receptive. "I think . . . there was a lot of positive feeling about a woman running for office," Holtzman said, "primarily because the voters thought that a woman was not a politician. She wasn't part of the back-room, cigar-smoke, wheeling-and-dealing atmosphere."

On June 15, five days before the primary election, the *New York Times* endorsed Holtzman. On election day, a spokesman for

Celler predicted that he'd win, two to one. Instead, in a victory the *Times* called "the most surprising upset of all," Holtzman won by about 600 votes out of 35,000. In staunchly Democratic Brooklyn, getting the Democratic nomination was virtually the same thing as being elected, and though Celler ran in the general election as the candidate of the Liberal party, Holtzman beat him easily.

Liz Holtzman went on to become famous during the congressional hearings on impeaching Richard Nixon, when she grilled President Gerald Ford about why he had pardoned Nixon. In the late 1970s, she gave up her House seat to run for the Senate and lost by one percent of the vote. During the 1980s, she became Brooklyn District Attorney and then New York City Comptroller. Over the years, her political fortunes reflected the fact that it had become increasingly difficult for women to beat the male-dominated system at the top levels.

HIGH HOPES AND STRONG BEGINNINGS

In 1972, as Liz Holtzman triumphed over Emanuel Celler, feminists in politics were on a roll. Shirley Chisholm ran for President that year; she was a New York congresswoman, an early member of NOW. Forty percent of the delegates at the Democratic convention were women, up from just 13 percent four years earlier, and as a result another feminist, Frances Farenthold, almost won the Democratic vice-presidential nomination. At the Republican convention, 30 percent of the delegates were female.

That year, more women ran for election to the House and to state legislatures than ever before. Meanwhile, Rutgers University had established a research center charged with examining women's status in politics and government. Called the Center for the American Woman and Politics (CAWP), it would play a significant role in the coming years in studying and organizing political women.

In the early 1970s, legislators were paying attention to women's demands. Feminists were in the news almost daily, and lawmakers were afraid if they didn't pay attention, there would be consequences at the polls. Before the 92nd Congress adjourned at the end of 1972, it passed a record number of women's rights bills. Many people expected steady progress for women in legislation and in politics.

Instead, women forged ahead in local politics, but made hardly any headway in achieving high office. In 1971, males filled almost 98 percent of the seats in Congress; in 1991, twenty years later, 94 percent. State legislatures were over 95 percent male in 1971, 82 percent in 1991. There were no women governors in 1971; in 1991, there were three.

Those figures don't reflect enormous public reluctance to elect women. They're explained largely by the fact that campaign practices changed during the seventies. It now cost much more to run for higher office. In addition, powerful political action committees (PACs) had become the major source for campaign funds, and they generally favored incumbents. As a result, women running for Congress in the 1980s faced different obstacles than before. Over the same period of time, women in Western Europe who ran for seats in parliament did much better.

To American feminists, electing more women to high office seemed a matter of simple justice. In addition, they assumed that once in office, most women would represent women's interests better than most men did.

FROM PRECINCT WORKER TO CANDIDATE

During the forty years between the first and second waves of feminism, very few women ran for office. Of the handful who were elected to Congress, many came in via the "coffin route": They were the widows of congressmen, appointed to fill a husband's seat when he died and elected by the voters after that. Both political parties had a women's division, but the vast majority of the women involved in party politics were low-level volunteers. They did the clerical work while men ran for office.

In 1972, galvanized by the second wave, feminists flooded into the political arena, demanding equal treatment for women. The flood was organized by the National Women's Political Caucus (NWPC), which had been founded in July of the previous year. Many of NWPC's first members belonged to NOW, for the NOW leadership felt that the task of opening up the political system was so big that there should be an organization to work on it full time. The Caucus had separate internal Task Forces for Democratic and Republican women, and local chapters as well.

At its organizing conference, NWPC officially recognized that candidates must shape their platforms to reflect the needs of their constituents, but stated that nevertheless "women have a clear community of interest. . . ." NWPC's founders then assembled a list of priorities that went beyond equal pay, the ERA, and support for abortion. They committed themselves to fight racism as well as sexism; they were for withdrawal from Vietnam, preservation of the environment, and an adequate income for all.

POLITICAL CONVENTIONS: NEVER THE SAME AGAIN

While NWPC's local chapters concentrated on local and state elections, at the national level the Caucus almost immediately turned its attention to presidential politics. In 1972, the Democratic party's system for nominating a presidential candidate was under reconstruction, and feminists had good reason to expect concessions for women. At the Democrats' 1968 national convention, huge antiwar demonstrations outside the convention hall had forced party liberals to face the fact that some groups were being excluded from the political process. Afterward, a commission appointed to study the problem issued new guidelines: At future conventions, state delegations were to include minorities, women, and the young in reasonable numbers, based on their proportion within each state's population. Under pressure from women in the party, the commission ultimately put teeth into its guidelines and required compliance.

The Republicans, too, were somewhat open to change, and a party committee advised states to increase the number of women and minorities in their delegations. However, its recommendations weren't binding.

Seizing the opportunity offered by both parties, the fledgling NWPC held seminars around the country to teach women about party rules so that they could try to become convention delegates. Those who succeeded were then bombarded with information and position papers. The goal was to empower the women: They were to come to the convention better informed than their male colleagues, so that they'd have the confidence to speak out for women's interests.

As the Democratic primaries proceeded, the Caucus challenged virtually every state delegation in which women were underrepresented. (The Republican "recommendations" offered no basis for similar challenges.) That year, when the Democratic credentials committee met two weeks before the start of the convention, 40 percent of the delegates were challenged, most by feminists or groups representing people of color. No one had ever seen anything like it. Clearly, the Democratic convention in July of that year was going to be very different. Not only were almost 1900 women attending as delegates and alternates, but 15 percent of the delegates were African-Americans, up from 5.5 percent in 1968. In Miami Beach, where the convention was to be held, people worried aloud about being invaded by hippies.

Shirley Chisholm was still in the race for President as the Miami Beach meeting opened. Unlike Elizabeth Holtzman, Chisholm knew she couldn't win; that was part of the reason she ran.

"[S]omeone had to do it first," she wrote after the election. "In this country everybody is supposed to be able to run for President, but that's never been really true. I ran *because* most people think the country is not ready for a black candidate, not ready for a woman candidate."

Chisholm was also hoping to play power politics: to accumulate enough votes so that if the Democratic convention deadlocked, she could bargain with the front-runners. "I am your instrument for change . . ." she had told voters, focusing her campaign on people of color, white women, and others outside the system. "Give your vote to me instead of one of those warmed-over gentlemen who come to you once every four years. . . . I belong to you." She wanted to remind the Democrats that they couldn't take the black vote for granted.

Within the Democratic party, Chisholm's candidacy presented both feminists and blacks with a classic political dilemma. Those smart enough to back a winner in the primaries might be on the inside track with the next administration or might at least influence the issues raised in the campaign. Because Chisholm had no chance of winning, in backing her they would be throwing away an opportunity to have that kind of influence. In addition, many feminists wanted to make a commitment to Senator George McGovern, who opposed the war in Vietnam and seemed to have taken women's issues to heart. Thus, though some feminists campaigned for Chisholm, overall the women's movement surprised her by its coolness.

The African-American community was no better. Wherever Chisholm went, its leaders were divided over her candidacy and sometimes openly hostile. Black politicians, too, wanted to back a winner, and they didn't want to do anything that would help reelect Nixon. In addition, many black men were outraged that a woman had stepped into the race while they were still standing around, "peeing on their shoes," as a Chisholm aide put it—arguing over which black male candidate to back.

Chisholm's campaign, like Holtzman's, was a shoestring operation, and the volunteers who worked for her included black women, white women, and black men. There was often friction between the white feminists and the black males. Chisholm recalled that "the women were hard, tireless workers . . . but [t]hey wanted to talk of little but abortion, day care, equal rights and other women's issues. Disgruntled blacks complained to me that they could not relate to [the women]." Some of the men were afraid that Chisholm was simply a front for the feminists. One black politician noted that "the specter of white women bargaining in the Democratic convention with white men on behalf of the black community was a frightening thing."

TWO STEPS FORWARD, ONE STEP BACK

For Democratic women who had never been to a national convention before, the meeting in Miami Beach was an intense experience. Delegates spent all their time on the convention floor or closeted in caucuses; on three nights, the evening session lasted almost until dawn. Even well-to-do delegates lived on hot dogs and soda because there wasn't time to go out for dinner.

Though McGovern won the nomination on the first ballot, Chisholm made a respectable showing. Afterward, feminists asked if they could nominate her for Vice-President. When she declined because she felt that McGovern had a right to choose his own running mate, Gloria Steinem, one of the NWPC members attending the convention, nominated Frances ("Sissy") Farenthold, a former member of the Texas legislature. During the balloting, Farenthold rolled up so many votes that she was on her way to victory when the McGovern camp realized what was happening and pulled its people back into line. In the end, she was the runner-up in a field of four, second after McGovern's choice, Senator Thomas Eagleton.*

By the time the convention ended, many feminists were disillusioned with McGovern, who had let them down on issues that mattered to them, including an abortion-rights plank. McGovern's strategists felt the abortion issue was too controversial

---

* Ten days later, Eagleton revealed that he'd been hospitalized during the 1960s for "nervous exhaustion and fatigue," and on July 31 he withdrew from the campaign. In replacing Eagleton, the McGovern forces never even considered runner-up Farenthold —proving that women still had a long way to go.

to include in the platform, and some feminists agreed. Actress Shirley MacLaine, who had taken time off from her career to work for McGovern, explained, ". . . with Richard Nixon as the opposition, it seemed to me a strong abortion plank would hurt not only George McGovern—but the issue itself. . . . In my opinion [Nixon] was mercilessly political on the subject and might fan the emotional flames surrounding it so much that other important issues in the fall campaign could become forgotten." On the other hand, Congresswoman Bella Abzug insisted that Nixon would make abortion a campaign issue anyway, and that the laws needed changing so badly that politicians mustn't avoid the subject.

The reproductive-rights plank was defeated, roughly 1570 to 1100, after the McGovern forces lobbied against it. Nevertheless, the Republicans set out to paint McGovern as a left-wing extremist and, among other things, accused him of favoring abortion—just as Abzug had predicted they would. The charge proved damaging, just as MacLaine expected.

When any group bent on changing society begins to act within the political system, the system presents one hard choice after another. Should activists press their demands no matter what, or is that self-defeating? When is a compromise a sell-out? A social movement needs both pragmatists and idealists, but inevitably they clash, and a movement also needs to present a united front.

In 1972, the Republican nominating convention, too, had a record number of women delegates. However, the only real gain for Republican feminists was a plank in the party platform that supported federally funded child-care centers. This was a hard-won victory, because Nixon, who was running for reelection, had vetoed the 1971 child-care bill. Congresswoman Margaret Heckler actually redrafted the plank ninety-six times before it was accepted.

Though McGovern was much better on women's rights than Nixon, after the nominating convention he stopped talking about feminist issues, so most voters weren't aware that the candidates had different attitudes. Nevertheless, the vote showed a modest gender gap, a difference in the way women and men voted: 38 percent of women cast their ballots for McGovern, compared to just 32 percent of men. The gap might have been larger if the Democrats had courted the women's vote. The same basic scenario was repeated every four years throughout the seventies and eighties: During the presidential primaries, Democratic candidates were more supportive of feminist issues than Republicans, but once nominated the Democrats rarely spoke of those issues again.

Nixon won a landslide victory, and, interpreting it as a mandate for his policies, promptly ordered new bombing raids on North Vietnam while drastically reducing social programs. Chisholm and others were convinced that racism was at least partly responsible for his victory, particularly resistance to school busing. In fact, fundamental changes were occurring within the white electorate as the southern states, once solidly Democratic, gradually turned to the Republicans, apparently rejecting the Democrats because they supported civil rights.

In the wake of McGovern's defeat, the old guard within the Democratic party set out to regain control. Backlash was probably inevitable, because many elected officials had been edged out of the nominating process by women, men of color, and the young. In addition, party moderates felt that in McGovern they'd been stuck with a left-wing candidate. One politician told the *New York Times*, "It's a crime against democracy that we had a candidate who didn't represent the Democratic party. . . . We don't want a party that just consists of Bella Abzug on one hand and Jesse Jackson on the other."

In short order, a new commission was appointed to reconsider the guidelines on choosing convention delegates. Robert Strauss, who chaired the Democratic National Committee (DNC), warned commission members that the DNC would go to court, if necessary, to block anything resembling quotas for women and minorities.

The 1972 presidential conventions drew a number of women into politics and motivated some to go out and run for office themselves. Throughout the seventies and eighties, many women got their first taste of politics as delegates to a national political convention.

THE TUG-OF-WAR OVER EQUAL DIVISION

For the next decade and more, the Democrats kept changing the rules that governed delegate selection as factions within the party won or lost ground. From 1976 on, equal division was the top priority for political women: They insisted that half the delegates at presidential conventions must be female. The DNC agreed to this in 1978, but what the party gave with one hand, it immediately began to take away with the other—by reserving a percentage of delegate seats for elected officials, who were, of course, mostly white males. Throughout the 1980s, the DNC kept tinkering with the system. Sometimes it increased the number of seats saved for the party elite (now called "superdelegates"), and sometimes it succumbed to pressure and reduced their number.

At the 1980 Democratic convention, women proved that, given equal division, they could win in a floor fight. A little over 49 percent of the voting delegates were women, and most of them supported two resolutions—on the ERA and on abortion—that feminists wanted incorporated into the party platform. Over vehement opposition from President Jimmy Carter's campaign, both resolutions were adopted. This demonstration of political muscle may well have influenced the party elite in 1984 when they were confronted by a feminist demand for a woman vice-presidential candidate.

Despite the superdelegates, women were much better represented at Democratic political conventions in the 1980s than they were in 1972. Feminists who lobbied the 1980 convention for the ERA and abortion resolutions found it an easy task, because half the delegates were women, compared to lobbying largely male state legislatures for the ERA. The lesson wasn't lost on the second wave's leaders, and they became more determined than ever to increase the number of women elected to office.

Over the same period of time, the Republican party became increasingly antifeminist, to the distress of Republican feminists and Democratic women as well, because there was now some danger that the Democrats might take feminist support for granted. At the 1976 Republican convention, incumbent President Gerald Ford narrowly defeated right-winger Ronald Reagan. For the first time, antifeminist women spoke out strongly, and feminists were forced to fight a rear-guard action to prevent party conservatives from repudiating the ERA. They were unable to prevent the convention from adopting a plank that called for a constitutional amendment banning abortion. In 1980, with Reagan the nominee, the platform made no mention of the ERA. It not only supported the amendment on abortion, but stated that only abortion opponents should be appointed as federal judges. At that convention, 29 percent of the delegates were women.

As Reagan battled Carter for the presidency, some feminists were in a quandary: Reagan would be a disaster for women's rights, but they had little use for Carter. Though he had appointed a record number of women to government posts and was committed to enforcing the laws against discrimination, he had backed restrictions on Medicaid funding for abortion and had cut social programs on which women and children depended, even as he increased the military budget. He had failed to support child-care legislation and had done very little to help pass the ERA.

Some feminists backed third-party candidate John Anderson, while others stayed home on election day. Many Republican women reluctantly voted for Reagan because they believed in what their party stood for and wanted it to regain the presidency. Some actually suggested that an enemy in the White House might be better than a friend like Carter, who divided feminists because he was for them in some ways and against them in others.

When Reagan won the election, exit polls suggested that most of those who voted for him were reacting to the fact that under Carter the economy had gone sour or to the hostage crisis in Iran, where U.S. embassy personnel were being held prisoner. However, this time most voters were aware that the candidates differed on women's rights, and exit polls revealed substantial gender differences: 56 percent of male voters cast their ballot for Reagan, but only 47 percent of female voters did. During the 1980s, feminists would parlay this gender gap into a slot on the Democratic presidential ticket.

HAVE WOMEN MADE A DIFFERENCE?

Feminists, concerned about advancing their agenda, gambled that they could do it by electing more women to office. However, at first, most political women were afraid to be identified as feminists, and even those who were concerned about women's issues were often unwilling to discuss them except when they spoke privately to women's groups. Sometimes, experience in office changed attitudes. New Jersey Congresswoman Marge Roukema, for example, eventually found herself working with other women on women's issues because male legislators simply weren't interested. "If we don't do it, no one else will," she said.

As the gender gap made news in the 1980s, it lent new legitimacy to feminist concerns, and political women became less defensive about pursuing them. Surveys conducted by CAWP showed that women who'd been elected to office were usually more liberal than men, whether they were Democrats or Republicans. Women also hired and promoted other women to a much greater extent than men did, and they represented women's interests better. In the fifteen states that failed to ratify the ERA, for example, 76 percent of the female legislators were for it, compared to 36 percent of men. Of all public officials, black women were the most liberal and the most likely to belong to feminist organizations.

CAWP worked hard to promote a feminist consciousness among women legislators. Susan Carroll, senior research associate at CAWP, observed that, once women were elected, they were under pressure to conform to male norms and forget they were women. Noting that British Prime Minister Margaret Thatcher had done little for women, Carroll speculated that, as Thatcher moved up and was integrated into the male world, her links to other women were broken.

"We have to maintain the links between women," said Carroll. She suggested that feminists outside political institutions needed to be both support system and conscience for the women they elected. CAWP, in fact, was both. It gave political women a place to go where they were listened to, and it constantly reminded them of the feminist agenda. As CAWP's surveys confirmed that women lawmakers were different from men, they became self-fulfilling prophecies: The women learned that they weren't alone in caring about women's issues and also came to appreciate their responsibility to other women. When they needed help, CAWP linked them to women in other state legislatures working on the same problems and to organizations with expertise to share. It also regularly brought them together across party lines.

THE BARRIERS TO PROGRESS

Through the years, the number of feminist organizations focused on politics kept growing. Women running for office often turned to such groups for advice, training in campaign skills, useful contacts, or funds. In the eighties, women of color organized their own groups. They were dissatisfied because they'd made less progress on the political scene than white women and because the existing feminist organizations often failed to represent their interests. Meanwhile, inside legislatures, women began to form alliances that operated across party lines to promote women's issues.

Despite all these efforts, the U.S. Congress remained stubbornly just 5 percent female. In most countries in Western Europe, women made greater gains. By 1987, for example, the Dutch parliament was over 20 percent female; women filled more than one third of the seats in the Norwegian parliament. Why did American women lag so far behind? Back in 1972, the major barriers in the United States were the attitudes of male politicians and voters of both sexes plus the political system itself. During the next decade, even as attitudes improved, the system threw up new obstacles.

Men in politics, like men in business, were generally not pleased in the seventies when women began to compete for political office, and they typically used an informal quota system to try to keep females out. Thus, a woman was apt to be told that she couldn't be a candidate because "we already have a woman on the ticket"—though an all-male ticket never seemed to bother party bosses. When the bosses did encourage a woman to run, it was often as a "sacrificial lamb" against an opponent considered unbeatable.

Accused of prejudice, politicians would generally argue that women simply weren't electable. Though they exaggerated voter resistance, many voters *were* prejudiced against women. Especially in the 1970s, a married woman running for office was apt to be asked over and over again what her husband thought about her candidacy, and how her children would manage without her. Single women had to survive rumors that they were lesbian or were having affairs. When Barbara Mikulski first ran for the Baltimore city council in 1971 (she later became a U.S. senator), rumor had it that she was sleeping with the Black Panthers—*all* of them.

Because both sexes had had it drilled into them that women were supposed to be subservient to men, many voters seemed particularly reluctant to elect women to positions where they would have authority over men. When Liz Holtzman ran for Brooklyn District Attorney in 1981, people sometimes told her, "You know, Liz, we voted for you for Congress, but this is not a job for a woman." Both men and women would ask, "How are men going to work for you?"

Women in politics had to tread a fine line between acting tough and not acting too tough. Where a man had to take strong stands to avoid looking like a wimp, when a woman was too strong it was held against her. Yet if she was quiet, warm, "womanly," that was also held against her—obviously, she wasn't tough enough to hold office. This double bind haunted Bella Abzug, according to Ruth Mandel, director of CAWP. Opponents often accused Abzug of being too abrasive or too ambitious; Abzug herself believed that if she'd been a man, the same qualities would have been seen as signs of strength. Mandel noted that, "Defeated between 1976 and 1978 in senatorial, mayoralty, and congressional races by three men who could hardly be termed 'soft-spoken,' Bella Abzug more than any other female candidate has been seen as a warning about what happens when a woman cannot escape a negative image after having been labeled as 'too ambitious' and 'too aggressive.' " Some women candidates were actually advised not to wear a hat while campaigning, to avoid being associated in the public mind with Abzug, who was famous for her hats.

Eventually, men in politics became more open to women candidates. Though after 1980, Republicans in the White House tried to undermine some of the progress women had made toward equality, surprisingly, the Republican party made more of an effort than the Democrats did to recruit, train, and fund women candidates. Evidently, GOP leaders were concerned about the gender gap. However, in both parties, the improvement in attitude was spotty—some cities and states were better for women than others—and, according to Liz Holtzman, candidates who were frankly feminist still didn't get party support.

Though voter resistance also eased over the years, the bias against women didn't disappear completely; the remnants went underground. By the mid-1980s, most voters, when polled, said they were willing to vote for a woman, even for President. Were they really? When researchers asked subtler questions—about men's and women's strengths, for example—the old sex stereotypes turned out to be alive and well. Many Americans still assumed that women were more honest and compassionate than men and that men were tougher and better in a crisis.

AS OLD BARRIERS FELL, NEW ONES AROSE

In some ways, the American political system opened up to women and to men of color during the 1970s. Party decisions were less often made in the privacy of back rooms by cliques of powerful men; in many places, candidates were now chosen by the voters in direct primary elections, rather than by conventions dominated by the bosses. These and other changes accompanied a decline of the major political parties that was probably good for women overall. "Women have seldom been given anything much by the political parties," said Susan Carroll of CAWP.

However, as the parties declined, other obstacles arose. The major problem was the astronomical increase in the cost of campaigning, added to the fact that it was next to impossible to unseat legislators once they were elected to Congress.

When Liz Holtzman ran for Congress against Emanuel Celler in 1972, she spent $36,000 on the primary race and an inconsequential amount on the general election.* In 1988, the average cost of winning a seat in the House was over $300,000, while the cost in the Senate was nearly $4 million.† It was no longer possible to run a grass-roots campaign for Congress and have any chance of winning. That hit women harder than men, because women were less likely to be tied into the male networks from which campaign contributions flowed.

If costs skyrocketed, it was largely because in politics, as in many other areas, technology had taken over. Where ward bosses used to recruit volunteers who telephoned people in the district on election day to get out the vote, politicians now relied on television commercials to motivate voters. In the New York area in the late eighties, it wasn't unusual for a candidate, during the last weeks of a campaign, to spend more than $500,000 a week just for TV. Polls had become increasingly important, and the bill for a statewide poll could come to as much as $30,000.

The political parties contributed to some campaigns, but the bulk of the expense was borne by the candidates themselves, who did their own fund-raising. Some politicians (generally, incumbents) were spectacularly successful at raising money, and they then publicized the fact that they had a huge campaign war chest in order to discourage opposition. In 1986, Liz Holtzman considered running for the U.S. Senate against Republican Senator Alfonse D'Amato, but decided against it largely because D'Amato had accumulated over $6 million to spend on the race.

For women and other outsiders, the problem of incumbency was at least as difficult as the money problem, and the two were connected. In 1990, about 96 percent of incumbents running for Congress were reelected. Getting elected to Congress was now like achieving lifetime tenure: Short of a major scandal, most

---

* As the Democratic candidate, running in a traditionally Democratic district, she could coast once she'd won the primary.
† To raise $4 million, a senator must somehow bring in $1800 a day, seven days a week, for the whole six years between campaigns.

politicians stayed in office for as long as they liked. In state legislatures, incumbents also had an advantage, but it wasn't as great.

What made congressional incumbents so hard to beat? They had name recognition and opportunities to be of service to constituents. They had a staff and a travel allowance, and when it was time to redraw the boundaries of election districts, they could often persuade state legislatures to include in their district the neighborhoods where they ran strongly.

These advantages weren't new, but campaign reforms instituted during the midseventies made the situation worse. The new laws, which were meant to prevent rich campaign contributors from "buying" elections, limited the amount of money an individual could give to a political campaign in a given year. Though they also set limits for groups such as political action committees (PACs), they left so many loopholes that the PACs immediately began to proliferate and soon became the major source of funds for most congressional candidates. The PACs favored incumbents. In the 1990 congressional elections, for example, PACs gave twelve times as much money to incumbents as they gave to the candidates who challenged them. The incumbent advantage meant that white males were likely to dominate the highest levels of government for years to come.

THE TROUBLE WITH PACS

A PAC is an organization that solicits money from individuals who want to contribute to political campaigns; it pools that money and distributes it to candidates. Corporations have PACs; so do unions, trade groups, and organizations such as the National Rifle Association.

The PAC system was an invitation to influence buying and influence peddling. However, it existed, and so, unable to change the system, some pragmatic feminists created their own PACs. The Women's Campaign Fund was established in 1974. By 1989, there were thirty-five women's PACs and a few had state and local chapters around the country. Some gave money only to women candidates; others would also contribute to a male who supported women's issues. Over the years, they helped to elect many women by giving them funds when party officials were indifferent or hostile and other PACs simply weren't interested.

In the 1980s, many feminists, busy juggling job and family, found it easier to give money to the movement than to invest time. By contributing to a feminist PAC, they could help elect other women and call attention to women's issues at the same time, because candidates who received money from the PAC knew it came from a group with a particular agenda.* Nevertheless, during the 1980s the PAC system seemed to have few redeeming features for feminists. The money women's groups were able to contribute was generally inconsequential compared to the funds amassed by other PACs, including ultraconservative groups.

The right-wing PACs were a menace to feminists. They raised money through national campaigns, then spent it on expensive media attacks on moderate and liberal candidates. The National Conservative Political Action Committee, in particular, was known for attacking the candidates it opposed without supporting anyone else in the race. In 1980, these tactics helped defeat Senators George McGovern and ERA-champion Birch Bayh, among others.

Though feminist and conservative PACs were primarily interested in influencing the outcomes of elections, most PACs didn't care who won. What they were "buying" with their contributions was access to candidates after the election. Thus, because incumbents were more likely to win, they backed incumbents, contributing even when a politician was running unopposed or was ahead by a huge margin. Sometimes PACs gave money to both sides in a race, and sometimes if they'd backed a loser, they contributed to the winner *after* the election.

When legislation came up that affected a PAC's interests, its officials contacted the dozens or even hundreds of candidates they'd given money to and made their case, explaining how they hoped the lawmakers would vote. (Feminist PACs didn't do that kind of lobbying. The amount of money they contributed was too small to provide much clout.) Some PACs were so powerful that there was no way to persuade Congress to pass legislation if they opposed it. For instance, thanks to insurance industry PACs, there was very little chance of getting a bill through Congress that would forbid sex discrimination in insurance.

Did PACs discriminate against women candidates? Some surveys done in the 1980s showed that women could raise as much PAC money as men in comparable races. However, the studies didn't analyze how much effort it took women and men to raise

* According to Ruth Mandel, by the 1990s women's money had begun to play a significant role in some highly competitive contests, such as Ann Richards's successful campaign for Governor of Texas.

the same amount of money, nor did researchers look at the primary elections, and women often failed to make it through the primaries for lack of funds. To overcome that obstacle, in 1984 feminists founded a PAC called EMILY's List; EMILY was an acronym for Early Money Is Like Yeast. The group provided both funds and technical support to Democratic women running for Congress.

The experience of Congresswoman Claudine Schneider may have been typical. When Schneider first ran for Congress in 1978, most PACs wouldn't back her. She was told there were two reasons: First, she was a Republican, running in traditionally Democratic Rhode Island; second, she was a woman, campaigning in a district with many older Italian voters, who were expected to feel that she should be home having babies. Once Schneider was elected, PAC money flowed in. In subsequent elections, the bigger her margin of victory, the more money she was able to raise afterward.

For women, then, "equal treatment" from PACs boiled down to this: Because most elected officials were males, women candidates usually ran as challengers and could expect the PACs to fund their opponent; men who ran as challengers faced similar problems. In races for open seats where there was no incumbent, men were more likely to get both the party nomination and sufficient funding. A woman elected in spite of this system might find afterward that she now had as much PAC-appeal as a male.

In 1988, Liz Holtzman said, "I thought when I was first elected that there'd be lots of young women running for Congress after me. And yet sixteen years later there's only one woman in Congress from New York State." The major problem, she said, was the enormous cost of campaigning, together with the fact that women, especially feminists, had a tougher time raising campaign funds than men did. "It's much harder now for people who are mavericks . . . to get into the system," she explained. If she herself were starting over as a young idealist with little money, she couldn't hope to run for Congress. Holtzman was encouraged by the fact that there was now a women's political community organized to provide support, but she said, "Change is taking far too long."

THE DIFFICULTIES OF REVAMPING THE SYSTEM

It wasn't difficult to imagine an electoral system more democratic than the one that existed in the 1980s. Public funds, which already paid for presidential campaigns, could be used to pay for the campaigns of all candidates for Congress, both incumbents and challengers. Congress could set limits on how much candidates could spend. As for PACs, many political experts felt that they should be banned outright. If incumbents were deprived of their ability to outspend challengers, they would still have enormous advantages, but the system would open up somewhat. However, only the members of Congress—incumbents, all—could reform the system, and because they benefited so mightily from it, the prospects for meaningful change weren't good.

When the nation's founders drafted the Constitution, they were as suspicious of power as the women in the early women's liberation groups were. One of the founders, George Mason, said, "From the nature of man, we may be sure that those who have power in their hands will not give it up while they can retain it. On the contrary, we know they will always, when they can, rather increase it." Thus, the Constitution provided for elaborate checks and balances, and power was distributed through layers of government—local, state, and federal.

As the years passed, the political system proved to be enormously stable. It allowed outsiders just enough entrée so that armed revolt made little sense. However, groups that wanted to get into the system had to wait a very long time. Eventually, many Americans came to distrust both politicians and the system that made it so hard to turn them out of office. In the 1990 elections, voters in three states and one city approved measures that set a limit on how many terms lawmakers could serve.

The European Advantage: Quotas

As noted earlier, by the 1980s women in Western Europe were being elected to high office in much greater numbers than American women. The explanation is complicated, but the structure of the U.S. political system was largely responsible for the difference.

Typically, in most West European countries, a number of major and minor parties had seats in parliament. In some nations with

successful minor parties, European feminists developed a strategy that worked quite well. They began by persuading one of the
smaller parties to adopt a quota: to agree that henceforth a certain
percentage of its seats in parliament (usually, 40 percent) must go
to women. Soon, the major parties started to worry about the
women's vote, and women in those parties demanded a similar
quota.

The strategy paid off first and most impressively in Norway.
By 1988, women occupied 34 percent of the seats in the Norwegian parliament and almost half of all cabinet posts; the prime
minister was a woman. In most other nations in Western Europe,
at least one of the major parties set a women's quota, but progress
was slower. In 1988, the European Parliament endorsed quotas
and affirmative action for women for all nations that were members of the EEC, the European Economic Community.

In America, feminists wouldn't accomplish much by persuading a minor party to set a quota. Though the United States did
have such parties, they rarely won seats in Congress, because
American congressional elections were winner-take-all: The candidate who achieved a simple majority won. It was almost impossible for someone from a minor party, running in most cases
against both a Republican and a Democrat, to succeed. By contrast, many European countries had proportional representation.
Though some seats in parliament were reserved for members
who were elected by a district, there were also at-large seats,
which were filled according to the proportion of the vote that
each party won nationwide. With proportional representation, it
was much more likely that minor parties would gain some seats.

In the absence of smaller parties that could provide leverage, it
would take a long time to persuade American politicians to adopt
quotas. For one thing, even if the national leadership of one or
both major parties agreed to endorse more women candidates
during primaries, in some places they would be blocked by a state
law that prohibited such endorsements. State and local party organizations, which were often quite autonomous, might well resist quotas set on the national level.

Feminists continued to press party officials to nominate more
women, but prospects weren't good. By the late 1980s, the whole
concept of quotas had become unacceptable to those in power.
On the job front, conservatives were fighting affirmative action
on the grounds that it amounted to discrimination against white
males. Affirmative action didn't even call for quotas—only for
goals and timetables.

204 · *MOVING THE MOUNTAIN*

THE FUTURE

In 1990, women filled 5.6 percent of the seats in Congress. According to Susan Carroll of CAWP, that put the United States "about on a par with Iraq and Sri Lanka." If change continued at the same pace, it would be more than 300 years before there were as many women in Congress as men. Even in the state legislatures, it would take about fifty years to achieve equality.

Few people expected the rate of change to be quite that slow. As more women entered politics at ground level and worked their way up—and as male politicians retired or expired—more women were bound to be elected. However, unless there were reforms in the political system itself, their numbers would increase very slowly. There wouldn't be progress at all unless feminists kept pressing for it.

Politics was the ultimate power game, and political women confronted, in intensified form, the dilemmas that faced women of achievement in other walks of life. Those who were feminists had to decide whether they were in the game for themselves, to better the lot of all women, or for both reasons. They often had to walk a narrow line because a woman who was openly a feminist, or who became narrowly identified with women's issues, was less effective.

Yet experience had proved that women in office *were* different from men. In fact, if by some miracle women suddenly occupied half the seats in Congress, government policy would be very different. Among other things, it would be more liberal, less inclined to military spending and the use of force, and more supportive of social programs.

If, instead, it took a hundred years or more to elect men and women in equal numbers, would there still be a distinctly female point of view when political equality was finally achieved? Could women compete with men on men's terms without losing sight of feminist values? Or would they inevitably "take on the pinstripes of the oppressor," to quote the late Barbara Boggs Sigmund, Mayor of Princeton, New Jersey, who sometimes felt she saw this happening.

In the 1990s, such questions loomed large for many women because the feminist vision of the future no longer began and ended with gender equality. The goals instead were a society that was, in a much broader sense, just and compassionate, and a political system that was truly open to all.

chapter 11

Changing Education

⟶

*I*n the early 1970s, feminists set out to change American education. Activists tackled it at every level from kindergarten through graduate school, from the content of textbooks to the way colleges hired faculty. Thousands of women were involved, and their efforts were vital to the second wave.

Some feminists attacked sexism in education directly. In 1972, women in Washington persuaded Congress to pass a law banning sex discrimination in public schools and most colleges. However, what should have been a happy ending was only the beginning of the struggle, for once the law was on the books, opposition to enforcing it grew steadily.

Moreover, women needed more than just access to schools and teaching jobs. Over the long run, they needed to change sexist attitudes and raise a generation of women prepared to stand up for women's rights; that meant they had to change what students were taught. Thus, in the early seventies, activists began to establish women's studies programs at colleges around the country. Eventually, feminist scholars challenged basic premises in almost every academic discipline: They wrote women into history, turned literary criticism on its head, disputed social theories that reflected male biases, and more. As researchers and theorists, women in academia also provided a kind of scaffolding for the rest of the movement, an intellectual structure that helped define its shape and direction over the years.

The women's education movement eventually spun off feminist groups at every level of the educational system; umbrella organizations linked them when joint action was necessary. In Washington, for example, the National Coalition for Women and Girls in Education (NCWGE) coalesced in 1974. It began modestly enough with seven or eight women who made it a point to lunch together regularly to discuss education issues, but it soon grew into an alliance of more than thirty women's groups. Another major step was taken in 1977, when feminist scholars founded the National Women's Studies Association (NWSA) to foster the growth of women's studies programs. The education movement also included student groups, women's centers on college campuses, women's caucuses in academic associations, groups intent on achieving equity for women's athletic programs, and many other organizations as well.

AMERICAN EDUCATION BEFORE FEMINISM

Until well into the 1970s, one of the first lessons taught in American schools was a subtle contempt for females. In the stories in children's first readers, boys outnumbered girls by more than two to one, and the girls were usually meek and slightly stupid. Often, they were younger sisters—feminists came to call this the "ninny sister syndrome." Textbooks for older students ignored both the achievements of individual women and the history of the first wave of feminism.

In high schools, advanced math and science classes were sometimes closed to girls, and teachers and guidance counselors discouraged them from pursuing subjects that weren't traditionally feminine. So did aptitude tests. The Strong Vocational Interest Blank, for example, was issued in blue for boys and pink for girls. The blue version suggested that boys with certain interests become doctors, while the pink advised girls with exactly the same interests to consider nursing. Vocational training courses also treated boys and girls differently. Boys learned the rudiments of a skilled trade in industrial arts classes that were almost always closed to females; girls learned sewing, cooking, and perhaps typing.

At the college level, to get into the top schools women had to be better qualified than the men who were accepted. Graduate and professional schools often set quotas for females. Only 10 percent of law students and 11 percent of medical students were women.

The sex bias in athletics was even more blatant. Most school districts spent far more on boys' teams than they did on girls'. In 1971, one Texas district budgeted $250,000 for athletics but the only sport girls were allowed to play was tennis; the budget for tennis that year was $970. At universities, women's athletics often received 1 or 2 percent of the money available for men.

Women educators also faced discrimination. In 1970, women were 66 percent of all public school teachers, but only 13.5 percent of school principals. Brilliant women with PhDs often had to teach at junior colleges or lower-status four-year schools because even women's colleges preferred to hire men. Furthermore, many universities had rules against employing both husband and wife. If two members of the faculty married, it was assumed that the wife would lose her job.

Women who became pregnant weren't welcome in public schools or colleges, whether they were teachers or students. Almost all school districts made pregnant teachers stop teaching several months before their baby was born. Pregnant high school students were expelled, and some colleges also asked pregnant students to leave.

Astoundingly, before about 1970 women were blind to many of the prejudices operating against them. No one had compiled statistics like these, and students who applied unsuccessfully to colleges and women trapped in lower-level jobs often concluded that they themselves simply weren't good enough.

The women's movement tackled the problem of sex bias in education in four major ways: Washington feminists filed charges against colleges and universities; they also steered two antidiscrimination bills through Congress; on college campuses, women's studies took root and flourished; and at all levels of the educational system, girls and women began to demand equality in athletics.

FACULTY WOMEN FILE CHARGES

Dr. Bernice (Bunny) Sandler took on the education system almost singlehandedly in the early 1970s; her story is one of the movement's Doris-and-Goliath sagas. Sandler originally turned to feminism out of personal outrage. In 1969, she was teaching part-time at the University of Maryland when seven new full-time faculty positions opened up. She was never even considered as a candidate because—as a male friend told her—"Let's face it, Bunny, you come on too strong for a woman." However, it didn't occur to Sandler that she'd been a victim of sex discrimination until she was turned down for other jobs as well.

Her consciousness belatedly raised, Sandler joined WEAL and began to read up on the civil rights laws, searching for a way to do something about her situation. None of the laws seemed to apply to academics. Title VII exempted schools and colleges; the Equal Pay Act didn't cover professionals, which meant academics; Title VI, which laid down rules for all programs that received federal assistance, banned discriminating on the basis of race, color, or national origin, but said nothing about sex discrimination.

Finally, Sandler came across a book that described Executive Order 11246, a federal regulation that applied to major government contractors. It said they couldn't discriminate on the basis of race, color, religion, or national origin.* The Order had been amended in 1968 to include sex discrimination, but the authors had consigned this information to a footnote. As an academic, Sandler habitually read footnotes, and when she read this one, she immediately made the connection: Because many colleges and universities had federal contracts, presumably they were covered under the Order.

Hardly able to believe her eyes, Sandler called the OFCC (Office of Federal Contract Compliance) at the Department of Labor. The OFCC was charged with setting policy for the Executive Order, though other agencies actually enforced it. To her consternation, she was immediately put through to Assistant Director Vincent Macaluso, who asked her a lot of questions and then suggested that she come and see him. The conversation was so one-sided, with Macaluso asking all the questions and volunteer-

---

* Government contracts were so widely distributed that the Executive Order actually covered about one third of the U.S. labor force.

ing little information, that Sandler couldn't help wondering "whether he was serious or whether he was making a pass." As it turned out, Macaluso had just been waiting for someone to come along and use the sex-discrimination provision of the Executive Order. After the Order was amended to include sex in 1968, he had been assigned to draft new guidelines for it. He knew better than anyone what it could do.

The Order wasn't a law. It was the latest in a series of regulations issued over many years by U.S. Presidents, which spelled out what companies must do if they wanted federal contracts. Macaluso explained to Sandler that not only could she file charges against the University of Maryland under the regulation, but she could file a class-action complaint against all American colleges and universities. Two features made the Executive Order almost ideal for Sandler's purposes: It applied to the whole university, not just to the departments that had the federal contracts; and it required contractors to develop a written affirmative-action plan. Macaluso gave Sandler advice on how to draw up the complaints, then read them for her when she'd finished and suggested improvements.

With WEAL's enthusiastic backing and behind-the-scenes support from Macaluso, in January 1970, Sandler filed a historic class-action complaint on behalf of WEAL against every college and university in the United States, charging an industry-wide pattern of discrimination against women, a charge supported by more than eighty pages of data. She filed the complaint with HEW—the Department of Health, Education and Welfare—which was primarily responsible for applying the Executive Order to colleges and universities. She also sent copies to key members of Congress and to the press.

The response was good and in the months that followed, Sandler's campaign generated considerable publicity. WEAL began to look like a powerful organization. Appearances were deceiving. "I had a title," Sandler said. "I was the head of WEAL's Action Committee for Federal Contract Compliance. I was also the whole committee."

As word of Sandler's activities spread, faculty women began to write to her about their own experiences with sex discrimination. Sandler would write back, offering to file charges for them. Under the Executive Order at that time, one person could file on behalf of others without actually naming them or citing specific incidents—it was enough if she could show a pattern of sex bias. That was important, because a university couldn't retaliate against women who initiated a complaint if it couldn't identify them.

The initial class-action complaint had been primarily an attention-getting device. Over the next few years, WEAL followed up by filing individual charges against more than 250 colleges and universities. Other feminist organizations, including NOW, got involved, too. Drawing up a complaint soon became so easy for Sandler that she could do it on the back of an envelope. All she needed were a few basic facts: How many women and men were instructors in the departments in question, how many were assistant, associate, and full professors, and at each level what percentage of the total number employed were women. She put this together with information she'd already gathered about the number of women "in the pipeline"—how many held PhDs in economics, for example, and so might be available for posts in an economics department.

Sandler developed an ingenious way to use the press to pressure the universities. "When I filed a charge, I sent a notice to the student newspaper," she said. "I never sent it to the president of the university, so he was caught unawares. The newspaper would . . . call up the president and say, 'It looks like you have no women in the psych department,' and he would often blurt out stupid things. There would be a lot of fuss in the student paper, and the press would pick it up."

At first, officials at HEW took no action on WEAL's complaints —they seemed to assume that if they waited long enough, feminists would lose interest. At Macaluso's suggestion, Sandler "held their feet to the fire." She asked the women behind the complaints to get as many people as possible to write their members of Congress. They were to say that charges had been filed against a particular university but that HEW wasn't following through, and they were to urge the legislators to write to the Secretary of HEW or the Secretary of Labor and ask them why HEW wasn't enforcing the Order. This strategy required minimal effort on anyone's part, and the members of Congress didn't even have to take a stand on sex discrimination—all they had to do was ask a question. "It was fairly easy to generate several hundred letters from Congress," said Sandler. Soon, HEW had to assign one person to do nothing but answer this mail. Sandler noted that "if anything moves the bureaucracy—and not much does—it's a series of inquiries from Capitol Hill." The strategy worked, and in the spring of 1970 HEW reluctantly lumbered into action.

The WEAL campaign against the academic establishment was masterminded by a very small number of Washington women and men with grass-roots support on campuses across the country. Sandler estimated that the whole effort probably cost a few hundred dollars, mostly for postage and phone calls, because she herself was an unpaid volunteer. Yet it led to significant changes in the American system of higher education. Though HEW never pursued complaints with much enthusiasm, the very fact that university policies and practices *were* being investigated, and that in some instances federal funds were delayed because a college was uncooperative, forced most institutions to reconsider the way they treated faculty women and make some "voluntary" adjustments.

Sandler's activities had three other unforeseen consequences. They galvanized feminist groups on many campuses; they drew more women into WEAL; and they gave attorney Phineas Indritz, the mentor of NOW's legal committee, the ammunition he needed to persuade Congresswoman Edith Green to hold hearings on sex discrimination in education. Green, who chaired a House education subcommittee, had been hesitating because she wasn't sure enough people would come forward to testify. In fact, the hearings, which were held in 1970, not only documented widespread discrimination against women but legitimized it as an issue. Afterward, Green asked Sandler to edit the testimony; then she had it published. Six thousand copies were printed and sent to every member of Congress, to education associations, and to the press.

THE BATTLE FOR EQUITY IN EDUCATION

In the early 1970s, feminists winkled two important education bills out of Congress, Title IX and the Women's Educational Equity Act (WEEA). Each presented a different strategic problem, though in both cases the problem boiled down to the fact that Congress wasn't inclined to do anything about gender bias in education. In order to pass Title IX, feminists kept a low profile. They didn't want to call attention to the bill, because if more people understood just how broadly it would affect education, the opposition would grow. WEEA, on the other hand, wasn't controversial but it nearly died because its sponsor couldn't stir up enough interest to get it out of committee. The solution was to include it in a huge, complex education bill where it passed virtually unnoticed.

Title IX

In 1970, the House had three education subcommittees, and Oregon Democrat Edith Green chaired the one with jurisdiction over higher education. Green saw the need for new laws to combat sex bias in education. Though the Executive Order gave faculty women a weapon, it was no help to students, and a hostile administration could easily revoke it. Green was already sponsoring a bill that increased federal funding for colleges. She added a section (Title IX) prohibiting sex discrimination in any federally assisted educational program or activity. Because virtually all public schools and colleges received some federal money and most private colleges did, too, the bill would cast a wide net.

Title IX also had a provision that closed the loophole in the Equal Pay Act, but it was cleverly hidden—just a few lines of type, giving the numbers of certain sections of the Fair Labor Standards Act that were now to be deleted. There was no indication that those sections were in the Equal Pay Act, which was itself part of the Fair Labor Standards Act, nor that they were the particular sections exempting administrative, executive and professional employees. Sandler recalled that "the Labor Department was quite surprised after the passage of Title IX that they had had the Equal Pay Act amended under their noses."

Green's bill finally reached the floor of the House in early November 1971. There, debate focused almost entirely on college admissions policies. Several powerful Ivy League schools* lobbied for an exemption—they had quotas for women, because they wanted to keep their student bodies predominantly male. They prevailed in the end, and when Title IX passed the House, it exempted the admissions policies of private undergraduate colleges.

In March 1972, the bill was consigned to a House-Senate conference committee to be reconciled with a similar bill passed by the Senate. Green shrewdly advised feminists not to lobby for Title IX. Opponents had evidently lost interest in it once they got the exemption for private undergraduate admissions. Apparently, few people realized that Title IX would affect such things

---

* The universities were Harvard, Princeton, Yale, and Dartmouth. The first three had quotas for women, while Dartmouth was still all-male.

as athletics, particular classes that didn't admit women, policies on maternity leave, and the whole question of whether a school had the right to expel pregnant students. "They didn't see those things as discrimination," Sandler explained.

In the end, the committee approved the bill, and Title IX became law in June 1972. Then the battle *really* began—but more about that later.

WEEA

WEEA—the Women's Educational Equity Act—was drafted by a handful of feminists who had little or no experience in drawing up legislation. Most of them were convinced, even as they worked, that there was little chance that Congress would pass their bill; they knew that only about 10 percent of all the bills introduced each year were even reported out of committee.

Originally, WEEA was the bright idea of a young woman who was doing clerical work—despite her college degree—for one of the House education subcommittees. Arlene Horowitz had seen many bills passed that provided relatively small sums for special projects such as consumer education. Why not a bill to fund women's studies? Horowitz first approached Bunny Sandler, who recalled that "Arlene eventually convinced me and other people that it would be worth [trying] if only to get a hearing on the bill. If we had testimony on how bad and sexist the textbooks were . . . then the publishers would be nervous . . . and they might produce better books."

Soon, seven Washington feminists began meeting in the evenings and on weekends to work on the bill. Horowitz produced the first rough draft, sometimes lifting whole sections from similar legislation to get the language right. The basic concept behind the bill changed with time. In the end, it provided funds not just for women's studies, but for a variety of model programs—from efforts to revise sexist textbooks to seminars designed to sensitize teachers. WEEA would also establish an advisory council within HEW to watchdog the position of women in education.

In March 1972, Representative Patsy Mink, a Democrat from Hawaii, agreed to sponsor the bill. She was a senior member of another of the House education subcommittees. The hearings on WEEA were held in the summer of 1973, and when very few members of the subcommittee bothered to attend, Mink concluded that probably the bill wouldn't even be brought up for a vote. She decided that the best way to pass WEEA—and perhaps the only way—was to incorporate it into a catchall education bill that was then being considered. The House version was so close to passage that there wasn't time to add to it, but Walter Mondale, who had agreed to sponsor WEEA in the Senate, could still offer an amendment there. Thus, WEEA was simply absorbed into the Senate's education bill and was never really debated. WEEA wasn't a major piece of legislation. No one would have predicted then that during the 1980s the right wing would make determined attempts to scuttle it, proving by their very opposition just how effective the law was (see chapter 20).

Attempts to Undo Title IX

As people began to realize what Title IX might accomplish, it became the center of a firestorm of controversy. In Congress, a well-organized opposition mounted a campaign to weaken the law, while feminists put together a coalition to defend it. Meanwhile, federal agencies stalled, first on issuing regulations for Title IX, then on enforcing them. The burgeoning opposition proved that Edith Green was right: The law would never have been enacted if educators had realized just how far-reaching it was.

Because opponents knew they had little hope of repealing Title IX outright, they attempted to weaken it by amending it. While some pressed for an exemption so that males and females needn't be treated equally in school sports, others tried to prohibit HEW from gathering information about sex discrimination; without this data, it would be impossible to enforce the law. Both groups used the element of surprise and introduced their amendments without warning, hoping to catch Title IX's advocates off guard. Several times, one house of Congress passed an amendment that would have undermined Title IX, and women then had to work hard to get the other house to undo the damage.

Overall, feminists held their ground. By the midseventies, the women's network in Washington included a broad spectrum of organizations, some focused exclusively on education. For instance, monitoring the enforcement of Title IX was the primary purpose of PEER, the Project on Equal Education Rights, which was founded in 1974 thanks to foundation grants. That same year, Holly Knox—director of PEER—Bunny Sandler, and others organized NCWGE, the National Coalition for Women and Girls in Education. This highly effective alliance had an initial roster of thirty to thirty-five groups, but it kept growing, and because several mass-membership organizations were included, it represented literally millions of women.

Title IX and the Sex Bias in Sports

Though Title IX covered educational institutions in a very broad way, many Americans came to think of it as a law that applied only to athletics because in the beginning there was so much vocal opposition from the sports establishment. The NCAA (National Collegiate Athletic Association) conducted an emotional campaign, insisting that if college athletics departments had to spend as much on women's sports as they spent on men's, the big intercollegiate games would suffer.

High school administrators also complained that the money to upgrade girls' sports programs would have to come from boys' sports. Some coaches didn't even want girls' teams competing for school facilities. Ron Wied, a coach at a Wisconsin high school, said in 1973, "We've got a boys' gym and a girls' gym. Before, we could use the girls' gym for wrestling and B team basketball a lot more than we can now. I think girls have a right to participate but to a lesser degree than boys. If they go too far with the competitive stuff, they lose their femininity."

In addition, coed gym classes drew the fire of sexual conservatives, who couldn't bear the thought that boys and girls might play "contact" sports together. Many men were also concerned about protecting the male ego. Charles Maas, secretary of the Indiana State Coaches Association, explained that "there is the possibility that a boy would be beaten by a girl and as a result be ashamed to face his family and friends. I wonder if anybody has stopped to think what that could do to a young boy."

In the early 1970s, those who saw athletics as a male preserve were under siege. In 1974, the Little League, beset by lawsuits brought by girls and their parents in over a dozen states, agreed that females could play. Meanwhile, women in professional sports were demanding a new deal. In tennis, golf, and every other sport in which both sexes competed, women had always earned much less in prize money than men did. The drive for change climaxed in 1973 in the match that pitted tennis hustler Bobby Riggs, a former world champion, against women's champion Billie Jean King. Billed as "the battle of the sexes," it was held in the Houston Astrodome, and 30,000 spectators turned out to see it—the biggest crowd in U.S. tennis history. Though the odds out of Las Vegas were five to two in favor of Riggs, King won easily.

However, the campaign against sex bias in athletics soon developed some unexpected complexities, for the old equality-difference dilemma surfaced once again. Title IX mandated equal treatment, and that was exactly the right approach when it came to schooling. Activists simply wanted girls and women to get an education equal to (meaning, the same as) the education boys and men got. In athletics the problem was muddier. Few females are as strong as males, and most sports were invented by males as a test of physical strength. Thus, a gender-neutral approach—treating girls exactly the way boys were treated—would simply ensure that most girls didn't make the team.

In the context of Title IX, some feminists argued that "equality" meant that women must have their own teams with an equal budget and facilities; others believed in literal, equal treatment because women who were good enough to compete with men deserved the chance to try. To complicate things further, women coaches and others who belonged to AIAW—the Association for Intercollegiate Athletics for Women—were reluctant to see women's sports turned into an income-producing "industry" like intercollegiate football, with all the pressure to win. For a time, AIAW actually opposed athletic scholarships for women.

By 1990, most of these issues had been worked out. In marathons, for example, women and men ran in the same races but there were prizes for the best woman and the best man. Many people now simply assumed that women athletes who were good enough should have the chance to compete with men, that few women would do so, and that the rest were entitled to have their own teams and tournaments.

Foot Dragging by Federal Agencies

Though Congress passed Title IX in 1972, HEW didn't release proposed regulations for almost two years. When they were finally published in June 1974, they were a mixed bag, especially for athletics. On the negative side, they didn't require equal funding for men's and women's programs, merely "basic equality," and they were vague about what that meant. On the positive side, they allowed a number of options: Coed gym classes were mandatory, but single-sex teams were permitted as long as they were treated equally; coed teams were allowed as well, provided they weren't used as a way to exclude most women by making them compete with men for places on the team.

Sandler and others prepared a detailed analysis of the regs, translating them into language a lay person could understand and recommending changes. They urged feminists around the country to lobby HEW. In the end, the department was deluged with mail both from Title IX's backers and from the opposition. Ten thousand letters poured in; ordinarily, when regs were released, they brought in anywhere from 10 letters to 400. With no clear mandate on what changes to make, HEW set about revising the regs—and spent another year doing it.

Meanwhile, though Title IX had been on the books since 1972, there had been no effort at enforcement. HEW had said it wouldn't enforce until the regs were in place, though schools and colleges were doing things that—even without regs—were clearly against the law. In 1974, National Women's Law Center attorney Marcia Greenberger, representing WEAL and others, filed a law suit against HEW and the Department of Labor that charged them with failing to enforce Title IX. The suit dragged on for years.

Title IX regulations finally went into effect in July 1975. Afterward, very little changed. OCR—the Office of Civil Rights within HEW—was responsible for enforcement, and according to Marcia Greenberger, OCR "was an agency without any resources. They were a mess administratively. They lost claims, or if they investigated and school authorities were recalcitrant, they just let them drop. There was no will to enforce."

By 1976, feminists were fed up and PEER set to work to analyze HEW's records of complaints that had been filed. Focusing on elementary and secondary schools, the researchers found that over a four-year period HEW had resolved just 179 complaints— 20 percent of its caseload for schools. Two- and three-year delays were common. Most investigations were handled by mail. Though HEW claimed it was overburdened, PEER learned that the department had received an average of just six complaints per year for every staffer assigned to investigate discrimination in the public schools. Furthermore, it had left scores of staff vacancies unfilled and had returned millions in unspent funds to the Treasury.

In one area only, HEW had acted with alacrity. When academic men charged that because of pressure from HEW, educational institutions were practicing reverse discrimination and hiring women and minorities over better-qualified white males, HEW promptly appointed an ombudsman to deal with the problem on a priority basis.

By June 1976, OCR was in such chaos that all efforts at enforcing Title IX ground to a halt. After Jimmy Carter was elected President, his administration found it had inherited an OCR backlog of 3000 to 4000 cases.

Why was HEW so slow to act on Title IX? The PEER report noted that staffers apparently didn't feel that sex discrimination warranted a serious effort. The vast majority of the top professionals on the staff were males, and that undoubtedly had something to do with it. The report also said, "Some observers feel it is part and parcel of a long retreat from the federal commitment to equal rights. . . ."

Despite poor enforcement, sex discrimination eased significantly in schools and colleges during the 1970s. Women acting on the local level were a major force for change. Because so many girls and women were now interested in sports, individuals and groups filed suits in state courts all over the country. As a result, a number of schools were ordered to integrate boys' and girls' programs for noncontact sports. Other schools, presumably reading the handwriting on the wall, also improved their programs for women. In areas other than athletics, some institutions responded to pressure, while others voluntarily changed rules that treated the sexes differently—dropping policies that had set different financial-aid standards for women and men, for example. Meanwhile, the lawsuit filed by Marcia Greenberger resulted in a court order requiring the government to enforce Title IX. The court actually kept the case open for a number of years to ensure that federal agencies complied, and that made a difference.

Over the years, women made solid progress in athletics and education. At the Olympic Games in 1984, three-quarters of the American women who competed said they wouldn't have been there if it hadn't been for Title IX. In the late 1980s, women filled about one third of the seats in medical schools and law schools. They had also made inroads into architecture, dentistry, engineering, and other male-dominated professions.

Nevertheless, female students in the nineties still face obstacles in many areas. Legally, girls have the same access to math and science classes as boys do, and many take advantage of that. In high schools, 60 percent of female students take four years of math, up from just 38 percent in 1975. Yet girls are still less likely to sign up for math and science courses than boys are. Walteen

Grady Truely, director of PEER, speaks of a "climate of discouragement" for girls that is worse in some schools than in others. With their female students, too many teachers emphasize compliant behavior and make little effort to encourage intellectual curiosity. In 1991, Truely also had the impression that guidance counselors still tend to steer girls toward traditionally female occupations.

As for textbooks, a recent study of books that were published in the 1980s for grades one through eight found that the language had consistently improved—it was generally nonsexist—and that the majority of math books now used girls and women as frequently as men and boys in their illustrations and in laying out problems. However, most story books were still riddled with sex stereotypes—the boys in the stories had more adventures and did more problem solving than the girls—and history books were even more imbalanced and devoted very little space to women's history or point of view. In high school texts, change was also uneven. Nonsexist approaches had become popular by the late 1970s, but interest in them declined after about 1987 partly because of a surge of conservatism in the schools. Nevertheless, in the early nineties at every level, from children's readers through college texts, there are now many more nonsexist books for teachers and professors to choose from.

In general, women students now get a better break than faculty women do. Sandler noted that "the more power involved [and] the more money, the harder it is to make changes. . . ." Women scholars are still much less likely than men to receive tenure—or, for that matter, to find full-time teaching positions.* In sports, gains are also mixed. Women's athletics programs in schools and colleges are much better funded in the 1990s than they were in the early 1970s, but they still receive a good deal less money than men's programs, and colleges probably spend twice as much on athletic scholarships for males. Worse, as funding improves, male coaches move in. Men now coach more than half of all female college teams; in 1972, they'd coached 10 percent.

In 1981, a report on education examined women's status in many areas, from high school sports to acceptance in graduate schools and the likelihood that faculty women would receive ten-

* In 1981, fewer than 50 percent of women who were full-time faculty had tenure, compared with 70 percent of the men. By 1987–88, women had not improved their position in relation to men and the tenure rate had dropped for both sexes: 45 percent of the women were now tenured, compared with 65 percent of men.

ure. The report concluded that for women, the glass could be called half empty or half full. Ten years later, feminists are still using the same analogy.

ACADEMIC ACTIVISTS AND THE BIRTH OF WOMEN'S STUDIES

While some women were pursuing legal solutions in Washington, others were tackling the education issue in other ways. In 1969, academic feminists began to organize within their professional groups, beginning with the American Sociological Association. By the end of the year, five independent women's caucuses and four advisory councils had sprung up in various organizations; two years later there were nearly fifty such groups, each committed to raising the status of women within a particular discipline.

Women's studies also exploded onto the American scene in the early seventies, and in the process universities became vital centers for the women's movement. In the fall of 1969, American colleges offered only about 17 courses concerned with women. A year later, there were over 100 women's studies courses, and by 1973, there were over 2000. No feminist organization could take credit for this—the courses cropped up spontaneously all over the country. On some campuses, students and faculty held sit-ins to demand them. In other places, faculty women privately pressured their departments.

Women's studies pioneer Catharine R. Stimpson noted that for both faculty and students the discovery of women's studies often "began with a sense of rupture and estrangement from accepted knowledge. . . ." Historian Joan Kelly recalled an experience that may have been typical. In 1971, Kelly received a letter from Gerda Lerner, another historian, suggesting that she develop a women's course. Kelly wrote back to say, "Since I was in Renaissance history, there was nothing much I could offer. . . ." Lerner insisted on seeing her anyway, and talked for hours about the potential for women's history. Kelly wasn't convinced, but promised to think about her field and how it related to women.

"That turned out to be the most exciting intellectual adventure I can recall," she wrote later. "It was like a very rapid repetition of the confusion into which I had been plunged in adolescence: the profoundly frightening feeling of all coherence gone, followed by restoration, if not of a new order, at least of a new direction. . . . I knew now that the entire picture I had held of the Renaissance was partial, distorted, limited, and deeply flawed. . . . All I had done was to say . . . [s]uppose we look at the Renaissance from the vantage point of women?" From that perspective, the Renaissance was not a renaissance for women; in fact, they had more freedom during the Dark Ages.

Stimpson observed that feminist scholars often had to deconstruct what they thought they knew and then reconstruct it again. Perhaps the best-known example was the work of Harvard psychologist Carol Gilligan, which became a touchstone for feminists who believed that sex differences were important. In the early 1970s, Gilligan was a junior member of the Harvard faculty. Interested in the turning points in people's lives, she began to study young women who were trying to decide whether or not to have an abortion. As they spoke of their moral dilemma and the choice they had to make, it struck her that they spoke with "a different voice."

It was almost a truism in psychology that women were morally immature. Freud had said so, and Gilligan's Harvard colleague, psychologist Lawrence Kohlberg, who studied the development of moral values in children, had concluded that youngsters passed through six stages, but that moral development in girls was usually arrested at stage three. Kohlberg noted that women saw the moral choice as the one that helped or pleased others, while men passed through that stage to a higher one where they understood that morality was a matter of justice, of abstract rules and people's rights. Actually, Kohlberg constructed his scale by studying the moral development of eighty-four boys; he accepted them as the norm for both sexes. Once she realized this, Gilligan asked the obvious question: What if girls were not inferior but simply different in the way they developed values? Her own studies suggested that that was the case.

Gilligan believed that sex differences in values had their roots in early childhood; she cited the work of another feminist, Nancy Chodorow. According to Chodorow, a boy growing up under a mother's care needed to separate himself from her before he could feel truly male, while a girl could identify with her mother, remain attached to her, and still feel female. That was why, as adults, men needed emotional space (separation), while women needed closeness. Chodorow suggested that it also explained why men often feared intimacy, and what women dreaded was isolation.

Gilligan's research on women's values meshed seamlessly with

Chodorow's theories. According to Gilligan, because relationships were so important to women, they tended to judge whether something was right or wrong by looking at how it affected other people. They thought in terms of responsibilities, and for them, morality arose from the particular context of a situation. Men, on the other hand, were more apt to focus on individual rights and to rely on abstract ideas of justice.

Most men saw life in terms of hierarchies; it was very important to them which rung of the ladder they were perched on. Women more often saw relationships as a supportive network. The view from the ladder of hierarchy offered a very different perspective than the view from the web of connection.

Some researchers who tried to replicate Gilligan's findings reported that boys and girls were apparently not as different in their ethical development as her work had suggested. Gilligan herself agreed that the "different voice" she heard was usually— but not always—female. Be that as it may, her insights touched off an avid feminist reexamination of old studies. Many researchers had used only males as subjects, on the assumption that they were representative of both sexes. Gilligan's work was also eagerly embraced by difference feminists committed to preserving women's values.

Of course, Gilligan and those who touted women's values had their critics. Some argued, for example, that women's values were originally produced by male oppression. As men's dependents, women *had* to care about relationships and responsibility; they were bound to fear isolation. Thus, no one knew what women were really like, or what they could be like if they were raised differently. The same thing was true of men.

As feminist scholars began to do research on women and to reexamine every subject from literature to ethology, many academics were skeptical or openly hostile. Then and later, whenever there was a budget crunch, women's studies courses were apt to be the first cut. Nevertheless, they not only survived but began to reach down into the secondary schools. In 1983, Peggy McIntosh of the Wellesley College Center for Research on Women began to lead monthly seminars for high school teachers. Over a period of a year, she would explore with them ways of integrating new scholarship on gender, race, and class into the secondary school curriculum. In 1987, McIntosh and Emily Jane Style found a way to expand the project's reach: During one-week summer sessions, they prepared groups of interested teachers so that they could return to their schools and hold monthly seminars for other teachers. By 1991, the National S.E.E.D.* Project on Inclusive Curriculum had prepared 135 seminar leaders. As a result, more than 2000 teachers in thirty states and several foreign countries participated in S.E.E.D. seminars.

In 1990, more than two thirds of all universities offered women's studies courses. There were many feminist scholarly journals and dozens of research centers. The National Women's Studies Association (NWSA), founded in 1977, had about 3000 members. Most important, the insights of feminist scholars had challenged the entrenched male perspective in practically every discipline.

Women's Studies and Multiculturalism

During the 1980s, feminist scholarship underwent major changes, becoming more inclusive as many feminists realized that in the past, women's studies had too often meant white-women's studies. By 1990, secondary schools and universities all over the country were making similar efforts to make their curricula "multicultural," and they began to mainstream feminist scholarship along with material chosen to reflect the histories and perspectives of people of color.

Both feminists and scholars of color were divided about whether mainstreaming was a good idea. Women's studies sometimes fostered pride and a sense of solidarity in women students; black studies did the same sort of thing for African-Americans. Some felt it was too soon to give that up. Feminists were also afraid that radical insights would be defanged and that "equal treatment" for feminist scholarship would mean it was absorbed into the male canon with barely a ripple to show where it went down.

Different problems have been in the offing, however, for suddenly in the early nineties controversies erupted at schools and colleges around the country. As the interest in multicultural, non-sexist courses and curriculums grew, so did a conservative backlash. Some right-wingers undoubtedly have felt threatened by the fact that on many campuses the faculty and student body have been transformed—they are no longer largely male and almost entirely white. In 1991, just 30 percent of the students at the University of California at Berkeley were white. By the year 2000, one third of elementary and high school students will be youngsters of color.

* Seeking Educational Equity and Diversity.

As conservatives and other traditionalists reacted to the changes on campus, the debate centered on affirmative action in admissions and in hiring, and on the new multicultural courses and curriculums. Traditionalists insisted that colleges were sacrificing quality—in the student body and the professoriate and on reading lists—for dubious political ends. They were particularly upset because the "canon"—the generally accepted roster of the greatest works of all time—was being challenged. On the other hand, multiculturalists denied that standards were slipping in admissions or on the faculty and argued that when it came to the curriculum, "greatness" had always been in the eye of the beholder—an eye that wore cultural blinders.

At stake was the nature of education—and more. The debate *was* political, as some on both sides admitted: it was about power. White males had always had an inestimable advantage, for their own experience was reflected back to them at every level in their education, from their first readers to college courses in great books—virtually all written by European men and American men of European ancestry. At the same time, the contributions of women, of other American racial and ethnic groups, and of non-Western cultures were ignored. Multiculturalists were intent on opening up the canon.

On another level, the controversy was about what it meant to be an American. Traditionalists felt that the very identity "American" was being eroded by the emphasis on diversity, that the nation's central values were being undermined. Multiculturalists responded that it was time to explore that identity in all its diversity and complexity and redefine it as necessary.

Beginning in the fall of 1990, students and faculty also argued about "political correctness." In response to racial incidents and the verbal harassment of women and gays, some colleges and universities had drawn up codes of acceptable and unacceptable behavior. At least one student was expelled for shouting insults aimed at blacks, Jews, and gays, and some faculty members were rebuked for making biased comments or apparently lost their bid for tenure because of things they'd said. Conservatives charged that a new kind of "political correctness" was being required on campus and that it threatened the right to free speech. The other side responded that female students and men of color had a right to an education and a right to equal protection and that a hostile environment on campus interfered with both.

Through all the conflict, many feminists and other civil rights activists were certain that the real issue was that white heterosexual men were determined to preserve their own privileges and power. Multiculturalists were also convinced that if schools and colleges didn't begin to provide students with an education that mirrored—and valued—the experiences of all races and both sexes, the nation had little chance of surviving as a peaceful and productive society.

Bias in the Classroom

By the 1990s, sex discrimination in education had become less open, less common—but was in some ways harder to deal with. For instance, though women no longer had to have higher grades than men to get into top colleges, the faculty still treated them differently. According to Bernice Sandler, studies done between 1978 and 1982 showed that in the classroom women students were called on less often than men and were interrupted more. Instructors who went to great pains to draw out male students simply passed over what females said with no comment. Nobody defined such behavior as discrimination and it was seldom intentional. Most women weren't even aware of it, but that actually increased the impact, because each student assumed that she was simply getting the treatment she deserved. Researchers found that the longer women stayed in college, the less self-esteem they had. Women's colleges provided a more supportive atmosphere and gave more women a chance to exercise leadership, because they didn't have to compete with men, but women's colleges had become an endangered species: In 1969, there were over 200; in 1989, just 94.

Meanwhile, new studies by Carol Gilligan indicated that most females began to lose their self-confidence even before they reached college age. From 1981 through 1985, Gilligan and a team of researchers studied girls who attended private schools and others who were in public school, some in the inner city. They found that at around the age of eleven, many experienced "a moment of resistance"—of almost perfect confidence in what they knew and in their own integrity. Then they came up against "the wall of Western culture," which embodied male values and a relentlessly male perspective. By fifteen or sixteen, most girls had become hesitant and apologetic and tended to qualify many of their statements with "I don't know."*

A 1990 survey of 3000 children confirmed Gilligan's findings.

* As in, "I thought it was, like—I don't know—a little unfair."

Though both girls and boys were less confident in high school than in elementary school, for girls the drop in self-esteem was much larger. However, there were some intriguing differences among females. Black girls were far more likely to retain their self-confidence than either whites or Hispanics. Janie Victoria Ward, an advisor on the study, pointed out that in African-American communities, girls grew up surrounded by strong women who were good role models. In addition, black parents often taught their children to blame racism rather than themselves when they experienced rejection. However, self-esteem didn't correlate with academic achievement for black girls; it appeared that in gaining themselves, they might be losing a chance to acquire skills and knowledge that would be important in the future.

Gilligan's work suggested that it might be possible to intervene during early adolescence to forestall the loss of confidence in girls, and in the 1990s she and her colleagues are busy researching possible strategies. They had discovered already that writing helped—for example, journal writing is a way for a girl to stay in touch with her own inner voice and opinions in a world in which others often fail to listen to her. Activities that involve group efforts rather than individual competition also seem to be confidence-building. Nevertheless, there are no quick fixes in sight, because basically adolescent girls are responding to the fact that it is still a man's world—though that is changing slowly, thanks to the efforts of activists.

In the 1990s, the feminist movement for equality in education is stronger than ever. The National Coalition for Women and Girls in Education (NCWGE) has fifty member organizations, and their representatives continue to meet once a month. Women's studies programs are thriving, and there are feminist research institutes, scholarly journals, and women's caucuses in various academic and professional associations. Many campuses have women's centers, and as abortion becomes an urgent issue, new feminist groups are springing up among students.

chapter 12

The Women's Health Movement

In the early 1970s, feminists became acutely aware of the sex biases that warped the American medical system. The vast majority of doctors were men and they often treated women patients high-handedly. Activists skimming medical-school textbooks found them sprinkled with condescending statements about female masochism and passivity—assumptions that encouraged a kind of medical chauvinism.

As health activists organized, the issues that galvanized them tended to involve reproduction. It was there that medical men seemed the most wrong-headed, perhaps because it was, above all, the female ability to bear children that made women seem so alien to many men. They couldn't imagine what it would be like to be perpetually bogged down (as they assumed women were) in the business of the body: menstruating, being pregnant, bearing and then breastfeeding babies. Thus, in the eighteenth century, after the early feminist, Mary Wollstonecraft, died from childbed fever, the Reverend Richard Polwhele observed that she "died a death that strongly marked the distinction of the sexes, by pointing out the destiny of women, and the diseases to which they are peculiarly liable."

In addition, there had always been men (including physicians) who felt that they had a right to use women's bodies and control women's fertility. Some were determined to dictate female behavior as a means of population control or for the sake of eugenics. A gynecologist put it bluntly back in about 1920, when birth control activist Margaret Sanger asked him why he favored abortion rather than contraception. He told her:

> We will never give over the control of our numbers to the women themselves. What, let them control the future of the human race? With abortions it is in our hands; we make the decisions, and they must come to us.

That attitude was still alive seventy years later, though it was less often stated openly.

The women's health movement took root in the late sixties and early seventies as women who belonged to a NOW chapter or a consciousness-raising group, or who had become caught up in the second wave in some other way, got together to form new groups focused on particular health issues. The first feminist health conference was held in 1971. Eight hundred women attended, and among other things they discussed abortion techniques and drug safety—subjects long considered too technical for anyone except medical experts. By 1973, there were dozens of health groups scattered around the country that provided women with services (information and referrals to doctors with enlightened attitudes, for example) or lobbied for changes in the laws. In 1975, the National Women's Health Network (NWHN) was founded and became an umbrella for the whole health movement. Both individuals and groups joined NWHN, which linked everyone by providing vital information; it also monitored proposed legislation and the actions of government agencies.

During the 1970s, health activists raised the alarm about dangerous contraceptives and also challenged the tendency of doctors to treat natural processes such as pregnancy as if they were diseases. From the beginning, feminists took the position that the patient had a right to all the facts. The drive to demystify medicine was basic to the women's health movement and it gave rise to self-help groups, information hotlines, books like the feminist classic *Our Bodies, Ourselves,* and feminist clinics where the medical staff went to great lengths to explain procedures to patients.

In the 1980s, there were several major new developments in the women's health movement: Women of color began to organize their own separate groups focused on health issues, and some feminists opposed the new technologies that were moving reproduction into the laboratory, where babies were conceived in test tubes. The feminist divide opened up once again as a controversy developed over surrogate motherhood. Meanwhile, fetal rights had become an issue, and there was a growing tendency to put the rights of the fetus ahead of those of the pregnant woman.

UNNATURAL CHILDBIRTH

Philosophically, the women's health movement had its roots in the campaign for natural childbirth and the struggle to legalize abortion. Activists in both causes shared the conviction that women must be the ones to decide what would happen to their bodies.

Throughout most of human history, women gave birth at home, attended by a midwife. However, during the twentieth century, childbirth in the United States was medicalized when it gradually moved from home to hospital. By the late 1940s, the typical American woman gave birth while drugged into a state called "twilight sleep." She was confined to bed in a room with other laboring women, most of them moaning and tossing, drugged and groggy. Her memory of the whole experience was apt to be fragmented and nightmarish. Small wonder, then, that many women were avidly interested when two physicians independently developed ways to train women to cope with childbirth with little or no medication.

In 1951, Doris Haire was among the first Americans to have a baby by natural childbirth. "That was the beginning of my ego," she said, "because for the first time in my life, I did something that I thought was really wonderful and courageous. . . . [I]t takes courage to have natural childbirth, but women who have it come out with such a sense of power."

Haire happily devoted the next fifteen years of her life to raising children. Then, in 1966, she connected with ICEA, the International Childbirth Education Association, a group formed to promote natural birth, which was still highly controversial. By 1970, she was co-president of the organization and had undertaken an ambitious study of childbirth practices that took her to hundreds of maternity hospitals around the world. She also audited the core course in obstetrics at a medical school.

Haire's report on her research, *The Cultural Warping of Childbirth*, was published in 1972 and marked a turning point in obstetric care. In a meticulously documented indictment of the American way of birth, she pointed out that, compared with other industrialized nations, the United States had a higher rate of infant mortality and of babies harmed during childbirth. The reason, she said, was that American obstetricians interfered too much during childbirth. In other countries, midwives managed normal deliveries and they were inclined to let labor run its course. Doctors were called in only when something went wrong.

Nor were infant mortality and obvious morbidity the only problems. Haire believed that the amount of medication given American women during childbirth often produced some degree of brain damage in babies. She also pointed out that each intervention in the normal birth process tended to make other interventions necessary. For example, epidural anesthesia made it difficult or even impossible for the woman to bear down, so that the doctor often had to use forceps to deliver the baby. Then again, using drugs to induce labor caused unusually intense, prolonged, painful contractions that subjected the baby's head to great pressure. The drugs also shortened the recovery intervals between contractions and that could diminish the infant's oxygen supply—sometimes to the point where an emergency Cesarean section was necessary. Virtually all drugs given to a laboring woman could affect her fetus, but for a long time, many doctors were reluctant to believe this. They clung to the belief that the placenta filtered out harmful substances.

Thanks to ICEA and other women's groups, by the early 1970s some hospitals were encouraging natural childbirth; they allowed husbands to be present during labor and delivery and offered "rooming in" as an option: The baby could stay in the mother's room, rather than in the hospital nursery. By the late 1970s some cities had birthing centers where a woman could give birth attended by a midwife and surrounded by family or friends, with a physician on call for emergencies. Many hospitals, driven to compete, also set up "home-style" birthing rooms. The number of midwives grew, and more women had their babies at home.

However, even as feminists won on some fronts, they lost on others. New devices were developed, and, though they saved lives in the 10 percent of cases where problems occurred, doctors also used them routinely for births that were entirely normal. For example, purely as a precaution, a laboring woman was often hooked up to a fetal monitor. However, since the monitors weren't always accurate, and some doctors didn't have the skill to interpret them even when they were,* the result too often was an unnecessary Cesarean section, done because the baby seemed to be in trouble, when in fact it wasn't. Partly as a result of the misguided use of the new technology, the number of C-sections soared, until in the late 1980s nearly one quarter of all births in the United States were by Cesarean, the highest rate in the world. According to the World Health Organization, there was no justification for a rate higher than 10 to 15 percent.

Many obstetricians contended that it was the fear of malpractice suits that made physicians resort to fetal monitors and overtreat patients in other ways. However, Doris Haire maintained that doctors were ignoring a very simple alternative. Haire had drafted a virtually ironclad consent form to be filled in by the patient. It began: "I, . . . , understand from my health care provider, . . . , that my condition has been diagnosed as . . . and that he/she has proposed the following treatment . . . I understand that there are known risks inherent in the proposed treatment, which are . . ." And so on. The two-page document was made up mostly of blank spaces. By the time a patient understood enough to fill out the form, she knew a great deal. When Haire showed the form to doctors, most objected that if they used it, they'd have to spend too much time explaining things to patients. To Haire, the issue was the patient's right to know and to make her own decisions.

In the 1980s, doctors in other countries began to do more C-sections, following in American footsteps. In an effort to counteract to overuse of Cesareans, women formed the Cesarean Prevention Movement in 1982. By the early 1990s, CPM had eighty chapters in the United States and individual members in at least seven other countries.

SELF-HELP GROUPS AND FEMINIST HEALTH CENTERS

To health activists, it was an article of faith that women must take charge of their own medical destiny. The Boston *Our Bodies,*

---

* In 1990, researchers reported that the use of fetal monitors didn't improve a premature infant's chances of survival and might be linked to cerebral palsy.

Ourselves collective popularized the idea, as did author Barbara Seaman's early books. At about the same time, some feminists went a step farther and formed self-help groups to diagnose and treat simple gynecological problems. One woman also invented a device that women could use to do abortions for one another.

The first self-help group was founded in the early 1970s by two California women. At the time, Carol Downer and Lorraine Rothman belonged to a Los Angeles consciousness-raising group that had decided to do abortion referrals. Abortions were legal in the state at the time, but were expensive and unavailable in many areas. Because Downer and Rothman realized that they didn't know what a good abortion was, they arranged to observe procedures at several places. They came away convinced that abortions were surprisingly simple to do and that most doctors were dilating the cervix more than was necessary.

The two women set out to learn more about gynecology. In the process, they discovered that by using a flashlight, a mirror, and a physician's speculum, a woman could examine her own vagina and cervix; they began demonstrating the technique to other women. To most, it was a revelation: It simultaneously demystified the female body and medicine itself, for they soon found that they could recognize early signs of pregnancy and symptoms of vaginal infection or syphilis. By experimenting, they discovered that vaginal yeast infections could sometimes be cured simply by applying yogurt.

Then, in 1971, Lorraine Rothman invented the Del-Em, a simple suction device that could be used to perform an abortion. She took a Mason jar (the kind used for home canning) from her own cupboard, plugged the top with a wide stopper, pierced the stopper in two places, and attached two lengths of thin aquarium tubing. She connected one tube to a syringe, the other to a plastic cannula. By pumping the syringe, she could suck air into the jar through the other tube. The cannula was so slender that it wasn't necessary to stretch the cervical opening before sliding it into the uterus; it was so soft and flexible that it was unlikely to damage the uterine walls. Pumping the syringe created enough gentle suction to empty the uterus into the jar. The Del-Em was, in short, an improvement on the traditional abortion method, a surgical scraping of the womb, and an improvement, too, on the suction devices then in use. The whole apparatus cost just a few dollars to assemble.

The California feminists were prepared to set up an underground abortion clinic, as the women of Jane had done in Chicago, but in the end the clinic wasn't necessary because California hospitals began rapidly expanding their abortion facilities. Instead, in the fall of 1971, Downer and Rothman set off across the country to demonstrate self-examination during a whirlwind tour of twenty-three cities. Over 2000 women attended their clinics and demonstrations, and self-help health groups began to spring up everywhere.

On their return to Los Angeles, Downer and Rothman founded the Feminist Women's Health Center (FWHC), a gynecological clinic controlled and staffed entirely by women. The clinic cheerfully demystified medical procedures and involved patients in diagnosis and treatment. It became a model for many other women's clinics. In 1972, the FWHC also became, briefly, a cause célèbre, when ten policemen burst in and arrested Carol Downer and Coleen Wilson for practicing medicine without a license. They charged Downer with applying yogurt to a vaginal infection and tried to seize a container of yogurt as evidence. They were forced to hand it back when someone identified it as her lunch.

Wilson pleaded guilty and was released on probation, but Downer chose to stand trial. Feminist publications issued appeals for money to pay her legal expenses. During the trial, Downer's attorney raised many questions about how the law defined "medical practice." Was it practicing medicine to tell someone she had a cold sore on her lip? If not, how could it be practicing medicine to tell her she had a sore (cervicitis) on her cervix? Would it be a crime to apply yogurt to the cold sore? If not, how could it be criminal to apply yogurt to the cervix? The jury found Downer not guilty.

Because abortion restrictions were wiped out by the 1973 Supreme Court ruling, the Del-Em was not widely used by the feminist abortion underground. However, self-help groups around the country taught themselves to use the device to do menstrual extraction (ME). A woman plagued by heavy flow or severe cramps could gently empty her uterus in twenty to thirty minutes; so could a woman who didn't want her period to interfere with an athletic competition or a trip.

Women learned ME over a period of months or even years as part of a group that included members with more experience. Menstrual extraction was always done in a group, because it wasn't possible for a woman to insert the tubing by herself and because it seemed safer. Some groups, when they'd had enough practice with menstrual extraction, graduated to doing early abortions, which were trickier because there was more risk of infection. Though ME wasn't against the law, groups were legally harassed, so most operated more or less underground. Over the years, as the anti-abortion movement grew stronger, many self-helpers acquired another reason for doing ME: They felt that it made sense for women to be prepared, in case abortion became illegal again.

By 1976, there were about fifty feminist health centers in the United States and an estimated thirty menstrual extraction groups. The centers generally had a conventionally trained medical staff who handled abortions and routine care, such as Pap smears and pregnancy tests, for fees set according to what women could afford to pay. They tried to provide a new model of medical care, for feminists dreamed of a relationship between patient and medical professional that would replace mystery with self-knowledge, a relationship in which information would be shared and self-help, encouraged.

Doctors who worked for the feminist clinics had to be committed to participatory health care and willing to work long hours. According to Lorraine Rothman, from the beginning most of the physicians involved were men, and they worked at the clinics and had their own private practices as well. In the 1990s, though there are many more women in medicine, it is still hard for feminist health centers to recruit women doctors. Rothman notes that female gynecologists are in great demand everywhere. In addition, they probably have even less time available to do clinic work than men do, because they spend more time on child care and housework than their male colleagues.

Women's health centers were hard hit in the 1980s by a wave of violence against abortion facilities.* They had to pay for additional security staff and equipment, and insurance became so expensive that it drove some out of business. The higher premiums bore no relationship to the risks of abortion, which was safer than childbirth, or to the safety records of the clinics. Throughout the 1980s, the number of feminist health centers kept dropping. In the early nineties, there were only ten to fifteen left, according to Lynne Randall, executive director and cofounder of the Feminist Women's Health Center in Atlanta.

Throughout the 1980s, menstrual extraction remained a controversial procedure. Then, in July 1989, the Supreme Court handed down the *Webster* decision, which permitted Missouri to intro-

---

* Events in the abortion struggle are discussed in chapter 21.

duce major new restrictions on abortion. For the first time, it seemed possible that the Court's conservative majority might overturn *Roe* v. *Wade*. There was a dramatic revival of interest in ME, as feminists began to talk of organizing an abortion underground, if that became necessary.

Downer and her organization, the Federation of Feminist Health Centers (FFHC), were swamped with inquiries about the Del-Em. The women of the Federation had made a decision: Rather than becoming part of a possible abortion underground, they would provide the information other groups needed in order to operate. They began with a videotape that demonstrated how to do a suction abortion, which was widely distributed to women's groups. Interviewed in the press in 1989, Downer estimated that since 1971, 20,000 to 30,000 menstrual extractions had been done in the United States. Though some medical authorities still insisted that using the Del-Em was risky, others acknowledged that safety depended entirely on the skill and experience of the self-help group. Over the years, Rothman had heard of just ten cases in which an infection developed.

In the early 1990s, the leaders of the Federation knew that their method was no substitute for legal abortion. The Del-Em had to be used in the first weeks after conception. In addition, "We're realistic about the fact that this is not going to reach everyone," said Shireen Miles, Associate Director of FFWC. "Our insistence that women join a group and learn self-help is going to limit it to those who are very motivated." A woman couldn't wait until she was pregnant to find a group and learn ME. However, for women who *were* motivated, a self-help group would be safer than a back-alley abortionist.

Meanwhile, Downer and others had been teaching abortion techniques to women in Guatemala, Nicaragua, and Venezuela, and there was a growing self-help abortion movement in Mexico.

DANGEROUS CONTRACEPTIVES

Beginning with the 1960 contraceptive breakthrough known simply as "the pill," American women became guinea pigs for experimentation on a massive scale. Throughout the 1970s and 1980s, the women's health movement fought rearguard actions against a number of dangerous contraceptives.

Theoretically, dangerous drugs should never get past the FDA (Food and Drug Administration). However, the drug-approval system had problems, as Doris Haire discovered when she did a study of the way the agency operated. She found that when a company submitted reports of its research on a new drug to the FDA, the agency often accepted much of the company's data in good faith. What's more, the FDA didn't do systematic follow-ups on drugs it approved but depended on the manufacturer to report adverse effects. Predictably, drug companies weren't eager to expose problems that might cost them sales and leave them open to lawsuits.

In addition, because many FDA officials hoped to move on eventually to highly paid positions in the pharmaceutical industry, it wasn't in their best interests to antagonize the companies they regulated. (Other regulatory agencies had a similar problem.) During the 1980s, matters grew worse as the Reagan administration, in its enthusiasm for deregulation, cut the FDA's staff and pressed the agency to be even less adversarial. By 1991, the situation had gotten so out of hand that pharmaceutical companies themselves were lobbying to have the agency strengthened.

The FDA's inadequacies were partly responsible for the contraceptive tragedies of the 1970s and 80s. Corporate carelessness and greed also played a role, as did an insidious form of racism.

The Rise and Fall of the Pill

"The pill" provided the first chapter of the long and disillusioning story. It should have been tested even more carefully than most drugs because it was intended for long-term use by healthy women who had other options in birth control. Instead, the FDA approved it after just 132 women had used it for a year or more. Three of them died with symptoms suggesting blood clots, but they weren't even autopsied.

By the time the pill had been on the market for two years, 1.2 million American women were taking it. Throughout the 1960s, there were scattered reports in the medical literature questioning its safety, and in 1968, British researchers reported that it could cause potentially fatal blood clots. Few American physicians were willing to believe that, and for the next couple of years U.S. scientists who questioned the safety of the pill sometimes lost their federal funding. The widespread reluctance to face facts was due partly to concern about the population explosion taking place in the Third World—a concern fueled by deep-seated prejudices. Similar worries had developed at the turn of the century, when

many Americans, in the name of eugenics,* advocated sterilization of the poor. Jarred by a flood of immigrants, they wanted to
make sure the "right" women (white, native-born, middle- and
upper-class) had more children than the "wrong" ones did.

In the 1960s, the intellectual heirs of the eugenicists were intent
on finding new, longer-lasting contraceptives that could be used
by women who were "underprivileged" and "unmotivated"—in
other words, poor and nonwhite. Thus, the chairman of an FDA
advisory committee explained during congressional hearings on
the safety of the pill in 1970 that his committee had concluded
that the pill was safe, despite evidence to the contrary, after
weighing its risks against its benefits—not the benefits to individual women, but its benefits in controlling population growth.

Feminist author Barbara Seaman was the first to call the pill
into question in ways that got the public's attention. Her influential 1969 book, *The Doctors' Case Against the Pill*, described the
little-known studies that linked oral contraceptives to blood clots,
strokes, cancer, and a long list of other, less serious problems.
When the Senate held hearings on the pill in 1970, Alice Wolfson
and other activists disrupted them, demanding that women be
allowed to speak; the resulting media coverage further publicized
their arguments against the pill.† The FDA drafted a package
insert describing the possible side effects of oral contraceptives,
but the wording was watered down because of pressure from the
AMA (American Medical Association).

During the 1970s, researchers developed safer versions of the
pill by reducing the dosages of the hormones it contained. However, the original high-dose pills, which were pulled from the
market in Europe in the early 1970s, weren't discontinued in the
United States until 1988, and during the 1980s, 900,000 American
women continued to use them. It took years of prodding by the
National Women's Health Network and other groups to get them
banned.

DES: A Medical Time Bomb

In 1966, Boston gynecologist Arthur Herbst treated a fifteen-
year-old girl for a rare and deadly form of vaginal cancer that was

---

* The eugenics movement sought to improve the human species genetically through se-
lective mating.
† Seaman, who had helped the Senate staff plan the hearings, got together with Wolfson
and activist Belita Cowan afterward; the group that would become NWHN was born.

virtually unknown in women under twenty-five. Within the next three years, half a dozen other very young women with the same type of cancer came to his attention, and Herbst and a colleague began to look for some factor that linked them. They found that in all cases the teenagers' mothers had taken a drug called DES during pregnancy.

DES, diethylstilbestrol, is a form of estrogen. Between 1945 and 1970, it was prescribed for about three million American women to prevent a miscarriage, despite research that showed that women given DES were actually *more* likely to miscarry, and animal studies indicating that it might be a carcinogen.

Herbst published his findings on DES in 1971, but the FDA waited seven months to send out a warning bulletin. In the years that followed, it became apparent that the daughters of women who had taken DES were also prone to another, less deadly type of vaginal cancer, that many of them were infertile, and that some DES sons had genital abnormalities.

The feminist press covered the DES story in depth, as did the mainstream media. Unfortunately, the news failed to reach many women because their mothers had never been told the name of the drug they were given while pregnant. Outreach could have saved lives—the cancer was more likely to be cured if caught before it produced obvious symptoms—yet no public health agency was willing to mount a national campaign to contact the women. In July 1974, the AMA recommended that all doctors who had used DES warn patients; few complied. Some had kept poor records; others were undoubtedly afraid they would be sued for malpractice. In the midseventies, two feminist groups, the Coalition for the Medical Rights of Women and DES Action, were formed to alert DES daughters and doctors to the need for cancer screening.

Despite the revelations about DES, sales of the drug actually mounted in the early 1970s. It was now being marketed for use in massive doses as a "morning-after" pill, though it didn't have FDA approval as an abortifacient* and was risky for DES daughters. Studies done by Belita Cowan revealed that some college health services offered the pill to students without asking if their mothers had taken the drug. Some hospitals gave DES to new mothers to dry up their milk, though estrogen promotes blood clots, a potential hazard after childbirth. Doris Haire badgered the FDA for more than five years before it finally agreed to ban

---

* Though the FDA only approves drugs as treatments for specific conditions, doctors are generally not prohibited from using them for other purposes.

the use of DES to suppress lactation. However, in 1991 the drug was still being used (though infrequently) as a morning-after pill, according to the National Women's Health Network.

During the 1980s, many DES daughters filed lawsuits against the companies that marketed the drug, and attorney Sybil Shainwald represented a number of them.* She noted that unfortunately the women were often thwarted by state laws that set a time limit on claims for damages. The damage from DES didn't become obvious for twenty to thirty years, and by that time it was often too late to file a claim.

The Dalkon Shield Disaster

The Dalkon Shield was an IUD (intrauterine birth control device). It was a small, harmless-looking piece of white plastic, shaped like a crab, that dangled a length of string, and between 1970 and 1974 it was inserted into the wombs of 2.2 million American women to prevent conception. Thousands of users suffered a perforated uterus, had a miscarriage or a stillborn child, or developed a raging infection that left them permanently sterile; at least seventeen women died from septic miscarriages.

Before the Dalkon Shield was put on the market in 1970, an employee of A.H. Robins, the manufacturer of the device, warned company executives that the product's tail string might be dangerous. The string dangled from the uterus into the vagina to give doctors something to pull on when it was time to remove the IUD, and because it was made of absorbent material, it was like a wick. Vaginal bacteria could travel up it into the uterus, which is normally bacteria-free, causing an infection. Robins executives ignored the warning.

By mid-1972, Robins was getting reports that the Shield had a substantial pregnancy rate, was difficult and painful to insert and remove, and had caused massive infections. The company made no move to investigate and denied that its IUD was to blame. The FDA did nothing. FDA officials may have been influenced, once again, by the fact that IUDs were touted as virtually foolproof birth control that would work even for "unmotivated" poor women.

In June 1974, after an article in a medical journal linked the Dalkon Shield to several deaths, Robins finally took the product

---

* Shainwald was president of the National Women's Health Network for four years in the early eighties—years during which NWHN burgeoned into a large, mass membership organization.

off the market at the request of the FDA. However, neither Robins nor the FDA made any move to recall the devices still being worn by hundreds of thousands of women. For the next ten years the National Women's Health Network campaigned for a worldwide recall of the Dalkon Shield.

In 1975, Robins lost the first of a series of lawsuits brought by women injured by the Shield. Eventually, thousands of women filed claims, but many others chose to settle for whatever the company would give them rather than face humiliation in court. Because pelvic infections could also be sexually transmitted, lawyers for Robins asked the women detailed questions about their sex lives and personal hygiene. Some women were actually asked for the names of every sexual partner they'd ever had, ostensibly so that the lawyers could track the men down to see if they'd had a venereal disease.

The legal cases dragged on into the 1980s, and there had still been no recall. Late in 1984, the Network notified the FDA that there had been three more deaths linked to the Shield between 1981 and 1984. The FDA began an investigation. Meanwhile, an attorney once employed by Robins had testified in court that ten years earlier, on instructions from company officials, he had destroyed documents that proved that top executives knew about potential problems with the Shield. A district court judge publicly reprimanded Robins executives, urging them to stop the "monstrous mischief" and recall the Shield. Robins finally announced a "removal program" for women still wearing the Shield.

In 1985, the company declared bankruptcy. Some women injured by the Dalkon Shield believed this was a ploy to reduce what the company would be ordered to pay them. Almost 200,000 claimants were suing Robins for damages, and several different groups had tried to organize them, including a grassroots feminist organization called the Dalkon Shield Information Network (DSIN), headed by Karen Hicks. The bankruptcy case dragged on in the courts while Robins's top officers dickered with corporations interested in buying the company. In the spring of 1988, the women suing Robins were finally asked to vote on a complex reorganization plan that would establish a trust fund of $2.5 billion to pay their claims. Though DSIN opposed the settlement, most voted to accept it. Hicks felt that Robins had emerged the victor. She noted that company officials voted themselves a healthy year-end bonus afterward, and stockholders made a fourfold profit on their stocks.

During the long legal battle, DSIN received less help from the women's health movement than Hicks would have liked. She concluded that feminist support for her cause had been undercut partly by abortion politics. Women's groups, defending the right to choose, were besieged by religious fundamentalists who opposed most forms of birth control. Anti-abortion leaders often referred to the Dalkon Shield tragedy, implying that other contraceptives were equally unsafe. Feminist leaders were well aware that American research on birth control had practically ground to a halt, partly because drug companies were concerned about possible lawsuits over new products. Under the circumstances, some women's groups undoubtedly wished the Dalkon Shield case would just go away.

In 1991, IUDs were back in the news. One and a half million American women were still wearing them, down from three million in 1982. Their popularity had dropped because of publicity over the Dalkon Shield and because of studies published in the early 1980s. Analyzing data on women who had been hospitalized with pelvic infections, scientists had concluded that wearing an IUD increased a woman's chance of developing an infection and that the Dalkon Shield was substantially riskier than the other devices studied. Now, researchers had reanalyzed the data from that earlier study, criticized its methodology, and announced their own contradictory conclusion: that there was no increased risk from IUDs in general—though they didn't completely exonerate the Dalkon Shield itself. NWHN was skeptical, according to Cindy Pearson, its program director, partly because two of the three researchers involved in the new study had been consultants for Robins in the past. The authors of the original study defended their methods, and other scientists suggested that the data should be re-examined by a third, "disinterested" party. Pearson said, "We believe that all IUDs raise the risk of pelvic infection somewhat and that the Dalkon Shield raised the risk more because of the design of its string."

UNNECESSARY SURGERY

Over the years, American women have been subjected to a great deal of unnecessary surgery, thanks to a fee-for-service medical system that puts money in surgeons' pockets every time they operate, combined with male prejudices about women and the fact that many women hesitate to challenge medical authority. The women's health movement has campaigned not only against unnecessary Cesareans but against the common practice of treating breast cancer with a radical mastectomy, despite evidence that when the cancer is caught early enough, survival rates are the same if the surgeon simply removes the tumor.

Health activists have also tried to reduce the number of hysterectomies. The United States has an exceptionally high hysterectomy rate—by the 1990s, half of all American women could expect to have their uterus removed before they reached age sixty-five. Doctors often present the operation to patients as a threefold solution: a way to cure a gynecological problem such as pelvic pain, while preventing cancer of the uterus and ending the need for birth control. Thus, a Connecticut gynecologist, making the case for the surgery in a medical journal, wrote that once a woman had completed her family, it was better to remove her uterus rather than to tie her tubes, because the uterus was now a "useless, bleeding, symptom-producing, potentially cancer-bearing organ." Yet some women die from hysterectomies; for birth control, tying the tubes is much less risky though it's still not risk-free.

Similarly, doctors have sometimes recommended removing the ovaries (oophorectomy) to prevent cancer. According to Nora W. Coffey, president of the HERS Foundation (Hysterectomy Educational Resources and Services), ovarian cancer is deadly but rare, and afflicts less than one percent of all women. Coffey founded HERS after her own hysterectomy/oophorectomy produced unexpected side effects. Among other things, she suffered from bone and joint pain, was chronically fatigued, and experienced a loss of sexual sensation. She spent two years in medical libraries reading gynecological textbooks and medical-journal articles, and concluded that women advised to have hysterectomies needed somewhere to turn for information.

HERS opened its doors and its telephone hotline in 1982. By 1991, staffers had counseled 62,000 women; they sent out information, including medical-journal articles, and referred women to particularly skillful physicians—those who made a specialty, for example, of removing benign fibroid tumors while leaving the uterus intact. Nora Coffey believes that many women are victims of a conspiracy of silence: they aren't given all the facts. Women have a right to the facts, she says, so that they can make informed decisions.

FETAL RIGHTS

During the 1970s, the controversy over abortion began to change people's attitudes toward pregnant women. Anti-abortion groups succeeded in personifying the fetus for many Americans who had never before thought of it as an unborn baby, and at about the same time doctors proved that they could treat certain conditions even before birth. Some physicians now saw the fetus as their primary patient, and referred to the woman involved as "the maternal environment," as if she were a mere container. There was also a new tendency to treat a woman and her fetus as two beings with potentially conflicting interests. This was fostered partly by anti-abortion rhetoric and partly by the knowledge that if a pregnant woman smoked, took legal or illegal drugs, or drank even moderately, her fetus might be affected.

In the 1980s, as drug addiction reached epidemic proportions and produced a generation of "crack babies," damaged before they were born, in many parts of the country prosecutors became determined to control—or punish—pregnant addicts. Many were creative in adapting old laws to the new situation. Thus, in 1989, a Florida twenty-three-year-old was convicted of "transmitting prohibited drugs to minors." She was a cocaine addict; the minor was her fetus; and transmission supposedly took place in the minute or two between the baby's birth and the clamping of the umbilical cord, because according to state law the fetus only became a child at the moment of birth. The judge who sentenced the woman disregarded the fact that she'd been turned away by a drug treatment program.

The American Civil Liberties Union (ACLU) Reproductive Freedom Project filed the appeal in the case. Among other things, the brief argued that it was unconstitutional for criminal laws to treat pregnant women differently from everyone else. It also pointed out that few drug and alcoholism programs were willing to accept pregnant women, and that threatening women with legal action actually made it less likely that they'd seek help. In addition, attempts to regulate women's behavior during pregnancy were apt to become a legal quagmire. How many drinks did a woman have to consume, for example, to have committed a criminal act? Could the law force her to give up smoking? And what about fathers? Several studies showed that men who had two or more drinks a day had babies that were smaller than average, and animal research indicated that heavy consumption of alcohol could damage sperm and cause birth defects.

By the summer of 1990, more than fifty women had been brought up on criminal charges for using drugs while pregnant. Eighty percent of them were women of color, though studies showed that white women were as likely to use drugs during pregnancy. Some of the women who were charged were jailed, while others lost custody of their children. Most feminists argued that pregnant addicts should be treated, not punished, but some were more ambivalent because they'd seen the suffering of infants born to addicts. They reasoned that even if treatment were widely available, many addicts wouldn't come forward. It was a difficult and urgent problem: Researchers estimated that 15 percent of pregnant women were on drugs.

There were other legal actions based on fetal rights as well. Some cases seemed ridiculous but ominous: One father successfully sued the mother of his child, on behalf of the child, because she took an antibiotic (tetracycline) while pregnant and it affected the baby's teeth—they grew in discolored. More often, the circumstances were tragic. By 1990, several dozen women who were seriously ill had been forced by the courts to have their baby delivered by Cesarean section.

One of the worst cases involved a dying woman compelled to have the surgery to "save" her twenty-six-week fetus, against her wishes and those of her family and her doctors, who were certain the fetus couldn't survive. Mother and baby both died soon after the operation. Her family sued, and an appeals court ultimately ruled that a pregnant woman couldn't be forced to undergo a Cesarean, even if she was dying and the fetus was likely to live. The court pointed out that there was no legal precedent for forcing one person to undergo a medical intrusion for the sake of another. A man couldn't be forced to donate a kidney to a sibling, for example, even to save the sibling's life.

During the late 1980s, some corporations adopted "fetal protection policies" and began excluding women from jobs that would expose them to chemicals such as lead that might cause birth defects in a fetus. Johnson Controls, for example, refused to hire female production workers unless they could prove they'd been sterilized. The company stated that "the issue is protecting the health of unborn children," but it was also concerned about being sued if an employee had a baby with birth defects. The union went to court, arguing that the company policy was sex discrimination and that women had the right to decide for themselves whether to take jobs that posed a risk if they became pregnant. In 1991, the Supreme Court declared that fetal protection policies violated civil rights laws. Some estimated that if the union had lost, 20 million industrial jobs could have been closed to most women.

The fetal-protection issue was both new and old. Johnson Controls' statements about "unborn children" suggested spillover from the abortion controversy. However, feminists pointed out that, historically, whenever men wanted to keep women in their place, the excuse they used was that women produced the next generation. Females were treated as walking wombs, continually on the brink of pregnancy.*

WOMEN OF COLOR ORGANIZE THEIR OWN HEALTH GROUPS

During the 1970s, the women's health movement was almost entirely white and middle class, largely because its priorities were white and middle class. Natural childbirth, self-help groups, and even the battle against dangerous contraceptives didn't speak to the needs of low-income women concerned primarily about simply finding and paying for adequate medical care. During the eighties, women of color began to form their own health organizations. They had the support and encouragement of some of the primarily white groups—particularly of the Our Bodies, Ourselves collective and the National Women's Health Network.

The National Black Women's Health Project, based in Atlanta, Georgia, was the first of the new national organizations for women of color. It was founded in 1981 by Byllye Avery, a remarkable African-American feminist. She was working with black women in a CETA (Comprehensive Employment Training Act) project when she began to wonder why so many of them were in poor health. Medical statistics on African-Americans sketched a dismal picture. They were twice as likely as white women to die from diabetes in middle age, and three times as likely to be killed by cervical cancer. Though they didn't develop breast cancer as often, if they did get it, they were less likely to survive, and if they had high blood pressure, they were more apt to suffer kid-

* The company, unconcerned about male employees, apparently ignored research indicating that male rats exposed to relatively low levels of lead produced offspring with brain defects.

ney damage. In addition, black infants were twice as likely as white babies to die before they were a year old.

In part, these vulnerabilities reflected the quality of the medical care low-income Americans received, but that wasn't the whole story. According to Avery, black women's health problems were also produced by the stress of living with racism, sexism, and classism: "I'm talking about the way racism makes us feel we're less than white people, the way sexism makes us the very sad victims of abuse and violent mistreatment by men, the way economic discrimination leaves us with the worst-paying jobs. . . ."

To tackle the problem, Avery organized a self-help group for women who wanted to share health information and mutual support and take action on local problems. She also presented a paper on black women's health needs at a meeting of the National Women's Health Network. NWHN subsequently helped her put on the First National Conference on Black Women's Health Issues —and launch a new organization, the National Black Women's Health Project. By 1989, NBWHP had nineteen full-time staffers and 2000 members, organized into ninety-six local self-help groups. It had produced a film and videotapes on teenage pregnancy, and schools were using them to encourage teens to discuss the problem. The organization also had a number of ongoing pilot projects: one aimed to educate women about cancer; another, to teach them about the causes of infant mortality; a third focused on the health of homeless women; a fourth had established a wellness center in a housing project. That year, Avery received one of the MacArthur Foundation's twenty-nine "genius" awards in recognition of her work.

NBWHP quickly became a model for other groups. In 1986, Luz Alvarez Martinez had it in mind when she and three other Latinas* cofounded the National Latina Health Organization, headquartered in Oakland, California. Their group, too, held a major conference, and by the late 1980s they were offering classes that provided health information and functioned as support groups as well. Ultimately, Martinez hoped to have local chapters around the country.

Martinez noted that Latinas also had their own health issues. For instance, the language barrier made it difficult for some to get adequate medical treatment at clinics and hospitals that didn't have Spanish-speaking staff. Because Latinas were generally

---

* Some Americans with roots in Spanish-speaking countries find the term Hispanic objectionable because it's a reminder of Spanish imperialism. For others, Hispanic is no problem. Consequently, I've used both terms.

Catholic, abortion was a potentially devastating experience for them, and some made that choice and then never told their husbands or mothers. "They need a place where they can talk about it, so they don't need to carry that all by themselves," said Martinez. She also insisted that a woman should never be in a situation where abortion was her only option—that reproductive rights must include a right to information about sexuality and contraception and access to birth control, regardless of cost.

"Many Latina women who have had abortions complain that they weren't given any family planning information afterward," said Martinez. Some hospitals offered two different films: The one in English described various methods of birth control, while the one in Spanish emphasized sterilization. Martinez noted that "so often doctors think, when we have so many children, that there's something deviant about it. . . . Without asking, they direct us toward the kind of birth control (sterilization) that they feel we can handle. You talk about choice," she added. "What choices do we have?"

Native American women also became health activists during the 1980s. One dynamic group took root in 1985, when Charon Asetoyer organized the Native American Community Board on a South Dakota reservation where health was a continuing crisis. Eighty-five percent of those who lived on the reservation were unemployed; 70 percent of the adults over forty were diabetic; the infant mortality rate was 28.8 percent, five times the national average; and life expectancy on the reservation was just forty-five years of age. In addition, many young people died in alcohol-related accidents or as suicides. Alcoholism had long been a serious problem for Native Americans, yet in 1985 the Indian Health Service (IHS), the government agency responsible for providing medical care on reservations, spent only 3 percent of its budget to treat alcoholism.

For several years, Charon Asetoyer operated from an office in her own home, but her dream was to establish a health center. In January 1988, she made contact with the National Women's Health Network and began receiving support—in the form of health information, mentoring, and other resources—not only from the Network but also from the National Black Women's Health Project and the Latina Women's Health Network. Foundations contributed funds, Asetoyer bought a house, and before the year was out the Native American Women's Health and Education Resource Center had opened, with Charon Asetoyer as executive director. The Center provided the community with information on family planning, child development and nutrition, alcohol-related problems, and AIDS, among other things. Battered women turned to it in crisis situations and attended meetings of battered women's groups; children also came there for tutoring.

As the 1990s began, Asetoyer and her group were intent on preventing the reservation's only hospital from cutting services. The IHS planned to turn the hospital into an outpatients-only clinic in 1991, though it served an area roughly twice the size of Delaware. Already, women in labor were required to go to a hospital off the reservation to have their babies. Some had to travel over 100 miles, which contributed to the reservation's high infant mortality rate.

Asetoyer noted that American hospitals had a strong lobby in Washington, and that federal funds available to the Indian Health Service gave that lobby a financial incentive. In South Dakota, the IHS was paying one off-reservation hospital about $300,000 a year for delivering the babies of Native American women. For that money, Asetoyer pointed out, a hospital on the reservation could afford to bring in a midwife, an obstetrician, and an anesthesiologist, to upgrade the delivery room, and to establish a prenatal program to reduce the number of high-risk pregnancies.

REDEFINING ''REPRODUCTIVE RIGHTS''

In the 1980s, some predominantly white health groups, eager to reach more women, invited feminists of color to serve on their governing boards. However, Luz Alvarez Martinez remarked that women of color wanted more than tokenism; they wanted their issues addressed. As the abortion battle heated up in the late 1980s, some were afraid that it might monopolize the movement's resources.

Most women of color supported the right to choose—one poll reported that 80 percent of them were prochoice, compared to 67 percent of white women. Yet for several reasons, relatively few became prochoice activists. For one thing, talk of "defending the right to choose" alienated those who had no such right. Charon Asetoyer pointed out that the Indian Health Service wouldn't pay for abortions even in cases of rape or incest. Most low-income women had no "right to choose" without Medicaid. An abortion often cost more than a woman's whole monthly welfare check.

Though feminists were committed to restoring Medicaid funding, they made no headway.

Women of color also felt alienated because when some white feminists spoke of "reproductive rights," abortion was all they had in mind. Martinez, Asetoyer, and others insisted that rights must include good, affordable health care, especially prenatal care, information on contraception, protection from sterilization abuse, and more.

For most low-income women, access to decent medical care was *the* primary health issue. While families poor enough to qualify for Medicaid could get (often inadequate) health care, for those only slightly better off, a health crisis was always a financial crisis as well. The United States and South Africa were the only Western industrialized nations with no national health plan. In the late 1980s, more than 35 million Americans had no health insurance, and many more were underinsured. Over one quarter of all women of childbearing age had no coverage for prenatal care. Women's health groups were committed to changing that situation, but Congress was slow to act.

Sterilization Abuse

Over the years, the sterilization issue caused many misunderstandings between white middle class activists and women of color because their experiences with the medical profession were so different. Until the mid-1970s, white middle class women were often turned down arbitrarily when they asked to have their tubes tied to prevent conception. Some hospitals refused to do the surgery unless pregnancy would endanger the woman's life or health; some required the husband's consent. Many applied a formula suggested by ACOG (the American College of Obstetricians and Gynecologists): a woman could be sterilized only if her age, multiplied by the number of children she had, came to more than 120. In effect, she had to have done her reproductive duty. Feminists challenged such practices, and in the 1970s hospitals and physicians began to respond.

While white women were fighting for their right to be sterilized, women of color were being sterilized against their will. In 1973, newspapers headlined a particularly distressing case. An Alabama family planning clinic had sterilized two black girls, twelve and fourteen years old, after their mother gave consent by drawing an X on a form she couldn't read; no one told her what she was actually agreeing to. The Southern Poverty Law Center filed a class-action complaint on behalf of the girls and all other poor persons who had been involuntarily sterilized. As a result, in 1974 HEW was ordered to draw up guidelines to try to prevent such abuses. Among other things, the new rules mandated a seventy-two-hour waiting period between the time a woman signed a consent form and the surgery, and they required that she be told that the operation was permanent. However, the guidelines were poorly enforced and didn't go far enough—for example, a woman who spoke only Spanish could still be presented with a consent form written entirely in English.

When the Alabama case first came to light, fourteen feminist organizations held a joint press conference to demand action by the government. Nevertheless, in 1975, when health activist Helen Rodriguez-Trias spoke on sterilization at a national conference on women's health, she discovered that many middle class feminists still couldn't imagine how anyone could force a woman to be sterilized.

Women of color knew that it happened all the time and that it was a form of racism. Some women signed a sterilization consent form because a doctor urged it on them while they were in labor and were partially drugged. Others agreed because they were told that it would kill them to have another baby, when that wasn't true; or that the surgery was reversible, when it almost never was; or that they'd lose their welfare benefits if they didn't give consent. There was also coercion of a subtler sort in the fact that Medicaid paid for sterilization but not for contraceptives or abortion. Under those conditions, many women who couldn't afford another pregnancy in the near future opted for sterilization even though they were far from certain that they'd never want another child.

Charon Asetoyer noted that proof of coercion was hard to come by because there was no record of what doctors told patients to persuade them to have surgery; there was only the woman's word for it. However, statistics reflected the racist biases involved. By the 1980s, 16 percent of white women had undergone sterilization; 24 percent of black women; 25 percent of Chicanas; and perhaps one third of Native American women. Puerto Rico had the highest rate of female sterilization in the world: 35 percent.

By the late 1970s, health activists were hard at work on the problem of sterilization abuse. In 1977, radical and socialist feminists in New York City founded the Committee for Abortion

Rights and Against Sterilization Abuse (CARASA), formally linking the two issues. In 1978, CARASA, the National Women's
Health Network, and other groups persuaded New York City
to issue sterilization guidelines stronger than those issued by
HEW in 1974. Afterward, they pressured HEW until it revised its
guidelines, using New York City's as a model. Despite feminist
efforts, however, women of color had no doubt that the abuse
continued.

Activists acquired a new worry late in 1990 when the FDA
approved Norplant, a new birth control device that offered a way
to control the fertility of poor women for long periods without
actually sterilizing them. Surgically implanted under the skin,
Norplant contained hormones that were released gradually and
could prevent conception for a full five years. It wasn't safe for
every woman, nor was it free of side effects, but it was barely on
the market when the Kansas legislature began considering a
scheme to pay welfare recipients $500 if they'd use it. Then a
California judge told a woman who had been convicted of abusing her child that if she wanted probation, she must agree to have
the device implanted. Obviously, drug addicts and retarded
women were likely candidates for similar treatment. The right to
privacy promised by the *Roe* v. *Wade* decision implied that a
woman had a right to choose whether or not to use birth control,
but by 1990 the *Roe* decision itself was on shaky ground.

Questioning the New Reproductive Technology

Back in 1970, radical feminist Shulamith Firestone noted that
someday medical technology might free women from their biological destiny. Pregnancy, she said, was barbaric; it deformed a
woman's body for the sake of the species. Conception in a test
tube, gestation in an artificial womb, might be preferable. Over
the next twenty years, Firestone's fantasy began to come true:
Doctors learned how to achieve conception in a laboratory dish,
transfer embryos from womb to womb, freeze them for future
use. And feminists challenged the new technology, in 1984
founding an international network to monitor it.

However, the women's movement was far from united in its
response. In fact, the feminist divide surfaced once again. Equality feminists argued that a woman had a right to try test-tube
fertilization or surrogate motherhood if she wanted to; the choice
should be hers. Difference feminists, convinced that women
needed special treatment (in this case, protection), insisted that

some of the new technologies should be banned or at least recognized for what they were—men's latest attempts to control female fertility and make use of women's bodies. They were primarily concerned about four new developments: prenatal testing, *in vitro* fertilization, embryo transfer, and surrogate motherhood.

Prenatal testing made it possible to identify congenital defects before birth, so that a woman could choose whether or not to carry a pregnancy to term. In amniocentesis, the test most often used, the physician inserted a long needle through the pregnant woman's abdomen into her uterus and drew out amniotic fluid, which was then analyzed for signs of problems such as Down's syndrome or sickle cell anemia. The baby's sex could be determined as well.

Amniocentesis was an important medical advance, but feminists were concerned about it for several reasons. First, some doctors overextended the technology. Although it was originally intended primarily for use with older women, because their babies were more at risk, by 1990 it was being urged on thirty-two- and thirty-three-year-olds, though it was costly and there was some risk of miscarriage. In addition, some feminists feared that prenatal testing might encourage people to feel that all babies should be perfect; women might be pressured into aborting fetuses with relatively minor problems. Disabled women pointed out that life wasn't necessarily a tragedy for an individual born with Down's syndrome, for example, or cerebral palsy. The determination to produce only perfect babies, like the old eugenics, was dangerous.

Feminists were also concerned because prenatal testing was already being used in other countries by couples who wanted to choose the sex of their baby—and the sex they chose was almost always male. In India, where amniocentesis was relatively inexpensive, thousands of abortions were done during the 1980s so that couples could have sons. One study found that of 8000 fetuses aborted after prenatal testing, 7999 were female. Female abortion was also practiced in other Asian countries. Many feminists worried because women's numbers and their willingness to organize were about the only advantages they had in male-dominated societies.

Health activists also raised questions about *in vitro fertilization* (IVF), a high-tech therapy for infertility. A woman undergoing IVF was first given hormones in massive doses so that a number of ova would mature. Then a surgeon retrieved the eggs by inserting an instrument either through her vagina or through an incision in her abdomen. The eggs were mixed with sperm in a laboratory dish, and if embryos resulted, several were transferred to the woman's womb, while the spares were frozen for possible future use.* IVF was expensive, painful, and had little chance of success. Nevertheless, during the 1980s many couples eagerly tried it. Though it was first used only for women with blocked oviducts, soon those who were infertile for no obvious reason were also being treated, sometimes before it was certain that the couple wouldn't conceive without help.

As IVF caught on in the 1980s, the American media reported that infertility had reached epidemic proportions and blamed it on career women who waited too long to have babies. In fact, the infertility rate hadn't changed, though the number of people using infertility services had tripled as more couples sought help. Furthermore, though it was true that older women didn't conceive as easily, infertility was more often caused by other factors, such as sexually transmitted diseases. The media's focus on the older women's infertility "epidemic" seemed to reflect lingering hostility to career women.

Feminists who opposed IVF pointed out that it was risky and expensive, and it was being oversold—it actually worked for only about 10 percent of those who tried it. One of the most successful U.S. clinics provided these figures: Of every 100 women treated, 93 responded when "superovulated" with hormones; 84 had eggs retrieved; in about 70 cases, one or more ova were successfully fertilized and transferred to the uterus; 14 women became pregnant; 4 miscarried; and 10 actually had a baby. The drugs used all had side effects, ectopic pregnancies were a substantial risk, and the Cesarean rate was about 50 percent.

IVF technology took another long step forward in the 1980s (and created another issue for feminists) when scientists learned how to do *embryo transfers*: to flush an embryo out of the uterus of one woman and implant it in another. By 1987, transfers had begun to produce live babies. Thus, it was now possible for a woman who didn't ovulate to give birth to a child, even if it wasn't genetically hers. Embryo flushing had other possibilities as well. One researcher suggested to health activist Gena Corea that someday it might be done routinely during pregnancy to make sure the embryo had no genetic flaws. Another scientist offered this scenario: In the future, young women would come to

---

* Physicians liked to transfer several embryos because that made it more likely that one would "take." Of course, it also resulted in multiple births at times.

a clinic to have a few embryos flushed out and frozen. The women would then be sterilized for birth control. Afterward, whenever they wanted a child, they could simply have an embryo defrosted.

Activists noted that the whole high-tech approach to conception encouraged people to think of a woman as a means to an end and a baby as a product, with quality control a possibility. Already, there were couples who came for infertility treatment who asked if fertilization could be done with donor sperm or eggs rather than their own. Though presumably they'd come to the clinic instead of trying to adopt because they wanted a child of their own, they were unhappy with some aspect of themselves and willing to consider using someone else's genes to produce the perfect baby. Some health activists wanted *in vitro* fertilization banned. Feminist sociologist Barbara Katz Rothman simply felt that Americans should be warned that, so far, it embodied the worst in medical care: It was available only to the wealthy and it seldom worked.

Surrogate motherhood was another development hotly protested by difference feminists. A mother was a "surrogate" if she was paid to have a baby for someone else. Usually, a broker made the arrangements for a married couple, and the surrogate was artificially inseminated with the husband's sperm.

Artificial insemination (AI) itself wasn't new. It was a simple technique: A man ejaculated into a container, and the semen was drawn up into a syringe and injected into a woman's vagina. Since 1954, it had been possible to freeze and store sperm, and men who had vasectomies for birth control often had this done, so that if they changed their minds, they could still father a child. When a woman's husband was the source of the sperm, the method was known as AIH (artificial insemination by husband); when the donor was an anonymous male, it was known as AID (AI by donor sperm). AID obviously had possibilities for women who wanted a child but didn't have—and perhaps didn't want to have—a husband. Beginning in the mid-1970s, lesbians and single heterosexual women in their thirties began using AID, sometimes with the help of a feminist health center.

AI raised no troubling questions for feminists until it was used to impregnate surrogate mothers. The controversy within the women's movement was ignited in 1987 by the Baby M case. Mary Beth Whitehead, a young married woman already the mother of two children, agreed to have a child for William and Elizabeth Stern. After the baby was born, Whitehead couldn't bear to give her up. She succeeded in keeping the infant for over a month, but then the Sterns persuaded a judge that Whitehead was unstable. Police raided her house in an unsuccessful attempt to seize the baby, and the Whiteheads fled to Florida and went into hiding. Eventually, detectives located them and brought the baby to the Sterns.

The Baby M trial took place in New Jersey in the winter of 1987. At the end of it, Judge Harvey R. Sorkow gave William Stern custody, citing the surrogacy contract Whitehead had signed. Calling her "manipulative, impulsive and exploitive," he stripped her even of visitation rights. In response to defense arguments that surrogacy was baby-selling, Sorkow stated that "at birth, the father does not purchase the child. It is his own biological genetically related child. He cannot purchase what is already his."

Whitehead appealed, and a year later the New Jersey Supreme Court ruled that commercial surrogacy contracts couldn't be enforced in a court of law, and that the state's adoption statute applied to such cases; it allowed a woman a grace period after a baby's birth in which to change her mind about giving the child away. The decision was a blow to surrogacy, at least in New Jersey, but it didn't return the baby to Whitehead. Though the court rebuked Judge Sorkow for judging her "rather harshly," it approved his decision to give the child to the Sterns, because Whitehead's family life was "anything but secure." By that time, she had become pregnant by a man other than her husband, and had divorced her husband and married the father of the child she would bear the following spring.

The Baby M case divided feminists, and once again the issue was equality versus difference. Women speaking from the equality side of the divide insisted that a surrogate had a right to make decisions about her own body, and that a ban on surrogacy contracts would imply that she wasn't competent to decide. They argued that she knowingly accepted some risks when she signed the contract, and must live with them. According to equality feminists, those who wanted to protect surrogates were reinforcing the notion that females were too emotional and irrational to be trusted, especially while pregnant, and also the idea that they were born victims.

Difference feminists responded that women often *were* victims. Medical ethicist Janice Raymond said, "We all know women collude in our own oppression." She argued that that wasn't the same as free choice. Activists pointed out that society programmed women to feel that if they couldn't have children they'd failed, and that motherhood was their highest calling. Thus, infertile women would do almost anything to have a baby. As for surrogates, Mary Beth Whitehead, who already had two children, turned to surrogacy because once the children were in school all day, her life seemed empty. She felt that mothering was the one thing she was good at, and she couldn't have another baby because her husband had had a vasectomy. She thought she could give an infertile couple the ultimate gift, but she was unprepared for her own fierce love for the child.

Difference feminists maintained that surrogate mothers weren't exercising their right to do as they liked with their bodies—they were signing away that right. According to Sybil Shainwald, Whitehead's contract required her to have amniocentesis done, so that the Sterns could opt out if the fetus had congenital defects. Most surrogacy contracts also stipulated that a woman must not smoke or drink, or take any drugs, including aspirin, without a doctor's written permission. If the woman had a miscarriage before the fifth month of pregnancy, she typically received nothing; if she miscarried after that, she was entitled to just $1000; if the baby was deformed or retarded, the couple could back out and keep most of their money. (Some equality feminists agreed that surrogates shouldn't sign away control over their pregnancy.) Author Phyllis Chesler also pointed out that in business it was common to renegotiate contracts or buy them out, and that Whitehead never accepted the $10,000 payment that was due her.

Exploitation was a final, major concern. Some feminists were afraid the day might come when middle class women, intent on their careers, would hire poor women to bear babies for them just because that was more convenient. If embryo transfers became more common, women of color would be especially vulnerable, because many were low-income. White parents who wanted a child to pass off as their own would no longer be limited to white surrogates—almost any female would do. Ethicists pointed out the irony of a situation in which well-to-do white couples were already ignoring thousands of babies of other races, older children, and children with disabilities, who were available for adoption, to spend enormous sums on surrogacy and *in vitro* procedures.

In the wake of the Baby M trial, laws on surrogacy were proposed in twenty-seven states. Some legislators wanted to legalize commercial surrogacy but require court approval for every contract; others were determined to limit clients to married, heterosexual couples who could prove the wife was infertile. In the end, most states took no action because there was no consensus about what they should do, and the surrogacy business continued to thrive, unaffected by the Baby M decision. In 1990, experts estimated that in the United States over the past three years, there had been almost 2000 "traditional surrogate" births (like Baby M, based on artificial insemination) and about 80 "gestational surrogate" births, where the surrogate provided a womb for an embryo that wasn't genetically hers.

Over the years, it often seemed as if health activists had barely solved one problem when another flared up—for example, by the 1990s new groups had formed to protest the way medical researchers ignored women who had AIDS. Despite continuing problems, however, there was no doubt that the health movement had accomplished a great deal.

Aside from the specific victories described in this chapter, there had been major changes in the way medicine was practiced. For one thing, there were now many specialized nurses who provided well-woman care—an indirect response, Cindy Pearson suggested, to women's angry demands for better treatment. Perhaps more important, physicians were less autocratic—less likely to duck explanations and simply tell a patient what to do. Many doctors, especially the younger ones, now assumed that it was their role to help patients make their own medical decisions. That was always a primary goal of the women's health movement.

Of course, there were still many high-handed, paternalistic doctors. Nevertheless, the overall change in attitude could be found at every level, from the kind of information provided before major surgery to the way routine pelvic exams were performed. Today a woman having a pelvic was much more likely to be told, step by step, what the doctor was doing as the exam progressed, and there was even a good chance she'd be offered the opportunity to see her cervix.

Obviously, medical schools were teaching their students rather differently. In fact, in one of the most surprising developments, students in many med schools now performed their first pelvic exams not on a woman who had been anesthetized to avoid embarrassment (common practice in the sixties) but on health activists from a group under contract to the school. With no doctors in the room, these women taught the students the difference—from the patient's point of view—between a good pelvic exam and a bad one.

In the early 1990s, in most ways the women's health movement is more vigorous and more diverse than ever. Five hundred feminist groups and health organizations belong to the National Women's Health Network, which has thousands of individual members as well. As it has done from the beginning, the movement serves as a kind of anchor for the larger feminist community, a reminder of basic body issues. Often more uncomfortable to deal with than legal or economic rights, body issues are seen to be at the root of the age-old prejudices against women.

chapter 13

Lesbian Feminism

———

When the gay rights movement caught fire in 1969, many lesbians already belonged to NOW chapters or women's liberation groups. Most had kept their sexual preference secret. Now, as gay pride blossomed, they came out within the women's movement and began to raise their own issues. During the period that followed, there were fierce conflicts in many groups between gay and straight women as heterosexual feminists insisted that lesbian issues had nothing to do with feminism.

Up to a point, the conflicts resembled arguments that cropped up some years later when feminists were accused of ignoring the issues that were priorities for women of color. Obviously, feminists weren't immune to the biases that warped the thinking of most Americans. In addition, during the 1970s, many feminists, the majority of whom were "straight" and white, wanted to define "women's issues" quite narrowly, both for practical reasons (activists were already spread thin) and because gay rights were so controversial that they were afraid if feminism became associated with them, the movement would suffer. Some believed that feminists should take one thing at a time—should pass the ERA, for example, and secure other legal rights before broadening their agenda to include more controversial demands.

Thus, many activists tried to push problems like homophobia under the rug. For a long time, they failed to see the parallels between sexism and heterosexism.* Ironically, the right wing connected women's rights and gay rights almost from the beginning. To conservatives, both movements were threats to morality and the traditional family. The danger from the right finally convinced most gay and straight feminists that they must work together.

THE ROOTS OF THE GAY RIGHTS MOVEMENT

During the 1950s and 1960s, lesbians were "isolated and separated—and scared," according to Del Martin and Phyllis Lyon, who co-authored the book *Lesbian/Woman*. In the fifties, Senator Joseph McCarthy launched investigations of the U.S. State Department that led to the firing of hundreds of women and men for homosexuality, sometimes based merely on suspicion. President Eisenhower decreed that the federal government couldn't hire gays and they were purged from the military. Gay bars were frequently raided by the police, and sometimes local newspapers published the names of those rounded up during a raid. The possibility of exposure was a constant worry for lesbians, because if they were discovered, they were apt to be fired from their jobs, and those who were divorced could lose custody of their children.

In 1955, a handful of San Francisco women founded the Daughters of Bilitis† (DOB) as a kind of social club for lesbians, a place to go where they didn't have to pretend to be heterosexual. During the first year, there was a split within the group, and those who felt that secrecy must be preserved at all costs resigned. Afterward, DOB tackled the task of trying to educate Americans out of their homophobia. The organization began to hold once-a-month meetings that were open to the public and that featured discussions of lesbianism. Soon there were chapters in other cities as well. Del Martin was DOB's first president, and Phyllis Lyon, the first editor of its newsletter.

When the second wave of the women's movement emerged in

---

* Heterosexism is the conscious or unconscious assumption that only heterosexuality is "normal."

† Bilitis was immortalized in *Songs of Bilitis*, by the lesbian poet Sappho.

the midsixties, it attracted a number of lesbians, including some DOB members. The women were particularly drawn to NOW because of its emphasis on employment issues. For most lesbians, a job was a necessity—they never expected to be supported by a husband. Some became officers of NOW, and a few were quite open about their lifestyle. In 1968, Del Martin and Phyllis Lyon of DOB joined NOW as a lesbian couple at the reduced rate permitted for couples; they had been living together at that point for about fifteen years. Afterward, Martin was elected secretary of San Francisco NOW. She made no secret of her relationship with Lyon, and there were no repercussions. However, most lesbian NOW members were still in the closet.

For gay men and lesbians all over the country, the whole atmosphere changed dramatically in 1969. New gay and lesbian groups had been springing up all' over the country, and unlike the older, more cautious organizations, they sometimes mounted demonstrations in the streets. Then, on June 28, New York City police raided the Stonewall Inn, a gay bar in Greenwich Village, and gays fought back. Harassed inside the bar, pushed out onto the sidewalk, they began to throw things at the police. Soon, they were setting up barricades in the streets. The rioting continued sporadically for three days.

In the aftermath, a militant new movement was born. Many gay people had concluded that American attitudes would never change as long as they stayed in the closet; that they had to identify themselves as gay and fight for their civil rights as blacks and feminists were doing. It was partly a matter of self-respect, for with secrecy came shame. One lesbian wrote that ". . . the worst part of being a homosexual is having to keep it *secret*. . . . the daily knowledge that what you are is so awful that it cannot be revealed."

The gay rights movement paralleled the women's movement in some ways. It had both a liberal civil rights branch and left-leaning gay liberation groups that were more militant. By the late 1970s, most of the gay liberation groups had disappeared; they were survived by liberal gay rights organizations focused primarily on legislation and by groups and networks organized within professions, religious denominations, and so on.

NEW YORK NOW: THE FIRST LESBIAN PURGE

In the women's movement, the gay-straight conflict seems to have surfaced first in the New York chapter of NOW. In the late 1960s, lesbians who belonged to the chapter were beginning to find their situation intolerable. Though NOW was not yet organizing consciousness-raising groups, many members—reacting to what they'd heard and read about C-R—had begun to discuss their personal lives at meetings, sharing intimate details about husbands and male lovers. It was a time and a place in which all "normal" people were expected to *have* a heterosexual love life, and under the circumstances some lesbians reluctantly invented one. Others rebelled. "It was bad enough to have to hide from colleagues in the office, but to hide from other women in the movement was too much," Sidney Abbott and Barbara Love wrote in a 1972 book that chronicled NOW's gay-straight tribulations.

Gradually, some lesbians in New York NOW began to come out. According to Jean Faust, the first president of the chapter, "Suddenly people started announcing themselves as lesbians while they were sitting around in someone's house, waiting for a committee meeting to begin. . . . Our first reaction was: What's that got to do with anything?" Rita Mae Brown was one of the first to raise the lesbian issue. In 1969, at a rap session for new members, she asked why the women spent all their time talking about men, and why they avoided talking about lesbianism. According to Brown, feminists in the room responded first with outrage, then with curiosity. There were other lesbians present, but none of them spoke up, and Brown was angrier at them than at the straight women.

Soon Brown became the chapter's "token lesbian," as she put it, and the editor of its newsletter. Articulate, always outspoken, and sometimes very funny, she managed to antagonize quite a few members. "Now I can laugh," said Dolores Alexander years later, "but at the time Rita Mae was something of a troublemaker, all in the name of her idealism, of course." Alexander, who was active in the New York chapter, became NOW's first national Executive Director in 1969.

For many NOW members, lesbianism was a sensitive subject because they had had to defend themselves against accusations that all feminists were gay. As the few out-of-the-closet lesbians in New York began to press the organization to take a position on lesbian rights, the word got around that Betty Friedan herself considered the lesbian issue a "lavender herring"—and lesbians, a "lavender menace."

Friedan was afraid for the women's movement. She was just beginning to realize, as she wrote later, that "some of the best, most hard-working women in NOW were in fact lesbian." She worried that if the enemies of the movement succeeded in equating feminism with lesbianism, they'd discredit the drive for women's rights. Born and raised in the Midwest, Friedan was convinced that the fact that she came from Peoria, Illinois, was "part of whatever political wisdom I may have. . . . For me . . . for most women, surely, . . . the equality we now demand, [has] nothing whatsoever to do with lesbianism."

Some lesbians who were members of NOW agreed with Friedan that the movement was too new and vulnerable to take a position on gay rights. "They felt that the most important issue was employment," according to Noreen Connell, later president of New York State NOW. They also felt that though they were lesbian, that wasn't the most significant thing in their lives.

As the decade spun to a close, the conflict within NOW escalated. Late in 1969, Friedan spoke out strongly about the dangers of the lesbian issue during a meeting of the National Executive Board. She also spoke against Executive Director Dolores Alexander, "in such a way that the two issues were linked in the minds of those present," according to Abbott and Love. Rumors began to fly to the effect that Alexander was a lesbian.

In January 1970, Rita Mae Brown and two confederates put out the NOW-New York newsletter for the last time and featured in it their own angry letter of resignation, in which they observed that "lesbianism is the one word which gives the New York N.O.W. Executive Committee a collective heart attack." Later that year from San Francisco, Del Martin wrote both to Friedan and to Kay Clarenbach, who chaired the National Board of Directors, asking that NOW take a stand on the lesbian issue. Martin got no reply from Friedan and a negative one from Clarenbach.

At the next Board meeting, Ivy Bottini, president of NOW-New York, proposed an amendment to the organization's Bill of Rights that would have guaranteed "sexual privacy." She was forced to withdraw it because the Board didn't want to go on record either for or against such a proposal. At the same meeting, Dolores Alexander was fired. Recalling the incident many years later, Alexander said, "I got fired primarily for crossing Betty. I was also accused of being a lesbian, although I wasn't." Among lesbians, the whole sequence of events, including Brown's resignation and the ouster of Alexander, came to be known as NOW's first lesbian "purge"; there was to be a second one.

THE LAVENDER MENACE

NOW was not the only organization to struggle with the gay-straight split. After Rita Mae Brown resigned from NOW, she joined Redstockings. "I became the token lesbian once more," she wrote. Again, she left "with recriminations and blow-ups." Turning to the Gay Liberation Front, she introduced lesbian members to consciousness-raising, but she soon found that gay men were as chauvinistic and as uninterested in women's issues as straight males were. Ultimately, Brown said, the GLF lesbian caucus decided that "we are no longer willing to be token lesbians in the women's liberation movement nor are we willing to be the token women in the Gay Liberation Front." The group set to work to draft a position paper on how lesbianism related to the women's movement. Before long, they hit on the perfect place to present it and force the issue: a conference billed as the Congress to Unite Women, to be held in New York City on May 1 to 3, 1970.

Four hundred feminists from all over the East Coast turned up for the Congress. On the first evening, while all were assembled in the auditorium, the lights suddenly went out. When they came on again, twenty women were lined up at the front of the room, facing the audience. They all wore T-shirts inscribed with the words "Lavender Menace," and they demanded the microphone. When someone passed it down from the stage, one woman began to read their position paper, which was entitled "The Woman-Identified Woman."

It was one of those rare, pivotal moments in the history of the movement: Afterward, many things would never be quite the same again, for the ideas presented in the paper gripped the imagination of many feminists. Determined to play a role in the movement, heartily sick of the emphasis on their "deviant" sexuality, the Lavender Menace group chose to present lesbianism as a political, rather than a sexual, choice. Their paper began:

> What is a lesbian? A lesbian is the rage of all women condensed to the point of explosion. She is the woman who, often beginning at an extremely early age, acts in accordance with her inner compulsion to

be a more complete and freer human being than her society . . . cares to allow her. . . . She is forced to evolve her own life pattern, often living much of her life alone, learning usually much earlier than her "straight" (heterosexual) sisters about the essential aloneness of life (which the myth of marriage obscures). . . . As long as the label "dyke" can be used to frighten a woman into a less militant stand . . . to that extent she is controlled by the male culture. Until women see in each other the possibility of a primal commitment which includes sexual love, they will be denying themselves the love and value they readily accord to men, thus affirming their second-class status.

The Menaces ended by asking for a show of support from lesbians and straight women. According to Abbott and Love, "Most Lesbians in the audience were really torn. Some came slowly forward. Others never budged." In the end, thirty women joined the group at the front of the auditorium.

The next day, when the lesbian contingent offered workshops, they were jammed, though they weren't on the conference agenda. At the closing session, the lesbians presented the following resolutions, which had been drawn up by their workshops:

1. Be it resolved that Women's Liberation is a Lesbian plot.
2. Resolved that whenever the label "Lesbian" is used against the movement collectively, or against women individually, it is to be affirmed, not denied.
3. In all discussions on birth control, homosexuality must be included as a legitimate method of contraception.
4. All sex education curricula must include Lesbianism as a valid, legitimate form of sexual expression and love.

Most of the lesbians who had come to the Congress had never said anything in their own feminist groups about their sexual preference, and Abbott and Love note that "nothing in their lives had prepared them for a group of radical gay women openly, warmly, and with humor affirming their Lesbianism. . . ." Some were embarrassed or frightened. They believed that their secret was safe as long as straight women were fooled by the stereotype and assumed that all lesbians were mannish, truck-driver types. If too many lesbians emerged from the closet, that stereotype would be in danger.

The straight, liberal feminists who attended the meeting varied in their reactions. A New Jersey NOW member reported in her chapter's newsletter that she had felt out of place.

I . . . went to a discussion on lesbianism. I attended to find out about this alternative life-style. However, I was told that by living with a man, I was fraternizing with the enemy. . . . I'm in Women's Lib to be liberated, and I don't want to be forced into another set of stereotypes prescribed by my revolutionary sisters.

However, some straight women not only acknowledged that lesbians had raised a legitimate issue when they accused the movement of discriminating against them, but were intrigued by the notion of a brand-new, radical, political stance. On the first night, when the Lavender Menaces asked for a show of support, one young heterosexual woman was among the thirty women who filed to the front of the room. Afterward, she asked a lesbian friend why she didn't come forward, too. The friend said it would be too dangerous. "That made me want to be a Lesbian even more," the young woman said. Later, she was denounced as a false lesbian by a member of the Gay Academic Union; she answered indignantly that "sleeping with men doesn't make me not a Lesbian."

In the months that followed, the Lavender Menaces attracted a host of new members. The Menaces changed their name to Radicalesbians and began to spin off C-R groups. Meanwhile, many feminist groups were dealing with new tensions because with the stereotype stripped away, everybody was wondering which women were lesbians. This was frightening both to those who were still in the closet and to straight women, who wanted to talk about their own uneasiness but couldn't distinguish those who might share it from those who would be offended to hear about it. A few heterosexual women complained that they'd been propositioned by lesbians. Some lesbians wondered why they were so outraged—why they couldn't just say no, as they did with men. Other out-of-the-closet lesbians were furious because straight women treated them as if they were men and flirted with them.

The gay-straight conflict surfaced in many groups. Noreen Connell, who belonged at various times both to women's liberation groups and to NOW, noted that the issue seemed to pop up naturally, as if at a certain stage in the evolution of a group— often in its third or fourth year—somehow the lesbian issue had to be dealt with. On the West Coast, where the sexual atmosphere was more relaxed, there was much less animosity. That was true in the conservative South and Midwest, too, because lesbians there were more hesitant about pushing their demands.

After May 1970, in some cities including New York, gay and

straight feminists began the effort to reach an understanding. Movement newsletters and anthologies started to carry articles on lesbianism written by lesbians. In New York, Chicago, Los Angeles, and San Francisco, NOW and DOB chapters exchanged speakers. Trust came hard. Many straight women felt they were being pressured to become lesbian or at least to stop consorting with the enemy (men). According to a hardening lesbian political line, bisexuality was a copout, and celibacy just wasn't realistic.

EARLY EFFORTS TO END THE GAY-STRAIGHT SPLIT

For most of 1970, the gay-straight issue simmered beneath the surface in women's groups. Late in the year, the conflict became public knowledge when Kate Millett was pilloried by *Time* magazine. The attack temporarily united much of the women's movement.

On November 12, Millett was on a panel at Columbia University that included both gay rights and women's liberation activists. A stringer from *Time* magazine was in the audience to cover the meeting. In her remarks, Millett listed her pertinent credentials almost as if she were making a joke: She was a founding member of Columbia Women's Liberation and a bisexual. After she'd spoken, she was challenged from the floor by a gay activist, demanding that she say whether she was lesbian. Millett recalled,

> Five hundred people looking at me. . . . Everything pauses, faces look up in terrible silence. . . . I know what she means. The line goes, inflexible as a fascist edict, that bisexuality is a cop-out. Yes I said yes I am a Lesbian. It was the last strength I had.

Later, a *Time* reporter came to Millett's home to ask whether she'd really said that. "The *Time* people feel a wonderful solicitude that my statement 'will hurt the women's movement,' " she noted. "I cannot, must not hurt the movement. But the movement cannot sell out on gays, cringe before the dyke-baiting, shuffle into respectability."

In its next issue, *Time* attacked Millett in a short feature that began by quoting at length from a particularly vitriolic review of her book. (In August, *Time* itself had called the book "remarkable" and had admired its "articulate rage.") After mentioning that several intellectuals had recently criticized Millett and the women's movement, the story continued, "Ironically, Kate Millett herself contributed to the growing skepticism about the movement by acknowledging at a recent meeting that she is bisexual. The disclosure is bound to discredit her as a spokeswoman for her cause, cast further doubt on her theories, and reinforce the views of those skeptics who routinely dismiss all liberationists as lesbians."

Both gay and straight feminists were outraged and they got together to hold a press conference. Gloria Steinem, Flo Kennedy, Ti-Grace Atkinson, and Susan Brownmiller were among the well-known women who were present. Bella Abzug, recently elected to Congress from New York, sent a statement supporting the group's action, and so did Wilma Scott Heide, who chaired NOW's national Board, and NOW president Aileen Hernandez. The news coverage, for once, was fair, and at least in New York City, lesbian-baiting virtually ended.

In retrospect, Noreen Connell was convinced that at that point the women's movement had to meet the gay-straight issue head-on. She recalled that at the height of the NOW controversy over lesbianism, she herself was the union shop steward for a day-care center. During a planning meeting for a pro-day-care rally, Connell suggested inviting Betty Friedan to speak: "Everybody piped up—and these were some of the leading lights of the day-care movement in New York City—'Oh no, we can't have Betty Friedan. She's a lesbian.' " Obviously, feminists were going to be called lesbians no matter what they said or did.

Nevertheless, the gay-straight conflict continued to divide both New York NOW and the organization's national board. In fact, the New York chapter effectively purged both lesbians and their straight supporters in January 1971, by voting them out of office. (That was the chapter's second lesbian purge.)

However, later that year at NOW's annual convention, the whole membership tackled the controversy head-on and surprised almost everyone by voting overwhelmingly in favor of a strong pro-lesbian resolution. It admitted that NOW had been "evasive and apologetic" about the lesbians in its midst and stated firmly that the oppression of lesbians was indeed a legitimate concern for all feminists.

POLITICAL LESBIANS

Over the next few years, the gay-straight conflict continued, coming to a head in various groups at different times. At the center of it were the women who insisted that lesbianism was not just a sexual choice but was, in fact, primarily a political choice—the line originally taken by the Lavender Menace group. They argued that if everyone felt free to love anyone of either sex, male supremacy couldn't last; they urged true feminists to seek love and affection from other women, and they also held up lesbians as model feminists.

"The lesbian . . . is freed of dependence on men for love, sex, and money," Martha Shelley wrote. "She does not have to do menial chores for them (at least at home), nor cater to their egos, nor submit to hasty and inept sexual encounters. She is freed from fear of unwanted pregnancy and the pains of childbirth, and from the drudgery of child raising."

Some feminists, convinced by such arguments, became gay as a political choice. Because they were "instant Lesbians," as Martin and Lyon put it, theirs was a very different experience from the process of slow recognition that had previously brought almost all lesbians to the same point. For some radical women, the very danger and forbiddenness of lesbianism were part of its appeal: Here was the ultimate chance to burn their bridges and demonstrate the commitment they'd made to feminism. To others, emerging from shattered marriages, an all-woman environment seemed to promise a refuge where they could find intimate relationships that were truly equal. The lesbian-feminist community was often presented as a kind of utopia in which women's values prevailed.

Many lesbians of the older generation were critical of political lesbians. "I was repelled by them . . ." wrote one woman. "They hadn't suffered like me. . . . They didn't live a lie, with the fear and self-loathing I had. Their lesbianism must be a gimmick."

As for straight women, some became defensive about their own sexual preference. Diane Balser of Boston's Bread and Roses noted that for a time, a married woman didn't dare say to her women's group, "I like my husband." She continued, "I think a lot of heterosexual women got nervous that they wouldn't be able to work out their relationship with men. Some of my closest single women friends left Boston because they felt in the Boston women's movement there were such strong pressures against men."

The pressure to become lesbian gradually receded. However, in the meanwhile, some groups had split into gay and straight factions, while others had been decimated as members dropped out to return to leftist politics, to have a nervous breakdown, or to join a collective and become lesbian separatists.

LESBIAN SEPARATISM

Beginning in 1971 in several cities, lesbians who were refugees from the women's movement connected with others who had abandoned the gay rights movement because of its male chauvinism. They founded new groups and identified themselves as lesbian separatists. The most famous of these groups, The Furies, was formed in Washington, D.C., by twelve women, including Rita Mae Brown and Charlotte Bunch, who ultimately became one of the major feminist theorists. The Furies set about developing a lesbian-feminist political analysis. As Bunch said, ". . . I belonged to a minority that was loathed. . . . I had to know why the simple act of loving other women sexually . . . was so taboo and threatening to others."

The Furies began by analyzing heterosexism. They defined it as a form of domination based on the assumption that heterosexual sex was the only "natural" kind. Equally important, heterosexism assumed that every woman was either bound to a man or wished she were. Women were seen as wives and mothers first, and The Furies pointed out that all the institutions that oppressed women were based on the assumption that women would always put men first. (The institutions they had in mind were the family, the workplace, the educational system, the media, and various religions.)

Charlotte Bunch argued that heterosexism was "a cornerstone of male supremacy." She noted that women who did bond with a man were rewarded with heterosexual privileges that included economic security and social acceptance. That gave them a stake in behaving as the male-dominated society said they should behave—a stake in maintaining the status quo. Bunch suggested that straight women who didn't understand what heterosexual privilege was should "try being a queer for a week."

Some years later, Adrienne Rich took these ideas farther. She suggested that because of the strong connection between mothers and infants, a female's first and most fundamental attachment was to other women. She asked: Why, then, would women turn to men? What societal forces could "wrench women's emotional and erotic energies" away from other women? Rich believed the wrenching was done by "compulsory heterosexuality," sexual choice compelled by methods that ranged from rape to visions of romantic love. Rich also conceived of lesbianism as a continuum that stretched from sexual relations at one end to intense nonsexual experiences such as "bonding against male tyranny" at the other.

Lesbian theory laid the groundwork for a lesbian counterculture that developed during the 1970s, as gay women began to affirm their pride in themselves as lesbians and as women. They poured their energy into hundreds of projects: They published journals, founded small presses, and opened bookstores; they organized women's music festivals and set up record companies. They were the ultimate difference feminists, certain that women and men were profoundly different and that women's values were superior.

The first wave of lesbian separatism peaked in about 1974, according to Charlotte Bunch. Some women, like Bunch, had always seen separatism as a political strategy—a temporary withdrawal from mainstream activism while they explored a lesbian identity and developed an approach to their issues that would guarantee that other activists finally paid attention. Eventually, said Bunch, they began to feel that "it didn't make sense to work in that much isolation." However, many lesbians remained committed to a women's culture. In the late 1970s, a second wave of lesbian separatism arose and was primarily oriented to the women's counterculture. The women of this second wave weren't as political; they were chiefly interested in creating their own space.

BACKLASH

Through the mid-1970s, both gay and straight feminists generally assumed that though social progress might be slow, progress was inevitable. In 1977, they were brought up short by two events that demonstrated just how strong the right-wing backlash was. These and other similar experiences convinced most activists that it was time to mend fences and form coalitions.

Some of the action that year focused on a local ordinance that

had been passed in Dade County, Florida, in 1976, which prohibited certain types of discrimination against homosexuals. Other
municipalities had adopted similar laws, but in Florida, evangelist singer Anita Bryant immediately mounted a vigorous campaign to repeal the ordinance. She had the backing both of
politicians and of religious groups. Fundamentalist churches supported her; TV evangelists invited her to appear on their programs and raised money for her. In a pastoral letter, the
archbishop of Miami urged Catholics to overturn the ordinance,
and twenty-eight rabbis also called for repeal. That June, voters
cast their ballots for repeal by a huge margin.

Feminists were also shaken by the right wing's strength as they
began organizing for the National Women's Conference in 1977.*
In the months before the conference, meetings were convened in
every state and territory to elect delegates and draft planks for a
National Plan of Action. In some states, right-wingers set out to
pack the meeting with conservatives in an effort to take over the
conference. They mobilized local Right-to-Lifers, fundamentalists, anti-ERA groups, and members of conservative fringe
groups such as the John Birch Society and the Ku Klux Klan. In
the end, eleven states elected delegations in which the majority
opposed most feminist goals. Feminists responded by forming a
coalition that linked forty major organizations.

Charlotte Bunch was part of the Washington, D.C., delegation,
and the experience persuaded her that the threat from the right
was real and wasn't going to go away. "Up until then, I had been
on the diplomatic edge of the radicals," she said. "I could be sent
out to talk to NOW or the other groups, unlike most of the people
I worked with, who were totally contemptuous of them. . . .
They made fun of us, too. Both sides were equally bad, in my
opinion. But I became convinced that if we didn't learn to work
together, it was all over."

While the National Women's Conference was meeting in Houston, Phyllis Schlafly, founder of the Eagle Forum, held a counter-
convention in the same city and formed a new conservative
coalition called the Pro-Family Movement. During 1978, it managed to overturn gay rights ordinances in St. Paul, Minnesota,
Wichita, Kansas, and Eugene, Oregon. In addition, the Oklahoma legislature passed a law calling for the dismissal of teachers
who practiced or simply defended homosexuality. The various

---

* The conference, which was held in Houston, Texas, in November 1977, was the United
  States government's response to International Women's Year sponsored by the United
  Nations.

right-wing campaigns repeatedly suggested that laws protecting the civil rights of lesbians and gay males were a license for child molesters—despite the fact that the overwhelming majority of molesters were heterosexual.

Before the end of the year, there was better news for feminists. California conservatives had set out to pass a referendum like Oklahoma's law, to rid the school system of gays and anyone who defended them. They organized a coalition in which evangelical churches played a major role, though the Ku Klux Klan and the American Nazi Party were also involved. In response, thirty organizations sprang up around the state to fight the so-called Briggs Initiative, and a number of unions and black and Chicano leaders joined forces with gay rights activists. Harvey Milk had just become San Francisco's first openly gay city supervisor, and he spoke against the Initiative on television and in town meetings. In the end, the Briggs Initiative lost. (Unfortunately, just weeks later, Harvey Milk was assassinated, together with San Francisco's liberal mayor, George Moscone.)

THE AIDS CRISIS

For gay rights activists, the 1980s were dominated by the specter of AIDS. The disease initially claimed the lives of so many gay men that it became associated with homosexuality in the minds of many Americans. Though lesbians ran a very low risk of getting AIDS, as members of the gay community many became involved in the struggle to force the government to fund research and medical care.

AIDS was first mentioned in a medical journal in 1981, but for a long time it was virtually ignored by the government and the media. In 1982, gays began to form support groups for themselves. The following year, the media carried stories that focused on the "innocent victims" of AIDS—children, people who got it through a blood transfusion, and the female partners of bisexual men who were infected. Then interest waned until 1985, when movie star Rock Hudson died of AIDS and it finally became a hot issue. By that time, it had killed 7000 Americans, 75 percent of them gay men.

The advent of AIDS increased the backlash against all gay people. Some conservatives almost welcomed the disease. TV evangelist Jerry Falwell announced that it was God's punishment for homosexuals, and other Americans also gave vent to their homophobia. From 1985 to 1988, opinion polls reported that for the first time in years the majority of those surveyed were against legalizing homosexual relations between consenting adults. In the meantime, violence against gay men and lesbians increased steadily. It finally leveled off in 1989—a year in which more than 7000 incidents of violence and harassment against gays and lesbians were reported, including sixty-two murders. The one bright spot during the 1980s was that, because of the AIDS crisis, the gay rights movement grew in size and strength. As activists pressed lawmakers to provide money for AIDS research, they were recognized in some cities as a potentially powerful voting bloc.

For most of the 1980s, AIDS issues were so urgent that gay rights groups relegated other problems to the back burner. Late in the decade, activists began to expand their agendas once again, taking on family issues, for example, partly because lesbians were finally assuming the leadership of some groups.

LESBIAN FAMILY ISSUES

For lesbian feminists, as for other women, family issues loomed large during the 1980s. Many lesbians wanted children but were prevented from adopting them by laws, regulations, or plain prejudice. The prejudice was usually expressed as a fear that children raised by lesbians would grow up to be gay, though a number of studies had been done comparing children raised by single heterosexual mothers and those raised by lesbians, and all had found that the children of lesbians were no more likely to be gay than other youngsters.

Prevented from adopting and often eager to have a baby themselves in any case, lesbians turned to artificial insemination (AI). By 1990, thousands had given birth to infants conceived through AI, and divorce courts in some states were beginning to deal with child-custody battles between lesbian couples. Often, the partner who was not the child's biological mother had been supportive throughout the pregnancy, present for the birth, and had shared the child-rearing, but legally she had no parental rights.

For lesbians who fell in love and formed a family together, the legal system had many pitfalls, and in the 1980s, the Kowalski case threw some of them into sharp relief. Sharon Kowalski and Karen Thompson considered themselves married; they bought a house together in St. Cloud, Minnesota. Then in 1983, Kowalski was severely injured in a car accident. Afterward, confined to a nursing home, she couldn't walk and could barely speak. Thompson spent hours with her, teaching her to type, helping her with reading and short-term memory skills, until she was able to answer questions by typing or by gestures.

Kowalski's parents had never been told that their daughter was a lesbian and they denied it now. Her father became her legal guardian and from 1985 on, he prevented Thompson from visiting her. Thompson went to court over and over again. In 1988, she finally succeeded in having Kowalski's condition evaluated, got her moved out of a nursing home to a rehabilitation center, and was permitted to visit her. However, in 1991, the legal battle over who was to be Sharon's guardian still continued.

The Kowalski case and others like it gave new meaning to the concept of "heterosexual privilege." A lesbian partner, who was neither a spouse nor a blood relative, had no rights in crisis situations, even if she and her lover had lived together for decades. If one partner wound up in intensive care in a hospital, as a nonrelative the other wasn't allowed to visit her. If one partner died, the other couldn't expect her own employer to grant her bereavement leave. One woman's health insurance didn't cover the other; they had no claim on one another's pensions; they couldn't apply for family memberships together—and so on. Employers and others, pressed to extend benefits to gays in long-term relationships, usually refused on the grounds that without a marriage certificate, it was impossible to tell a partner from a mere roommate. Some lesbians were eager for a legal option resembling marriage that would legitimize "domestic partnerships." Others were against it because they believed marriage was oppressive.

Pressed by gay rights activists, during the 1980s seven cities recognized domestic partnerships to the extent of granting the unmarried at least a few spousal rights—for example, in some places, city employees who had filed a domestic partnership affidavit could take bereavement leave. In November 1990, voters in San Francisco passed a local ordinance that established a system of registration. Couples who formally declared that they had a committed relationship, that they lived together, and that they had agreed to be responsible for one another's basic living expenses, were given an affidavit. For some, registering was purely a symbolic act, but others planned to present the affidavit to employers and others and to press for family benefits.

Meanwhile, some gay couples in California had begun to use a state law under which unincorporated nonprofit associations could register and receive a certificate; the couples simply identified themselves as a "family association." By December 1990, seven nontraditional families had registered under the law. They included two homosexual couples, an unmarried heterosexual couple, a stepfamily, a married couple with different last names, and a family that consisted of three refugee boys and their legal guardian.* Registering gave them no legal rights, but it did provide proof of their intention to live as a family. Similar laws were on the books in six other states.

GAY RIGHTS: A STATUS REPORT

As the gay rights agenda expanded in the late 1980s, activists also focused on the regulations that barred gay people from serving in the armed forces. Under the Uniform Code of Military Justice, which applied to all four services, homosexual acts were felonies. About 1400 men and women were forcibly discharged by the military every year for alleged homosexuality, and women were more apt to be dismissed than men.

Going into the 1990s, gays are the only minority still blatantly discriminated against by laws and government regulations. Not only are they banned from serving in the military, but in six states homosexual sodomy is a crime; in eighteen others, sodomy is a crime for heterosexuals as well. Though sodomy laws don't directly affect lesbians, they stigmatize all gays. The movement received a serious setback in 1986, when the Supreme Court ruled that the constitutional right to privacy didn't extend to homosexuals: In a state with an antisodomy law, they could be tried as criminals for having sex, even if they made love only in the privacy of their own homes. However, in 1990, courts in three states struck down similar sodomy laws, citing a right to privacy guaranteed by the state constitution.

In 1990, there were more than 3000 gay organizations. There were groups for gays who were recovering alcoholics, for those who were disabled, for older lesbians, for Asian lesbians living on the East Coast, and many, many more. Not all groups were politically active.

Though the activists made little progress in some areas, they

---

* In the late 1980s, only about one in four U.S. households still fitted the old Ozzie and Harriet model: two parents of opposite sexes, with children.

could point to significant gains in others. Despite the right wing's determined efforts, eighty municipalities now had laws prohibiting discrimination against gays in situations such as education or housing. Eleven states barred discrimination against gays in government jobs, and Wisconsin and Massachusetts banned it in the private sector as well. There were now fifty elected officials who were openly gay, up from about half a dozen in 1980. The Human Rights Campaign Fund, founded by gays, was one of the largest independent PACs in the country and it provided the community with a certain amount of political clout.

As for the relationship between gay and straight feminists, though it had definitely improved, there were still problems at times. Straight women occasionally complained about lesbian chauvinism, while lesbians were frustrated by continuing heterosexism in the women's movement. According to Charlotte Bunch, straight women still sometimes pressured lesbians to keep quiet about lesbian issues, or denied themselves lesbian leadership when a gay woman would have been the best choice, or shied away from joining a group just because it was predominantly lesbian. "Things *are* better, but not enough better, when you consider that we've been talking about this for twenty years," Bunch concluded.

chapter 14

Feminists and
Family Issues

*D*uring the 1980s, the women's movement was attacked by critics who blamed feminists for the plight of the mothers now doubly burdened with family responsibilities and a
full-time job. The critics pointed out that the United States was
almost the only industrialized nation where the government
didn't mandate maternity leave or subsidize child-care centers,
and that American divorce laws were a disaster for mothers and
children. They charged that the women's movement was responsible, that feminists had been so intent on achieving equality in
the job market that they ignored the needs of mothers, that the
movement had rejected the family. The trouble with feminists,
the argument went, was that they wanted to be just like men—
they denied that in significant ways women were different. The
critics pointed out that activists had pushed hard for gender-
neutral laws that would treat the sexes exactly alike, and those
laws had created new hardships for women.

Family issues were also raised within the women's movement
in the eighties, as activists argued strategy across the feminist

divide. Difference feminists maintained that because women bore children and usually handled most of the child care as well, mothers sometimes needed special treatment. They suggested that in some areas (particularly divorce) gender-neutral laws were a trap. They, too, sometimes blamed equality feminists for advocating such laws.

The truth was complex, but it boiled down to the fact that over the years feminists did what seemed doable. Their demands for child care and family leave met enormous resistance from conservatives, and they made little progress on those issues. As for divorce law, the history is muddier, but in defense of the movement it must be said that at first it seemed to almost everyone that no-fault, gender-neutral laws would be an improvement. When it became clear that women and children were being hurt, feminists led the fight for change.

In short, this chapter will argue that, if the double burden fell heavily on American women, the blame lay primarily with politicians who resisted European-style solutions, such as government funding for child-care centers. On a deeper level, it was the American tradition of rugged individualism that made progress so difficult.

Activists concerned about family issues didn't coalesce into a single, coherent movement. Instead, loosely linked networks of groups and individuals tackled each of the major family problems.

- The drive for federal support for child care was pursued from 1971 on by a shifting coalition that included most major national women's organizations.
- Because divorce was regulated by the states, local women's groups joined forces to lobby state legislatures for changes in the divorce laws. In addition, during the 1970s Washington feminists kept pressing the federal government to collect data on the consequences of divorce. When the information finally became available and demonstrated that divorce often impoverished ex-wives and children, national women's organizations were able to persuade Congress to act—to require the states to enforce child-support orders, among other things.
- In the 1980s and early 1990s, a coalition that included most of the same women's organizations, as well as other groups, fought for a federal family-leave law, while local groups pressed state legislatures for similar legislation.

CHILD CARE: A NEAR VICTORY

In the early 1970s, child care was a hot issue, and Congress actually voted to establish a national network of government-subsidized day-care centers Then right-wingers organized to oppose the bill and President Nixon vetoed it. For years afterward, child care on the European scale—affordable and widely available—was a dead issue.

From the vantage point of the 1990s, it's easy to forget how controversial day care was in the seventies. When feminists first began to demand government-subsidized child care, conservatives muttered darkly that they weren't about to give away taxpayers' money to women too irresponsible to look after their own children. Most middle class Americans weren't convinced that mothers had a right to hold jobs, or that children could be handed over safely to mother-substitutes. Many psychiatrists and psychologists insisted that they couldn't. In addition, there was a stigma attached to day-care centers, because at the time most of them served the very poor. Conceived as a way to get mothers off welfare by making it possible for them to work, the centers were inadequately funded and simply warehoused children. "Day care" eventually developed such a bad image that its backers began to speak of "child care" instead.

Nevertheless, by 1970 the pressure for government action was growing. A number of groups had become vitally interested in the child-care issue, though for different reasons.

Some conservatives backed day care solely as a way to get women off the welfare rolls. They favored the Family Assistance Plan (FAP) proposed by President Nixon, which would force welfare mothers to place their children in day care and find a job or lose their welfare benefits.

The National Welfare Rights Organization (NWRO), founded by welfare clients and liberals who supported them, wanted more federal money for child care but opposed the FAP. Most of the women in NWRO were eager to find work, but if the FAP passed, they would have to take any job they were offered and accept whatever child care the government provided, no matter how bad it was.

Many child-development experts wanted to expand Head Start, the preschool program for the poor. Convinced that the first five years of a child's life were critical for mental development, they hoped Head Start would give poor children the resources to lift themselves out of poverty as adults.

Feminists were concerned about the problems of working mothers. In 1967, NOW's Bill of Rights called for "child care facilities . . . established by federal law on the same basis as parks, libraries and public schools. . . ."

However, even among feminists there was some ambivalence about child care. Florence Falk-Dickler headed NOW's Task Force on Child Care during the late 1960s and early 1970s, and she recalled that most women in her own NOW chapter were more interested in employment issues, possibly because agitating for child care "was a very dangerous position to be in. . . . The whole social milieu said, how could you leave your children with strangers?"* Eleanor Smeal, later the president of NOW, pointed out that in addition there were many competing issues during the seventies and few feminists. "In 1970, NOW had between 3,000 and 4,000 members nationwide," she recalled. "We only had a handful of chapters. . . . In Pittsburgh, my phone was one of the NOW hotline numbers, and we were getting calls on job discrimination, on wife-beating, on rape. . . ."

Nevertheless, child care was the top priority for some activists. Smeal herself was one of the founders of the South Hills (Pennsylvania) NOW Day Nursery School in 1971 and was its administrator for a year. Like other feminists, she became convinced that good child care could actually be better for children than being tended by a single adult at home.

The Child-Care Coalition

In 1971, twenty-three groups that shared an interest in child care formed the Ad Hoc Coalition on Child Development, a powerful but fragile alliance of unions, church groups, civil rights organizations, groups organized to promote children's welfare, feminists, and the NWRO. The alliance was fragile because its members had different priorities and felt strongly about them.

Many believed that the right kind of child care could reshape the society. Marian Wright Edelman of the Children's Defense Fund, for example, was a strong advocate of community activism.

* Elizabeth Chittick, president of the National Woman's Party, believed that much of the opposition to the ERA after 1972 was generated by feminists' positions on lesbianism, abortion—and child care.

She pressed for child-care centers that would provide services for the entire family, in the hope that parents who became involved in such a center would be inspired to play a role in all of the local institutions that affected their lives. Liberals and feminists believed that racially mixed centers could help put an end to racism. Congresswoman Bella Abzug wanted ". . . a child-care system that would accommodate rich and poor alike, that would let our kids . . . learn that they can bridge the racial and economic gap that divides their parents."

Feminists also saw child care as a chance to combat sex stereotypes: In feminist-run centers, girls wouldn't be relegated to the housekeeping corner. And, of course, affordable child care would free women so that they could compete in the job market. From the beginning, the movement's leaders were convinced that the only hope for quality care was to include all classes. Good funding was important, too, so that child-care workers—almost always women—could be adequately paid and trained. Smeal noted that many people seemed to assume that anybody at all could be hired to care for children.*

The fact that funding was likely to be inadequate created tensions within the coalition. Groups concerned about the poor were afraid that if the government provided subsidies for middle class families, it would be at the expense of the poor.

The Comprehensive Child Development Act of 1971: The Child-Care Solution That Wasn't

In 1971, several members of Congress introduced child-care bills, including Walter Mondale in the Senate and John Brademas in the House. With input from the Ad Hoc Coalition, the Mondale-Brademas bill—known as the Comprehensive Child Development Act of 1971—evolved into a masterpiece of compromise. As Marian Wright Edelman said later, "[E]verybody got something." The bill would have established a network of child-care centers; local councils would have had a role in setting policy; care would be free for the poorest families and other families would pay fees set on a sliding scale. The bill authorized an expenditure of $2 billion for the first full year. Feminists knew that

---

* In the United States, child care simply wasn't respected. The *Dictionary of Occupational Titles*, put out by the U.S. Department of Labor, rated all occupations; the higher the rating, the lower the status of the job. In 1971, it gave a rating of 371 to barbers; 787 to sanitation workers; and 878, the worst possible rating, to jobs involving child care, such as homemaker or kindergarten teacher.

was too little to provide quality care on the scale they'd envisioned, but it would give them something to build on.

During the fall of 1971, while Congress was debating the bill, the right wing mounted a campaign against it. The anti-Communist John Birch Society joined with fundamentalist church groups and others to form a huge coalition, and conservatives wrote thousands of letters to Congress. Many described the bill as an invasion of the family; they called it radical and socialistic and likened it to the Soviet system of child care. In vain, Representative Brademas pointed out that no one would force families to enroll their children at a child-care center.

The coalition backing the bill tried to fight back. In their newsletters, women's organizations urged members to write to Congress, but there wasn't much of a response. In 1971, women's groups all over the country were deluging Congress with mail on the ERA, yet Washington lobbyists were unable to generate similar support for child care. At one point, the administration stated that for every letter the White House received that was pro-day care, it received 100 letters against.

Ultimately, the bill passed the Senate by a sizeable margin and squeaked through the House. Then Nixon vetoed it. His veto message deemed the legislation unworkable and fiscally irresponsible and complained of "family-weakening implications." It asserted that the bill would commit "the vast moral authority of the National Government to the side of communal approaches to child rearing [instead of] the family-centered approach." The veto message went on to say that ". . . good public policy requires that we enhance rather than diminish both parental authority and parental involvement with children—particularly in those decisive early years when social attitudes and a conscience are formed and religious and moral principles are first inculcated." Critics pointed out that Nixon's own FAP would force welfare mothers to leave their children. What was good policy for the middle class was apparently irrelevant for the poor.

Thanks to the furor stirred up by conservatives, Congress failed to override the President's veto. Jane O'Grady, a Washington lobbyist, believed that ultimately the legislation died because the child-care coalition couldn't generate enough grass-roots support. To O'Grady, this was proof that lobbying, important as it was, "is no substitute for mass action. . . ."

Later Child-Care Bills That Failed

During the 1970s, child-care advocates tried several times to get a federal law enacted but had no success. In 1975, Mondale introduced a scaled-down version of his 1971 bill. Feminist organizations were among those who testified in favor of the bill when hearings were held. However, by that time the child-care alliance had developed deep splits. Albert Shanker, head of the teachers' union, the American Federation of Teachers, had become involved and he wanted to locate day-care centers in the schools and staff them with teachers. Marian Wright Edelman and others objected. African-Americans didn't want child care taken over by white middle class educators, who sometimes behaved as if black children came from homes that were automatically deficient. Feminists supported Edelman, but their backing was largely rhetorical. The issue was not top priority for the women's movement, perhaps because it was clear that there was no way to get federal funding extended to include middle class families. In the end, Congress passed Mondale's 1975 bill, but President Gerald Ford vetoed it.

In 1979, Senator Alan Cranston introduced a bill that was even more modest. The Carter administration testified against it: HEW assistant secretary Arabella Martinez maintained that federal funds weren't necessary because mothers preferred to have their children cared for by relatives at home. The right wing once again produced a deluge of mail. Conservatives opposed social welfare services in general, but they were vehement about child care. As one woman explained it,

[The federal government] interferes by increasing inflation. That makes it necessary for women to leave their homes to go to work. . . . Then the government uses the fact that they are in the work force to create day care. Day care is powerful. A program that ministers to a child from six months to six years has over eight thousand hours to teach beliefs and behavior. The family should be teaching values, not the government or anyone in day care.

Some right-wingers once again raised the specter of Communism. "The red-baiting injured us terribly on this issue," Ellie Smeal said. In the past, conservatives had often used red-baiting to try to derail social movements. During the 1920s, they had accused women's organizations of Communism and succeeded in intimidating some. Throughout the 1970s they played on the

American fear of Communism once again to forestall the development of a federal child-care system.

In 1979, the result was that Cranston's bill never even got out of committee. He blamed opposition from the public and from the Carter administration and faltering support from child-care advocates.

The Irresistible Growth of Child Care

In the early 1970s, at the same time that feminists campaigned for a national day-care network, they fought for a child-care tax deduction. At the time, businessmen could routinely deduct as "ordinary and necessary" business expenses such things as a country club membership, but day care was classified as a personal expense, even when it was absolutely necessary before a parent could work. Only a fraction of it was deductible and only by low-income families.

The Revenue Act of 1971 raised both the size of the deduction allowed and the ceiling on family income. Over the next decade, Congress improved the deduction several times, in the process converting it to a tax credit, which made it worth more in terms of tax money saved. This eased the situation for the middle class, but because the poor paid little or nothing in taxes, a deduction or credit didn't help them.

The money provided for child care for the poor never met the demand and was dispensed unevenly. After 1974, under the program known as Title XX, the federal government gave the states block grants to cover all social services. A state could divide up the money any way it saw fit, and social-welfare programs had to compete with each other for funds. Some states set aside a reasonable sum for child care; some set aside nothing.

During the 1970s, despite the failure to establish a national day-care system, the need for child care was so great that federal funding kept growing. However, by the end of the decade, most of the money was going to the middle class; Title XX funding was in second place.

What Killed the Child-Care Initiative?

What made child care a dead issue after 1971? At least three different factors were involved. First, there was the right-wing opposition to "communal child rearing." Second, the pro-child-care groups were unable to maintain a united front. When organizations that presumably have common interests begin fighting among themselves, politicians are apt to ignore all of them, rather than favor one faction and risk being attacked by the rest. Third, in the seventies there wasn't the kind of public support for child care that materialized in the 1980s, as desperate parents began to demand help from the government.

It was 1990 before Congress finally passed a major child-care bill (the Act for Better Child Care, discussed in chapter 20). Long before that, most Western European countries had state-subsidized care. In many cases they had it not because feminists had agitated for it, but because after two world wars decimated the population, political leaders wanted to increase the birth rate so they made it easier for couples to support children. The strong public support for subsidized child care in Europe was also part of a consensus that backed broad social-welfare measures.

DIVORCE AND THE NOUVEAU POOR

During the 1980s, the United States had the highest divorce rate in the world—half of all new marriages failed. What's more, the American system of divorce was a disaster for women: In every state, the laws and the courts, between them, gave men enormous advantages. As a result, according to one study, after divorce a man's living standard rose by about 42 percent, while the standard of living of his ex-wife and children fell by 73 percent.

Obviously, a woman risked a lot when she married and had children, especially if she dropped out of the job market to become a full-time mother. In fact, divorce was partly responsible for the startling increase in the number of women living in poverty during the 1970s and 80s. Every year from 1969 to 1978, 100,000 more women with children fell below the poverty line. By the mid 1980s, at a time when 16 percent of all American families were headed by a woman, almost half of all *poor* families were female-headed. Many of these women were divorced, though some had never been married.

Some conservatives held the women's movement responsible for the epidemic of divorce that raged during the 1970s and 1980s. They claimed that wives were abandoning their marriages in droves, and they blamed feminists. However, the divorce rate began to rise before the second wave of feminism took hold, and the second wave was, in part, a response to the insecurity of marriage. In fact, as writer Barbara Ehrenreich pointed out, men rebelled against marriage long before women did. During the 1950s, movies and books often depicted marriage as a trap for husbands, who supposedly led a life of gray, meaningless toil so that their wives could enjoy a pampered existence in the sub-urbs.* *Playboy* magazine regularly lambasted money-hungry women in general and ex-wives who lived on alimony in partic-ular. The belief that housewives were privileged and that their contribution to the family was trivial shaped divorce reform in the 1970s.

No-Fault, No-Responsibility Divorce

The American divorce rate actually began to rise at the turn of the century, climbed fairly steadily until the 1960s, and then shot upward, increasing by 100 percent between 1963 and 1975. In 1963, one couple was divorced for every four couples who got married; by 1975 there was one divorce for every two marriages. In response to the change, a wave of divorce-law reform swept all fifty states, beginning with California.

At first, reform efforts focused primarily on the grounds for divorce. In most states in order to get a divorce, one spouse had to accuse the other of wrongdoing—of infidelity, perhaps, or mental cruelty. Because the law required that the guilty party be punished by the financial terms of the settlement, usually each side did its worst to smear the other. If both spouses wanted to end the marriage, they had to resort to collusion and trump up grounds. Those who could afford it often chose migratory divorce instead, filing papers in Nevada or Mexico, where marriages could be ended quickly and easily.

Many Americans believed that when a marriage died, it should be dissolved as painlessly as possible. Thus, in 1970 when Cali-fornia passed the first pure no-fault divorce law anywhere in the Western world, it seemed an improvement. To get a divorce, a couple simply asserted that their marriage had experienced an "irremediable breakdown." Only one of them had to say so—a reluctant spouse couldn't block a divorce. The financial settle-ment was to be based on the needs and resources of each; the property acquired during the marriage must be divided equally.

---

* Ehrenreich suggested that after industrialization, men came to see a family as a respon-sibility rather than an asset. Once work was no longer home-based—a farm, a shop, a craft, that engaged the efforts of the man himself *and* of his wife and children—woman's work somehow lost its legitimacy.

Because many wives were now employed, the new law assumed that most could support themselves. However, three types of women were to receive "spousal support" (formerly known as alimony): mothers with custody of young children; homemakers who needed retraining; and long-married, older homemakers. For the mothers and women in training, the support was to be temporary, but the legislators recognized that most long-married women had never expected to work outside the home and that it was unfair to change the rules so late in the game.

California's new law started a wave of reform. By 1980, there were only two states that had *not* adopted some form of no-fault divorce. Some did away with fault grounds altogether, while others simply added a no-fault option to traditional grounds for divorce. Though the new laws often sounded reasonable in theory, in practice they were grossly unfair to women.

GROUNDS FOR DIVORCE:

In an influential 1985 book, sociologist Lenore Weitzman argued that women lost their financial leverage with the advent of no-fault. Under the old laws, the partner who wanted to escape the marriage—most often the man—had to bargain to win freedom, and the wife could hold out for a decent financial settlement, provided he couldn't prove that she had done something wrong. Because most men had enormous financial advantages during a divorce, women needed all the leverage they could get.

ALIMONY:

During the 1970s, groups of divorced men all over the country lobbied successfully for an end to alimony. They convinced legislators that legions of women were living idle lives as "alimony drones," ex-wives who were quite capable of supporting themselves but were sustained instead by their alimony. The term implied that the women had done nothing as homemakers and mothers to deserve support from their ex-husbands.

Many people believed in alimony drones; some still do. Actually, only a fraction of divorced women were ever awarded alimony and it was always hard to collect. Nineteen percent of women divorced before 1970 were legally entitled to alimony, compared to 13 percent of those divorced since 1980—a small difference. However, other changes were devastating. Before reform, alimony was usually awarded for life or until the woman remarried; under the new laws like California's, payments almost always stopped after a few years. California legislators hadn't intended to limit alimony so drastically, but that was the way judges interpreted the law. They required virtually all ex-wives to support themselves, even mothers of small children and long-married homemakers who had never worked. They seemed to have no idea how difficult it was for such women to find jobs at decent pay.

PROPERTY:

Under the old divorce laws, when a marriage ended, property was retained by the person who had title to it. Consequently, a woman could emerge from a twenty-year marriage empty-handed. By the 1980s, eight states required that assets be divided fifty/fifty on divorce and the rest mandated equitable (meaning "fair") division. However, because the system everywhere gave the courts so much leeway in evaluating property (in assigning a value to a house or business, for example), the actual division was rarely fifty/fifty. On the average, wives received 35 to 40 percent. Even an equal split would mean, in the typical divorce, that one person (the husband) got half the family assets while three people (the wife and two children) shared the other half.

Because the average divorcing family had less than $20,000 to divide and often the husband could earn more than that in a single year, *his* earning power was actually their chief asset, together with his fringe benefits: a pension, health insurance, and various company perks. Even if the wife had a job, many women worked in occupations that didn't provide such fringes. Over the years, feminists made some progress in forcing courts to take into account the so-called "new property" (pensions, etc.). They persuaded Congress to pass legislation giving the ex-wives of foreign service officers a share of their husbands' pensions; afterward, a number of states adopted similar laws that applied to all couples.

CHILD SUPPORT:

During the early 1980s, half of all divorced mothers with custody weren't awarded any child support in the first place; the rest usually discovered that the support they were entitled to paid for less than half of the children's expenses. American courts rarely ordered a man to give more than a third of his net income to his ex-wife and children because judges claimed they must leave him enough so that he'd be motivated to earn. Lenore Weitzman called this the "father first principle," contrasting it to the system in England, which provided for the children's needs first, then divided the remaining income between the parents.

In setting child support, American courts almost never built in an automatic adjustment for the rising cost of living, nor did the amount of money increase as the children grew older. Theoretically, a woman could go back to court to ask for more money, but many women couldn't afford to hire a lawyer, and judges were often unsympathetic in any case.

Default was another serious problem. In 1985, only half the mothers who were supposed to be receiving child support were getting it; one quarter got partial payments and another quarter got nothing. When an ex-husband defaulted, a woman's only recourse was to drag him into court. His lawyer would then negotiate endless delays, and when the case was finally heard, the judge would simply issue a reprimand or order a token payment. Studies repeatedly found that most fathers could afford to pay—if they didn't, it was because they knew they could get away with it. In places where judges sent defaulters to jail, there were many fewer defaulters. Some men actually said they'd prefer to have the support deducted automatically from their paychecks, so they wouldn't be tempted to spend the money.

CHILD CUSTODY:

Most of the old divorce laws stipulated that while the children were young, custody should normally go to the mother. The new laws were gender-neutral. Statistically, that made little difference: Women still had custody about 90 percent of the time, because that was what both parents wanted. However, by the 1980s, in the 10 percent of cases where the father fought for custody, he now won more than half the time.

Though judges who sided with the father were sometimes simply choosing the better parent, at other times they made the decision on questionable grounds. "Some judges get excited about a father who shows the slightest interest in parenting," said feminist attorney Lynn Hecht Schafran. Judges also chose the father because he could provide a higher standard of living—though with adequate child support, the mother could do as well—or because he'd remarried and had a stay-at-home wife, while his ex-wife must work full-time to survive.* In the worst cases, judges gave custody to men known to be wife beaters. They failed

* The older a divorced woman was, the less likely she was to remarry; divorced men tended to remarry at every age.

to understand that the children were also likely to become his victims, and that even if they didn't, they were probably terrified of him. Schafran pointed out that, in addition, giving custody to wife beaters was a signal to all concerned that battering was acceptable. Thus, the man might feel free to continue his assaults on the woman—battering often actually escalated after divorce— while the children were more likely to grow up to be batterers or batterers' victims themselves.

In the 1970s, fathers' rights groups pressed hard for gender-neutral laws that would award custody according to the best interests of the child. Later, they lobbied effectively for joint custody. Both the best-interests standard and joint custody initially sounded reasonable, even to many feminists. However, the new laws gave all fathers, good and bad, one more weapon to add to an already formidable arsenal. "Some of these born-again fathers are only interested in their own rights, not in what's best for the children," said Harriet N. Cohen, head of the matrimonial law department of a New York City law firm. "For others, the fight for custody is part of a power struggle with the wife. Some men threaten to go for custody when they don't really want it, just to get the woman to settle for less financial support. Many mothers will agree to almost anything rather than risk losing their children."

Joint custody increased women's financial problems because usually the children lived with their mother, though the custody arrangement gave the father an equal say in all major decisions affecting them. In such situations, the courts set child-support payments at even less than the usual inadequate norm, on the assumption that the father would pay directly for some of the children's expenses, whereas often he contributed little or nothing.

State laws that favored joint custody sometimes required divorcing couples to submit to mediation before they could be heard in court. Some feminists failed to understand at first that mediation, too, was often bad for women because it was most often the woman, who was unused to negotiating, who knuckled under in the process. What was worse, though a woman could appeal a judge's decision, there was no way to appeal an agreement arrived at by mediation.

The one ray of hope in the custody situation was the primary-caretaker rule, which was established in West Virginia in 1981 by the state Supreme Court. The rule asserted, as a strong legal preference, that custody should go to the parent who had provided most of the day-to-day child care. Usually, that parent was the mother.

Needless to say, all ex-wives weren't paragons of virtue, nor were all ex-husbands irresponsible opportunists. Nevertheless, male-dominated legislatures and the predominantly male judiciary created a system so biased against women that it brought out the worst in many men.

Divorce, European Style

While American divorce laws were being transformed, similar changes were taking place in Western Europe, but they were generally less damaging to women because most European nations built in safeguards for dependents. In England, France, and West Germany, for example, if one spouse didn't want a divorce, the law prescribed a waiting period of several years, and in hardship cases the court could deny the divorce altogether. Such laws contradicted the notion that a person had a "right" to walk out of a marriage at any time, scot-free. They also gave a dependent wife some bargaining power when her husband was eager to end the marriage.

As for child support, in the 1980s enforcement was better almost everywhere in the West than it was in the United States. Some European countries now had standard formulas for calculating support in realistic amounts and deducted payments automatically from the father's wages. In other countries, the state paid the support directly to the mother and then collected it from the father, so that mother and children needn't go short if he missed a payment. In France, West Germany, and Sweden, child support rose automatically with the cost of living.

Yale law professor Mary Ann Glendon, who compared divorce in Western Europe and the United States, noted that the United States was unique in the Western world because it didn't provide for the economic casualties of divorce, either by insisting that the former spouse assume the responsibility or through public welfare. In England, where the divorce laws treated women and men differently, older housewives still got lifelong alimony. In Sweden, the divorce laws were strictly gender-neutral, but the government provided subsidies for single mothers and long-time homemakers who had trouble supporting themselves.

Glendon wrote of a "mythology of self-reliance" in America that contrasted with a "politics of compassion" on the continent. Women were better off in most of Western Europe, not only because divorce was not quite so unfair, but because social welfare policies provided them with a safety net. Glendon suggested that the American reluctance to pay for a safety net was rooted in discomfort with the nation's racial and ethnic diversity. A Swede in Stockholm was apt to feel genuinely concerned about the welfare of a Swedish child in Malmö; Sweden had a homogeneous population. White middle class Americans apparently didn't feel that kind of concern about black children in the ghetto, for example, or mothers on welfare.

The Divorce Wars: An Uphill Battle

In all fifty states, women's coalitions worked to change divorce laws that harmed ex-wives, but they had so little success that even some feminists questioned whether they tried hard enough. Joanne Schulman, for example, was staff attorney for the National Center on Women and Family Law from 1980 to 1986, and she felt that some women's organizations didn't understand the risks involved in the new laws. They mistakenly backed—or simply failed to oppose—damaging divorce reforms such as the laws California passed in the early 1980s making mediation mandatory and joint custody the preferred type. Once it became clear how badly those laws were working, NOW and other groups fought to change them, but in the meantime harm was done.

In fact, many feminists *did* fail to see what was coming when the laws began to change. Most of the reforms looked reasonable at first—the courts could have interpreted them so as to be fair to both sexes—but very few people understood how biased many judges were, not just in handling divorces but in other cases as well. In 1969, attorney Sylvia Roberts conceived the idea of a program to educate judges, and the following year she proposed it to the newly formed NOW Legal Defense and Education Fund. However, according to Lynn Hecht Schafran, when NOW LDEF asked foundations to fund a project to try to change the attitudes of judges, "the response was, 'There's no bias against women in the courts. Judges are impartial.' NOW LDEF spent ten years proving that a program *was* needed."

Proof wasn't easy to come by at first, because the U.S. Census Bureau hadn't collected data on the impact of divorce since 1922. Alerted by the few studies that had been done—and sometimes by their own experiences in getting a divorce—some women tried to sound the alarm, but they were largely ignored by the media and by legislators. The National Commission on the Observance of International Women's Year kept pressing the federal government to collect data on alimony, child support, and property settlements. Finally, in 1978, the Census Bureau complied. The results confirmed what feminists had been saying—for instance, that only a small percentage of wives was awarded alimony, and that many husbands failed to pay court-ordered child support.

In the early 1980s, other factors combined to make divorce a national issue. Research showed that a growing number of single mothers were living in poverty. Divorce had always impoverished women, but as long as they were from blue-collar backgrounds or were women of color, no one paid much attention. Once white middle class mothers began applying for welfare in significant numbers, people took note. Meanwhile, sociologist Lenore Weitzman completed her landmark study of the impact of the divorce reforms. Ultimately published as *The Divorce Revolution*, it led to some changes in the laws. National women's organizations also pressed for better laws, and at about the same time, grass-roots self-help groups were springing up around the country, as women fought to get their child-support orders enforced.

Eventually, Congress became involved. Legislators responded because they were concerned about the gender gap—the fact that women were voting differently from men and were evidently concerned about different issues. Lawmakers knew that child support was a hot issue for women. In addition, several congressmen had daughters whose ex-husbands had defaulted, and some conservatives finally realized that, via welfare, federal money was supporting the ex-wives of well-heeled men.

In 1984 and again in 1988, Congress passed bills that toughened child-support enforcement. The new federal laws made a number of improvements. The support was now to be deducted automatically from the noncustodial parent's paycheck, beginning immediately after the divorce. The states were required to set formulas specifying how much support a judge should order for one child, how much for two, and so on. Courts were ordered to review and adjust the awards every three years for families on welfare and for others who requested such a review. States that failed to comply with the federal requirements would lose their welfare funding. By 1989, enforcement was beginning to improve but according to Lynn Hecht Schafran, it had a very long way to go.

Re-educating Judges

Why was it so difficult to do anything about the divorce situation? "In my opinion, the courts are the chief reason," said Harriet N. Cohen. State laws gave judges a lot of room to exercise discretion. There were still very few women on the bench in the 1980s and even fewer feminists.

For almost ten years, the idea of educating judges had been on the back burner at NOW LDEF—it was sometimes referred to as the "impossible project." In 1979, Norma Wikler, a California sociology professor, put together a proposal that helped persuade funders to support the effort. Wikler's approach was based on the premise that women who asked for equal justice weren't trying to impose a feminist agenda on the judiciary; they simply wanted judges to be true to their own ideals—to be objective and impartial. Therefore, the task was to provide them with facts and try to sensitize them to the realities of women's lives.

In 1980, NOW LDEF launched the National Judicial Education Program to Promote Equality for Women and Men in the Courts (NJEP) and invited the newly formed National Association of Women Judges to become the program's cosponsor. Wikler served as NJEP's founding director. Knowing that the judiciary would find it hard to believe that courts were biased against women, NJEP's seminars used local cases and information whenever possible to demonstrate to judges that gender bias was a problem in their own state's courts. However, too little information was available. In 1982, New Jersey Judge Marilyn Loftus asked the state's Chief Justice to appoint a group to study gender bias in the courts, and the first Task Force on Women in the Courts was born. It became a catalyst for similar efforts in other states. By the 1990s, more than half the states had task forces; all found that gender bias was pervasive.

NJEP's programs designed to counter that bias were well received by some judges, while others were indifferent or downright hostile, according to Lynn Hecht Schafran; in 1981, she succeeded Wikler as director of NJEP. Schafran conducted seminars for judges around the country, sometimes in tandem with Wikler. She noted that some judges genuinely believed that women were now on an equal footing with men in employment. Others apparently acted out of malice: "They seemed to have the attitude, 'You want equality, lady? I'll give you equality,' " said Schafran. Still others favored the husband because they didn't feel that a woman who was "just a housewife" contributed as much to a marriage as her husband, the breadwinner. In this, they shared the assumptions of the larger society, which had always devalued "women's work." Schafran pointed out that nurses and teachers were underpaid and child-care workers earned less than parking-lot attendants.

Roadblocks in State Legislatures

In the state legislatures, too, the struggle was difficult. The issues were complex and at times feminists were divided. In 1980 in New York, for example, the legislature indicated that it was finally ready to replace the old divorce law that awarded property to the spouse who had title to it. Some women's groups, led by NOW, would accept nothing less than equal division. Other activists were convinced that the Senate committee considering the legislation would never agree to fifty-fifty and felt they should take what they could get. "There were members of the committee who were themselves in the midst of divorces and they weren't looking to rock the boat," said Lynn Hecht Schafran. Equitable division became the law. Afterward, feminists tried unsuccessfully to pass an amendment establishing a legal presumption that property division would be equal. Some activists still believed it would have been better to hold out for fifty-fifty.

The Drawbacks of Gender-Neutral Laws

Before 1970, divorce laws, presumably drafted to protect dependent wives, often worked to their disadvantage. If a man kept all the property in his own name, for example, on divorce it belonged to him. Alimony awards were supposed to compensate for this, but the courts rarely ordered men to pay alimony.

The old gender-specific laws were interpreted to favor husbands, but so were the new gender-neutral laws. In treating women and men alike, the divorce laws ignored both inequalities that marriage created and sex discrimination in the job market. Wives would never be on an equal footing with husbands as long as most mothers had the primary responsibility for child care and housekeeping, even when they also had a job; as long as they subordinated their own career to their husband's; as long as women earned so much less than men. Divorce laws that ignored these realities put women at a profound disadvantage.

One solution would be to campaign for gender-specific laws that protected women. Joanne Schulman, for example, believed that child-custody laws should give mothers the preference. Other feminists favored West Virginia's primary-caretaker rule, a gender-neutral approach that would have much the same effect, theoretically, because the mother was usually the primary caretaker. Schulman supported that approach in principle but was leery of the West Virginia law itself because it left too much to the judge's discretion. "I don't trust judges to define primary caretaking," she said.

Schulman pointed out that many judges already applied a double standard in child-custody cases. They considered a man who had changed two diapers a week the best father in the world, though of course a mother who changed two diapers a week would be neglecting her child. "That's not equal treatment," said Schulman. "That's ignoring reality to give special treatment to men."

Obviously, it would be difficult to persuade state legislatures to pass divorce laws that favored wives at the expense of husbands, and there was a good chance such laws would be declared unconstitutional, anyway. In 1979, the Supreme Court ruled that statutes allowing alimony for women but not for men violated the equal protection clause of the fourteenth amendment. In addition, many feminists felt that the equality approach was still the best strategy. Lynn Hecht Schafran noted that some fathers really were the better parent. For the child's sake, gender-neutral laws would be preferable if judges weren't so biased. Schafran also believed, as other equality feminists did, that it was dangerous for women to ask for special treatment.

It was possible to improve the situation for women within the framework of gender-neutral laws. To mention just a few suggestions that Lenore Weitzman made: The laws could say that the judge's goal must be to produce two households with equal standards of living; parents who were late with support payments could be charged interest or an automatic penalty; joint custody could be permitted only when both parents wanted it.

It was also possible to draft laws that allowed judges much less discretion, and some believed this should be done. States could mandate a fifty-fifty property split, for example. However, while that would reduce the amount of damage biased judges could do, Lynn Hecht Schafran pointed out that it would tie the hands of other judges, who were trying hard to be fair. *Should* judges have less leeway? It was a hard call to make.

Schafran argued "we must give up the illusion that law is pure, rational, objective, abstract, and principled, and recognize that although the vast majority of judges are committed to fairness, the vast majority of judges are upper-middle-class white men whose perception of fairness is filtered through the lens of that particular life experience. . . ." Thus, judges must be educated, but in the long run the best way to protect women—particularly homemakers—was to get more feminists onto the bench and into the legislatures, a long-term project.

FAMILY LEAVE: FOR WOMEN ONLY?

By the late 1980s, the United States and South Africa were the only industrialized Western nations that didn't require employers to give women time off for childbirth. In Western Europe, the average working woman got five months of *paid* leave when she had a baby, with her job guaranteed. In contrast, in most states in the United States, businesses could do as they liked. Thus, in the 1980s one major study reported that only 40 percent of the women in the work force were permitted to take as much as six weeks of paid leave when they had a baby.

A handful of states, acting where the federal government had failed to, had mandated some type of unpaid maternity leave. California was among them, and feminists made headlines because NOW and some other groups actually opposed the California law. NOW's action was vigorously debated within the movement, and people outside generally misunderstood it. The controversy was never a repudiation of maternity leave per se—it was primarily a debate about the best political strategy.

The argument was perhaps the quintessential conflict between the special-treatment and equal-treatment approaches. Difference feminists felt that women couldn't hope to compete with men in the job market unless they could wring concessions, such as maternity leave, from employers. The equality side felt just as strongly that it was dangerous to ask for special treatment because businesses, forced to make concessions for mothers, might be reluctant to hire, train, or promote younger women. Predictably, the equality feminists were accused of ignoring mothers' needs. Meanwhile, many people lost sight of the fact that pregnant women owed the sparse maternity benefits they *did* have to steady pressure from the women's movement.

The Campaign for Maternity Benefits

Until the 1970s, women were often fired the minute it became obvious that they were pregnant. Health insurance plans covered almost everything except childbirth, or else offered meager payments. As for disability insurance, most plans limited the benefits for pregnancy and childbirth or refused to cover them at all. Employers insisted that pregnancy was different from other medical conditions because it was voluntary, but in fact, policies covered vasectomies, hair transplants, plastic surgery, and other voluntary conditions without a murmur.*

The real reason for denying maternity benefits was that the men who set the policies believed that women—especially pregnant women—didn't belong in the work place. Pregnancy was, in fact, the ultimate excuse for excluding them. Before Title VII, many businesses claimed they couldn't hire or promote women because women would only get pregnant and quit. Though most women had only two or three children in a lifetime, males in authority seemed to assume that all women were perpetually on the verge of pregnancy. In that atmosphere, if women were going to compete in the job market, they were obviously going to have to do it on men's terms. Thus, in the beginning, most feminists simply argued that employers must treat pregnancy and childbirth like other disabilities: They should be covered by a company's health insurance and disability plans and by its normal policy on sick leave.

In 1976, the Supreme Court handed down a decision on maternity leave that galvanized the women's movement. The case was a class-action suit brought by seven women who worked for General Electric. They argued that GE's disability plan discriminated on the basis of sex because it didn't cover pregnancy or childbirth. Around the country, federal district courts and appeals courts had been ruling in favor of women in similar cases. The Supreme Court supported GE on the grounds that its disability plan didn't treat men and women differently—it simply distinguished between pregnant women and nonpregnant persons.†

Within a week of the Court's decision, angry feminists, civil rights groups, unions, and church groups had formed a broad

---

* At one point, General Electric's disability policy excluded pregnancy and childbirth, but would cover injuries incurred because of attempted suicide or during the commission of a crime.

† "When I heard about that," said Leslie Wolfe, director of the Center for Women Policy Studies, "I started advocating sex education for elderly men."

coalition and began to lobby Congress for a law to undo the decision. In 1978, Congress responded by passing the Pregnancy Discrimination Act (PDA). An amendment to Title VII, it stated clearly that pregnancy discrimination *was* a type of sex discrimination. The PDA didn't say that companies had to offer maternity benefits or leaves only that they must treat pregnancy the way they did other disabilities. Because many American employers made few concessions for illness, most women still didn't get adequate maternity leave. "[The PDA] was simply the best that was possible at the time in our legal and political environment," said Catherine East.

During that same year, 1978, California passed maternity-leave legislation. The new law said that all businesses in the state except small ones must grant sick leave to women who had to take time off from work because of pregnancy or childbirth. The leave could be unpaid, but the woman had a right to get her job back. She was supposed to return to work as soon as she was physically able—within four months at the outside. In short order, a bank sued the state, claiming that the new law was invalidated by the PDA, which said pregnancy must be treated like other disabilities. California had no laws mandating leave for employees disabled for other reasons.

The women's movement came down on both sides of the case. Difference feminists backed the California statute. Equality feminists maintained that it *was* in conflict with the PDA, but that the solution was to extend it to cover both sexes and other medical problems as well (a gender-neutral approach). The Court could have directed the state to do that. The women envisioned a law, like those common in Western Europe, that would guarantee sick leave for all employees; maternity leave would be included.

Lynn Hecht Schafran noted that singling out mothers for special leave didn't seem to move women forward toward a day when fathers would participate fully in child-rearing. In addition, the California law was a complex piece of legislation consisting of nine related measures, and seven of them actually discriminated against pregnant women—for example, by saying that employers could refuse to hire them. "In its totality, it was a terrible law," said Schafran. It proved that when a legislature singled out pregnancy for special treatment, the results were as likely to be bad as good.

It took years for the California case to rise through the appeals system. In 1987, the U.S. Supreme Court finally ruled that in passing the PDA, Congress intended to prohibit discrimination against pregnant workers, but not discrimination in their favor, and that the California law actually promoted equal job opportunity because it "allows women, as well as men, to have families without losing their jobs."

While the California case was pending, feminist lobbyists began to work for a different kind of solution, a federal family leave law that would apply so broadly that employers couldn't single women out as a problem. Early in 1984, a committee began drafting a bill that would require companies to provide job-protected, unpaid leave for employees (male or female) who were very sick or who needed time off to take care of a new baby, a newly adopted child, a seriously ill child, or a parent who was seriously ill. The employer must maintain the employee's medical insurance coverage, pension rights, and seniority during the leave.

The bill was fiercely opposed by the U.S. Chamber of Commerce, which coordinated a flood of protests from small businesses. Among other things, the Chamber argued that the law's gender-neutral language would not be enough to prevent the backlash feminists feared, and that the legislation would hurt women because mothers, rather than fathers, would take the leaves, and as a result, employers would hesitate to hire or promote women.

Family Leave in Europe: The Trade-offs

Because the Chamber of Commerce was also making wild charges about the damage American businesses would suffer if they had to grant family leave, the Women's Research and Education Institute (WREI) asked researcher Susanne A. Stoiber to study leaves systems in Europe, to see how they affected both employers and women.

Stoiber's report, published in 1989, noted that over the last sixty years, every nation in Western Europe had evolved laws mandating some form of paid, job-protected maternity leave. In contrast, in the United States, both state and federal governments were reluctant to regulate the work place. There were no federal laws setting minimums for vacation time or sick leave, as there were in Europe, and American unions had generally been more interested in increasing wages than in winning fringe benefits.

West Germany's leaves system was more or less gender-neutral but, according to Stoiber, it was designed to encourage *mothers* to stay home while their children were small. It guaranteed a woman up to fourteen weeks of maternity leave with benefits that almost always replaced her normal income. At the end of that time, either parent could stay home and collect a child-raising allowance, available from the government until the child was three. However, the money was just enough that the average woman, if she also took a part-time job, could count on an income that was about 85 percent of what she used to earn. Because most men earned a great deal more, and because Germans had traditional ideas about roles within the family, very few men stayed home with the children. Some German employers complained about the leaves system and said it made them reluctant to hire or promote women.

In Sweden, a government-financed leaves system guaranteed parents nine months off at full pay to stay home with a baby. At the end of that time, there were ways to extend the leave at partial pay or without pay, or by working part-time, for another nine months or more, and still have a job waiting at the end. As in West Germany, either parent could take the leave, but usually mothers did. Because men earned more, few couples could afford to have the husband stay home once the nine months of fully paid leave were over. Many mothers were glad to spend time at home because they had boring jobs; yet women probably wound up doing boring, underpaid work partly because they cared for the children and couldn't make a wholehearted commitment to a job.

Both West Germany and Sweden set out to create a "soft" labor market for women: to make it easy for them to have babies (considered important, because the birth rate was dropping), fulfill their family responsibilities, and still hold a job. Gender equality was not the primary concern. In both countries, mothers seldom faced the kind of stress, juggling work and family, that American women dealt with. However, women in West Germany had very little job mobility, and while Swedish women were somewhat better off, they had fewer opportunities than American women.

Stoiber concluded that for women, every leaves system represented a trade-off between long-term security and job mobility. Everywhere in the industrialized world, women who dropped out of the job market to raise children tended to reenter it in lower-status jobs that paid less. Many never built up enough credits for a pension, and divorced women often faced an impoverished old age as a result. When mothers could take long leaves with a guarantee that their jobs would be held, they not only gained security but their lifetime earnings were higher. However, if a leaves system was too generous, their mobility was inevitably reduced. They were less likely to rise through the ranks, and fewer women worked in better-paid, traditionally male occupations.

Summarizing her findings, Stoiber concluded that "protected leave periods in Germany and Sweden are excessive and place too great a burden on employers. Quite predictably, employers respond by reducing their exposure—which in effect means reducing employment opportunities for women." However, she also concluded that the family leave bill being considered by the U.S. Congress was so modest that it would do employers no damage and was unlikely to harm women's job opportunities. On the basis of the European experience, she believed that most businesses could hold positions open for employees for four to six months with no ill effects.

That still left the question about whether businesses would be reluctant to hire women because they were more likely than men to take family leave. There were ways to get around that. For example, the law might mandate three months of parental leave per parent, per child—in other words, each parent could have three months to stay home with a child, for a total of six months per couple, and the leave couldn't be transferred between the parents. In 1983, the European Parliament recommended such a law in a draft of a directive to the nations of the EEC (European Economic Community). The directive was blocked by the United Kingdom.

A leaves system such as the one the European Parliament recommended would limit a couple's choices. If one spouse couldn't take time off to care for the baby, and the other longed for six months at home, they'd be forced to settle for three months all the same, while parents with more flexibility were getting six. Were such limits a good idea? That depended on whether one's ultimate goal was freedom of choice for individuals in the short run, or a change in sex roles that in the long run would allow women the kind of career choices men took for granted.

In 1990, Congress passed the feminist-backed family leave bill, but it died when President Bush vetoed it (see chapter 20). However, the battle was far from over. Activists immediately began urging state legislatures to pass similar legislation.

THE MOMMY-TRACK CONTROVERSY

The controversy over special treatment for mothers in the work place came up in another context in the late 1980s, centered on the notion of a "Mommy track." In 1989, the *Harvard Business Review* published an article by Felice N. Schwartz, president and founder of Catalyst, an organization that had been working with corporations since 1962 on issues concerning women. Schwartz proposed that corporations distinguish between two types of women, those who were career-primary and the career-and-family sort. The first group never married, she said, or chose not to have children, or were satisfied to have their children raised by someone else. They would play by men's rules and deserved an open road to the top. Most women, however, wanted to spend more time with their children, and "are willing to trade some career growth and compensation for freedom from the constant pressure to work long hours and weekends." For this group, Schwartz advised businesses to build in flexibility: to permit the women to take a long parental leave or to come back to work part-time.

Feminists leapt to attention, because clearly Felice Schwartz was suggesting that corporations institutionalize the so-called "Mommy track." Though she never used the term, a few months before her article was published, the *New York Times* had reported that some law firms had informally established a special "track" for mothers, assigning them less demanding work. The catch was that they would never make partner. Many feminists were sure businesses would use the concept of a Mommy track as an excuse to keep women out of top positions. Why couldn't Schwartz have spoken of a "parent track," they demanded—of the need to offer concessions to fathers as well as mothers?

Once again, equality feminists felt the best—and most practical —approach was gender-neutral. Lynn Hecht Schafran, for example, noted that lawyers notoriously worked long hours and had a high divorce rate. The men, too, were concerned about the toll on their families, and many hoped that, as more women entered the profession, its demands would lessen. So far that hadn't been true.

"The model of the American work place," Schafran said, "is that the employer owns the man. It is free to set his hours, move him and his family to any location at any time, and demand that its interests be his highest, if not only, priority." If businesses made concessions to mothers but not to fathers, that was apt to cost women their job mobility. Schafran felt it was important for employers to make changes for women and men at the same time.

EQUAL TREATMENT VERSUS SPECIAL TREATMENT

During the late 1970s, the feminist divide surfaced once again within the women's movement as activists debated whether women needed to be treated exactly the same way men were or whether in some circumstances they needed different—special— treatment. The question kept cropping up in different contexts, but the controversy was particularly intense where family issues were concerned. The equality-difference debate occurred on at least two levels: It was argued in terms of ultimate goals and strategic choices. What kind of world did feminists want? And what were the best strategies for achieving it? The feminist divide sometimes turned up as a fissure in the thinking of particular women who leaned one way on goals and the other on strategy. They might long for a world that reflected women's values—one that made it easier for parents to raise children, for example— and yet believe that demanding equal treatment for women was the best way to get there. Sometimes, too, women crossed the divide from one issue to the next: They might argue for different treatment in one situation and for strict equality in another— illustrating Carol Gilligan's point that most women looked for justice within a particular context, rather than in abstract princi- ples.

The debate over strategy—over equal versus special treatment —was difficult and divisive. Those on the difference side of the divide were convinced it was a mistake to treat women just like men when there were real differences between the sexes—when only women bore children and mothers still did most of the child care. They argued that gender-neutral laws often weren't at all neutral in their outcome, because they treated women and men alike on the assumption that both had the same opportunities when, in fact, men started out with distinct advantages. For in- stance, divorcing husbands and wives were seldom on an equal footing in their ability to support themselves, especially if the wife had shouldered most or all of the responsibility for raising their children.

Another problem with the equality approach, said the difference feminists, was that it condemned women to playing by men's rules. Universities, businesses, government, the justice system—all dominated by men—operated according to rules and standards that developed to fit males, and no one seemed inclined to adapt them to fit females.

On the other side of the divide, equality feminists were convinced that it was dangerous for women to ask for special treatment, especially on reproductive grounds. They pointed out that men used women's maternal role and feminine "nature" for centuries to justify keeping females in their place, and that the laws that supposedly benefited women almost always worked to their ultimate disadvantage, as California's maternity leave legislation did.

Some activists maintained that in any case the basic equality approach—the commitment to treat women and men alike—often wasn't to blame when gender-neutral laws hurt women. For example, Lynn Hecht Schafran argued that in divorce cases the real problem was that the courts failed to distinguish between mechanical equality and realistic equality. It was mere mechanical equality to split a couple's property in half and call it equal treatment even if the wife had been out of the work force for years.

In the opening stages of the second wave, most feminists had argued that the law must treat women and men alike. That was the obvious strategy in the 1960s, because most of the laws that treated women differently did put them at a disadvantage. In addition, in demanding equality, feminists were building on the successes of the civil rights movement. Blacks had initially focused on the Constitution's guarantees of equal rights in order to end laws and customs that treated blacks and whites differently. The courts had invalidated some of those laws, and Congress was prepared to ban racial discrimination in certain contexts. Feminists seized their opportunity and demanded laws against sex discrimination that were often simply amendments to legislation that prohibited other kinds of discrimination and required that everyone be treated alike.

However, even if there had never been a civil rights movement, 1960s feminists would probably have pursued change in the shape of equal rights. Belief in equality was deeply ingrained in the American tradition. That made it both the strategy most likely to succeed and the one most likely to be used.

The trouble with debating strategy in terms of equality/difference was that both sides were right: Women seemed to lose either way. When the laws treated women and men differently, it was generally to women's disadvantage. Under feminist pressure, most statutes were rewritten to be gender-neutral, and though women gained in some ways, they lost in others.

Americans tended to believe they could solve almost any problem by throwing legislation at it; unfortunately, many problems weren't that simple. State legislatures could decree that divorcing husbands and wives must be treated equally, for example, but that left a conservative, mostly male judiciary to define "equal." The problem wasn't so much gender-neutral laws as the fact that male domination was so deeply embedded in the system. Ultimately, women really needed to have it both ways: They had to achieve the same rights as men without completely plowing under their needs—and identity—as women.

Why were family issues so hard to resolve in the United States? The ultimate explanation may lie in the American tradition of extreme individualism, which undercut the commitment to the community, to the common good, and even to the family. Europeans not only had a stronger sense of community, but preferred a life-style that was less single-mindedly work-oriented. Noting that Americans had always put a priority on high disposable income rather than on time off, Stoiber remarked that "when family time becomes really important to us, we'll get it."

The family issues fitted together like the pieces of an interlocking puzzle:

- With an adequate leave system, more mothers could retain their jobs and divorce would be less devastating.
- If good, affordable child care were available, shorter leaves might suffice in most cases.
- If the United States did a better job of supporting the family —with benefits like child care and parental leave—divorce might not be so common.

chapter 15

Violence Against Women

⟶

*U*ntil the 1970s, most Americans assumed that rape, incest, and wife-beating rarely happened. The women's movement revealed that they were common occurrences.

The statistics were chilling. An American woman stood one chance in three of being sexually abused before the age of eighteen—usually by a relative or friend of the family. When she reached college age, the chances were one in five that she'd be raped on a date. Nine female employees out of ten had been sexually harassed on the job. Every year, about 7 percent of American women were kicked, punched, or choked by the man they lived with; some were beaten repeatedly.*

Most people assumed that rapists and men who beat their wives were simply sick individuals. However, feminists saw vio-

---

* Estimates of how many women are battered vary with the way ''battering'' is defined. According to researcher Murray A. Straus, if it includes slapping with an open hand, almost two thirds of American couples, married or cohabitating, report at least one incident of battering during their life together. If slapping is left out and battering is defined instead as assaults more likely to cause injury—punching, kicking, and choking —then in any given year about 7 percent of American women are victims.

lence against women as an ancient evil, long tolerated by societies that treated women as the property of their husbands or fathers. Though legally women were no longer property, some men still felt that they were. Others believed that males were helpless to resist their own sexual urges and that women who tempted them deserved to be raped. The tendency to blame the victim was one of the unifying threads that connected the violence issues.

Beginning in the early 1970s, feminists established rape crisis centers and shelters for battered women and lobbied for changes in the laws that would make it less difficult to prosecute rapists and batterers. Efforts had to be mounted community by community and state by state, because most laws on rape and battery were passed at the state, not the federal, level. The women who became involved developed their own specialized networks, and those networks grew to be social movements in their own right —the antirape and the battered women's movements. Activists also worked on the issues of sexual harassment, incest, and prostitution, and in the late 1970s an antipornography movement coalesced. During the 1980s, feminists split over pornography, as some women campaigned for legislation to put a damper on porn while others opposed them.

For most Americans, including many feminists, the violence issues were disturbing. They revealed women at their most vulnerable and men at their worst.

MAN AND WIFE: WOMAN AS PROPERTY

Throughout recorded history in most cultures, females were legally the property of their father until marriage and afterward they were the property of their husband. This fact was reflected in the rape laws. Among the ancient Hebrews, for example, if an unmarried virgin was raped, her attacker was required to marry her and pay her father fifty silver shekels as compensation for her bride price. In England in the Middle Ages, rape was taken seriously only if the victim was young, a virgin, and came from a family with property. It wasn't until the end of the thirteenth century that the law recognized rape as a crime against public order in the same sense that robbery and murder were crimes.

Because a wife was a man's property, most people believed he had a right to beat her if she misbehaved, provided he didn't do her serious injury. In the United States in 1824, a North Carolina court acquitted a man who had whipped his wife because the switch he used was no thicker than his thumb—a limit commonly accepted in those days. It wasn't until 1871 that two states made wife-beating illegal for the first time. Even then, except in cases of extreme cruelty, when battered wives went to court they got little satisfaction; judges maintained that the government shouldn't trespass on the privacy of the family.

RAPE: THE UNMENTIONABLE CRIME

Rape became an issue for feminists in 1971. Susan Brownmiller, who later wrote *Against Our Will*, a feminist classic on rape, recalled that one evening someone in her NYRF (New York Radical Feminists) consciousness-raising group brought in a feminist newspaper that had a first-person account, written by a woman who had been gang-raped. "We read this and then in our usual fashion went around the room and started to talk," said Brownmiller, "and two of the women in the room had been raped." At first, Brownmiller didn't see it as a feminist issue; it was simply the victim's misfortune—like being mugged. Nevertheless, by the end of the evening someone had proposed a speakout and Brownmiller suggested a conference. In the months that followed, other NYRF consciousness-raising groups also discussed rape. Feminists gradually realized that the crime was quite common. "You'd get a group of seven and out of that group, maybe two, maybe three, had been raped," said Noreen Connell.

Most Americans would have said that they didn't know anyone who had been sexually assaulted. Women who had been raped were reluctant to talk about it, and most never even reported it. Experts estimated that only one out of every five rape victims went to the police, or perhaps only one out of twenty—nobody really knew.

The NYRF speakout on rape was held on a Sunday in January 1971. Three hundred women crowded into a small church in midtown Manhattan to share their experiences or simply to hear what others had to say. There were students in jeans, mothers carrying babies, older women who came out of taxis elbow-first, according to journalist Gail Sheehy, with "that special elbow action which tells you this is a woman accustomed to being handled by doormen like a precious egg."

Forty women actually spoke that Sunday, and they told chilling stories about being raped. Often, they had been terrified, certain they were going to be killed. Most had no idea how to defend themselves—they'd never been taught. And the way they were treated afterward by the justice system in many cases amounted to a second, psychological rape. The police were often indifferent or didn't believe the woman, especially if the man wasn't a total stranger. If she was older or unattractive, they sometimes implied that she was sex-starved and that her story was wishful thinking. Then again, some forced the victim to describe the attack in such minute detail that it was clear they were enjoying themselves.

Biased Rape Laws

The NYRF conference on rape, held in April 1971, included another speak out and papers based on research. Participants learned that rape laws all over the country were biased in favor of rapists and that New York's laws were among the worst. Before a rapist could be convicted in New York, the prosecution had to provide independent corroboration on three points: that penetration had occurred, that the woman didn't consent to intercourse, and on the identity of the rapist. If the man didn't ejaculate—and many rapists couldn't—and the woman wasn't a virgin, she couldn't corroborate penetration. If she was threatened with a knife or gun and therefore didn't put up a fight, without bruises or torn clothing to show, she couldn't corroborate the fact that she wasn't willing to have intercourse. And because there were no witnesses to most rapes, usually she was the only one who could identify the man.

There was no other crime for which the state required similar corroboration, not even murder. In cases of assault, when one person attacked another and there was no witness to the attack, the law assumed that the jury was capable of deciding who was telling the truth, and that the accused was adequately protected by a system that held that guilt must be proven beyond a reasonable doubt.

The impact of New York's corroboration law was reflected in these New York City statistics: In 1971, there were 2415 rape complaints that the police considered "founded" and worth pursuing; they made 1085 arrests; 100 cases were held to be solid enough to present to the grand jury; the grand jury subsequently handed down 34 indictments. In the end, there were 18 convictions—less than 1 percent of all the complaints.

In the early 1970s, fifteen states had laws that required some form of corroboration in rape cases. In a few others, the law didn't require it, but the courts had decreed that it was necessary.

Even where corroboration wasn't required by law or by the courts, women found that without it the police and the district attorney didn't believe them, nor did the jury if the case went to trial.

There was no question that juries tended to favor the accused in rape cases. Two law professors who analyzed 106 rape trials observed that jurors "weighed the conduct of the victim in judging the guilt of the defendant." The usual defense in a rape trial was to admit that there had been intercourse but to maintain that the woman was willing. Then the defense attorney would set out to discredit her, knowing that the jury was unlikely to convict if he could show that she'd been promiscuous in the past, had allowed herself to be picked up, had been drinking—or if she'd been raped while out on a date.

Myths about rape helped to shape both laws and jurors' attitudes. The most damaging myth was the notion that women often tried to get revenge on men by falsely accusing them of rape. The fear of being falsely accused was both widespread and ancient. During the seventeenth century, England's Lord Chief Justice, Matthew Hale, put it into language that was quoted for hundreds of years afterward by attorneys, judges, and legal scholars. Hale wrote, "Rape is an accusation easily to be made and hard to be proved, and harder to be defended by the party accused, tho never so innocent." Until the 1970s, it was standard procedure in the United States for judges to read the so-called "Lord Hale Instruction" to juries considering rape cases.

Because men feared false accusations, the law made it hard for a woman to prove she'd been raped. However, it was unlikely that women often falsely accused men—most rapes weren't even reported. Male anxiety about trumped-up charges probably represented the collective nightmare of all the men who ever used "a little force" to overcome a woman's objections.

There were other myths as well. Many people believed that males had an almost irresistible sex drive and couldn't be blamed if sometimes it got out of hand; and that, if a woman was provocative in dress or behavior, she was asking for rape and deserved what she got. Another myth held that females secretly enjoyed being raped, that they were naturally masochistic, as Freud suggested. Then again, some people were convinced that it was impossible to rape a woman who really struggled; hence, the old saw, "You can't thread a moving needle." Feminists, exploring the rape issue in the 1970s, quickly understood that the rape myths served male interests because they excused men and placed the blame on women.

African-American Women and Rape

After Susan Brownmiller's book on rape was published in 1975, black women began to speak out about the ways in which their experience with rape had been different. Some were angry at white feminists for ignoring the differences.

In the days of slavery, many white men didn't consider it rape when they assaulted black women. Feminist scholar Bell Hooks wrote that at the time, southern white women were held to be too pure to have sexual feelings, and black women were conveniently seen as "the embodiment of female evil and sexual lust." When white husbands raped their slaves, white wives often blamed the women for enticing them. Hooks noted that "contemporary sexist scholars . . . argue that white men used the rape of black women to further emasculate black men." She pointed out that this interpretation belittled the effect that being raped had on black women.

Many people saw a woman who had been raped as damaged goods, and Hooks maintained that in a somewhat similar way, black women were devalued because of the way they were sexually exploited during slavery. That attitude "has not altered in the course of hundreds of years. . . ," she wrote. "One has only to look at American television . . . to learn the way in which black women are perceived in American society—the predominant image is that of the 'fallen' woman, the whore, the slut, the prostitute."

The rape issue worried the black community for other reasons as well. In the South, black males had often been falsely accused of raping white women and had been tried and executed or simply lynched. Some blacks were concerned that the changes in the rape laws that feminists were demanding, to make it easier to convict rapists, would leave black men even more vulnerable than they already were.

Rape Crisis Centers and Political Action

The rape issue struck a nerve in many women. Whether or not they had ever been sexually assaulted, they'd been taught to fear it. Some believed, with Susan Brownmiller, that rape was "a conscious process of intimidation by which *all men* keep *all women* in a state of fear."

During the early 1970s, feminists in various cities began to set up rape crisis centers. Most operated as collectives and maintained a hotline, so that a woman who had been raped could telephone and get advice, and perhaps find someone to accompany her to the hospital and the police station. Some centers also sponsored self-help groups for women who had been raped in the past and had never managed to put the incident behind them; some offered classes in self-defense; others got involved in the struggle to change state laws.

The feminist actions that focused on rape were a model of the women's movement at its most effective. Radical feminists raised the issue, and women's rights and socialist feminists joined them in challenging rape laws. In the midseventies, under pressure from women, almost all states rewrote their rape laws, doing away with corroboration and changing the rules of evidence so that defense lawyers were no longer permitted to bring up a woman's past sexual history in a rape trial. In the process, the laws were made gender-neutral: Now they also covered cases where men raped men, or the rare instances where a woman raped a man.

The antirape movement made other gains as well. Some cities set up sex crimes units, staffed by women police officers, to handle sexual assault cases. Police departments began turning to feminists for help in dealing with rape victims and so did some hospitals. In the past, hospitals had been insensitive at times in the way they handled women who had been raped. A Chicago doctor recalled medics who would yell across the emergency room, "I got a rape for ya, Charlie."

In the middle 1970s, the Justice Department and other federal agencies began to fund antirape projects. Though many rape crisis centers were struggling to survive financially, much of the money went to the criminal justice bureaucracy instead, or to universities to do research and produce reviews of the literature. When crisis centers did receive grants, there were apt to be strings attached: The women were told they couldn't provide services for victims who decided not to bring charges against the rapist, for example. Antirape collectives found that to get funds they had to establish a hierarchy and hire mental health professionals. By 1976, there were 1500 antirape projects in the United

States, and only about 400 of them were autonomous, feminist, rape crisis centers.

Two Steps Forward, One Step Back

Though all over the country the rape laws were rewritten, the justice system itself didn't change nearly enough. Whether the courts handled a rape case well or badly now depended almost entirely on the kind of rape involved. Violent rape by strangers was more successfully prosecuted than many other violent crimes, but "simple" rapes (sometimes called "date rapes" or "acquaintance rapes") were often not prosecuted at all, and juries still failed to convict.

Most rapes were simple rapes—by one estimate, 82 percent. Many people believed that rape was less traumatic for a woman if her attacker was someone she knew, but in fact it could be more traumatic. Assaulted unexpectedly by a man she trusted who had suddenly turned brutal and threatening, the woman was often terrified that she'd be hurt or even killed, and of course she could become pregnant. Afterward, she found it difficult to trust any man again. If she brought charges, the police and the prosecutor's office were apt to suggest that she led the man on. Even if they believed her story, they might advise her not to press charges. Some prosecutors claimed it was a waste of the state's money to try a simple rape, because a jury was unlikely to convict. If the case did go to trial, the defense was certain to argue that she had sex with the rapist willingly, and though state law might prohibit asking questions about her sexual history, the defense attorney would ask them anyway, attempting to discredit her. The judge would tell the jury to disregard such questions, but they made an impression.

In addition, though many states no longer required proof that the woman resisted sex, they did require evidence that the man used force, and that wasn't much of an improvement in the law. Juries didn't seem to understand that it took a lot less force to overcome the average woman than it did to pin down the average man. Rape was different from other types of assault not only because the man was virtually always bigger and stronger than the woman, but because most women had no experience in defending themselves.

During the 1980s, many Americans began to realize that rape —including gang rape—was a serious problem on college campuses. Studies showed that many men believed there was nothing wrong with using a little force to get sex; they didn't see that as rape. Many young women weren't sure they had a right to say no. As more rapes were reported, a growing number of colleges set up special programs for students to deal with the rape issue.

Wife Rape

If a woman raped by her date had little chance of justice, a wife raped by her husband had even less. Until the late 1970s, there were few states in which marital rape was against the law. Most defined rape as "the forcible penetration of the body of a woman *not the wife of the perpetrator,*" which meant it was legally impossible for a man to rape his own wife. For a long time, state legislators resisted feminist efforts to make wife rape a crime. Most were married men, and some probably shared the sentiments of the California state senator who asked "But if you can't rape your wife, who can you rape?"

In 1977, Oregon became one of the first states to drop the marital exemption for rape. In 1978, John Rideout was indicted for rape under the new law, and the case made headlines around the country. His wife, Greta, testified that he had forced her to have sex two or three times a day; that once a week he wanted violent sex; that he often hit and kicked her.* She left him three times and returned each time because she couldn't support herself and her infant daughter either on welfare or on what she could earn. In October 1978, Rideout demanded sex and when his wife refused, beat her into submission. Afterward, she went to the police and charged him with rape.

In December, a jury acquitted Rideout. Two weeks later, newspapers reported the couple's reconciliation. Apparently, Rideout convinced his wife that he'd learned his lesson. For most Americans, the story ended there because the press lost interest after that. Actually, less than three months later, the Rideouts separated for good. The following summer, John Rideout was charged with breaking into his ex-wife's home and received a suspended sentence; he was eventually jailed for harassing her.

Press reports on the Rideout case were often highly critical of Greta Rideout and of the law that made it possible for her to charge her husband with rape. Nevertheless, the publicity helped

---

* Though wife rape and battering often went together, some women who were never battered were repeatedly raped.

the efforts to reform rape laws in other states, perhaps because the details of the case showed how terrifying marital rape could be. Research suggested that though it was less traumatic than stranger rape, it was much worse than being assaulted by an acquaintance or a date, probably because it was so much more likely to be repeated.

Changes in the laws on wife rape were extremely slow in coming. By 1991, however, there were only four states left where it was still perfectly legal for a man to rape his wife. In twenty-nine others, it was a crime but was treated differently from other types of rape—the penalty was less or it was legal in certain circumstances, for example. In seventeen states, a rape was a rape, whether the man and woman were married or not.

Feminists also had to fight for the repeal of laws that in some states had extended the marital rape exemption to cover other situations. According to the National Clearinghouse on Marital and Date Rape, which spearheaded the drive for change, in 1980 there were thirteen states in which a man couldn't be charged with raping a woman if they were living together, even if they weren't married. By 1991, only five states still had such statutes. However, in Delaware—one of the five—the law also prescribed a lesser penalty for rape if the woman had simply been the man's "voluntary social companion" at the time.

When states changed their laws on rape in marriage, they generally avoided the term "wife rape," and spoke instead of "marital" or "spousal" rape. Feminists agreed that men should be protected from sexual assault, and gender-neutral terminology was probably necessary to conform to equal rights laws and state ERAs. Nevertheless, talk of "spousal rape" conveniently neutered the issue, obscuring the fact that it was almost always women who were assaulted.

INCEST

In the 1970s, as the antirape movement made it easier for women to admit that they'd been raped, incest victims began to come forward. Americans reluctantly realized that incest happened much more often than anyone had thought and that it devastated children. Feminist therapists in Boston, working with women so disturbed that they were hospitalized, found that many of them had been traumatized by incest. Some had developed multiple personalities or had found other ways to dissociate from the experience—to send their minds away whenever they were raped. Most blamed themselves for what happened and believed that they were abused because they were fundamentally bad. That was less threatening than believing that a parent was evil, and it gave them some hope of control: If they could just change themselves, the assaults would stop. Research indicated that many women who became prostitutes had been sexually abused as children.

In the 1980s in many places, the justice system failed women who were trying to protect their children from sexual abuse. Incest was regarded with such horror that when a wife reported that her husband was abusing their child, she often found that the authorities weren't willing to believe her, especially if the man was middle or upper class. The situation was especially difficult in divorce cases. If the wife charged incest and had no proof, the judge was apt to give the father custody to punish her for her supposedly vindictive behavior. Even if she won custody, the husband was almost never denied visitation rights.

In one case that caught the attention of the press, Dr. Elizabeth Morgan, a plastic surgeon, argued in court that her former husband mustn't be allowed to spend time alone with their daughter, Hilary, because he had been sexually abusing the child. Though thirteen out of sixteen experts who testified in the case said they'd found evidence of abuse, Judge Herbert Dixon ordered Morgan to turn the five-year-old over to her father for a two-week visit. Instead, Morgan hid her. In August 1987, Dixon sent Morgan to jail, vowing that she'd stay there until she revealed where Hilary was. Morgan stubbornly remained in jail for more than two years; she was finally released after Congress passed a bill that forced the judge either to free her or put her on trial. Five months later, Hilary's father located the child and her grandparents, living in New Zealand, and went to court there to get her back. In December 1990, the New Zealand court awarded custody to Elizabeth Morgan instead.

The Underground Railroad

By the late 1980s, there had been many similar cases in which courts refused to believe mothers. As a result, a kind of underground railroad sprang up to hide women and children. Hundreds found refuge in a secret network of private homes or else moved quietly from one battered women's shelter to the next, staying only a few days in each, because local police regularly checked the shelters for missing persons. Groups were organized with outposts in about half the states to provide the fugitives with money, advice, contacts, and sometimes with fake identification.

THE BATTERED WOMEN'S MOVEMENT

In the early 1970s, as women's centers and rape crisis centers were established in many communities, calls from battered women began to flood in. Feminists discovered that, like rape, wife-beating was distressingly common.

At the time, there were no shelters for battered women, and a woman who was beaten by her husband often had no place to go. She couldn't hide indefinitely with friends or family and might not be able to earn enough to support herself and her children. In some places, battered women who applied for welfare were turned down on the grounds that their husband's income made them ineligible. When women *were* able to get welfare benefits, the first check didn't arrive for weeks.

The police, reluctant to arrest batterers, claimed they didn't want to interfere in a family squabble. In many places, it was official police policy to discourage women from filing a complaint, and if they filed anyway, nothing was done, for district attorneys weren't eager to prosecute.* If a woman went to court and got a protective order that required her husband to stay away from her, the police often failed to enforce it. Sometimes the man threatened her and she reported it, only to be told that nothing could be done until he actually attacked her.

"Why Doesn't She Just Leave?"

From the beginning, the question that was a hurdle for the battered women's movement was: Why did women stay when they were being beaten? Over the years, police and prosecutors often excused their own failure to act by pointing out that battered women frequently refused to press charges. In the middle seventies, as shelters began to open around the country, feminists themselves discovered that many of the women who took refuge in a shelter returned to their tormentor just a few days or weeks later.

---

* In Washington, D.C., during 1966, 7500 women charged their husbands with beating them; the city issued only 200 arrest warrants.

Researchers have found that women stay in violent relationships for a number of reasons. Most often, they simply can't
support themselves and their children. However, some are afraid
to leave because the man has threatened to kill them if they do—
and the danger is real. Others stay because they have traditional
ideas about the wife's role and feel that if their marriage is failing,
it must be their fault. Batterers generally tell their victim that they
only beat her because of things she has done wrong. However,
when a woman is beaten, it's often for resisting the man's demands.

Some women stay because they hope the man will change. He
may be overcome with remorse after each assault, may break
down and cry and promise that it will never happen again. Other
women hesitate to seek help because they're sure no one will
believe the man is violent—batterers are often likable, popular
members of the community.

Wife-beating is typically accompanied by psychological abuse
that destroys the individual's self-confidence. In addition, the
batterer usually sets out to isolate his woman from family and
friends; he also threatens even worse beatings if she tells anyone
about his violence. When friends do know or guess what is going
on, sometimes the woman begins to avoid them because she can't
bear to see herself through their eyes: to feel their pity or to know
that they are judging her at a time when she either is choosing
not to get out of the relationship or is so demoralized she is no
longer capable of making choices.

"Leaving is a process," said Barbara Hart, staff attorney for the
Pennsylvania Coalition Against Domestic Violence. Most women
return to their batterer several times before they separate from
him permanently. The first time, a woman may simply hope that
if she leaves, the man will finally get psychological help. The
second time, she may be testing, trying to learn what resources
would be available to her if she left. She may return to the man
resolved to find a job or to continue her education so that she'll
be in a better situation if she's forced to leave again. Most battered
women do eventually leave for good.

The First Shelters

Internationally, the battered women's movement surfaced first
in London in 1971, when a group of women opened a shelter. In
the United States, the movement got under way not long afterward in St. Paul, Minnesota. A feminist collective there had set

up a legal-advice hotline and received so many calls from battered women who had no place to go that some members began to take women and children into their own homes. It took the group until October 1974 to raise enough money to buy a house and refurbish it as a shelter; the minute it opened it was filled to capacity. By that time, several shelters had been established in other parts of the country as well. In some places, local NOW chapters took on battering as an issue; in others, shelters were started by social workers or by women who had once been battered themselves. Some didn't consider themselves feminists.

As the new movement attracted media coverage, it grew rapidly. The women involved soon began to form statewide coalitions, driven by the need to change state laws. A national network linking the groups, the National Coalition Against Domestic Violence (NCADV), was founded in 1978.

During the late 1970s, shelters began to receive funds from state and federal sources, and the money turned out to be a mixed blessing, just as it was for the rape crisis programs. Shelters were expensive to run, and battered women needed the services. On the other hand, feminists believed it was important to identify battering as a by-product of male domination and the macho mentality, and those ideas weren't popular with funders.

As money became available, nonfeminist social workers and other professionals began to compete for grants and for the control of some shelters. Feminist collectives, committed to operating without a hierarchy, found that to get funding they had to appoint a professionally trained administrator and a board of directors, and to hire social workers rather than grass-roots activists. Some of the new administrators and directors then insisted that the issue of sexism shouldn't be confused with the problem of "family violence." During battles for control at a few shelters, feminists were accused of being lesbians; some of those who were accused were gay and some weren't. Lesbians had been active in the battered women's movement since the beginning. As one woman said, they "were able to look at violence . . . and not freak out about its meaning for their relationships with men."

Shelters run by nonfeminists sometimes became like any other social work agency—the emphasis was entirely on providing services. Feminists had always felt that a shelter should do more: It must somehow empower battered women, help them feel they were part of the feminist struggle and of a community of women who could help each other. That way, when they left, they'd be strong enough not to return to the batterer. If, during their time in the shelter, everything was done *for* them, they wouldn't have a chance to learn that they were resilient human beings who could control their own lives.

Despite the problems that came with funding, the money was necessary, and so feminists were pleased when the Carter administration introduced a bill that would have funded shelters, research, and a federal agency concerned with family violence. However, right-wingers vehemently opposed the bill, and during the summer of 1980, they organized a drive to defeat it. Some conservatives claimed that the bill would prevent them from spanking their children; others argued that shelters would only accept women if they promised to divorce their husbands, and that they were staffed by feminist missionaries poised to attack traditional family values. In the end, a Senate filibuster killed the bill, and after 1980 it became a dead issue as the Reagan administration cut deeply into the limited funds that had previously been available.

For activists in the battered women's movement, the early 1980s were a gloomy period. They had created shelters and reformed the laws, but the police response and court procedures had changed very little, and federal funds had been cut. In addition, in some places the women's community was preoccupied with the need to defend abortion in the state legislature. "Politically, it felt as if we were at a standstill," said Susan Kelly-Dreiss, executive director of the Pennsylvania Coalition Against Domestic Violence.

In 1984, the stalemate ended. Over the objections of the Reagan administration, Congress passed the Family Violence Prevention and Services Act, which provided funds for shelters and family violence programs. That year, there had been a flurry of interest in the problems of crime victims. To finance services for them, Congress created an ingenious mechanism: Fines were collected from people convicted of federal crimes, and the money was combined with forfeitures and funneled into a victims' fund. Some of that money went to shelters. A few states also began to fund family violence programs through similar systems of fines, while others added a surcharge to their marriage license fee. The money came in automatically, which meant that activists didn't have to campaign anew for funding year after year.

According to Barbara Hart, the Reagan administration was actually helpful in some ways because it took a hard line on crime, including domestic violence. Feminists had been saying for years that batterers should be evicted and had pressed for this change.

Finally, even conservative Phyllis Schlafly supported the idea that battered women shouldn't have to leave their homes. Presumably, like most right-wingers, she didn't want them in shelters where they might be influenced by feminists. At any rate, the Reagan administration ruled that to qualify for federal funds under the 1984 bill, states must permit eviction of the batterer. Of course, evicting him also cost less than maintaining the woman and children in a shelter.

The Good News and the Bad

By 1991, there were approximately 1600 battered women's programs around the country—shelters, individual "safe" homes that would take in families, hotlines, and advocacy projects. Overall, the police were more likely to arrest batterers, partly because of pressure from activists, but also because they were afraid of being sued. In a few places, women had won huge settlements when they took the local police department to court for failing to protect them. Battered women also had easier access to protective orders. In almost every state, a woman could now get a court order requiring her husband to move out of their home, to stay away from her, to enter treatment, to pay child support, or some combination of these things.

That was the positive side of the picture. On the negative side, women still had trouble finding help. For lack of space, shelters were forced to turn away 40 percent of the women who contacted them. Protective orders were still poorly enforced, and, thanks to court backlogs, cases were often postponed for months. Judges were reluctant to put batterers in jail because of prison overcrowding.

In addition, some well-intended changes in the judicial system had turned out to be dangerous. In more and more states, a prosecutor could bring a batterer to trial even if the victim was unwilling to press charges. The theory was that if the woman had no control over the decision to prosecute, the man was less likely to blame her and abuse her further. (Such laws also meant that the district attorney's office didn't have to cope with women who changed their minds.) However, the woman herself generally had the best sense of what was dangerous. Though for most, safety lay in leaving the man, for some the opposite was true. Batterers were most likely to kill *after* the woman had left them. When a woman refused to testify against her batterer, sometimes the district attorney, attempting to coerce her, had her arrested for filing a false police report, or put her on the stand knowing that, for fear of retaliation, she'd perjure herself and deny that she was beaten. Some women were then arrested and jailed for perjury. Whether she went to jail or not, an arrest record could someday cost the woman custody of her children.

Like reform laws on rape, the new laws on battering were sex neutral and spoke of "domestic violence" or "spouse abuse." The battered women's movement originally substituted "domestic violence" for "wife-beating" because it wasn't only wives who were beaten; women who lived with violent men or simply dated them were battered as well. Legislators were also more responsive when the issue was framed as domestic or family violence rather than as wife-beating. Unfortunately, the sex-neutral terms again obscured the nature of the violence, just as talk of "marital rape" hid the reality of wife rape.

Sociologist Diana Russell noted that when she began doing research on rape in 1971, she was astounded at how often she was asked, especially by men, why she wasn't studying the rape of men. When she turned her attention to battered wives, there were a lot of questions about battered husbands. Some people began to say that husband-beating was widespread and comparable to the problem of battered wives. In fact, husband-beating was rare; in cases of "spouse abuse," the batterer was the man 95 percent of the time.

During the 1980s, counseling programs for batterers proliferated. Typically, court proceedings were suspended if the batterer agreed to counseling, and charges might be dropped if he completed the treatment. According to Barbara Hart, women often expected much too much of the treatment programs. Because they assumed the man would make a good-faith effort to change, they returned to him as soon as he entered the program, rather than insisting that he complete it and change his behavior before they'd consider a reconciliation.

How often did treatment actually cure batterers? Reliable estimates were hard to come by, but battered-women's advocates agreed that it helped only a very small percentage of batterers. Though most men refrained from physical violence as long as they were in counseling, very few gave up verbally abusing the woman, and what they did after they finished the program depended primarily on local police policy. In a few places, where the man knew that if he assaulted his wife again he'd definitely go to jail, the beatings might never resume, but the woman's life could still be miserable.

"There are a variety of batterers," Hart explained, "and while some are clearly homicidal, the substantial majority are not intentional killers." They beat their wives not because they can't control their anger, but to get their way. Their violence gives them absolute, tyrannical control over another human being. "If you don't care about intimacy and trust," said Hart, "it's very nice on some level to have your every need anticipated and met, to know that nobody will voice an objection to anything you do.

"Every batterers' program that ever existed is a school for non-violent control," she continued. For most batterers, the desire to control others is almost irresistible. Thus, thrown into a group, the men learn from one another how to get their way without violence. One man might describe how he stalks his wife so that he knows her every move; another might tell how he clocks his woman when she goes to the store. If she is away too long, he flies into a rage—though he doesn't hit her—and seizes the excuse to slam out of the house and go drinking with his friends.*

Domestic violence isn't just physical assault, according to Hart. "It's the attempt to totally control the woman's life, so that she may not wear clothes he doesn't like, she may not attend church if he doesn't want her to. . . . It means she isn't allowed to make the independent decisions that any competent adult person should be able to make. And that usurpation of power is consolidated by violence. Some women are assaulted only once every two years; still, they're never free."

Battered Women and Self-Defense

Some battered women ultimately kill their tormentors. In fact, most women imprisoned for murder have killed their husbands, and in most cases the men were batterers. Typically, the woman had called the police any number of times and gotten little protection; yet when she struck out because she felt her life was in danger, she received a long sentence. Some judges claim that if they were more lenient, they'd be giving wives a license to kill.

By the 1990s, feminist attorneys in some states had persuaded the courts to accept testimony on the "battered woman syndrome" to help the judge and jury understand why battered women fear what they fear and act as they act when they take self-protective measures. Barbara Hart explained that it's critical

---

* Though drinking is often associated with battering, most researchers feel that it doen't cause the violence but is often used as an excuse for it. At any rate, usually the battering doesn't end if the man stops drinking.

for courts to recognize that women who have been terrorized by a man over a long period of time can't be judged by the usual self-defense standards, which are based on men's reactions. In self-defense cases, the law generally demands that the person who was attacked respond only with reasonable force and only if death or serious injury seem imminent. Unfortunately, judges and juries often seem to expect that a 130-pound woman facing a 200-pound man in a homicidal rage will behave the way a man might when faced with a mugger on the street. Feminists have pointed out that when a man comes at a woman without a weapon, intent on hitting and kicking her, she may legitimately fear for her life—many battered wives who are killed were beaten, choked, or kicked to death—and may reach for a weapon herself; or she may wait until he's off guard or even asleep to strike out at him to prevent him from trying to kill her later when she may not have the means to protect herself.

PROSTITUTION FROM THE FEMINIST PERSPECTIVE

Prostitution is often described as "the world's oldest profession"—implying that it's inevitable, given the nature of men and women. Myths about the happy hooker have a lot in common with the myths about women who enjoy being raped and wives who like to be beaten, though it took feminists longer to see the connection.

The first feminist conference on prostitution took place late in 1971. Sponsored by NYRF and other groups, it took an unexpected turn when a group of prostitutes showed up uninvited. Susan Brownmiller, one of the conference organizers, recalled that "there was an advance piece in the *Village Voice* and a lot of call girls and women working in the brothels came. Some of them had been organized by leftist women because at that time some of the Weather women were working in brothels to support the revolution.* They came to trash the conference. . . . They were screaming things at us, things like, '. . . you don't know how to make your men happy; that's why they go to us.' . . . They took the left line that all work is exploitative, and therefore to sell your

---

* When the SDS splintered, some members turned to real revolution and went underground. Hunted by the authorities, they were known as the Weather Underground.

body is no more exploitative than to sell your mind." Under the circumstances, there were a number of issues the conference failed to consider, but it raised the very basic question: Should it be illegal for men to buy women's bodies?

For a time, some feminists felt that in considering prostitution, it was necessary to distinguish between women who were forced into it and those who chose it. However, by the 1980s, many activists had concluded that prostitutes were usually driven into "the life" by a desperate need for money. In addition, studies indicated that many had been victims of incest or sexual abuse as children. Kathleen Barry, founder of the International Network Against Female Sexual Slavery, concluded that laws should punish pimps and clients, but not prostitutes, and that the government must provide training and job opportunities so that the women would have real choices. A UNESCO meeting held in Madrid in the mideighties incorporated Barry's recommendations into its report to the United Nations.

Feminists eventually organized around the issue of prostitution on a global scale—they had to, because the traffic in women crossed national boundaries. Thus in 1988 a conference held in New York City brought together women from all over the world. Speakers from South Korea and the Philippines described the thousands of prostitutes who lived in poverty and misery near American military bases in their countries, and the "sex tours" that brought in foreign men to use those women. The feminists wanted the bases gone and the sex tours ended. A speaker from Japan reported that thanks to a labor shortage, young women in her country could now get decent jobs, and few were becoming prostitutes. As a result, the Japanese sex industry was importing 100,000 women a year from the Philippines, Taiwan, and Thailand, where jobs were scarce. Often, the women came to Japan expecting to work as waitresses or models and were forced into prostitution. Some were only children.

A Norwegian woman described sex tours that took Norwegian males to the Far East, promising them passive Asian women as a relief from home-grown feminists. When the Norwegian Women's Front demonstrated at an airport to call attention to a sex tour destined for Thailand, the travel agency sued. Feminists from other countries, including Thai women, testified at the trial, and the Women's Front won. Meanwhile, Norwegian women were organizing other joint actions: On one occasion, a sex tour took off from an airport in Norway where women were demonstrating and landed in the Philippines to find local demonstrators waiting. By 1988, only one Norwegian travel agency was still in the sex-tour business.

PORNOGRAPHY

Radical feminist Robin Morgan once wrote that "pornography is the theory, and rape the practice," suggesting that porn was responsible for male violence against women. Many feminists don't agree—historian Alice Echols dubbed this "the domino theory of sexuality." Over the years, pornography has proved to be a divisive issue.

Until the 1970s, obscenity laws curbed pornography; they also prevented bookstores from selling such classics as James Joyce's *Ulysses*. The U.S. Supreme Court modified the legal definition of obscenity in 1973, and as a result literary works that included passages of explicit sex could no longer be banned. In addition, pornography proliferated. In the process, it became increasingly sadomasochistic, fusing eroticism with violence against women.

In 1976, San Francisco women became the first to organize to combat porn. A few years later, New York feminists founded Women Against Pornography and began leading tours of the porno outlets around Times Square so that women could see what they were really like. Meanwhile, activists in other cities snapped pictures of men entering porn shops and made up "Wanted" posters, which they pasted up all over town.

In 1983, two feminists invented a controversial legal strategy to curb pornography. When activist Andrea Dworkin and feminist attorney Catharine MacKinnon were invited by Minneapolis city officials to draft an antiporn ordinance, they conceived the idea of a law that would permit women harmed by porn to sue the makers and distributors for sex discrimination. During hearings on the proposed ordinance, many people testified about the damage done by pornography. Linda Marchiano, who starred as Linda Lovelace in the blue movie *Deep Throat*, revealed that she had been virtually a prisoner throughout the making of the film. Professionals who worked with sexually abused children explained that porn was almost always involved: Abusers used it to show the children what they wanted them to do. Psychologists described research which demonstrated that at least in the short run, after watching or reading violent porn, many men behaved more aggressively toward women.

The problem with any kind of legislation on pornography had always been the difficulty of defining what was obscene or pornographic. The Minneapolis ordinance defined pornography as "the sexually explicit subordination of women, graphically depicted, whether in pictures or in words." It then went on to list many specific examples. Something was pornographic if it presented women as objects or commodities; as enjoying pain, humiliation, or rape; if it showed them tied up, cut up, mutilated, bruised, or physically hurt; in positions of display, or penetrated by objects—and so on.

Under the law, a woman who had worked in pornography could sue for damages if she felt she'd been harmed. So could anyone who had pornography forced on her, or who could prove she was assaulted because a man used porn. Finally, any woman acting against the subordination of all women could file a complaint, but again she had to prove that the pornography in question had caused some injury.

The Minneapolis City Council passed the ordinance twice, but each time the mayor vetoed it, and there weren't enough votes on the Council to override the veto. In May 1984, the city of Indianapolis passed a similar law, and a federal court struck it down, ruling that it was an infringement on freedom of speech. The U.S. Supreme Court let the decision stand. Dworkin and MacKinnon tried again in several other cities, without success.

After Minneapolis, the ordinance was opposed in most places by a feminist group called FACT, the Feminist Anti-Censorship Task Force. In legal briefs, FACT argued that porn often provided erotic pleasure for women as well as for men, even when it involved images of women "in positions of display or penetrated by objects." The women of FACT suggested that antiporn feminists were confusing harmless fantasies of sexual violence with violent acts themselves. They believed that if an antiporn ordinance passed, those who published hard-core porn wouldn't be the only ones to suffer. As they saw it, the law's definition of pornography was so vague that local courts could interpret it as they saw fit, and they were unwilling to trust those courts to decide what kind of pornography was bad for women. They pointed out that the ordinance could be used against women writers, who were just beginning to deal explicitly with sexuality.

In the controversy over porn, many feminists were caught in the middle. Though they deplored the brand of porn that eroticized violence against women, they were afraid the attempt to curb it might undermine free speech. Throughout the 1980s and into the 1990s, right-wingers were very active all over the country, pressuring schools and public libraries to remove books—some of them feminist classics—from their shelves. Obviously, conservatives would use any legal opening to try to censor feminist writing. In addition, many women were convinced that banning hard core porn wouldn't accomplish much because a kind of eroticized violence permeated ordinary films, television, and advertising. An evening of TV subjected the viewer to a steady stream of images of women being beaten, raped, and killed; rape was the theme of one out of every eight Hollywood movies. In the mass media, the underlying message wasn't explicit, the way it was in hard-core porn, but that made it all the more insidious.

Many feminists, like Lynn Hecht Schafran, opposed both the ordinance and violent porn. Schafran pointed out that people couldn't buy magazines devoted to the torture of Jews or of blacks at their corner newsstand; why should the torture of women be different? However, her solution was to raise public awareness. She credited Dworkin and MacKinnon with having done that quite effectively.

THE FEMINIST DIVIDE, REVISITED

The battle over pornography resurrected the familiar arguments about equality and difference. On one side, equality feminists insisted that women were adults, not perennial victims, and when they made choices, they had to live with them. If a woman freely chose to pose for pornography, for example, she had to take the consequences, just as surrogate mothers must once they signed a contract. On the other side, difference feminists argued that some women *were* victims, programmed by their upbringing and perhaps by sexual abuse in childhood to do self-destructive things. They deserved protection.

Faced with the prevalence of rape and battering, some difference feminists equated violence with maleness, and that had unexpected repercussions. Lesbians, like straight women, were occasionally battered by their partners. Some found that feminist friends refused to believe they were being assaulted because battering was supposedly something only men did. Ellen Bell, who was beaten by her lesbian lover, learned much later that her experience had been very much like that of most battered wives. She noted that violence was a way one person gained power over another. It wasn't inherently male, though society tolerated it in men and up to a point even encouraged it.

Feminists who organized against violence initiated far-reaching changes in the justice system. In addition, the rape hotlines, the shelters, the underground railroad, all made a difference in many individual women's lives.

There was no question that feminists had raised the nation's consciousness about the violence committed against women, and in the 1990s there is some evidence that attitudes are beginning to change. For example, because of concern about date rape, a number of colleges have set up special seminars for students to make sure they understood what rape is. In another new development, by early 1991 the governors of two states had granted clemency to women who were serving prison sentences because they'd attacked or killed the men who battered them. Feminists in other states pressed hard for similar action and for laws that would force the courts to admit evidence of abuse when battered women were on trial. Meanwhile, a bill known as the Violence Against Women Act has been introduced in Congress; among other things, it would toughen the penalties for sex crimes prosecuted in federal courts and provide a much-needed increase in funding for battered women's shelters.

However, the basic problem—the prevalence of violence against women—has actually grown worse. During the 1980s, the number of rapes alone had risen four times faster than the general crime rate, and experts, testifying at a congressional hearing in 1990, confirmed that there seemed to have been an increase in other types of violence against women as well. Few believed that women were simply reporting attacks more often.

Some feminists are convinced that the violence is a response to women's demands for change, but that probably isn't the whole explanation. Other types of hate crimes are also up, and there have been many attacks on men of color and a wave of violence against gays. The United States also now has a higher crime rate than most countries—and imprisons a bigger percentage of its population than any other nation in the world. The problem of violence in America is complex and deep-rooted, and since 1980 it has been exacerbated by right-wing administrations that tacitly condone white male backlash.

chapter 16

Equal Pay and the Pauperization of Women

$\longrightarrow$

*I*n 1978, sociologist Diana Pearce called attention to a phenomenon she dubbed "the feminization of poverty." She noted that almost two thirds of all American adults who were poor were women. Concluding that women were worse off financially in the late 1970s than they had been in the 1950s, Pearce connected the change primarily to the increasing number of single mothers.

Some feminists seized on the poverty issue. If single motherhood *was* impoverishing millions of women—if most women were just one man away from welfare, as some said they were—that vulnerability was potentially a bond, uniting women of all classes and races. However, many low-income women, especially women of color, weren't impressed. They noted bitterly that white feminists had only discovered the poverty issue after it began to affect white middle class women. They charged that feminists were exaggerating the vulnerability of more privileged women and minimizing the problems of those who had always been poor, and that they were ignoring the effects of racism and classism. They insisted that women weren't poor just because of the rise in the number of woman-headed families. The causes of poverty were more complex, and so were the possible remedies.

The women's movement did not develop a comprehensive plan for combating poverty and bettering women's lives economically, nor did it spin off a separate movement or central coalition focused on the problem of women's poverty. Instead, individual activists and groups took on different issues.

- The major national women's organizations worked hard to end sex discrimination in the job market. Though this was sometimes described as a middle class effort to benefit middle class women, it put money into the pockets of many low-income women, especially after it evolved into the pay-equity campaign to win fair wages for women's occupations.
- Some activists pressed for programs for "displaced homemakers"—housewives suddenly forced to support themselves after a divorce, or because their husband lost his job, was disabled, or died.
- OWL, the Older Women's League, spearheaded efforts to pass new laws governing pensions and social security.
- Welfare rights groups fought for the very poor, the women on welfare.

As poverty became more of a priority for the women's movement, white feminists, low-income women, and feminists of color did begin to work together more closely, though not without tensions. Some white activists revised their assumptions about what it meant to be poor.

WHO IS POOR AND WHY

Each year, government experts determine the poverty level: They figure out what a bare-minimum diet would cost per person over the course of a year and multiply that cost by three, on the assumption that most poor people spend one third of their income on food; then they multiply by the number of people in a family to establish the "poverty threshold" for a family that size. On this basis, in 1991 a family of three with an annual income a little over $11,000 was held to be living in poverty. Some experts argued that the figure was unrealistic because the cost of housing had gone up enormously since the formula was first developed, and the diet that was its key element was nutritionally inadequate in any case.

Many Americans, in effect, blamed the poor for being poor. That attitude had its roots in one of the nation's proudest traditions: the belief that in the United States anyone willing to work hard can achieve a decent standard of living. If that were true, then people who were poor must be lazy or inferior, and at least partly to blame for their own poverty.* Conservatives believed these things, and even liberals tended to buy into the common American stereotype of a poor person: a black welfare mother living in an urban ghetto with a brood of children, all supposedly trapped in a perpetual cycle of poverty because they were part of an "underclass," a subculture that distorted their values and sapped their motivation.

In fact, poverty was both more common and less persistent than most people believed. Back in 1968, researchers at the University of Michigan began a major study that recorded the economic fortunes and misfortunes of 5000 American families for more than twenty years. They found that 25 percent of those they studied fell below the poverty line at some point during a ten-year period. Most recovered within two or three years; less than 3 percent were chronically poor. The researchers also found that children who grew up in welfare families had the same values as other Americans.

Despite this research, the American myths about poverty persisted and shaped government policies, especially under conservative administrations. During the 1960s, the nation's general affluence, together with the Johnson administration's War on Poverty, boosted the incomes of many poor Americans, with white males benefiting more than any other group. Beginning in the mid-1970s, these gains were gradually erased. A faltering economy was partly responsible, but after 1980 its ill effects were compounded by the White House, which decimated social-welfare programs. By 1988, when Ronald Reagan left office, the United States had the highest poverty rate of any industrialized nation: 13.1 percent of Americans fell below the poverty line.

Through the 1970s and 80s, the rich grew richer, and the poor became poorer.† Meanwhile, the elderly fared somewhat better

---

* A 1989 Gallup Poll found Americans almost evenly split on whether people were poor because of "lack of effort" or because of circumstances beyond their control. The American poor have generally been less demanding than the poor in other industrialized nations, perhaps because many believe their poverty is their own fault.
† The income of the richest 20 percent of the population rose by more then 24 percent between 1973 and 1987, while that of the poorest 20 percent dropped by almost 12

than before because of Medicare and improvements in Social Security retirement benefits, while the very young were worse off. In 1969, 14 percent of children were poor. By the late 1980s, one American child in four lived below the poverty line—most supported by a struggling single mother.

However, these generalizations obscure important differences. In 1989, 17 percent of all white children under six were poor, but so were one third of all Hispanic children and half of all black children. People of color, only one fifth of the U.S. population in the 1980s, were one third of the poor.

Meanwhile, women—half of the adult poor in 1959—were almost two thirds of the adult poor by 1978. What accounted for the increasing poverty of women? Certainly, the fact that so many were single mothers was a big part of the explanation, not only for white middle class women but for women of color as well. In the 1980s, the income of African-American families with two parents was almost on a par with that of two-parent white families. The average black single mother, on the other hand, had an income only about half the income of the average white single mother—who earned little enough.

Nevertheless, to low-income women of color, it seemed absurd to suggest that women were poor just because they were single mothers. They blamed racism, not sexism, for their poverty—the racism that kept wages down and unemployment high in their community, and that made family life difficult to sustain. For instance, 56.3 percent of all black men were unemployed in 1990 —up from about 25 percent in 1960—despite the fact that African-Americans now spent almost as many years in school as whites. Male joblessness to a large extent explained why black women were more likely to be divorced than white women, less likely to remarry—less likely to marry at all.

Of course, sex discrimination helped to keep women poor, for the job market still shunted most females into the low-paid occupations traditionally considered "women's work." Feminists in the early days of the second wave had imagined women advancing in every type of job, but during the 1970s heavy industry declined. As decently paid factory jobs disappeared, they were replaced by poorly paid jobs in the service sector, such as waitressing or being a sales clerk in a store, which sopped up the influx of women into the labor market.

---

percent. The salaries of working wives were all that prevented many families from tumbling out of the middle income category.

The welfare system also trapped women in poverty. Benefits were well below the official poverty line in every state, even taking extras like food stamps into account.* Few welfare mothers could afford child care so that they could look for work. In the early nineties, there were programs that supposedly trained women and paid for some work-related expenses during a transition period, but they were generally underfunded. Therefore, the training was minimal; the jobs, marginal; and the women were soon laid off and back on welfare.

SEX BIAS IN THE JOB MARKET

By the early 1970s, thanks to feminists, women who faced discrimination on the job could bring charges under four federal laws or the Executive Order, which applied to all government contractors. Over a dozen different government agencies were involved in enforcement.

Several features combined to make American antidiscrimination laws potentially more powerful than many of the laws passed in Western Europe during the 1970s. In the United States, class-action suits were possible, whereby a single individual or group filed a complaint on behalf of everyone in the same situation.† Affirmative action also made a huge difference: Under the Executive Order, government contractors were required to set flexible goals for increasing the number of women (and men of color) hired and promoted and to develop timetables for achieving those goals. In addition, if a company lost a case, it could be required to provide back pay for all employees unfairly treated in the past. Thus, the landmark 1973 AT&T settlement produced more than $38 million in higher wages and back pay for 13,000 women employees and 2000 men of color.

Faced with the threat of government action, many companies changed their employment policies in the 1970s. Women made real gains, and so did men of color. Of course, sometimes discrimination simply went underground: Supervisors went through the motions of interviewing women, for example, even when determined to hire a man. Many firms hastily moved a few

---

* In 1989, welfare benefits for a family of three ranged from $118 a month in Alabama to more than $800 in Alaska. The poverty threshold for a family of three that year was about $824 per month.

† For example, a flight attendant could challenge an airline on behalf of all flight attendants who had been fired after they became pregnant.

"token" women into higher positions, while continuing to limit most women to low-level jobs.

There were problems with enforcement as well. During the Nixon/Ford years, most of the enforcement agencies were underfunded and had high staff turnover, and there was no real push from the administration to pursue cases. Huge backlogs of complaints developed. In addition, by the early 1970s, backlash had begun, and the agencies also had to deal with thousands of charges filed by white males who argued that, thanks to affirmative action, they were victims of "reverse discrimination."

Attorney Marcia Greenberger of the National Women's Law Center, an expert on sex-discrimination cases, noted that poor women and women of color rarely filed complaints. The process was risky and complicated, and most weren't connected to feminist groups that could provide advice and support. Nevertheless, many benefited from victories such as the AT&T settlement, from affirmative action plans, and from the new ideas about women's roles that influenced most employers to some extent.

The Carter administration made a major effort to improve enforcement, but four years weren't enough to solve the problem. Roughly a dozen different agencies had been charged with enforcing the Executive Order, and Carter consolidated them all into one office within the Department of Labor. That office made the first concerted efforts to reform particular industries, with important results affecting banks, coal mining companies, and construction jobs. Meanwhile, women's groups had campaigned to have feminist Eleanor Holmes Norton made head of the EEOC. After Norton took charge, the agency made great progress in clearing up its backlog of cases. Greenberger said, "She brought in some very good people, boosted morale enormously, developed new systems for handling complaints, but was not able to get the part of the agency that was supposed to deal with big class-action efforts organized before she left."

After 1980, the Reagan administration deliberately set out to turn the clock backward (chapter 20). During two terms in office, Reagan filled almost half the seats on the federal bench with conservative judges, many opposed to further civil rights progress. By the late 1980s, very few class-action suits were being filed because the courts were now so unreceptive. Greenberger said in 1988, "It's harder now to get a group recognized as a 'class' and harder to get attorney's fees if you prevail. It's possible to be slapped with the other side's costs if you lose, and it's harder to win on the merits."

Meanwhile, the Justice Department had persuaded the Supreme Court to cut the heart out of Title IX and several other civil rights laws. In 1988, Congress undid the damage by passing the Civil Rights Restoration Act, but then in 1989 the Court gutted several more laws. According to Eleanor Holmes Norton, "Those decisions wiped out the 1964 Civil Rights Act and more."

Despite the roller-coaster history of civil rights enforcement, American women made considerable progress. Law schools and medical schools began graduating females in record numbers, and many women now worked as bartenders, bus drivers, police officers, and in a few other traditionally male blue-collar occupations. Nevertheless, throughout the 1970s, the gap between women's earnings and men's yawned as wide as ever, because most women still did low-paid "women's work"—they were jammed into just 20 of the 420 occupations listed by the U.S. Bureau of Labor Statistics.

THE CAMPAIGN FOR PAY EQUITY

Feminists were convinced that women's work was underpaid precisely because it had always been done by women, and that the problem boiled down to the way men valued work. They cited as an example the *Dictionary of Occupational Titles*, published by the U.S. government, which ranked jobs from the most important and valuable to the least. Thousands of employers referred to it when setting wages. In 1986, the latest edition still placed kindergarten teachers well below dog trainers, and general-duty nurses below hotel clerks.

By the mid-1970s, feminists had adopted pay equity (also known as comparable worth) as a strategy: They argued that women were entitled to be paid as much as men who did jobs of approximately equal value. If it took about as much training and effort to be a registered nurse as to be a teacher of vocational education, for example, then nurses and teachers who worked for the same school system should be paid comparable wages.* Conservatives raised three principal objections to pay equity:

* In the 1980s, the state of Minnesota paid the registered nurses in its employ about $20,700 a year, while the vocational education teachers on the state payroll had an annual income of approximately $27,000. Studies done around the country indicated that, in general, jobs filled mainly by women paid between 5 and 20 percent less than comparable male jobs.

- Right-wingers insisted that the free market—supply and demand—must be allowed to determine wages. Feminists responded that the free market actually did no such thing. They pointed out that nurses were scarce, but their wages didn't begin to rise until many hospitals were in crisis. Furthermore, employers sometimes conspired to set wages: In Boston, various companies met once a year to agree on pay scales for their clerical workers.
- Conservatives maintained that it was impossible to compare different jobs and determine their value, that the whole exercise was subjective. Feminists pointed out that job evaluation systems had been around since 1924, and that most big corporations and state agencies routinely used them to divide jobs into categories and then establish a range of pay for each category. The women argued that an employer could easily use such a system to analyze all jobs that were filled almost entirely by one sex or the other. For example, the work that registered nurses did could be assigned points on the basis of four factors: the effort the job required, the skill needed, the responsibility it entailed, and working conditions. The work pharmacists did could be evaluated in the same way. Afterward, if it turned out that the nurses had a total point count approximately equal to the point count for the pharmacists, and the nurses were paid less, their wages could be raised.
- The conservatives' third argument held that women were paid less mainly because they freely chose occupations that happened to be poorly paid. Basically, this was another version of blame-the-victim; it ignored the fact that sex and race discrimination left many women with very few options.

The conservative and feminist points of view on the question of choice were set forth in detail in the Sears case by two noted women historians who took opposite sides of the argument. The Sears lawsuit began during the Carter administration, when the EEOC charged the giant retailer with sex discrimination because so few of its women employees held high-paying commission sales jobs or positions in management. The court action continued into the Reagan years.

In defending itself, Sears insisted that most women didn't want demanding jobs. Historian Rosalind Rosenberg testified that women were raised to be less competitive than men, and that security and the social aspects of the work were more important to them than making the maximum pay; in addition, because most had to manage housework and child care at home, they preferred the easier sales jobs. Appearing for the EEOC, historian Alice Kessler-Harris argued that given a chance, women had always eagerly moved into better-paying, traditionally male jobs—as they did during both world wars. She insisted that it was mainly discrimination that held them back. Nevertheless, in February 1986 the courts ruled in favor of Sears.

Many Routes to Pay Equity

Around the country, women fought for pay equity through lawsuits, legislation, collective bargaining, and sometimes by going on strike. In many places, the state Commission on the Status of Women led the way, but unions were at the heart of the effort, and progress was possible largely because during the 1970s and 80s women's influence within the labor movement grew, especially after jobs in heavy industry began to disappear and male membership in unions declined as a result.

The battle for pay equity began in 1973 and focused primarily on government jobs, because local and state governments were politically vulnerable to union pressure in a way that businesses were not. In 1973 in the state of Washington, AFSCME (the American Federation of State, County, and Municipal Employees) persuaded Governor Dan Evans to have a study done comparing government jobs in which men predominated with those that were predominantly female. The researchers found that women's jobs paid about 20 percent less than comparable men's jobs and recommended raises for the women. However, progress stalled when Dixie Lee Ray became governor; her administration refused to carry out the study's recommendations.

In 1981, AFSCME sued the state of Washington. Two years later, Judge Jack Tanner of the U.S. District Court not only ruled in AFSCME's favor but ordered the state to hand over more than ten years of back wages to those who had been underpaid. In 1985, an appeals court reversed Tanner's decision, and AFSCME accepted an out-of-court settlement. However, in the meantime, in the light of Tanner's ruling, government officials all over the country had become nervous about possible lawsuits, and Minnesota had actually become the first state to mandate pay equity for employees of state and local governments.

After Ronald Reagan was elected President in 1980, there was little chance of federal action on pay equity. Reagan appointee Clarence Pendleton, head of the Civil Rights Commission, dubbed comparable worth "the looniest idea since Looney Tunes." In an obvious attempt to divide pay equity's supporters, right-wingers argued that it was a strategy designed to help white middle class women at the expense of blue-collar minority-group males. "The maintenance man will be paid less so the librarian can be paid more," said Michael J. Horowitz of the Office of Management and Budget. In fact, the pay-equity principle was being used to raise the wages of men of color as well as all women. Furthermore, though middle class feminists had been active on the issue, so were pink-collar clerical and service workers, and they were reaping most of the benefits.

As Reagan filled seats on the federal bench with conservatives, the courts rejected pay equity in case after case, until lawsuits no longer seemed a promising tactic. Instead, activists focused primarily on legislation and labor negotiations, still targeting state and local governments. By 1991, twenty states had begun to make pay-equity wage adjustments for state employees; half a dozen, like Minnesota, were making changes on a broad scale, while others had upgraded wages in a few occupations, sometimes as a result of a lawsuit. On a local level, more than 1700 municipalities, counties, and school districts had taken some steps toward equalizing wages. In addition, feminist scholar Frances Hutner reported that at business conferences, most big corporations no longer greeted sessions on pay equity with open hostility; some were quietly making changes.

Experience had proved that pay equity wasn't likely to cause major financial problems for an employer and that it did put money into the pockets of the lowest-paid women. In Minnesota, for example, about 8500 state employees got pay-equity raises that averaged $2200 each, spread over four years. The full cost of these raises came to less than 4 percent of the state's annual payroll.

As a strategy for change, pay equity turned out to have both advantages and disadvantages. On the positive side, it challenged the assumption that the value of work was whatever the market would pay, and it made people conscious of their own presumptions about what women's work was worth. On the negative side, there were problems with the job evaluation systems used. For one thing, they assessed women's work according to traditional male values. Abilities that were part of the female stereotype, such as skill at nurturing, sometimes weren't mentioned at all in awarding points—women got no credit for things they supposedly did well "naturally." The systems also tended to value responsibility for money (a male administrator's job) more than responsibility for people (a head nurse). In addition, they reinforced job hierarchies. That was hardly surprising; evaluation systems were originally developed to help managers exert control by defining their subordinates' jobs more precisely. However, as explained in chapter 5, many feminists believed in a flattened hierarchy, in which authority was more widely shared. In the end, women wound up both criticizing the commercial job evaluation systems and defending their use, because, flawed as they were, they did lead to higher wages for women.

Pay-equity activists hoped that their issue would draw more women into the movement, and sometimes, when women sat down to think about the real value of their own work, they did develop a sense of solidarity and a need for action. However, Sara Evans and Barbara Nelson, who studied comparable worth in Minnesota, concluded that as an issue, it would never rival the ERA. The process of achieving equity was complex and technical and was generally managed by experts. In addition, activists faced a difficult choice. If they publicized the drive for equity, they might stir up formidable opposition, but if they worked quietly for change, they were unlikely to make converts to the cause. In Minnesota, where the union deliberately played down the issue, only a little over half the state employees who got a pay-equity raise even realized they'd received one. Though women benefited financially, feminists didn't get either the credit or the converts they'd worked so hard for. Evans and Nelson concluded that pay equity would undoubtedly become more widespread in the future, but that it must be combined with other strategies if women were to close the wage gap.

DISPLACED HOMEMAKERS

In 1972, California housewife Tish Sommers was divorced after twenty-three years of marriage and confronted the problems that older women often faced when they were divorced or widowed. Sommers had been an unpaid community organizer, active in the civil rights movement, but when she applied for jobs, she was told either that she had no experience that counted or that she was overqualified. Meanwhile, she had lost her medical insurance, which had been provided through her husband's employer, and she had trouble getting credit, because all their credit records were in her husband's name. Aware that she was being discriminated against because of her age as well as her sex, in 1974 Sommers founded the Alliance for Displaced Homemakers, together with Laurie Shields, a recently widowed former ad executive. The term "displaced homemaker" captured the sense many older homemakers had that they were like refugees, displaced persons. When they lost their husbands, they not only lost their livelihood but were forcibly exiled from their chosen occupation.

In the early days of the second wave, many feminists tended to look down on full-time housewives and to feel that dependency was demeaning. Sommers and Shields raised their consciousness: They argued that marriage was an economic partnership, and that a woman's work at home contributed to her husband's career and entitled her to an equal share of the family assets. Their ultimate goal, in the words of Laurie Shields, was ". . . to have homemaking and child-rearing recognized as a viable occupation for both sexes. . . ."

Because for most displaced homemakers the most urgent problem was getting a job, in 1975 the Alliance set out to establish a pilot program to train such women and help them find work. Sympathetic California legislators agreed to introduce a bill to fund the project on a modest scale, but the bill met a surprising amount of resistance. Governor Jerry Brown wanted to know why former homemakers couldn't simply turn to "religious institutions, friends, and relatives" for support. Even lawmakers who backed the bill sometimes did it for the wrong reasons. One supporter explained himself by noting that "if we can get these women retrained, ex-husbands won't get socked with all that alimony."

Ultimately the bill passed, and the first center for displaced homemakers was established in Oakland. The following year, several religious denominations supplied financial backing to pay Shields's travel expenses while she toured the country advising women who wanted to lobby for similar laws in their own states. Soon there were centers in Iowa and Maryland as well. Operating on bare-minimum budgets, they provided job counseling, referrals, and self-help groups, often using women who had been displaced homemakers themselves to do counseling.

In 1977, Sommers and Shields began lobbying for federal funds for the centers, against opposition from right-winger Phyllis Schlafly. Schlafly's newsletter, the *Eagle Forum*, claimed that displaced homemaker programs were nothing but feminist indoctrination centers. She urged her readers—primarily conservative Republican women—to write letters to Congress opposing federal funding. In the end, the government did provide money through CETA (the Comprehensive Employment Training Act), and by late 1979 there were about 300 displaced-homemaker programs around the country. The Reagan administration cut their funds in 1982, and a number of centers closed, but two years later Congress provided new money. In 1990, there were over 1000 programs.

THE OLDER WOMEN'S LEAGUE

Meanwhile, Shields and Sommers had moved on to new issues as others assumed the leadership of the Displaced Homemakers Network, which had succeeded the Alliance for Displaced Homemakers in 1978. That same year, the two women founded OWLEF, the Older Women's League Educational Fund, and set out to document the problems of older women with a series of "gray papers." In 1980—noting soberly that one out of every four women employed that year would be poor in her old age—they organized OWL (the Older Women's League), a national organization with headquarters in Washington, D.C., and chapters around the country. It had evolved out of the smaller, more specialized OWLEF.

Pensions, social security, and health insurance were primary issues for OWL. Half the women in the work force had jobs with no pension plan; most of the rest had access to a plan that discriminated blatantly on the basis of sex. Either it demanded higher contributions from women than from men, or it paid them lower benefits on the grounds that on the average they lived longer and would ultimately collect more from the pension fund. Eventually, the Supreme Court ruled—in decisions handed down in 1978 and 1983—that such policies amounted to sex discrimination.

However, the whole system was stacked against women in other ways. Because they earned less than men and benefits were based on earnings, their benefits were generally smaller. In addition, pensions were designed to reward long-term, full-time employees, and women were less likely than men to stay with one company long enough to earn a pension. Many dropped out temporarily to raise children or gave up a job to move to another city with a husband who was transferred. In 1987, retired women received only 54 percent as much income from their pensions as retired men did.

In addition, divorced women generally had no claim on their husband's retirement benefits, and only 2 percent of all widows received benefits from their husband's pension. Many pension plans paid nothing to the spouse if the worker died before age fifty-five, and most plans also gave employees a choice: They could have higher monthly payments that stopped when they died or could agree to lower payments so that their spouse would continue to receive benefits after their death. The spouse had no say in the matter. As of 1979, more than 64 percent of federal civil service retirees and 95 percent of military retirees had decided against survivor's benefits; the figures for the private sector were only slightly better.

In the early 1980s, under pressure from OWL, NOW, and other women's groups, Congress passed several bills that improved the situation. Legislation that applied to the Foreign Service and the military set precedents and created a formula for dividing a pension when a couple divorced; some states adopted similar laws. Then, in 1984, Congress passed REA, the Retirement Equity Act. It required the written consent of both husband and wife before a worker could refuse survivor benefits, and it guaranteed that benefits would be paid to a wife even if her husband died before he could retire; it also required that pension coverage be maintained for employees who took a few years off to stay home and raise children. Unfortunately, for many older women, such changes came too late. In the early 1990s, two out of five older women lived in poverty or had incomes just above the poverty line.

Feminists also succeeded in changing some of the rules governing social security. Back in the 1930s, those who designed the system assumed that virtually all women were dependents of a breadwinning husband and would collect retirement benefits as wives rather than in their own right as workers. The planners also seem to have assumed that a homemaker's contribution to a marriage was worth very little—certainly, it wasn't comparable to her husband's contribution as breadwinner. At any rate, a wife was entitled to a monthly check half the size of the one her husband received, whether or not she had ever held a job and paid social security taxes herself. Because the benefit was based on earnings—roughly speaking, it was determined by the worker's average annual income over the years—and because many women earned very little, most found that they were entitled to more social security as a wife than as a worker. In the early 1990s, 62 percent of women collected benefits as their husband's dependent rather than in their own right. The percentage hadn't changed since 1960, despite the fact that so many women were now in the labor force.

In a number of ways, the social security system put women workers at a disadvantage. For one thing, a woman who dropped out of the job market to stay home while her children were young accumulated years of zero income, which brought down the average on which her benefits would be based. For another, a divorced woman couldn't collect social security based on the taxes her ex-husband had paid unless they'd been married for at least ten years. (The requirement was twenty years until 1979, when feminists persuaded Congress to make it ten.)

Even lifelong homemakers were shortchanged by the system. The woman who received a monthly benefit as a dependent that was half the size of the benefit her husband received certainly wasn't being treated as an equal partner in the marriage—someone whose work in the home helped her husband earn his salary. To feminists, the basic principle seemed wrong, and women's groups pressed for a new system of "earnings sharing." They proposed that the social security administration maintain a separate record for every individual. For the duration of a marriage, a couple's earnings would be totaled every year, and each spouse given credit for half the total, to produce the record of earnings on which retirement benefits would eventually be based.

Health care was also high on OWL's agenda, because many women worked in jobs that didn't offer group health insurance. Though some were covered through their husband's policy, if a divorce occurred, the woman generally found that her health insurance had ended with the marriage. In 1986, Congress passed a law that gave such women the right to continued coverage for a few years, assuming they could pay the premiums themselves.

In the early 1990s, OWL had 120 chapters and an agenda for change focused primarily on economic issues. Those issues were urgent, because two out of five older women were poor or near-poor, and the situation wasn't improving. Twenty years earlier, many people simply assumed that if women were in the labor force for most of their adult lives, they would be able to retire, as so many men did, with a pension and social security benefits that would allow them to live comfortably. Instead, in the nineteen years between 1970 and 1989, women's social security benefits increased only marginally in relation to men's: where women had once received 70 cents on the male dollar, they now received 73 cents. As for private pensions, for unknown reasons the situation had actually worsened. In 1974, older women's pensions were 73 percent of men's; in 1987, they were just 58 percent. Furthermore, more than three out of four women workers had no pension when they retired, often because they had worked for a company without a pension plan; men were almost twice as likely to have a pension.

WELFARE RIGHTS

The history of the National Welfare Rights Organization (NWRO) is a lesson in the politics of poverty. It also highlights race and class issues that haunted the women's movement.

Welfare benefits were introduced during the Depression so that women who had no husband could stay home with their children. Ironically, not much more than a generation later, many Americans began to insist that welfare mothers should be forced to go out to work. As more women joined the labor force, the argument that poor children needed their mothers at home was undercut. However, the push for a work requirement was fueled primarily by images, conjured up by conservatives, of black ghetto mothers too lazy to take a job, having babies just to increase the size of their welfare check. With welfare benefits so meager, it was an unlikely scenario.

In the United States, relatively few people applied for welfare before the 1960s because of the stigma attached to it, and about half of those who did apply were turned away. Administrators and caseworkers, determined to keep the welfare rolls down, made it difficult for poor women to find out whether they were eligible and arbitrarily rejected claims.

For women who needed help, the system was an endless Catch-22. Though Congress expanded AFDC* in 1961 so that two-parent families with unemployed fathers could also receive benefits, the states weren't required to adopt the new program and many decided not to. Thus, if a man couldn't support his family, often the best way to put food on the table was to desert them, to make them eligible for welfare. If a woman who had been abandoned by her husband or perhaps had never married had a live-in "boyfriend," she lost her benefits—it was assumed that the man should be supporting her. Officials sometimes staged midnight raids on welfare families to find out whether

* The Aid to Families with Dependent Children (AFDC) program was what people generally meant when they spoke of "welfare."

there was a man in the house. Welfare officials were also quick to prosecute for fraud. It was fraud if the welfare department mistakenly sent a woman more money than she was entitled to and she cashed the check, even if only a few dollars were involved, and it was fraud if a friend gave her cast-off furniture and she forgot to declare it.

During the late 1960s, the situation began to change. Riots in the inner cities in the North had made urban poverty an issue; the War on Poverty had legitimated the grievances of the poor; and new federal programs provided funds for community action. Some Americans began to think of welfare as a basic right: to argue that everyone was entitled to a share of the nation's wealth, and that if society couldn't provide people with jobs, it should at least see that they had enough income to survive.

In this atmosphere, the National Welfare Rights Organization (NWRO) was born. It began as a grass-roots movement, but liberals soon stepped in to organize it from the top down. Because its leaders came from such different backgrounds, NWRO was beset by internal tensions almost from the beginning.

The movement's rank-and-file members were low-income women, mostly African-American, and they were led by the charismatic Johnnie Tillmon. In 1963, Tillmon was unemployed, ill, and had six children to support. When she had trouble getting AFDC benefits, she decided to organize welfare mothers in her area, the Watts section of Los Angeles. Local welfare rights groups were also forming in other parts of the country.

However, it was George Wiley, a young black college professor, who first saw the need for an effort on the national level. In June 1966—at about the same time that NOW was being formed —he began to organize demonstrations for welfare rights. These protests, staged around the country, marked the birth of a movement. Wiley had just founded the Poverty Rights Action Center (PRAC), which became the headquarters for a new organization, the NWRO.

In addition, two white social scientists, Frances Fox Piven and Richard A. Cloward, had a strong influence on the welfare rights movement. Research they did in the 1960s proved that at least half of all families eligible for welfare benefits weren't receiving any; furthermore, most of those who *were* on welfare didn't realize that they were also entitled to special grants for emergencies and for basic needs such as winter coats. In a paper called "A Strategy to End Poverty," which circulated widely among liberals in 1965 and 66, Piven and Cloward suggested that if all the families eligible for benefits and grants were to demand them, there would be such a crisis that the government might be forced to revamp the system and establish a national minimum income standard.

At NWRO's founding convention in 1967, elections were held and Johnnie Tillmon became the new organization's chair, while other women were elected to an executive committee, which hired George Wiley as executive director. The other elected officers, like Tillmon, were welfare mothers, as were 85 percent of the members. The officers met intermittently between annual conventions, but the organization's real leaders were Wiley and his paid staff, who were mostly young white middle class males. Locally, the staff organized welfare rights groups (called WROs); nationally, they ran the Washington office. Wiley was a skillful fund-raiser and soon generated financial support from churches, foundations, and the federal government.

The local WROs handled grievances for women who joined the organization and staged demonstrations, such as sit-ins in welfare offices. According to sociologist Guida West, who wrote the definitive history of NWRO, the local groups were of two types. Some were started by organizers (usually men), who instructed the women and masterminded protests. The men were primarily interested in confronting the system, and West felt that they often used welfare mothers as a means to an end. Other WROs were initiated and run by the women themselves, and though they mounted political actions, they insisted that members also needed services—needed support when a welfare check was lost in the mail, for example, or when they were facing eviction.

To West, who spent eight years studying the welfare rights movement, NWRO was a mass of contradictions: a women's movement led by men, a movement of the poor financed by middle class liberals, a black movement supported mostly by whites. Race and gender biases limited its membership. Poor white women avoided NWRO because they saw it as a movement for militant blacks; poor males ignored it because they believed it was dominated by women.

How does a stigmatized minority, which has no resources to speak of, change the system? That was NWRO's essential, overwhelming problem. There were only about three million welfare mothers in the whole country, and, as Johnnie Tillmon put it, "We're the worst educated, the least skilled and the lowest paid people there are." Piven and Cloward believed the answer was to destroy the welfare system, so that the government would have to make a fresh start. Wiley was concerned that if NWRO succeeded in breaking down the system, it might be replaced by something even worse. He believed that the poor needed a national organization to lobby Congress and prevent repression.

In the late 1960s, NWRO achieved a great deal. More of the families who were eligible began receiving welfare: Between 1965 and 1970, benefits provided to the poor rose by 69 percent. Many welfare departments developed procedures for negotiating grievances and invited welfare recipients to serve on advisory councils. One of the worst abuses ended in 1968, when the Supreme Court ruled that benefits could no longer be denied to a woman caught with a man in her house, thus ending the midnight raids. Ultimately, NWRO managed to reshape the food stamp program and expand other nutritional and health programs for poor children and mothers.

With each success, membership grew, until it peaked in 1969 at 22,000. There were now more than 500 WROs, and some local leaders became celebrities. Johnnie Tillmon, in particular, proved to be feisty, direct, and highly articulate, and she made a deep impression on some feminists. In a 1972 interview published in *Ms* magazine, she noted that "welfare's like a traffic accident. It can happen to anybody. . . ." Anticipating the poverty that would be generated by divorce, she warned middle class activists that "every woman is one man away from welfare."

Inevitably, NWRO's successes generated backlash. In 1969, President Nixon, calling the welfare system a "colossal failure," proposed the Family Assistance Plan (FAP). Among other things, it would force all welfare recipients except mothers of children under six to accept employment, though it made very limited provisions for child care. Tillmon pointed out that under the FAP, a woman would have to accept any job she was offered and any child care, no matter how inadequate. In addition, the Nixon administration launched highly publicized investigations of welfare fraud, sometimes targeting local and national welfare rights leaders for harassment. Faced with rising welfare costs, a number of states also reacted. They reduced benefits and stiffened rules for eligibility, and now, when welfare mothers staged protests, there were arrests. For the women, that escalated the cost of being involved in the movement.

After 1969, NWRO's membership declined dramatically, partly because of the backlash but also because, with local WRO leaders serving on welfare advisory boards, the groups no longer mounted protests and membership seemed superfluous. Piven and Cloward noted that "the sense of participation in something larger than oneself . . . was gradually lost."

Meanwhile, at the national level there were conflicts over NWRO's goals, aggravated by class and gender differences. The male organizers, including Wiley, wanted more jobs in the ghettos for men, so that they could assume their roles as breadwinners. NWRO's female leaders had different priorities: higher benefits, child care, and more jobs and training for welfare mothers themselves.

Increasingly, the women insisted on having more of a say about policy and demanded paid jobs in the organization. The staff at first resisted, citing limited funds. Guida West noted that underneath, unstated, was "the feeling that the poor women on welfare did not possess the educational level, skills, or sophistication needed to lead a national protest movement." Wiley, like many of the organizers, believed in participatory democracy. He had always said that someday NWRO's members would run their own organization, but he felt it was too soon. Nevertheless, in 1969, a few token women were given minor jobs in Washington, and in 1971, after continued pressure, Tillmon was hired as Wiley's associate director.

In the fall of 1972, Congress rejected the FAP, a major victory for NWRO. However, by that time the organization had a sizeable deficit and new conflicts had erupted between Wiley and the women leaders. At a bitter meeting in November 1972, they accused him of usurping their policy-making role. He subsequently resigned, and Johnnie Tillmon succeeded him. In January, a press release aligned NWRO for the first time with the feminist movement. It asserted that "NWRO views the major welfare problems as women's issues and itself as strictly a women's organization."

Unfortunately, Wiley had taken most of the funding with him. Foundations and churches weren't interested in backing a movement led by poor black women. The male organizers also disappeared, and the grass roots had already withered. NWRO struggled on for several years, but in 1975 was forced to file for bankruptcy and close its Washington headquarters.

In retrospect, Piven and Cloward blamed the demise of the organization on its female leadership, noting that they came from the lowest origins, were lifted to "heights of recognition and deference," and eventually put all their efforts into securing their own hold on those heights.*

* According to a classic theory in sociology, called the "iron law of oligarchy," in social movements people in leadership positions eventually come to care only about maintain-

"There were elements of truth in this," said West, noting that a lot of money went into meetings, social functions, and maintaining the Washington office. "But remember, these were women who were barely surviving from day to day. Asking them to be involved politically, to fight for their rights, was another burden. . . . You had to have some incentives to keep people interested in the movement."

Welfare Rights and Women's Rights

Throughout most of its history, NWRO had the backing of white liberals, particularly Protestant churches. In contrast, it received little support from black women's groups. Though they had always been concerned about the poor, the NWRO, with its sit-ins, may have been too militant for middle class African-Americans. Attitudes changed in the late 1970s as black feminists began to organize. The new groups included some former leaders of NWRO, and from the beginning they were concerned about welfare, but by that time NWRO was defunct.

As for predominantly white feminist organizations, for a long time they didn't see welfare as a women's issue—like AFDC women themselves, they thought of it as a poor people's issue. In addition, there were misunderstandings on both sides. NWRO's African-American leaders found it hard to forget the racism they'd experienced in the past from white women, and feminists resented Wiley's attitude. In 1970, invited to speak to NOW's national board, he stated that NWRO's goal was to put black males back where they belonged at the head of the family, and that the organization wasn't concerned about economic independence for women.

The dependency issue was a major source of controversy between feminists and welfare activists. Middle class feminists, already in the labor force themselves or eager to join it, couldn't understand why women on welfare would want to stay home and collect benefits. Tillmon, on the other hand, insisted that welfare mothers must have a choice about whether to take a job. She pointed out that for poor women, decent child care was often unavailable or unaffordable, and the only jobs open to them were menial and low-paid. NWRO's members wanted more education, training, and better jobs, but their children were their priority.

---

ing the organization and their own power; they refuse to take risks to achieve the goals of the movement.

However, in the end, significant cross-fertilization did take place. Tillmon and others, influenced by feminism, declared themselves part of the women's movement. Meanwhile, NWRO convinced many feminists that welfare *was* a women's issue. Though NWRO never achieved its primary goal—an adequate income for all those in need—it did have a lasting impact on the welfare system. It also proved that it was possible for poor women to have an impact, and that became a taking-off point for a revitalized welfare rights movement a few years later.

Welfare Rights: The Second Wave

In the 1980s, the welfare issue revived as legislators proposed new laws designed to get families off public assistance and welfare rights groups sprang up once again around the country. The legislative effort started in 1981, when policymakers began to argue that AFDC needed a complete overhaul. Supposedly, by providing families with their basic needs, it encouraged women to have children without marrying and discouraged them from looking for work.

Some authorities argued that female-headed families were responsible for the growth of an "underclass" in America, because they had produced a generation of fatherless youngsters whose attitudes and behavior didn't reflect the American work ethic. The women and their children were said to be trapped in a cycle of poverty, with each new generation supported by welfare. The solution—or so the argument went—was to require AFDC mothers to work and to keep benefits so low that no one would prefer welfare to holding a job.

Those who advocated such welfare "reforms" ignored the University of Michigan's long-term study, mentioned earlier, which painted a different picture of the typical welfare family. The study tracked a representative sample of 5000 American families from all income levels for decades, and it found that most women weren't on welfare for long. Many went in and out of the work force, resorting to AFDC between jobs because they weren't eligible for unemployment benefits. There was no evidence that the system itself somehow destroyed their motivation. Instead, their problems seemed to be caused by inadequate education, a shortage of jobs that paid decent wages, and by discrimination in the job market. The research also demonstrated that very few families remained on welfare generation after generation. There were young women in the study population who had grown up in long-term AFDC families, and as they reached their twenties, only one out of five became, in turn, heavily dependent on welfare.

However, the research was unable to uproot welfare mythology. In 1988, to a fanfare of platitudes lamenting the families trapped on welfare for generations, Congress passed the Family Support Act of 1988. Its effects were to be phased in during the early 1990s, and they were a mixed bag. On the positive side, all states would now have to give welfare benefits to eligible two-parent families and must step up efforts to collect child support from absentee fathers. They must also provide a child-care subsidy and medical coverage for a transition period of one year for a parent who entered the work force. On the negative side, the new law failed to raise benefits, and it forced women with children over three out of the home. They must take a job, participate in a training program, or return to school, or else lose their benefits, and there was no guarantee that either the job or the child care offered would be adequate.

According to Guida West, though some of the principles behind the new law were good, the basic problem was money. She noted that the legislation was based partly on a New Jersey program called REACH, which had been a disaster in practice because it was inadequately funded. Women were given the sketchiest sort of training and thrust into dead-end, high-turnover jobs, where they were soon let go. "Then they're back on welfare," said West. "The system is like a revolving door." The shortage of affordable child care was also a major problem. It was likely that at the end of a year, when their child-care subsidy dried up, many women would have to quit their jobs.

As the welfare rights movement revived during the 1980s—it had never died completely—it assumed a substantially different form. When new groups were organized, some NWRO old-timers were involved, but so were many younger women, and many more of them were white. The National Welfare Rights Union brought a few of the groups together into a loose coalition, but the movement remained primarily grass roots.

The local groups faced severe new problems. With the federal government demanding reductions in the welfare rolls, some welfare departments resorted to a practice known as "churning." Families were dropped from the program on almost any excuse —because the woman forgot to sign a single form, for example. She could reapply and be reinstated, but in the meantime the welfare department could claim that it had reduced its caseload. Left without rent money, some families became homeless.

During the late 1960s, welfare benefits in many states maintained families a little above the poverty threshold. By the early 1990s, families often struggled to survive on benefits well below the poverty line. In New York City, where AFDC grants were relatively high compared with other places, a family of six could receive a *maximum* of about $815 a month—the average grant was less. Roughly $350 of the $815 was supposedly for rent, though it was virtually impossible to find housing in the city for that price. However, assuming the impossible, that left $465 for everything else, or $2.50 per person per day to cover utilities, clothing, transportation, baby bottles, diapers, laundry, and items such as soap and toilet paper. The family would also receive food stamps, but they would provide less than two weeks per month of nutritionally adequate meals. Yet politicians still talked as if women chose to be on welfare and were simply too lazy to go out to work.

Feminists continued to debate how best to change the system. Some, like Guida West, envisioned a social service system that would empower, rather than control, poor women. Caseworkers would function as enablers, informing women of their rights and encouraging them to define their own problems and possible solutions. The ultimate purpose would be to help them gain control over their own lives. Theresa Funiciello, a one-time welfare mother turned writer and activist, advanced a more radical proposal. She pointed out that much of the money spent on welfare each year went to pay the salaries of social workers and administrators, when it could be better spent furnishing an adequate income for the poor. Funiciello noted that many other countries provide automatic allowances for families or for children, which keep people out of poverty in the first place. She acknowledged that women do sometimes need the services provided by social workers, but argued that those services shouldn't be required. If the women were allowed to choose what kind of help they wanted, on a market model, the services that actually helped would survive.

Meanwhile, some feminist legal scholars were arguing that food, shelter, and medical care should be considered "enabling rights" under the Constitution, because without them the so-called fundamental rights, such as free speech and the right to vote, were meaningless. Unfortunately, a Supreme Court dominated by conservatives was unlikely to agree.

chapter 17

Diversity: From the Melting Pot to the Salad Bowl

*T*he second wave of feminism was sometimes derided as a white women's movement. Though women of color were among the founders and leaders of some of the major feminist organizations, from the beginning most activists were white and middle class. This became a major issue in the 1980s, as women of color organized their own groups and demanded that the women's movement address their issues. They were linked by umbrella groups such as the National Institute for Women of Color and the Women of Color Leadership Council, and at the same time many were part of the major coalitions formed originally by predominantly white organizations. In a sense, women-of-color groups were a movement within the feminist movement.

The concern about diversity could be seen not only in the women's movement but in the nation. The "browning" of America provided some of the impetus, for whites were beginning to realize that in the future they might no longer be the majority of the population. There was also belated recognition that the old notion of the American melting pot had done a great deal of damage. Europeans might blend comfortably into an American stew, but other ethnic groups did not, partly because of racial prejudice. More to the point, it was naive to assume that people of color would *want* to give up their ethnic identities, and short-sighted not to recognize the potential strength and richness of a truly multicultural society.*

As white feminists began to focus on diversity, they found that it was tougher to achieve than most had expected. Women of color were tired of being marginalized—of being the token African-American or Latina on a board of directors or a conference panel. There were misunderstandings and confrontations, often despite the best intentions of all concerned. Nevertheless, by 1990 there had been a significant change in American feminism. The groups formed by women of color were making their presence felt, and most of the predominantly white organizations were groping for new ways to connect with women of color. The movement ran broader and deeper than ever before.

THE "WHITENESS" PROBLEM FROM THE WHITE POINT OF VIEW

In the early days of the second wave, women of color were sparsely represented in both branches of the women's movement —liberal feminism and women's liberation—and the reasons were somewhat different in each case.

Most liberal feminists simply assumed they were building a movement that would serve women of all races and ethnic groups. When the National Women's Political Caucus (NWPC) was founded, for example, racial integration was one of its goals. The twenty-one-member steering committee included, among others, American Indian activist LaDonna Harris, Beulah Sanders of the NWRO, and Fannie Lou Hamer, the SNCC field secretary who was one of the founders of the Mississippi Freedom Democratic Party. Harris, who was also the wife of Senator Fred Harris, was on the boards of many organizations in those days. She didn't see herself as the token Native American—or as the token female on the boards of male-dominated organizations—because her very presence represented a breakthrough. Most people assumed that more changes would follow. However, years rolled

---

* During the 1980s, *integration* became a word to be avoided because it suggested not a mixing of equals but the absorption of minorities into the mainstream, where their racial and ethnic identities would be erased. In the early nineties, the preferred terms were *diversity* and *multicultural*.

by and women of color continued to occupy only one or two chairs on the boards of most white-dominated women's organizations. Few white feminists recognized that as a serious problem.

Another problem, more obvious, was that most of the women who joined organizations such as NWPC and NOW were white. Jean Faust of NOW–New York recalled that "we were all eager to have black women in NOW as officers and on committees, but few were interested." White activists concluded that women of color were either still locked into traditional ideas about sex roles or else were too involved in the struggle against racism to have time for the women's movement. In fact, as will become apparent, the problems were more complex than that.

NOW elected a black president, Aileen Hernandez, in 1970, and continued to have a few feminists of color on its board, but the membership remained overwhelmingly white. A panel discussion during the annual conference in 1989 touched on some of the stumbling blocks. Women of color explained that they resented it when white activists descended on them wanting to know how they could recruit more minority women; it made them feel that the feminists simply wanted to use other women. They suggested that if NOW worked with women-of-color organizations on the issues that mattered to them, better relationships would follow. However, the "whiteness problem" was at least partly self-perpetuating, a vicious circle: The members of an organization determined its priorities, and then those priorities determined who joined the organization, which meant that new members seldom challenged the old priorities.

As for the women's liberation wing of the movement, in 1968, radical women fresh from SNCC and the New Left actually debated whether or not to invite black activists who were involved in civil rights but not women's liberation to the first national women's liberation conference. They decided not to. Afterward, some feminists felt that was an important missed opportunity; others were convinced that the black women wouldn't have come in any case (see chapter 4).

In retrospect, it was clear that white feminists had made a mistake when they assumed that all women were essentially alike and suffered at the hands of men in the same ways. According to Ann Snitow, a member of New York Radical Feminists, "The dream was that underneath our differences, our oppression unified us in a very fusing way." However, because feminists glossed over issues of race and class, many women of color felt excluded and angry. As feminist philosopher Elizabeth Spelman observed, white women behaved as if a shared viewpoint were somehow a given, rather than a difficult achievement.

In an influential 1988 book, *Unessential Woman: Problems of Exclusion in Feminist Thought,* Spelman argued that by ignoring differences—by speaking as if all women were white and middle class—white feminists made women of color feel invisible, much as men had made women feel invisible by speaking of "mankind," for example. Men insisted that of course "mankind" included women, but feminists were angrily aware that the language reflected the power structure. Similarly, when feminists and others spoke of "women and blacks," African-American women understood that the phrase often meant white women and black men—or perhaps white women and black people. Either way, "women" obviously didn't include black females. Women of color who were not African-American often felt even more marginalized. Because blacks were the biggest U.S. minority group, people sometimes made statements about "minority women" that obviously referred only to blacks, as if no other groups existed.

In short, feminists, like other Americans, took the white middle class heterosexual woman as the female norm, much as men had always taken males as the human norm. Spelman observed that "the problem with the 'story of man' was that women couldn't recognize themselves in it." Similarly, when white women took what they understood of themselves to be "some golden nugget of womanness," they were excluding all other women. Though some white feminists felt it was a mark of prejudice even to mention race or class, Spelman argued that it was actually racism to assume that there was nothing different or valuable about having a racial history and identity that didn't happen to be white.

Of course, there *were* white feminists who recognized very early that the women's movement couldn't afford to homogenize the identities of women. One of the most significant was Leslie Wolfe, who began her career in Washington in 1973 as deputy director of the women's rights program of the U.S. Commission on Civil Rights. The job shaped her perspective. Rather than set up a separate unit to deal solely with women's rights, the Commission assigned Wolfe and her staff to act at the highest levels of the agency and infuse an awareness of sexism and women's concerns into all the studies then being done—on minorities and federal contracting, minorities and housing, minorities and television, and so on. At a time when "women's rights" automatically meant white women, Wolfe learned a great deal from women of color and took every opportunity to pass on what she'd learned to others.

"I always thought I was doing missionary work to white feminists," she said. "Not because they were racists—they weren't." However, Wolfe saw that they needed more than good intentions to forge bonds with women of color. Specifically, they needed to do homework on the history, traditions, and concerns of other groups of women. Wolfe explained, "It's not enough to say to Native American women, for example, 'Come and join us, because our issues are the same,' without knowing something about where those women have come from and what's important to them."

In 1979, Leslie Wolfe was appointed director of the WEEA program (Women's Educational Equity Act) just in time to draw up the final guidelines for distributing federal grants to women's education projects. Because women of color felt that whenever projects were designed to serve all women, their particular needs were submerged, Wolfe made it one of WEEA's five official priorities to fund programs specifically for them; another priority was to support programs for women with disabilities. In addition, all those who applied to WEEA had to explain what their project would do for diverse groups of women.

Thus, while Wolfe headed WEEA, money went to a program to teach disabled women about their legal rights; to a group that produced a directory of Native American and Native Alaskan women working in education—so that heads of government agencies could no longer say that they'd love to give an appointment to a Native woman if they just knew of one who was qualified; to a project that provided education and training for southern black women moving from rural areas into cities; and to many other activities that would never have been funded in the past.

If there was a turning point during the 1970s—a point at which concern about diversity began to accelerate—it was the huge national women's conference held in Houston in 1977 in connection with International Women's Year (IWY). In preparation for the conference, roughly 130,000 women attended meetings held in every state and territory to draft recommendations for a national Plan of Action and elect delegates to the conference. When the delegates finally assembled in Houston, 2000 strong, they were the most diverse group ever elected in the United States: rich and poor, young and old, straight and lesbian, drawn from almost every racial and ethnic group and religious background.

More than one third of the delegates were women of color, and their numbers gave them a strong voice. Even before the conference, some groups had been meeting to try to hammer out their own plank for the twenty-five-point Plan of Action, to replace the homogenized three-paragraph version originally proposed. During the conference, representatives of those groups met in exhausting, nonstop sessions. When their plank was adopted almost unanimously, many women felt it was the most important —and the most moving—event of the conference.

WOMEN OF COLOR FIND WAYS TO CONNECT

What does a black academic have in common with a Native American woman living on a reservation, or an Asian-American working in a garment factory? The conviction that such women did have common ground produced the "minority women" plank in Houston, which listed—among other shared experiences—sexism, racism, sterilization abuse, high infant and maternal mortality, ghettoized housing, culturally biased tests, health services that made no provision for those who couldn't speak English, and more. In other words, for women of color, the priority issues had to do with survival. Most also came from traditions that put the needs of family and community ahead of those of individuals, and that urged individuals to achieve partly or primarily so that they could help the community.

In 1981, Sharon Parker and Veronica Collazo, two women of color who had dropped out of NOW, founded the National Institute for Women of Color (NIWC) to try to forge connections among black, Hispanic, Native American, Alaska Native, Asian-American, and Pacific Islander women. Parker became NIWC's chair. Her first project was to try to revamp the American vocabulary and replace the phrase "minority women" with "women of color." *Minority* not only meant fewer in number, but to many it implied second-class status. Parker argued that the phrase encouraged a "minority mentality" in a nation that prided itself on majority rule, a mentality that could be self-defeating. She also wanted to emphasize the links between American women of color and women of color around the world, because on the global scale, people of color were, in fact, the majority.

Determined to build on the strengths of diversity, NIWC gradually linked women's groups around the country into a loose network. By 1990, it had over 8000 affiliates—task forces, committees, organizations, and other networks, including a few predominantly white groups, such as Illinois-NOW. The Institute supplied its affiliates with publications, fact sheets, "Brown Papers" on issues, and other types of assistance. It held conferences that drew a rainbow of women eager to discuss their issues, and that served as a model for local groups who wanted to use a conference to open up a dialogue among women. NIWC also joined established coalitions and helped to start new ones—such as the Women of Color Leadership Council in Washington, D.C.

In 1990, most women-of-color organizations were at the same stage that organizations such as NOW were at during the 1960s. They had no paid staff and in some cases no central office; they operated on shoestring budgets and were led by women who also had full-time jobs. Nevertheless, they were vigorous and creative, and they were changing the face of the women's movement. Some organizations, like NIWC, called themselves feminist; others felt the term was irrelevant, and some avoided using it. Sharon Parker noted that women of color, like white women, often prefaced their remarks with "I wouldn't call myself a feminist, but. . . ." All of the groups were concerned about women's issues, and when they joined forces, they spoke from a new position of strength.

BLACK WOMANISTS

Some of the strongest groups in the women-of-color alliance came out of the black* community. African-American women were, in a sense, natural feminists, though many were uncomfortable with the word because it conjured up an image of a white women's movement. Ultimately, some began to refer to them-

---

* Some American writers capitalize *Black* but not *white* to emphasize that there is a black (African-American) culture, while *white* refers to so many different ethnic groups that it can't be considered a culture. Others point out that, in fact, African-Americans, too, belong to more than one culture—the history and traditions of West Indians, for example, are different than those of Ghanaian-Americans or of African-Americans whose familes have been in the United States for generations. I have chosen not to capitalize.

The arguments over what to call various groups are far from over and they *are* important. The naming of something empowers the namer; that's one reason why when activists organize, sometimes one of the first things they do is rename themselves.

selves as "womanists," a term suggested by Alice Walker, who defined it this way:

> *Womanist* . . . A black feminist or feminist of color. From the black folk expression of mothers to female children, "You acting woman-ish," i.e., like a woman. Usually referring to outrageous, audacious, courageous or *willful* behavior . . . Responsible. In charge. *Serious.* . . .

Overall, black women supported feminist goals long before the white mainstream did. As early as 1972, polls showed that 67 percent of African-American women were in sympathy with the efforts of women's liberation groups; only 35 percent of white women agreed. In the mid-1980s, white women still hadn't quite caught up. However, despite feminist *attitudes*, during the sixties and seventies relatively few African-Americans became feminist activists. Historically, there were a number of reasons.

Many black women simply distrusted white women: They knew that racism wasn't confined to white men. Some, watching feminists capitalize on gains made by the civil rights movement, were afraid that under pressure from the government, employers would hire or promote white women rather than black women or men. At various times, government agencies did try to play off one group against the other—by declaring women a minority, for example, and encouraging them to compete for the limited number of jobs or contracts already reserved for racial minorities.

The fact that for generations white women had employed African-American women as domestic servants added to the legacy of resentment. In 1971, writer Toni Morrison observed that many black women regarded white women as:

> . . . willful children, pretty children, mean children, ugly children, but never as real adults capable of handling the real problems of the world.
>
> White women were ignorant of the facts of life. . . . They were totally dependent on marriage or male support (emotionally and economically). . . . Those who could afford it gave over the management of the house and the rearing of children to others. (It is a source of amusement even now to black women to listen to feminist talk of liberation while somebody's nice black grandmother shoulders the daily responsibility of child rearing and floor mopping, and the liberated one comes home to examine the housekeeping, correct it, and be entertained by the children.) If Women's Lib needs these grandmothers to thrive, it has a serious flaw.

Many black women were inclined to activism, even attuned to feminism, but as the second wave got under way they felt that feminist leaders weren't talking to them. Betty Friedan's book urged middle class, suburban housewives to seek a career as the answer to their problems. Most black women grew up assuming they'd be in the work force, as their mothers had been before them, because the family needed the income. To them, Friedan's advice "seemed to come from another planet," as historian Paula Giddings put it. Middle class white women were struggling to achieve the independence that racism had forced upon black women.

In the early 1970s, when radical feminists attacked the patriarchal family, many African-Americans were alienated still further, for the family was their bulwark against a racist society. In any case, they had other priorities—they put their energy into combatting racism. Many were incensed when white feminists began to claim that sexism was just like racism. Dorothy Height, president of the National Council of Negro Women, noted with asperity that white women had had the right to vote for fifty years but "it took lynching, bombing, the civil rights movement and the Voting Rights Act" to get that right for black people. Pam Allen, an early white women's liberationist married to a black activist, suggested that feminists were attempting to relieve their own guilt by saying that "we're oppressed too and therefore not really responsible." They wanted to believe that only white *men* were guilty.

Most black women felt that their first loyalty must be to their community, and they were under pressure from black men not to desert the civil rights struggle for feminism. They were also under pressure to be less assertive, thanks to the Moynihan report, a study done by Daniel Patrick Moynihan that was published in 1965 which concluded that "at the heart of the deterioration of the fabric of Negro society is the deterioration of the Negro Family." Slavery and racism had supposedly been harder on black males than on females because "the very essence of the male animal, from the bantam rooster to the four-star general, is to strut." Black men were prevented from strutting because there had been role reversal within the black family. The report went on to argue that female dominance was not only destroying black families but was creating widespread welfare dependency. Moynihan urged the government to see to it that every able-bodied black man had a job, even if that meant taking jobs away—not from white men, but from women.

The talk of black matriarchy encouraged black males to redefine their problem: It wasn't just racism, but their own natural need to assert their manhood (a need, incidentally, shaped by a mainstream culture that equated manhood with the ability to make money). Black power advocates, in particular, insisted that it was the black woman's duty to be submissive and to stay home and have babies to perpetuate the race. Though black women were well aware that their men had privileges they themselves didn't have, many believed the men's chauvinism stemmed from their frustration. Dorothy Height stated that "the major concern of the Negro woman is the status of the Negro man and his need for feeling himself an important person." (White women, too, were brought up to believe that women must protect men's egos, though white men were less vulnerable.)

Some black women resisted the pressure to take a backseat. Writer Michele Wallace recalled that in 1970 when she was in college and becoming a feminist, ". . . when the brothers talked to me, I talked back. . . . My social life was like guerrilla warfare." Her women friends were dropping out of school because men had persuaded them that it was "counterrevolutionary" for them to do anything except have babies and keep house. Meanwhile, African-American men she knew were "doing double time —uptown with the sisters and downtown with the white woman whom they always vigorously claimed to hate. Some of the bolder brothers were quite frank about it. 'The white woman lets me be a man.' "

Beyond the pressures that black women experienced, perhaps the stubbornest problem dividing black and white women was simply that their issues and priorities were different. While many white middle class women were hungry for a career and focused mainly on employment issues, the reality for most working-class black women was that a poorly paid, dead-end job neither liberated them nor gave them financial independence.

There were other differences as well. Homophobia was even stronger among people of color than it was in the white middle class, and lesbians were a visible presence in the women's movement, beginning in the 1970s. The rape issue was also divisive. For generations, white men had been raping black women with impunity, while black men accused—often unjustly—of raping white women were being lynched. That made rape a loaded subject for black women, and many white feminists didn't understand that. The issue became more complicated when black power advocates, such as Eldridge Cleaver, began to suggest that when black men raped white women, it was a justifiable political act. Black women were slow to protest.

Abortion also caused conflicts. Many black churches were not only anti-abortion but regarded it as a form of genocide, and religion played a central role in the lives of black women. Equally important, like other women of color, African-American women objected to white feminists' single-minded focus on abortion. They wanted predominantly white organizations to tackle sterilization abuse, infant mortality, access to prenatal care—reproductive rights in a much broader sense.

Beyond issues and priorities, the very theories with which white feminists made their case were often a problem. In the early days, black women were offended when radical feminists insisted that all oppression was rooted in male supremacy, not white supremacy, and that sexism was the oldest form of domination, the model for all others, and therefore must be dealt with first. Racism could wait its turn.

Audre Lorde, who described herself as a black, lesbian, feminist, socialist poet, argued that there could be no hierarchies of oppression. "Within the lesbian community I am Black, and within the Black community I am lesbian," she wrote. "Any attack against Black people is a lesbian and gay issue, because I and thousands of other Black women are part of the lesbian community. Any attack against lesbians and gays is a Black issue because thousands of lesbians and gay men are Black."

Sometimes, white feminists seemed to assume that racism was a kind of add-on, an extra burden of oppression that black women carried on top of their basic oppression as women. However, one couldn't describe black women's problems by adding together the problems of black men and those of white women. Though sexism affected all women in some similar ways, there were also important differences—for example, the survival issues that were top priority for many black women.

Nevertheless, there were always feminists in the black community. As early as 1971, Kathleen Cleaver, an officer in the Black Panther Party and the wife of Eldridge Cleaver, argued that women must join forces if they were ever to be free of male domination. However, she didn't believe that white and black feminists could work together in the same organizations. She favored coalitions of white and black feminist groups—and, of course, coalitions eventually flourished.

In 1973, with black militancy fading and male chauvinism rampant, the National Black Feminist Organization (NBFO) was founded.* Within a year, NBFO had spawned ten chapters and sponsored a conference. By the late 1970s, it had succumbed to the familiar conflicts between lesbians and heterosexuals, and between middle class and low-income women. However, in the meantime, a splinter group created after that first conference had begun to describe the way various systems of oppression interlocked: The black lesbians who formed the Combahee River Collective committed themselves to political struggle against racism, sexism, heterosexism, and class oppression.

Black feminists also organized around issues such as women's health and politics—for example, mobilizing and registering voters were top priorities for the National Coalition of 100 Black Women. In 1990, in a development that seemed to hold the seeds of a new unity among feminists, black women formed a coalition called African-American Women for Reproductive Freedom. The press conference announcing the new organization featured speakers ranging from Dorothy Height to Faye Wattleton, the dynamic president of Planned Parenthood. The issue hadn't changed—women of color still felt that reproductive rights must mean more than just abortion—but as the threat to *Roe* v. *Wade* mounted, some believed it was time for black women to unite and take a stand.

CREATING A VOICE FOR LATINAS

During the 1980s, Hispanics† were the fastest-growing segment of the U.S. population—experts predicted that by the year 2000, they would be the country's largest minority group. Most (62 percent) were of Mexican origin; 13 percent had their roots in Puerto Rico; 12 percent, in Central or South America; and 5 percent, in Cuba. Hispanics shared the Spanish language, some traditions, and the Catholic religion, but were otherwise very different. Some grew up in prosperous families that had been in the United States for generations; others were recent immigrants

---

* Historian Jacqueline Jones suggested that black feminism arose at least partly in response to the militants who urged black women to efface themselves.
† Some Americans of Latin origin prefer the term *Latina* (*Latino* for men) because *Hispanic* is a reminder of Spanish conquest; others see nothing objectionable about *Hispanic*. Therefore, I've used both terms. Some Mexican-American women prefer to be called *Mexican-American*, while others call themselves *Chicanas*. In general, *Chicana* has political overtones and is often associated with activism.

with little training, entering a labor market that offered few jobs for the unskilled. More and more Latino families were headed by a single mother—almost one in four by the late 1980s—and more than half of those families were poor.

Latinas had always been activists at the community level. Veronica Collazo recalled that "back in Texas when I was growing up, Mexican women and Mexican-American women were very much part of the union leadership and were active in social and political ways. We have a long history." In the 1970s, Latinas began to form their own nationwide women's organizations. Though there were a few umbrella groups, mostly they organized separately—as Mexican-Americans or Puerto Ricans, for example.

MANA, the Mexican-American Women's National Association, founded in 1974, was one of the oldest and most influential groups, and it defined itself from the beginning as a feminist organization, part of the women's movement. MANA's founders lived in Washington, D.C., and as Mexican-Americans far from home, they often got together on weekends. The women's movement was developing an agenda for change at the time, and the dialogue was dominated by Anglos and to some extent by black women. Meanwhile, male-dominated organizations spoke for Hispanics of both sexes to Congress and to the press. The women decided they needed their own organization to give Chicanas a voice. MANA had other goals, as well: to provide leadership opportunities for Chicanas and promote public awareness of their issues, to work for parity between women and men in the Mexican-American—and the larger—community, and to serve as a communications network for Latinas around the country.

By 1990, MANA had chapters in sixteen states and members in thirty-six. Latinas who were not Mexican-American often joined the organization, and some chapters elected presidents who weren't Chicanas. "We've always had leadership that was across the Hispanic spectrum," said Elvira Valenzuela Crocker, author of a forthcoming history of MANA.

MANA's unpaid and necessarily energetic leaders in Washington handled all the tasks done by paid staff in many white feminist organizations: They testified before Congress, planned strategy, and attended meetings of the various feminist and civil rights coalitions. Over the years, they campaigned for everything from the ERA to family leave.

The leaders of the male-dominated Hispanic organizations "tried to tell us you couldn't be both a Chicana and a feminist," said Crocker. She added that MANA undoubtedly aggravated both the men and some predominantly white feminist groups that simply wanted MANA to hop on the bandwagon on every issue.

MANA was prochoice almost from the outset, despite the fact that most members had grown up Catholic. Crocker recalled that "we had some real debate about abortion . . . but we viewed it as an important health option for women." Though a few members resigned because of the organization's stand on abortion, there seemed to be no hard feelings; they respected the group's work in other areas.

However, the women of MANA always defined reproductive rights more broadly than Anglo groups did and sterilization abuse was a major issue for them. Well aware that women who spoke little English sometimes agreed to be sterilized without understanding what the procedure would do or that it was permanent, MANA's leaders testified before Congress on the need for regulations that would require doctors and clinics to explain sterilization to every woman in her primary language. They were subsequently invited to work with HEW officials in drafting regulations and guidelines.

Many Hispanic feminists were pleased when the women's movement increasingly turned its attention to family problems in the 1980s. "Hispanic women have always had a family focus," said Crocker. They were also deeply concerned about their own community. In fact, it was part of MANA's tradition to analyze any issue by asking two key questions: "How does this affect our women?" and "How does this affect our people?"

From the beginning, education was one of MANA's top priorities. In 1987, only half of all adult Latinas had finished high school, compared to more than 75 percent of non-Hispanic females. The dropout rate for Hispanic youngsters was 50 percent in many areas and rose as high as 70 percent in some inner-city schools. Many Hispanic students were held back by the language barrier, but women like Elvira Crocker were convinced that low self-esteem, caused partly by racism, also contributed to the high dropout rate. Crocker recalled that when she herself was in first grade, she had a teacher who often made disparaging remarks to her about "your people." Her third grade teacher sometimes said indignantly to other children in the class, "Even the Mexican kid did better than you did." Crocker noted that "throughout my schooling, I was a constant surprise to teachers, because they had no expectations of me."

To encourage students to stay in school, MANA developed a project called *Hermanitas* (little sisters) through which members reach out to girls in junior high and high school. They help students explore their career options and advise them on what the requirements are for high school graduation (school guidance counselors often haven't told them) or on how they might be able to go on to college, if they're interested. The MANA women are not only advisors but role models. Perhaps most important, they listen and take the girls seriously; that alone can boost self-confidence. MANA also awards college scholarships annually.

PAN ASIAN GROUPS

American women of Asian and Pacific Islands descent (sometimes called API women, for short) organized at the national level both as separate ethnic groups and across ethnic lines. For instance, a Chinese-American woman could join the Organization of Chinese-American Women, which had chapters all over the country, and/or the Organization of Pan Asian American Women —known as Pan Asia—which was founded in 1976 expressly to bring API women together so that they could have an impact on public policy. There were many local, grass-roots groups as well. In addition, in the 1980s, API organizations that served both sexes were increasingly staffed and even led by women, because, like most nonprofit groups, they couldn't afford to pay employees as much as men could earn in the private sector.*

In 1980, there were almost two million API females in the United States. The majority traced their ancestry to India, China, Japan, the Philippines, Korea, Vietnam, Guam, Samoa, or Hawaii. Some Chinese- and Japanese-Americans came from families that had been in the United States since the nineteenth century. Recent immigrants included thousands of Southeast Asians who arrived during the 1980s.

To many people, Asian-Americans seemed a model minority: well-educated, affluent, socially accepted. In fact, partly because U.S. immigration policies favored college-educated professionals, API women were better educated overall than any other group of American women. They had inherited a strong work ethic—most families had several wage earners—and were more likely to be in the labor force than other women. Nevertheless, the women av-

---

* Most groups still had a largely male board of directors.

eraged just fifty-two cents on the white male dollar, and those who worked for corporations had even less chance of penetrating the "glass ceiling" than white women did. The model-minority stereotype created problems for APIs. Because most seemed to be doing well, there were few special programs for them. Irene Lee, president of Pan Asia, noted that "there are also low-achieving Asians who speak very little English."

What were "women's issues" for APIs? Pan Asia had to address that question, because its goal was to influence public policy on behalf of *all* API women. Thus, over the years, it combined many of the usual feminist priorities with specifically Asian issues and a concern for recent immigrants. Because most members were professional women, the organization had to struggle with the same problem that dogged predominantly white feminist groups: how to do outreach to low-income women.

During the late 1970s and 1980s, Pan Asia was involved in most significant feminist events, from the Houston conference to the effort to mobilize women voters in 1984. Its ongoing concerns included affirmative action and pay equity, family leave and child care. Pan Asia members, globally oriented, also joined demonstrations against apartheid and worked in the peace movement. Nuclear testing was a major concern for Pacific Islanders who came from places used as test sites.

According to Irene Lee, there were a few feminist issues on which API women were apt to be ambivalent. Like other women of color, many felt alienated when white feminists spoke as if reproductive rights began and ended with abortion. On lesbian rights—another issue that was often problematic for women of color—groups such as Pan Asia were supportive in a low-key way. To most API women, rooted in cultures in which sex was not discussed in public, sexual preference was not a comfortable subject.

As for the major Asian-American issues that Pan Asia became involved in, the 1990 census was of particular importance. Not only had APIs been undercounted in the past, but the data made available to the public often lumped them with Native Americans in the category called "other" and didn't even separate the sexes. That made it difficult to build a case about the likely impact of proposed laws and government policies.

In 1990, Pan Asia had no paid staff and no central office, and that limited how much it could accomplish. Irene Lee was increasingly concerned about the problems of low-income women. She had discovered, for example, that, as an issue, pay equity simply didn't "resonate" with API women who worked on electronic assembly lines and in garment factories. Their priorities were more apt to be health insurance and getting access to language classes and other training programs.

Pan Asia was also concerned about mail-order brides. A number of agencies were bringing in women, mostly from the Philippines, to marry American men. The men chose a bride from photos and descriptions published in catalogs, which often made a point of Asian women's supposed submissiveness. The brides arrived in the United States with no support system, often spoke little or no English, and lived with the threat that they might be deported if they displeased their new husbands.

Irene Lee, struggling to make sense of Pan Asia's diversity, felt that the organization's single biggest challenge was to find ways to include low-income women so that they could speak for themselves on public policy matters. That meant she must somehow raise the funds to hire a staff—there was no way volunteers could do outreach on the scale that was necessary.

NATIVE AMERICANS: NATIONS WITHIN A NATION

In 1980, American Indians* and Native Alaskans together made up one half of 1 percent of the U.S. population. Vastly outnumbered, they fought to preserve their heritage, while working—and otherwise participating—in the larger society. There were hundreds of tribes and they had different languages and traditions; about half of all Native Americans lived on reservations. Nations within the nation, the tribes were political units of government. They provided their members with services, which were partly supported by the federal government under arrangements established by treaty when the Indians agreed to give up tribal lands.

Native American women were organized almost entirely on the local level, and they were less likely than other American women to form groups separately from men, partly because women were more accepted as leaders within most Indian tribes than they were in the white world. Historically, Native American women

---

* Though *Native American* is the term preferred by some activists, others refer to themselves as *American Indians*. I've used both terms.

and men were on a fairly equal footing before white settlers came. During centuries of white dominance, women's status declined, but in the 1960s it began to improve again. LaDonna Harris estimated that by 1990, one quarter of the members of most tribal councils were women, and women filled half the seats on many. They were also among the top tribal administrators and were included in the leadership of Indian rights groups.

Though American Indian women didn't organize explicitly as feminists, many became grass-roots activists focused largely on women's concerns. For those who lived on reservations, health care and unemployment were generally the most urgent issues. On a few reservations, women who became activists because of health issues moved on to tackle other problems. For example, on the Pine Ridge reservation in South Dakota, the Oglala Women's Society began by forcing the Indian Health Service to provide a new village well; then it turned its attention to electoral politics. The Society made alcoholism an issue in the 1988 tribal elections, successfully appealing to voters to "pick the person who is sober this election over your relative who is not." The new council, with a majority of nondrinkers, began to tackle alcohol-related problems such as child abuse and wife-beating.

Domestic violence was a major issue, and on reservations all over the country, women's groups sprang up during the 1980s to protect women and children. The White Buffalo Calf Society and Women of All Red Nations both had a number of chapters in the Midwest that served battered women. Loretta Webster, an Oneida, recalled that a group she was involved with eventually decided that nothing would really change unless they found a way to reach the men as well. As they began to work with groups set up for male batterers, they focused on a powerful argument. "We told the men domestic abuse is not part of our heritage," said Webster. For those who honored the traditional ways, the statement was eye-opening.

In Webster's view, both wife-beating and alcoholism were largely the result of government practices that undermined the American Indian family. Up until the 1950s, Indian children were often removed from their families as soon as they were six or seven years old and placed in special boarding schools, often against their parents' wishes. The schools punished the children for speaking their own language and taught them nothing about their heritage. In that sterile environment, they had only older children to turn to for the kind of nurturing their parents had provided. "It was the end of families as we knew them," said Webster, "and it happened for a couple of generations in the Indian community."

Native American women worked alongside men on issues such as treaty rights. In Wisconsin, after the Menominee lost their tribal status, Ada Deer led the fight to make them a federally recognized tribe again. Meanwhile, around the country, American Indians were demanding that various states not only honor ancient treaties but accept Native Americans as partners in managing natural resources like fish, game, and timber. According to Loretta Webster, who was associate vice chancellor for the Advancement of Cultural Diversity at the University of Wisconsin, a survey of a number of states found that wherever tribes had gained a say in how fishery resources were handled, those resources were better managed afterward.

LaDonna Harris was one of the few American Indians with national visibility. An activist since the 1960s, she worked in the civil rights and women's movements and for Indian rights. In the early 1970s, she became the founder and president of Americans for Indian Opportunity (AIO). Washington-based, AIO had a national board of directors composed of twenty-five women and men from different regions and tribes. It pressed for administrative changes in the federal agencies that handled Indian affairs, but it was also a Native American think tank. "We try to take issues that are on the cutting edge and develop some strategy," said Harris, "then take that out to the community and lay it out so that grass-roots groups can use the ideas as they see fit."

Thus, in 1990, AIO was studying traditional tribal methods of governing, approaching from an American Indian point of view some of the questions about leadership that also interested feminist theorists. Harris, a Comanche herself, noted that in Comanche society when people came together to make a decision, they were expected to approach the problem in different ways. Not only was everyone allowed to speak, but no one challenged anyone else's point of view—it was seen as information the group needed to incorporate before it could develop a collective sense of the problem. Leadership was seen as shared responsibility, rather than as an opportunity to have power over others. Most tribes ultimately adopted the American majority-rules approach, said Harris, and that caused a great deal of infighting. The goal of the AIO study was to look at ways to mesh the two traditions. Harris suggested that perhaps society needed to reorganize in smaller units, so that people could have more say in decisions that affected them and would feel responsible for their actions and relationships. She spoke of "retribalizing" people in the inner cities, for example.

THE DISABILITY RIGHTS MOVEMENT

In the 1980s, women who were disability rights* activists challenged the women's movement to address their issues. Feminists must begin, some said, by making their meetings accessible to women who used wheelchairs and those who were deaf or visually impaired.

The disability rights movement, like the second wave of feminism, evolved out of earlier efforts by activists. The parents of disabled children laid the groundwork during the late 1940s and 50s, when they organized to demand schooling and jobs for their children.† Those involved were primarily mothers.

In the early 1970s, the first independent living centers (ILCs) were established and they became a springboard for the disability rights movement. ILCs, which were run by disabled people themselves, provided services so that people with disabilities could live independently in the community and could gain or regain a sense of self-respect. Someone who used a wheelchair, for example, could turn to an ILC for help in finding accessible housing and a personal attendant; equally important, the centers provided peer support and a philosophy that emphasized pride, autonomy, and activism.

There are striking parallels between the events that triggered the disability rights movement and those that touched off the second wave of feminism. In 1973, Congress passed a law with a key provision, known as Section 504, that banned discrimination against the disabled in all federally funded programs. By 1977, the law still hadn't gone into effect because the Ford and Carter administrations delayed issuing regulations. As with Title VII, the law that prohibited job discrimination, the government had

* The disability rights movement represented the interests of Americans with both physical and mental disabilities (cognitive impairments or mental illness). In the early 1990s, activists were still debating terminology. Some didn't want to be called *disabled*. In Michigan, the preferred term was *handicappers*, while in other places activists called themselves *handicapables*. In the women's movement, the terms *differently abled* and *physically challenged* were sometimes used. However, according to Patrisha Wright of the Disability Rights Education and Defense Fund, "On the political left of the movement, we refer to ourselves as disabled. . . ."

† Until 1975, there was no law requiring that disabled children be given an education.

passed legislation, legitimated a cause, then stalled—and ignited a movement.

Throughout the 1970s, grass-roots groups sprang up, and disabled people staged demonstrations around the country. These protests brought together people with different disabilities, just as the ILCs did. In April 1977, groups acting under the umbrella of American Coalition of Citizens with Disabilities (ACCD) mounted protests in ten cities. Most were short-lived, but in San Francisco 150 people, led by activists from the Berkeley Center for Independent Living (CIL), staged a sit-in at the HEW building that lasted for twenty-seven days. Thanks to the CIL, the Bay Area's disabled were already semi-organized; they also had a great deal of support from the community, including civil rights groups and unions. During the sit-in, food and other supplies were provided by the Salvation Army, the Black Panthers, the local Safeway, and gay rights groups, among others, and San Francisco's mayor actually had showers rigged up for the protestors at the city's expense. When the federal government still failed to act, the San Francisco demonstrators sent a deputation to Washington. It joined forces with an East Coast ACCD contingent to stage further demonstrations. On April 28, the regulations for Section 504 were finally issued. Meanwhile, disabled people all over the country had been fired up.

During the 1980s, disability rights groups joined the civil rights coalition in Washington. By that time, an astonishing one in six Americans had some disability. The numbers had grown because people were living longer, and medical advances often saved lives but left individuals with chronic problems.* The disability movement now encompassed independent living centers, and organizations of the disabled, for the parents of the disabled, and for rehabilitation professionals. As AIDS groups sprang up around the country, they were included. There were also grass-roots activists who didn't belong to any group but would readily join a protest. "My job is to hold the groups together for long enough to pass a bill," said Patrisha Wright, director of government affairs for DREDF, the Disability Rights Education and Defense Fund.

Many groups were headed by disabled women, partly because disabled men more often landed better-paying jobs in business or government service. Most organizations were disability-specific. However, the ILCs and a few other groups, such as DREDF and

---

* In the long run, most people are only temporarily able-bodied.

the World Institute on Disability (WID), addressed the issues of all disabled people.*

In the late 1980s, disability rights activists scored two major victories. The Fair Housing Act was amended to require that all new multifamily housing must be either accessible to the disabled or constructed so that it could be made accessible: Doors must be wide enough for a wheelchair, for example. Then in 1990, Congress passed the Americans with Disabilities Act (ADA). Where Section 504 had prohibited federally funded programs from discriminating against the disabled, the ADA extended the ban to all employers. It was the most sweeping new civil rights law since 1964.

The ADA covered not only job discrimination but access to office buildings and public places, because an antidiscrimination law was meaningless if disabled people couldn't even get into the building to apply for a job. Among other things, the ADA required all new or renovated buildings—including stores, restaurants, doctors' offices, and so on—to be accessible to people using wheelchairs and those with other types of disabilities. Experts estimated that this would add less than 1 percent to the cost of construction.

"The ADA says . . . no longer will we build a society that's inaccessible . . . ," said Judy Heumann, cofounder and vice-president of WID. She pointed out that if society were designed with disabled people in mind, many could support themselves totally or partially. However, she noted that "we should not have to prove that we are cost-neutral. . . . We believe that regardless of the apparent severity of one's disability, an individual is capable of making contributions."

The ADA was just a first step. It forbade job discrimination except in cases where hiring someone with a disability would be an undue hardship for a company. However, in reality a business was unlikely to employ a woman who was legally blind, for example, if it must also pay someone to read to her. Some disabled people could function only if they had physical assistance. Those who could afford it hired assistants through an independent living center, and that enabled them to take a job and live on their own. Paid attendants helped them dress, feed, and bathe themselves, did housecleaning or shopping, fed and diapered babies

* DREDF developed legislative strategy, drafted bills, and provided training and technical assistance for people and groups concerned about disability rights; it also handled legal cases. WID was a public policy research organization. Both were spin-offs from the independent living movement.

for disabled parents, interpreted for those with hearing and speech problems, wrote checks for the intellectually impaired— in short, handled whatever tasks a person couldn't manage without help.

In the late 1980s, disability rights activists began pressing for federal personal-assistance legislation. As matters stood, people were often institutionalized because funds were available to pay for nursing home care but not for services in the community. A few people, given no option other than a nursing home, had actually petitioned the courts for the right to die. There was no national policy on personal assistance and every state was different: California provided it for more than 130,000 disabled people, while in Virginia a pilot program reached 36 individuals. Most state programs, where they existed at all, paid for attendants only for the very poor. There weren't enough programs, and many disabled people couldn't afford an attendant, and so they were unable to go to work.

Disability rights activists pointed out that nursing home care was much more expensive than personal assistance programs in the community, and that many people currently institutionalized could be released and could go to work if such programs were widely available. Some could pay part of the cost of the attendant themselves, if the states charged sliding fees based on the individual's income *after* all disability-related expenses were deducted. To Judy Heumann, personal assistance was very much a women's issue. Women were not only more likely than men to be disabled because they lived longer, but they were the ones who currently provided disabled people with services as low-paid workers or unpaid family members. In fact, it was largely because of the efforts of families that only two million of the nation's nine million disabled citizens lived in nursing homes.

The concerns of disabled women overlapped those of feminists on many issues—for example, equal pay.* However, disability activists disagreed with many feminists about the right to live. Judy Heumann, for example, explained that she was strongly prochoice and believed every woman had a right to decide whether to bear a child; yet she questioned the practice of aborting fetuses that might be born with a disability. Many such abortions seemed based on the assumption that it was impossible for someone with a disability to live a quality life—that it was better

* On the average, for every dollar able-bodied white men earned, disabled men earned 48 cents, disabled women made 27 cents, and women of color with disabilities earned just 12 cents.

to be dead. Disabled people don't see their lives as tragedies, Heumann said. The tragedy is "society's unwillingness to accept us as equals" and to remove barriers that prevent disabled people from realizing their own potential.

Heumann was also concerned about genetic research, because its ultimate goal was to rid society of disabled people—and *disability* was becoming more and more broadly defined. Some ethicists predict that in the future women might be urged to abort fetuses that had only a genetic *tendency* to a disease, such as cancer.* "The goal is to make the perfect person," said Heumann. "Disabled people are not perfect." In fact, the more significant the disability, the more they remind the (temporarily) able-bodied of their own vulnerabilities and frailties.

THE STRUGGLE FOR DIVERSITY

In the 1980s, concern about diversity was obvious at virtually every feminist conference and in feminist publications. However, coalitions that linked women-of-color groups with predominantly white groups were much more common than multicultural organizations. In Washington and in various state capitals, the groups formed alliances to press for legislation. Yet the women found that achieving diversity within a single organization was both difficult and risky.

The problems and the potential of diversity were illustrated by a meeting that took place in November 1989, when 500 young women gathered in Washington, D.C., for the first national feminist conference for women in their twenties. That same weekend, 300,000 marchers descended on the capital to demonstrate for reproductive rights. Surprisingly, throughout the young women's conference, the need for diversity in the women's movement was at least as hot a topic as abortion. The discussions were sparked by the fact that the speakers and panelists included many women of color, lesbians, and disabled women. The conference was sponsored by CWPS, the Center for Women Policy Studies, and Leslie Wolfe—now director of CWPS—explained that the Center made a point of looking at any issue from the differing perspectives of all the groups of women who had been marginalized in the past.

---

* People with identifiable genetic tendencies were already finding that even though they weren't sick, they couldn't get health insurance.

Most of the young white women who came to the conference seemed delighted that the panels were multicultural. During a discussion period, one of them stood up to say just that; she also invited women of color from the audience to take the microphone. A black woman responded angrily, calling this "white woman's do-goodism." She was quite capable of speaking out whenever she wanted to, she said—she didn't need a special invitation. (Black feminist Bell Hooks once observed that white women sometimes behaved as if they owned the women's movement.)

On the last morning of the conference, during a plenary session, women of color brought up that incident and other instances of subtle racism that they'd experienced during the weekend. As the discussion progressed, several black woman said that they didn't want to sit and listen to white women talk about their own guilt; that it wasn't their responsibility to educate white women about racism—enough had been written on the subject and there were books they could read. At times during the morning, confrontations were so heated that they brought tears to the eyes of those involved. Some white feminists obviously felt intimidated. A few black women were openly contemptuous of those whose sensitivity lagged on racial issues.

Leslie Wolfe noted that there was a big difference between the contempt expressed that day by those few women of color and the frustration of some others, which was coupled with an expectation that the other party might be willing to learn. The confrontation wasn't a bad thing, she said. "A few years ago, the whole discussion would have been shut off or would never have happened and things would have festered. This way they got to have an explosion together. . . . Afterward, there was some genuine reaching across the gulf."

During the 1980s, as feminists struggled to bridge that gulf and create multicultural organizations, some groups and individuals experimented with creative strategies. The YWCA, one of the oldest women's organizations, provided a model to prove that diversity was possible. In 1970, the YWCA made a decision: to use its collective power to eliminate racism both in the nation and within the organization. Women on nominating committees and at all other levels made a conscious effort to bring in women of color in substantial numbers, as members and as leaders. Changes didn't happen overnight, but by 1990 women of color filled nearly half the seats on the YWCA's seventy-five-member

National Board and held many of its top offices. In a major way, Dorothy Height, a National YWCA staff member for almost thirty years, provided leadership in the transformation.

As for other feminist organizations, the National Women's Health Network and the *Our Bodies, Ourselves* collective nurtured several health groups founded by women of color. The Network subsequently invited some of those women to serve on its board. The AAUW (American Association of University Women), long known as an organization for older, elite white women, also undertook a serious struggle to diversify in the late 1980s.

In 1989, a handful of NOW activists in Dallas, Texas, founded NOW's first truly multicultural chapter. The way they went about it created a model for other groups. They began by doing a survey of women living in a black and Hispanic neighborhood to find out what their issues were; then they started to hold meetings in a neighborhood church. They soon discovered that homelessness and child care were bigger concerns for the women of the community than abortion rights, and that discrimination clinics, which brought in lawyers and counselors to advise the women, were obviously helpful.

During its first year, Dallas Rainbow NOW worked on several projects that reflected members' priorities—for instance, it joined forces with the SCLC (the Southern Christian Leadership Conference) to open up abandoned housing projects for homeless people. When the chapter was a year old, its membership was 45 percent Anglo, 45 percent African-American, and 10 percent Latina. There had been difficult times—votes that fell along racial lines, arguments because some Anglo members felt the chapter wasn't doing enough to defend abortion. Nevertheless, chapter president Karen Ashmore, one of the founders, said, "From a selfish point of view, this has enriched my life more than anything I've ever done."

It was probably easier to build a multicultural organization from the ground up than to diversify the membership of a small group that was already established, but that, too, was possible. In the early 1980s, the members of New York Women Against Rape (NYWAR)—mostly white—decided that they must achieve a better racial mix because there was no point in doing antirape work in a city like New York if they weren't reaching women of color. Their initial strategy was to establish affinity groups within NYWAR for women of color, lesbians, and older women. Those groups were asked to meet and discuss their issues separately, defining them so that the whole membership could talk about them afterward. The women in the affinity groups felt that collectively they had new strength and influence.

The effort to change NYWAR was unexpectedly time-consuming, according to the group's director, Danette Wilson, because the issues raised had to be dealt with on a daily basis, not just in occasional discussions. Some of the original members left, and because NYWAR had stated publicly that it would address racism and all other isms head-on, new members came into it with high expectations. "The reality," said Wilson, "is that it's a continuing struggle. . . . Dealing with racism on an everyday level has tremendously challenged the organization."

In the 1980s, some women also took steps as individuals to promote a multicultural movement. Peggy McIntosh, a white feminist educator much in demand as a speaker on curricular diversity, let it be known that she would talk about her work on white privilege only if she could copresent with a woman of color. Because the copresenter was generally someone from the community that had invited McIntosh to speak, that brought the issues home to the audience. Guida West, a well-known white welfare rights activist, decided that she would go to conferences only when she could afford to pay for someone else to go as well. Thus, in 1989, she told the organizer of a major meeting in San Franciso that she'd contribute money so that a welfare mother could attend, and then *if* she could afford it, she'd come herself.

Despite these strong but scattered efforts, as the nineties began, the women's movement still had a long way to go to eliminate racism. Charon Asetoyer, director of a Native American women's health group, argued that it wasn't enough for white feminist groups to include women of color on their boards of directors if their priorities remained unchanged. Leslie Wolfe suggested that white women must be willing to be more than just partners with women of color; they must be willing to be led by them and to have their issues defined by them at times. Luz Alvarez Martinez, who headed a Latina health organization, maintained that the major feminist groups had nothing to fear even if a majority of their board members were women of color, because "we wouldn't overlook their issues—their needs are part of our needs." In other words, women of color had the same issues that white women did, and more besides.

THE SALAD BOWL REPLACES THE MELTING POT

In the 1980s, some women began to reframe feminist theory to reflect the life experiences of women of color as well as those of white women. In the process, they defined women's basic problems somewhat differently.

Black scholar Bell Hooks wrote that "to me feminism is not simply a struggle to . . . ensure that women will have equal rights with men; it is a commitment to eradicating the ideology of domination that permeates Western culture on various levels—sex, race, and class, to name a few. . . ." Hooks believed that nothing would really change if feminists fought only for a share of the power and privileges currently monopolized by white males. Though some women might succeed, they would immediately acquire a vested interest in preserving the hierarchy and their own position in it, and other women would gain little or nothing.

Hooks observed that, like men, women both dominate others and are dominated. ". . . [I]t is first the potential oppressor within that we must resist—the potential victim within that we must rescue. . . ." She argued that women must attack both the assumption that human interactions should be based on hierarchies, and the assumption that it was acceptable to maintain power by coercion.

White theorist Charlotte Bunch argued along similar lines. She noted that the idea that difference justified domination was deeply embedded in the American psyche. Most people simply assumed that there would always be poor people, that those who were smarter, harder-working, more competitive, simply rose to the top, while others sank to the bottom. People who believed that hierarchies were inevitable were easy to manipulate, Bunch suggested. It wasn't hard to persuade them that people who were different (and lower in the hierarchy) must be a threat to their own position. Thus, they tended to see race, class, and ethnic differences in terms of degrading and menacing stereotypes.

The feminist struggle against racism was important not only for the future of the women's movement but as a possible model for the nation. Like it or not, whites were going to have to shed their racism or face a future of escalating conflict as resentful "minorities" jointly came to constitute the majority of the population. Experts predicted that by the year 2000, 85 percent of those entering the American labor force would *not* be white males; by 2020, at least one third of the nation would be nonwhite; by mid-century, whites might no longer be the majority. Would they cling desperately to power in the United States, or be replaced in the power structure by others equally determined to preserve their own newly won privileges? Could Americans of all races belatedly learn to accept, even to value, diversity?

Some traditionalists feared a loss of identity. They argued that a nation couldn't exist without shared values, and that minority groups must conform to American norms as generations of European immigrants had done. However, Emily Style, codirector of a program for multicultural and gender-fair high school curriculums, suggested that the United States had always been more like a salad bowl than a melting pot. Furthermore, the idea that it *should* be a melting pot helped to keep people of color down.

As feminist attorney Lucinda Finley neatly put it: "The American melting pot has been a cauldron into which we have put black, brown, red, yellow, and white men and women, in the hope that we will come up with white men. The ideal of homogeneity . . . blinds us both to the fact and to the value of our diversity."

The task for the 1990s was to learn to appreciate differences and yet to eliminate them as the basis for distributing power and privilege. The change was bound to be difficult, perhaps especially on the personal level where it had to begin. The complexity of the problem was caught in the opening lines of a poem by Pat Parker:

For the White Person Who Wants to Know How to Be My Friend

The first thing you do is to forget that I'm Black.
Second, you must never forget that I'm Black. . . .

chapter 18

Why the ERA Lost

*F*or ten years, from 1972 to 1982, the struggle to ratify
the ERA consumed the energy of the women's movement; it
gripped most liberal feminists as no other issue had since the
fight for suffrage. Their commitment grew out of their belief in
equality, their rage when they realized that the only right women
had under the Constitution was the right to vote, and their frustration with the slow pace of social change.

The ERA was one of those issues that touched off a movement
of its own. Though most of the major national women's organizations were involved in the drive to ratify the amendment, so
were many groups and individuals who weren't part of the larger
feminist movement. Religious and professional organizations,
unions, and civic groups joined forces with feminists. After the
first few years, efforts were coordinated by an umbrella organization in Washington called ERAmerica and by affiliated coalitions in varous states.

Throughout the ratification campaign, feminists and antifeminists argued about what the ERA really meant. The amendment
was, perhaps, the ultimate gender-neutral statement. In the

1920s, women who opposed it referred to it as the "blanket amendment" because they believed it would invalidate all laws that treated females and males differently. That was more or less what second-wave feminists predicted as well; they often cited an article published in the *Yale Law Journal* that became part of the amendment's legislative history and hence would help to determine the way it would be interpreted. The article stated that if the ERA passed, laws that treated women and men differently would be unconstitutional with just two exceptions: statutes protecting the right to privacy, and those involving physical characteristics unique to one sex (the state could regulate sperm banks, for example).

Antifeminists insisted that it would be disastrous to treat women just like men and fought to preserve the laws that supposedly protected women. ERA supporters maintained that those laws actually held women back. Ultimately, difference feminists began to suggest that—in certain, limited circumstances primarily related to pregnancy—women *did* need laws that treated them differently than men. However, unlike the ERA's opponents, the difference feminists were simply arguing strategy. The antifeminists wanted to return women to their traditional role. Difference feminists were determined to set them on an equal footing with men, and they believed that could happen only if the law gave mothers a few special breaks.

The ERA's defeat left many feminists confused and angry. How could the amendment lose, they asked, when the polls showed that a solid majority of the public—63 percent—supported it? As scholars began to suggest answers to that question, a complex picture emerged. At least half a dozen major factors were involved in the ERA's defeat. A handful of powerful misogynist politicians, too well entrenched to care about public opinion, played a decisive role, as did a determined opposition; feminists were slow to organize in support of the amendment; and there were other, even more basic factors as well.

Though in the end the amendment was defeated, the ratification campaign itself had enduring consequences. In most ways, they were good for the women's movement.

A SHOO-IN TURNS CONTROVERSIAL

When the Senate passed the ERA in March 1972, it seemed that ratification would be quick and easy. Hawaii approved the amendment within the hour and before the week was out, five other states acted. By early 1973, thirty states had ratified; only eight more were needed. At first, there was little opposition—in some legislatures the vote was unanimous.

Feminists were understandably optimistic and—partly for that reason—the pro-ERA campaign got off to a slow start. In August 1972, eighteen women got together in Washington to form the ERA Ratification Council, a coalition of thirty groups. It was to serve as a central clearinghouse to help groups in various states form coalitions and exchange information. However, it had no paid staff and a very small budget. As Washington activist Bernice Sandler pointed out, in the early 1970s the women's movement was still young and struggling. "We were an incredibly small band of people with very limited money and not much experience in state politics," she said.

In contrast, antifeminists were quick off the mark. Phyllis Schlafly, who would become their leader, discovered very early that the ERA was an emotionally loaded subject. Schlafly published a newsletter ordinarily focused on the dangers of Communism, which was mailed primarily to conservative Republicans. In November 1972, she devoted an entire issue of the newsletter, the *Phyllis Schlafly Report*, to an attack on the amendment and immediately heard from many readers who agreed with her. Obviously, women who were passive when lectured about the Communist menace could be moved to outrage when warned of changes in their own lives that might be wrought by the ERA.

Schlafly, long active in the Republican party, was known for her hard-line position on Communism. Back in 1967, she had lost the presidency of the National Federation of Republican Women partly because many people believed she was involved with the John Birch Society, a semisecret, far-right organization that insisted that the United States was already 50 to 70 percent Communist-controlled. Schlafly denied being a member, but she spoke at Birch-sponsored events. To mainstream Republicans, the Birchers sounded paranoid, and Schlafly had been tainted by her association with them. Her opposition to the ERA gave her a respectable issue on which to build support.

The struggle over the ERA not only made Phyllis Schlafly famous but helped create and shape the New Right, the social movement that would win the presidency in 1980. For ten years, the amendment served as a lightning rod for the conservative backlash. Political scientist Jane Mansbridge noted that "it allowed the New Right to talk about issues that were really close to people's lives, just the way we got into feminism . . . the personal is political." The anti-ERA campaign mobilized people who hadn't been involved in politics before and gave them something concrete to do. Conveniently, the action was in the states, not far away in Washington.

If antifeminists hadn't organized, the ERA would have passed in 1973 or 74. As it was, in January 1973, as state legislatures reconvened all over the country, the *New York Times* reported that "well-organized and seemingly well-financed opposition groups have appeared. . . ." They were part of a new organization, headed by Schlafly, called STOP E.R.A. Spokeswomen concentrated on two points: They argued that if the ERA passed, women would be drafted, and they claimed that it would mean the end of laws requiring men to support their families. Feminists agreed that both sexes would be drafted but denied that homemakers were in danger of losing their support.

Early in 1973, the draft was abolished, letting some of the steam out of that issue. In October, the AFL-CIO admitted defeat on the protective labor laws and announced that it would join the campaign for the ERA. Though some feminists felt that victory must be near, they couldn't have been more mistaken. By the end of 1973, the ratification drive had lost much of its momentum as the amendment became more and more controversial. At that point, only a few states had active ERA coalitions, while in Washington the ERA Ratification Council was still operating on a shoestring.

During the first five weeks of 1974, three more states ratified. There were now just five to go, but the backlash was building. That year, the Tennessee legislature voted to rescind its earlier ratification of the amendment after hearing claims that the ERA would send pregnant women to the battlefront in future wars. Most legal experts agreed that states couldn't undo their decisions to ratify, but that didn't stop Tennessee and three other states from trying. Rescissions might not hold up legally, but they gave the impression that Americans were changing their minds.

ANTIFEMINISTS DEFINE THE ISSUES

When Congress first passed the ERA, many people simply assumed that it would benefit all women. Doubts arose when homemakers, organized by Schlafly, began to pepper legislators and local newspapers with anti-ERA letters. A few years later, fundamentalist churches got involved. Male ministers organized busloads of women and delivered them to state capitals to lobby legislators. Phyllis Schlafly seemed to be everywhere, claiming to speak for the beleaguered housewife. Martha Griffiths and others were convinced that the ERA would actually do more for the homemaker than for women who were employed,* but they had trouble getting their message across. Throughout the early years of the campaign, men were more apt to support the ERA than women.†

Feminists believed that as a matter of principle, women should be included in the Constitution, and that the ERA would rid the nation of a hodgepodge of discriminatory laws. The opposition brought up a host of other issues, and ERA backers felt the debate slipping through their fingers, as it was framed—disastrously—in someone else's terms.

The heart of the antifeminist argument was a defense of traditional sex roles. Schlafly argued that equal rights would actually be a step down for women because they already had special privileges, such as the right not to take a job; she claimed that if the amendment passed, wives would be forced to provide half the family's income. Feminists emphatically (and correctly) denied this. They pointed out that the right to support, in states where such laws existed, was actually unenforceable. The only way a woman could make her husband provide for her was to file for divorce or separation, because the courts refused to interfere in a marriage as long as it was intact.

Antifeminists also insisted that the ERA would abolish laws that gave mothers custody of young children and would cost women their right to alimony. Feminists acknowledged that women might indeed lose their automatic custody preference but insisted that little else would change. If, under the ERA, divorce laws were rewritten to be gender-neutral, alimony would be awarded to a "dependent spouse" rather than to the wife, but it was almost always the wife who was dependent. In fact, even without the amendment, the laws were rewritten (see chapter 14).

In describing the possible consequences of the ERA, antifeminists made a number of unlikely, even outrageous predictions.

---

* For example, in the sixteen states that had an ERA in their constitution, divorce courts were required to recognize the economic value of a homemarker's contribution when they divided a couple's property.

† In 1975, for example, 63 percent of men who were polled backed it, compared to 54 percent of women.

They charged that the ERA would abolish rape laws and legalize homosexual marriages. Feminists responded that rape laws, made gender-neutral, would simply extend to men and boys the same inadequate protection females had. On the question of gay rights, the amendment's legislative history made it clear that the ERA would merely ensure that the laws treated gay men and lesbians the same way: If same-sex marriages were permitted for men, they must be allowed for women, too.

The conservatives also declared that the amendment would require that public toilets and prisons be unisex. Feminists replied that such facilities were protected by the constitutional right to privacy. Scholars, canvassing state legislators, found that anti-feminists damaged their own credibility with their emphasis on "potty politics." However, ERA opponents kept harping on uni-sex toilets, apparently because for many antifeminists they symbolized the way women would lose protection under the ERA. In the South, the bathroom issue was also a reminder of the civil rights struggle that put an end to the racial segregation of public toilets.

The two arguments against the ERA that its supporters took most seriously were the claim that it would require that tax money be used to pay for abortions, and the statement that women would be drafted and would have to serve in combat. In both cases, feminists disagreed among themselves about how the amendment would and should be interpreted. These issues will be explored more fully later in this chapter.

To feminists who debated Phyllis Schlafly in the media and during public meetings, her charges were a maddening blend of facts and distortions. Many concluded that because she was obviously a very astute woman, the distortions must be deliberate. Long-time ERA proponent Catherine East, who debated her a number of times, said, "When I first saw her newsletter, I thought she wasn't very smart . . . but after I got to know her, I saw she knew exactly what she was doing."

If antifeminists succeeded in convincing many people that their predictions were accurate, it was partly because press coverage was poor. When Catherine East analyzed approximately 2200 news stories about the ERA that were published in the 1970s, she found that only about 30 percent referred to its legal effects at all, and of that 30 percent, less than 8 percent provided information from reliable sources. Most reporters simply repeated the wildest and most colorful statements of both sides and made no attempt to find out whether there was any basis for such claims. In interpreting the amendment, the courts would refer to its legislative history—the reports of congressional committees and the statements of its supporters during floor debates. Only three news stories used the ERA's legislative history to clarify competing claims, though hundreds of thousands of copies of background material on that history had been distributed to the press. Reporters could also have turned to constitutional experts, but very few did.

THE ERA STALLS; THE WOMEN'S MOVEMENT GROWS

One state ratified the ERA in 1975, and one in 1977, but they were to be the last. Though victory was now just three states away, the outlook was grim. The remaining unratified states were deeply conservative, either southern or else Mormon-dominated, except for Illinois, which required a three-fifths majority in both houses of the legislature to pass constitutional amendments (most states required a simple majority).

Nevertheless, the opposition to the amendment was actually fueling the growth of the women's movement, just as opposition had done in the past. By mid-1974, there were statewide pro-amendment groups in most of the unratified states. After July 1975, money was no longer as tight, because BPW voted to earmark $1.50 of every member's annual dues for the ERA drive for the duration of the campaign. Early in 1976, Washington feminists founded ERAmerica to promote the amendment on the national level. ERA supporters all over the country could contribute to the new organization, and it would funnel the money to the states where it seemed likely to do the most good.

In September 1977, with the deadline for ratification still about eighteen months away, NOW stunned other groups by proposing that they ask Congress for an extension. Eleanor Smeal, president of NOW, called a meeting of the leaders of women's organizations and laid out a detailed analysis of the fifteen nonratified states, summarizing the voting record of each legislator. On the basis of this analysis, NOW had concluded that the amendment couldn't be ratified before the deadline, March 22, 1979. The campaign for extension lasted for months, culminating in July 1978 with a march in Washington by 100,000 activists. The following month, Congress pushed the deadline back, but only to June 30, 1982.

After that, pro-ERA groups redoubled their efforts. They were learning a lot about state politics, sometimes the hard way. In Florida, for example, feminists campaigned to elect several legislators because they promised to support the ERA; they subsequently voted against it. Dempsey Barron, chairman of the Rules Committee in the Florida Senate, used parliamentary tactics several times to defeat the ERA and bragged afterward that he had killed the amendment single-handedly. Feminists found it significant that his law firm represented over a dozen insurance companies. The insurance industry opposed the ERA, in the belief that it would end the practice of charging women more than men for insurance.*

Because state pro-ERA coalitions brought together many, very different women's groups, inevitably there were conflicts at times over strategy. At the national level, some feminist organizations were particularly aggravated with NOW, which had decided in 1978 that it would no longer join ongoing coalitions, though it would work with other groups on specific actions. NOW's leaders had concluded that they would alienate their own membership of ardent activists if they had to compromise continually with other organizations.

Several times between 1978 and 1982, the ERA vote in a state legislature was too close to predict, but ratification remained just out of reach. Nineteen eighty was a particularly difficult year. It had barely begun when President Carter announced plans to resume draft registration so that conscription could proceed quickly if it ever became necessary; he asked Congress for the authority to register young women as well as men. Congress refused. Not long after that, a district court ruled, in a suit brought by several young men, that it was unconstitutional to draft men but not women. The Supreme Court quickly agreed to hear the case.

Feminists were thrown into confusion. Many were Vietnam-era veterans of the antiwar movement and they were opposed to war and the draft. Yet WEAL and BPW, in particular, had been pressing for equal rights for women in the armed forces; it would be inconsistent to urge a draft exemption for women. Furthermore, virtually all ERA supporters believed that if the amendment passed, women would have to be drafted whenever men were. In the end, NOW opposed the registration of either sex, but argued that if there *were* registration, women and men should be treated the same way, even when it came to combat.

---

* NOW estimated that, thanks to gender-based insurance rates, women typically paid about $16,000 more than men did, over a lifetime, for all types of insurance combined.

After Carter brought the draft into the limelight, Schlafly and other ERA opponents focused increasingly on the issue of women in combat. Polls showed that in 1980 fewer than one out of every four Americans favored sending women into combat, although most believed women should be allowed to volunteer for it.

As 1980 wore on, the ERA's prospects looked increasingly dim. The Republican convention picked antifeminist Ronald Reagan to run for President, and at his insistence, the party—which had supported the amendment at least nominally for forty years—dropped the ERA plank from its platform. When Reagan won, Schlafly claimed that her Pro-Family Movement had given him the election, while NOW's leaders insisted that his opposition to the ERA had, in fact, cost him the votes of many women—for the first time, there was a substantial difference in the way women and men voted, a "gender gap." Although in retrospect it seems likely that economic issues, rather than social issues, gave Reagan the presidency, NOW set out to use the threat of a gender gap to persuade state legislators that they were risking their seats if they rejected the ERA. Ultimately, the gender gap proved to be a potent weapon, but too late to save the ERA.

In June 1981, the Supreme Court ruled that Congress could refuse to draft women without violating the Constitution. Historically, the Court had almost always deferred to Congress on military matters. The decision indicated that the ERA *wouldn't* require women to be drafted, let alone be sent into combat. Yet the opposition continued to hammer away at the combat issue, and feminist leaders never backed down on their assertion that women who could qualify for combat should be expected to fight.

On both sides, the struggle over the ERA consumed enormous amounts of money and energy. Feminists believed, though they could never prove it, that the insurance industry was pouring funds into the coffers of anti-ERA groups. By the early 1980s, organizations and individuals were showering money on the pro-ERA forces, as well. Near the end, NOW—which spearheaded the ratification drive in most states—was receiving about $1 million a month and spending vast sums for pro-ERA television ads.

Many new activists were drawn into the women's movement by the ratification campaign. They demonstrated, lobbied legislatures, and went door-to-door to raise funds and get petitions signed. Some college students dropped out of school for a year to become missionaries, campaigning for the amendment on campuses all over the country. Older women also took sabbaticals from their jobs and personal lives to work for the cause. By 1982, more than 450 organizations, with a combined membership of over 50 million, had come out in favor of the ERA. Meanwhile, polls showed that women were now more likely than men to support the amendment, and that homemakers were as likely to support it as women in the work force. Nevertheless, in many of the unratified states, the opposition had actually grown stronger.

THE FINAL THROES

During the final months of the campaign, national attention focused on Illinois and Florida, the two states where there was still some hope of passage. In mid-May, Illinois feminists made headlines when a group of eight women began a fast that lasted for thirty-seven days. Growing visibly thinner and weaker, they appeared at the state capitol in Springfield every day that the legislature was in session. Antifeminists, calling them "dieters," came and ate pizza and hotdogs in front of them.

Then on June 3, seventeen women who identified themselves as the Grass Roots Group of Second Class Citizens chained themselves to the railings in the Illinois Senate chamber. They remained there for four days until police, armed with chain cutters, staged a dawn raid and carried them out of the chamber; they were not arrested. Some legislators were infuriated by such tactics, while others were sympathetic.

Polls showed that 62 percent of the people in Illinois supported the ERA. Nevertheless, on June 22, a vote in the lower chamber of the legislature fell four short of the necessary three-fifths majority; another try on June 24 also failed. On June 21, the Florida Senate had voted against the ERA, taking Florida out of the picture. With the deadline upon them, feminists acknowledged defeat.

In her victory statement, Phyllis Schlafly announced that her organization would now turn its attention to a campaign against sex education, because she believed it was a principal cause of teenage pregnancy. She would work against a nuclear freeze, as well. "The atomic bomb is a marvelous gift that was given to our country by a wise God," she said. She was also determined to purge school textbooks of feminist influence because "the way it is now, you can't show a picture of a woman washing the dishes."

ANATOMY OF A DEFEAT

Many activists felt that the will of the majority—as reflected in the polls—had been thwarted by a handful of men. Catherine East, for example, stated that the ERA was defeated by twelve powerful legislators in seven key states. She pointed out that in state legislatures the speaker of the lower House controlled committee assignments and the fate of bills lawmakers introduced. Thus, these men virtually controlled a legislator's future.

In some states, a few men succeeded in blocking the amendment through a combination of political pressure and parliamentary maneuvers. They were able to do so because it was such a close fight—a switch in just a few votes would have changed history. However, as noted earlier, the amendment wasn't defeated solely by a few powerful men. Other factors were involved as well—for one thing, there weren't enough women in the legislatures. If there had been more, the ERA would probably have passed. In the unratified states, 79 percent of women lawmakers supported the amendment, compared with just 39 percent of the men.

The ERA also failed because the odds were against it. The founding fathers deliberately made it difficult to change the Constitution, and controversial amendments are seldom ratified. To succeed, an amendment needs a two-thirds vote in Congress and approval by three quarters of the states. In effect, this gives veto power to any substantial minority strongly opposed to change, for the odds are with the minority. Where pro-ERA forces needed to persuade thirty-eight states to ratify, the opposition only needed to persuade thirteen states to vote no. Not surprisingly, social movements out to make major changes have taken decades to pass an amendment: fifty-seven years to free the slaves, seventy-two years to give women the vote.

There were other, even more basic reasons for the amendment's defeat. A minority of women saw feminism as a threat and made their stand against it on the issue of the ERA. There was a genuine conflict of interests involved. Feminists were determined to put significant numbers of women into positions of power, where they could better the lot of all women. They were unlikely to succeed if most wives dropped out of the job market to raise children. Women who played the traditional role made it harder for others to combat the old stereotypes.

On the other hand, homemakers lost status because of feminism. As educated women in growing numbers insisted on escaping from the home, many full-time housewives began to feel they had to defend the choice they'd made. Furthermore, as traditionalists saw it, men and women had long ago made a bargain: The husband supported the household and the wife maintained it with her labor. Feminist author Barbara Ehrenreich suggested that

> what was at stake in the battle over the ERA was the *legitimacy* of women's claim on men's incomes. . . . By simply asserting women's right to enter the labor market on an equal footing with men, feminism undercut the dependent housewife's already tenuous "right" to be supported. If some women can "pull their own weight" . . . then why shouldn't all of them?

All around them, traditional women saw marriages crumbling and ex-husbands defaulting on child support. They blamed feminism and the sexual revolution, and they believed that if the old rules were just reinforced, their own marriages would survive. Schlafly herself said that it was duty, not love, that tied a man into a marriage; romantic love wasn't apt to survive in the long run. Many of the women concerned about abortion believed that sex without consequences (pregnancy) was undermining men's loyalty to their wives; with the divorce rate soaring, it was no time to scuttle traditional values. Ehrenreich speculated that "from the vantage point of the antifeminists, the crime of feminism lay not in hating men, but in trusting them too well."

Both traditional women and feminists were concerned about the insecurity of marriage, but they were committed to diametrically opposite solutions. Traditionalists wanted to go back to the old ways, while feminists were fighting to make women independent. Though many of the antifeminists' statements about a woman's right to support seemed irrational, they expressed real fears. As long as feminists lacked the power to change the legal system so that women whose marriages failed had some real protection, they had no way to address those fears.

The Most Damaging Issues

After the amendment's defeat, some feminist critics argued that it might have passed if women's groups had handled certain issues differently. The pro-ERA forces could have explained, according to the critics, that the courts would never order women into the front lines against the will of military leaders and the Congress (which was almost certainly true), and that the ERA would not expand women's abortion rights (probably true). Some said that feminists should also have downplayed their commitment to lesbian rights until the amendment was safely in place.

If the movement seemed to court controversy at times, the basic dynamics of social movements were partly responsible. As Jane Mansbridge observed, disillusioned activists might have withdrawn in disgust if movement leaders had deserted their principles even temporarily, as a matter of strategy. Sometimes the leaders tried to tread warily on an issue, and other activists immediately staked out a stronger position, providing the enemy with ammunition. Furthermore, in the heat of battle, some decisions weren't consciously made—as Mansbridge put it, they "simply flowed from earlier decisions and premises."

The movement's stand on combat was like that, according to Mansbridge. The leaders of NOW, the most prominent pro-ERA organization, just assumed that the ERA would, and should, mean that some women would fill combat positions. In part, this assumption grew out of equality feminists' conviction that if women wanted equal rights, they would have to shoulder equal responsibilities. As Bernice Sandler of WEAL put it, "We can't say, 'We're equal except in combat.' Small women who aren't strong enough . . . shouldn't be in combat, but neither should small men. Equality is about making distinctions, not on the basis of gender, but on the basis of who can actually do the job."

Feminists were also offended by the arguments for keeping women out of combat—for example, by the general who said sarcastically, ". . . [I]magine, if you will, a news photo distributed worldwide showing American diplomats cowering behind their desks while women marines try to defend them." Though Phyllis Schlafly kept insisting that females needed male protection, many women now had a different self-image. Once, at a women's college, Martha Griffiths debated an Indiana state legislator who opposed the ERA. Griffiths recalled that "she [the legislator] told the audience, 'If the ERA passes and there is a war, you will be drafted and your husband will stay home with the children.' All 1200 women in the audience arose as one woman and applauded. I nearly fell off the platform. You could just see them thinking, 'I'll be in Paris, and he'll be home with those darn kids.' "*

In addition, feminist leaders felt that they had to be consistent, and they had campaigned hard for equality in the military as the number of women in the armed forces rose during the 1970s.† Many women were eager to enlist because the pay was typically 40 percent more than they could earn as civilians, but most soon found that their opportunities were limited because Congress had decreed that women couldn't be assigned to combat-related jobs. Though the top brass kept redefining "combat-related," it was always clear that they weren't just concerned about hand-to-hand fighting. Women weren't permitted to be fighter pilots, either, or to hold a host of other choice, well-paid positions. In 1980, 73 percent of the jobs in the military were closed to females. Under the circumstances, few women had any chance of being promoted into the top ranks.

To feminists, there seemed little reason to keep women out of combat. Females hadn't as much upper-body strength as males, but the Vietnam War had proved that, thanks to modern lightweight weapons, small, agile fighters could be a match for big, muscular ones. Furthermore, during the 1970s, police and fire departments and the military academies—ordered to lower the barriers to women—had revised their requirements for upper-body strength, and no disasters had occurred. In the services themselves, when both sexes were tested on combat skills at the end of basic training, women did as well as men.

Public attitudes toward combat seemed irrational to ERA proponents. One survey reported that 94 percent of those polled thought it was fine for a woman to be a nurse in a combat zone (where she could easily be killed), while only 59 percent believed women should be air defense missile gunners based in the United States. Apparently, many Americans had a gut reaction to any suggestion that women could be aggressive and powerful. Public opposition to women in combat was strong, and in retrospect, some feminists believed the movement should have insisted that the ERA would never put women on the

---

* In 1990, when the Pentagon sent 11,000 women to the Middle East after Iraq's invasion of Kuwait, a number of them confessed to reporters that they'd told their husbands and children they had to go, when in fact they had volunteered.

† After Congress ended the draft, Pentagon officials and conservative Congressmen, afraid black men would come to dominate the new, all-volunteer services, set out to recruit women, both black and white, as a way to dilute the expected influx of African-American males.

front lines—especially because that was probably true.* Others disagreed.

Jane Mansbridge concluded that by the late 1970s, women's legal position had improved so much that at that point it was probably better "to lose fighting for a good symbol than to win fighting for a bad one." In fact, Mansbridge suggested that both sides in the ERA debate zeroed in on the combat issue after 1980 largely because they could come up with so few other dramatic examples of immediate changes that the ERA would bring about. Many doors had been opened to women during the ten-year ratification campaign (more about that shortly). By the 1980s, though the amendment's long-range effects would still have been profound, in the short run it would have changed very little. Because the leaders on both sides needed to keep their activists motivated, they tended to exaggerate what the amendment would do.

Abortion was another issue that may have hurt the ERA. In the late 1970s and early 1980s, half of those who supported the amendment in public polls opposed abortion on demand, and so did many state legislators. Antifeminists maintained that the ERA would require the government to pay for abortions for the poor. Feminists responded that abortion law was based on the right to privacy, and it was unlikely that the Supreme Court would abandon earlier precedents and cite the ERA in order to broaden abortion rights.

Many pro-ERA feminists felt that it would be a strategic error to associate the ERA with the abortion issue, but others disagreed. Marjorie Pitts Hames, who argued the companion case to *Roe* v. *Wade*, believed that there was enough public support for abortion that the drive for the ERA might actually benefit from the connection. In any case, the connection was made. At the time, feminist attorneys were bringing cases in both federal and state courts to try to restore Medicaid funding for abortions. Though NOW president Eleanor Smeal and others urged them to avoid linking the ERA to abortion, after the Supreme Court upheld *federal* restrictions on abortion funding in 1980, ACLU attorneys decided they couldn't afford to hold back. They pulled out all stops, and in some courts argued that state funding must be

---

* During the Gulf War in 1990–91, many women reservists were sent to Saudi Arabia (without benefit of an ERA), where they were so close to the front line that they ran most of the same risks men did; a few were killed or taken prisoner. It was unclear how this would ultimately affect the ERA's chances.

restored because the state's constitution had an ERA. The opposition promptly cited these arguments as proof that the federal amendment would expand abortion rights.

Homophobia also played a role in the ERA's defeat. Many lesbians worked hard for ratification, as they had for other feminist causes. At times, their visibility in the campaign caused controversy. When the National Women's Conference was held in Houston in 1977, feminists hoped it would provide a shot in the arm for the ERA. However, some were concerned about a resolution backing lesbian rights that delegates were scheduled to consider, because they were afraid the ERA and lesbian rights would be connected by the media and in people's minds. Martha Griffiths begged other feminists not to raise lesbian rights issues. "I said, 'Get the ERA through first,'" she recalled. Phyllis Schlafly predicted that the Houston meeting would finish the women's movement. "It will show them off for the radical, antifamily, prolesbian people they are," she said.

During floor debate, a Georgia feminist called the lesbian rights plank an albatross, noting that the states that still hadn't ratified were very conservative. Then, unexpectedly, Betty Friedan spoke in favor of the resolution. "I am known to be violently opposed to the lesbian issue," she said. ". . . I have had trouble with this issue. Now my priority is in passing the ERA. And because there is nothing in it that will give any protection to homosexuals, I believe we must help the women who are lesbians."

The resolution passed by a comfortable majority, and the media, predictably, featured it. In fact, there was probably very little feminists could have done to prevent gay rights from becoming an issue in the ratification drive, because antifeminists had never hesitated to call all feminists lesbians.

WHY THE ERA IS STILL NECESSARY

The defeat of the ERA was an enormous setback. However, as mentioned earlier, its passage would have had little *immediate* impact on women's legal rights. In 1972, the amendment's sponsors could list many reforms they expected it to accomplish. To mention just a few: Graduate schools would no longer be permitted to set quotas for women; laws that required wives to use their husband's surname would be abolished; community property states could no longer give husbands complete control of the couple's property (including, in some states, the wife's salary). Most laws would have had to become gender-neutral.

During the 1970s, the legislatures and the courts, between them, made all of these changes and more, and by 1982 the ERA no longer offered many immediate benefits. That didn't mean the ratification campaign was a wasted effort. On the contrary, many legal changes happened *because* of the campaign, which called attention to discriminatory laws. Nor did it mean the ERA was no longer necessary. Women remained at a disadvantage. Domestic violence was a bigger problem than ever; most women were still trapped in low-paying jobs; divorce had plunged many mothers into poverty. Feminist leaders believed that if the ERA had passed, the attitudes of courts and legislatures would have been different after 1982—not instantly transformed but improving as women, taking advantage of their constitutional rights, brought suits.

THE (PARTIAL) EDUCATION OF THE SUPREME COURT

For feminist legal scholars, what made the ERA vital was the stall-out in their campaign to persuade the Supreme Court to apply the same standards in sex discrimination cases that it applied to racial discrimination. Though the High Court had come a long way since the 1960s, it hadn't come far enough.

To recapitulate material covered in earlier chapters: In the 1950s and 60s, when the Supreme Court began, belatedly, to use the equal protection clause of the fourteenth amendment on behalf of African-Americans, some feminists argued that if the Court could be persuaded to extend equal protection to women as well, the ERA wouldn't be necessary. The problem was to get the justices to declare gender a "suspect" category.

Historically, laws that treated blacks differently from whites were the backbone of racial discrimination—for example, in the South they had ensured that generations of black children would be educated separately from whites. Beginning in the 1950s, the Supreme Court began to consider all such laws *suspect* and to judge them by a tougher standard than it used for most laws that *classified* people in some way (to use the legal terminology). Many statutes classified: They distinguished between thieves and honest citizens, or between adults and children. However, those that singled out people of a particular race, religion, or ethnic group for special treatment were almost always discriminatory.

To distinguish between laws that classified on a legitimate basis and those that didn't, the Supreme Court developed two different standards of analysis, called the *two-tiered* approach. In practice, almost any law could meet the first-tier standard. Very few survived second-tier analysis, known as *strict scrutiny*. Laws were subjected to *strict scrutiny* only if they involved certain fundamental rights, such as the right to vote, or if they classified people in ways the Court had deemed *suspect*—according to their race, religion, or national origin.

- Statutes that were analyzed according to the first-tier standard simply had to be *rationally* related to a *permissible* government objective for the Court to uphold them.
- Statutes judged by second-tier *strict scrutiny* were considered unconstitutional unless the state could prove that it had a *compelling* or overriding need for such a law, and that the classification was *necessary* for the law to achieve its objective.

Because the Supreme Court rejected virtually every effort to overturn laws that classified people by gender and treated females and males differently, by 1970 most feminists were convinced that the ERA was the only solution. Nevertheless, in the early 1970s, perhaps prompted by media attention to the revitalized women's movement, the Court began to overturn some laws that treated the sexes differently. Except in the 1973 abortion decision, the justices made no large waves. However, within a remarkably short time it was generally accepted that most laws must be gender-neutral.

Lawyers who litigated sex discrimination cases in the 1970s had no grand plan or firm philosophy as their guide. Their approach was pragmatic. According to Ruth Bader Ginsburg, the brilliant constitutional scholar who argued key cases before the Court, "We were attacking a series of closed doors, and to the extent that there was an overall strategy . . . we simply used the approach most likely to persuade the decision-makers to change." Though on the surface, some of the laws that treated women and men differently seemed to benefit females, almost all actually put women at a disadvantage. The logical tactic, then, was to argue that such laws must treat the sexes alike and to object to classification by gender. For example, in an era when most women were fired as soon as they became pregnant, arguing for paid maternity leave would have been a waste of breath, so instead feminist leaders maintained that pregnancy should be treated like any other disability, "reserving judgment," said Ginsburg, "about whether in the end that was the right place to go."

It was also part of the feminist legal strategy to challenge sex stereotypes. Feminists needed to convince the justices that laws that appeared to protect women actually held them back. Ginsburg noted that she was addressing her arguments to nine men, "all of whom thought they'd been terribly good to their own wives and daughters, and who didn't really grasp what women were complaining about." In effect, in a series of cases, she attempted to educate the Court.

Civil rights precedents were a tremendous help, and Ginsburg and others piggybacked on earlier racial discrimination cases. "Courts are much more comfortable taking a baby step than a giant step," Ginsburg explained. Lawyers were more likely to be successful if they could argue that they were only asking the Court to extend an established doctrine to people in a similar situation—from race discrimination to sex discrimination, for example. However, feminist attorneys also had a sense that they were part of a worldwide women's movement, and they sometimes cited equal rights guarantees in other nations and international human rights documents.

In 1971, before Congress passed the ERA, Ginsburg and her colleagues won their first Supreme Court victory with a case known as *Reed* v. *Reed*. It was a turning point for women's legal rights. Ginsburg acted, on this and other cases, for the ACLU Women's Rights Project.

Sally Reed had separated from her husband, Cecil, when their son, Richard, was quite young. For the first few years she had custody of Richard, but as soon as he was in his early teens, a court turned him over to his father.* At the age of nineteen, while in a severe state of depression, Richard shot himself with his father's rifle. Ginsburg recalled that Reed blamed her estranged husband for the boy's death, deeply resented the fact that he had been given custody, ". . . and then, to top it off, she found she couldn't be the administrator of Richard's estate." Cecil Reed had also applied to do the job, and according to Idaho law, when a man and a woman both wanted to administer an estate and both

---

* Until the mid-1970s, state custody laws often gave legal preference to mothers, but only while children were "of tender years." Once they were able to do most things for themselves, they could be transferred to their father's care. That was more often done with boys.

bore the same relationship to the deceased, the court must appoint the man. Sally Reed sued.

Ginsburg felt that *Reed* was the perfect case to advance women's constitutional rights because a law that automatically favored men over equally qualified women was flagrantly unfair. The state's only defense was that it was a matter of convenience: It saved probate courts from having to hold hearings. In the end, the justices voted unanimously to overturn the Idaho law. They found it arbitrary, rather than reasonable, ostensibly using first-tier standards. However, Court-watchers agreed that the justices behaved as if sex, as a classification, was at least somewhat suspect.

The next Supreme Court decision on sex discrimination that dealt with equal protection issues was *Frontiero* v. *Richardson*. Sharron Frontiero, an Air Force lieutenant married to a college student, sued the government when she was refused the extra housing allowance and medical benefits that male officers received automatically if they were married. As a female, Frontiero could have the benefits only if she could prove that she was supporting her husband. She couldn't quite do that, because as a veteran he received a small GI benefit. Obviously, the statute in question presumed that wives were normally dependents and husbands weren't—a sex-role stereotype.

Eight of the nine justices found the statute unconstitutional, but they disagreed as to why, and the ERA played an ambiguous role in their reasoning. In January 1973, when the Supreme Court heard arguments on *Frontiero*, Congress had passed the amendment and twenty-two state legislatures had already ratified it. Justice Brennan, in an opinion joined by three of his colleagues, stated unreservedly that sex should be a suspect classification; he noted that Congress had evidently come to the same conclusion, because it had approved the ERA. However, in a separate opinion, Justice Powell also voted to overturn the law but argued against making sex suspect at that point in time. With the ERA pending, he said, the Court would be preempting a major political decision if it accepted strict scrutiny as the proper standard for sex discrimination cases. Because two other justices joined Powell in his opinion, there was no majority for changing the Court's standard of review for sex-based classifications.

In retrospect, Ruth Ginsburg felt that Brennan had moved too fast. "The Court should have held for Sharron Frontiero, but on about the same basis as *Reed*," she said. Brennan was able to persuade only three of his colleagues that sex should be declared suspect. One more justice (for a total of five, including Brennan) and the "strict" standard, accepted by a majority, would have been in place. Ginsburg believed that if Brennan had waited until the Court had decided half a dozen more sex discrimination cases before pressing for strict scrutiny, he might have had a convert. Apparently Stewart, for example, simply wanted to move more slowly. As it was, once some of the justices had formally refused to go along with suspect classification, they would find it difficult to change their position without seeming inconsistent.

Over the next few years, the Supreme Court wavered, sometimes insisting that laws must be gender-neutral, sometimes not. Then in 1976, the Court took another step forward. The fact that the ERA seemed to have stalled may have influenced some of the justices; there was now less chance that the matter would be resolved quickly in the political arena. The case involved, *Craig* v. *Boren*, was not one that resonated with drama: It challenged an Oklahoma law that permitted girls to buy 3.2 percent beer at eighteen and required boys to wait until they were twenty-one because males were more likely to drink and drive.

Several years earlier, in her brief on *Frontiero*, Ginsburg had not only argued that sex should be a suspect classification but had suggested an alternative, in case the justices weren't willing to go that far. She had noted that some previous decisions of the Court seemed to reflect an intermediate level of scrutiny, tougher than the first tier but not as tough as the second. In the *Craig* decision, the Court took up her suggestion. Seven justices held that Oklahoma's beer law was unconstitutional; six of them signed onto an opinion written by Brennan, which acknowledged that previous cases had established a new, intermediate standard. As he summarized it, to be constitutional, classifications by gender must be *substantially related* to *important* government objectives. (Under strict scrutiny, they would have had to be *necessary* to some *compelling* government purpose.) It was clear that there were deep divisions within the Court. Powell, who agreed that the law was unconstitutional, wrote in a separate opinion that he couldn't endorse a new, middle tier.

Predictably, with the Court divided, the justices used intermediate scrutiny over the next few years in ways that feminists found inconsistent. Thus, in 1979 they overturned an Alabama law that said that only husbands were required to pay alimony, but in 1981 they upheld a California law that said that only men could be charged with statutory rape for having intercourse with someone who was underage. In upholding the California statute, the Court concluded that the state had a "strong interest" in preventing "illegitimate" teenage pregnancies; because only females became pregnant, treating the sexes differently was permissible.*

By 1982, the feminist campaign to teach the justices to recognize and reject sex stereotypes had had mixed results. It had produced a number of highly satisfactory opinions. However, in the statutory rape decision and others, the Court majority had failed to see that sex stereotypes were involved. The rape law was based on the assumption that males were sexually aggressive and females were passive, and it also reflected the old double standard. Legally, a male could begin having intercourse at any age, provided he confined himself to females over seventeen, while a girl couldn't (legally) have sex with anyone until she was at least eighteen. The justices also ignored the fact that a gender-neutral alternative was possible. Some states penalized adults, male or female, who had sex with adolescents if those adults used some form of coercion or if there was a substantial age gap.

Clearly, some of the justices had had their consciousness raised —by Ginsburg and her colleagues, by the cases themselves, and by changing times—but others on the Court still had a 1950s mind-set. In addition, though the Court was now better at spotting the more obvious stereotypes (breadwinner/homemaker), it backslid whenever "real" biological differences entered the picture, as in the statutory rape decision. One faction within the Court often saw "real" differences where feminists were convinced none existed that were relevant to the case.

Throughout the 1980s, the Supreme Court's record on sex discrimination cases provided proof that American women still needed the ERA—despite the legal progress they'd made. The justices still refused to apply strict scrutiny; they used intermediate scrutiny unevenly (some of them didn't believe in it); and— perhaps most important—they upheld some gender-neutral laws that harmed women.

WHEN GENDER NEUTRAL IS FAR FROM NEUTRAL

By the 1980s, it was clear to many American women that gender-neutral laws could sometimes be just as damaging as stat-

* The boy who was convicted in the case was seventeen; the girl involved was sixteen.

utes that singled women out for special treatment. Back in the early 1970s, the EEOC passed regulations under Title VII forbidding practices that were gender-neutral but that had a "disparate" and negative effect on women. For example, regulations requiring that all prison guards meet minimum height and weight standards eliminated many women without even mentioning sex. In 1977, the Supreme Court affirmed that Title VII did indeed prohibit such laws and practices. However, in disparate-impact cases that involved the constitutional equal protection issue rather than Title VII, the justices set a tougher standard: They insisted on proof that the laws or practices involved were actually *intended* to discriminate.

The case that set the standard for women was *Personnel Administrator of Massachusetts* v. *Feeney*. Helen Feeney was a Massachusetts resident who had done so well on civil service exams that she ranked second or third in the state. However, when she applied for jobs in the state government, she lost out again and again to male veterans because Massachusetts had a law that gave veterans an absolute, lifelong preference in the civil service. One quarter of the state's population were veterans, and less than 2 percent of the veterans were women (hardly surprising, because the military had always had quotas for women). As a result, though the veteran's preference law said nothing about males and females, men who were barely able to pass the civil service tests were hired or promoted because they were vets, while women with nearly perfect scores, like Feeney, were passed over. Men held almost all the top government jobs in the state.*

In deciding the case in 1979, the Supreme Court conceded that the law had had a severe impact on the job opportunities of women, but upheld it on the grounds that there was no proof that the legislature had *intended* to discriminate against women; it simply wanted to reward veterans. It was extremely difficult to prove what lawmakers' intentions were—often, they acted out of mixed motives. In addition, unintentional discrimination could do a great deal of harm.

Thus, an increasingly conservative Supreme Court had virtually stymied feminist efforts to undo the damage caused by some gender-neutral laws. Movement leaders believed the ERA could solve the problem by forcing the Court to reject harmful gender-neutral statutes even when the harm was unintended.

* Other states, less extreme, gave vets an advantage in the civil service for a limited number of years or gave them a modest permanent edge by automatically adding a few points to their scores on civil service tests.

THE AFTERLIFE OF THE ERA

Not long after the ERA's defeat, House Speaker Thomas P. (Tip) O'Neill Jr. announced that he planned to reintroduce it in the next session of Congress. Despite undiminished enthusiasm for the amendment, many feminists were dismayed. Nothing had changed—there was little likelihood that they could persuade thirty-eight states to ratify. They needed time to regroup, but they couldn't very well object. Determined to shape the legislative history of the amendment so that if it did pass, there could be little doubt about the way it was to be interpreted, women's organizations got together to hammer out their positions on various issues. If those positions were adopted by the chief sponsors of the amendment, it would be hard for the Supreme Court to ignore them.

As they worked, feminists laid down the framework that they hoped to use to achieve legal equality for women. According to that framework:

- The ERA would invalidate all laws that treated women and men differently (a tougher standard than strict scrutiny) except those that involved the constitutional right to privacy and laws designed to remedy past sex discrimination. (In other words, unisex bathrooms would not be required, and affirmative action would be permissible.)
- Laws that dealt with physical characteristics unique to one sex would also be permitted but would be subject to strict scrutiny. For example, if a legislature passed a statute that had to do with pregnancy, it must prove to the courts that the state had a compelling need for such a law, and that the only way it could meet that need was by singling out pregnancy.
- Gender-neutral laws that had a disparate impact on one sex or the other must also be given strict scrutiny if they could be traced back to discriminatory patterns or if they served to perpetuate sex discrimination. Thus, the *Feeney* decision would be overturned because giving such an absolute preference to veterans perpetuated a gender hierarchy in the civil service, and because other, less discriminatory alternatives were available.

In testimony before Congress, attorney Ann Freedman—speaking for a coalition of women's organizations—explained in detail how she believed the ERA would and should be interpreted. According to Freedman, among other things it would mean that gender-neutral divorce laws would have to be treated to strict scrutiny if they clearly disadvantaged women. The social security system would also have to be re-examined because, though it was now gender-neutral, it was still based on the old assumption that men were breadwinners and women were their dependents, and it operated to the disadvantage of many women in the work force. Freedman stated that the amendment would have no effect on abortion statutes.

The ERA never made it through Congress. Opponents insisted that it was a can of worms. "The problem with the ERA, of course, is that no one has the slightest idea what it really means," said Senator Orrin Hatch, the conservative who presided over the Senate hearings on the amendment. Anti-ERA legislators especially objected to the amendment's impact on gender-neutral laws and the fact that it would allow affirmative action to make up for past discrimination. At one point, Hatch asked an ERA supporter, "Would it be fair to say, then, that . . . the ERA requires equality unless women have the advantage?" He accused feminists of demanding equal results rather than just equal opportunity. To activists, aware that "equal opportunity" was a farce as long as society was overwhelmingly male-dominated, it seemed fair enough to ask for temporary measures to compensate for past discrimination.

By November 1983, Speaker O'Neill had come to doubt that even in the House the ERA could be passed unadulterated. Opponents were vehemently demanding various amendments. In the end, House Democrats voted to suspend normal rules, limit floor debate on the ERA to forty minutes, and bar amendments. Because the rules were normally suspended only when legislation was noncontroversial, opponents were furious and some lukewarm supporters were alienated as well. The ERA was defeated: It fell six votes short of the two-thirds majority it needed. Privately, many feminists were relieved. Now they had more time to elect sympathizers to state legislatures.

In January 1985, the amendment was reintroduced in Congress, but women's groups had an understanding with their congressional supporters that it wouldn't reach the floor to be voted on because there was still no hope of ratification. They wanted to keep the issue alive but temporarily on the back burner.

THE ERA AND THE FEMINIST DIVIDE

In the 1980s, after the ERA's defeat, feminists began to debate old and new issues among themselves with renewed vigor. Jane Mansbridge suggested that with the ERA out of the picture, it was no longer so important to present a united front, and a lot of energy was released as a result. Feminist attorneys, in particular, carried on a vehement debate in legal journals over old, unsettled business. Did women need equality or difference, gender-neutral laws or special treatment?

In general, lawyers from the difference side of the divide argued that a totally gender-neutral approach to the law was assimilationist—a good solution only for women who were willing to play by men's rules and be treated like men. They also maintained that the Supreme Court had failed to address adequately the real, biological differences between the sexes, such as pregnancy, and they blamed attorneys like Ginsburg because they had downplayed sex differences. In addition, they pointed out that in a society where one group holds most of the power, "neutral" laws usually benefit the powerful.

Attorney Wendy Williams, a primary spokesperson for equality feminists, responded that the Supreme Court justices were unlikely to understand that laws based on biological differences could oppress women. Williams argued that *all* sex-based classifications, including those grounded on biological differences, deserved strict scrutiny. Just as some antifeminists believed that the ERA's supporters trusted men too much, Williams apparently felt that difference feminists placed too much trust in male-dominated courts. Emphasizing that special treatment had always been used to keep women in their place, she concluded that "to settle for [that] now would be to sell equality short."

AN END AND A BEGINNING

In significant ways, the ERA ratification campaign was far from a failure. State laws were changed that wouldn't have changed otherwise. Even after the ERA was rejected, some bills were apparently passed out of guilt or for fear of voter retaliation—for example, in 1983 Illinois made marital rape a crime. Meanwhile, the polls had traced a gradual shift in public opinion after 1972, as women and men began to understand just how pervasive sex discrimination was.

The struggle over ratification created a new, highly organized antifeminist movement and helped polarize the American political scene. However, it also fueled the growth of many feminist organizations—for example, NOW's membership surged from 55,000 in 1977 to 210,000 in 1982; over the same period, its annual budget climbed from $700,000 to $8,500,000.

Many women who had campaigned for ratification came away committed to feminism. Some went into politics afterward; others lobbied state legislatures, using what they'd learned in the ERA campaign. In Florida after the amendment lost, a team from national NOW stayed on in order to recruit women to run for the legislature and prove to politicians that it could be costly to oppose the ERA. Nine women won seats in the Senate, more than doubling that body's female membership.

Meanwhile, many of the women's organizations in Washington had been professionalized. Longtime NOW activist Nancy Stultz recalled that "when Ellie Smeal went to Washington, she was the only president of a national women's organization who was full-time and paid." A number of groups followed NOW's lead, she said, when they saw how much NOW could accomplish after the change.

Feminist scholars, analyzing the long campaign, suggested one final, ironic benefit: If the ERA had passed, grass-roots feminists might have retired from the fray, assuming their job was done, as many abortion activists did after *Roe* v. *Wade*. Instead, the women's movement tooled up energetically to try to exploit the gender gap.

PART THREE

Confronting the Political Realities

chapter 19

The Eclipse of the Gender Gap

———✐———

In July 1984, the Democratic national convention nominated Geraldine Ferraro for Vice-President of the United States. She told the cheering delegates: "By choosing an American woman to run for our nation's second-highest office, you send a powerful signal to all Americans. . . . If we can do this, we can do *anything*."

That moment was an all-time high for many American women. For a dedicated few, it was also the culmination of a campaign that began over a year earlier, when they set out to secure the second spot on the Democratic ticket for a woman. They succeeded because they made political capital out of the fact that women were voting differently from men—the phenomenon known as the gender gap.

Yet in November of that year, 57 percent of the women who voted cast their ballot for Republican Ronald Reagan. Though fewer women than men voted for him, politicians had expected a bigger difference, and the gender gap was largely discredited. Feminists had to face the fact that most women apparently preferred Reagan, though Reagan had spent the last four years trying to turn back the clock on women's rights, while Democrat Walter Mondale not only supported those rights but had chosen a woman as his running mate.

For the feminist movement, the outcome of the 1984 election revived some troubling questions. Blacks voted as a bloc; why didn't women? In 1984, seven million more women voted than men. If they had used their ballots to reward the candidate who supported women's equality, Reagan would have lost the election. In fact, because women were the majority, theoretically they could have their way with Congress: If they voted only for politicians who favored an adequately financed national child-care system, for example, the nation would soon have decent child care.

Did the fact that most women didn't seem to base their vote on a candidate's record on women's rights mean that American women weren't vitally interested in equality? If women were really different from men in their values, wouldn't their votes reflect that difference? During the 1980s, more and more feminists became concerned about such questions as the movement's major national organizations became increasingly involved in politics in response to the threat from the New Right.

THE DREAM THAT DIED: THE ''WOMAN VOTE''

When the gender gap first made news in 1980, it seemed that American women were finally about to acquire the kind of political power that some feminists thought they'd won almost sixty years earlier. In 1920, after the suffrage amendment passed, many people assumed that a "woman vote" would immediately materialize and that feminists would use it to fight political bosses and press for new laws protecting women and children. Anticipating just such pressures, in 1920 the Democratic platform incorporated twelve out of fifteen planks that the League of Women Voters (LWV) was backing, while the Republican platform adopted five of them. Over the next few years, Congress passed several major pieces of legislation that women's organizations were demanding, and state legislatures were also responsive.

However, by the midtwenties magazines were running articles suggesting that woman suffrage had been wasted. In the elections of 1920 and 1924, voter turnout for women was supposedly 25 percent lower than it was for men and no strong voting bloc was apparent. A Chicago survey of women who failed to vote was widely quoted: Almost one third of those interviewed said they simply weren't interested in politics. In fact, the 25 percent estimate was almost pure guesswork, for real evidence of women's voting behavior was skimpy, to say the least. Illinois was the only state that kept its voting records by sex, and exit polls had yet to be invented. Some historians now argue that though it was probably true that fewer women voted than men, the difference was exaggerated.

Be that as it may, the widespread assumption that women weren't interested in politics cost the women's movement dearly. Some laws recently passed to please women were actually repealed, and feminists lost much of their political credibility. Many people said they'd oversold the power of the women's voting bloc.

During the 1980s, second-wave feminists found that at any point in time their reception in Congress depended partly on whether recent elections seemed to have registered a sizeable gender gap or not. In 1984, women were accused of overselling the gap in much the same way that suffragists were blamed for overselling the woman vote.

THE CRAFTING OF THE GENDER GAP

Second-wave feminists understood, as the suffragists had before them, how much a women's voting bloc could accomplish if politicians could be persuaded that one existed. In fact, as the women's movement mushroomed after 1970, Congress responded just as it had fifty years earlier, anticipating that feminist sympathies *would* influence voters. Between 1970 and 1980, it passed more bills that addressed women's issues than the sum total of all such bills passed in the previous history of the nation.

However, until 1980 the women's vote remained a shadowy possibility rather than a force to be reckoned with. In 1972 and again in 1976, more women than men voted for a Democrat for President, but in both elections the difference was small—perhaps because the candidates largely ignored women's issues—and there was no fanfare about a women's vote. Then in 1980, exit polls showed that fewer women than men had voted for Republican candidate Ronald Reagan. This time, the difference was a solid 8 to 10 percent. Nevertheless, the gender gap would have remained an interesting anomaly if feminists hadn't seized on it and promoted it.

It wasn't immediately obvious *why* the sexes voted differently in 1980. After the election, some suggested that women were disturbed by Reagan's "warmonger image" or were concerned about social issues. The leaders of NOW concluded that the ERA and other feminist goals must lie at the heart of the difference. At the time, NOW was totally caught up in the hard-fought campaign for ratification of the ERA, and the exit polls did show that those who supported the amendment were less likely to have voted for Reagan. Though that was true whether they were male or female, feminists assumed that because the ERA was more important to women than to men, they were more likely to have based their vote on it. In 1980, the amendment was stalled. NOW decided to use the fact that there was finally something that could be called a women's vote to try to convince lawmakers that they were risking their political futures if they opposed the ERA.

Over the next few months, NOW produced a booklet that described President Reagan's problem with women and named the problem "the gender gap." The NOW national office began a coordinated effort to make sure political pollsters paid attention to gender differences and to publicize polls that reflected those differences. By 1982, the polls were showing that the majority of American women didn't like the way Reagan was handling the presidency. In the congressional election that year, their displeasure translated into votes for the Democrats: In races for open seats where there was no incumbent, the gender gap was a stunning 16 percent. The gap wasn't enough to save the ERA, but the publicity about it influenced press coverage of the amendment's defeat, and that had been one of NOW's goals from the beginning. Feminists were afraid the newspapers would run banner headlines: "Women Reject Equality." Instead, most press reports quoted predictions that the loss of the ERA would politicize American women.

The defeat of the amendment had an enormous impact on feminist leaders. NOW president Ellie Smeal observed that "at every step of the ERA fight, we felt women were regarded as politically expendable." The campaign demonstrated that even with public opinion behind them, women's groups couldn't win the most important item on their agenda. The obvious solution was to fill the state legislatures with ERA supporters, and that meant electing more women, because even the most sympathetic males seldom cared as much about the amendment as women did.

By 1982, NOW had succeeded in defining the gender gap as a profeminist vote, though surveys done in the early 1980s reported other, major differences in attitudes between the sexes. Women were more concerned than men about peace and social welfare; they were less militaristic and cared more about the environment and about checking the growth of nuclear power; they were more supportive of programs to help the poor and of racial equality. No one was sure which issues were most signficant at election time.

However, several things *were* clear about the gender gap that would soon be obscured. It was obvious that it was a small difference in voting patterns—merely a gap—and that it could change the outcome of an election only in a close race. The gap also appeared to be related to issues, not to a tendency for women to vote for other women. Probably, those issues included both the "traditional" concerns of women, such as peace, and the feminist agenda.

THE GENDER GAP PAYS OFF

The Reagan administration wasn't blind to its problem with women. Soon after the 1980 election, a White House memo warned that the women's vote "could prove dangerous for Republicans in 1984." Reagan responded with symbolic gestures rather than by dealing with the issues. He appointed one woman, Sandra Day O'Connor, to the Supreme Court and another, Jeane J. Kirkpatrick, to the United Nations. When the gender gap showed up strongly in the 1982 election, he appointed Elizabeth Dole and Margaret Heckler to Cabinet posts. However, the day Heckler was sworn in, leaders of the National Federation of Republican Women delivered a statement to Reagan which warned that he must demonstrate "some tangible evidence of concern for women." By July 1983, the gender gap yawned twenty-one points wide: Asked whether Ronald Reagan deserved a second term, only 62 percent of *Republican* women said yes, compared to 86 percent of Republican men.

Over the next few years, Republicans in Congress, wary of the gender gap or genuinely concerned about women's issues, joined forces with Democrats to pass a number of bills that benefited women. Reagan signed them. As a result, in the coming years some women would find it easier to collect child support, and states would be allowed to consider a military pension a form of marital property in divorce cases. The Republican leadership in the Senate also supported a pension-reform bill that was high on the feminist agenda. These and a few other pieces of legislation were dividends produced by the gender gap.

There were other benefits as well. Some women candidates who had been closet feminists no longer felt they had to avoid women's issues. Once it was assumed that a substantial number of voters were concerned about such issues, male candidates also began to address them.

The gap was at least partly the result of the increasing feminization of poverty. After 1980, as 2.5 million women dropped below the poverty level, Reagan cut the social programs that would have helped them. That not only devastated poor women, but it threatened the jobs of women who worked for social agencies. At the time, there were 4 million women on welfare but there were over 17 million human services workers, and 70 percent of them were female.

A WOMAN FOR VICE-PRESIDENT

In 1983, movement leaders began to focus on the 1984 election. For months, feminists held discussions about running a woman for President or Vice-President. One key group included two congressional staffers, the executive director of NARAL, the director of the bipartisan Women's Vote Project, and Mildred Jeffrey, a feminist who had been active in the Democratic party since the 1950s. By November 1983, they had analyzed the political records and backgrounds of all the women who might be a candidate, and had settled on Geraldine Ferraro. Over dinner one night, they proposed to her that she run for Vice-President, and she agreed that they could put their best efforts into getting her the nomination.

In the summer of 1983, the National Women's Political Caucus (NWPC) invited the six declared male candidates who were pursuing the Democratic presidential nomination to address its biennial convention. Always before, candidates had responded by sending position papers or sometimes their wives. This time, apparently impressed by the gender gap, five of them agreed to come. One Caucus member called it "a quantum leap" in feminist influence. All the candidates supported the women's agenda: They were prochoice and pro-ERA; they were for pay equity and against wasteful defense spending; they deplored the federal policies that were pauperizing women.

The Caucus had always been bipartisan, but by 1983 Reagan

had so alienated feminists that during the NWPC convention Kathy Wilson, Caucus chair and a Republican herself, referred to him as "a dangerous man." "We want our party back," she said, "and we make a distinction between Ronald Reagan and the rest of the Republican Party."

The feminists who had been discussing the possibility of running a woman for President met again during the convention. Time was now short and they still hadn't been able to agree on a candidate, so they set their sights instead on the vice-presidency, which seemed a more achievable goal. In fact, several of the male candidates had said they'd be willing to consider a woman as their running mate. They may not have been serious, but the press seized on those remarks.

Not everyone agreed that feminists should focus on the vice-presidency. Betty Friedan argued that "a lot of women would not vote for a woman just because she's a woman. . . ." It was vital to defeat Reagan, she said, and to do that the Democratic nominee must choose the running mate, male or female, who would make the biggest difference to the ticket. After the election, sociologist Carol M. Mueller suggested that in shooting for the vice-presidency, feminists had shifted from the pursuit of one symbolic goal—the ERA—to the pursuit of another. Most U.S. Vice-Presidents have had little or no real power.

Jesse Jackson was the only Democratic candidate who actually promised to choose a woman as a running mate. Nevertheless, in December 1983, NOW's executive board formally endorsed Walter Mondale, who had merely promised to "consider" putting a woman on the ticket. NOW president Judy Goldsmith explained that the board had chosen Mondale because he had a better chance of defeating Reagan. She emphasized that the decision was not a rejection of Jackson. All the same, Jackson *had* antagonized some feminists. He was personally against abortion, and he'd complained that the women's movement was led by a narrow constituency of upper middle class white females.

Some members of NOW felt the Mondale endorsement was a mistake, but the leadership hoped it would give them access to Mondale's campaign and a chance to provide some input on issues and tactics. However, after the endorsement Mondale's staff generally ignored NOW, and the candidate had little to say about women's issues. NOW had sacrificed any leverage it might have had with the other candidates, and it wasn't at all clear what, if anything, it had gained.

Meanwhile, NOW had stopped bombarding reporters with

analyses of polls showing the gender gap, and as a result the gap began to take on a different meaning. The media always emphasized the "horse race" aspects of a presidential campaign, focusing on who was ahead and on strategy rather than on issues. Thus, it was perhaps predictable that the press would begin to treat the gap as a measure of women's tendency to vote for a woman. When new surveys reported a positive public response to the idea of a woman on the ticket, and pollsters suggested that including a woman would affect the outcome of the election, the media responded enthusiastically.

Some feminists were personally convinced that a woman would make a huge difference, but others were dubious. Millie Jeffrey recalled that "we tried to tell reporters, 'Look, you're exaggerating this.' It made us very uncomfortable, because women are anything but monolithic, and we knew that Reagan was going to be reelected." Jeffrey feared that, after all the hype, the gender gap would be discredited.

Nevertheless, women's organizations pushed forward. On June 18, the Caucus presented Mondale with a memo analyzing the electoral votes the Democrats might win with a woman on the ticket. NWPC also spent $20,000 to poll Democratic convention delegates and organized about 600 delegates into an elaborate whip system. Using the information from the poll, the whips would know, if it came to a floor fight, which delegates were likely to support a woman for Vice-President. It was the most powerful political machine feminists had ever put together for a convention, but NWPC's leaders were prepared to use it to trade, if necessary: They would give up the vice-presidency for other concessions.

NOW, typically, took a more confrontational approach. Rumors were flying that summer that John R. Reilly, Mondale's man in charge of the running-mate selection process, believed there was little real public pressure for a woman on the ticket. NOW's annual convention reacted by passing a resolution urging that a woman be nominated from the floor of the Democratic convention if Mondale picked a man.

Other feminists immediately denounced the resolution. Caucus chair Kathy Wilson said that while she wouldn't rule out a floor fight (indeed, the Caucus was organized to mount one), "We don't want to make threats at this point." A few days later, twenty-three political women met with Mondale to assure him that he had their backing even if he picked a man. The women were afraid that if Mondale were pressured into choosing a woman and then lost the election, feminists would be blamed. Mondale himself told one of his advisors that if women's organizations kept pushing him, they might make it impossible for him to choose a woman. He had already been accused of being the candidate of special interests, and the press had portrayed him as someone so weak that he gave in to every demand. In selecting a running mate, he wanted to be seen as "a man strong enough to make history," he said, not as a man who gave in.

On July 9, NWPC hand-delivered to Mondale the results of its survey of convention delegates. The survey reported that fully 82 percent had either very positive or somewhat positive feelings about having a woman on the ticket.

In the end, Mondale conducted a series of highly publicized interviews with seven vice-presidential candidates. He talked to two blacks, one Mexican-American, three women, and only one white male. Some Democrats warned that this wouldn't endear him to white males, and that it gave the impression the party was controlled by special interests. The women were Congresswoman Geraldine Ferraro, San Franciso Mayor Dianne Feinstein, and Governor Martha Layne Collins of Kentucky.

On July 12, before the convention opened, Mondale named his running mate: little-known New York Congresswoman Geraldine Ferraro. First elected to the House in 1978, Ferraro was Italian-American, Roman Catholic, and represented a blue-collar district. Married, with children who were almost grown, she had a clean-cut image. She seemed to exemplify family values, and Mondale was planning to emphasize those values during his campaign.

On July 19 at the Democratic convention, Geraldine Ferraro was nominated by acclamation. For women delegates, that moment was unforgettable, but some male Democrats questioned whether the country was ready for a woman Vice-President, and whether the ticket would win more votes among younger women than it would lose among middle-aged men.

Black feminists came away from the Democratic convention disillusioned. NOW's leaders initially backed planks that Jesse Jackson wanted included in the party platform, then changed their minds. The Caucus abandoned its whip system as soon as Mondale picked Ferraro, though black women had hoped to use it to line up support for their issues. Because there were hard feelings between black women who had backed Mondale and those in the Jesse Jackson camp, each faction met separately with Geraldine Ferraro to urge her to appoint black women to her campaign staff. Ferraro was torn, but felt she had to reward those who had worked for Mondale. A month later, out of general frustration black feminists founded the National Political Congress of Black Women, with Shirley Chisholm as its first chair.

The Republican Response

In 1984, the Republicans belatedly set out to compete for the women's vote. Party officials went out of their way to recruit women to run for local and state offices, on the theory that that would encourage women to vote a straight party ticket. The GOP also recommended, as an informal goal, that 50 percent of the delegates to the Republican nominating convention should be women.

Many feminists stayed away from the GOP convention. On opening day, which had been planned as "women's day" with a parade of women scheduled to speak, NWPC chair Kathy Wilson held a press conference elsewhere and released a fifty-page document that indicted the Reagan administration for decimating social programs and cutting the number of discrimination cases brought on behalf of women and people of color. Wilson also noted that only 3 percent of the convention delegates were black and one percent were Hispanic. In September, the Caucus endorsed Mondale, temporarily setting aside its bipartisan principles.

The 1984 Campaign

After Geraldine Ferraro's nomination, thousands of American women suddenly developed an avid interest in politics. For days, the NWPC phone lines in Washington were jammed as women called in to ask how they could work on the campaign. Yet Mondale's staff never did supply women's groups with the funds they needed to mount a massive voter-registration drive, and it was September before the campaign got around to setting up a hotline that women could call if they wanted to volunteer. As Betty Friedan remarked after the election, once the Mondale team had nominated a woman, they seemed to develop cold feet—worried, perhaps, about male backlash.

What was worse from the feminist point of view, Mondale's advisors told Ferraro not to focus on women's issues. Actually, that suited her. She said, "I wanted people to vote for me not because I was a woman, but because they thought I would make the best Vice President." Everyone seemed to have forgotten that the gender gap was issue-related.

For Ferraro, the campaign often posed problems that a male candidate wouldn't have faced. At the outset, Mondale strategists seemed to assume that they could simply order her around, and she objected strenuously. They would not have been so presumptuous in dealing with a man, she said, and she suggested to Mondale that his staff "should pretend every time they talk to me . . . that I'm a gray-haired Southern gentleman, a senator from Texas."

The stereotypes that had always shaped the way press and public saw political women haunted Ferraro. When she appeared on *Meet the Press*, Marvin Kalb asked her if she was strong enough to push the nuclear button. It wasn't the first time she'd had to answer that question, and Ferraro noted that

> it was so endlessly annoying to be presumed as weak and indecisive simply because I was a woman. . . . The discussion was never about whether force should be used only when every other avenue is exhausted, or whether or not I had the knowledge and the intelligence and the fortitude to move toward arms control negotiations so that pushing the nuclear button never would become a necessity. No. My "strength" in ordering the destruction of the world dominated the controversy.

Almost from the beginning, the opposition targeted Ferraro for personal attacks. Two weeks after the convention, she was challenged to explain her family's financial affairs. Throughout the difficult period that followed, she was held to higher standards than a male candidate would have been—for instance, the media put pressure on her to release the tax returns of her husband, John Zaccaro, when she released her own. Nobody had asked to see Elizabeth Dole's tax returns when Robert Dole became the Republican candidate for Vice-President in 1976. Several of Zaccaro's real estate transactions were subsequently questioned. Meanwhile, the ultraconservative Washington Legal Foundation, an organization with ties to the White House, filed a complaint against Ferraro with the House Committee on Standards of Official Conduct. The Foundation charged that on congressional disclosure forms she had failed to list her husband's assets along with her own. In fact, the rules allowed a "spousal exemption" if a couple kept their finances separate, and many members of Congress took the exemption. None had ever been challenged.

There were other charges as well. Eventually, long after the election, Ferraro and her husband would be exonerated of virtually all of them. In the meantime, there were the usual ugly rumors about a Mafia connection that almost always surfaced when Italian-Americans ran for high office.

Finally, in mid-August, Ferraro released both her own tax returns and her husband's. The next day, she faced 250 journalists alone, submitted to a ninety-minute grilling, and carried it off well. However, by that time the Democrats, who had finished their convention roughly even with Reagan in the polls, had lost 15 percentage points, and some blamed that entirely on Ferraro. Though the charges against her had an effect on the campaign, Mondale's position on taxes probably had more of an impact. He was telling Americans something they didn't want to hear: that because of the federal deficit, taxes would have to be raised.

Everywhere Ferraro went, huge crowds gathered, and everywhere she was shadowed and heckled by anti-abortion demonstrators. Finally, NBC news carried a story linking California hecklers to the Reagan campaign. Reaganites denied that there was a connection, but immediately afterward the protestors became less disruptive.

Ferraro had said that as a Catholic she herself would never have an abortion, but she felt that other women had a right to decide differently. Speaking of Ferraro, Catholic Archbishop John O'Connor stopped just short of telling Catholics not to vote for her: He said during a televised news conference that "I do not see how a Catholic in good conscience can vote for an individual expressing himself or herself as favoring abortion." The church hierarchy had never taken such a strong stand against male politicians who were Catholic and prochoice. Ferraro noted that "I was a dangerous prochoice spokesperson. . . . It was one thing for Catholic men to speak in the abstract about a woman's right to abortion. . . . I could actually have one."

Throughout most of the campaign, Ferraro put little emphasis on women's issues. However, by October, with polls showing Reagan far ahead, the Mondale campaign was apparently ready to try a new strategy. In the final weeks, Ferraro began to talk more about the ERA and the House pension bill she cosponsored to protect widows, and about the fact that her candidacy was historic, but by that time it was too late. The Democrats had lost the chance to ride the crest of women's enthusiasm over her nomination.

How Republicans Captured the Women's Vote

Meanwhile, the Republicans had been wooing the women's vote in their own way. Back in the summer of 1983, party strategists had asked Republican women for advice about the gender gap. The women, quoting census reports and national surveys, challenged the men's stereotypes: They pointed out that only 7 percent of U.S. families now fitted the traditional pattern of male breadwinner, full-time housewife, and children; that by 1990, 40 percent of family income would come from the paychecks of wives; that there were now more women enrolled in colleges and graduate schools than men.

Presidential pollster Richard B. Wirthlin responded by conducting a survey of 45,000 women. Afterward, he broke them down into eight different categories, using criteria such as their age, marital status, and whether or not they were employed, and gave each category a woman's name, using the first eight letters of the alphabet: Alice, Betty, Carolyn, and so on. Wirthlin found that each group had somewhat different concerns and thus a different response to Reagan. The "Helen" group, for example, were unmarried, unemployed, under twenty-five, and mostly anti-Reagan.

Writing off the women who seemed hopelessly opposed to Reagan's policies, the Republicans devised direct mail campaigns and television ads aimed at the groups considered likely prospects, focusing on women as members of the work force who had a stake in a healthy economy. For example, mailings sent to older women stressed that the Reagan administration had curbed inflation; those sent to young, married, working women emphasized that during the Reagan years the tax credit for child care had been increased. *Washington Post* writer Bill Peterson concluded that the Republican strategists understood the women's vote better than the Democrats *and* did more to cultivate it.

Postmortem on the 1984 Election

In November, Ronald Reagan was reelected by a wide margin. To the distress of feminists, 57 percent of the women who voted chose Reagan, up from 47 percent in 1980. The gender gap survived—fewer women than men voted for Reagan—but it was narrower now, somewhere between 4 and 9 percent in various polls. Because most people had expected more, many reacted as if the gap had disappeared. The press announced that women had suffered a major setback, noting that some who ran for Congress lost as well. In fact, female incumbents kept their seats, as incumbents almost always did, and most female challengers were defeated, as challengers usually were.

CBS estimated that Ferraro contributed 1 percent to Mondale's total vote, about what vice-presidential candidates normally contributed. However, some Democrats were quick to blame Mondale's defeat on Gerry Ferraro. A member of the campaign's inner circle insisted that "the party got a gun put to its head by the women to choose a woman for Vice-President. They overpromised what they could not deliver: the sweep of the women's vote, millions of unregistered women voters, millions of volunteers. The truth of the matter is they didn't bring in anything. . . . After this performance, I don't think the women should come running up to the table demanding more very soon."

Democratic consultant Patrick Caddell warned that "we can't afford to have a party so feminized that it has no appeal to males." In some districts where women ran and lost, male political bosses were now saying that women made bad candidates. Meanwhile, Republican politicians were gloating about the "anti-female backlash" reflected in the vote. They maintained that the real gender gap was the Democratic party's problem with men. Worst of all, in Congress women's issues were no longer taken as seriously, though some congressmen were probably using Ferraro's defeat as an excuse for refusing to support bills they wouldn't have voted for in any case.

Responding to the barrage of criticism, feminists noted indignantly that voters go by the top of the ticket. Historically, the vice-presidential candidate never made more than a marginal difference. The women also pointed out that the gender gap had decided several Senate races and elected Madeleine Kunin Governor of Vermont. They charged that the Mondale staff blew their chance by providing women's groups with so little in the way of resources; and they pointed out that despite the lack of support, Ferraro brought in 10,000 volunteers and raised as much money for the ticket as Mondale. Furthermore, a coalition consisting mostly of women's groups had organized a voter registration drive and registered 1.8 million women. As a result, in 1984 for the first time women voted at a higher rate than men did.

The feminists complained bitterly that Ferraro was not allowed to talk about women's issues until the last two weeks of the campaign. As usual, the election was dominated by the competition for the white male vote. Columbia University political scientist Ethel Klein wrote that "by not focusing on the substantive concerns of women, the Democrats provided a vacuum in which the Republican message could diffuse the women's vote."

In retrospect, there was no question that some feminists, swept along by the media's avid interest in the subject, oversold the benefits of having a woman on the ticket. The price for the feminist venture into presidential politics was high: Women temporarily lost the clout that the gender gap had provided, for they had squandered their political capital on the campaign for a woman Vice-President.

For Geraldine Ferraro herself, the campaign had been agonizing at times. In the book she wrote afterward, she said, ". . . [W]hat I wasn't prepared for was the depth of the fury, the bigotry and the sexism my candidacy would unleash. I didn't expect the antiabortion protests to be so vicious, to be politically orchestrated and funded on the national level." Though she insisted that overall the campaign was worth it, she also admitted candidly that ". . . if God had shown me a videotape the day Fritz asked me to be his running mate of what the next months would be like, I would have said, 'Thanks, God, but could you do me a favor and choose Dianne [Feinstein]?' "

It's easier to count the costs of the Ferraro campaign than it is to measure the benefits, which were less tangible. Summing up the whole adventure, sociologist Carol Mueller noted that in order to influence the Democrats, feminists had to wage a public campaign through the media; that their influence had its limits, and so did the party's willingness to meet their demands. However, just getting a woman onto the ticket was a considerable achievement that "has changed forever the limits of the possible for American women."

Aftermath

The 1984 election results puzzled and frustrated liberals and feminists alike. As Gloria Steinem saw it, ". . . [A] large majority of men and a slender majority of women went to the polls and voted for a President whose major positions—from disarmament talks to deficit spending for arms, from illegal abortion to reduced environmental controls—a majority of Americans don't share." Sure enough, two weeks after the election a Gallup poll confirmed that public opinion was still heavily in favor of a mutual, verifiable nuclear freeze and of increased spending for social programs, that Americans wanted pollution controls enforced, and were in favor of the ERA.

According to exit polls, the state of the economy was the pivotal issue in the 1984 election, as it had been in 1980 when voters turned against Carter largely because of high inflation. In 1984, by nearly two to one, those who were polled rejected Mondale's position that a tax increase was needed. Ferraro suggested that, in fact, they rewarded Reagan for telling them only the good news, and punished Mondale for bringing them the bad. Most women voters were no different in this than men. Furthermore, as Millie Jeffrey said, American women were not monolithic. Republican strategist Richard Wirthlin had wooed them brilliantly, playing to their disparate interests.

The election also reflected profound changes in the way voters saw the major parties. The GOP had long been the party of the privileged, but now it also attracted many working-class whites, who felt that the Democrats had supported special treatment for people of color.

After 1984, the press no longer ballyhooed the power of the gender gap, but news reports did register the fact that it was there. Most political observers now saw it for what it was: a consistent difference in the way men and women voted, big enough to decide the outcome in a close race.

In the 1986 election, the gap cost the Republicans nine seats in the Senate. The Democrats who were elected each received less than 50 percent of men's votes, but won because they received 50 percent or more of women's. As a result, the Republicans lost control of the Senate for the first time since 1980. Because the House, too, was in Democratic hands, women's votes effectively derailed the Reagan agenda.

The 1988 presidential campaign was, in some ways, a throwback to the politics of the 1970s, and feminists played a less significant role in it. When the Democratic party's leaders met to draft a platform, Eleanor Holmes Norton was there to represent Jesse Jackson, the only candidate still contesting the nomination against Michael Dukakis. With Jackson's blessings, Norton also looked after the interests of feminists: She spelled out what the platform should say on women's issues such as the ERA and abortion, and then refused to budge from her position. In the end, she wore down the opposition. Nevertheless, once the general election campaign got under way, both Dukakis and Republican George Bush presented themselves as middle-of-the-roaders and more or less ignored women's issues. Once again, the Democrats seemed primarily concerned about winning back white male voters.

In 1988, some feminist leaders were already preparing for the 1992 election. Ellie Smeal, now head of the Fund for the Feminist Majority, toured the country in an effort to persuade as many women as possible to run for election. Many would lose, but if they gained name-recognition, they were apt to do better the next time, and some feminists were now setting long-range goals. They had concluded that the only way to pass the ERA was to elect more women to state legislatures and to Congress. Though incumbents had a huge advantage, the census would be taken in 1990, and afterward state legislatures would reapportion districts. That meant there would be open seats both on the state level and in Congress, where California, Florida, and Texas were expected to gain seats to reflect population growth. Feminists wanted the maximum number of women in a position to run for open seats in 1992, because if enough of them were elected, women's groups could revive the ERA and have some chance of winning.

By 1990, feminists were also testing another political strategy. The previous year, in the wake of the Supreme Court's anti-abortion decision in the *Webster* case (see chapter 21), NOW gained many new, young recruits. Enraged at the threat to abortion, they took the leadership by surprise during NOW's annual convention and passed a resolution calling for a commission to investigate whether NOW should form a new political party. Other women's organizations thought it was a wild idea. The very notion of founding a new party seemed quixotic at a time when abortion rights had to be defended in virtually every state. How could feminists do that without working with Democratic and Republican politicians? However, the women of NOW believed that, at a minimum, the threat might force the Democrats and moderate Republicans to deal with women's issues and others they were neglecting. And in the end, the Commission might simply recommend major reforms in the political system—reforms many Americans believed were long overdue.

Thus, in 1990, NOW invited approximately forty prominent Americans to serve on a Commission for Responsive Democracy. It was to hold hearings in major cities around the country to discuss "the political health of the nation and steps that might be taken to build a more representative democracy." In assembling the Commission, NOW's leaders discovered that many groups outside the women's movement were fed up with the political status quo and eager to explore options for changing the system.

In fact, public cynicism had reached a new high, thanks to years of negative campaigning, the pernicious influence of PACs, and the fact that it had become almost impossible to defeat incumbents. People were disgusted with politics—in 1990, fewer than 40 percent of those who were eligible to vote bothered to go to the polls. NOW's Commission would be tapping into that widespread dissatisfaction.

THE ELUSIVE WOMEN'S VOTING BLOC

During the late 1980s, the gender gap became a modest but well-established factor in American elections.* In 1990, a gap of at least 4 percent registered in more than half the races where exit polls were taken. Three new state governors owed their victories to the women's vote, and in some major races that vote went strongly to female candidates.

Surprisingly, in most countries in Western Europe there was still no significant difference in the way women and men voted. Some political scientists suggested that the United States was different because American women were in many ways worse off than European women, and because a strong feminist movement had raised their consciousness. Americans had no parental leave nor state-subsidized child care, and the courts had impoverished thousand of divorced wives. Yet in the United States women's expectations were higher and they believed more vehemently in equality. Going into the 1990s, there was an additional factor: Legal abortion was in jeopardy in America (see chapter 21), and that had politicized many women.

---

* On opinion polls, it showed up at times as a gender gulf. In the fall of 1990, 73 percent of women opposed using force in the Persian Gulf. compared with 48 percent of men.

chapter 20

The New Right and the War on Feminism

⟋‿⟍

*I*n the late 1970s, many feminists believed that American women were finally coming into their own. They had made gains in almost every field. Though there was a long way to go, and some activists felt that the glass was half empty, others already saw it as half full.

The election of Ronald Reagan abruptly stalled progress for women, and feminists spent the 1980s defending ground they thought they'd won. Given the strength of their opposition—the social movement known as the New Right—it's remarkable that they were able to succeed as well as they did.

On the eve of the 1980 election, remarks by Howard Phillips, national director of a group called the Conservative Caucus, provided a disturbing clue to the mind-set of some right-wingers then on the brink of power. Phillips told a "pro-family" rally that "it has been a conscious policy of government to liberate the wife from the leadership of the husband and thus break up the family unit as a unit of government." He wasn't talking about policy in the 1960s and 1970s; his complaints went back further than that. The first mistake, he said, was that in the 1800s women were given property rights; then they got the vote. "You know," Phillips said, "it used to be that in recognition of the family unit as a basic unit of society, we had one family, one vote. And we have seen the trend instead toward one person, one vote. The ultimate extension of this philosophy has been the sexual liberation of the woman from her husband." That liberation in turn led to adultery and promiscuity, he told his audience.

Phillips's remarks weren't widely reported. Probably, most people who voted for Reagan had no idea just how reactionary some right-wingers were. Determined to defend the traditional male privileges of their race and class, they were angry at the women who had challenged them. They were also out of touch with the reality of most Americans' lives.

Phillips was far from the only one. As Reagan took office a few months later, the word got out that George Gilder's *Wealth and Poverty* was recommended reading for members of the new administration—the President himself had endorsed it. Gilder's conservative credo denied that sex discrimination existed; it admitted that there was still some residue of racial discrimination, but maintained that it only affected black males. How could such men achieve upward mobility? Gilder believed what they needed was greater incentive—in the form of a totally dependent wife.* The New Right had its head in the sand—and its hands on the reins of power.

THE RISE OF THE REACTIONARY RIGHT

The New Right brought together four major groups: avid anti-Communists; economic conservatives for whom the free market was an article of faith; predominantly Catholic anti-abortion activists; and Protestant fundamentalists and evangelicals. The conservative movement actually began in the 1950s when anti-Communists joined forces with free-marketers. Both groups felt marginalized, elbowed out of the American mainstream. The excesses of McCarthyism and of the John Birch Society had pretty much discredited hardline anti-Communism, and free-marketers were often treated as an eccentric minority because the Depres-

---

* Gilder was also the author of *Sexual Suicide*, which argued that woman's place *was* in the home, and *Naked Nomads*, which warned that society was being threatened by tribes of unmarried men, created in part when women refused to do their duty; their duty, as Gilder saw it, was to sustain family life and civilize men.

sion had convinced most economists that laissez-faire—a completely unregulated market—simply didn't work.

As conservatives saw it, a liberal establishment controlled both political parties and, indeed, the nation, via a network of think tanks, foundations, and the liberal media. Thus, they set out to create a counterestablishment of right-wing institutions: to supplant the influence of the *New York Times* with that of the *Wall Street Journal*, and the research of the Brookings Institute with that of the American Enterprise Institute; to match the financial power of the Ford Foundation with funding from their own foundations. Their ultimate goal was political power, and "regular" Republicans were as much their enemy as the Democrats.

The right wing's first triumph occurred when conservative Barry Goldwater won the Republican presidential nomination in 1964. Though Goldwater was trounced by Lyndon Johnson and some felt the ultraright had been discredited, in fact it had established a beachhead within the Republican party. The campaign also thrust Ronald Reagan into the spotlight. The best-known Hollywood personality to support Goldwater, he gave an impassioned television speech that attracted the attention of right-wing leaders. With their backing, he was elected Governor of California.

Reagan was to become indispensable to the conservatives. Always optimistic, he seemed both forceful and sincere, and he took their abstract theories and turned them into images that seized the imagination of the public. His backers included CEOs —the chief executive officers of powerful corporations—eccentric millionaires, and Sunbelt entrepreneurs, as well as right-wing intellectuals.

The Religious Right

For the most part, the religious right—Catholic and Protestant —didn't become politically active until the 1970s. Anti-abortion Catholics organized first. Soon after the Supreme Court legalized abortion in 1973, the Catholic church launched the National Right to Life Committee (NRLC) to coordinate the activities of anti-abortion groups. Though NRLC was officially a separate organization,* in fact the church provided local activists with meeting

---

* It was risky for any church to become too directly involved in politics, because a federal regulation prohibited religious organizations from endorsing political candidates on pain of losing their tax-exempt status.

rooms, office supplies, transportation, a communications network, and funds. From the beginning, the church focused on electoral politics. Thus, in 1975, the National Conference of Catholic Bishops (NCCB) produced the Pastoral Plan for Pro-Life Activities, a blueprint for organizing millions of Catholics into a vast pressure group. Its primary goal would be to elect members of Congress who would vote for a constitutional amendment banning abortion.

A few years later, right-wing Protestants turned their attention to politics. The United States had experienced a religious revival during the 1970s as Americans by the thousands joined fundamentalist and evangelical churches, subscribed to conservative Christian publications, and enrolled their children in religious schools and colleges. By the end of the decade, fundamentalists and evangelicals owned over a thousand radio stations and forty local TV stations, as well as a cable television network. Some televangelists—television preachers like the Reverend Jerry Falwell—had huge followings.

In the past, Protestant preachers had insisted that it was sinful —or simply a waste of energy—to focus on social reform rather than on "saving" individuals. During the 1970s, some began to have second thoughts. They had been stunned by the sexual revolution, appalled by the Supreme Court's abortion decision and the banning of school prayer. When the Internal Revenue Service threatened to cancel the tax exemptions of religious schools that refused to integrate, that was the last straw. Many felt that they were losing control of their children, their families, and their lives. While some responded by withdrawing into their own Christian counterculture, others organized politically, forming hundreds of single-issue groups to oppose sex education, gay rights laws, or other types of social change.

Gradually, links developed between anti-Communists, freemarketers, and the religious right, both Catholic and Protestant. Richard Viguerie, a conservative who owned a direct-mail business, was one of the first to understand that the New Right could use particular issues as hooks to draw groups and individuals into the movement. Their votes and financial contributions could help to elect conservatives even as they gave the movement a broader base. The abortion issue seemed especially promising because it symbolized feminism and the sexual revolution, and many Americans were uncomfortable with both.

In the late 1970s, Ronald Reagan's advisors set out to cement the budding alliance between the political New Right and the

religious right. A few men began to crisscross the country, introducing evangelical and fundamentalist preachers to leading local
conservatives. In January 1979, one such meeting so inspired
evangelist Jerry Falwell that afterward he founded a new national
organization, the Moral Majority. Its purpose was to encourage
evangelical and fundamentalist Christians to play an active role
in the political process.

Feminists suspected that conservative politicians were simply
using the religious right and its issues to gain power—that they
didn't really care one way or the other about abortion or school
prayer, for example. Religious conservatives themselves wondered at times how sincere some of the other right-wing activists
were. Clearly, the various factions had different priorities. Some
were moved by a powerful nostalgia for small-town America, for
a time of simple moral certainties and stable, devout communities; others, by a belief in a wide-open economic system—the free
market—in which no holds were barred. Few pointed out the
contradiction.

CONSERVATIVES WIN THE WHITE HOUSE

Ronald Reagan's 1980 campaign broke new ground in several
ways. American corporations spent enormous amounts supporting conservative candidates, and many based their campaign contributions on ideology, rather than party, for perhaps the first
time. Negative campaigning was also widespread, as New Right
PACs set out to defeat particular liberal senators by attacking
them directly, rather than simply supporting their opponents.
The formidable NCPAC—the National Conservative Political Action Committee—spent nearly $2 million on negative campaigns.
Meanwhile, the Moral Majority used the churches to mobilize
voters. Volunteers set up voter-registration tables in Protestant
churches every Sunday morning for months, visibly mixing religion and politics.

Reagan lambasted the Democrats for high taxes and wasteful
spending, and condemned school busing and affirmative action.
He promised to build up the military and restore the nation's
"place in the sun." Not only was he elected, but at the same time
a handful of well-known liberal senators were defeated. Many
people concluded that the public supported the right wing on key
issues. In fact, because so many voters stayed home on election
day or weren't registered to vote, Reagan was actually elected by

26 percent of adult Americans. The turnout *was* higher than usual in the South, where there were many evangelicals, but when researchers asked conservative Christians who had backed Reagan to give their reasons, they generally cited the state of the economy and foreign policy, like most other Americans who voted Republican that year.

THE RICH GET RICHER, THE POOR GET POORER

Reagan's economic policies vastly increased the number of women living in poverty, first by plunging the nation into a recession that began in August 1981, then by decimating the social programs that kept poor families afloat. During Reagan's first term, the American poverty rate climbed past 15 percent for the first time in 20 years.

During his campaign, the President had promised to build up the military, cut everyone's taxes, *and* balance the budget. His advisors—primarily budget director David Stockman—insisted that it really was possible to do all three. According to the theory known as supply-side economics, tight control of the money supply would reduce inflation; meanwhile, taxes would be cut for everyone, but especially for corporations and the wealthy. They would invest the money they saved, and that would lead to a boom. As a result, government revenues would actually grow and the budget would be balanced. Supply-side economics had been tried before unsuccessfully and was widely regarded as a pie-in-the-sky panacea. However, supply-siders believed the governments involved had never given it enough time.

The administration's economic proposals were presented to Congress in February 1981. By June, Reagan's top advisors had concluded that their economic forecasts had been much too optimistic, but they decided that it wouldn't be politically expedient to admit their mistake. *After* Congress had approved a 25 percent across-the-board tax cut, they told Reagan that the country was about to experience a recession and that there was bound to be a huge federal deficit. He flatly refused to believe them and rejected their suggestion that he reduce military spending. The recession that followed lasted until early 1983 and was the worst since the Great Depression of the 1930s.

Despite the recession, the administration proceeded to cut the very social programs intended to help people weather hard times

—the conservatives simply didn't believe in a welfare state. Thus, budget director David Stockman set out to pay for both the tax cuts and the defense budget—the biggest peacetime military buildup in the nation's history—by cutting domestic spending to the bone.

In the end, Stockman didn't get everything he wanted. For example, though he tried to eliminate WIC, the Women, Infants, and Children Program, feminists and liberals in Congress were able to save it. However, funds were cut drastically, and as a result 100,000 low-income pregnant women and young children lost the food supplements and health care they'd been receiving through WIC.*

Other social programs suffered worse damage. Hundreds of thousands of families were declared ineligible for welfare or had their benefits reduced. Medicaid funds were cut. More than one million people could no longer get food stamps, and three million children were dropped from school lunch programs. Fuel assistance, housing assistance, and funds for housing development were cut. Three quarters of all day-care centers were forced to scale back, because federal funds that helped low-income families pay for child care were repeatedly slashed. More than 300,000 people who had been receiving federal disability benefits were suddenly told they were no longer eligible and would have to find a way to support themselves.

Despite the cuts in social programs, within a short time Reagan's economic policies, combined with the recession, produced a record deficit. Many liberals were convinced that the administration deliberately created the deficit to force Congress to reduce social spending still further, and David Stockman more or less admitted that that was true. At any rate, the deficit had a lasting effect: Even after Reagan's departure, it tied the hands of the Democrats, making it impossible for them to introduce substantial new programs.

By the spring of 1983, the economy had begun to recover, and the administration took the credit, though it was the deficit that made short-run prosperity possible. At the end of Reagan's second term, for a variety of reasons including a regressive tax reform, many American families had less income in real money than they had had in 1977. Over the same period of time, the rich grew richer while the poor sank deeper into poverty. Nowhere

---

* WIC was intended to head off health problems. Experts estimated that for every $1 spent through WIC on food for pregnant women, taxpayers saved $3—the cost of the medical care WIC recipients would have required in the future.

was the disparity between rich and poor more obvious than in the growing number of people, including women and children, who were homeless. Rents had been going up faster than income for some time, but the situation grew worse in the 1980s because the Reagan administration made deeper cuts in housing programs than in any other area. The money for new, federally aided housing dried up almost completely.

SETBACKS IN CIVIL RIGHTS

Once conservatives gained the White House, they set about undermining antidiscrimination laws. The New Right had argued all along that such laws amounted to "reverse discrimination" against white men and that they forced employers to set quotas —they were referring to the goals and timetables required by affirmative action plans. As the New Right saw it, civil rights laws were just one more instance of government interfering with the free market. David Stockman explained that equality was basically unjust because it took state power to achieve it.

On the other side, feminists and other civil rights activists had no doubt that affirmative action was both fair and necessary. Wilma Scott Heide, an early president of NOW, once remarked dryly, "We've had affirmative action programs for white men for centuries; we just haven't called them that." As for goals and timetables, liberals pointed out that the government began to require affirmative action plans only after trying unsuccessfully to enforce antidiscrimination laws without them, and that very few employers had ever treated them as quotas. Many companies actually wanted the government to go on requiring affirmative action. Some said it had been good for business; others were afraid that without a firm, federal requirement, they might be whipsawed between lawsuits charging discrimination and suits brought by white males charging reverse discrimination.

The right-wing campaign to turn back the clock on civil rights got under way in 1981. One of the first targets was the Executive Order, issued in 1969, that required federal contractors to draw up affirmative action plans; its regulations exempted small companies and those with modest contracts. Reagan officials simply broadened the exemptions until over 70 percent of government contractors were no longer required to do affirmative action. Another new rule stated that complaints filed under the Executive Order must now identify "all known victims of discrimination."

That meant that women's groups could no longer file a complaint for employees and shield their identities. The administration also began pressuring cities, counties, and states to drop affirmative action plans that had already opened up police and fire departments and other agencies.

On another front, Justice Department officials announced that instead of mounting class-action suits—the most effective way to fight discrimination—they would now proceed on a case-by-case basis. Meanwhile, the administration slashed the budgets of the agencies charged with enforcing antidiscrimination laws, left positions in those agencies unfilled, or filled them with conservatives. Right-wing appointees turned the Civil Rights Commission into such a travesty that by 1986 some members of Congress wanted to put it out of business.

The New Right also used the courts effectively. Twice during the 1980s, a conservative administration persuaded the Supreme Court to gut major civil rights laws, and activists turned to Congress to try to restore the legislation. First, the Justice Department attacked Title IX, the 1972 law designed to give women equal opportunity in education. A key section of Title IX banned sex discrimination in any "program or activity" receiving federal financial assistance. The wording was borrowed from Title VI of the 1964 Civil Rights Act, which was also the model for laws that prohibited discrimination against minorities, the disabled, and the elderly. Though all four statutes had always been taken to mean that if an institution received federal funds in any form, the whole institution was forbidden to discriminate, Justice Department lawyers argued before the Supreme Court that discrimination was illegal only in the particular "program or activity" receiving the funds. If a college took federal money solely for student loans, for example, the financial aid office couldn't discriminate, but the athletics department—or any other department—could.

In February 1984, the Supreme Court handed down a decision in *Grove City College* v. *Bell* that cut the heart out of Title IX. Henceforth, most educational institutions would be a kind of patchwork, with some departments forbidden to discriminate on pain of losing their federal funds, while others were free to do as they liked. The other three statutes were affected as well. By April, a bill had been introduced in Congress to change the wording in all four laws to make it clear that they covered whole institutions or companies.

Unfortunately, the legislation soon bogged down in controversy. Some legislators insisted on saddling the bill with an anti-abortion amendment, which said that educational institutions couldn't be required to provide or pay for abortions as a condition for receiving federal funds.* Feminists were outraged at the attempt to hitch an anti-abortion rider onto a major civil rights bill. The coalition lobbying for the bill, which was known as the Civil Rights Restoration Act (CRRA), tried hard for three years to change anti-abortion votes. Women's organizations finally gave up in 1988 and pushed for passage of the bill, knowing that the abortion amendment would be included. Congress passed the CRRA, and Reagan vetoed it, but the lawmakers overrode his veto.

After George Bush replaced Reagan, the Justice Department continued to attack civil rights laws. The strategy paid off for the second time in 1989, when a new, conservative majority on the Supreme Court—almost all, Reagan appointees—handed down a series of decisions undercutting antidiscrimination statutes. Civil rights lawyers were stunned. Liberals in Congress immediately introduced a bill to undo the damage. Known as the Civil Rights Act of 1990, it was highly technical, because the loopholes the Court had opened up in the antibias laws were devastating but highly technical. The bill was vetoed by the Bush administration on the same old grounds—that it would force employers to set quotas—and this time Congress failed to override the veto.

The Campaign Against WEEA

Right-wingers opposed to antidiscrimination laws also trained their sights on the WEEA, or Women's Educational Equity Act, program, which provided grants for educational projects designed to help women achieve equality. Leslie Wolfe, who was WEEA's director when Reagan took office, recalled that "WEEA was tiny, barely a blip in the federal education budget." Yet it was anathema to the New Right. Richard Viguerie's *Conservative Digest* described it as a "money machine for a network of openly radical feminist groups." Wolfe felt it was a lightning rod for the same hostility that conservatives directed against textbooks that supposedly taught feminism. "They considered the effort to change the way schools treat children . . . an incredible threat to the way of life that they'd like to preserve," she said.

---

* Under a long-standing Title IX regulation, some colleges that already provided faculty or students with health insurance or comprehensive health care had been required to include pregnancy and abortion in their coverage.

The Reagan administration began its attack on WEEA by asking Congress to end it as an independent program; when that strategy failed, Reagan officials tried to get Congress to zero-fund it—to vote it no budget at all. Thanks to intensive lobbying by feminists, though WEEA's funds were reduced, the program survived. In 1982, the administration transferred Leslie Wolfe temporarily to another position, and then saw to it that the outside experts brought in to judge grant proposals were drawn from Phyllis Schlafly's Eagle Forum, an organization of right-wing Republican women, and other conservative groups. Many had traditional ideas about a woman's place; most had no relevant experience. A year later, Wolfe was forced out of her job at WEEA. However, in 1984 feminists persuaded Congress to rewrite the original WEEA legislation, incorporating new criteria that would make it difficult for those administering the program to ignore its basic purposes. In Wolfe's view, the administration's attempt to damage or destroy WEEA failed.

The White House also targeted an advisory council that had been created by the WEEA legislation to give women a voice on education policy. NACWEP, the National Advisory Council on Women's Educational Programs, had twenty members, all appointed by the President. It had always been bipartisan and independent, and the executive director, Joy Simonson, was a feminist.* The Reagan administration not only appointed twenty conservatives to the Council but stage-managed their dramatic first meeting. The women had barely settled in their seats when someone moved to fire Simonson on the spot and set up a search committee to interview candidates for her job. "I, of course, was sitting there as friendly as could be, having invited them all to dinner at my house that night," Simonson recalled. Over the objections of a few women, the deed was done.

"When we broke for lunch," Simonson continued, "the secretary in the outer office said that a woman had come in during the morning and announced that she was there for the job interview. That was before they had even gotten to voting me out." That afternoon, half a dozen applicants—several from out of town—turned up to be interviewed, sent over by the White House, which somehow knew that the supposedly independent Council would be in the market for a new director that day. The woman who stepped into Simonson's shoes, like the head of the search committee, was a member of the Eagle Forum.

---

* Simonson was one of the group of women who originally drafted the WEEA bill.

The ideological fervor of the conservatives had changed the whole atmosphere in Washington. Bernice Sandler, one of the architects of WEEA, recalled that when Nixon was in office, "The Republicans would meet with us . . . and you could convince them on political grounds that something was necessary. The Reagan administration was not even interested in meeting with us." Under the circumstances, compromise was rarely possible.

TRANSFORMING THE POWER STRUCTURE

Whenever the White House changes hands, the new administration has the chance to fill key federal jobs with its supporters, to reward them for their loyalty. The conservatives had another agenda in mind as well: They were determined to burrow into the Washington bureaucracy so that they could hang on to power after Reagan was gone. Thus, the administration went out of its way to fill jobs, not with mainstream Republicans, but with those whose ideology passed muster. The computer at the Heritage Foundation, a right-wing think tank, disgorged hundreds of names of people who had demonstrable connections with conservative groups. Few who were appointed to high-level jobs were female.

However, the conservatives' real hold on the future—besides the deficit—was the judiciary. The President has the right to appoint judges not only to the Supreme Court but to federal district and appeals courts. Because Congress expanded the federal judiciary, before the Reagan administration left office it was able to fill about half of the seats on the federal bench with conservatives, carefully chosen for their right-wing views on issues such as abortion and affirmative action. A bipartisan standing committee of the American Bar Association rated them less qualified overall than judges appointed by previous administrations. Their decisions were also more often proprosecution, antigovernment regulation, and antiwomen, according to one survey. There was irony in the fact that the conservatives, who had long insisted that the courts should simply interpret the laws and not make policy, resorted to packing the courts with ideologues. After George Bush became President, he continued to appoint right-wingers to the bench.

Change came more slowly to the Supreme Court. Reagan had the opportunity to fill three seats on the Court with conservatives, beginning in 1981 with Sandra Day O'Connor—who probably owed her selection at least partly to Republican nervousness about the gender gap. O'Connor was a moderate conservative, and the Moral Majority and anti-abortion groups actually lobbied against her, based on dubious evidence that she had prochoice sympathies.

In 1986, when Chief Justice Warren Burger retired, Reagan appointed right-winger Antonin Scalia to the vacant seat—in effect, replacing a conservative with a conservative—and made William H. Rehnquist, the Court's most right-wing member, the Chief Justice. Feminist and civil rights groups opposed Rehnquist's promotion—to no avail; the Republican-dominated Senate supported Reagan's choice.

Nevertheless, the Court still didn't have a totally consistent, conservative majority. Reagan's third chance to tip the balance came in June 1987, when Justice Lewis F. Powell Jr. resigned. Powell had occupied the middle ground between the conservative and liberal factions, often providing the swing vote on important decisions; he'd supported abortion rights and civil rights. To replace him, Reagan nominated Judge Robert H. Bork, a legal scholar who had built his reputation by attacking Supreme Court decisions that expanded individual rights, including *Roe* v. *Wade*.

The battle over the Bork nomination quickly became a major crusade for both sides. The loosely organized coalition opposing Bork included hundreds of groups—some said it was the largest coalition ever mobilized by a battle in Congress. The struggle lasted for three months and came to a head as Bork was questioned in televised Senate hearings for five grueling days. Public opinion polls showed a sharp rise in anti-Bork sentiment afterward. It was obvious that he was unlikely to support antidiscrimination precedents, and he also insisted that the Constitution didn't include a right to privacy, let alone a right to abortion. Surveys showed that most voters supported abortion. Thanks to a sophisticated media and direct-mail campaign waged by the anti-Bork coalition, Bork became a symbol of right-wing ideas. The Senate, which now had a Democratic majority, responded by rejecting his nomination by a vote of 58 to 42.

The White House complained bitterly that the opposition had politicized the nomination process. However, Bork was a highly political choice to begin with, the culmination of Reagan's campaign to change the federal bench. What's more, the Senate's Democratic majority was created after an election campaign during which Reagan stumped the nation urging voters to elect Republicans because they would help him replace liberal judges with conservatives.

After Bork's defeat, Reagan nominated Judge Douglas H. Ginsburg to the High Court, but Ginsburg withdrew as a candidate when it came out that he had smoked marijuana during the 1960s and 70s. For his third choice, Reagan nominated Judge Anthony Kennedy, a more distinguished and apparently more moderate conservative. The ultraright was not happy; the liberal opposition was confused. Ten days before the Senate hearings, organizations such as NARAL and the ACLU had still not decided what stand to take. Catherine East recalled that "most women's organizations didn't want to take Kennedy on. They figured he was the best we would get from Reagan, and anyway there was no chance to defeat him." NOW, almost alone, opposed Kennedy. In the end, the Senate confirmed Kennedy, 97 to 0.

That was in February 1988. Reagan left office that year, but the 1988–89 Supreme Court term proved that he'd accomplished what he set out to do: The Court now had a solid, conservative majority—as demonstrated by the set of decisions that made job discrimination suits much harder to win and others that gave the states greater leeway to restrict abortions. In each case, the final tally was 5 to 4, and Justice Kennedy's vote made the difference. Bork's defeat seemed a hollow victory after all.

The one bright spot for feminists was that in response to the increasing conservatism of the Supreme Court, the top courts in some states began to cite the state constitution to protect or expand individual rights. Liberal Justice William Brennan called this probably the most important recent development in constitutional law.

CONGRESS: WINS AND LOSSES

During the 1980s, the few gains that women achieved on the national level were made through Congress, almost always against the opposition of the Reagan administration. Though feminists relied primarily on Democrats, they needed the support of some Republicans to succeed on any issue.

The situation on Capitol Hill had changed in many ways since the early 1970s, when a handful of feminists turned up to lobby on every women's issue that came along. Now the lobbyists were mostly seasoned professionals, employed by various women's organizations. Feminists in Congress had long since organized a caucus of their own; most congresswomen belonged, and congressmen were accepted as associate members. Beginning in 1981, in each session of Congress, the Congressional Caucus for Women's Issues introduced a package of bills focused on women's economic needs.

To a striking extent, women's legislative fortunes in Congress rose and fell according to the way politicians thought women might vote. Thus, because the 1980 election was widely taken to be a repudiation of feminism and the civil rights movement, afterward lobbyists for women's organizations and groups like the NAACP found they had lost much of their political clout. When the gender gap registered clearly in the election of 1982, politicians suddenly became concerned again about women's issues. Congress passed an important pension reform law and strengthened the system for collecting child support. The White House actually supported both measures. In fact, the 98th Congress (1983–84) passed more new laws for women than any other Congress since the early 1970s. Feminists were even able to muster enough votes to enact a law that provided funds for battered women's shelters, despite determined opposition from the Reagan admininistration.*

The gender gap was discredited by the 1984 election, and once again it appeared that women's issues had been buried. Then in 1986, the Democrats regained control of the Senate with the help of a gender gap that had actually been there all along. However, if women's issues were again recognized as legitimate, they often fell victim to insider trading. According to Patricia Reuss, legislative director of WEAL, virtually every feminist-backed law that passed had its downside. The CRRA restored Title IX, as mentioned earlier, but carried an anti-abortion amendment; a welfare reform bill had some good features, but was punitive and underfunded, and it was financed in part by reducing the tax credit that helped middle-income families pay for child care—and so on.

When George Bush assumed the presidency in 1989, the rhetoric from the White House became somewhat less hostile to feminism. However, some of Bush's closest advisors were

---

* Conservatives fought the domestic violence law, especially a $625,000 grant to NCADV, the National Coalition Against Domestic Violence, an umbrella group for shelters all over the country. Right-wingers claimed NCADV was a front for feminists and lesbians, and after the law was passed, Attorney General Meese withheld the NCADV funds for months. He finally released them, after pressure from the Congressional Caucus for Women's Issues, after cutting them by $50,000.

conservative ideologues, and in any case even the Democrats now hesitated to back ambitious new programs because of the deficit.

PARENTAL LEAVE AND CHILD CARE

With most mothers now in the work force, parental leave and child care became the two major feminist initiatives in the late 1980s. They had so much public support that for a time action on both fronts seemed likely. However, both bills were threatened by the basic ideological conflicts between liberals and conservatives that had been tearing the nation apart since the 1970s. By the end of 1990, though a child-care act had passed, family leave was apparently a dead issue, at least at the national level.

Family Leave Defeated

The family leave bill was originally drafted in 1984 by half a dozen Washington feminists. Gender-neutral, it would require companies to give male and female workers a job-protected leave of absence if they needed it to care for a newborn, newly adopted, or seriously ill child, or for seriously ill elderly parents, or for a medical problem of their own. The leave could be unpaid, but the employer must continue medical insurance coverage and maintain other benefits, such as seniority. The women who drafted the bill realized that low-income workers couldn't afford to take an unpaid leave, but they knew there was absolutely no chance of passing legislation that required time off with pay. At least, if minimum-wage employees were forced to go on leave, they could get their jobs back afterward.

The coalition formed to lobby for family leave included more than seventy organizations, ranging from NOW to the U.S. Catholic Conference. Though 74 percent of the public were in favor of family leave, President Bush opposed the legislation, as Reagan had before him. He maintained that the federal government had no right to tell businesses what to do. In 1990, Bush vetoed the bill and Congress failed to override his veto. Angry but undeterred, the groups that had backed family leave began planning campaigns in the states to pass similar legislation. By June 1991, twenty-five states, the District of Columbia, and Puerto Rico had passed some type of leaves law but only six had taken a comprehensive approach similar to the proposed federal legislation; thirteen mandated maternity leave only.

The final version of the Family and Medical Leave Act was so watered down that it was hard to understand why anyone was against it. The feminists who drafted the original proposal had wanted the law to cover all businesses; a later version exempted those with fewer than five employees, which would have meant that most workers benefited. The final bill would have applied to just 10 percent of the nation's businesses. However, the modest nature of the bill made no difference to the opposition. Conservatives, like feminists, knew that it was a foot in the door, likely to lead to further changes.

The Child-Care Dilemma

Feminists had been demanding federal support for child care since the early 1970s, and by the 1980s, the need was obvious and urgent. Yet the decade began on a note of disaster, as Reagan made drastic cuts in the programs that helped low-income parents pay for child care. In 1984, in the shadow of the gender gap, Congress passed a relatively modest bill that provided funds for referral services to help parents find child care and for after-school programs to serve "latchkey" youngsters, who would otherwise go home to an empty house.

In 1988, with public pressure for action building and Reagan on the way out, the child-care issue finally took off. Suddenly, dozens of competing bills circulated in Congress. Most feminists backed the ABC bill (the Act for Better Child Care). Eclectic in its approach, it would give the states federal money, which could be used in various ways: to expand the Head Start program, for example, or to establish new child-care centers or renovate old ones; to train staff or set up referral services. The states would be required to adopt health and safety standards for child care that reflected federal guidelines. Other bills introduced that year took different approaches.

The ABC bill became caught up in the usual ideological conflicts. Conservatives were against setting federal standards for day care; that would create a new bureaucracy, they said, and they believed in minimum government. Liberals replied that children's safety was at stake. An even tougher problem was posed by the Constitution's requirement that church and state remain separate. By the 1980s, one third of all youngsters in day care went to a church-run center. The government had never funded religious schools; how could it now pay for church-run child care? There were other questions as well. If a church did receive public money for its child-care center, should the center be allowed to accept children and hire staff on the basis of their religion, in defiance of antidiscrimination laws?

In 1990, Congress finally passed a bill that was a hard-fought compromise. To begin with, it provided $15 billion in tax credits for low-income working parents who were paying for child care. In addition, grant money was earmarked for child care for families on welfare or on the verge of welfare. The states were also given other, discretionary funds to use as they saw fit—to train providers or renovate centers, for example. In a victory for conservatives, the legislation said that parents could be given vouchers and could spend them at day-care centers run by churches; those centers were permitted to hire staff on the basis of religion. As a concession to liberals, the states must establish health and safety standards.

Like the failed family leave bill, the child-care legislation was a foot in the door. It just might lead eventually to the sort of support for working parents that was common in Western Europe. However, some feminists were concerned that it might prove to be a foot in the door in other ways as well—a threat to the constitutional wall between church and state that was all that held back the demands of the religious right. In January 1991—with the law scheduled to take effect the following September—child-care advocates complained that the Bush administration was taking too long to write the regulations, and that it was off to a bad start because it had assigned a welfare agency to run the program, rather than a child-development agency.

THE FUTURE OF THE RADICAL RIGHT

Periods of great social change, like the 1960s and early 1970s, are almost always followed by periods of backlash or stagnation. When the backlash is extreme, eventually the pendulum must swing back in the other direction.

Thus, by 1990, it seemed clear that the New Right had passed its peak. In some ways, it was suffering from events that it had helped set in motion. Reagan's economic policies had produced a speculative boom, rather than a healthy economy, and the stock market crash of 1987 showed just how vulnerable the economy was. Americans were concerned and no longer trusted conservatives to come up with the right answers. In addition, the Communist threat had evaporated. Right-wingers greeted this with mixed feelings. On the one hand, they claimed the credit, insisting that American pressure had forced the Soviets into an arms race that ruined their economy. On the other hand, conservatives were uneasy because anti-Communism had been the glue that held the various factions of the New Right together. Furthermore, as liberals were quick to point out, thanks to the arms race, the U.S. economy, too, was in trouble. Instead of spending money to support plant expansions and modernization or social programs, the nation had spent it on the military. American exports suffered, and American children and the U.S. labor force now tested at the bottom of the scale on almost everything, compared to other industrialized nations. Author Christopher Lasch argued that, in fact, the Soviet Union and the United States had destroyed one another.

The conflicting agendas of the factions that made up the New Right were now more obvious than ever. Religious conservatives were primarily concerned with morality and had often found the free-marketers too materialistic. The free-marketers, on the other hand, were uncomfortable with the puritanism of the fundamentalists. David Stockman once noted that he didn't believe in economic regulation *or* moral regulation. As he saw it, Reagan was aligned with ". . . the anti-gun-control nuts, the Bible-thumping creationists, the anti-Communist witch-hunters, and the small-minded Hollywood millionaires to whom 'supply side' meant one more Mercedes."

For the conservatives, signs of troubled times were to be seen everywhere. By 1990, the once formidable National Conservative Political Action Committee (NCPAC) had lost much of its financial support and political power, and direct-mail specialist Richard Viguerie had had to sell his magazine, *Conservative Digest*, and lay off employees. Meanwhile, the major television ministries had been discredited by sexual and financial scandals. The Moral Majority had gone out of business, its credibility and financial support undermined when it failed to have a major impact on the 1986 congressional election. Though the United States was the most religious of all the industrialized nations, if religiousness was measured by the proportion of the population that attended services regularly, the tradition of the separation of church and state was deeply ingrained. Many Americans believed that churches and religious leaders shouldn't become involved in politics, and the audience for Falwell's television show actually declined after he became political.

In 1990, conservative columnist Kevin Phillips, who once forecast the rise of the New Right, predicted that the pendulum would now swing back in the liberal direction, partly because wealth had become too concentrated in the hands of a few. Polls showed that low and middle income whites were almost as disillusioned as African-Americans—over one third no longer believed that hard work was any guarantee of success in the United States. People were fed up with politics-as-usual: The majority identified the Republicans with "monied interests," and many also felt that the Democrats were incompetent.

However, no matter what political turn the nation took, the Reagan legacy was bound to last a long time. His administration had created a deficit that would limit social programs for years to come. It had weakened unions through deregulation and anti-labor rulings. It had created a tax system that rewarded the rich at the expense of everyone else. Because for eight years it had the support of the electorate and Americans seemed to have become more conservative, even the Democrats had moved to the right.

Though some of the major conservative organizations had been through hard times, the New Right had succeeded in creating a sprawling infrastructure. There were now dozens of local and regional right-wing think tanks and publications. Foundations had endowed chairs at universities for conservatives, and whole college departments had come to be dominated by right-wingers. Funders had also created a network of right-wing student newspapers—a conservative group in Washington, D.C., supplied them with money and story ideas, and they campaigned against affirmative action and opposed the spread of women's studies and ethnic courses, demanding a return to a more traditional curriculum. Meanwhile, top jobs in the federal bureaucracy and seats on the federal bench were increasingly filled by conservatives.

Where did that leave the women's movement? Congresswoman Patricia Schroeder summed up the position succinctly: "We have made no gains over the decade. If anything, we've marched backwards."

Schroeder made that remark in April 1989. In the months that followed, the movement was revitalized by the threat to legal abortion (see the next chapter). Nevertheless, on the abortion front and almost everywhere else, it seemed that the struggle for equality would rage on for all of the foreseeable future.

chapter 21

The Unending Struggle over Abortion

$$\longrightarrow$$

*D*uring the 1980s, abortion often seemed to over-shadow all other issues for feminists and conservatives alike. It was, of course, a highly personal matter that had a major impact on people's lives, but beyond that, abortion was symbolic. For both sides, it stood for women's freedom and independence, especially the sexual freedom that conservatives found so threatening.

Thus, though many prolife activists genuinely believed that abortion was a form of murder, for some men the primary issue was control. Were women really to be allowed to decide for themselves how many babies to have and when? In a revealing comment on the subject of birth control, conservative author George Gilder wrote:

When the women demanded "control over our own bodies," they . . . were in fact invoking one of the most extreme claims of the movement. . . . For, in fact, few males have come to psychological terms with the existing birth-control technology; few recognize the extent to which it shifts the balance of sexual power in favor of women. A man quite simply cannot now father a baby unless his wife is fully and deliberately agreeable. There are few social or cultural pressures on her to conceive.

In addition, a woman who could resort to abortion had almost as much sexual freedom as men traditionally had, because she needn't fear pregnancy. Contemplating that fact, eyeing their wives and daughters, some males found it intolerable.

As for feminists, abortion was the biological bedrock on which their demands were based. A woman who was unable to control when and whether she would have babies had no control over her own life. Feminists insisted that a woman's body was her own and that she could not be treated as a means to an end— even if her husband (and the human race) couldn't procreate without her.

The New Right tried a number of different strategies in its efforts to outlaw abortion, and feminists, on the defensive for most of the decade, were spread thin as attacks came from all directions. Then in 1989, the Supreme Court's new conservative majority indicated that they were on the verge of reversing the *Roe* v. *Wade* decision. Suddenly, there was a massive response from thousands of Americans who had previously been indifferent because the right to choose seemed to have been guaranteed by the courts. In the space of about three months, the situation changed radically.

THE DIMENSIONS OF THE ISSUE

During the 1980s, American women had more unwanted pregnancies—and more abortions—than the women in most other Western nations. One out of three American pregnancies ended in abortion, compared to one in ten in the Netherlands, for example. To feminists, the reasons for the difference seemed obvious. To begin with, women in the United States had fewer contraceptive choices available,* and sex education was often badly handled, partly because it was under attack by conserva-

---

* American research on birth control had virtually dried up: The number of U.S. companies doing contraceptive research dropped from seventeen in the 1970s to just one in the late 1980s. Apparently, American drug companies were afraid of lawsuits since the Dalkon Shield debacle, and were intimidated by the anti-abortion climate and deterred by the difficulty of getting FDA approval. For the same reasons, they were unwilling to market new methods that had already been researched in Europe.

tives. In addition, women who found themselves unintentionally pregnant could expect little help if they decided to have the baby, whereas in most of Western Europe, social programs helped pay for prenatal care and child care, and family leave was readily available.

The net result was that in the United States, half of all pregnancies were accidental, with contraceptive failure to blame almost 50 percent of the time. Of the women who were reluctantly pregnant, roughly half chose to have an abortion. That added up to 1.6 million abortions per year. About 90 percent were done in the first trimester of pregnancy, more than half within the first eight weeks.

To many Americans, including most feminists, the way to reduce the number of abortions seemed obvious: develop better contraceptives, improve sex education, and provide support for women who chose to continue with an unintended pregnancy. However, religious conservatives had a different answer: They wanted to outlaw abortion altogether.

The American public was both divided and ambivalent. Polls showed that a consistent majority believed that abortion should remain legal and that the government shouldn't interfere in it because it was a private decision. Yet in the next breath, responding to further questions, many people indicated that abortion should be an option in some circumstances but not others. Most felt it should be legal if pregnancy endangered the woman's life, if she was a victim of rape or incest, or if the fetus had a severe birth defect. Less than half favored legal abortions for women who didn't want a baby because they were unmarried, couldn't support a child, or already had as many children as they could manage.

Before Reagan was elected, some women from both sides of the abortion controversy believed that compromise might be possible. Thus, in February 1979, NOW sponsored a meeting in Washington for leaders of major pro- and anti-abortion groups. The women who attended came despite opposition from other activists in their own movements. In the end, they were able to agree that more research should be done on male contraceptives and on making all types of birth control safer, and that men should take more responsibility for the consequences of sexual activity. They even agreed that there should be more sex education. Then, as the meeting was drawing to a close, the whole discussion was derailed. Three young women from Cleveland got to their feet. One of them announced that "out of respect for

NOW we came in good faith and not to disrupt this meeting. However, for those of us who love the unborn and for those who do not know the unborn, here is our sister killed by abortion." The woman standing beside her opened a bundle she was holding to reveal the body of a female fetus. The meeting ended abruptly in pandemonium.

Afterward, some of the anti-abortion women wrote a letter of apology, explaining that they had no idea what the Cleveland women were planning. Others capitalized on the publicity to re-iterate that all abortions were murder and must be banned. The incident put an end to any further discussions, and after Reagan was elected, in the polarized, angry atmosphere of the 1980s, no one felt inclined to re-open the dialogue.

THE CAMPAIGN TO UNDO ROE

Soon after the Supreme Court legalized abortion in 1973, con-servatives drafted a constitutional amendment to reverse the de-cision. Called the Human Life Amendment (HLA), it was short and simple: "The paramount right to life is vested in each human being from the moment of fertilization without regard to age, health or condition of dependency." If the Constitution stipu-lated that life began at fertilization, then legally all abortions would be considered murder.

Several similar but competing amendments were also intro-duced. One allowed abortion if the woman's life was in danger; one would also permit it in cases of rape or incest; another said life began at implantation rather than at fertilization. That was a crucial difference because contraceptives such as IUD's, the so-called morning-after pill, and even, many said, the widely used combination pill acted after the ovum had been fertilized—they prevented it from becoming implanted in the uterus. Thus, those types of birth control, too, would be considered murder under the HLA.

The conflicts over which amendment to support revealed schisms within the religious right. The Catholic hierarchy rejected all amendments except the HLA because, according to Catholic doctrine, life began at fertilization and abortion was never per-missible, even to save the life of the mother. The church also opposed all forms of birth control except the "rhythm method." This left anti-abortion organizations in a quandary. Because they were sure that a constitutional amendment outlawing all abortions would never pass, most believed that, like it or not, a few exceptions would have to be permitted. However, they disagreed about which ones. Meanwhile, 57 percent of rank-and-file, self-described conservatives actually opposed any amendment.

Contraception was an even stickier issue because the American public—including the majority of Catholics—believed in birth control. The HLA, by drawing the line at the instant of fertilization, would not only ban many contraceptives but in effect would mean that anyone using those contraceptives was committing murder. Clearly, that wouldn't sit well with the public. Yet many anti-abortion activists were almost as strongly opposed to birth control as they were to abortion. Some believed that a ban on contraceptives could undo the sexual revolution. Judie Brown, president of the American Life Lobby, noted that "birth control is at the core of that desire of our society to be sexually permissive." Others seemed motivated by revulsion for sex itself. Joe Scheidler, founder of the Pro-life Action League, said, "Most people in the pro-life movement have a certain morality and believe sex is not for fun and games. . . . I think contraception is disgusting—people using each other for pleasure." The leaders of the NRLC, on the other hand, tacitly acknowledged the public acceptance of birth control by refusing to take a public position on contraceptives. However, they often worked behind the scenes to try to limit their availability.

Except for a few organizations such as NARAL, throughout the 1970s feminists were slow to understand just how serious the threat to legal abortion was. The *Roe* decision seemed to provide a bulwark, and Congress resisted the pressure for a constitutional amendment. Groups like NOW were preoccupied with the ERA in any case, and reluctant to link it to the abortion issue.

Alarmed by Reagan's election in 1980, some women's groups began to campaign against the HLA via newspaper ads and direct mail, emphasizing that it would outlaw many contraceptives as well as abortion. Activists repeatedly attacked the logic of the right-to-life position. Federal Trade Commissioner Patricia Bailey noted that if the nation, via the HLA, conferred the status of "person" on all fertilized eggs while a woman was still not recognized under the Constitution as a "person," something was wrong. Bailey asked, "Would all unborn beings then be constitutional persons until the moment of birth, after which point only those who were male would continue to be 'persons,' while those who were female would not?" Others pointed out that most Americans felt abortion was justified in cases of rape, yet they would be horrified if anyone suggested that infants born as a result of rape be put to death. In some muddled way, a fetus was *not* the same as an unborn child in the minds of most people.

ANTI-ABORTIONISTS TAKE A PIECEMEAL APPROACH

When conservatives failed to pass a constitional amendment, they set out to restrict abortions in any way they could. Thus, beginning in the late 1970s, they persuaded Congress to cut off federal funding for abortion for 40 million of the most vulnerable Americans: poor women, Native Americans, Peace Corps volunteers, federal workers, and military personnel and their dependents. The funding restrictions were accepted by the courts, and until the late 1980s polls indicated that the majority of Americans agreed that the government shouldn't pay for abortions.

Right-to-life organizations attacked birth control as well. After Reagan was elected, family-planning clinics lost about one quarter of their federal funding under Title X, the program that provided contraceptive and infertility services for low-income women and others. Paul Brown of the American Life Lobby explained that "we want to totally dismantle Title X. There are better places for taxpayers' dollars than IUDs and pills for our kids."

The administration also tried to undermine family planning abroad. At a conference in Mexico City in 1984, the United States announced that it would no longer contribute to international family-planning agencies that provided abortions or counseled women to have abortions, even if those agencies carefully set aside American money so that it wasn't spent for those purposes. In addition, the administration dropped its support for International Planned Parenthood because in some countries its programs included abortion services. As a result, birth control efforts faltered, and by 1988 in many Third World countries the number of abortions had actually increased, and so had mortality rates for young women, as they attempted to end their pregnancies themselves.

State Laws Restricting Abortion

Right-to-life groups were at least as active in the states as in Washington, and they bombarded legislatures with bills that attempted to restrict abortion. Thus, during the 1970s and 1980s, state laws were passed that decreed that a woman must have her husband's permission to get an abortion; must sign a consent form and then wait twenty-four hours; must have the procedure done in a hospital if she was more than three months pregnant, whether that was medically necessary or not. (It was seldom medically necessary and hospital abortions were much more expensive.) There were also laws requiring that doctors deliver a spiel about the dangers of abortion and the "perceptual abilities" of the fetus—some statutes said the doctor must show the woman photos of fetuses.

Increasingly in the late 1980s, legislators focused on teenagers. In more and more states, minors couldn't have an abortion without the consent of one or both parents, or couldn't have it until one or both had been notified. Some states offered an alternative known as a judicial bypass—a girl could go to court and get a judge's permission instead, a daunting procedure. More than one quarter of all abortions performed in the United States every year involved teenage girls. By 1991, in seventeen states parental notification or consent laws were in effect.

Conservatives maintained that parents had a right to know about it when their children had medical treatment. In vain, feminists pointed out that more than half of all minors who had abortions voluntarily told their parents. Many of the rest came from violent families or had parents who were alcoholics or drug abusers, or else the pregnancy was the result of incest. It could be dangerous to force a young woman to tell her parents that she was pregnant, and requiring her to tell both parents made no sense with divorce so common—in some cases, she would be forced to track down a father she hadn't seen in years. However, polls showed that a majority of Americans were in favor of restricting teenagers' access to abortion, and that was all the encouragement state legislators needed. Many undoubtedly hoped that if young people knew they couldn't fall back on abortion, they might forgo sex.

By the late 1980s, horror stories had begun to accumulate. A thirteen-year-old Idaho girl who was pregnant by her father told him—in compliance with state law—that she wanted an abortion, and he shot her to death. Becky Bell, an Indiana seventeen-year-old, couldn't bear to tell her parents that she was pregnant, as state law compelled her to do if she wanted a legal abortion. Her attempt to end the pregnancy herself killed her. Afterward, her father and mother traveled the country, speaking out against parental consent laws.

Over the years, many state abortion laws were appealed to the Supreme Court, and its rulings delivered a mixed message. On the one hand, the justices affirmed parental notification and consent laws, provided a judicial bypass was available, and ruled that federal and state governments could refuse to spend public money on abortion. On the other hand, they overturned a law that required a husband's consent, and in 1983 strongly reaffirmed *Roe* in a decision that struck down an Akron, Ohio, ordinance requiring that all abortions beyond the first trimester be done in a hospital and imposing a twenty-four-hour waiting period. After the *Akron* decision, many anti-abortion activists felt extremely frustrated, and opposition to abortion became more vocal—and more violent—as a result.

Throughout the late 1970s and the 1980s, groups such as NARAL, Planned Parenthood, and the ACLU lobbied in Congress and in state legislatures to defend abortion rights; they took key cases to court and mounted media campaigns. Some feminist legislative strategies were creative, to say the least. In 1982, the Florida Senate was considering a bill that would require that a husband be notified if his wife sought an abortion. Senator Patricia Frank proposed an amendment stipulating that a man must notify his wife if he impregnated another woman and that woman decided to have an abortion. When her amendment failed overwhelmingly on a voice vote, Frank demanded a roll call. That time around, she lost by just two votes because many senators left the floor rather than go on record. The original bill was subsequently withdrawn—some said because the president of the Senate thought the Senate was being made to look foolish.

Abortion Clinics Under Siege

After the Supreme Court's *Akron* decision, right-to-life extremists declared war on abortion clinics. Their campaign began in earnest in 1984: That year, there were twenty-four bombings and arson attacks on abortion and birth control facilities, and eighteen clinic directors received death threats. Patients, too, were deliberately intimidated. In Everett, Washington, for example, they had to run a sidewalk gauntlet of protestors who videotaped them and ostentatiously wrote down their car license numbers.

In defense of militant tactics, some anti-abortion activists argued that the bombings and arson damaged only property. They took place at night when the clinics were empty, so that no one would be hurt. However, that wasn't always the case. In December 1985, an alert receptionist at a feminist abortion clinic in Portland, Oregon, spotted a letter bomb in time to call the bomb squad; three other letter bombs were discovered (and defused) at a local post office. In October 1986, a bomb exploded in a Manhattan abortion clinic, injuring passersby. Two months later, the bomb squad arrived at the Manhattan headquarters of Planned Parenthood just in time to prevent an incendiary device from setting off fifteen sticks of dynamite, enough to collapse the front of the building and shatter windows a quarter of a mile away.

In 1988, militants Joe Scheidler of the Pro-Life Action League and Randy Terry, head of Operation Rescue, invented a new strategy: They led demonstrations in which activists blockaded a clinic and refused to move, deliberately provoking arrest. Once arrested, they wouldn't give their names, which meant they couldn't be arraigned and the city had no choice but to keep them in jail. The jailings caught the attention of the press and created new martyrs for the movement. Meanwhile, the militants clogged the courts and confounded cities whose jails were already overcrowded. By the end of 1988, roughly 9500 arrests had been made, though about 2000 individuals accounted for most of them. Some of the core group traveled the country as full-time demonstrators, their expenses presumably paid by Terry's organization.

Abortion clinics were hard hit. Some now had trouble finding doctors, and staff turnover was high because of the strain. Clinics also had difficulty getting malpractice insurance, because antiabortion groups had been pressuring insurance companies to drop coverage for abortion providers. Meanwhile, many doctors not affiliated with clinics had given up doing abortions after their offices and even their homes were picketed by militants.

Mobilized by the threat to abortion clinics, local women's groups were kept busy escorting frightened patients through blockades, while feminist attorneys went to court to get injunctions against the demonstrators. At first, the injunctions were often ineffective: The fines handed out were minimal, and some demonstrators were jailed many times and were still undeterred. However, by 1989, women's groups began to see results from lawsuits that had been mounted against the militants in the middle 1980s. Some were filed under the RICO law (Racketeer Influenced and Corrupt Organizations Act). In a typical RICO case, a clinic sued the militants for conspiring to destroy its business and property, citing a pattern of activity that included intimidation and threats; it asked for heavy damages. Some clinics also successfully used a Reconstruction Era law known as the Ku Klux Klan Act.

By 1990, Randall Terry had announced that he was disbanding Operation Rescue, which was supposedly almost bankrupt because of fines levied by various courts. However, Ann Baker—editor of a newsletter that was a vital link in the prochoice community—strongly suspected that groups fronting for Terry were still taking in contributions, which were being hidden away in bank accounts out of the reach of officials charged with collecting the fines.

Nevertheless, Terry was now finding it harder to recruit demonstrators. In most places where blockades happened repeatedly, city authorities eventually lost patience, and fines and jail sentences became so severe that they were a real deterrent. As a result, clinic blockades were much smaller, and thanks to feminist escort services and quick police action, few women were actually prevented from having an abortion. However, the demonstrators still succeeded in intimidating patients and making life miserable for clinic staff.

The Webster Decision

In 1989, a Supreme Court decision once again marked a major turning point in the struggle over abortion. The case was *Webster* v. *Reproductive Health Services*, and it involved a Missouri statute that banned the use of public funds or public facilities to perform abortions except to save a woman's life. Because virtually all hospitals received some public funding, presumably the law would drastically reduce the number of places where Missouri women could have an abortion. It also required doctors to conduct tests if the woman had been pregnant for twenty weeks or longer, to make sure the fetus was not viable.* In addition, the preamble to the statute stated that life began at conception.

The *Webster* decision, handed down in July 1989, upheld the Missouri law. Even the preamble was acceptable to the Court's new conservative majority—Rehnquist wrote that it had no legal impact and was simply a value judgment by legislators. Yet lawyers on both sides of the abortion controversy agreed that the

---

* According to most medical experts, twenty-four weeks was the earliest point at which a fetus might be able to live outside the womb, because before that its lungs were undeveloped. Less than 1 percent of U.S. abortions took place at or beyond twenty-one weeks.

preamble had been intended to have legal consequences—it could be used, for example, to prevent doctors in public hospitals from prescribing contraceptives, such as the IUD, because they acted after fertilization. Feminists also pointed out that the preamble endorsed a theological doctrine held by some faiths but not others, thus violating the First Amendment, which said that the government must not "establish" any religion.

The *Webster* decision almost overturned *Roe*. Four of the justices wanted to undo the 1973 decision that legalized abortion, but Justice O'Connor resisted. Though she, too, upheld the Missouri law, and she described *Roe*'s trimester framework as "problematic," she argued there would be time enough to "revisit" it when it clashed unavoidably with a state law restricting abortion. In other words, the *Webster* decision was an open invitation to the states to draft new laws that directly contradicted *Roe*. Some political analysts predicted that *Roe* would be past history within the year. When that happened, the states would once again be able to regulate abortion in any way they saw fit, and the nation would have a patchwork of laws, with abortion freely available in some states and banned partially or altogether in others. As always, low-income women would suffer the most because they couldn't afford to go where abortions were legal.

The NRLC immediately set about drafting a model bill that states could use to challenge *Roe*. Because the Supreme Court seemed unlikely to uphold a law that permitted abortion only to save the life of the woman, the bill allowed abortion also for victims of rape or incest (provided they reported the rape within seven days) and in cases where the fetus was severely deformed. In some states, the NRLC model was subsequently adapted to fit a new strategy: Anti-abortion lawmakers introduced a supposedly modest bill that merely outlawed abortion as a means of birth control. However, the fine print in the Alabama version, for example, stated that all abortions were a form of birth control except those done because the pregnancy endangered the woman's life or because she was a victim of rape or incest. In other words, 95 percent of abortions would be banned.

In the first year after *Webster*, more than forty states considered anti-abortion laws, including some truly draconian measures. The Louisiana legislature, for example, outlawed all abortions except those necessary to save the woman's life; it mandated up to ten years at hard labor and up to $100,000 in fines for anyone who performed an illegal abortion and apparently for any woman who had one (the penalty for having an abortion was somewhat unclear). Louisiana's governor, who considered himself prolife, vetoed the bill, saying that it was too severe. In Idaho, the governor rejected a bill that was almost as harsh.

As right-wingers drafted all-out abortion bans for the first time since *Roe*, they had to face the issue of penalties. Before *Roe*, abortionists were sent to prison but the women themselves almost never were. That approach suited many right-to-life leaders, because they assumed that women were overly emotional, weak, and easily manipulated. Dr. Jack C. Willke, head of NRLC, said, "A woman kills under emotional strain. Always." He noted that "it's my firm position I don't think any woman should ever be punished for having an abortion. Any more than we ever know of a cuckolded husband being punished for shooting his wife's lover in the bedroom when he walked in and found them there." Men like Willke seemed primarily concerned with controlling the behavior of wives and daughters—without sending them to prison.

In November 1989, Pennsylvania became the first state where prolifers actually succeeded in enacting a law designed to overturn *Roe*. Some provisions in the law directly challenged previous Supreme Court decisions—for example, the new statute required that every woman be "counseled" by a doctor, who was to deliver a state-prescribed talk and present her with a pamphlet filled with pictures of fetuses; in 1983, the Supreme Court had rejected a similar provision in an Akron, Ohio, city ordinance. In addition, the law required women to notify their husbands before they could have an abortion, despite a 1976 High Court ruling that a state couldn't force a woman to get her husband's consent. Thus, Pennsylvania presented the Court with an opportunity to reverse several earlier decisions and perhaps go farther and actually overturn *Roe*. The legislation also banned most abortions at public hospitals and prohibited abortion after twenty-four weeks, except to save the woman's life or to prevent "irreversible impairment of her major bodily functions." Minors would now need the written consent of one parent or a judge before they could have an abortion, and the parent must first listen to a lecture from a doctor. Prochoice groups promptly challenged the law, and it was stayed temporarily while the case worked its way up through the appeals system to the Supreme Court.

In March 1990, the U.S. territory of Guam in the western Pacific also challenged *Roe*. Its legislature acted after a Catholic archbishop threatened to excommunicate any Roman Catholic who voted against the bill in question; all of the lawmakers were Catholic except one. Guam's new statute permitted abortion only to save the life of the woman or if it would "gravely impair" her health to continue the pregnancy. Even then, she needed the approval of two doctors, whose decision must be reviewed by a committee. The penalty for having an abortion (or helping someone else obtain one) was as much as a year in jail and a $1000 fine; the penalty for performing an abortion was up to five years in jail.

The action on Guam took prochoice forces by surprise. Janet Benshoof of the ACLU's Reproductive Freedom Project immediately flew out to try to persuade the governor to veto the bill but found that he wouldn't see her. One provision of the law prohibited anyone from "soliciting" a woman to have an abortion, and Benshoof chose to challenge that provision immediately. Speaking at the Guam Press Club the day after the Governor signed the bill, she advised women that they could still get legal abortions in Hawaii, 3000 miles away. Three hours later, she was charged with the crime of soliciting. The charges were later dropped so that prosecutors could concentrate on overall constitutional issues as the challenge to the law headed for the Supreme Court later that year.

Abortion foes made a few other gains in 1990 as well. South Carolina passed a parental consent bill, and the Supreme Court handed down two more decisions upholding state parental-notification laws. More important, Justice William Brennan, a defender of abortion rights, retired from the Court, giving George Bush an opportunity to appoint another conservative. His choice was David H. Souter, a federal appeals court judge whose views on abortion weren't on record, making it hard for prochoice groups to oppose him—or even to decide whether all-out opposition was worthwhile, because if they defeated him, Bush's next candidate might be worse.

A NEW CLIMATE OF OPINION

Despite anti-abortion gains, by the summer of 1990 feminists were feeling decidedly encouraged. When the *Webster* decision was first handed down, political analysts generally agreed that in short order at least sixteen state legislatures would pass laws that challenged *Roe*. Yet, in the end only Pennsylvania and Guam did so, because *Webster* unexpectedly changed the political climate.

In April 1989—before *Webster* but at a time when the peril was clear—NOW organized a march in Washington for abortion rights. An astounding 300,000 people* descended on the city for one of the biggest demonstrations it had ever seen. NOW vice-president Sheri O'Dell estimated that 40 percent of the demonstrators were men, and young marchers arrived by the busload from college campuses—much to the delight of older activists. In the past, most Americans (74 percent, according to a 1985 poll) hadn't believed that abortion could ever again be outlawed. Now, with the right to choose clearly in danger, many people were galvanized. Between the Washington demonstration in April and mid-July, just after the *Webster* decision was announced, NOW's membership increased by 40,000 to more than 200,000 members. Local chapters were inundated with volunteers. NARAL, Planned Parenthood, the ACLU, and the Fund for the Feminist Majority all reported that their phones, too, were constantly ringing with calls from agitated women and men, who wanted to know how they could help defend abortion rights. Paradoxically, *Webster* had (literally) rejuvenated the women's movement.

As a result, by September the media were noting a striking change in the political climate. In the past, anti-abortion groups had wielded a great deal of influence because right-to-lifers supposedly cared enough to base their votes solely on a candidate's stand on abortion, while many people who were prochoice were proud of the fact that they weren't single-issue voters. After *Webster*, when lawmakers suddenly began to hear from agitated prochoice constituents, many re-examined their positions. Thus, in the fall of 1989, for the first time in eight years, the House of Representatives approved Medicaid funding for abortions in cases of rape or incest (the bill died when Bush vetoed it). And when Florida's governor called a special session of the legislature to consider new ways to restrict abortion, lawmakers—deluged with letters and calls from prochoice voters—rejected all the restrictive bills he proposed.†

The 1989 election provided the first test of whether prochoice Americans would use their votes to elect prochoice candidates. Many feminist organizations—including NARAL and NOW—

---

* The march's organizers put the crowd at about 600,000, while the United States Park Police estimated 300,000.

† The prochoice victory in Florida was due partly to public support for abortion and partly to the fact that women chaired key committees in both houses. In addition, the Florida Senate now had a significant number of women, and nine out of ten of them voted prochoice. Women first gained a foothold in the legislature thanks to NOW's efforts back in 1982: Because Florida played a key role in defeating the ERA, a team of NOW organizers stayed on after the amendment's defeat to help elect more women.

committed their resources to key political campaigns, and their efforts paid off. The media duly noted the fact that not only were candidates who supported abortion rights elected, but exit polls showed that abortion *was* the major concern of many voters.

The election left anti-abortion activists in a state of shock, and some Catholic bishops and priests immediately began to take punitive action against Catholic politicians who supported the right to choose. The first target was Lucy Killea, a California assemblywoman running for the State Senate in a special election in December 1989. Killea had emphasized her prochoice stand partly as bait, according to her campaign manager; she was expecting an overreaction from a militant group such as Operation Rescue. Instead, a Catholic bishop suddenly announced that she was to be barred from receiving communion. Killea won a squeaker of an election—she was a Democrat running in a notoriously conservative Republican district—and afterward political analysts agreed that the bishop's action had helped her.

However, when the 1990 election rolled around, in most places abortion was no longer as hot an issue. In some races where there was a clear choice between prochoice and prolife candidates, the abortion rights candidate won, but most right-to-life politicians were now deliberately playing down their anti-abortion stand, and voters were evidently no longer as concerned about the issue. Many had expected the worst after *Webster*, and when very little happened, they were once again lulled into complacency— ignoring the fact that it had taken a mighty effort by prochoice groups to stall anti-abortion bills in most state legislatures.

RU-486: A PRESCRIPTION FOR COOLING THE CONTROVERSY?

In the late 1980s, many feminists believed the only hope of shortening the abortion struggle was a drug called RU-486 that had been available in France since 1988. It was 95 percent successful in bringing about an abortion when combined with a prostaglandin (another type of drug) and used during the first three months of pregnancy. Feminists felt that RU-486 might change the whole context of the debate, because as it replaced surgical procedures, it would make abortion a truly private decision. A ban would be more difficult to enforce.

Anti-abortion groups tried to prevent the release of RU-486 in France, where it was developed, but they failed. By 1990, one third of French women who had to have an abortion were choosing the drug over the surgical procedure. However, there were no signs that American women would have the benefit of RU-486 in the near future. NRLC and other anti-abortion groups had notified U.S. pharmaceutical companies that they would boycott all of a company's products if it marketed the drug. Many in the medical community were furious, because RU-486 showed great promise in areas other than abortion. It was an effective treatment for one form of Cushing's disease, an adrenal gland disorder, and it looked promising as a way to treat endometriosis, breast cancer, and a type of benign brain tumor that was sometimes fatal. Because it could soften and dilate the cervix, it might also reduce the need for Cesarean sections during childbirth. Despite these potential benefits, anti-abortion groups wanted RU-486 banned entirely because once a drug was approved by the FDA for any purpose, a doctor could legally prescribe it for some other purpose.

Feminists were determined to bring RU-486 to the United States. However, the FDA ruled in 1989 that individuals couldn't carry the drug into the country or receive it through the mail. In any case, the French company that owned the patent—apparently nervous about a right-to-life boycott—was reluctant to export it to the United States even for research. Eleanor Smeal, president of the Feminist Majority Foundation,* predicted that RU-486 would eventually be available in the United States, either legally or on the black market, but she emphasized that feminists wanted lawful access. "We want it properly tested and used with medical supervision to ensure its safety for women," she said. Though the drug seemed to be very safe, if it failed to cause an abortion (which could happen, without the prostaglandin), it might cause birth defects.

AN UNCERTAIN FUTURE

Throughout the 1980s, liberals and conservatives—prochoicers and prolifers—were locked in a desperate battle that surged back and forth over the supine body of the American public, which often seemed indifferent to the struggle. The *Webster* decision got the attention of the public and changed the priorities of many feminist groups; it galvanized people who hadn't really thought

* Smeal was president of NOW from 1977 to 1982 and again from 1985 to 1987.

about abortion for a long time. Once again, feminism had been revitalized by opposition to rights that many people took for granted.

By 1991, reproductive rights were under siege almost everywhere in the United States. Abortion opponents in state legislatures had introduced twenty-five new restrictive laws in 1989 after the *Webster* decision, four hundred in 1990, and two hundred in the first half of 1991. The prochoice forces were able to hold their ground in some places, and Connecticut and Maryland passed statutes, based on the *Roe* v. *Wade* decision, that protected abortion rights. A referendum in Nevada approved a similar law. By mid-1991, however, ten states had passed parental consent laws and seven required parental notification, while others had placed new restrictions on abortion funding or had decreed that women who wanted an abortion must listen first to a state-prescribed anti-abortion spiel. At least four new restrictive laws, including those passed by Pennsylvania and Guam, were in the judicial pipeline, headed for the Supreme Court.

If the Supreme Court actually overturned *Roe*, it was bound to be a shot in the arm for the women's movement. However, very few feminists wanted that to happen—the price in women's lives was bound to be too high. Ann Baker believed that the Court would allow *Roe* to stand but would permit the states to restrict abortions more and more, until *Roe* was virtually meaningless. Either way, a titanic battle would be fought in the state legislatures for years to come. The nation would become a patchwork of laws, as it was before 1973, with abortion virtually banned in some states and freely available in others. Women who couldn't afford to travel across state lines to have an abortion would once again resort to back-alley abortionists.

In 1991, activists had already begun to discuss the measures they might take if *Roe* were overturned. Some talked of organizing a kind of pony express with cars, to drive poor women from states that prohibited abortion to those where it was available: One woman might provide transportation for the first fifty miles, another for the second, and so on. Other activists compared notes on ways to induce abortions using herbs or acupuncture. Many sent for information on the Del-Em, the menstrual-extraction device invented by California feminists in the early 70s (see chapter 12). Obviously, if abortion was widely banned in the United States, a feminist underground would not be far behind. The women's movement would move into a new and more dangerous phase.

As the 1992 paperback edition of this book was going to press, the U.S. Supreme Court handed down an ambiguous decision on Pennsylvania's abortion law. Though the Justices voted, five to four, to reaffirm *Roe*, they also changed the rules. Abortion would no longer be treated as a fundamental right; instead, the Court declared that states could try to persuade women to choose child-birth over abortion as long as their efforts didn't impose an "undue burden" on women.

Next, the Justices approved most sections of the Pennsylvania law. Women in that state would now be required to listen to a prolife lecture and then wait twenty-four hours before having an abortion; minors must have the consent of one parent or a judge. The only part of the law the Court rejected was husband notification. Though statutes that made almost all abortions a crime weren't likely to pass the "undue burden" test, many other restrictions obviously would.

Both antiabortion and abortion-rights groups immediately condemned the decision. Antiabortion leaders wanted *Roe* overturned; four of the Justices were prepared to do that—one short of a majority. Prochoice leaders argued that laws like Pennsylvania's *were* an undue burden for many women. For example, a twenty-four hour waiting period might sound harmless, but some women have to travel hundreds of miles to the nearest clinic. They must now take two days off from work and pay for an overnight stay or for two trips to the clinic. The added expense could put abortion out of reach financially.

While some on the prochoice side welcomed the reaffirmation of *Roe*, others insisted that the Court had gutted the 1973 decision. However, everyone agreed that the important thing was that *Roe* had survived by just one vote. It was more vital than ever to elect a prochoice president who would appoint liberals as Justices, and yet the Court's new ruling had muddied the waters and might lull prochoice voters into complacency.

Feminists were determined to elect both a president and a Congress that were prochoice, so that they could pass legislation that would write *Roe* into federal law. Even if they succeeded, anti-abortion activists were unlikely to concede defeat. The battle over reproductive rights would continue for the foreseeable future—until some technological fix, similar to RU-486, finally made an abortion ban unenforceable.

chapter 22

The Women's Movement in the 1980s

After the defeat of the ERA in the early 1980s, the women's movement reached its lowest ebb. Some of the major national organizations were in trouble financially, and many Americans were blaming the movement for the bind women were in as they struggled to do justice to both job and family. An analysis published in *Ms* in the mid-80s noted that even among those who had been the movement's allies, there seemed to be a consensus that the nation had "tried feminism and it didn't work." Meanwhile, supposedly, feminism itself was dead. According to journalist Ann Taylor Fleming, writing in the *New York Times Magazine* in 1986, there was "no discernible women's movement left. . . ."

Of course, that wasn't true. In fact, by the end of the decade the movement was broader than ever before, for throughout the eighties it continued to expand, spinning off new groups and even new submovements. There were major shifts in emphasis: Some of the big national organizations became more focused on politics (see chapter 19); most were very concerned about diversity (see chapter 17); and abortion replaced the ERA as *the* major issue for many (see chapter 21). In addition, difference feminism gained strength and the women's movement became globalized (these developments are discussed in this chapter).

When social movements are totally stymied they're apt to die, because activists have been deprived of hope. On the other hand, movements that are partly successful sometimes put themselves out of business prematurely, at a point where they've resolved only the most urgent issues.* Neither of these things happened to feminism during the 1980s. The second wave maintained enough headway to avoid death by discouragement, and it was in no danger of expiring from a surfeit of success. As the 1990s began, it was clear that feminism would be around for a long time to come.

THE DARKEST DAYS

Where did Americans get the idea that the second wave had petered out? It was true that the defeat of the ERA discouraged many activists and left certain groups in a financial bind. By mid-decade, some of the major national feminist organizations had had to lay off employees. NOW was $1 million in debt and its membership was down to 130,000 from a peak of 200,000. Meanwhile, under Reagan, government funding had dried up as far as most feminist projects were concerned, and the major foundations had new priorities—as social programs were slashed, they focused on the needs of low-income Americans.

The graying of the women's movement was another problem. Sex discrimination in education and employment had lessened just enough that many young, white middle class women believed the battle was over—according to the press, they saw themselves as the "postfeminist" generation. Of course, some young women *were* active in the movement. Ellie Smeal noted that in 1986, four anti-abortion referenda were defeated at the polls partly because of the efforts of college students, and she estimated that college-age women were one third of the marchers at major demonstrations held in 1986 and 1989. Nevertheless, many feminists who taught women's studies courses felt that they were doing well if, by the end of an introductory course, they had simply convinced most of the students that sex discrim-

---

* The suffrage movement is a case in point: Though the basic thrust for women's rights survived after women won the vote, most of the first wave's momentum subsided.

ination still existed. Laurie Crumpacker, director of the women's studies program at Simmons College, suggested that women students were cool to feminism largely because the men they knew were openly hostile to it. The young women were not only reluctant to alienate the men, but may have been afraid that if they listened to what feminists said, those same men would begin to look less attractive.

Once women were exposed to the job market, many learned the hard way that the battle wasn't over. However, it often seemed that by the time they could see the need for feminism, they were fully occupied with job and family. Ironically, in many cases the job was open to them because of the women's movement. At any rate, by the 1980s most women had less time for activism.

Reporting the ''Death'' of Feminism

The media were the other reason so many Americans believed feminism was a dead issue. The press exaggerated the very real problems that activists were facing and often suggested that the women's movement was on its last legs. Granted, it wasn't easy to gauge the strength of feminism in the 1980s. The women's movement was wonderfully diffuse—there were now women organized as feminists almost everywhere, from unions to universities, from black women's health groups to the legislatures. The media, defining the movement narrowly as a few organizations with nationwide memberships, failed to see what was in front of their eyes.

In fact, elements in the press seemed eager to write the movement's obituary. Thus, the 1970s media-created image of the modern superwoman who "had it all"—husband, kids, and career—was rapidly replaced with the image of the working mother, driven to desperation by the competing demands of job and family. Newspapers, magazines, and even advertising featured stories about women who had seen the light and were staying home to raise the children. Many working mothers *were* desperate, and some women who could afford to *had* dropped out of the job market temporarily. However, activists questioned the shift in emphasis, from stories about the gains women were making in employment and the obstacles they faced, to the feminism-has-been-a-disaster scenario, implied or spelled out.

Many men apparently resented the fact that women were competing in the job market, and men were still the "gatekeepers" of the press. Though two thirds of the students in journalism schools were now female, males ran the newsrooms and made the decisions about which stories were worthwhile and how much space or air time to give them. Thus, in 1986 when researchers reported that women who postponed marriage to pursue a career were finding that the marriage market had passed them by, the media had a field day with the news. The researchers became instant celebrities: They appeared on the Phil Donahue show on television and were featured in major publications ranging from *People* magazine to the *Wall Street Journal; Newsweek* observed that a forty-year-old woman had a better chance of being killed by a terrorist than of getting married. Many feminists were infuriated by the news coverage, which often managed to suggest that educated women were paying for their independence.

The media also blamed the women's movement for the strains that beset the American family in the 1980s. The strains were real enough: the lack of adequate child care and maternity leave, the fact that a woman could lose her job if she had to stay home with a sick child. Stories in the press implied that all this was the fault of feminists who lured housewives out of the home in the first place; some writers claimed that the movement, despising the family, had paid no attention to the needs of mothers.

Several major books by feminists published in the 1980s lent support to that argument. In 1981, Betty Friedan's *The Second Stage*, which focused on the job-and-family dilemma, caused an uproar among feminists because Friedan, too, blamed radical feminists' early antifamily rhetoric for the current crisis, and because the new agenda she proposed for the movement seemed narrowly focused on family issues. Lenore Weitzman's study of the devastating impact of divorce on women and children was published in 1985 (see chapter 14), and many took it as proof that the feminist insistence on gender-neutral laws had backfired. Then, in 1986, economist Sylvia Ann Hewlett weighed in with *A Lesser Life*, which argued that the movement had stripped American women of their traditional support systems and left them vulnerable to the high divorce rate, inadequate child care, the lack of maternity leave, and so forth. Hewlett, like many others, indicted "the strident feminism of the seventies with its attempt to clone the male competitive model."

In the words of sociologist Arlie Hochschild, American women were "stuck midway" in the feminist revolution. Second-wave activists hadn't anticipated the stall-out, or the high price that a whole generation of women would pay. Many shared the dismay of Laudie Porter. In the mid-80s, Porter, a feminist in her fifties, would watch from her own house each morning as the woman next door left for work and day care, balancing a baby on one hip and carrying a briefcase, with a toddler clinging to her suit skirt. Porter wanted to charge out the door, shouting, "Stop! It wasn't supposed to be like this!" Nevertheless, it was the conservatives who stalled further progress, and feminists deserved credit for the fact that the stall-out never became a real retreat.

THE REVIVAL OF DIFFERENCE FEMINISM

The feminist debate over equality and difference heated up during the 1980s, and for a number of reasons, difference feminism grew stronger. It flourished because of what women had achieved since the beginning of the second wave; because some feminist theorists led the way; and because many activists had arrived at a point in their own lives where they were rethinking their values and the choices they'd made.

In retrospect, it seems inevitable that the second wave would eventually shift from an almost universal insistence on equality to a widespread celebration of difference. In the late sixties and early seventies, women were intent on destroying the narrow stereotype that had defined them as not only different from men but inferior to them.

For a time, androgyny was a common goal in the movement. Men were supposed to become more like women, even as women became more like men. Thus, psychologist Sandra Bem, creator of the Bem Sex-Role Inventory, a personality test that threw out the old sex stereotypes, felt that "a healthy sense of maleness or femaleness involves little more than being able to look into the mirror and to be perfectly comfortable with the body that one sees there. . . . one's gender need have no other influence on one's behavior or life style."

However, in practice many women set out to purge themselves of the harmful effects of female socialization—in other words, to become more like men—and few men returned the compliment. Women signed up by the thousands for courses in assertiveness training and modeled their behavior on the job on the men they saw around them. Because men had always made the rules, they were the norm, so it was women who made most of the adjustments. The problem with androgyny was that it ignored the realities of power. It also suggested to women that they could overcome sex discrimination just by changing themselves.

Nevertheless, the old sex stereotypes *were* gradually being undermined, and as a result feminists became less defensive. Consciousness-raising also fostered new self-esteem in many.

Difference Feminism: Theory and Practice

As stereotypes paled and women's confidence grew, feminist theorists led the revival of difference feminism. Working on the assumption that women and men really *were* different in significant ways, some proceeded to re-examine women's traditional values, while others plumbed the depths of the experience of motherhood.

Several theorists concluded that many of the supposedly negative aspects of the female stereotype were actually quite positive. Psychologist Jean Baker Miller, for example, argued that certain character traits crucial to a healthy society had been "assigned" to women and then had been devalued. Though those traits could be unhealthy and helped keep women in their place, they could also be an asset, according to Miller. For instance, women were supposed to be weak, and because that was considered "feminine," some were actually afraid to be strong. However, women also readily asked for help when they needed it and weren't ashamed to admit it when they felt vulnerable. Men believed they must be strong in every situation; that was a burden and led to bluster and conflict.

Carol Gilligan's research on women's values triggered a surge of interest in the "different voice" of the female ethic (see chapter 11). It not only influenced other academics but inspired activists and legal scholars as well. Meanwhile, Mary Daly carried the work of reclaiming women's values to its logical extreme: She argued that women were superior to men, and advocated female bonding and spiritual change. She also maintained that the women's movement had made only token gains.

Daly's work was controversial, as were the theories of all the difference feminists. Critics charged that Daly, in particular, was encouraging a retreat from the struggle against male domination. Inevitably, the difference feminists were accused of reinforcing sex stereotypes. Some opponents also suggested that values such as concern for others helped to keep women mired down, feeling they must always put others' needs ahead of their own. Nevertheless, the celebration of women's values resonated irresistibly for many activists. Perhaps women, raised to be nurturers, could never really shed that perspective. There was also the question of what kind of world it would be if both sexes opted for the highly competitive *macho* model that was the male stereotype. Of course, to many of the difference theorists, that was exactly the point.

One of the most significant new developments in feminist theory occurred when a number of scholars began to reevaluate motherhood. Feminists had traveled a long road since 1970, when Shulamith Firestone wrote of the need to free women from "the tyranny of their reproductive biology. . . ." Several theorists suggested that the experience of mothering gave women unique skills and valuable perspectives. Others examined the consequences of the fact that women provided virtually all of the child care in most families. In the intensity of the relationship between the all-powerful mother and the helpless infant, they found the roots of certain destructive responses in adults—the male fear of intimacy, for example, and the adult male's anger at women and need to control them. The theorists suggested that children—and the society—would be much better off if fathers shared the child care.

Parenting was so exclusively associated with women that the assumption was built into the language. As sociologist Nancy Chodorow pointed out, though a man could be said to "mother" a child, a woman could never "father" one. Yet mothering no longer defined women's lives—it was no longer who they were. In 1900, a twenty-year-old white woman could expect to be widowed at fifty-two and to die herself at about the age of sixty-four. Especially if she had a large family, most of her adult life would be devoted to child-rearing. In 1980, a white woman could expect to have an empty nest by forty-eight and to live to the age of seventy-nine. There was almost a 50 percent chance she'd be divorced.* The prospect was, then, that for two thirds of her adult life she would have no children in the household, and for half to two thirds of it, she'd have no husband. The drama of family life—the whole script for earlier generations—was now only the subject of the first act, with two more to follow.

* Women of color also lived longer than earlier generations, were likelier to be divorced, and so on. The numbers were different but the changes since 1900 were generally in the same direction. For example, a nonwhite infant born in 1900 could be expected to live about thirty-three years, a white infant, forty-eight years; at the time, more than 90 percent of nonwhite Americans were black. African-American babies born in 1988 had a life expectancy of 69.2 years, compared with 75.6 years for white babies. Life expectancy kept increasing for both whites and blacks until the mid 1980s; after that it began to drop for blacks.

Americans were still struggling to adjust to these and a multitude of other changes. The difficulty of the task gave an added impetus to the debates over equality and difference within the women's movement, for feminists, too, were re-examining their choices. In their personal lives, they faced the same problems as other American women—sometimes complicated by the fact that they were involved in the movement. Many women who were activists in the late 1960s and early 1970s delayed marriage and childbearing, as did others of their generation. As feminists, they were very much aware of society's pronatalism (the belief that all women should become mothers), and some were determined to resist the enormous pressures on women to have children. In the 1980s, now well into their thirties, some began to rethink the choices they'd made. Those who had delayed marriage and childbearing and then found conception difficult wondered if they'd made all the wrong decisions. Others, who had had babies and then had become less active in the movement because they were absorbed in career and family, often felt they'd betrayed the cause.

Speaking at a conference in 1990, feminist scholar Ann Barr Snitow noted that she had been re-evaluating the pronatalism not only of society, but of the women's movement in the 1980s. She suggested that during the second wave, feminists' attitudes toward motherhood had gone through three distinct periods. From the beginning until the middle 1970s, activists challenged pronatalism and in most movement groups ecstatic descriptions of motherhood were pretty much taboo. From the mid- to the late seventies, a kind of neutrality prevailed, as feminists simultaneously criticized the institution of motherhood and explored mothering as an experience, theorizing about its implications. In the 1980s pronatalism revived, said Snitow. During a reactionary political period that was a time of retrenchment and sorrow for many feminists, pregnancy, childbirth, and child-rearing were once again romanticized.

"The feminist hope of breaking the iron bond between mother and child seems gone. . . . We have embraced nurturance . . . ," Snitow later wrote in an article published in *Ms.* Yet she noted that at the same time many women had become cynical and no longer believed that mothers would ever get help from men or from the government. As a result, women were "voting with their feet" by marrying later and having fewer children.

Snitow raised the questions: Do feminists want women's identity as mothers to expand or contract? Do they want men to become mothers too? Noting that women disagreed on this, she touched on the psychological power that mothers have. "We give up something, a special privilege wound up in the culture-laden word 'mother' that we will not instantly regain in the form of freedom and power. We're talking about a slow process of change," she wrote. It was hard even to imagine how women would progress from control over parenting to parenthood shared with men, but she felt that it was time for feminists to talk more about it and to structure their demands as they sought new identities for women.

At the end of her presentation at the 1990 conference, Snitow received a near ovation, and during the animated discussion period that followed, it was clear that her remarks had struck a chord with most women in the room. Clearly, feminists weren't finished with the task of re-evaluating women's traditional role and the values that sustained it. Many Americans, including feminists, were still groping for ways to make sense of their lives, caught as they were in a time of transition.

Equality, Difference, and the Law

During the 1980s, legal scholars on both sides of the feminist divide carried on a debate, using various law journals as their forum. Their arguments focused primarily on equal treatment versus special treatment and on issues such as maternity leave and pornography.

On the equal rights side, some feminists argued that the women's movement had responded to the rise of conservatism in the 1980s by retreating from demands for equality and arguing for protection instead. Attorney Wendy Kaminer suggested that some women felt threatened by the whole idea of equality, which promised "choice and the unsettling search for identity that goes with it." In some ways, the traditional female role was easier, less demanding. As for the renewed emphasis on women's values, Kaminer saw it as an outburst of female chauvinism. Others argued that demands for special protection for women were based on a view of women as eternal victims, unable to fend for themselves.*

Some difference feminists, in turn, argued that it was those on the other side of the divide who saw women as victims. Equality feminists, they said, assumed that females had had their tradi-

* The basic equality argument is laid out in more detail in chapter 18.

tional role forced on them. Though to some extent that was true, it was also a role that many women freely chose and one that was vital to families and communities. Difference feminists believed it was possible to fight for women's traditional values and challenge male domination at the same time. Finally, they argued that women couldn't hope to compete with men in the work place unless some concessions were made for childbirth and child care.

In a nation committed, at least in principle, to equal rights for its citizens, a demand for equality was the argument most likely to succeed, and indeed American women had made great strides in education and employment, for example, because activists took advantage of laws and attitudes based on a vision of equal rights. However, that vision was linked to a tradition of extreme individualism, and eventually some feminists began to suggest that the tradition had gone too far.

Thus in 1984, Kenneth Karst, a law professor at the University of California, Los Angeles, adopted Carol Gilligan's metaphor that contrasted the (male) ladder of hierarchy with the (female) web of connection.* Arguing that the U.S. Constitution reflected only the view from the ladder, Karst suggested that women's perspectives might eventually reshape constitutional law. He pointed out that the founding fathers assumed that society was composed of individuals driven by self-interest and struggling for power in a zero-sum game, where one person's gain was inevitably another's loss. Suspicious of the appetite for power, they believed that safety lay in rules that protected the individual from interference by others or by the government. Therefore, the Bill of Rights focused mainly on negatives—on the ways government was not allowed to intrude.†

Karst argued that the view from the web of connection was different: The power to dominate seemed less important than the power to provide care for others. Relationships weren't free of conflict, but the solution was to negotiate, to compromise, and if possible to redefine goals so that all could share them. In constitutional law, these philosophical differences meant that, for ex-

---

* Gilligan suggested that men tended to see human relationships in terms of a hierarchy and a competition for status, while women saw them as a supportive network (see chapter 11).

† In the late 1970s, some legal scholars developed a school of thought called Critical Legal Studies (CLS). They argued that legal theory was too often used to justify the status quo, and they challenged liberal legalisms, particularly the belief that society was composed of individuals who acted in their own self-interest, limited only by notions about rights. For the "fem crit" wing of CLS, in particular, the goal was to develop a more complex image of justice.

ample, from the ladder, the central issue in discrimination cases was the need to protect individual rights, and affirmative action was a device intended to remedy past acts of deliberate discrimination, whereas from the web, the issue was society's responsibility for all its citizens, and affirmative action was necessary not to punish past evil, but to promote future participation by all.

Karst suggested that if women had had a voice in drafting the U.S. Constitution, the nation might have gone beyond a "jurisprudence of rights." Agreeing with him, his UCLA colleague Carrie Menkel-Meadow maintained that under a different Constitution based partly on women's values, feminists might not have been forced to argue that pregnancy must be treated like any other disability; they might have had a legal and philosophical basis for insisting that society must acknowledge its collective responsibility for childbearing and its medical costs. Menkel-Meadow suggested that perhaps Americans had a right to be connected to others and cared for, as well as a right to be let alone.

Every society must strike a balance between individual rights and the needs of the community. Many feminists felt that the United States had gone much too far in the direction of rugged individualism—especially during the 1980s. Many believed—or simply hoped—that as more women moved into positions of power, the nation's priorities would change, and that Americans would eventually combine their traditional insistence on individual rights with a new ethic of responsibility. Some pointed out that in Western Europe, rights and responsibility together had produced policies such as parental leave that supported the family and were better for women and ultimately for the nation.

Meanwhile, both legal scholars and political activists were asking questions about the basic concept of equality. The American tradition of equal rights was based on an ancient principle: that likes must be treated alike—in other words, if two groups were similar enough, they rated equal treatment. Though that sounds self-evident, and it provided the basis for ending segregation in the South, the insistence on similarity was also problematic, because it tended to preserve the status quo. Those in power could protect their privileges in some cases by maintaining that others were so different that they didn't merit equal treatment—for example, women could be kept out of so-called combat positions in the armed forces. In other cases, courts or legislators could decide to ignore vital differences and, by treating people equally, could actually rob them of an equal chance. That sometimes happened in the work place, too, when employers made no concessions for the fact that it was women who bore children.

Another difficulty was that a system that rested on treating likes alike was geared to produce equal opportunity, not equal results.* Feminists and civil rights activists had learned through experience that situations that supposedly provided equal opportunity often failed to, and some favored an equal-results approach. At a minimum, it would judge laws not solely by whether they applied a purportedly neutral rule, but by their outcome as well. It would assume not that people were similar, but that they were very different; that they seldom started out on a truly equal footing, especially in a society where wealth and privilege were so unevenly distributed; and that steps might have to be taken (such as affirmative action) to set them on a more nearly equal footing.

Americans were deeply committed to the ideal of equal opportunity—many felt that it was all that should be necessary. They saw creeping socialism in any attempt to ensure equal results instead, and they feared a kind of leveling and the loss of individual freedom. If everyone got the same rewards, that was (in theory) communism, or at least socialism, and it might kill people's initiative. Nevertheless, a more just society lay somewhere on the continuum between a system based on a myth of equal opportunity and one that rigidly prescribed equal results.

During the 1980s, the New Right paid lip service to the principle of equal opportunity and took the American traditions of rugged individualism and the individual's right to be free from government interference to the extreme, with disastrous consequences for the nation. As the century drew to a close, the United States desperately needed new ways to think about differences, and not just about sex differences. People of color were challenging the myth of the American melting pot, and they, too, demanded the right to be different—to be themselves and still receive both political and (much harder) economic justice. By the middle of the twenty-first century, whites would probably be just one American minority among many. Rethinking equality—what it was based on, what it consisted of—was becoming a matter of

---

* An equal opportunity approach treats everyone exactly the same way according to strict rules, leaving them to sink or swim according to their own aptitude. Employers do this, for example, when they make hiring decisions on the basis of (supposedly) objective tests. A strategy aimed at producing equal results judges by the outcome and adjusts policies accordingly—partially discounting test scores, for example, if studies show that people of color perform better on the job than their test results would predict or if the company simply wants to achieve a multicultural work force.

survival for everyone. Yet in 1990, most of those in power weren't dealing with the problem; many still wanted to march backward into the past rather than face the challenges ahead—including the need to find ways for people to be both different *and* equal.

Ultimately, women needed both equality and difference: They needed equal treatment most of the time, and different treatment in the special circumstances where they were genuinely different from men. For the present, the sexes were very different in many ways—not just in reproductive biology but in their upbringing and the kind of life it prepared them for, and in the fact that an old-boys' network still existed almost everywhere and gave white males a decided advantage.

With time, and as more feminists achieved positions of authority, the nonbiological gender differences were bound to lessen. Many feminists were concerned that women's values—the view from the web—might be lost in the process. They assumed that those values were not innate but persisted because of the way women were brought up and because the whole culture reinforced certain attitudes in females. Though some stereotypically "male" values were useful, most feminists—on both sides of the divide—agreed that politics largely unleavened by "female" values had made the world a very dangerous place for all living beings.

As the 1990s began, it seemed likely that the debate in the women's movement over equality and difference would continue for the foreseeable future. However, the voice of difference feminism was strong, and fused goals were emerging: Some activists now argued for equal treatment as the best short-term strategy, even as they spoke of the need to change society radically in the long run to reflect women's values.

ECOFEMINISM AND WOMEN'S SPIRITUALITY

As mentioned earlier, the women's movement not only survived the 1980s but continued to expand. In Washington and other parts of the country, it had become institutionalized: There were now a number of well-established feminist organizations led by women who had managed to make a career of feminism. Equally important, the second wave still had its grass roots, with new groups and whole new networks springing up around particular issues.

The ecofeminist movement was one such offshoot that developed during the 1980s. It blended feminist and environmental concerns, and it originally surfaced partly in response to the near disaster at the Three Mile Island nuclear plant in 1980. Afterward, feminists held a conference to discuss environmental issues. The following year, a different group of women sponsored a similar conference; in typical movement fashion, they hadn't heard about the first meeting. Starhawk, a California activist, later formed WomanEarth Institute, the first national ecofeminist organization.

By the late 1980s, some mainstream environmental groups had feminists in leadership positions, and women had also organized their own groups to work on environmental issues—to demonstrate outside missile bases and nuclear power plants, for example. There was a flowering of new theory. Basically, ecofeminists opposed all forms of domination: Whites over people of color, men over women, humans over animals and nature. They believed that all creatures were part of an interconnected web of life. Feminists of color—and many white feminists—also now spoke of domination, rather than patriarchy, as the fundamental problem.

Throughout the second wave, feminists addressed the issue of domination as they struggled to enlarge the liberal notion of "equality." In the early days, women's liberation groups tried to create radical equality within the group by operating without formal leadership (see chapter 5). Some stuck too rigidly to their principles and that helped to kill various groups. Nevertheless, a commitment to radical equality survived within the movement, though as time passed women became more relaxed about it. When activists gathered, it was still the custom to sit in a circle if possible—symbolizing the fact that all were equal. By and large, feminists who taught women's studies courses tried to treat students with the respect due to colleagues. Even in business during the 1980s, there were now those who argued that women had a different, more egalitarian leadership style and that it was highly effective. In fact, it resembled participative management, the teamwork approach that was much discussed because it was the norm for Japanese corporations.

Women's spirituality was another offshoot of the movement and, like ecofeminism, it celebrated women's values. During the eighties, women's spirituality groups sprang up all over the country. The women who formed them were intrigued by archaeological indications that long before the Judeo-Christian tradition took root, people worshiped a nurturant goddess. The women met to explore the histories of male-dominated religions and assess their impact on women's lives—a form of consciousness-raising for the eighties and nineties.

Some spirituality groups began to create their own goddess-centered, feminist rituals to celebrate the seasons, the earth, the milestones in women's lives. Starhawk became known for combining such ceremonies with political demonstrations—for example, when Reagan was re-elected, she led a Political Despair Ritual: At the end of it, participants lit candles to symbolize a renewed pledge to work for a better future. Meanwhile, at feminist conferences, panel discussions on religion had become extremely popular. In every generation of feminists, there have been women who felt the need to purge religious traditions of their misogyny and reclaim them for women. As they turned to goddess rituals, the current generation created what scholar Mary Jo Weaver called "a new myth of origins"—they believed in an ancient world where human beings lived in peace with one another and women and men were equally valued. Did it ever exist? Weaver noted that "utopias need not have connections to a real past in order to provide hope for a real future."

GLOBAL FEMINISM

For American feminists, one of the most significant developments during the 1980s was the growth of global feminism. The international women's movement first began to take shape in the midseventies. Ironically, it was the United Nations—a bastion of male privilege—that midwifed the birth of it by declaring 1975 International Women's Year and staging a major conference. Delegates to that first meeting, which was held in Mexico City, agreed that a year wasn't enough, and persuaded the UN to declare a Decade for Women (1975–1985) and to schedule two more international meetings. One was held in Copenhagen in 1980, the other in 1985 in Nairobi.

The Mexico City conference set an important precedent, because the nongovernmental organizations related to the UN (called NGOs), which over the years had become like a community, jointly sponsored a Tribune—a kind of international convention for women—that was held at the same time. According to Rosalind Harris, one of the Americans who organized the Tribune, its purpose was to give women and their organizations some access to the United Nations, together with a chance to discuss their issues. Thus, while the official government delegates wrangled over world problems in one part of Mexico City, across town 6000 women, including many American feminists, attended sessions at the Tribune. Anyone who wanted to give a workshop or to get together with others interested in a particular issue had only to fill out a form and ask for a room, and in the end, over 200 workshops were offered.

By 1980, when the second UN conference was held in Copenhagen, many people were becoming aware of problems that women shared, worldwide. The UN itself summed up the situation with these statistics: "Women, 1/2 the world's population, do 2/3 of the world's work, earn 1/10 of the world's income and own 1/100 of the world's property." Everywhere, married women shouldered a double burden: Whether they worked in the fields or in a skyscraper, they went home at night to do most of the housework and child care. There was no nation where women earned as much as men, yet globally they were the sole support of one third of all households. Two thirds of the world's poorest families were headed by a lone woman.

Nevertheless, during the official conference at Copenhagen, many delegates found ways to avoid dealing with women's issues. Third World governments restated their grievances about Western imperialism, while glossing over the question of women's rights in their own countries. Western delegates expressed concern for the plight of Third World women, while ignoring the fact that Western governments and multinational corporations were partly to blame for women's continuing poverty, both abroad and at home. In the end, the conference was virtually paralyzed by the Palestinian question.

Meanwhile, 10,000 women attended the unofficial Forum (the Tribune had been renamed). There, an enormous amount of networking went on, though at times there were fierce arguments between those who wanted to concentrate on "women's issues," narrowly defined, and those who felt that all issues were women's issues. Rosalind Harris noted that "if you're a South African or Palestinian woman, to be told that apartheid or the plight of refugees in the Middle East aren't 'women's issues' is the greatest put-down I can imagine."

The Decade for Women culminated in 1985 with a final conference and Forum held in Nairobi, Kenya. Delegates to the conference were supposed to produce a document setting goals and strategies for women until the year 2000—a task that was fraught with problems. Some Moslem countries objected to paragraphs in the proposed document that called for full equality for women. Western nations protested the emphasis on apartheid and Palestinian refugees. Only a last-minute agreement to drop language that equated Zionism with racism averted an American walkout. Nevertheless, the final document, called "Forward-Looking Strategies," went well beyond existing laws and customs. Among other things, to the chagrin of the Reagan administration, it recommended that governments ensure equal pay for work of equal value (pay equity), as well as child care and flexible schedules for working parents. Acknowledging the priorities of rural women in Africa and other parts of the world who spent hours each day fetching water, it called on governments to construct wells, dams, and other devices to catch water. "Forward-Looking Strategies" also proposed that governments fund women's organizations. It noted the natural continuum from violence in the home to conflict between nations and recommended that studies be done on the effect of toys and publications that promoted the idea of war, and on the impact women might have if more of them participated in peace conferences. Meanwhile, about 16,000 women from at least 130 countries descended on the University of Nairobi to attend the Forum, a mammoth undertaking that lasted ten days and offered more than 1000 workshops.

Over the course of the Decade for Women, there were significant changes in the UN meetings. The number of female delegates increased dramatically—at Nairobi, over 80 percent were women. Though they expressed the official views of their male-dominated governments, many were personally determined to have something constructive emerge, and that probably helped to create a climate where compromise was possible. In addition, the Tribune/Forum grew enormously in size and importance. Whereas in Mexico City most women at the Tribune were very concerned about what was happening at the official conference, the women who came to Nairobi for the Forum were completely caught up in the Forum. Many delegates also attended its workshops—some delegations actually assigned members to do so.

On a number of issues, attitudes changed during the Decade. When lesbians spoke out at the Tribune in Mexico City, many heterosexual women considered it an outrage. In Copenhagen, half a dozen lesbian workshops were scheduled but the women were marginalized, left to discuss their issues among themselves. At Nairobi, lesbians held informal outdoor gatherings every day in a much more relaxed atmosphere.

By 1985, most Western women agreed that virtually all issues were indeed women's issues. At the Forum in Nairobi, many were impressed by a group called DAWN (Development Alternatives with Women for a New Era Project), which ran ambitious sessions on world development. DAWN had produced a book—written by twenty women from five continents—that argued that most Third World women were worse off than ever at the end of the Decade, partly because of the development process. DAWN pointed out that women, doing subsistence farming to feed their families, produced more than 60 percent of the food consumed locally in low-income countries. Yet development money for agricultural technology and training almost always went to the men. Thus, increasingly, development meant that farmlands were used for cash crops (known in some places as "men's crops"), and women, trying to feed their families, were hard hit. Meanwhile, in many countries technology had been misapplied and had destroyed forests and fertile land. As a result, men were forced to migrate to the cities. Women were either left behind to scratch a living from the land or else had to migrate, too, to urban slums where they wound up in the worst-paid jobs.

Just as Western feminists revamped their definitions of a "women's issue," Third World women also expanded their agendas. At Copenhagen, when Europeans expressed concern about the poverty of older women, participants from Third World countries asserted that where they came from, the extended family was alive and well, and such problems didn't exist. Five years later at Nairobi, women from the same countries came to workshops to lament the way older women were being left behind as societies changed.

Women's attitudes to feminism had also evolved by 1985. At the two earlier conferences, the very word *feminist* was often enough to provoke an argument. At Nairobi, workshops discussed how to organize women, whatever they called themselves. Feminists were still outside the mainstream in every country in the world, and Rosalind Harris was sure that most of the women who came to Nairobi didn't consider themselves part of a worldwide feminist movement. Nevertheless, women's networks had expanded mightily.

In some ways, the Decade ended amid ominous signs. Nairobi's Forum offered more than 100 workshops on religion, and at some of them Islamic attorneys from South Asia and Catholics from Latin America exchanged stories about the problems of life under a patriarchal religious system. Women all over the world were confronting rising fundamentalism. In the twentieth century, human beings everywhere were hammered by massive social changes—by wars, new technologies, and a kind of globalization of Western ideas, via the media. Disoriented, frightened, angry, some people in almost every country mounted a defense of traditional values, to the detriment of women.

Unfortunately, after 1985 few governments acted systematically to carry out the plan of action adopted at Nairobi. However, on the positive side, women's awareness and activism had grown as more women came to understand how important it was to organize and how much they could learn from one another.

International Networks

During the Decade, feminists themselves also organized international conferences. In 1976, over 2000 women met in Brussels for the International Tribunal on Crimes Against Women, a kind of global speakout about violence and sexual exploitation; that same year, women concerned about development met in the United States at Wellesley College. In time, global conferences were also held to discuss reproductive rights, women's health, lesbian rights, religion, and other issues, while in Latin America, Southeast Asia, and elsewhere, feminists organized regional meetings.

Global feminism, as it emerged, was a conglomeration of informal networks, each focused on a particular area of concern. The range of issues was quite extraordinary—from DAWN, for those interested in development, to the International Feminist Network Against Female Sexual Slavery, founded in 1983 to combat sex tourism and trafficking in women.

There was no question that women needed to organize internationally—their problems weren't confined by national boundaries, and the male-dominated policies and practices of one country could devastate the women of another. During the Vietnam War, for example, widescale prostitution developed in Thailand and the Philippines to service the American military; it became an important factor in the economies of both countries. When the war ended, sex tourism was invented to take up the slack. Japanese businesses pioneered its development, sending out planeloads of men to visit foreign brothels. Japanese feminists pioneered the opposition to this practice (see chapter 15).

Similarly, American feminists found that when they succeeded in getting harmful contraceptives, such as the Dalkon Shield, banned in the United States, the devices were offered to unsuspecting women in the Third World. When Americans elected Ronald Reagan, an anti-abortion President, family planning efforts all over the globe suffered as the Reagan administration withheld funds. Meanwhile, the U.S. government failed to use its money and influence on behalf of Third World women—for instance, it funded schools for the children of Afghan rebels, apparently without raising an eyebrow over the fact that those schools were closed to girls. RU-486, the French abortion pill, first spoken of as a boon to women in the Third World, was held back by its manufacturer because of pressure from Western anti-abortion groups and fear of what the U.S. administration might do.

During the late 1980s and early 90s, *global* was a major buzz word in American feminist circles. Some foundations were beginning to take an interest in funding women's projects that had an international aspect. Global feminism also acquired an academic base when Rutgers University established a Center for Women's Global Leadership at Douglass College with Charlotte Bunch as director. Among other things, the Global Center would gather women from around the world for annual meetings.

The globalization of feminism was just one facet of a much larger phenomenon: Many things were now happening on a global scale. In the 1990s, the United States, where the multinational corporation was invented, was uneasily adjusting to the fact that foreign corporations now owned huge chunks of American property—from Rockefeller Center in New York to some of the major Hollywood studios and book publishers. Meanwhile, jobs were going abroad, because in other countries labor was cheaper, more skilled—or both. Tremors in the stock market in Tokyo could conceivably affect the lives of Americans. Human beings all over the planet were interconnected in ways they had never been before.

Some said the world was becoming a global village, but that image seemed too peaceful—the planet was more like a vast, brawling global megalopolis. International politics were as confrontational as ever. As feminists, working across national boundaries now themselves, began to share information, resources, and visions of a better world, many fervently believed that if women could just make their voices heard, the course of history might be different.

chapter 23

The Future of Feminism: The 1990s and Beyond

*F*or the women's movement, the nineties began with an exhilarating explosion of activism. Fearing the overturn of *Roe v. Wade* (chapter 21), feminists organized two huge marches on Washington. Many were also up in arms over the news that medical research had largely ignored women's diseases.

Then, in 1991, the Clarence Thomas/Anita Hill hearings galvanized even nonfeminists. After Thomas was nominated to the Supreme Court, Hill reluctantly told investigators that he had sexually harassed her years earlier. During televised hearings, members of the Senate Judiciary Committee bluntly questioned Hill's motives and character. The image of that all-male committee was burned onto the retinas of American women. When Thomas's nomination was confirmed, the fact that there were only two females in the 100-member Senate suddenly took on new significance. Feminist PACs were inundated with contributions—EMILY's List, which supports prochoice Democratic women candidates, raised $6.2 million. The following year, so many women were elected to Congress that 1992 became known as "the year of the woman."

Social movements sometimes thrive in times of adversity, only to lose momentum when the threat is removed. Thus, much of the movement's energy dissipated when the Supreme Court's 1992 *Casey* decision appeared to guarantee core abortion rights. The election that same year gave the country a prochoice President and Congress. The Family and Medical Leave Act soon became law, and 37 percent of President Clinton's first 500 appointments were women. Many activists heaved a sigh of relief and withdrew to the sidelines.

The 1994 election turned the tables. Described by some as "the revenge of the white male," it produced a Congress dominated by conservatives. The rest of the decade resembled the 1980s, as activists were forced to defend women's gains against a powerful backlash.

This is a broad-brush sketch of the nineties. Actually, each of the submovements that made up the women's movement had a different experience. Given the rising power of the right wing, most did surprisingly well, though prochoice organizations were caught in a downward spiral.

THE DOWNSIDE: REPRODUCTIVE RIGHTS

The Supreme Court's 1992 *Casey* decision (p. 470) ostensibly upheld *Roe*, but it was also an open invitation to the states to restrict abortion. Thus, while President Clinton issued executive orders demolishing obstacles to choice at the federal level, state legislatures passed laws (often drafted by antichoice groups) that made it more difficult for women to get abortions. After the 1994 election gave the House of Representatives an antichoice majority, Congress, too, began to legislate restrictions.

In mid-1995, abortion opponents launched a new strategy. In Congress and state legislatures, they moved to ban "partial birth" abortion. As they defined it, this was a procedure in which the doctor partially delivered the fetus, only to kill it. Prolifers claimed this was done to healthy babies just days away from normal birth.

The method in question, called dilation and extraction (D&X), is one of several used in the second and third trimesters of pregnancy.* Prochoice activists pointed out that a ban on D&X wouldn't save a single fetus's life; it would simply force doctors to use a different procedure that was riskier in some circumstances.

However, antichoice leaders had more in mind than saving lives.

---

* Just one percent of abortions are performed after twenty weeks. They're usually done because of severe fetal abnormalities or a threat to the woman's health.

By focusing on "partial birth," they had found a way to bring home to the public the reality of late-term abortions. In addition, the bills they drafted were so broadly written that they would actually ban all the most common surgical abortion procedures, even early in pregnancy. That was not accidental.

"It's interesting to read through the legislative histories of those bills," said Elizabeth Cavendish, legal director and general counsel for NARAL. "Amendments were almost always offered that would clarify which procedure the bill was talking about, but they were rejected. The legislators knew what they were doing. They wanted to ban all abortions and they went about it in a diabolically crafty manner." They also refused to permit an exception if a D&X was necessary for a woman's health.

Because the "partial birth" ban was so broad, in most states courts refused to allow it to go into effect. Nevertheless, Cavendish said grimly, "It's been an uphill battle. Prochoice forces have had to fight this in 47 state legislatures so far."

Clinic Violence Escalates

Throughout the 1990s, antichoice demonstrators continued to harass abortion providers. The situation improved initially and then worsened.

It improved because prolife militants could no longer turn out hundreds of followers and successfully block access to clinics. Most abortion providers had obtained court injunctions against the demonstrators, which meant substantial fines, and fewer people were willing to risk arrest. In addition, clinic administrators fed the names of blockaders who were arrested to the National Center for the Pro Choice Majority (NCPCM), where Ann Baker had compiled arrest data on 14,000 individuals. When the protestors came to trial, the clinic's lawyer—using information supplied by NCPCM—told the judge how often these particular individuals had been arrested in the past for besieging medical facilities. That, too, increased fines. In addition, local prochoice activists regularly defended clinics, escorting patients inside and, if necessary, shielding them with their own bodies.

Frustrated, some hard-core militants resorted to murder; others encouraged them. The first killing took place in March 1993, when Dr. David Gunn was shot outside a Florida clinic. Afterward, Operation Rescue split, divided between those who condoned the murder and those who didn't. A horrified Congress passed FACE, the Freedom of Access to Clinic Entrances Act. It prohibited using obstruction, property damage, force, or threats against abortion providers, though peaceful demonstrations were permitted.

Between 1993 and early 1998, anti-abortion extremists committed six murders, yet the media treated them with kid gloves. In late 1993, militant Paul Hill appeared on TV's *Nightline* and advocated killing doctors. Host Ted Koppel noted solemnly that he posed a "very, very difficult moral question." Seven months later, Hill himself murdered a doctor and a clinic escort. In 1995 on the *Geraldo* show, Father David Trosch not only argued that it was justifiable homicide to murder doctors but called for killing all women who used IUDs or took birth control pills.

In the early 1990s, it appeared that medical abortions (using drugs such as RU-486) might eventually take the heat off clinics because doctors could give patients the drugs in privacy. The Feminist Majority deluged the French developer of RU-486 with hundreds of thousands of petitions and letters, urging it to market the drug in the United States, but anti-abortion groups threatened a boycott. In 1994, the company donated the U.S. patent rights to the nonprofit Population Council. Four years later, RU-486 was still awaiting final FDA approval, and Congress was considering a law that would prevent the agency from approving any abortifacient.

Meanwhile, the National Abortion Federation had issued guidelines on how to do medical abortions using methotrexate and another drug already on the market. Some physicians probably did begin discreetly to do methotrexate abortions in their offices. However, prochoice leaders were far from certain that this would ultimately ease the pressure on clinics. NARAL's Elizabeth Cavendish feared that the threat of violence, on top of onerous state regulations, would keep most doctors from doing medical abortions. Some state legislatures had passed laws laying down burdensome abortion regulations that affected doctors' offices as well as women's clinics. Other statutes required providers to register, giving anti-abortion groups a way to target physicians for harassment.

There was some good news in 1998. After twelve years of litigation, NOW won a civil law suit against anti-abortion militants. Under the RICO statute (chapter 21), NOW had charged that antichoice groups and their leaders had conspired to drive clinics out of business, using intimidation, extortion, and violence. A Chicago jury unanimously agreed. The defendants were required to pay triple the cost of the damage they'd done to providers. NOW received none of the money but got what it asked for: a nationwide injunction against the militants.

Roe: *An Empty Promise?*

In framing his dissenting opinion in the 1992 *Casey* decision, Supreme Court Chief Justice William Rehnquist knew what that decision would do to abortion rights. Observing that the Court should have overturned *Roe* altogether, rather than pretending to respect its central tenets, he wrote: "*Roe* continues to exist, but only in the way a storefront on a Western movie set exists—a mere facade to give the illusion of reality."

By the mid-nineties the number of physicians willing to do abortions was shrinking. In thirty states, a woman who wanted an abortion had to listen to a prolife lecture from the doctor and then come back twenty-four hours later. In twenty-eight states, teenagers couldn't have the procedure without telling their parents first. Most states wouldn't pay for abortions for poor women. Health care facilities in women's prisons weren't permitted to do abortions, nor were military hospitals overseas or the Indian Health Service, primary provider of health care on reservations.

Elizabeth Cavendish noted that when prochoicers celebrated the twenty-fifth anniversary of *Roe* in 1998, "we had some fairly grim and dark conclusions about where we are right now." Yet the prochoice public remained complacent about abortion rights. In 1996, fewer saw it as an important political issue than in 1992. The majority still believed abortion should remain legal and saw it as a private matter, but higher percentages were willing to accept stricter limits on access.* Once again, a presidential election could prove crucial. Ann Baker said, "If we elect a President in 2000 who appoints antichoice justices to the Supreme Court, that could set the stage for reversing *Roe* completely."

POLITICS: DIZZYING UPS AND DOWNS

Throughout the 1990s, feminists worked hard to elect politicians who cared about women's issues and to increase the number of women in office. In the 1992 election, women ran for Congress in record numbers. Ever since the defeat of the ERA, feminist organizations had been urging their supporters to go into politics; many

* In January 1998, 32 percent of those polled said that abortion should be generally available, down from 40 percent in 1989; 45 percent said it should be available but with stricter limits (up from 40 percent); 22 percent said it should not be permitted at all (up from 18 percent).

women had done so and were ready to move up. Before the election, women comprised 5 percent of Congress; afterward, they comprised 10 percent.

In 1994, the Christian Coalition targeted feminists and other liberals in Congress, pouring millions into pivotal races. Sixty-two percent of white males voted for conservative or Republican candidates that year. Voter turnout was low, and 33 percent of those who voted were Evangelical Christians. A half dozen of the feminists elected in 1992 lost their seats—in some races to women opposed to women's rights. The Republicans, now in the majority, soon defunded the Congressional Caucus for Women's Issues. Members continued to meet but because they had no staff, coordinating action was difficult, said Debra Dodson, senior research associate at CAWP, the Center for the American Woman and Politics.

Preparing for the 1996 election, more than a hundred women's organizations worked together to persuade women to vote. "One byproduct of that effort," said Dodson, "was that candidates from the President on down, particularly on the Democratic side, made a real effort to talk about issues in a way that would resonate with women." That may explain why the gender gap in the race for the presidency was the biggest ever—an 11 percent difference. With the male vote divided almost evenly between Bob Dole and Bill Clinton, women's support kept Clinton in office.

Feminist incumbents in Congress won their races, and half a dozen more women were added to their number. After the election, women filled almost 12 percent of the seats.* It was progress, but slow and incremental. Meanwhile, conservatives dominated both houses.

In the 1980s, studies had indicated that women elected to office were much more likely than men to care about women's issues. By the late 1990s, some feminists questioned whether that was always true; conservative women in Congress often spoke for the right wing. However, Dodson noted that women, overall, remained more supportive than men on feminist issues like abortion.

"IS FEMINISM DEAD?"

Time magazine asked the question on its June 29, 1998, cover. *Time* wasn't quite prepared to publish an obituary. Instead, writer Gin-

---

* Before the 1994 election, NOW estimated that if women continued to gain seats in Congress at the same pace as in 1992 (which didn't happen), they would not comprise 50 percent of Congress until 2068.

ia Bellafante mourned the end of the old feminism, focused on social change, which had supposedly been replaced by a new pop
culture "of celebrity and self-obsession." Among Bellefante's prime
examples of the new feminism were television's Ally McBeal—
young, single, neurotic, and fictional*—and nonmovement wom-
en who *called* themselves feminists.

The media had declared the movement dead so often that to many
activists the latest attack was a yawn.† Feminists obviously had no
control over how pop culture portrayed women. However, the *Time*
article did reflect a problem new in the 1990s: the mainstream media not only ignored movement leaders but welcomed right-wing
women. Some claimed to be feminists, though they didn't sound
it. Self-described feminist Christina Hoff Sommers, for example,
author of *Who Stole Feminism?* berated the movement for embrac-
ing "victimhood." She was particularly down on women's studies.
"There are a lot of homely women in women's studies," said Sommers. "Preaching . . . anti-male, anti-sex sermons is a way for them
to compensate for various heartaches—they're just mad at the beautiful girls." While writing her book, Sommers received financial
support from three right-wing foundations.

"GENERAL-INTEREST" GROUPS

General-interest feminist organizations worked hard and thrived
in the nineties, despite some ups and downs. NOW members, for
example, marched, picketed, lobbied, defended abortion clinics,
and worked in political campaigns. The organization's membership
soared after the Hill-Thomas hearings, declined once Bill Clinton
was elected, and surged again after the 1994 election debacle. Patricia Ireland, president of NOW, said, "It's a real irony that, in terms
of membership, we prosper in adversity." In 1998, NOW had
225,000 members and about 550 chapters, with a growing number
on college campuses, a few in high schools, and one on an Indian
reservation.

For Ireland, the low point of the decade was losing the fight to
preserve welfare. NOW and other women's organizations demonstrated and lobbied hard against the bill that gutted welfare. Congress slashed federal funds for the poor by $55 billion over five
years. The bill also required welfare recipients to work for their

---

* The protagonist of a TV series that bears her name.
† NOW estimated that since the early 1970s the media had announced the movement's demise roughly once every eighteen months.

benefits after two years and limited aid for most to just five years over a lifetime. The new law didn't provide adequate health care, child care, education, or training.

"It was not just a legislative loss," said Ireland. "It was a public opinion loss. It played to the public's frustration over the widening income gap. It's easy to scapegoat. People think, 'If I'm having trouble, it must be because of that undeserving welfare woman who's taking my taxes.'" In fact, welfare accounted for less than 1 percent of the federal budget in the mid-1990s. However, for many people money apparently wasn't the real issue. Republicans harped on the immorality of welfare mothers, stereotyping women on welfare as promiscuous black teenagers.

After the new welfare law took effect, as young mothers who had depended on benefits were forced to drop out of college and take dead-end jobs, the Center for Women Policy Studies (CWPS) helped draft a bill that would allow women to count two years of postsecondary education as their required work activity. CWPS had argued for years that higher education is a viable route out of poverty for almost half of all women on welfare. "Even one year of postsecondary education makes a difference," said Leslie Wolfe, president of CWPS. When women actually graduate from college, 79 percent land jobs that pay more than $20,000 a year.

The Feminist Majority

The toughest campaign of the nineties for the Feminist Majority was the battle over affirmative action in California. "It was really a campaign of orchestrated lies," said Ellie Smeal, the organization's founder and president. Voters were asked to approve an amendment to the state constitution that would end racial and gender "preferences." The words "affirmative action" were never used, and polls indicated that if they had been, the measure would have been defeated. Supporters of the initiative focused on race, claiming that thanks to "preferences," unqualified black students were being admitted to state universities. In fact, the initiative also outlawed affirmative action in public contracts, and Smeal believed that was the real concern of its sponsors. Under affirmative action, 22 percent of government contracts in California had been going to women and to men of color.

Voters approved the initiative by a narrow margin. The right wing managed to roll back affirmative action in several other states as well.

Meanwhile, Smeal's organization was busy working with college students. It ran a summer training institute and had created study plans—on how reproductive rights laws evolved, for example—that would earn students course credits *and* lead to action. In 1999, the Feminist Majority's Web site developed a virtual campus community, with chat rooms, conference centers, and an online newsletter for students (http://www.feminist.org).

Feminism's Next Wave

In the 1980s, activists worried about the graying of the women's movement. That became a nonissue in the nineties as young women not only joined existing organizations but created new ones of their own.

New York City had three very active groups for young women in the early 1990s. WAC, the Women's Action Coalition, mounted frequent demonstrations, picketing art galleries where women were underrepresented, for example. WHAM, Women's Health Action and Mobilization, often defended abortion clinics. Unlike WHAM, which had dissolved by 1998, and WAC, which was unlocatable, the third organization, the Third Wave Foundation, kept growing. As their first project in 1992, its leaders had recruited 110 young women and men who rolled across the country in three buses, registering new voters in inner city communities. The Third Wave eventually developed a network of 3000 members around the country, mostly women in their twenties. It offered leadership training and funded specific projects.

Women of Color

"In the nineties, women of color were still reluctant to join predominantly white feminist groups," said Aileen Hernandez, the African-American activist who had been NOW's second president. "They chose instead to create and strengthen their own organizations." Hernandez conceded that during the decade there were a few issue-oriented conflicts between feminists of color and their white counterparts. However, she noted that new relationships were built among groups through coalitions designed to share resources and develop joint strategies.

The National Council of Negro Women (NCNW) often spoke for African-American women in the national and international arenas. Founded in 1935, by 1998 NCNW represented 38 national organizations for African-American women and 250 community-based "Sections." It had an outreach to four million women.

According to Dorothy Height, NCNW's president and chief executive officer, the nineties brought gains and losses. The African-American middle class grew, more African-Americans and women were elected to public office, and there were advances in employment. However, white backlash resulted in threats to affirmative action and a rise in hate groups and violence. "Before we have been able to achieve full enforcement of the Civil Rights Act or move to a full measure of achievement, some of the tools that further equality are being lost," said Height. NCNW fought to preserve affirmative action in public policy.

The organization had offices in three African nations, where it worked with local women's organizations on leadership development and issues such as literacy. In the 1990s, some of those groups turned their attention to domestic violence, women's health, and AIDS.

In 1994, the Mexican-American Women's National Association (chapter 17) officially became a pan-Latina organization and changed its name to MANA, a National Latina Organization. In 1995, it opened a Washington, D.C., office with a paid staff.

Leadership development was still one of the organization's top priorities. Elisa Sanchez, MANA's president and CEO, said, "We help our members develop so they can become representatives for the Latino community on boards and commissions or become elected officials." The other major ongoing project was the Hermanitas mentoring program, developed to keep young girls in school and to help them avoid pregnancy, and to encourage them to go on after high school to a trade school or college.

Wilma Espinoza, a former MANA president, noted that during the 1990s Latinas often faced open racism. "The talk about our demographic growth has scared people," she said. At the same time, the ballot initiative that killed affirmative action in California meant that Latinas at many state colleges felt unwelcome and isolated. MANA planned campus chapters.

Asian Women United of California (AWU) was a different type of organization. Located in San Francisco's Bay Area, it produced books and videotapes by and about Asian-American women, using the revenues from each product to fund the next. Rather than join AWU, most women simply signed onto a committee to work on a particular project.

"We try to know what's happening in our various communities, to figure out key issues so that we can do something on them," said AWU co-founder Elaine Kim. In 1998, AWU was beginning work on an anthology for thirteen-year-old Asian-American girls. Virtually invisible in mainstream magazines like *Seventeen,* these young teens are at an age when their bodies become racialized as well as sexualized, said Kim; others begin to see them as foreign. The book would reassure its young readers that they were not alone and that they were dealing not with a personal shortcoming but with a social phenomenon.

ACADEMIC FEMINISTS THRIVE

Women's studies grew during the nineties, offering more programs than ever at the undergraduate, master's, and Ph.D. levels. "In addition, feminist scholarship is becoming an absolutely integral part of higher education," said Bonnie Zimmerman, 1998–99 president of NWSA (the National Women's Studies Association). "The sense that we're an experiment and just here for a little while is gone."

Women's studies also became much more inclusive during the 1990s because academic women of color insisted on it. Their issues and perspectives were incorporated into curricula and courses, even as their numbers grew on the faculty and in the student body.

At some universities, gender studies replaced or supplemented women's studies. Reflecting the influence of postmodernism, gender studies deconstructs the way gender is reproduced within social systems and individuals and how it affects both men and women. Academics who had been activists in the 1970s often saw this change as depoliticization. "They feel it's taking the women out of women's studies," said Zimmerman.

Women's studies were challenged repeatedly by conservatives. The attacks generally came from outside the universities, from the organized right wing, and from state legislators, who insisted that feminists were trying to force "politically correct" views down students' throats. Feminist philosopher Martha Nussbaum noted that, in fact, traditional scholarship "reflected the highly political judgment that it was more important and more interesting to study the activities, bodies, and experiences of men."

As for secondary schools, feminists remained concerned about girls' low self-esteem, as several studies confirmed subtle sex discrimination in the classroom (chapter 11). In response, the *Ms* Foundation launched an annual Take Our Daughters to Work Day (TODWD) in 1993. In its second year, 25 million parents took their daughters with them to work. By the third year, the right wing had organized a backlash, attacking TODWD as discrimination against boys.

In athletics, Title IX had transformed opportunities for girls and women. Between 1971 and 1997, the number of girls playing high school sports increased by 800 percent. In 1996, more American women than ever before competed in the Olympics, and two women's professional basketball leagues were formed.

Students of the 1990s often denied that they were feminists. However, they resonated to the same issues that had galvanized previous generations—violence against women, for example. "Of course, some young women are concerned about being accepted and about not threatening men," said Zimmerman. "They're resistant to calling themselves feminists but they're not resistant to what feminism means. It makes sense to them."

NEW RESOURCES FOR BATTERED WOMEN

In 1994, feminists achieved a major victory when Congress passed the Violence Against Women Act (VAWA). Among other things, it substantially increased funding for battered women's programs and for training sessions to teach police, prosecutors, and judges about domestic violence. "That training has really helped them do a better job," said Rita Smith, executive director of NCADV, the National Coalition Against Domestic Violence. The new law also had a vital—and controversial—civil rights provision. When violent crimes such as battering or rape were motivated by misogyny—in other words, when they were hate crimes—women could sue their assailants for violating their civil rights. If the criminal justice system failed them, they now had another legal remedy.

Another of VAWA's provisions rewarded the states for mandating arrest when domestic violence occurred. However, some activists questioned whether mandatory arrest was the best policy. Police officers apparently resented being told what to do and frequently arrested both parties or sometimes just the woman. Increasingly, women who had simply defended themselves were ordered to complete programs designed for batterers; some wound up with a criminal record. NCADV had always favored policies that allowed police officers some discretion on whether to make an arrest.

During the nineties, battered women's advocates often found themselves working at the intersection of domestic violence and other issues—deportation, welfare benefits, and child custody, for example. Battered women who were undocumented aliens were often afraid that if they called the police, they'd be deported. In

Washington, D.C., a group called Ayuda created a clinic for battered immigrants that provided one-stop legal and social services.

According to some studies, 60 percent of women on welfare are survivors of domestic violence. Many use the benefits to get back on their feet, but that takes time. Some find it almost impossible to keep a job because they are being beaten or stalked and perhaps harassed at work by their batterers. Under pressure from a coalition of women's groups spearheaded by the NOW Legal Defense and Education Fund (NOW LDEF), Congress gave states the option of easing the welfare time limit for battered women.

As for child custody, Rita Smith estimated that a batterer who fought for custody got it 70 percent of the time. Many judges still didn't understand that children who lived with violence suffered emotional damage even if they were never beaten themselves.

VAWA delivered vast new resources to battered women's programs. "But the need is so great, a huge number of people still need services we cannot provide," said Sue Osthoff, director of the National Clearinghouse for the Defense of Battered Women. Ironically, since the 1970s the number of batterers killed each year by their partners had decreased steadily, probably because battered women now had other options. However, there had been no corresponding drop in the number of women killed by husbands or boyfriends.

IN THE COURTS: MIXED SUCCESS

During the nineties, feminist attorneys went to court for women in cases involving everything from abortion rights to child custody. With mixed success, they defended the civil rights provision of VAWA, which was challenged in courts around the country, and tried to overturn the "family caps" on welfare that some states established. The caps prohibited any increase in benefits when a woman on welfare had another baby.

There were important sexual harassment cases as well. According to surveys, half of all American women have been sexually harassed either on the job or in school. Feminist litigators "did well on the job side but not on the school side," said Lynn Hecht Schafran, director of NOW LDEF's judicial education program, NJEP (the National Judicial Education Program to Promote Equality for Women and Men in the Courts; see chapter 14). On the job side, the Supreme Court ruled that a company could be held responsible if a supervisor sexually harassed an employee, even if the employee wasn't fired or otherwise penalized for resisting. (However, the company could *not* be held responsible if it had made reasonable efforts to prevent sexual harassment and the employee had acted unreasonably by failing to make a complaint.)

On the school side, the Court decreed that a school district couldn't be held liable when a teacher sexually harassed a student unless a school official with authority to take action actually knew what was happening and deliberately did not act. "A teacher harassed by another teacher now has more protection than a student harassed by a faculty member," said Schafran.

For many in the feminist legal community, the most satisfying news of the decade was the appointment of Ruth Bader Ginsburg to the Supreme Court. The most satisfying Supreme Court decision was the one that opened the all-male Virginia Military Institute to women. Written by Ginsburg, the decision subjected sex discrimination to "skeptical scrutiny," a new and tougher standard. Justice Ginsburg wrote that the state must demonstrate an "exceedingly persuasive justification" whenever it treated women differently from men. Though this still wasn't quite strict scrutiny (chapter 18), afterward some suggested that the VMI decision had virtually enacted the ERA.

The ERA: Stalled But Still Alive

Many feminists had not given up on the amendment and, despite VMI, were not about to. A group called ERA Summit was pursuing a three-state strategy. The ERA was just three states short of ratification when time ran out in 1982. Nothing in the Constitution said that proposed amendments must have a time limit, and once before Congress had amended the ERA's preamble to extend the deadline. Thus, ERA Summit set out to persuade three more states to ratify. If it succeeded, Congress would have to act as well.

However, NOW and some other groups wanted a different, more powerful amendment that would, among other things, forever protect abortion and lesbian rights as part of women's equality. In 1998, as a first step, the Feminist Majority began drafting a federal women's rights bill that would do what the ERA would have done and more. No one expected the current Congress to pass it, and no one wanted to substitute a mere law for a constitutional amendment. However, as NOW's Patricia Ireland said, "It's a vehicle to start to talk about equality and why we don't have it, and a first step perhaps toward a new ERA."

HOT ISSUES IN HEALTH

In the early 1990s, indignation over the government's failure to fund women's health research launched a new wave of activism. Breast cancer, in particular, was a big issue. Baby boomers were reaching their late forties, the age at which the disease becomes more common; one in nine would get it. Breast cancer groups sprang up around the country, some materializing in the wake of Dr. Susan Love's 1990 book tour. Love, the author of a book on breast disorders, recalled later that at the end of one talk she wisecracked, "Maybe we should march topless on the White House." When some of her listeners asked where to sign up for the march, she realized how angry women were.

The National Breast Cancer Coalition, formed in 1991, lobbied hard for more money for research. When advocates couldn't pry enough out of the domestic budget, they persuaded the Department of Defense to fund studies—and to involve advocates in decisions about how the money would be spent. Later, other health agencies also agreed that women could play a role in decision making, and the Coalition began to train its members in basic science so that they could represent women's interests effectively.

Breast cancer wasn't the only disease that had been neglected. At a 1991 press conference, a group of women scientists and doctors revealed that less than 14 percent of the funding of the National Institutes of Health (NIH) was spent studying disorders unique to women. Research on diseases that affected both sexes was done almost entirely on men. Congresswoman Patricia Schroeder noted that "NIH had even conducted its breast cancer studies on men" and that in the research it funded "even the lab rats were male."

"That press conference led to lasting changes," said Cynthia Pearson, executive director of the National Women's Health Network. NIH established an Office of Research on Women's Health and began to insist that clinical trials include women. President Bush appointed a woman, Bernadine Healy, to head NIH, and Healy pushed through a huge study addressing the health issues of women.

When President Clinton proposed health reform, many feminists believed that universal access to medical care was within reach. The subsequent failure of the Clinton bill was a bitter blow. After Republicans took control of Congress in 1995, funding for research on women's diseases survived, but feminists could no longer shape the debate. Lawmakers threw an occasional sop to women—telling health maintenance organizations (HMOs) they couldn't eject new mothers from the hospital just twenty-four hours after childbirth, for example—but ignored most other issues.

Long-acting contraception was a concern for many groups. The Food and Drug Administration approved Norplant in 1990 and Depo-Provera in 1992, despite opposition from feminists. An injection of Depo-Provera prevents pregnancy for three months; Norplant prevents it for up to five years by implanting hormone capsules under the skin. Policymakers considered these ideal birth control methods because they were foolproof—in other words, under the control of the provider—but serious side effects were possible. Women's groups demanded that consent forms with information about side effects accompany the drugs; they succeeded with Norplant.

AIDS was another concern. The Center for Women Policy Studies and other groups struggled to ensure that women were included in programs for HIV prevention and had access to health care. CWPS, the first national women's organization to address these issues, created the National Resource Center on Women and AIDS Policy in 1987.

Top Priorities for Women of Color

During the nineties, the health organizations founded by women of color (chapter 12) grew, and new ones formed. The National Black Women's Health Project (NBWHP) moved its headquarters to Washington, D.C., and continued to support self-help groups all over the country. "What we're really about is wellness and empowerment," said Julia Scott, director of NBWHP. "However, from time to time we take on special illnesses because the numbers affecting us are so alarming." In the 1990s, the organization focused on AIDS and breast cancer. It argued against mandatory HIV testing of pregnant women and for more drug treatment centers to reduce the spread of HIV; it demanded funding for research to find a better breast cancer screening technique than mammography. Many women of African descent develop a particularly aggressive form of breast cancer in their late twenties or early thirties. In younger women, breast tissue is so dense that mammograms aren't helpful.

In 1998, the National Latina Health Organization (NLHO) was busy planning two binational conferences—in conjunction with Mexican and Cuban health groups—as well as three intergenerational conferences to encourage mothers and daughters to explore the problems of Hispanic adolescents. Teenage Latinas were a special concern because they were at risk for neglect, abuse, educational deprivation, and pregnancy, said NLHO cofounder Luz Alvarez Martinez. When Latinas went to clinics for birth control, they often had Norplant or Depo-Provera foisted on them; neither offered any protection against sexually transmitted diseases. At most clinics that served adolescents of color, long-acting contraceptives were the first method offered, though they had never been tested on women under eighteen and side effects included amenorrhea and osteoporosis. "How can this be safe for girls whose bodies are still developing?" asked Martinez.

Native American women, too, took issue with the way long-term contraceptives were dispensed. Charon Asetoyer, director of the Native American Women's Health Education Research Center in South Dakota, found that the Indian Health Service (IHS) had issued no medical protocol requiring informed consent and spelling out how Depo-Provera and Norplant should be used. The drugs were risky for women with certain medical conditions; providers weren't warning those women or monitoring them. The center pressured the IHS until it established a protocol, thus benefiting every reservation. Asetoyer's organization also fought a largely successful battle against outside groups determined to use reservation land to dump everything from chemicals to nuclear waste. One case went to the Supreme Court after the state government challenged the tribe's jurisdiction over its land. The Court affirmed the jurisdiction but exempted the particular landfill site the state had targeted.

Founded in 1993, the National Asian Women's Health Organization (NAWHO) had 3000 individual members by 1998 and over 100 organizational members—mostly groups that served the Asian-American community. NAWHO did research and education on issues such as tobacco use, offered leadership training, and addressed public policy questions on the national level. For instance, Mary Chung, NAWHO's founder and president, advocated strongly for federally funded research and prevention programs that would address the needs of specific ethnic groups. Working with specific groups is important, said Chung, because Asian-Americans come from more than thirty countries and have very different health profiles. Vietnamese women, for example, have the highest rate of cervical cancer in the nation, while Japanese-Americans have a comparatively high breast cancer rate. Due to NAWHO's efforts, the federal government began to allocate more resources to Asian-American women's health issues.

LESBIAN RIGHTS UNDER FIRE

Lesbian activists fought a bitter battle with the right wing throughout the 1990s. Religious conservatives challenged every gain they made.

By the early nineties, the GLBT (gay, lesbian, bisexual, and transgender) community had won basic civil rights guarantees in some cities and states—statutes that banned discrimination based on sexual orientation in employment and housing, for example. In 1992, a right-wing campaign persuaded Colorado voters to amend their state constitution in order to repeal gay rights ordinances in three cities, while prohibiting similar ordinances in the future. The Supreme Court declared the Colorado amendment unconstitutional, but the religious right simply reverted to a piecemeal strategy. With mixed success, it set out to repeal, one by one, all existing gay rights laws.

Same-sex marriage was another hot issue. In 1993, Hawaii's Supreme Court ruled that refusing to marry same-sex couples violated the state's constitution, which prohibited discrimination based on sex; however, the state could still show in new court proceedings that it had a "compelling interest" in preserving the status quo. The high court in Alaska made a similar ruling. While these cases dragged on, Congress passed the Defense of Marriage Act, which defined marriage for federal purposes as something that could only involve a man and a woman. Conservatives also persuaded more than two dozen states to pass laws stipulating that the state wouldn't recognize same-sex marriages performed elsewhere.

In another setback, President Clinton's 1993 attempt to drop the longstanding ban on gays in the military stalled because of a furious outcry from conservatives and the military. In the end, the administration agreed to a compromise, the "Don't Ask, Don't Tell" policy. If lesbians and gay men kept silent about their sexual orientation and abstained from sexual activity (except, presumably, the heterosexual kind) while in the service, military commanders would leave them alone. Commanders ignored the directive, and over the next few years the number of gays and lesbians discharged by the military actually increased.

Going into the 1998 election, lesbians and gay men became a prime target of the right wing. "We've been vilified in a way that no other community really could be in this day and age," said Rebecca Isaacs, political director of the National Gay and Lesbian Task Force (NGLTF). Senate majority leader Trent Lott publicly condemned homosexuals as sinners. Right-wing organizations placed full-page ads in seven major newspapers; the ads featured "former homosexuals" who supposedly overcame their sexual orientation through prayer. "It's kinder, gentler bigotry," said Isaacs dryly.

While these battles raged, public attitudes were slowly changing. Though the majority of Americans in 1996 still disapproved of homosexuality, 84 percent now favored equal rights in employment for gay men and lesbians. Though almost two-thirds of those surveyed opposed same-sex marriages, more than half favored extending to gays some of the practical benefits of marriage—for example, the spousal right to inherit. Meanwhile, 5 percent of voters now identified themselves as gay in exit polls. The GLBT vote could conceivably tip the balance in some races.

THE WORLDWIDE WOMEN'S MOVEMENT

In the 1990s, the global women's movement grew exponentially. Women had organized in many countries, and three major UN conferences gave them the opportunity to form both informal networks and international coalitions, even as they thrust women's issues onto the world's agenda. Before each conference, women's advocates strategized across national boundaries and pressured their own governments to address women's concerns.

In 1993, global feminists took up the issue of women's human rights. The United Nations Universal Declaration of Human Rights, adopted in 1948, supposedly applied to both sexes, yet many violations of women's rights, such as rape in wartime, were ignored. The UN convened a World Conference on Human Rights in Vienna in 1993 to develop a future agenda for human rights. An international coalition of women's groups and individuals, led by the Center for Women's Global Leadership at Rutgers University, had been preparing for the meeting for two years.

As the conference began, delegates were aware that in Bosnia 20,000 Muslim women had been raped by Serbs as a deliberate strategy to impregnate the women and dilute their children's ethnic identity. "The campaigning we had done helped people recognize that this was a human rights violation," said Charlotte Bunch, founder and executive director of the center, "and the news reports about Bosnia helped the world to understand what 'women's rights are human rights' really means." In the end, the Programme of Action explicitly recognized violence and other abuses against women as human rights violations. Afterward, some countries began to grant asylum to women who were fleeing gender-based persecution—for instance, pressed by feminists, the United States gave asylum to a woman from Togo because if she returned home her family would force her to submit to genital mutilation.

In 1994, concern about world population growth brought delegates and women's advocates to Cairo, Egypt, for the fourth UN International Conference on Population and Development. Two days of the nine-day meeting were spent trying to overcome the Vatican's opposition to a single paragraph on abortion. Also hostile to women's rights were population control enthusiasts who advocated programs to sterilize women in developing countries.

Nevertheless, as a result of women's lobbying, the final document produced by the delegates recognized that the true cornerstones of development were education for girls and empowerment for women, who must be enabled to control their own fertility. Leslie Wolfe, president of the Center for Women Policy Studies, remarked that the document read like a feminist agenda.

In 1995, women gathered in Beijing, China, for the Fourth World Conference on Women, the largest UN conference ever held. Despite obstacles placed in their way by their own governments and by the Chinese, 30,000 women attended the NGO Forum. To many American activists, discouraged by media indifference and right-wing successes back home, Beijing offered proof that they were part of a vast, worldwide movement. The twelve-point Beijing Platform for Action, adopted by the delegates, expanded commitments to women made at previous conferences. Knowing that their governments might do nothing if not pressed, activists returned home determined to turn the platform's general principles into specific actions.

By the late 1990s, the Internet had begun to provide an easy way for women around the world to keep in touch, sometimes with startling results. Patricia Ireland recalled that a NOW member came to work one day to find that she had e-mail from women in Mongolia. The message began: "We are the daughters of Genghis Khan, and we will not be easily suppressed."

HALF A REVOLUTION

From the 1960s to the end of the century, the American women's movement accomplished an enormous amount. Americans had only to look back to add up the score. At midcentury, women were limited in the courses they could take in high school; kept out of graduate schools, medical schools, and law schools by quotas; barred from many occupations; automatically fired when they became pregnant; and routinely denied credit. Battered wives had nowhere to turn, sexual harassment was a dirty secret, abortion was illegal, and a woman who was raped had to produce a witness if she wanted the rapist brought to justice. Women of color were virtually invisible in politics, the media, and elsewhere.

The list could go on, but the message is clear: the movement had transformed society. In the process, feminists had raised the consciousness of the nation. Many of their ideas were now so broadly accepted that they were no longer even labeled "feminist." They shaped most people's beliefs about what women were like and what they could expect to do with their lives.

In the late 1990s, the women's movement was alive and well, as this chapter demonstrates. It was broader, more deeply rooted, and more diverse than ever. However, there was still much work to be done. Activists had proved that the mountain could be moved, but they hadn't yet moved it far enough. Every chapter in parts 2 and 3 of this book is an unfinished story that describes both the gains feminists made and the tasks that remain.

In short, by the late 1990s American feminists had pulled off just half a revolution, and it had taken the combined energy and determination of hundreds of thousands of activists to do it. Meanwhile, antifeminists had dug in for the long haul, and that meant slow progress. However, each new generation of women would do better than the last as long as a strong women's movement persevered.

Passing the Torch

In the summer of 1998, thousands of women descended on Seneca Falls, New York, to celebrate the 150th anniversary of the first U.S. women's rights convention. NOW took the opportunity to hold its annual membership meeting in nearby Rochester and to draft a statement embodying a vision for women in the next century.

During a plenary session, as the document was taking shape, eleven-year-old Lauren Penoyer, a delegate from South Carolina, approached the microphone, followed by nine-year-old Rachel Prehodka-Spindel from New Jersey. Lauren offered an amendment, seconded by Rachel, to change one line in the document so that it acknowledged girls as well as grown women.

Watching while Lauren read her amendment, Patricia Ireland thought about the first women's rights convention and the fact that because it took so many years to get the vote, those who launched the struggle died before victory was won. "I thought that in some ways we're simply bridges so that Lauren and Rachel can get across," said Ireland. "The work itself is what counts, whether we live to see all the results or not."

The final paragraphs of NOW's vision statement reflect that insight:

> Even when progress seems most elusive, we will maintain our conviction that the work itself is important. For it is the work that enriches our lives; it is the work that unites us; it is the work that will propel us into the next century. We know that our struggle has made a difference, and we reaffirm our faith that it will continue to make a difference for women's lives.
>
> Today we dedicate ourselves to the sheer joy of moving forward and fighting back.

Acknowledgments

This book would not have been possible without the generous help of many people who made time in their busy schedules to share their memories with me. Catherine East, in particular, gave me the benefit of her years of experience as a Washington insider and contributed in some way to almost every chapter in the book. She dug through her files for me, as did Jean Faust, who provided a wealth of material produced during NOW's first years. Jennifer Macleod lent me her archives, including stacks of feminist newsletters, clippings, and correspondence from many sources. I relived the late 1960s and early 70s through her files and through the 1960s Women's Liberation Archives for Action, the Redstockings' collection.

I want to thank all those I interviewed: Dolores Alexander, Charon Asetoyer, Ann Baker, Diane Balser, Anna Bexell, Libby Bouvier, Susan Brownmiller, Charlotte Bunch, Carol Burris, Susan Carroll, John Mack Carter, Jane Chapman, Nora Coffey, Harriet N. Cohen, Veronica Collazo, Nancy Collins, Noreen Connell, Flora Crater, Elvira Valenzuela Crocker, Laurie Crumpacker, Joetta Cunningham, Florence Falk-Dickler, Vilunya Diskin, Deborah Dodson, Carol Downer, Catherine East, Jean Faust, Muriel Fox, Ruth Bader Ginsburg, Marcia D. Greenberger, Martha Griffiths, Doris Haire, Marjorie Pitts Hames, LaDonna Harris, Rosalind Harris, Barbara Hart, Nancy Hawley, Judy Heumann, Karen Hicks, Elizabeth Holtzman, Phineas Indritz, Mildred Jeffrey, Susan Kelly-Dreiss, Ann Kolker, Larry Lader, Irene Lee, Alice Levine, Myra Lewinter, Vincent Macaluso, Jennifer Macleod, Ruth Mandel, Jane Mansbridge, Luz Alvarez Martinez, Shireen Miles, Marcia Neiman, Judy Norsigian, Janet Nudleman, Lynda Oswald, Sharon Parker, Roslyn Pulitzer, Marguerite Rawalt, Dusty Roads, Kris Rosenthal, Lorraine Rothman, Bernice Sandler, Kathie Sarachild, Lynn Hecht Schafran, Betty Schlein, Carol

Schmidt, Joanne Schulman, Sylvia Seaman, Sybil Shainwald, Joy Simonson, Eleanor Smeal, Murray Straus, Nancy Stultz, Emily Jane Style, Eileen Thornton, Betsy Warrior, Loretta Webster, Guida West, Danette Wilson, Leslie Wolfe, Denise Fuge Wood, Patrisha Wright, and Laura X. Naturally, any errors in fact or interpretation are solely my responsibility.

At an early stage in the project, Catharine Stimpson gave me advice and encouragement. In addition, I learned an enormous amount as a participant in the 1989 Seminar on Feminist Perspectives on Leadership, Power and Diversity, conducted by Charlotte Bunch at Douglass College, Rutgers University. The women's studies programs at Douglass, Rutgers, and Princeton University were a wonderful source of information and inspiration throughout the time that I was researching the book.

Laurie Crumpacker read early drafts of some sections of the book and made suggestions, and Kay Klotzburger gave me a great deal of valuable advice over the years. Patricia Burns, who helped with the research, brought skill, ingenuity, and immense patience to the task. As press time approached and the whole manuscript needed to be fact-checked to meet a tight deadline, Virginia Stuart pitched in and saw me through the worst of the job; Maggie Sullivan, Caroline Champlin, Teresa Stevens, Kathy Haynie, Linda Provenza, Julie Staats, Margaret Thorpe, and Charlotte Person worked with us. Judith Dzelzkalns helped not only with the checking but also with last-minute research. Laura Waldron and Gary Kramer gave up one of the most beautiful spring weekends in decades to cope with word processing tasks on a rush basis.

I will be forever grateful to my agent, Emilie Jacobson, who believed in the book and worked hard on its behalf in the early 1980s, when many publishers were apparently convinced that the women's movement had run its course and was old news. Marie Arana-Ward, my editor at Simon and Schuster, was thoughtful, insightful, wonderfully supportive, and never cringed (visibly) when I sent her sections of the book that ran almost twice as long as they were supposed to.

I also owe a great deal to the members of my writers' group. Over a period of six years at our bimonthly meetings, they listened to almost every word of the manuscript and made suggestions. The group was my touchstone, and I must thank Anne Barry, Sally Branon, Caroline Champlin, Paula Cullen, Hanna Fox, Janet Gardner, Kay Klotzburger, Irene Lynch, Meg Pinto, Janet Stern, Virginia Stuart, and Maggie Sullivan.

My daugher, Rebecca Davis, launched me on this project originally. As a junior in high school, she began to ask questions about the women's movement. When I realized how little she knew about what life was like for women when I was growing up, and how little she'd been told about the massive effort it had taken to bring women as far as we'd come, I knew I *had* to write this book. By the time it was in its final stages, Rebecca was an editor at a New York publishing house and had become my toughest critic and most sympathetic listener. My son, Jeffrey Davis, listened, too, with an open mind and a sense of humor. (I wish I could have back all the energy I wasted, worrying about what kind of man he'd become, in the days when he was an eight-year-old Super Heroes fan.) My stepdaughter, Tara Tayyabkhan, taught me a lot over the years about how young people perceive the movement; she was often ahead of me in what she knew about issues ranging from pornography to the feminist art world.

Last, but far from least, I want to thank my husband, Mamu Tayyabkhan, who willingly went out on a financial limb with me back in 1985, because he understood how much this book meant to me. He never complained, even when the work took years longer than it was supposed to.

In preparing new material for the 1999 edition, I find myself indebted once again to a number of people who made time in their busy schedules to answer my questions. I am especially grateful to Leslie Wolfe and Laurie Crumpacker for their suggestions. In addition, many thanks to all those I interviewed: Luz Alvarez Martinez, Charon Asetoyer, Ann Baker, Charlotte Bunch, Elizabeth Cavendish, Mary Chung, Debra Dodson, Wilma Espinoza, Dorothy Height, Aileen Hernandez, Patricia Ireland, Rebecca Isaacs, Elaine Kim, Vivien Labaton, Sue Osthoff, Cindy Pearson, Elisa Sanchez, Lynn Hecht Schafran, Julia Scott, Ellie Smeal, Rita Smith, and Bonnie Zimmerman.

Abbreviations Frequently Used

ACLU   American Civil Liberties Union
AIO   Americans for Indian Opportunity
ALSSA   Air Line Stewards and Stewardesses Association
BPW   National Federation of Business and Professional Women's
        Clubs
CACSW   Citizen's Advisory Council on the Status of Women
CAWP   Center for the American Woman and Politics
CWPS   Center for Women Policy Studies
DREDF   Disability Rights Education and Defense Fund
DSIN   Dalkon Shield Information Network
ECOA   Equal Credit Opportunity Act
EEOC   Equal Employment Opportunity Commission
ERA   Equal Rights Amendment
FFHC   Federation of Feminist Health Centers
FRB   Federal Reserve Board
FWHC   Feminist Women's Health Center
HERS   Hysterectomy Educational Resources and Services
ICEA   International Childbirth Education Association
LWV   League of Women Voters
MANA   Mexican American Women's National Association
NACW   National Association of Colored Women
NACWEP   National Advisory Council on Women's Educational
             Programs
NARAL   National Abortion Rights Action League
NAWL   National Association of Women Lawyers
NAWSA   National American Woman Suffrage Association
NBFO   National Black Feminist Organization
NBWHP   National Black Women's Health Project
NCADV   National Coalition Against Domestic Violence
NCNP   National Conference for New Politics
NCNW   National Council of Negro Women

NCWGE   National Coalition for Women and Girls in Eduation
NIWC   National Institute for Women of Color
NJEP   National Judicial Education Program to Promote Equality for
      Women and Men in the Courts
NOW   National Organization for Women
NWHN   National Women's Health Network
NWP   National Woman's Party
NYRF   New York Radical Feminists
NYRW   New York Radical Women
NYWAR   New York Women Against Rape
PCSW   President's Commission on the Status of Women
PEER   Project on Equal Education Rights
SDS   Students for a Democratic Society
SNCC   Student Nonviolent Coordinating Committee
WEAL   Women's Equity Action League
WEEA   Women's Educational Equity Act
WID   World Institute on Disability
YSA   Young Socialist Alliance
YWCA   Young Women's Christian Association

Notes

These notes are intended for readers who want to explore particular subjects in more depth. Most books and some particularly relevant articles are noted here in abbreviated form; see the bibliography for full details. News reports, government documents, and most articles are cited here in full the first time they are mentioned.

introduction

10 For more on recent social movements, see *Social Movements of the Sixties and Seventies*, Jo Freeman, ed.

chapter 1: *The Opening Salvos*

15–25 Story of the American Airlines stewardess union based mostly on interviews with Dusty Roads and Nancy Collins; other sources are noted specifically. All quotes from Roads and Collins are from an interview by the author, 5 August 1985, Los Angeles, CA. Joetta Cunningham also provided background information. For the history of another union's campaign against its airline, see Georgia Panter Nielsen, *From Sky Girl to Flight Attendant*.

17n Stewardesses become "flight attendants": Independent Federation of Flight Attendants, personal communication, 20 May 1991.

17 Details on how stewardesses were hired: Nielsen, 20, 82.

17 ". . . not getting married," from Fredric C. Appel, "Airlines Vie With Cupid for Stewardesses," *New York Times*, 26 April 1965, p. 33.

17 Social pressure to marry described in Betty Friedan, *The Feminine Mystique*, 12. See also interview with Radcliffe President Mary Bunting, "One Woman, Two Lives," *Time*, 3 November 1961, pp. 68–71.

18 ". . . hostess at home," quoted in Appel, "Airlines Vie," *New York Times*, 26 April 1965, p. 33.

18 Fact that fifteen of thirty-eight airlines dismissed stewardesses in their thirties: From Fredric C. Appel, "Unions Want Airlines to Break Age Barrier for Stewardesses," *New York Times*, 8 December 1965, p. 49.

18 ". . . was catch-22." Lynda Oswald, telephone interview by author, 16 June 1985.

19 Stewardesses' secret marriages reported: Tania Long, "Airline Will Rehire 75 Married Stewardesses," *New York Times*, 27 May 1967, p. 62.

19 During EEOC hearings, the IATA (International Air Transport Association) representative kept stressing the stewardess image. Roads, author's interview.

21 Older stewardesses were better cooks, etc.: Art Buchwald, "Age Limit on Stewardesses? Let's Be Adult About This," *Los Angeles Times*, 25 April 1963.

21 Complaint filed: For news report, see Fredric C. Appel, "Unions Want Airlines to Break Age Barrier for Stewardesses," *New York Times*, 8 December 1965, p. 49.

21 ". . . dimensions of the problem." Quoted in "House Panel Hears Complaint of Stewardesses," *New York Times*, 3 September 1965, p. 12.

21 ". . . sore for a month" and ". . . less sensitive after thirty. . . ." Quoted in "House Panel Hears Complaint of Stewardesses," *New York Times*, 3 September 1965, p. 12.

21 Resolution of stewardesses' case in New York reported in "Age Limit on Air Hostesses Upheld," *New York Times*, 26 January 1968, p. 94.

22 Aileen Hernandez described her experience on the EEOC in Aileen C. Hernandez, "E.E.O.C. and the Women's Movement 1965–1975."

23 "unauthorized gesture," Hernandez, 26.

23 ". . . to overthrow sex discrimination." Betty Friedan, *It Changed My Life*, 93.

23 Court injunction against EEOC's stewardess ruling reported in "Judge Bars Ruling on Stewardesses," *New York Times*, 25 February 1967, p. 54.

24 EEOC rulings on the marriage issue described in Nielsen, 86.

24 Congresswoman Martha Griffiths's role in preventing strike at American Airlines: Martha Griffiths, interview by author, Lansing, MI, 3 December 1985.

24 See "Air Stewardesses Win Over-Age Fight," *New York Times*, 10 August 1968, p. 27. Also: "Hostesses Agree to an Airline Pact," *New York Times*, 11 August 1968, p. 74.

24 One of the class-action suits against United dragged on until 1984, when the Supreme Court finally settled it. See "Supreme Court Roundup: Justices to Consider Enforcing of Surgery to Remove a Bullet," *New York Times*, 17 April 1984, p. A17.

24 Later history of flight attendants' challenges to sex discrimination recounted in David Martindale, "Flight Attendants," 65.

25 ". . . smooth enough any more." Lynda Oswald interview.

25 Situation of cabin crew in 1985 described: Martindale, 65–74.

chapter 2: *The Resurgence of Liberal Feminism*

26 ". . . high-button shoes." Robert Coughlan, "Changing Roles in Modern Marriage," *Life*, 24 December 1956, p. 110.

26 Social movements develop out of existing networks: Doug McAdam, *Political Process and the Development of Black Insurgency 1930–1970*, 15.

27 Americans didn't begin to speak of "feminism" until the 1910s; nineteenth-century activists referred to "the woman movement" or "woman's rights." See Nancy F. Cott, *The Grounding of Modern Feminism*, 3.

27 For an account of antifeminism in the 1920s and the Spider-Web Chart, see Cott, 242–67; also Amy Swerdlow, "Women's Activism Undercut," 12–13.

27–8 The "failure" of suffrage described: Cott, 99–114.

28 Proliferation of women's groups in the 1920s described in Cott, 86–97.

28 Reactions of African-American women noted in Leila J. Rupp and Verta Taylor, *Survival in the Doldrums*, 153–54. See also Cott, 69–70.

28 Women's denial of feminism: Rupp and Taylor, 53.

29n ". . . account of sex." Harrison, *On Account of Sex*, 16.

29 For more on the ERA in the 1920s and attitudes of women's groups, see Cott, 120–42. Black women split: Cynthia Harrison, *On Account of Sex: The Politics of Women's Issues 1945–1968*, 11–12.

29–30 The evolution of the debate over equality/difference is described in Hester Eisenstein, "Introduction," in Eisenstein and Jardine, *The Future of Difference*, xv–xxiv. See also: Deborah L. Rhode, ed., *Theoretical Perspectives on Sexual Difference*; Anne Phillips, ed., *Feminism and Equality*. Equality feminism is defended in Wendy Kaminer, *A Fearful Freedom: Women's Flight from Equality*.

30 Ann Barr Snitow coined the term "feminist divide" in a 1989 article that explored the complex issues involved. See Ann Snitow, "Pages from a Gender Diary: Basic Divisions in Feminism," 205–24.

30 Nineteenth-century attitudes to equality/difference are described in Cott, 19–20. See also Elisabeth Griffith, *In Her Own Right: The Life of Elizabeth Cady Stanton*, 205.

30 The "social housekeeping" argument is discussed in Ethel Klein, *Gender Politics: From Consciousness to Mass Politics*, 29–30.

30–1 Old enmities that fueled dispute over ERA described in Cott, 59–60, 122; Rupp and Taylor, 62.

31 ". . . vigor of the race." *Muller* v. *Oregon*, 208 U.S. 412 (1908). See Leslie Friedman Goldstein, *The Constitutional Rights of Women*, 8–22.

31 Protective laws in 1925: Cott, 135.

31 Dispute between the NWP and other women's organizations over ERA is described in detail in Cott, 120–40.

31–2 Wisconsin ruling on employing women in legislature: Cott, 120–21, 124–25.

32 ". . . in our everyday life." Quoted in Rupp and Taylor, 60.

32 For a brief discussion of pros and cons of the protective laws, see Norma Basch, "The Emerging Legal History of Women in the United States," *Signs* 12, no. 1 (Autumn 1986): 113–15.

32–3 ERA and protective laws in the 1940s: Harrison, *On Account of Sex*, 15–23, 44.

33 History of the Status Bill: Harrison, *On Account of Sex*, 26–30; Rupp and Taylor, 62–63. For history of the Hayden rider: Harrison, *On Account of Sex*, 30–33. Also Rawalt, "The Equal Rights Amendment," 52–54. Celler's opposition: Harrison, *On Account of Sex*, 32, 205.

33 ". . . or social function." Quoted in Harrison, *On Account of Sex*, 27; Rupp and Taylor, 62.

33 ". . . persons of the female sex." Marguerite Rawalt, "The Equal Rights Amendment," 53.

33–4 Description of the NWP in the 1960s in Carl M. Brauer, "Women Activists, Southern Conservatives, and the Prohibition of Sex Discrimination in Title VII of the 1964 Civil Rights Act," 37–56. See also Rupp and Taylor, 38–40.

34 Activists of 1960 described: Rupp and Taylor, 45–52. BPW became pro-ERA in 1937, the General Federation of Women's Clubs in 1943. Other prominent pro-ERA organizations included Zonta International, the National Association of Women Lawyers (NAWL), and the American Medical Women's Association (AMWA). See Rupp and Taylor, 59. BPW's role: John T. Mason, Jr. (interviewer, oral history), "The Reminiscences of Marguerite Rawalt," 369–70.

34 Complaints about younger women noted: Rupp and Taylor, 81.

34–8 The history of the Kennedy Commission is presented in Katherine Pollak Ellickson, "The President's Commission on the Status of Women." Also, Esther Peterson, "The Kennedy Commission," 21–34; Rupp and Taylor, 166–74; Harrison, *On Account of Sex*, 109–65; Judith Paterson, *Be Somebody*, 130–45.

34 ". . . hurt working women." Peterson, 25.

34 ". . . agitation about the 'equal rights amendment.' " Quoted in Harrison, "A 'New Frontier,' " 638.

35 For background on Kennedy Commission, see Rupp and Taylor, 169; Harrison, *On Account of Sex*, 115–21; Harrison, "A 'New Frontier,' " 638–39. Also the Commission's report: President's Commission on the Status of Women, *American Women*, 85; referred to hereafter as PCSW report.

35–6 Activities of the Committee on Civil and Political Rights and Murray's proposed compromise described in Harrison, *On Account of Sex*, 125–30.

36 For Rawalt's description of the Commission's final meeting, see Mason, 372–76; Paterson, 143–44.

36 ". . . not *now* be sought." PCSW report, 45.

36 Assessment of the Commission's impact on ERA: Harrison, *On Account of Sex*, 131–34, 137, 183–84, 202–5.

36 ". . . a lonely time." Marguerite Rawalt, interview by author, Washington, D.C., 19 November 1985.

36 ". . . in tennis shoes." Catherine East, interview by author, Arlington, VA, 23 November 1985.

36–7 ". . . the art of the possible." Peterson, 29.

37n Gap between women's and men's pay in 1960: PCSW report, 38. Pay gap was bigger in 1960 than in 1956, when women earned 63.3 percent of what men did, and it would continue to grow—in 1966, women would be paid only 58.2 percent on the male dollar: See Harrison, *On Account of Sex*, 90–91, 171.

37 Sales of PCSW report noted in Mason, 366.

37 Proposal that marriage be considered an economic partnership: PCSW report, 47.

37 ". . . cook the meals." Rawalt, author's interview.

37 Recommendations on child care, etc.: PCSW report, 20, 37, 43, 30.

37 ". . . intensive consciousness-raising." Quoted in Rupp and Taylor, 173.

37 Kennedy's directive to federal agencies reported: PCSW report, 32. Also Catherine East, author's interview.

37–8 Equal Pay Act: Harrison, *On Account of Sex*, 89–105. See also Fern S. Ingersoll, "Former Congresswomen Look Back," 201–3.

37–8 PCSW accomplishments summarized in Harrison, *On Account of Sex*, 159–65, 182.

38 Catherine East's comments on PCSW from interview by author. For more on state status of women commissions and Citizens' Advisory Council, see Judith Hole and Ellen Levine, *Rebirth of Feminism*, 24–25. Also Catherine East, "Newer Commissions," 35–44; and Irene Tinker, "The Federal Government Considers the Status of Women," 17–20. Jo Freeman, *The Politics of Women's Liberation*, 52–53. Myra Marx Ferree and Beth B. Hess, *Controversy and Coalition: The New Feminist Movement*, 53–54.

39–40 The history of the NWP's role in the passage of Title VII is recounted in Brauer, 37–56.

39 ". . . will of steel," "Master in the House," *Newsweek*, 20 January 1964, pp. 19–20.

39 ". . . in modern times." Don Oberdorfer, " 'Judge' Smith Moves With Deliberate Drag," *New York Times Magazine*, 12 January 1964, p. 13.

40 Griffiths's strategy noted in D. A. Robinson, "Two Movements in Pursuit of Equal Employment Opportunity," 413–33. Also, Martha Griffiths, " 'Make No Heroines' May Be Newspapers' Attitude," *Press Woman*, November 1985, p. 7; Martha Griffiths, author's interview; Fern S. Ingersoll, interview with Martha W. Griffiths for Former Members of Congress.

40 ". . . to leave Congress." Griffiths, " 'Make No Heroines,' " 8.

40 How congressional careers were made: See Rochelle Jones and Peter Woll, *The Private World of Congress*, 27. Also Ingersoll, interview with Griffiths, 63.

40–1 Description of floor debate on civil rights bill, strategies of both sides: Richard L. Lyons, "Long House Wrangle On Fair Employment Puts Off Rights Vote," *Washington Post*, 9 February 1964, p. A1. Fate of Dowdy's amendments from Brauer, 8. See also Caroline Bird, *Born Female*, 1–7.

41-3 The debate in the House on the sex amendment is recorded in U.S. Congress, *Congressional Record*, 1964, 2577–84.

41 ". . . the majority sex" and ". . . the minority sex." Sex amendment, *Congressional Record*, 2577.

41 ". . . especially in this election year." Sex amendment, *Congressional Record*, 2577.

42 ". . . 'Yes, dear.' " Sex amendment, *Congressional Record*, 2577.

42 Rawalt's observations: Mason, 395.

42 ". . . you're lost." Quoted in Ingersoll, interview, 74.

42 ". . . would have proved it." Sex amendment, *Congressional Record*, 2578.

42 ". . . most of them, and listened." Mason, 395.

43 ". . . with no rights at all." Sex amendment, *Congressional Record*, 2579.

43 Griffiths believed legislators gave no thought to black women: Martha Griffiths, unpublished article, included in microfilm with Ingersoll interview, 3.

43 ". . . against the Negro," "clutter up" and ". . . who today support it." Sex amendment, *Congressional Record*, 2581.

43–4 Senate filibuster and behind-the-scenes activity described in Robinson, 417–418; Brauer, 52–55; Paterson, 154; Harrison, 176–81.

44 ". . . voted against [the amendment]," Martha Griffiths, unpublished article, 13.

44 Rawalt's observation that sex amendment should be called the Griffiths amendment: Rawalt, author's interview.

44 Griffiths didn't know NWP had been lobbying Smith: Griffiths, author's interview.

45 Brauer on chivalry: 45, 56.

45 " '. . . offered it as a joke.' " Griffiths, author's interview.

45 ". . . and repeated them." Martha Griffiths, unpublished article, 13.

45–6 How EEOC operated described in Robinson, 421–22; Harrison, *On Account of Sex*, 187–91; Hernandez, 1–9. Sex discrimination complaints summarized: Brauer, 1.

46 ". . . out of wedlock." Also comment about secretaries: Griffiths quoted Edelsberg in her speech to the House, 20 June 1966. U.S. Congress, Congresswoman Griffiths on the EEOC, *Congressional Record* 112: 13689–94.

46 "bunny law." See, for example, "De-Sexing the Job Market," editorial, *New York Times*, 21 August 1965, p. 20.

46 White House conference reported in "Problems on Job Rights of Women," *U.S. News & World Report*, 30 August 1965, p. 77. See also Bird, 13; Hole and Levine, 34.

46n Playboy Clubs' male rabbits reported: William E. Geist, "About New York," *New York Times*, 2 October 1985, B3. Also Michael Gross, "Big Cities Kiss Playboy Bunnies Goodbye," *New York Times*, 27 June 1986, p. A26.

46–7 EEOC guidelines reported in "The Official Word on Job Rights for Women," *U.S. News & World Report*, 22 November 1965, p. 90. See also Bird, 13. The EEOC's early guidelines and opinions are in its *Digest of Legal Interpretations Issued or Adopted by the Commission*, 9 October 1965 through 31 December 1965. Citizens' Advisory Council suggestions incorporated into guidelines: *Report on Progress in 1965 on the Status of Women*, 2nd Annual Report of Interdepartmental Committee and Citizens' Advisory Council on the Status of Women (Washington, D.C.: 1965), 25–26.

47 EEOC's enforcement powers: Robinson, 421; Freeman, *Politics*, 179.

47 ". . . least of all?" Martha Griffiths, unpublished article, 17.

47 Griffiths's speech, reprinted, used by East: Griffiths and East (1985), author's interviews; Paterson, 164.

chapter 3: The Founding of NOW

50 For a contemporary profile of Betty Friedan, see Jane Howard, "You're a Freak If You Have a Brain," *Life*, 1 November 1963, pp. 84–88.

50 Friedan's Smith College survey described: Betty Friedan, *The Feminine Mystique*, 2, 7, 345.

50 The mystique defined: Friedan, *Mystique*, 37.

50n "Cult of true womanhood": Rupp and Taylor, 14.

51 ". . . the diapers" and ". . . man and boy," quoted in Friedan, *Mystique*, 53–54.

51 On the collapse of the breadwinner ethic: Barbara Ehrenreich, *The Hearts of Men: American Dreams and the Flight from Commitment*, especially 11–12, 20, 37–39.

51 ". . . a parasite. . . ." Ehrenreich, 100.

51 *The Feminine Mystique* was published during a New York City newspaper strike and received little attention at first from the press or reviewers; personal communication from George Brockway, Friedan's editor.

51 Photos of Friedan accompanied profile by Jane Howard.

51–2 Friedan describes her ostracism: *Mystique*, 366. Recommends nurseries, maternity leave: 360–61.

53 ". . . makeshift, hassles." Friedan, *Changed*, 60.

53–4 Friedan's account of the conception of NOW: Friedan, *Changed*, 77–83. See also Paterson, 165–66. Catherine East's recollections: Interview by author, 1985.

53 BPW's refusal to become an NAACP for women: Hole and Levine, 81. Its membership in 1966: National Federation of Business and Professional Women's Clubs, *1990 Handbook of Policies and Procedures* (Washington, D.C.: National Federation of Business and Professional Women's Clubs, 1990).

53 ". . . point of impatience." Friedan, *Changed*, 81.

53 ". . . women I had met," Friedan, *Changed*, 80.

54 ". . . shut off debate." Quoted in Mason, 407.

54 ". . . mainstream of American society," Friedan, *Changed*, 83.

55 ". . . between 1965 and 1975." Aileen C. Hernandez, "E.E.O.C. and the Women's Movement 1965–1975," 9.

56 NOW's founding conference: Friedan, *Changed*, 84–86, 95–96; Paterson, 169–170; Hole and Levine, 84–87. Other sources: Muriel Fox, author's interview, Tappan, NY, 8 July 1985.

56–7 NOW would become one of the largest feminist organizations: See Joyce Gelb and Marian Lief Palley, *Women and Public Policies*, 48–50. NOW as a select group: Paterson, 167. Fact that 126 of founding members lived in Wisconsin: Kathryn Clarenbach, personal communication, 24 April 1991.

57 Accounts of NOW's first year: Friedan, *Changed*, 85, 92–103; Paterson, 171; Mason, 450–54; Freeman, *Politics*, 75–80; Hole and Levine, 86–88, 405. Also, author's interviews with Rawalt, Fox, East (1985).

57 ". . . power than they actually had." East, author's interview, 1985.

58 ". . . a very good idea," and ". . . had really counted correctly," Fox, author's interview.

58 ". . . marching millions." East, author's interview, 1985.

58 ". . . own priorities. . . ." Friedan, *Changed*, 95.

58–9 ". . . they believed in." Jennifer Macleod, interview by author, Princeton Junction, NJ, 28 May 1985.

59 Growth of female labor force described in William Chafe, *The American Woman*, 218–19. Job discrimination: Bird, 61–83; Friedan, *Changed*, 87–91. Quotas: See Pamela Roby, "Institutional Barriers to Women Students in Higher Education," in *Academic Women on the Move*, Alice S. Rossi and Ann Calderwood, eds., especially 43–44; Cynthia Fuchs Epstein, *Woman's Place* (Berkeley: University of California Press, 1971), 60; Mary Roth Walsh, *Doctors Wanted: No Women Need Apply* (New Haven: Yale University Press, 1977), 242–43. Married women denied credit: See chapter 8. Pregnant women fired: chapter 14.

59n Status and attitudes of African-American women: See Paula Giddings, *When and Where I Enter*, 299.

59–61 Details of NOW's campaign to change the want ads from: Jean Faust, interview by author, New York City, 7 November 1985; Noreen Connell, interview by author, New York City, 15 June 1985; also author's interviews with Muriel Fox; Jennifer Macleod. Written sources: "Special Edition #2: NOW Vs. Segregated Help-Wanted Ads," *NOW Acts* 2, no. 1 (Winter/Spring 1969): 24–27, at Schlesinger Library, Cambridge, MA. "Accuse EEOC of Double-Standard Discrimination Against Women," NOW press release in the files of Jean Faust at Schlesinger Library, Cambridge, MA. Gerald H. F. Gardner, "Want-Ads Tomorrow"; Harrison, 187–91; Hole and Levine, 40–44; Robinson, 423–24; Mason, 398–400; Griffiths, unpublished article; Friedan, *Changed*, 94; Freeman, *Politics*, 77–79. Financial hardship didn't amount to much: "Memo from: Don Gross, Research Analyst in Advertising Sales for Newsday," dated 31 July 1969, reported that there was "no effect on the employment classified lineage" after *Newsday* integrated its male and female want ad columns; in Jean Faust's files.

61 Statement about the tyranny of women noted by Jean Faust at the time; author's interview. In court hearings, Charles H. Volk, attorney for the *Pittsburgh Press*, raised the specter of unisex bathrooms, etc. "NOW vs. The Pittsburgh Press," booklet (Pittsburgh, PA: Know Inc., 1971), 11.

61 News stories and editorials complaining about unisex clothing and integrated classifieds excerpted in memo from Jean Faust to Grace Jackson and Jerry Fox, dated 22 October 1968, Faust's files.

61–2 For a summary of protective labor laws in the late 1960s, see Thomas H. Barnard, "The Conflict Between State Protective Legislation and Federal Laws Prohibiting Sex Discrimination," 41–43. The first article by feminist lawyers dealing with Title VII: Pauli Murray and Mary Eastwood, "Jane Crow and the Law," published in 1965 in *George Washington Law Review* and reprinted in *Radical Feminism*, ed. Anne Koedt, Ellen Levine, and Anita Rapone, 165–77.

62 Details of how NOW legal committee operated: Marguerite Rawalt, author's interview; also Mason, 456–57, 685–86.

62 ". . . wasn't there any more." Mason, 412.

62–4 Lorena Weeks case: Marguerite Rawalt, author's interview. See also Barnard, 54–55, 58–59; Mason, 423–26; Eleanor Humes Haney, *A Feminist Legacy*, 76–77; Paterson, 184, 195; Hole and Levine, 36–37. News report of victory: "Woman Wins Job Suit," *New York Times*, 25 April 1971, p. 32. The case citation: *Weeks* v. *Southern Bell Tel. & Tel. Co.*, 408 F.2nd 228 (5th Cir. 1969).

63 ". . . big law firms," Rawalt, "Equal Rights Amendment," 61.

63 ". . . equal footing," quoted in Rawalt, "Equal Rights Amendment," 61.

64 Rawalt's comment on male lawyers: Mason, 522.

64 For more on the EEOC's handling of complaints involving the state protective laws, see Hernandez, 15–20.

64 ". . . civil rights groups . . ." Hernandez, 20.

64 ". . . because of Betty Harragan," Fox, author's interview.

64–6 The Jane Daniel case: Phineas Indritz, telephone interview by author, 2 October 1985; also author's interview with Rawalt. See also Phineas Indritz and Marguerite Rawalt, "Brief of American Veterans Committee, Inc. (AVC) and National Organization for Women, Inc. (NOW), as Amici Curiae for Jane Daniel" in the Supreme Court of Pennsylvania, Eastern District, January Term, 1968, Nos. 150 and 187. Also, James J. Calloway, "Constitutional Law—Indeterminate Sentences for Women," *Arkansas Law Review* 22: 524–30; Hole and Levine, 406–7; and Marguerite Rawalt, testimony at hearings on ERA, 5 May 1970, in *Women and the Equal Rights Amendment*, Catharine Stimpson, ed., Hearings, U.S. Congress, Senate Subcommittee on Constitutional Amendments, 91st Congress, 2nd Session (New York: Bowker, 1972), 79.

65 ". . . of prolonged confinement." Katherine Bement Davis, "Treatment for Women Offenders," 4 *Journal of Criminal Law and Criminology*, 402, 403, 407–8 (1913), quoted in Indritz/Rawalt brief.

65–6 ". . . severely than men." Indritz, author's interview.

66 ". . . the same offense. . . ." Marguerite Rawalt testimony, ERA hearings, 1970, p. 79.

66–7 NOW's 1967 conference: From author's interviews with Fox, Rawalt, Faust. See also Friedan, *Changed*, 97–106; Mason, 460–66.

66 ". . . would break apart." Fox, author's interview.

66 "as God and motherhood," Fox, author's interview.

67 ". . . sat the United Automobile Workers." Mason, 461–62.

67 ". . . narrow job issues." Friedan, *Changed*, 105.

67 ". . . courageous stand. . . ." Fox, author's interview.

67 ". . . views and actions" and "patient, determined and diplomatic." Boyer quoted in "WEAL: Ten Years of Action for Equity," program for WEAL's 1978 Conference.

68 WEAL's founding described in "WEAL: Ten Years." Also: Eileen P. Thornton, interview by author, Princeton, NJ, 17 November 1985; author's interviews with Fox, Faust; Mason, 500–503; Hole and Levine, 95–98.

68 ". . . dignity—for all women. . . ." Friedan, *Changed*, 106.

chapter 4:   The Birth of Women's Liberation

69   Radical feminists a minority: See Alice Echols, *Daring to Be Bad: Radical Feminism in America 1967–1974*, 3.

69n   Feminism in Europe: Joyce Gelb, *Feminism and Politics*, 5–6.

69n   New Left: See Todd Gitlin, *The Whole World Is Watching*, 293.

71   For a brief biography of Ella Baker, see Charles Payne, "Ella Baker and Models of Social Change," *Signs* 14, no. 4 (Summer 1989): 885–99. Also Mary King, *Freedom Song*, 455–56.

72   Radical equality in SNCC: See King, 280–82, 306. Racial violence in the South: Doug McAdam, *Freedom Summer*, 32.

72n   Jane Mansbridge provides a brief history of participatory democracy in the Movement (she prefers the term *unitary democracy*). See Jane J. Mansbridge, *Beyond Adversary Democracy*, 290, 376n.

72   ". . . have ever encountered." King, 281.

72–4   The story of Freedom Summer is told in McAdam, *Freedom Summer*; see especially 33–39; Sara Evans, *Personal Politics*, 69–74; Harvard Sitkoff, *The Struggle for Black Equality*, 167–79; Emily Stoper, "The Student Non-Violent Coordinating Committee," 320–34.

72   ". . . in their lives." Evans, 82.

72n   Violent incidents during Freedom Summer: McAdam, *Freedom Summer*, 96.

73   Black women's experiences during Freedom Summer: Giddings, 261, 278, 284, 314–15; Jacqueline Jones, *Labor of Love, Labor of Sorrow*, 279–84.

73   Experience of white female volunteers: Giddings, 302; J. Jones, 283; Evans, 54; McAdam, 59–60, 107.

73   Black women's attitudes: At various times, Frances Beal, Ruby Doris Smith Robinson, Cynthia Washington, Kathleen Cleaver, and Angela Davis all spoke out against male dominance in SNCC—see Jones, 312–14; Giddings, 314–15.

73–4   ". . . other than female." Cynthia Washington, "We Started from Different Ends of the Spectrum," *Southern Exposure* 4 (Winter 1977), reprinted in Evans, 238–240.

74   Sexual relations during Freedom Summer: McAdam, 93, 106.

74   SNCC's problems after Freedom Summer: McAdam, 120–24. Giddings, 296–97.

74–5   The Waveland retreat and the King-Hayden paper: King, 442–53.

74–5   ". . . are to the Negro." King, 445; paper reprinted, 567–69.

74n   ". . . equal experience. . . ." King, 567.

75   ". . . peopled by women. . . ." King, 459.

75   King's remarks on purpose of King-Hayden position paper: King, 458–60.

75   ". . . better society itself." James Forman, *The Making of Black Revolutionaries*, 425; quoted in Echols, 32–33.

75   Hunger to be part of something bigger: McAdam, 137.

76   SNCC's turn toward black power: McAdam, 117. New Left: See Todd Gitlin, *The Sixties: Years of Hope, Days of Rage;* or for a brief account, Myra Marx Ferree and Beth B. Hess, *Controversy and Coalition: The New Feminist Movement*, 59–62. Role of women in SDS: Evans, 108, 139–41, 153–55. Explosive growth of SDS: Gitlin, *Watching*, 78–123.

76–7   The King-Hayden memo is recalled in King, 456–58. Reprinted, King, 571–74.

77   ". . . movement would develop." King, 458.

77   ". . . institutionalized by law." King, 560. "volitional," King, 461.

77   Workshops on the "woman question": Evans, 186.

77   NCPC convention described in Evans, 195–99; Forman, 497; Hole and Levine, 112–14; Gitlin, *The Sixties*, 245.

77   Growth of women's liberation in Chicago and elsewhere: Echols, 69; Freeman, *Politics*, 59; Hole and Levine, 114–15.

78   Details on formation of earliest women's lib groups in Freeman, "On the Origins of Social Movements," 21; Evans, 201, 207; Hole and Levine, 119–21.

78–9   The Jeannette Rankin Brigade demonstration: See Shulamith Firestone, "The Jeannette Rankin Brigade: Woman Power?" in New York Radical Women, *Notes From the First Year* (hereafter called *Notes 1*), 18–19. Also Marilyn Salzmann Webb,

"Call for a Spring Conference," *Voice of the Women's Liberation Movement* 1, March 1968, p. 4; Echols, 54–59; Hole and Levine, 117–19.

78 "tearful and passive," Firestone, "Rankin Brigade," 18.

78 "so that we can have independent lives." Kathie Amatniek, "Funeral Oration for the Burial of Traditional Womanhood," in NYRW, *Notes 1*, 20–22. (Kathie Amatniek later changed her name to Kathie Sarachild.)

78 "Sisterhood is powerful." Firestone, "Rankin Brigade," 18.

78–9 Groups and factions formed after Rankin Brigade demonstration: Evans, 209; Hole and Levine, 118–19. Note that some women who belonged to groups considered to be "politico" objected to the term, though it was acceptable to others; personal communication, Susan Brownmiller.

79 *Voice of the Women's Liberation Movement:* Chicago: Voice of the Women's Liberation Movement, available on microfilm as part of the Herstory series. The "Florida paper": Beverly Jones and Judith Brown, "Toward a Female Liberation Movement," was presented at the Sandy Springs meeting in August 1968 and widely distributed afterward. The Florida paper is available from Redstockings (see bibliography).

79–80 The Sandy Springs meeting: Echols, 104–8. See Echols, 369–77, for a partial transcript of the discussion over whether to contact radical black women.

80 Thanksgiving conference: Echols, 111–13; Hole and Levine, 130.

80 ". . . the white antiwar movement" and ". . . mistakes came later." Charlotte Bunch, interview by author, New Brunswick, NJ, 9 January 1991.

81 Fission in New York women's lib groups: Echols, 96–101, 186–97, 388.

81 Regional priorities in women's lib groups suggested by Bunch, author's interview.

81–2 For more on the division between politicos and radical feminists, see Hole and Levine, 109, 116, 121–22; Echols, 51–101 and 314, n. 2. Politico groups also had nonsocialist members: Kris Rosenthal, personal communication. Some radical feminists were strong socialists: Kathie Sarachild, personal communication. Radical feminist argument for a separate women's movement: Barbara Leon, "Separate to Integrate," in Redstockings, *Feminist Revolution*, 152–57.

82 "invisible audience": Marlene Dixon, "On Women's Liberation," *Radical America*, February 1970, p. 28, cited in Echols, 3.

82–3 Beginnings of women's liberation in Boston: Nancy Hawley, interview by author, Boston, MA, 2 June 1986.

82 ". . . worry about *that!*" Nancy Hawley, letter circulated to friends, 8 October 1970; recounts the history of the women's movement in Boston.

82 ". . . raised for me." Hawley, author's interview.

82–3 "about us, as women" and ". . . left feeling high." Hawley letter.

83 "just something you did" and ". . . had reached home." Hawley, author's interview.

83–4 Early history of Female Liberation Front: Betsy Warrior, telephone interview by author, 13 June 1986.

83 ". . . people of all ages . . ." Ad from Betsy Warrior's files. First meeting was on 18 July 1968.

83 ". . . what it was like." Warrior, author's interview.

83 The first issue of *No More Fun and Games: A Journal of Female Liberation* came out in September 1968 and was untitled; the name was adopted with the second issue, the following February. Some back copies available from: Archives, The Cambridge Women's Center, 46 Pleasant St., Cambridge, MA 02139.

84 ". . . like a circus," Warrior, author's interview.

84 ". . . made an impression." Hawley letter.

84 Editorial: "What Do You Women Want?" *No More Fun and Games*, Issue 2 (February 1969): 4–12.

84 ". . . their own doubts." Warrior, author's interview.

84 ". . . hadn't surfaced before." Hawley, author's interview.

84–5 Thanksgiving conference and growth of women's lib in Boston described: Nancy Hawley, author's interview; Hawley letter.

85 Spring, 1969, conference in Boston: Hawley letter; Kris Rosenthal, telephone interview by author, 21 May 1986.

85 ". . . bow after the movements." Julie Baumgold, "You've Come a Long Way, Baby," *New York* magazine, 9 June 1969, p. 27.

85 Karate's fringe benefits: "On Self-Defense," *No More Fun and Games*, Issue 6. (May 1973): 148–80.

85 Rush to join Cell 16: Warrior, author's interview.

85–7 Organizing of Bread and Roses: Rosenthal, author's interview. Also Kristine M. Rosenthal, "Women in Transition: An Ethnography of a Women's Liberation Organization as a Case Study of Personal and Cultural Change" (doctoral thesis, graduate school of education, Harvard University, 1972). Also Hawley, author's interview, and Hawley letter; Jane Mansbridge, interview by author, Princeton, NJ, 9 May 1986; Diane Balser, interview by author, Boston, MA, 2 June 1986.

86 ". . . coming and coming." Hawley letter.

87 "some pieces of paper" and ". . . brand-new things." Mansbridge, author's interview.

87 The first and most successful of the women's unions was CWLU, the Chicago Women's Liberation Union. See Echols, 136–37.

87 Politicos in the academic world: Bunch, author's interview.

88 " '. . . consciousness some more.' " Kathie Sarachild, "Consciousness-Raising: A Radical Weapon," in Redstockings, 144.

88 C-R as key to a mass movement: See Kathie Sarachild, "A Program for Feminist 'Consciousness Raising,' " in Shulamith Firestone and Anne Koedt, eds., *Notes From the Second Year: Women's Liberation—the Major Writings of the Radical Feminists* (hereafter *Notes 2*), 78–80.

88 Influence of Frantz Fanon, etc.: See Josephine Donovan, *Feminist Theory*, 137, 144. Similarly, Karl Marx wrote of "false consciousness"; see Alison Jaggar, *Feminist Politics and Human Nature*, 56–58.

88–9 Purpose of C-R: Sarachild, personal communication, May 1991; Kathie Sarachild, "Consciousness-Raising: A Radical Weapon," in Redstockings, 144–50.

89 How C-R session led to first speakout: Kathie Sarachild, personal communication (letter to author), 15 July 1986.

89 Founding of Redstockings: In 1968, women flocked to join NYRW. Meetings grew chaotic, partly because they now drew fifty to one hundred women. Late in 1968, the members voted to divide NYRW into three groups by drawing lots. The result left many dissatisfied, particularly some of the radical feminists who were split up among the new offshoots. NYRW became simply an umbrella for a growing number of groups, and six months later it died. See Echols, 96–101.

89n Origins of the name, Redstockings: Echols, 140.

89 Hearing on abortion reform: See Edith Evans Asbury, "Women Break Up Abortion Hearing," *New York Times*, 14 February 1969, p. 42. Sarachild, author's interview.

89–90 Abortion speakout: See Susan Brownmiller, " 'Sisterhood Is Powerful,' " *New York Times Magazine*, 15 March 1970, p. 27. Also Susan Brownmiller, "Red Stocking's Rap," *Village Voice*, 14 April 1969, p. 1.

90 Why the personal is political: Carol Hanisch, "The Personal Is Political," *Notes 2*, 76.

90 ". . . the persecution of women": Ti-Grace Atkinson, *Amazon Odyssey*, 43.

90 Protest at marriage license bureau: Echols, 170. For The Feminists' analysis of sexism, see "The Feminists: A Political Organization to Annihilate Sex Roles" in Firestone and Koedt, *Notes 2*, 114–18. The pro-woman line on marriage: Pat Mainardi, "The Marriage Question," in Redstockings, 120–22.

90n Kathie Sarachild's name change noted in Redstockings, 209.

91 ". . . what pleases men. . . ." Anne Koedt, "The Myth of the Vaginal Orgasm," in Firestone and Koedt, *Notes 2*, 37–38.

91 ". . . need to be changed." Friedan, *Changed*, 162.

91 "the male mystique" and ". . . being a man." Jones and Brown, 372.

91 Sex roles: Kate Millett, "Sexual Politics: A Manifesto for Revolution," in *Radical Feminism*, ed. Anne Koedt, Ellen Levine, and Anita Rapone, 365–67.

91 ". . . educate the chicken farmer," Marge Piercy, "The Grand Coolie Damn," in *Sisterhood Is Powerful*, Robin Morgan, ed., 482.

91 Male supremacy the root: For an overview of radical feminist theory, see Hester Eisenstein, *Contemporary Feminist Thought;* also Donovan, 141–69.

92 ". . . advantage of that. . . ." Ti-Grace Atkinson, "Radical Feminism," in *Notes 2*, 34.

92 ". . . child-rearing roles." Shulamith Firestone, *The Dialectic of Sex,* 72.

92 ". . . every means available. . . ." Firestone, *Dialectic,* 206.

92 For a concise summary of how feminists' positions on equality-versus-difference changed during the second wave, see Hester Eisenstein, *Thought,* xi–xii.

92 The pro-woman line: See Barbara Leon, "Consequences of the Conditioning Line," in Redstockings, 66–70. Sarachild, author's interview.

92 ". . . but to change men." Redstockings Manifesto, in Firestone and Koedt, *Notes 2*, 113.

chapter 5: Experiments in Radical Equality

95 Left-wing collectives: Jane J. Mansbridge, *Beyond Adversary Democracy,* 21.

95 Participatory democracy in SDS: Mansbridge, *Democracy,* 20–21; Gitlin, *The Sixties,* 172.

95 Mansbridge's comments on participatory democracy: Mansbridge, *Democracy,* 8–10, 20.

96 Size, structure of NOW-New York: Jean Faust, author's interview.

96 ". . . didn't believe in." Fox, author's interview.

96 ". . . sexy style," Marylin Bender, "The Feminists Are on the March Once More," *New York Times,* 14 December 1967, p. 56.

96 ". . . did unearth." Friedan, *Changed,* 109.

96–7 Atkinson's proposal for changing NOW described in Friedan, *Changed,* 109.

97 For Atkinson's account of the struggle over NOW-New York's bylaws, see Atkinson, *Amazon Odyssey,* 9–11. Also: "Excerpt from Minutes of NOW Board Meeting, 9/14/68" for discussion about whether NOW-New York's executive committee should be restructured; letter from Marguerite Rawalt to Ivy Bottini of the New York chapter, dated 9/18/68; minutes of the general membership meeting, NOW-New York, dated 17 October 1968; all in Jean Faust's files.

97 ". . . leadership positions." Faust, author's interview.

97 Atkinson's group was originally called the October 17th Movement to commemorate the battle within NOW, but was later renamed. See Echols, 167–69; also "The Feminists: A Political Organization to Annihilate Sex Roles," in Firestone and Koedt, *Notes 2*, 113–16.

97 ". . . world at large." Atkinson's letter of resignation, dated 18 October 1968, reprinted in Atkinson, 10.

98n Women's management style: Marilyn Loden, *Feminine Leadership or How to Succeed in Business Without Being One of the Boys.*

98 McCarthy era: See Hole and Levine, 160. The classic contemporary analysis of trashing: Joreen (Jo Freeman), "Trashing: The Dark Side of Sisterhood," *Ms,* April 1976, p.45. See also Kate Millett, *Flying,* 503–14.

98-9 For an analysis of media stars in the civil rights movement and New Left, see Gitlin, *Watching,* 146–79.

98 ". . . line about elitism." Kate Millett, *Flying,* 92–93.

99 ". . . incompetent in your own life." Quoted in Pauline B. Bart and Melinda Bart Schlesinger, "Collective Work and Self-Identity: The Effect of Working in a Feminist Illegal Abortion Collective," in *Workplace Democracy and Social Change,* ed. Lindenfeld and Whitt, 139–53.

99 ". . . open inside me. . . ." Morgan, *Going Too Far,* 120.

99 Story of *Rat:* Morgan, *Going,* 115–20.

99–100 Group process described in Jo Freeman, "The Tyranny of Structurelessness."

100 ". . . had articles printed." Susan Brownmiller, interview by author, New York City, 20 April 1987.

100 ". . . setbacks frequent." Joreen (Jo Freeman), "Trashing," 97.

100 "horizontal hostilities." Kennedy used the phrase, for example, in " 'It's Damn Slick Out There' " in Sohnya Sayres et al., eds., *The 60s Without Apology*, 352.

100 " . . . energy than anything." Brownmiller, author's interview.

100–3 History of the *Our Bodies, Ourselves* collective from author's interview with Nancy Hawley, Judy Norsigian, Vilunya Diskin, Boston, MA, 3 June 1986. All quotes by Hawley, Norsigian, and Diskin are from that interview. See also Wendy Coppedge Sanford, "Working Together, Growing Together: A Brief History of the Boston Women's Health Book Collective," *Heresies* 2, no. 3 (1979): 83–92. Judy Norsigian and Wendy Coppedge Sanford, "Ten Years in the 'Our Bodies, Ourselves' Collective," *Radcliffe Quarterly*, December 1979, pp. 16–18. "Going Strong: Boston Women's Health Book Collective," *Women and Environments International Newsletter* 2, no. 2 (Fall 1978): 1–5.

101 *Our Bodies, Ourselves* was revised and reprinted in 1984: The Boston Women's Health Book Collective, *The New Our Bodies, Ourselves: A Book By and For Women*.

103 Women are good at relationships: Mansbridge, author's interview.

103 ". . . wasn't transferable," Bunch, author's interview.

103–4 History of *Quest*: Bunch, author's interview. Also Bunch, *Passionate Politics*, 132, 230–39.

104 ". . . to other people," and ". . . they developed there." Bunch, author's interview.

104 On empowerment: See Bunch, 122–33.

chapter 6: The Media and the Movement

106 For more on deradicalization of social movements, see Gitlin, *Watching*, 291–292. Also: David Bouchier, "The Deradicalisation of Feminism."

107 ". . . ludicrous 'beauty' standards. . . ." From "No More Miss America!" flyer describing the proposed protest; Jean Faust's files.

107 Miss America protest: For a good, firsthand report, see Judith Duffett, "WLM vs. Miss America," *Voice of the Women's Liberation Movement* (October 1968): 1; Echols, 92–102; Kathie Sarachild, "The First Whack at the Miss America Edifice," *Newsday*, 12 September 1988, p. 89.

107 Bra-burning as a media invention: See Joanne Foley Martin, "Confessions of a Non-Bra-Burner," *Chicago Journalism Review* (July 1971): 11. An article in *Playboy* reported that "The demonstrators publicly remove[d] and burn[ed] their bras. . . ." Morton Hunt, "Up Against the Wall, Male Chauvinist Pig!" *Playboy*, May 1970, p. 96.

108 Clifton Daniel was the editor who explained failure to cover Rankin Brigade; reported in Gitlin, *Watching*, 182. In 1969 a Justice Department official explained his agency's inaction on sex discrimination this way: "We respond to social turmoil. The fact that women have not gone into the streets is indicative that they do not take employment discrimination too seriously." Quoted in Freeman, *Politics*, 79.

108 Media blitz described in Freeman, *Politics*, 114, 148–52; Hole and Levine, 266–270.

108 NOW membership figures cited in Haney, 73.

108 ". . . 'get the nuts.' " Steinem said this while she herself was a guest on the Dick Cavett show on ABC-TV in 1970; reported in "Post Policy Change," *NOW Acts* 3, no. 3, September 1970, p. 8.

108–9 ". . . bathing beauty figure." "Potential High Court Nominees," *New York Times*, 14 October 1971, p. 39.

109 ". . . crock of shit." Quoted in Sandie North, "Reporting the Movement," *Atlantic Monthly*, March 1970, p. 106.

109 Media's stabilizing role: Gitlin, *Watching*, 258–73. See also Gaye Tuchman, *Making News: A Study in the Construction of Reality*, especially chapter seven, "The Topic of the Women's Movement," 133–55.

109 Hostilities between women's liberation groups and press: North, 105–6.

109 ". . . normally get." Freeman, *Politics*, 114.

109 "militant man-haters." Quote from subhead of magazine article: "militant man-haters do their level worst to distort the distinctions between male and female and to discredit the legitimate grievances of American women." Morton Hunt, "Up Against the Wall, Male Chauvinist Pig!" *Playboy*, May 1970, p. 95.

110 Percentage of adult women employed in late 1960s: "Who's Come a Long Way, Baby?" *Time*, 31 August 1970, p. 17.

110 Stereotyping in the media: Gaye Tuchman, "Introduction: The Symbolic Annihilation of Women by the Mass Media."

110-1 *Newsweek* confrontation described: North, 106. Freeman, *Politics*, 114, fn; Hole and Levine, 259, fn. See also Henry Raymont, "As Newsweek Says, Women Are in Revolt, Even on Newsweek," *New York Times*, 17 March 1970, p. 30. Raymont's story is sprinkled with descriptions of the way the women were dressed.

111 ". . . soul of this story" North, 106.

111 ". . . 50 years." Quoted in Raymont.

111 Inspired by *Newsweek* case: See, for example, Eleanor Blau, "$2 Million Settlement Is Reported in Women's Bias Suit Against NBC," *New York Times*, 13 February 1977, p. 1.

111-13 The sit-in at the *Ladies' Home Journal* is described from a demonstrators' point of view in Vivien Leone, "Occupying the *Ladies' Home Journal:* My First Hurrah," reprinted in Beasley and Gibbons, 100–106. Lenore Hershey describes the action from *her* vantage point in Lenore Hershey, *Between the Covers: The Lady's Own Journal*, 79–92. Also: "Action for Change: The Sit-In," in Beasley and Gibbons, 98–99. Hole and Levine, 254–57. And: "Inside *Ladies' Home Journal*," a film produced by Janet Gardner and Jo Taverner.

111 ". . . shout at once" and ". . . for revolt." Hershey, 84.

111n Comment on Hershey's hat: Leone, 101.

112 ". . . marriage and family." Press release quoted in Hole and Levine, 255.

112 ". . . 'you get us.' " In Leone, 102.

112-3 ". . . in their coverage." Hershey, 87.

113 ". . . rid of us," Leone, 105.

113 Fact that radicals felt it was a sell-out: Echols, 195–97.

113 *Journal* supplement described: Beasley and Gibbons, 99; Hershey, 89; Hole and Levine, 256; Freeman, *Politics*, 231.

113n Women's Bureau used *Journal* list of women's lib groups: Freeman, *Politics*, 231.

113 ". . . magazine industry. . . ." Fox, author's interview.

113 ". . . dramatic way." John Mack Carter, interview by author, New York City, 23 April 1987.

114 For an analysis of the way three women's magazines—*Ladies' Home Journal*, *McCall's*, and *Redbook*—handled feminist issues from 1964 to 1971, see Sally Bolstad Wilson, "How Magazines Reflect Social Movements: A Case Study of the Women's Liberation Movement as Reflected in Three Women's Magazines" (master's thesis, University of Missouri, 1972).

114 ". . . and commercials." Quoted in Hole and Levine, 262.

114 Action in San Francisco noted: Hole and Levine, 263. In Washington: "Assault on the Media," *NOW Acts* 3, no. 2, July 1970, p. 8.

114 ". . . individual person." Quoted in Hole and Levine, 263.

115 Women's Strike for Equality: Friedan, *Changed*, 141–54; Hole and Levine, 92–93.

115 ". . . even we realized." Friedan, *Changed*, 141.

115 ". . . their oppression," Friedan, *Changed*, 144.

115-6 ". . . out of our way." Friedan, *Changed*, 151.

116 Official estimate of crowd size in New York: Linda Charlton, "Women March Down Fifth in Equality Drive," *New York Times*, 27 August 1970, p. 1. Feminist estimate: Friedan, *Changed*, 151. Dutch demonstration: Friedan, *Changed*, 150. Paris action described: Simone de Beauvoir, "Feminism—Alive, Well, and in Constant Danger" translated by Magda Bogin and Robin Morgan, in Morgan, *Sisterhood Is Global*, 230.

116 Chicago demonstration: "Thousands of Women Strike for Women," *The Spokeswoman* 1, no. 5 (30 September 1970): 1. The *Times* ran several stories on Strike Day, including: Grace Lichtenstein, "For Most Women, 'Strike' Day Was Just a Topic of

Conversation," and "Leading Feminist Puts Hairdo Before Strike," both *New York Times*, 27 August 1970, p. 30.

116 See bibliography for details of feminist best-sellers.

116 ". . . man's world," "Who's Come a Long Way, Baby?" *Time*, 31 August 1970, p. 16.

116 ". . . theoretician of the movement." Frank J. Prial, "Feminist Philosopher: Katharine Murray Millett," *New York Times*, 27 August 1970, p. 30.

117 Founding of *Ms* described: "*Ms* Magazine," in Beasley and Gibbons, 119–125. See also Bill Hieronymus, "For Some Feminists, Owning a Business Is Real Liberation," *Wall Street Journal*, 15 April 1974, p. 1.

117 Number of feminist journals, newspapers: Hole and Levine, 271.

118 Second complaint against *Newsweek*: "Women Renew Battle at Newsweek," *The Spokeswoman* 2, no. 12 (1 June 1972): 8. Women at *New York Times*: "Mrs. Chisholm Accuses Press of Racism and Sexism in Hiring," *New York Times*, 20 February 1972, p. 28.

118 Women employed by TV stations, their achievements: Georgia Dullea, "The Women in TV: A Changing Image, A Growing Impact," *New York Times*, 28 September 1974, p. 18.

119 Redstockings protests: Kathie Sarachild, author's interview. See Kathie Sarachild, "The Power of History," in Redstockings, 13–43. Also Kathie Sarachild, "Covering Up Women's History, An Example—Notes From the First, Second, and Third Years," *Woman's World*, July–September 1972, p. 22; Carol Hanisch, "The Liberal Takeover of Women's Liberation," in Redstockings, 163.

119 ". . . and speakers bureaus." Carol Hanisch, "The Liberal Takeover," 163–67.

119 ". . . sexual politics." Also, ". . . a class." And ". . . back at us." Betty Friedan, "Beyond Women's Liberation," *McCall's*, August 1972, pp. 136, 134, 134.

119–20 ". . . radical cause. . . ." Bouchier, 398.

120 ". . . practical possibility." Ellen Willis, "Radical Feminism and Feminist Radicalism," in Sayres, 100.

120 What makes news: See Tuchman, *Making News*.

chapter 7: *Congress Passes the ERA*

122 First-wave feminists and the fourteenth amendment: Eleanor Flexner, *Century of Struggle*, 146–47, 167; Elisabeth Griffith, 123. Women won the vote, nothing more: The case was *Fay* v. *New York*, 332 U.S. 261 (1947). Cited in Ruth Bader Ginsburg, address delivered at Symposium on "Feminism in the Law: Theory, Practice and Criticism," University of Chicago Law School, 14 October 1988, pp. 8–9.

122n Woman suffrage in the states: Griffith, 123.

122 ". . . nineteenth amendment." Quoted in Ginsburg, address at Symposium on "Feminism in the Law," 9.

123 Disruption of subcommittee hearings, UAW endorsement: Haney, 62–65; Catherine East, "The First Stage: ERA in Washington, 1961–1972"; Hole and Levine, 55–56.

123 ". . . martyrs out of us." Haney, 63.

123–4 1970 Senate hearings on ERA: Paterson, 205–6; East, "The First Stage"; Rawalt, author's interview.

124–6 Campaign for signatures on discharge petition: Ingersoll, interview with Griffiths, 18, 80–85. East, "The First Stage"; Paterson, 207–9. Also author's interviews with Martha Griffiths, Marguerite Rawalt.

124 In sixty years, 825 discharge petitions filed: East, "The First Stage." Griffiths on the difficulty of getting signatures: In Ingersoll, interview with Griffiths, 80. See also Paterson, 207.

124 Griffiths on trading her "credit": Ingersoll interview, 81, 116, 139.

124 ". . . we had lost," Griffiths, author's interview.

124 "apparently unteachable." Ingersoll interview with Griffiths, 82.

125 Need to get signatures quickly: Griffiths, author's interview.

125 ". . . what he was saying. . . ." Griffiths, author's interview.

125 Activities of Ad Hoc Committee: Flora Crater, telephone interview by author, 25 February 1987; and "Summary of the Activities of the Nat'l Ad Hoc Comm. ERA, June-November, 1970," memo dated 4 January 1971, from the files of Flora Crater (hereafter called Ad Hoc summary).

125 ". . . didn't say anything." Griffiths, author's interview.

125–6 BPW's Honolulu convention: Ingersoll, interview with Griffiths, 108; Mason, 737–78; Paterson, 208–9.

126 ". . . picked up immensely," Paterson, 208.

126 " '. . . petition on equal rights.' " Ingersoll, interview with Griffiths, 81.

126–7 1970 ERA debate in the House: Ingersoll, interview with Griffiths, 88; also Paterson, 208–9; Ad Hoc summary; Freeman, *Politics,* 218. Griffiths's speech summarized in East, "The First Stage." Because the parliamentarian turned off the clock at certain points—while one member was giving up the floor to another, for example—the debate actually lasted several hours; Mason, 741–42.

127 ". . . chestnut horse." Paterson, 209.

127 ". . . mischievous ambiguity." "The Henpecked House," *New York Times,* 12 August 1970, p. 40. Cited in East, "The First Stage," 9.

127 ". . . off their backs." Mason, 744.

127 ". . . should apply to women." Ingersoll, interview with Griffiths, 85.

127 Senator Ervin insisted on new hearings: Rawalt, author's interview. See Mason, 744–47.

127 Poll shows loss of ERA support in Senate: Paterson, 212.

127 September 1970 Senate ERA hearings: East, "The First Stage"; Paterson, 213. Senate vote in October: Ad Hoc summary.

128 Controversy over Bayh's substitute amendment: Paterson, 215–17; Mason, 750–57; East, "The First Stage." Feminist attitudes to the draft: Freeman, *Politics,* 215–16.

128–9 Founding of Women United: Paterson, 217–19; Mason, 758–59. Rawalt's connections to women's groups: Paterson, 721. Crater's Raiders: Author's interview with Flora Crater. The group was dubbed "Crater's Raiders" in retrospect, after the ERA passed Congress. Most of the women were members of NOW.

129 1971 modifications of ERA: Ingersoll, interview with Griffiths, 86; Paterson, 218–19. Alice Paul on seven-year limit for ERA: Amelia R. Fry, "Alice Paul and the ERA," in *Rights of Passage: The Past and Future of the ERA,* Joan Hoff-Wilson, ed., 8, 22.

129–30 1971 House hearings on ERA: Mason, 777–78. Ad Hoc Committee's approach to the women of George Washington University: Crater, author's interview.

130 Wiggins amendment: Mansbridge, *Why We Lost the ERA,* 11.

130 "kiss of death" and ". . . against the bill myself." Quoted in *Women Today* 1, no. 12 (12 July 1971): 4.

130 ". . . a lightning bug." East, "The First Stage," 10.

130 1971 House ERA debate: Mason, 783–88; East, "The First Stage"; Freeman, 219.

130 "triggers of cannons." Quoted in *NOW Newsletter,* Central New Jersey chapter, December 1971, p. 8.

131 Crater's Raiders lobbying system: Flora Crater, author's interview; Carol Burris, telephone interview by author, 18 February 1987. Isabelle Shelton, " 'Crater's Raiders' Pull Off Coup," *Washington Sunday Star,* 26 March 1971.

131 ". . . where to apply the pressure." Ingersoll, interview with Griffiths, 96.

131 Lobbying by Women United, etc.: Freeman, 217–18; Mason, 798–801; Rawalt, author's interview.

131 ". . . ten thousand letters." Freeman, *Politics,* 218.

131–4 1972 Senate debate: Paterson, 225–26. Also Eileen Shanahan, "Senators Bar Weakening of Equal Rights Proposal," *New York Times,* 22 March 1972, p. 1. Mason, 806–12.

132 ". . . shells of the enemy." Mansbridge, *ERA,* 66.

132n Ervin's list of weapons: Mansbridge, *ERA,* 66.

132 ". . . bastards she bears." Paterson, 225.

132 Draft most difficult issue, says Bayh: Eileen Shanahan, "Senators Bar."

132 ". . . tells you to go." Mansbridge, 172.

132–3 For a discussion of the draft/combat issues and Senate debate on them, see Mansbridge, *ERA*, 60–66. See also Shanahan, "Senators Bar."

133 ". . . objectives of the Amendment." Quoted in Mansbridge, *ERA*, 61.

133n ERA's exceptions: See Barbara A. Brown, Thomas I. Emerson, Gail Falk, and Ann E. Freedman, "The Equal Rights Amendment: A Constitutional Basis for Equal Rights for Women," *Yale Law Journal* 80 (1971): 890–92.

133–4 Ervin's arguments and the Senate debate: East, "The First Stage"; also Mason, 805–10; Paterson, 225; Mary Frances Berry, *Why ERA Failed: Politics, Women's Rights and the Amending Process of the Constitution*, 63–64.

133 ". . . sexual deviation." East, "The First Stage," 10.

133 "sense of possibility." Mason, 808.

134 First states ratify: Mansbridge, *ERA*, 12. Bayh's prediction noted: Eileen Shanahan, "Equal Rights Amendment Is Approved by Congress," *New York Times*, 23 March 1972, p. 1.

134 Deluge of mail: *Newsweek*, "The Senate: Woman Power," 3 April 1972, p. 28.

134 ". . . home during recess." In Shelton.

135 List of changes expected to occur post-ERA: Eileen Shanahan, "Equal Rights Amendment Is Approved."

136 ". . . moral climate for reform." Freeman, *Politics*, 222.

136 Feminists thought heaviest opposition to ERA would come from labor: "ERA Passed by Congress. 'Failure WAS Impossible!' " *NOW Acts* 5, no. 1 (1972): 1.

chapter 8: Turning Points

139 SWP's attempted takeovers: Freeman, *Politics*, 129–34. Reports on the 1970 Boston SWP meeting and the decision to target Cell 16 were found in the FBI's files on the Women's Liberation Movement; see Howard Husock, "The Feminist Papers: FBI Plays 'I Spy,' " *Boston Phoenix*, 15 February 1977, p. 7.

139–40 Cell 16's experience with SWP: Betsy Warrior, author's interview; Warrior's files are at the Schlesinger Library, Cambridge, MA. Note that the women of Cell 16 had actually dropped the group's name by summer, 1970, though for simplicity's sake I've continued to use it here. Betsy Warrior explained that after a political disagreement, the women disbanded as a formal entity rather than waste time in conflict with one another. Most of the group remained loosely affiliated as the Finance Committee that put out the journal *No More Fun and Games*.

140 ". . . and direct policy," ". . . don't deserve this" and ". . . in the right direction." Warrior, author's interview.

140 Warrior's warning letter: Hole and Levine, 164–65.

140 Only easy way to connect with feminist group: Mansbridge, author's interview.

140 Trot appeal: Susan Brownmiller, author's interview.

141 ". . . the doors open." Mansbridge, author's interview.

141 Intelligence agencies infiltrated social movements: See Frank J. Donner, *The Age of Surveillance*, especially 136, 160, 242. Also Dianne Dumanoski, "Feminists Suspected Feds Were Watching," *Boston Phoenix*, 15 February 1977, p. 7. Nicholas M. Horrock, "N.A.A.C.P. Checked 25 Years by F.B.I. No Illegal Activities Found—Women's Movement Also Monitored by Bureau," *New York Times*, 29 April 1976, p. 1.

141 ". . . and special agents . . ." Quoted in "Creeping Unfeminism," *NOW Newsletter*, Central New Jersey chapter, April 1972, pp. 8–9.

141–2 FBI file on women's liberation: Letty Cottin Pogrebin, "Have You Ever Supported Equal Pay, Child Care, or Women's Groups? The FBI Was Watching You," *Ms*, June 1977, p. 37.

141 ". . . never materialized." Donner, 151.

142 ". . . security of the United States." Pogrebin, 39.

142 FBI's problem spying on all-female groups: Donner, 135.

142 ". . . publication in Chicago . . ." Excerpts from FBI files were published in "Ms Gazette," *Ms*, June 1977, p. 71.

142 Bread and Roses said to be essentially Communist: Husock.

142 ". . . *agents provocateurs.*" Author's interview with Brownmiller.

143 ". . . larger than any of us." Balser, author's interview.

143 Outlandish questions: Mansbridge, author's interview.

143 ". . . breakthrough experiences." Mansbridge, author's interview.

143 Feminists who continued to work for the movement: In 1986, Diane Balser, formerly of Bread and Roses, was the director of a network of about eighty Massachusetts women's organizations that monitored state legislation affecting women. Jane Mansbridge, now a professor of political science at Northwestern, was the author of a book on the ERA. Betsy Warrior of Cell 16 had been the mainstay of a very active support group for battered women for fifteen years. She had also published two books, including *Battered Women's Directory*, which listed shelters and other resources and provided a wealth of practical information alongside chapters on feminist philosophy. Updated at intervals, the *Directory* had gone through nine editions.

143 Preserving the group wasn't a priority: Mansbridge, personal communication, June 1991. For more about the priorities of radical groups and what made them different, see Joyce Rothschild and J. Allen Whitt, *The Cooperative Workplace: Potentials and Dilemmas of Organizational Democracy and Participation* (Cambridge, England: Cambridge University Press, 1986), particularly chapters 4 and 5.

144 For more on the way NOW chapters operated, see chapter 3. WEAL: Gelb and Palley, 99, 167–68, 189, 205.

144 Founding of Cambridge Women's Center: On March 6, 1971, about 150 Boston feminists occupied a Harvard building that stood empty most of the time, and informed startled university administrators that they were there to stay until they were ceded that building or another like it for a women's center. The occupation lasted ten days—Jane Mansbridge remembered it as "one huge feminist slumber party." Eventually, an anonymous donor gave the women $5000 toward the cost of a women's center and promised to help them raise more money. With a police raid imminent, the protestors left the building. The Cambridge Women's Center opened early in 1972, but the building was partially destroyed by a fire just a few months later, and was virtually unusable for almost a year. It finally re-opened in April 1973. Mansbridge, author's interview.

144–5 History of Cambridge Women's Center: Libby Bouvier, telephone interview by author, 3 June 1986. Also author's interview with Mansbridge.

145 ". . . as men had." Bouvier, author's interview.

145 ". . . terrific tragedy," Mansbridge, author's interview.

145 Women's School moved back into Cambridge Women's Center: Bouvier, author's interview.

145–6 Women's counterculture: See Echols, 243–86. Also, Bill Hieronymus, "For Some Feminists, Owning a Business Is Real Liberation," *Wall Street Journal*, 15 April 1974, p. 1.

146 Critics of cultural feminism: See Brooke, "The Retreat to Cultural Revolution," Redstockings, 79–83; Eisenstein, xiv.

146 ". . . women's culture. . . ." Brooke, 79.

146–7 Transformation of radical feminism and rise of difference feminism regretted: Eisenstein, 136–45.

147 "the golden years," Jane Chapman, interview by author, Washington, D.C., 13 January 1988.

142–52 Campaign for credit legislation (ECOA): Chapman, author's interview; see Jane Roberts Chapman, "Policy Centers: An Essential Resource," in Tinker, *Women in Washington*. Gelb and Palley, 61–92.

148 Women's problems getting credit described: "Where Credit Is Due," *Ms*, October, 1972, p. 36. Also U.S. Congress, Hearings, Joint Economic Committee, *Economic Problems of Women*, 93rd Cong., 1st sess., 12 July 1973, pp. 152–53, 202–10. NOW and other groups received complaints: Chapman, author's interview.

148 Women's employment statistics: Gelb and Palley, 65.

149 ". . . never went back." Chapman, author's interview.

149 ". . . seed grant," Chapman, author's interview.
150 ". . . not like abortion," unnamed feminist quoted in Marylin Bender, "Women Equality Groups Fighting Credit Barriers," *New York Times*, 25 March 1973, p. 1.
150 ". . . law was passed," Chapman, author's interview.
150 ". . . women's organizations." Chapman, author's interview.
150 In the 1980s women still had trouble getting credit: Emily Card, *Staying Solvent: A Comprehensive Guide to Equal Credit for Women* (New York: Holt, Rinehart, 1985), pp. 2–4.
151–2 Role equity versus role change: Gelb and Palley, 5–6.
152 ". . . behind the curtain." Chapman, author's interview.
152–3 Foundation funding for feminists: Gelb and Palley, 44–48; Chapman, author's interview. Changes after Reagan's election: Author's interviews with Jane Chapman, Eileen Thornton, and Catherine East, 1985.
153 ". . . or bring lawsuits." Chapman, author's interview.
153–4 Dispersal of power: Gelb, *Feminism and Politics*, 20, 212–13.

chapter 9: *The Relegalization of Abortion*

157 Abortion in the 1960s: Lawrence Lader, *Abortion II: Making the Revolution*, 13, 22.
157n Annual legal abortions, 1980s: See Philip J. Hilts, "U.S. Is Decades Behind Europe in Contraceptives, Experts Report," *New York Times*, 15 February 1990, p. A1.
158–9 How theologians saw abortion: See Kristin Luker, *Abortion and the Politics of Motherhood*, 12–13, 59; James C. Mohr, *Abortion in America: The Origins and Evolution of National Policy*, 3, 187; Linda Gordon, *Birth Control in America: Woman's Body, Woman's Right*, 52–53, 57; Rosalind Pollack Petchesky, *Abortion and Woman's Choice: The State, Sexuality, and Reproductive Freedom*, 329; Barbara Milbauer with Bert N. Obrentz, *The Law Giveth: Legal Aspects of the Abortion Controversy*, 112. Quickening represented the earliest point at which a woman knew with absolute certainty that she was pregnant, because there were no pregnancy tests. In addition, people apparently reasoned that by moving, the fetus demonstrated for the first time that it was, in fact, an independent being.
159 Early history of abortion in the U.S.: Milbauer, 14; Mohr, 3, 22–23, 44, 78.
159 U.S. abortion after 1840: Mohr, 50, 86; Gordon, 53. Mohr estimates that during this period there was probably one abortion for every four live births in the United States. The rate in the 1980s was much the same—see Luker, 50–51.
159 Rise in abortion rate after 1840: Significantly, the U.S. birth rate, which began to drop in 1800, fell precipitously during the 1840s. Because the available contraceptives weren't very reliable, abortion was probably a more important factor. See Mohr, 79, 83, 86; Gordon, 48.
159–60 Physicians' anti-abortion campaign: Mohr, 33–37, 86, 147–70; Gordon, 59–60; Petchesky, 78–83; Luker, 20, 60; Milbauer, 122–24.
159 ". . . their competitors." Mohr, 160.
160 Courts and clergy slow to respond: Mohr, 182–85. Abortion laws in 1900: Luker, 15, 32–33.
160–1 Feminist case against abortion: Gordon, 90–91, 95–115.
160n Women never just victims: Gordon, xiii, 95–115.
161 ". . . her revenge." Gordon, 408.
161 Therapeutic abortions: Luker, 46, 54–56. Lader, *Abortion II*, 13. See also Lawrence Lader, "First Exclusive Survey of Non-Hospital Abortions," *Look*, 1 January 1969, p. 63.
161 ". . . her dirty underwear." Quoted in Lader, *Abortion II*, 22.
161 ". . . migraine headaches. . . ." Claudia Dreifus, "Abortion: This Piece Is For Remembrance," in *Seizing Our Bodies: The Politics of Women's Health*, Claudia Dreifus, ed., 139.
162 In 1971, Shirley Ann Wheeler of Florida became the first American woman to be convicted of the crime of having an abortion; she may have been the first such woman in the English-speaking world. Lader, *Abortion II*, 189.

162–3 Susan Brownmiller's story told in Dreifus, "Abortion," 137–38.
162 ". . . have an abortion." Dreifus, "Abortion," 138.
163 The Sherri Finkbine case: Luker, 62–65, 80. See also "Abortion—With the Future Dim, Should the Unborn Die?" *Life,* 19 August 1962, p. 32. Rubella epidemic: Luker, 80; also "Abortion and the Changing Law," *Newsweek,* 13 April 1970, p. 53.
163–4 Doctors urged reform: Milbauer, 38–39. ALI model abortion law described in Luker, 65; Hole and Levine, 282–83.
164 Growing demand for abortion: Petchesky, 103–4. Study of married women: Nancy Hicks, "1 in 3 Women Fail on Contraception," *New York Times,* 19 September 1973, p. 23.
164 Early male abortion reform activists and first reform laws: Lader, *Abortion II,* 42, 62, 66–70; Luker, 66, 85–92.
164 Lader's referrals: Lawrence Lader, interview by author, New York City, 11 August 1987. Lader's 1966 book was *Abortion* (New York: Macmillan, 1966).
164 ". . . engulfed in misery," Lader, *Abortion II,* 24.
164 "try to help women" and ". . . what I meant," Lader, author's interview.
164–5 For more on Patricia Maginnis, see Ninia Baehr, *Abortion without Apology: A Radical History for the 1990s* (Boston: South End Press pamphlet No. 8, 1990), 7–20. Also Lader, *Abortion II,* 27–34.
165 Clergy Consultation Service: Lader, *Abortion II,* 42–43; Cynthia Gorney, "Abortion, Once Upon a Time in America," in National Women's Health Network, *Abortion Then and Now: Creative Responses to Restricted Access* (hereafter called NWHN), 6–12.
165 ". . . principle of referral. . . ." Lader, *Abortion II,* 43.
165 Feminist "shock troops": Petchesky, 129.
166 ". . . by force." Luker, 97.
166 ". . . lovemaking and rape." Ellen Willis, *Beginning to See the Light* (New York: Knopf, 1981), 208. Cited in Petchesky, 19n.
166 ". . . 'safeguards against abuse.' " Lucinda Cisler, "Unfinished Business: Birth Control and Women's Liberation," in *Sisterhood Is Powerful,* Robin Morgan, ed., 309.
166 Inadequacy of reform laws: Lucinda Cisler, "On Abortion and Abortion Law. Abortion Law Repeal (Sort Of): A Warning to Women," in Firestone, *Notes 2,* 89–93. Also Hole and Levine, 287–88.
167–8 The Jane collective: See Pauline B. Bart and Melinda Bart Schlesinger, "Collective Work and Self-Identity: The Effect of Working in a Feminist Illegal Abortion Collective," in *Workplace Democracy and Social Change,* ed. Frank Lindenfeld and Joyce Rothschild White (Boston: Porter Sargent, 1981), 139–53. Also, Pauline B. Bart, "Seizing the Means of Reproduction: A Feminist Illegal Abortion Collective—How and Why It Worked," *Qualitative Sociology* 10, 1987, reprinted in NWHN, 31–40.
168 Founding of NARAL: Lader, *Abortion II,* 86, 88, 93; also Marcia Neiman of NARAL, telephone interview by author, 15 October 1986. In 1973, after the Supreme Court decision, NARAL changed its name but not its initials: It became the National Abortion Rights Action League.
168–9 Experience with reform laws: Lader, *Abortion II,* 85.
169 ". . . inhuman law." Lader, *Abortion II,* 85.
169–70 Abortion situation in Washington, D.C.: Lader, *Abortion II,* 113. In California: Luker, 88–89, 111, 134; Lader, *Abortion II,* 109.
169–70 ". . . medical politics." Lader, *Abortion II,* 111.
170 New abortion laws in Hawaii and Alaska: See Lawrence Lader, "A National Guide to Legal Abortion," *Ladies' Home Journal,* September 1970, p. 73. In Alaska, a woman must have been a state resident for at least thirty days to qualify for an abortion; in Hawaii, for ninety days. New law in state of Washington: Lader, *Abortion II,* 172–73.
170–1 Passage of New York's repeal bill: Lader, *Abortion II,* 122–47.
171 ". . . defeats this bill. . . ." Lader, *Abortion II,* 143.
171 Abortion in New York during first year or so after abortion repeal: Lader, *Abortion II,* 149–69. See also "New York Abortion Safety Record Termed 'Remarkable,' " *Women Today,* 12 July 1971, p. 2. Deaths related to pregnancy: "Birth Rate

and Maternal Deaths Down After New York Legalizes Abortion," *Women Today*, 17 May 1971, p. 3. Also, "U.S. Court Overturns Ban on Medicaid in Abortions," by Morris Kaplan, *New York Times*, 25 August 1972, p. 1. Michaels's defeat: Lader, *Abortion II*, 143.

171 ". . . fetus pictures." Lader, *Abortion II*, 198.

171–2 Campaign to repeal New York's liberal abortion law: Lader, *Abortion II*, 196–208. Also William E. Farrell, "Ruling Seems to Forestall Abortion Debate in Albany," *New York Times*, 23 January 1973, p. 1. Birth of feminist lobby in Albany: Linda Greenhouse, "In Albany, the Women Show Their Strength," *New York Times*, 29 January 1974, p. 28.

172 Abortion situation in United States in early 1970s: See Luker, 41, 127; Goldstein, 335–37; Marjorie Pitts Hames, personal communication, April 1991.

172 Polls on abortion and support from powerful groups: Lader, *Abortion II*, 186–187. Concern about overpopulation: Lader, *Abortion II*, 199.

172–3 The legal citation for *Roe* decision is *Roe* v. *Wade*, 410 U.S. 113 (1973). For a full account of the case, see Goldstein, 334–37; also, "Three U.S. Judges Rule Laws on Abortion Invalid in Texas," *New York Times*, 18 June 1970, p. 37.

173–4 Details about the *Doe* v. *Bolton* case from Marjorie Pitts Hames, telephone interview by author, 23 September 1987. See Goldstein, 336.

173–4 ". . . get it done," and ". . . additional plaintiffs." Hames, author's interview.

174–5 *Roe* v. *Wade* case: Goldstein, 334–37; Milbauer, 36–37. News report on McCorvey's revelation that she was never raped: Kenneth B. Noble, "Key Abortion Plaintiff Now Denies She Was Raped," *New York Times*, 9 September 1987, p. A23. Hames's statement: Author's interview.

174 ". . . thought was love." Quoted in Noble.

175 "the absolutist argument." Hames, author's interview.

175 The *Vuitch* case: Dr. Milan Vuitch, a Washington, D.C., physician, was arrested for performing abortions in 1969. Before that, he was the doctor to whom Larry Lader usually referred women. In 1969, a federal district court exonerated Vuitch and declared the District of Columbia's anti-abortion law unconstitutional on the grounds that it was too vague—it said only that abortions were permissible when necessary "for the preservation of the mother's life or health." In April 1971, the Supreme Court reversed the lower court and upheld D.C.'s law but at the same time said that its definition of "health" must include psychological well-being, and that doctors need not bear the burden of proving that the abortions they performed fell within the law. This was an early indication that the High Court might act against abortion restrictions. See Lader, *Abortion II*, 12–16, 26, 110, 115.

175 Precedents for right to privacy discussed: Goldstein, 298–332.

175–6 *Griswold* case: See Milbauer, 47; Goldstein, 310–21. A contemporary news report: "Test for an Ancient Law," *Time*, 18 December 1964, p. 44. In the early 1960s, Connecticut was the only state that actually forbade the use of contraceptives, though other states restricted birth control in other ways: by decreeing that contraceptives could only be distributed by medical personnel, or couldn't be distributed at all to the unmarried or to minors, for example. Lader, *Abortion II*, 12.

176 ". . . older than the Bill of Rights. . . ." See Goldstein, 314.

176 *Eisenstadt* v. *Baird*: Goldstein, 322–32; Lader, *Abortion II*, 54, 78–80; Milbauer, 51–52.

176 ". . . beget a child." Goldstein, 327.

176 Reason for Brennan's choice of words: Woodward and Armstrong, *The Brethren*, 206.

176–7 Derivation of right to privacy: Goldstein, 311–12

177 For a discussion of the various amendments used to argue abortion cases, see Milbauer, 35–36; also Hames, author's interview. Rationale for ninth amendment: Noted by Justice Arthur Goldberg in his concurring opinion in the *Griswold* v. *Connecticut* decision; in Goldstein, 314–16. Ninth amendment never used: "2 Suits Contest Bans on Abortion," *New York Times*, 14 December 1971, p. 21.

177 The "due process" argument: Hames, author's interview.

177–8 Hames's strategy: Author's interview with Hames. Blackmun's background described in Woodward and Armstrong, 241.

178 Oral arguments on *Roe:* Hames, author's interview. Also audio tape, *Oral Argument Before the Supreme Court, Case 70–18, Roe* v. *Wade,* argued 13 December 1971 (Washington, D.C.: National Archives, 1971). Goldstein, 337; "Constitutionality Case in Supreme Court," *The Spokeswoman* 2, no. 8 (1 February 1972): 3; "2 Suits Contest Bans on Abortion."

178 ". . . jurisdiction." Hames, author's interview.

178–9 Reporters' reconstruction of the *Roe* decision: "The Decision Blow by Blow," *Time,* 5 February 1973, p. 51.

179 ". . . potential for victory," Hames, author's interview.

179–80 The *Roe* decision in detail: Goldstein, 334–58; Milbauer, 316–19. See also Warren Weaver, Jr., "High Court Rules Abortion Legal the First 3 Months," *New York Times,* 23 January 1973, p. 1.

179–80 ". . . attending physician," ". . . with the physician" and ". . . to the answer." Milbauer, 318, 319, and 316.

180 ". . . abortion limitation." Hames, author's interview.

180 ". . . a void," Lader, author's interview.

181 ". . . laid to rest." Alfred F. Moran, quoted in Nadine Brozan, "Abortion Ruling: 10 Years of Bitter Conflict," *New York Times,* 15 January 1983, p. 17.

181n Right-to-Life in 1970: Petchesky, 241.

181 ". . . not a moral one." "Blackmun Accepts Aftermath of Writing Abortion Opinion," *New York Times,* 18 January 1983, p. A20.

181 Phone calls to hospitals within hours: See "A Stunning Approval for Abortion," *Time,* 5 February 1973, p. 50. ACLU and NARAL had to sue: John Sibley, "2 Groups to Challenge Hospitals That Resist Ruling on Abortions," *New York Times,* 2 July 1973, p. 11. Campaign for a constitutional amendment: Petchesky, 241–42.

182 Conservative backlash: See Gordon, 415–16.

182 ". . . women's lives." Luker, 194.

182–3 How Luker conducted her study: Luker, 194. World views of prolife activists: Luker, 159–75. Views of prochoice activists: Luker, 175–86. Abortion the tip of the iceberg: Luker, 200. Issues were not clear-cut for many: Luker reports polls over the years, 225–26. Feminists who oppose abortion: See Luker, 113. Women personally opposed to abortion who believe in choice: See, for example, Geraldine Ferraro with Linda Bird Francke, *Ferraro: My Story,* 215–18.

chapter 10: Women in Politics

185–6 Liz Holtzman's campaign for Congress: Elizabeth Holtzman, interview by author, Brooklyn, NY, 20 October 1988. See also B. J. Phillips, "Recognizing the Gentleladies of the Judiciary Committee . . ." *Ms,* November 1974, p. 70; Linda Charlton, "McGovern Victor in State; Celler Loses to Holtzman," *New York Times,* 21 June 1972, p. 1; "The Woman from Brooklyn Who Took on Gerald Ford," *People Weekly,* 4 November 1974, p. 12.

185 Celler's comment on monuments and toothpicks reported: B. J. Phillips, 74.

185 ". . . kind of representation," and ". . . wheeling-and-dealing atmosphere." Holtzman, author's interview.

185 *Times* endorsed Holtzman: "Time to Retire," *New York Times,* 15 June 1972, p. 40.

186 ". . . upset of all," "The New Politics," editorial, *New York Times,* 22 June 1972, p. 38.

186 Figures on female delegates at political conventions from Congressional Quarterly, *National Party Conventions, 1831–1984,* 120. See also Ruth B. Mandel, "The Political Woman," in *The American Woman 1988–89,* ed. Sara E. Rix, 115–16.

186 Record number of women's bills: Freeman, *Politics,* 202–5.

187 Male percentage in Congress: For 1971, see Geraldine A. Ferraro with Linda Bird Francke, *Ferraro: My Story,* 61. The situation in 1991: Ruth B. Mandel, personal communication, 17 April 1991.

187 Women in politics in Western Europe: See "Women in Government Around the World," fact sheet from CAWP, April 1987.

187 Women in U.S. politics between the waves: Ruth B. Mandel, *In the Running: The New Woman Candidate*, 9.

187–8 Founding of NWPC and its priorities: "Report of the Organizing Conference, National Women's Political Caucus," National Women's Political Caucus, Washington, D.C., 10–11 July 1971. Also: Gloria Steinem, "The City Politic: What Nixon Doesn't Know About Women," *New York*, 26 July 1971, p. 8; Friedan, *Changed*, 74; Jo Freeman, "Something DID Happen at the Democratic National Convention," *Ms*, October 1976, p. 74. NOW's attitude to the Caucus: Fox, interview by author; also Mandel, "The Political Woman," 82–83.

187 ". . . community of interest. . . ." NWPC, "Report of the Organizing Conference."

188 Campaign to increase number of women delegates at national conventions: Mildred Jeffrey, telephone interview by author, 30 January 1989. Also Congressional Quarterly, *National Party Conventions*, 119.

188 Republican delegations: Warren Weaver, Jr., "G.O.P. Will Open Doors to Women," *New York Times*, 23 July 1971, p. 31.

188 Empowering women delegates: Mildred Jeffrey, author's interview.

188–9 Caucus challenged state delegations: "NWPC Is Full-Blown Body Politic," *The Spokeswoman* 3, no. 2 (1 August 1972): 1. Also, Congressional Quarterly, *National Party Conventions*, 119.

189–91 1972 Democratic convention described: Jeffrey, author's interview. Also Chisholm, 112–31; Ethel Klein, *Gender Politics: From Consciousness to Mass Politics*, 144–51; Shirley MacLaine, "Women, the Convention and Brown Paper Bags," *New York Times Magazine*, 30 July 1972, p. 14; Jon Nordheimer, "Convention Life: Work, Not Play," *New York Times*, 15 July 1972, p. 13; Elizabeth Frappollo, "The Ticket That Might Have Been . . . Vice-President Farenthold," *Ms*, January 1973, p. 74; Congressional Quarterly, *National Party Conventions*, 119–22.

189 ". . . woman candidate." Shirley Chisholm, *The Good Fight*, 3.

189 ". . . belong to you." Stephen Lesher, "The Short, Unhappy Life of Black Presidential Politics," *New York Times Magazine*, 25 June 1972, p. 20.

189–90 Chisholm's campaign: Norman C. Miller, "Mrs. Chisholm Insists on Running, to Dismay of Many Politicians," *Wall Street Journal*, 14 February 1972, p. 1. Also: Chisholm, 8, 77.

189 "peeing on their shoes," Lesher, 12.

190 ". . . relate to [the women]." Chisholm, 66.

190 ". . . a frightening thing." Thomas A. Johnson, "Blacks, in Shift, Forming Unit for Mrs. Chisholm," *New York Times*, 4 February 1972, p. 10.

190n Eagleton's resignation: Frappollo, 119.

191 ". . . become forgotten." MacLaine, 19.

191 1972 Republican convention: Mandel, "Political Woman," 86. Heckler's role in drafting day-care plank reported: Abzug, 38.

191–2 Democrats' failures to court women's vote: Klein, 148–64.

192 Racism and changes in party loyalty: Chisholm, 132–39, 151. See also William J. Keefe, *Parties, Politics, and Public Policy in America*, 254–55.

192 ". . . Jackson on the other." Steven V. Roberts, "Democrats Face Fight for Control," *New York Times*, 9 November 1972, p. 1.

192 New Democratic commission: Abzug, 37. See also Christopher Lydon, "Democrats Name Panel on Delegates," *New York Times*, 22 September 1973, p. 14.

192 1972 conventions drew women into politics: Mandel, "The Political Woman," 86.

192–3 Equal division top priority for feminists: Jeffrey, author's interview. Campaign to achieve it: See Keefe, 94, 98. Also: Joseph A. Califano, "Tough Talk for Democrats," *New York Times Magazine*, 8 January 1989, p. 28. Superdelegates: Keefe, 94.

193 1980 Democratic convention: Jeffrey, author's interview. Eleanor Smeal, *Why and How Women Will Elect the Next President*, 11.

193 Antifeminism at 1976 Republican convention: Lambros. See also Congressional Quarterly, *National Party Conventions*, 131.

193 1980 Republican convention: Abzug, 81–82. Congressional Record, *National Party Conventions*, 134–38.

193–4 1980 presidential campaign, feminist dilemma: Thornton, author's interview. Ruth Mandel, author's interview, New Brunswick, NJ, 8 April 1988. See also Abzug, 54, 79, 86; Klein, 160–62; "The Gender Gap," CAWP fact sheet, July 1987.

194 Political women, closet feminists: Mandel, *In the Running*, 234–35. Also Susan Carroll, interview by author, 9 May 1988.

194 ". . . no one else will," Steven V. Roberts, "6 Republican Women and a Special Constituency," *New York Times*, 3 August 1983, p. A14.

194–5 Elected women more liberal, hired more women, etc.: Mandel, "Political Woman," 107–10.

195 ERA votes by women, men: Mandel, "Political Woman," 108. Black women most liberal: Mandel, "Political Woman," 79, 108.

195 CAWP's purposes: Susan Carroll, presentation, Seminar on Feminist Perspectives on Leadership, Power and Diversity, Douglass College, Rutgers University, New Brunswick, NJ, 15 March 1989 (hereafter, Seminar on Perspectives).

195 ". . . links between women." Carroll, author's interview.

195 Political organizations for women of color: For example, the National Political Congress of Black Women, and the Hispanic Women's Task Force. Alliances across party lines: Congresswomen's Caucus, which became the Congressional Caucus for Women's Issues in 1981—see Mandel, "Political Woman," 101. By 1987 there were eleven women's caucuses in state legislatures: See "Organizations of Women Legislators," *News & Notes about Women Public Officials*, CAWP, Winter 1988, p. 6.

195–6 Gains by women in politics in Western Europe: See "Women in Government Around the World," CAWP fact sheet, April 1987.

196 Barriers to U.S. women in early 1970s: Mandel, *In the Running*, 17, 84–91, 112.

196 Problems of married women: Mandel, *In the Running*, 66–70. Problems of single women and rumor about Mikulski: Mandel, *In the Running*, 67.

196 ". . . job for a woman" and ". . . work for you?" Holtzman, author's interview.

196–7 Image problem: Mandel, *In the Running*, 48. Abzug believed a man would have been seen as strong: Mandel, 41.

197 ". . . 'too aggressive.' " Mandel, *In the Running*, 47.

197 Party support for women candidates: Abzug, 175; Holtzman, author's interview.

197 Poll on woman for President: See Robin Toner, "Poll Shows Bias Against Women in High Offices," *New York Times*, 13 August 1987, p. A14.

197–8 Changes in political parties: Carroll, author's interview. See also Keefe, 25, 90–91.

198 ". . . by the political parties." Carroll, author's interview.

198 Holtzman's 1972 campaign spending: Holtzman, author's interview.

198n Cost of running for Congress, 1988: Richard L. Berke, "After Angry Debate, House Passes Bill to Restrict Campaign Costs," *New York Times*, 4 August 1990, p. 11; also Richard L. Berke, "For Political Incumbents, Loopholes That Pay Off," *New York Times*, 20 March 1990, p. A1.

198 Per-day cost of running for Senate: Michael Oreskes, "Modern Politicking Is Forcing Lawmakers to Devote More Time to Money," *New York Times*, 11 July 1989, p. A17.

198 Political technology: Frank Lynn, "In New York Quest for Campaign Money Never Ends," *New York Times*, 21 March 1988, p. B1.

198 How candidates raise money: Keefe, 117–18. Holtzman considers run: Maureen Dowd, "Women in New York Politics Find Fast Track Has Slowed," *New York Times*, 12 August 1986, p. A1.

198–9 Incumbent advantage: See R. W. Apple Jr., "The Big Vote Is for 'No,' " *New York Times*, 8 November 1990, p. A1. Also Keefe, 192; R. Darcy, Susan Welch and

Janet Clark, *Women, Elections, and Representation* (New York: Longman, 1987), 150–151.

199 Campaign "reform": Keefe, 135–38; Philip M. Stern, *The Best Congress Money Can Buy* (New York: Pantheon, 1988), 5, 170. PAC support for House incumbents in 1990: Richard L. Berke, "Bulk of $94 Million in Special Interest Gifts Goes to Incumbents," *New York Times*, 31 August 1990, p. 16.

199 Feminist PACs; Mandel, Carroll, author's interviews. See also Mandel, "Political Woman," 100–101.

200n Women's money helped Richards win: Mandel, personal communication, April 1991.

200 Right-wing PACs: Mandel, *In the Running*, 241; Smeal, 94–97; Stern, 167, 170. Buying access: Stern, 31–33. How feminist PACs lobby and power of insurance industry PACs: Catherine East, interview by author, Princeton, NJ, December 4, 1988. East noted that feminists had other ways of influencing Congress. When alerted by their lobbyists, the major women's organizations often contacted members, who then wrote letters to their legislators. Feminists who went to work in a political campaign made sure the candidate knew they were there because she (or he) had their organization's support.

200–1 PACs and women candidates: Mandel and Carroll, author's interviews. Also "Women Running for House Find Raising Money Is Easier," *New York Times*, 3 October 1984, p. A25; Rutgers News Service, "Susan Carroll on Women in Politics: Structural Barriers Are Still the Biggest Obstacle," *The Woman's Newspaper*, September 1986, p. 78. EMILY's List: Lucy Baruch, "Women's PACs: Update 1989," *CAWP News & Notes* 7, no. 1, Spring 1989, p. 24. For the 1990 campaigns, EMILY's List raised $1.5 million: See Peggy Simpson, "D.C. Lobby: Who's Minding the Store?" *Ms*, May/June 1991, pp. 88–89. Congresswoman Schneider's experience: Stern, 111–12.

201 ". . . from New York State," ". . . into the system," and ". . . far too long." Holtzman, author's interview.

202 Proposals for revamping electoral system: Stern, 179–90, especially 180–82.

202 ". . . rather increase it." William Peters, *A More Perfect Union* (New York: Crown, 1987), 113.

202 Voters limit lawmakers' terms: See Eleanor Smeal, Tamar Raphael, and Shauna Mulvihill, "1990 Elections: Breakthrough Year For Women," *National NOW Times*, November/December 1990, p. 4.

202–3 How European feminists gained political power: Strategy described by Eleanor Smeal in address to NOW-New Jersey conference, Trenton, NJ, 25 September 1988. See also "NOW, FFM Report on Feminist Movement in Europe," *National NOW Times*, October/November/December 1988, p. 14; "The Feminization of Power: An International Comparison," *The Feminist Majority Report* 1, no. 3 (Winter 1988–89): 1; "International Action by FFM," *The Woman Activist*, November/December 1988, p. 3.

203 How proportional representation helps minority parties: Keefe, 55–58. Problems of persuading parties to set quotas for women candidates: Mandel, author's interview. See also Keefe, 46.

204 ". . . Sri Lanka." Susan J. Carroll, "Looking Back at the 1980s and Forward to the 1990s," *CAWP News & Notes* 7, no. 3, Summer 1990, p. 9.

204 300 years to equality: Ellie Smeal, "Why I Support a New Party," *Ms*, January/February 1990, pp. 72–73.

204 How Congress would change with gender equality: See Mandel, "The Political Woman," especially 106–12.

204 ". . . pinstripes of the oppressor," Barbara Boggs Sigmund, speaking at "Women and Tradition" conference, Rutgers University, New Brunswick, NJ, 21 May 1985.

chapter 11: Changing Education

206 For more on NCWGE, see Gelb and Palley, 100–102.

206 The Central New Jersey chapter of NOW conducted the first feminist study of children's readers: Women on Words and Images, *Dick and Jane As Victims* (Princeton, NJ, self-published, 1972). For a summary of this and other, similar studies, see Andrew Fishel and Janice Pottker, *National Politics and Sex Discrimination in Education*, 8–9. High school textbooks: Jennifer Macleod, *"You Won't Do": What Textbooks on U.S. Government Teach High School Girls* (Pittsburgh: Know, Inc., 1973).

206–7 Sex discrimination in high schools and colleges: Fishel and Pottker, *National Politics*, 9–10. Also: National Advisory Council on Women's Educational Programs, "Title IX: The Half Full, Half Empty Glass," 25–26 (hereafter called NACWEP—the Council's acronym). Quotas: See National Organization for Women, "NOW Reports on Equity in Education," 1987 (hereafter called "NOW Reports"); admissions policies also discussed in Pamela Roby, "Institutional Barriers to Women Students in Higher Education," in *Academic Women on the Move*, Alice S. Rossi and Ann Calderwood, eds., 38–44; Cynthia Fuchs Epstein, *Woman's Place* (Berkeley: University of California Press, 1971), 168. The book that exposed med-school quotas was written under a pseudonym by Harvard Medical School Dean Mary Howell: Margaret Campbell, *Why Would a Girl Go into Medicine?* (New York: Feminist Press, 1973).

207 Sex discrimination in athletics: See Project on Equal Education Rights, "Stalled at the Start: Government Action on Sex Bias in the Schools," 14 (hereafter called PEER).

207 Women educators: Fishel and Pottker, *National Politics*, 12. See also Janice Pottker, "Overt and Covert Forms of Discrimination Against Academic Women," in *Sex Bias in the Schools: The Research Evidence*, Janice Pottker and Andrew Fishel, eds. (Rutherford, Madison, Teaneck, NJ: Fairleigh Dickinson University Press, 1977), 392–93.

207 Pregnancy discrimination: Fishel and Pottker, *National Politics*, 23, 400. Also, "NOW Reports."

208–11 Story of how Sandler discovered and used the Executive Order: Bernice Sandler, interview by author, Washington, D.C., 18 November 1986. Also Mary Ann Millsap, "Equity in Education," in Tinker, 91–119; Bernice Sandler, "A Little Help from Our Government: WEAL and Contract Compliance," in *Academic Women on the Move*, Alice S. Rossi and Ann Calderwood, eds.; Arvonne S. Fraser, "Insiders and Outsiders: Women in the Political Arena," in Tinker, 126–27.

208 ". . . too strong for a woman." Sandler, author's interview.

209 ". . . making a pass." Sandler, author's interview.

209 Macaluso's role described: Vincent Macaluso, telephone interview by author, 21 February 1987; Sandler, author's interview.

209 Details on Executive Order from Sandler's "A Little Help," 442.

209 ". . . the whole committee." Sandler, author's interview.

210 WEAL also filed a class-action complaint against every medical school in the country. Sandler, "A Little Help," 441.

210 ". . . pick it up." Sandler, author's interview.

210 ". . . feet to the fire" and ". . . letters from Congress," Sandler, author's interview.

210 ". . . inquiries from Capitol Hill." Sandler, "A Little Help," 443.

212–3 Passage of Title IX: Sandler, author's interview. Also Millsap; Fishel and Pottker, *National Politics*, 95–103, 105.

212 Amending the Equal Pay Act: Every federal agency follows the progress of bills that are of particular interest to it. However, because Title IX was part of an education bill, officials at the Department of Labor didn't bother to look at the committee reports or the testimony on it, which would have told them that amendments to the Equal Pay Act were being considered. Nevertheless, the changes in the Act shouldn't have come as a complete surprise. Morag Simchak, a feminist who worked for the Labor Department and had been involved in drafting the Equal Pay Act back in the early 1960s, had asked for and received the Department's permission to work with Congresswoman Green on the 1972 education bill. It was Simchak who produced the cryptic wording for the sections that dealt with the Equal Pay Act. Sandler, author's interview.

212 ". . . under their noses." Sandler, author's interview.

212n Universities that lobbied for an exemption: Sandler, author's interview.

213 ". . . as discrimination," Sandler, author's interview.

213–4 Passage of WEEA: Sandler, author's interview. Also Fishel and Pottker, *National Politics*, 67–70; Catharine R. Stimpson with Nina Kressner Cobb, *Women's Studies in the United States*, 49; Millsap, 97.

213 ". . . better books." Sandler, author's interview.

213–4 Patsy Mink described her involvement with WEEA in Fern S. Ingersoll, "Former Congresswomen Look Back," in Tinker, 205–6.

214–5 Attempts to undermine Title IX: Sandler, author's interview; Millsap; PEER, 5.

215 Founding of PEER: Gelb and Palley, 34, 44. NCWGE: Gelb and Palley, 101–2.

215 Athletic establishment's campaign against Title IX: See Project on the Status and Education of Women, "What Constitutes Equality for Women in Sport: Federal Law Puts Women in the Running" (Washington, D.C.: Association of American Colleges, n.d.), 14 (hereafter called Project/Status). Also Margaret C. Dunkle, "Women in Intercollegiate Sports," in *The American Woman 1987–88: A Report in Depth*, Sara E. Rix, ed., 230–31.

215 ". . . their femininity." Bil Gilbert and Nancy Williamson, "Programmed to Be Losers," *Sports Illustrated*, 6 June 1973, p. 62.

215 Opposition to coed gym classes: Brenda Feigen Fasteau, "Giving Women a Sporting Chance," *Ms*, July 1973, p. 56.

215 ". . . a young boy." Gilbert and Williamson, 60.

215 Little League accepts girls: Joseph B. Treaster, "Little League Baseball Yields to 'Social Climate' and Accepts Girls," *New York Times*, 13 June 1974, p. 26.

215 Bias against women in professional sports: See Bil Gilbert and Nancy Williamson, "Sport Is Unfair to Women," *Sports Illustrated*, 23 May 1973, p. 88.

215–6 The King-Riggs match: Billie Jean King with Kim Chapin, *Billie Jean* (New York: Harper & Row, 1974), 166–86. Also, Bud Collins, "The Intersexual Saga of Tennis," in *The Tennis Book*, Michael Bartlett and Bob Gillen, eds. (New York: Arbor House, 1981), 206–21.

216 Equality-difference debate in athletics: See Fasteau, 56; Project/Status, 10–12.

216 For more on AIAW, see Project/Status, 8, 10–12. Also ". . . And So Does UCLA," *Spokeswoman* 3, no. 1 (1 July 1972): 3.

216–8 General foot-dragging chronicled in PEER; Millsap. Also Marcia D. Greenberger, interview by author, Washington, D.C., 4 January 1988. For details of the Title IX regs, see Ellen Weber, "The Long March," *Womensports*, September 1974, p. 34.

217 Schools doing things against the law: For instance, in 1973 more than 200 school districts had different graduation requirements for boys and girls. HEW knew which districts were involved, but by the end of 1976 only one of the department's eleven regional offices had asked districts in its area to change graduation requirements. PEER, 28.

217 ". . . will to enforce." Greenberger, author's interview.

217–8 HEW ombudsman: U.S. Congress, Hearings, Joint Economic Committee, *Economic Problems of Women*, 93rd Cong., 1st sess., 11 July 1973, p. 121.

218 ". . . commitment to equal rights. . . ." PEER, 38.

218 For details of suits on athletics filed in state courts, see Fasteau. Some schools acted before the regs were enforced: Greenberger, author's interview.

218 Women at Olympics: "NOW Reports." Access to classes, behavior of guidance counselors: Walteen Grady Truely, director of PEER, by telephone, 6 June 1991. Study of texts for grades one through eight: See Christine E. Sleeter and Carl A. Grant, "Race, Class, Gender, and Disability in Current Textbooks," *The Politics of the Textbook*, Michael W. Apple and Linda Christian-Smith, eds. (New York: Routledge, Chapman and Hall, 1991), 78–110. Women in the professions: William R. Greer, "Women Now the Majority in Professions," *New York Times*, 19 March 1986, p. C1. Also, "Third of Medical Graduates Are Women," *New York Times*, 20 October 1987, p. C9.

219 ". . . make changes. . . ." Sandler, author's interview.

219n Statistics on tenure: 1988 National Survey of Postsecondary Faculty (NSOPF), U.S. Department of Education, National Center for Education Statistics.

219 For more on tenure, see National Advisory Council on Women's Educational Programs (NACWEP), *Title IX: The Half Full, Half Empty Glass*, 37. Radcliffe had considerable success with a special program to help women gain tenure: See "Faculty Tenure Program at Radcliffe Has 82% Success Rate," *Radcliffe News*, Winter 1989, p. 1. See also Elizabeth Kolbert, "Literary Feminism Comes of Age," *New York Times Magazine*, 6 December 1987, p. 110, especially p. 112.

219 Mixed gains in sports: Peggy Keller, Executive Director, National Association for Girls and Women in Sport, by telephone, 18 June 1991. Changes between 1977 and 1990: R. Vivian Acosta and Linda Jean Carpenter, "Women in Intercollegiate Sport: A Longitudinal Study—13-Year Update," unpublished study. See also Judith Jenkins George, "Women Coaches Are an Endangered Species," *New York Times*, 23 September 1988, p. A35.

219–20 The 1981 report: National Advisory Council on Women's Educational Programs, *Title IX: The Half Full, Half Empty Glass* (NACWEP).

220 For an account of feminist groups that developed within professional associations during the early 1970s, see Kay Klotzburger, "Political Action by Academic Women," *Academic Women on the Move*, Alice S. Rossi and Ann Calderwood, eds., 359–88.

220 Statistics on the growth of women's studies from Stimpson, 4. See also Mariam Chamberlain, "The Emergence and Growth of Women's Studies Programs," in *The American Woman 1990–91*, Sara E. Rix, ed., 315–24.

220 ". . . estrangement from accepted knowledge. . . ." Stimpson, 32.

220–1 ". . . vantage point of women?" "Author's Preface," in Joan Kelly, *Women, History, and Theory: The Essays of Joan Kelly*, xii–xiii.

221 More freedom in Dark Ages: Kelly, 19–50.

221 Scholars must deconstruct: Stimpson, 32.

221–2 Gilligan's groundbreaking book: Carol Gilligan, *In a Different Voice: Psychological Theory and Women's Development*; her analysis of Kohlberg's research, 18 to 23; Chodorow, 7–8. See also Nancy Chodorow, *The Reproduction of Mothering: Psychoanalysis and the Sociology of Gender*. And: Carol Gilligan, "Why Should a Woman Be More Like a Man?" *Psychology Today*, June 1982, p. 68; Stimpson, 32–33.

222 Legal scholar Kenneth Karst explored the contrast between the ladder and the web in Kenneth L. Karst, "Women's Constitution," *Duke Law Journal*, June 1984, pp. 447–508.

222 Gilligan's critics: See, for example, Catherine Greeno and Eleanor Maccoby, "How Different Is the Different Voice?" *Signs* 11 (1986): 310. Also Deborah L. Rhode, "Theoretical Perspectives on Sexual Difference," in *Theoretical Perspectives on Sexual Difference*, Deborah L. Rhode, ed., 5, 264; Alison M. Jaggar, "Sexual Difference and Sexual Equality," in Rhode, 239–54.

222 Women's values produced by oppression: See, for example, Catharine MacKinnon, *Feminism Unmodified: Discourses on Life and Law*, 38–39, 219–20. John Stuart Mill also made this point more than a century ago; see Harriet Taylor Mill, *Enfranchisement of Women*, and John Stuart Mill, *The Subjection of Women*, reissued together (London: Anchor Press, 1988), 27.

222 Academics were skeptical: For example, see "Scholars Attack Campus Radicals," *New York Times*, 15 November 1988, p. A22.

222–3 Founding of the S.E.E.D. Project (which was funded primarily by the Geraldine R. Dodge Foundation) described by Emily Jane Style, presentation, Seminar on Perspectives, 1 March 1989; further personal communication, April 1991.

223 Women's studies in 1990: Chamberlain, 315–24; Stimpson, 26–27.

223 New multicultural curriculums: Anthony DePalma, "The Culture Question," *New York Times* special report on education, 4 November 1990, sec. 4A, p. 22. Feminist wariness of mainstreaming: "Scholars Seek Wider Reach for Women's Studies," *New York Times*, 17 May 1989, p. B6.

225 For a history and discussion of the conflict over multiculturalism, see James Atlas, "The Battle of the Books," *New York Times Magazine*, 5 June 1988, p. 24.

Berkeley students were 70 percent nonwhite: Henry Louis Gates, Jr., "Whose Culture Is It, Anyway?" *New York Times*, 4 May 1991, p. 23. Students in the year 2000: Anthony DePalma, "Higher Education Feels the Heat," *New York Times*, 2 June 1991, sec. 4, p. 1. A defense of the canon and expression of concern about the American identity: Donald Kagan, "Western Values Are Central," *New York Times*, 4 May 1991, p. 23. The conflict over political correctness reported: Robert D. McFadden, "Political Correctness: New Bias Test?" *New York Times*, 5 May 1991, p. 32. The real issue is white male backlash: Frank Mulhern, "Backlash to Multi-Cultural Curricula," *NOW–New Jersey NewsBreaks* 10, no. 2 (April 1991): 1.

225 How women are treated in college classrooms: Sandler, author's interview. See *The Classroom Climate: A Chilly One for Women?* (Washington, D.C.: Project on the Status and Education of Women, Association of American Colleges, 1982). Dwindling of women's colleges: Edward B. Fiske, "Women's Colleges Are Dwindling, But Their Supporters Can Still Make a Case," *New York Times*, 14 June 1989, p. B8.

225–6 Gilligan on girls' fading self-confidence: Carol Gilligan, Nona P. Lyons, and Trudy J. Hanmer, eds., *Making Connections: The Relational Worlds of Adolescent Girls at Emma Willard School* (Cambridge: Harvard University Press, 1990). Also: Lindsy Van Gelder, "The Importance of Being Eleven: Carol Gilligan Takes On Adolescence," *Ms*, July/August 1990, p. 77; Francine Prose, "Confident at 11, Confused at 16," *New York Times Magazine*, 7 January 1990, p. 22.

225–6 Survey of 3000 children: Suzanne Daley, "Little Girls Lose Their Self-Esteem on the Way to Adolescence, Study Finds," *New York Times*, 9 January 1991, p. B6.

226 NCWGE in the 1990s: Ellen Vargas, Chair of NCWGE, by telephone, June 1991.

chapter 12: The Women's Health Movement

227 For an analysis of medical school textbooks, see Diane Scully and Pauline Bart, "A Funny Thing Happened on the Way to the Orifice: Women in Gynecology Textbooks," *American Journal of Sociology* 78, no. 4 (January 1973): 1045–1050. Feminist discussion of the patient-doctor relationship in Gena Corea, *The Hidden Malpractice: How American Medicine Treats Women as Patients and Professionals*, 74–85.

227–8 ". . . peculiarly liable." Sheryl Burt Ruzek, *The Women's Health Movement: Feminist Alternatives to Medical Control*, 147.

228 ". . . come to us." Quoted in Ruzek, 71; from Margaret Sanger, *Margaret Sanger: An Autobiography* (New York: Dover Publications, 1938, reissued 1971), 286.

228 How the women's health movement took root: See Ruzek, especially 33, 144–146, and 156. The five founders of the National Women's Health Network: Barbara Seaman, Alice Wolfson, Mary Howell, Belita Cowan, and Phyllis Chesler.

229 The medicalization of childbirth: See Adrienne Rich, "The Theft of Childbirth," in Dreifus, 146–63; Adrienne Rich, *Of Woman Born: Motherhood as Experience and Institution*, 166–79; Gena Corea, *The Mother Machine: Reproductive Technologies from Artificial Insemination to Artificial Wombs*, 305.

229 ". . . sense of power." Doris Haire, interview by author, New York City, 2 November 1989.

229–30 Haire's research on childbirth: Haire, author's interview. Her report: Doris B. Haire, *The Cultural Warping of Childbirth*, especially 4, 10. See also Corea, *Hidden Malpractice*, 188–211. Doctors reluctant to believe drugs reached fetus: see Doris Haire, "Drugs in Labor and Birth," *Childbirth Educator*, Spring 1987, p. 3.

230 Improvements in childbirth practices: Ruzek, 222–23.

230–1 Only 10 percent of childbirths develop problems: Esther Booth Zorn, Cesarean Prevention Movement, telephone interview by author, 29 April 1991. Fetal monitors: Haire, author's interview. Also Corea, 195–97. Statement by World Health Organization: Lin Nelson, "Challenging Obstetrics-as-Usual: The Cesarean Prevention Movement," *Network News* (published by National Women's Health Network), May/June 1987, p. 1.

231n 1990 report on fetal monitors: Lawrence K. Altman, "Electronic Monitoring Doesn't Help in Premature Births, a Study Finds," *New York Times*, 1 March 1990, p. B10.

231 Ironclad consent form: Haire, author's interview. Globalization of Cesarean problem: Nelson.

231 Cesarian Prevention Movement in the 1990s: Zorn, author's interview.

232 Seaman's early books: *The Doctors' Case Against the Pill; Free and Female* (New York: Coward, McCann, 1972).

232 First self-help group: History from Shireen Miles, Associate Director, Federation of Feminist Women's Health Centers, telephone interview by author, 21 November 1989. See Claudia Dreifus, "Introduction," in Dreifus, xxvi–xxviii; Ruzek, 54.

232 Invention of the Del-Em: Miles, author's interview. See Lorraine Rothman, "Menstrual Extraction," in National Women's Health Network, *Abortion Then and Now: Creative Responses to Restricted Access* (hereafter called NWHN), 67–69; Laura Punnett, "Politics," in NWHN, 69–75; Federation of Feminist Women's Health Centers, "Menstrual Extraction," in NWHN, 76–82.

233 Downer and Rothman's tour: Ruzek, 53–54; Rothman, 67; Phyllis Gapen, "Indisposed to Medicine: The Women's Self-Help Movement," *New Physician* 2, May 1980, reprinted in *Social Issues Resources Series: Women* 2 (1979–1983), Article 28. Founding of FWHC: Dreifus, "Introduction," xxviii. Downer's arrest and trial: Story in Ruzek, 57–58; Gapen, 20; Corea, *Hidden Malpractice*, 262–63.

233–4 Menstrual extraction: Miles, author's interview. Also Federation of Feminist Women's Health Centers, "Menstrual Extraction," in NWHN, 76–82; West Coast Sisters, "Self-Help Clinic Part II," in NWHN, 66; Gina Kolata, "Self-Help Abortion Movement Gains Momentum," *New York Times*, 23 October 1989, p. B12.

234 Feminist health centers in the mid-1970s: Gapen, 21; Ruzek, 144–46. New model of medical care: See Sheila M. Rothman, *Woman's Proper Place: A History of Changing Ideals and Practices, 1870 to the Present* (New York: Basic Books, 1978), 283.

234 Doctors in feminist health clinics: Lorraine Rothman, telephone interview by author, 31 May 1991.

234 Violence against clinics: Miles, author's interview. See also Committee for Abortion Rights and Against Sterilization Abuse, *Women Under Attack: Victories, Backlash and the Fight for Reproductive Freedom*, Susan E. Davis, ed., 57–58 (hereafter called CARASA); Gapen, 22–23; Corea, *Hidden Malpractice*, 264. Ten to fifteen clinics left in 1990s: Lynne Randall, telephone interview by author, 31 May 1991.

235 Revival of interest in ME: Miles, author's interview. Press interview with Downer: Gina Kolata, "Self-Help Abortion Movement Gains Momentum," *New York Times*, 23 October 1989, p. B12.

235 ". . . motivated." Miles, author's interview.

235 Self-help abortion movement in Latin America: Miles, author's interview.

236 Haire's study of the FDA was done for the National Women's Health Network; see Doris Haire, *How the F.D.A. Determines the "Safety" of Drugs—Just How Safe Is "Safe"?*, report released to the Congress of the United States (Washington, D.C.: National Women's Health Network, 1984). Drug companies lobby for stronger FDA: Cindy Pearson, author's telephone interview, 31 May 1991. See Philip J. Hilts, "A Guardian of U.S. Health Is Failing Under Pressures," *New York Times*, 4 December 1989, p. A1.

236–7 History of the pill: Seaman and Seaman, *Women and the Crisis in Sex Hormones* (New York: Rawson, 1977), 66–69; Corea, *Hidden Malpractice*, 15, 145; Boston Women's Health Book Collective, *The New Our Bodies, Ourselves*, 237–38; Dreifus, "Introduction," xxix; Ruzek, 36–38. Eugenicists and the pill: Corea, *Hidden Malpractice*, 126–30, 148; Dreifus, "Introduction," xxiv. The FDA committee: Corea, 145–46.

237 Seaman's challenge, FDA's response: Ruzek, 36–38; Seaman, "The Dangers of Oral Contraceptives," 79–80.

237 During the 1970s, researchers introduced new versions of the pill several times, each time reducing the amount of one of the hormones (estrogen or progestin) that it contained: Pearson, author's interview. High-dose pill discontinued in 1988: See "National Women's Health Network Highlights for 1988," *Network News*, November/December 1988, p. 3. See also: Boston Women's Health Book Collective, 237–238.

237–9 DES disaster: Sybil Shainwald, interview by author, New York City, 3 November 1989. See Seaman and Seaman, 1–59; Seaman, "The Dangers of Sex Hormones," in Dreifus, 167–71; Ruzek, 38–42, 169–71, 224–32. DES still occasionally used as morning-after pill: Pearson, author's interview.

238n FDA approves drugs for conditions: Haire, *How the F.D.A. Determines "Safety,"* 4.

239 Problems of lawsuits: Shainwald, author's interview. See also Linda Greenhouse, "Supreme Court Roundup: Product-Liability Ruling Left Standing by Justices," *New York Times,* 31 October 1989, p. D23.

239–41 Development of Dalkon Shield: Story of the Dalkon Shield debacle told in Susan Perry and Jim Dawson, *Nightmare: Women and the Dalkon Shield.* See also Sybil Shainwald, "Will $2.475 Billion Pay You For Your Hysterectomy?" *Network News,* May/June 1988, p. 6; Ruzek, 43–44; Mark Dowie and Tracy Johnston, "A Case of Corporate Malpractice and the Dalkon Shield," in Dreifus, 86–104. Also Shainwald, author's interview.

239 Septic miscarriages: Boston Women's Health Book Collective, 249.

239 FDA's interest in foolproof birth control: A 1968 report by an FDA advisory committee attributed the widespread interest in IUDs in part to the need to find contraceptives for underprivileged women that didn't require "recurrent motivation." See Corea, *Hidden Malpractice,* 148.

240–1 Efforts of DSIN: Karen Hicks, telephone interview by author, 13 January 1990. News report on outcome of damage claims: Linda Greenhouse, "Justices Reject Challenges to Dalkon Shield Settlement," *New York Times,* 7 November 1989, p. D1. U.S. birth control research derailed: Judy Foreman, "Fears Limit Birth Control Options in U.S.," *Boston Globe,* 23 April 1989, p. 1.

241 New controversy over IUDs in 1991: Pearson, author's interview. See Lawrence K. Altman, "Study Finds Doubt on Danger Arising from Use of IUD's," *New York Times,* 15 April 1991, p. A1.

241 "disinterested": Altman, p. B6. The suggestion was made by Dr. Thomas J. Petrick of Family Health International.

241 ". . . of its string." Pearson, author's interview.

242 Feminists question overuse of mastectomies: Seaman, *Free and Female;* Ellen Frankfort, *Vaginal Politics* (New York: Quadrangle, 1972); Kushner, *Breast Cancer: A Personal and Investigative Report* (New York: Harcourt, Brace, 1975).

242 Challenge to unnecessary hysterectomies: Nora Coffey, telephone interview by author, 29 December 1989. Also Shainwald, author's interview. See also Boston Women's Health Book Collective, 511–13; Sybil Shainwald, "Prescription for Your Legal Health," *Network News* 9, no. 2 (March/April 1984): 6. Vicki Hufnagel, M.D., *No More Hysterectomies* (New York: New American Library, 1988), 60. American hysterectomy rate: See Boston Women's Health Book Collective, 512. Some women die from hysterectomies: Deborah Larned, "The Epidemic in Unnecessary Hysterectomy," in Dreifus, 200.

242 ". . . cancer-bearing organ." Quoted in Deborah Larned, "The Epidemic in Unnecessary Hysterectomy," in Dreifus, 195–208.

243 "the maternal environment," terminology noted, for example, in Renate Duelli Klein, "What's 'New' About the 'New' Reproductive Technologies?" in G. Corea et al., *Man-Made Women: How New Reproductive Technologies Affect Women,* 66.

243–4 Woman convicted for transmitting drugs to fetus: Suzanne Shende of the ACLU Reproductive Freedom Project, telephone interview by author, 30 April 1991. See Jacqueline Berrien, "Pregnancy and Drug Use: The Dangerous and Unequal Use of Punitive Measures," *Yale Journal of Law and Feminism* 2 (1990): 239–50; Tamar Lewin, "Court in Florida Upholds Conviction for Drug Delivery by Umbilical Cord," *New York Times,* 20 April 1991, p. A6. A survey of seventy-eight drug treatment centers in New York City found that 87 percent of them refused to treat pregnant crack users; see Wendy Chavkin, "Help, Don't Jail, Addicted Mothers," *New York Times,* 18 July 1989, p. A21. Fathers and alcohol: Sandra Blakeslee, "Research on Birth Defects Turns to Flaws in Sperm," *New York Times,* 1 January 1991, p. 1. Animal studies reported in "Defective Offspring of 'Alcoholic' Rats," *New York Times,* 2 January 1990, p. C6.

244 Women brought up on charges: Jan Hoffman, "Pregnant, Addicted—and Guilty?" *New York Times Magazine*, 19 August 1990, p. 32; Gina Kolata, "Racial Bias Seen on Pregnant Addicts," *New York Times*, 20 July 1990, p. A13; Dorothy Roberts, "The Bias in Drug Arrests of Pregnant Women," *New York Times*, 11 August 1990, p. 25.

244 Father who sued over discolored teeth: Case cited by Barbara Katz Rothman, *Recreating Motherhood: Ideology and Technology in a Patriarchal Society*, 160.

244 Court-ordered Cesarean sections: Barbara Katz Rothman, 166. Appeals court ruling: Linda Greenhouse, "Court in Capital Bars Forced Surgery to Save Fetus," *New York Times*, 27 April 1990, p. A1. For a brief discussion of the common-law principle that one person can't be legally required to go to the aid of someone else, especially when providing aid involves a risk or significant cost, see Sylvia A. Law, "Rethinking Sex and the Constitution," *University of Pennsylvania Law Review* 132, no. 5 (June 1984): 1021–22.

244–5 "fetal protection policies": See Peter T. Kilborn, "Who Decides Who Works at Jobs Imperiling Fetuses?" *New York Times*, 2 September 1990, p. 1. Feminist analysis: See Jeanne Mager Stellman and Joan E. Bertin, "Science's Anti-Female Bias," *New York Times*, 4 June 1990, p. A23.

244 ". . . of unborn children," quoted in Kilborn, "Who Decides."

245 1991 Supreme Court decision on fetal protection policies: Linda Greenhouse, "Court Backs Right of Women to Jobs with Health Risks," *New York Times*, 21 March 1991, p. A1.

245n Effects of lead on sperm: Blakeslee.

245–6 National Black Women's Health Project: See Evelyn C. White, ed., *The Black Women's Health Book: Speaking for Ourselves*, especially Byllye Y. Avery, "Breathing Life into Ourselves: The Evolution of the National Black Women's Health Project," 4–10. Also Marilyn Milloy, "Taking Their Health into Their Own Hands," *Newsday*, 2 November 1989, p. 4. Medical statistics on African-American women: Milloy; also fact sheet from NBWHP, part of a news release dated September 1989.

246 ". . . worst-paying jobs. . . ." Milloy, 4.

246–7 National Latina Health Organization: Luz Alvarez Martinez, telephone interview by author, 24 January 1990.

247 ". . . by themselves" and ". . . do we have?" Martinez, author's interview.

247–8 Native American women's health: Charon Asetoyer, telephone interview by author, 21 November 1989. See also Daniel Golden, "The Most Desolate Place," *Boston Globe Magazine*, 19 November 1989, p. 52. Sara Miles, "Asetoyer-Rockboy: One Life at a Time, She Saves a Nation," *Mother Jones*, January 1990, p. 35.

248 Poll on reproductive rights reported: Alliance Against Women's Oppression, San Francisco, "Caught in the Crossfire: Minority Women and Reproductive Rights," AAWO discussion paper, January 1983 (hereafter called AAWO). Comments by Asetoyer, Martinez, from author's interviews.

249 Problems of access to health care and health insurance: Nancy Worcester, "Strange Bedfellows See Need for a National Health Plan," *Network News*, January/February 1990, p. 1.

249 Reluctance to sterilize white women: Ruzek, 46. Or see "Mother of 3 to Fight Sterilization Ban," *New York Times*, 29 August 1971, p. 50.

249–50 Alabama black girls sterilized: Ruzek, 47; Corea, 134. HEW guidelines and their limitations: Claudia Dreifus, "Sterilizing the Poor," in Dreifus, 105–20, especially 110 and 112.

250 Feminist press conference: Bill Kovach, "14 Organizations Urge the Government to Stop Providing Funds for the Sterilization of Minors," *New York Times*, 10 July 1973, p. 31. Helen Rodriguez-Trias recalled feminist disbelief at a conference on "The Sexual Liberals and the Attack on Feminism," New York City, 4 April 1987 (hereafter called "Sexual Liberals" conference). She became president of the American Public Health Association in 1993.

250 How sterilization was coerced: Claudia Dreifus, "Sterilizing the Poor," in Dreifus, 105–20; Corea, *Hidden Malpractice*, 133–36. Medicaid funds for abortion were cut off in most states, but Medicaid would still pay 90 percent of the cost of sterilization; see AAWO.

250 Asetoyer, author's interview. Statistics on sterilization from AAWO; see also U.S. Congress, House, Subcommittee on General Oversight and Investigations, *Use of the Drug, Depo Provera, by the Indian Health Service*, 100th Cong., 1st sess., 6 August 1987, p. 123.

250–1 Founding of CARASA: See CARASA, 1–6, 14. Successful campaigns for stronger sterilization guidelines: Pearson, author's interview. No doubt that abuse continued: Martinez, Asetoyer, author's interviews.

251 Norplant: News reports tracked the development of the issue: Philip J. Hilts, "U.S. Approves 5-Year Implants to Curb Fertility," *New York Times*, 11 December 1990, p. A1. Tamar Lewin, "Implanted Birth Control Device Renews Debate Over Forced Contraception," *New York Times*, 10 January 1991, p. A20. Michael Lev, "Judge Is Firm on Forced Contraception, but Welcomes an Appeal," *New York Times*, 11 January 1991, p. A17. Isabel Wilkerson, "Wisconsin Welfare Plan: To Reward the Married," *New York Times*, 12 February 1991, p. A16.

251 Shulamith Firestone, *The Dialectic of Sex*, 197–200. The international network was FINNRET, the Feminist International Network on the New Reproductive Technologies; see Janice Raymond, "Preface," in Corea et al., eds., *Man-Made Women*, 9.

251–2 For the equality point of view on reproductive technology, see Carmel Shalev, *Birth Power: The Case for Surrogacy*, especially 3, 13, 17–19. For the difference viewpoint: Corea, *Mother Machine*, especially 213–45.

252 Prenatal testing: For a feminist critique, see CARASA, 38; Boston Women's Health Book Collective, 356. Urged on thirty-two-year-olds: Nadine Taub, "Abortion, Sterilization and the New Reproductive Technology: Making Choice a Reality," lecture, Rutgers University, New Brunswick, NJ, 31 October 1989.

252 Sex selection: Corea, *Mother Machine*, 188–206; Robyn Rowland, "Motherhood, Patriarchal Power, Alienation and the Issue of 'Choice' in Sex Preselection," in Corea et al., *Man-Made Women*, 83; Sarah Blaffer Hrdy, "Sons Versus Daughters: How They Fare in Different Human and Animal Societies," *Radcliffe Quarterly*, September 1988, pp. 11–12. See also Steven R. Weisman, "State in India Bars Fetus-Sex Testing," *New York Times*, 20 July 1988, p. A1.

252–3 IVF procedure described: David E. Larson, ed., *Mayo Clinic Family Health Book* (New York: William Morrow, 1990), 1136. Success rates: Corea, *Mother Machine*, 179–80. Embryo freezing: Corea, *Mother Machine*, 130–32. IVF sometimes recommended before infertility is certain: Corea, *Mother Machine*, 120. For a collection of feminist writing on infertility, see Renate D. Klein, ed., *Infertility: Women Speak Out About Their Experiences of Reproductive Medicine* (London: Pandora Press, 1989). Also Robyn Rowland, "Technology and Motherhood: Reproductive Choice Reconsidered," *Signs* 12, no. 3 (4 April 1987): 519.

253 Infertility "epidemic": CARASA, 31–32. News story noting that infertility rate hasn't actually increased since 1965: Philip J. Hilts, "New Study Challenges Estimates on Odds of Adopting a Child," *New York Times*, 10 December 1990, p. B10.

253 For a feminist analysis of IVF, including success statistics: Andrea Boroff-Eagan, "Baby Roulette," *Network News*, March/April 1988, p. 3. See also Philip J. Hilts, "U.S. Urged to End Ban on In Vitro Birth Research," *New York Times*, 3 December 1989, p. 37.

253–4 Embryo transfers: Corea, *Mother Machine*, 80–95, especially 90, and 128–29. Also Gena Corea, presentation at "Sexual Liberals" conference; Renate Klein, "Resistance: From the Exploitation of Infertility to an Exploration of In-Fertility," in Klein, 249.

254 High-tech conception: Corea, *Mother Machine*, 126, 219–21. Barbara Katz Rothman, 148.

254 Artificial insemination: Described, Corea, *Hidden Malpractice*, 24, 42–46. See also "A Feminist Sperm Bank Offers Catalogue Shopping to Singles," *Chicago Tribune*, 24 October 1982, sec. 1, p. 13.

254–5 The Baby M case got its name from the fact that the Sterns called the child Melissa; the Whiteheads had named her Sara. See Mary Beth Whitehead with Loretta Schwartz-Nobel, *Mary Beth Whitehead: A Mother's Story* (New York: St. Martin's Press, 1989). Also CARASA, 34–36.

255 ". . . exploitive," and ". . . already his." Robert Hanley, "Father of Baby M Granted Custody; Contract Upheld," *New York Times*, 1 April 1987, p. A1.

255 ". . . harshly," and ". . . but secure." Robert Hanley, "Surrogate Deals for Mothers Held Illegal in Jersey," *New York Times*, 4 February 1988, p. A1.

255 For two different viewpoints on surrogacy from the equality side of the feminist divide, see Shalev, 121, and Kaminer, 157–61.

255 ". . . own oppression." Janice Raymond, presentation, "Sexual Liberals" conference.

256 Whitehead gives her reasons for becoming a surrogate: Whitehead, 89.

256 Difference feminists on surrogacy: Corea, *Mother Machine*, 213–45. Surrogacy contracts: Sybil Shainwald, at graduate students' conference, Princeton, NJ, 28 March 1987; also Corea, *Mother Machine*, 241–42; Whitehead, 9. Equality feminists agreed: Barbara Katz Rothman, 240–45. Chesler, author of *Women and Madness* (New York: Doubleday, 1972), made her point at "Sexual Liberals" conference.

256 Danger of exploiting women: CARASA, 35–36; Corea, *Mother Machine*, 214–219, 245. Ethicists on irony: For example, Dr. Arthur Caplan of the Hastings Center —see Robert Hanley, "Seven-Week Trial Touched Many Basic Emotions," *New York Times*, 1 April 1987, p. B2.

256–7 Surrogacy after Baby M: Shainwald, author's interview; CARASA, 35; also Robert Hanley, "Legislators Are Hesitant on Regulating Surrogacy," *New York Times*, 4 February 1988, p. B7. By 1989, four states had banned commercial surrogacy, two allowed it but required strict judicial review, and Indiana had stipulated that its courts couldn't uphold surrogacy contracts if they were challenged; see Robert Hanley, "Jersey Panel Backs Limits on Unpaid Surrogacy Pacts," *New York Times*, 12 March 1989, p. 38. Statistics on surrogacy, 1990: Carol Lawson, "Couples' Own Embryos Used in Birth Surrogacy," 12 August 1990, p. 1.

257 New groups concerned about women with AIDS: Wolfe, author's interview. Changes in doctors' attitudes, in the way pelvic exams are done, and in medical school training: Pearson, author's interview. For more on how medical students learn to do pelvic exams, see Robert M. Kretzschmar and Deborah S. Guthrie, "Why Not in Every School?" *Journal of the American Medical Women's Association* 39, no. 2 (March/April 1984): 43–45; the same issue, S. M. Guenther, "There Is No Excuse," 40–42. Dr. Lila Wallis of Cornell Medical School campaigned for this change.

chapter 13: Lesbian Feminism

260 ". . . scared," Del Martin and Phyllis Lyon, *Lesbian/Woman*, 244.

260 Situation of gays in the 1950s: John D'Emilio, "Capitalism and Gay Identity," in *Desire: The Politics of Sexuality*, Ann Snitow, Christine Stansell, and Sharon Thompson, eds., 147. Founding of DOB: Martin and Lyon, 238–79. See also Allen Young, "Out of the Closets, into the Streets," in *Out of the Closets: Voices of Gay Liberation*, Karla Jay and Allen Young, eds., 25–28.

260–1 Lesbians in early second-wave groups: Freeman, *Politics*, 135. A survey of 15,000 women, including a large number of feminists, by the magazine *Psychology Today* (March 1972) estimated that up to 20 percent of the women in some feminist groups were lesbians. Cited in Joan Cassell, *A Group Called Women: Sisterhood and Symbolism in the Feminist Movement*, 72. Martin and Lyon join NOW: Martin and Lyon, 286–88. Fact that most lesbians in NOW were in the closet: Sidney Abbott and Barbara Love, *Sappho Was a Right-on Woman: A Liberated View of Lesbianism*, 109.

261 Birth of gay rights movement: See Barry D. Adam, *The Rise of a Gay and Lesbian Movement*, 73–79; Young, in Jay and Young, 25–26.

261 ". . . be revealed." Martha Shelley, "Gay Is Good," in Jay and Young, 32.

261 Evolution of the gay rights movement: Adam, 79–83.

262–4 The gay-straight conflict in NOW is described in detail in Abbott and Love, 107–34.

262 ". . . too much," Abbott and Love, 110.

262 ". . . with anything?" Faust, author's interview.

262–6 Brown tells her own story: Rita Mae Brown, "Take a Lesbian to Lunch," in Jay and Young, 185–94.

262 According to Jean Faust, other lesbian members of NOW-New York also urged the chapter to deal with lesbian issues; personal communication, April 1991.

262 ". . . idealism, of course." Dolores Alexander, interview by author, New York City, 6 November 1986.

263 ". . . in fact lesbian." Friedan, *Changed*, 141.

263 Friedan's viewpoint: Friedan, *Changed*, 140–41.

263 ". . . do with lesbianism." Friedan, *Changed*, 159.

263 ". . . was employment," Connell, author's interview.

263 ". . . minds of those present," Abbott and Love, 112.

263 ". . . a collective heart attack." Abbott and Love, 112.

263 Martin asks NOW to take a stand: Martin and Lyon, 289.

263 ". . . wasn't." Alexander, author's interview.

264 NOW's first lesbian purge: Abbott and Love, 120–27; Gay Revolutionary Party Women's Caucus, "Realesbians and Politicalesbians," in Jay and Young, 177.

264 ". . . lesbian once more," ". . . blow-ups" and ". . . Liberation Front." Brown, 192, 193, 194.

264 Congress to Unite Women: See Brown, 194; Friedan, *Changed*, 137–38.

264–5 "Lavender Menace" action described: Abbott and Love, 113–15; Hole and Levine, 239–40.

264–5 ". . . second-class status." Radicalesbians, "The Woman-Identified Woman," in *Radical Feminism*, Koedt et al., eds., 240–43.

265 ". . . never budged." Abbott and Love, 114.

265 "expression and love." Resolutions in Abbott and Love, 115.

265 ". . . affirming their Lesbianism. . . ." Abbott and Love, 115.

266 ". . . revolutionary sisters." Danielle Bernstein, letter to the editor, *NOW Newsletter*, Central New Jersey chapter, June 1970, p. 5.

266 Straight feminists' reactions to "lavender menace" action: Abbott and Love, 115.

266 ". . . not a Lesbian." Miriam G. Keiffer, "Coming In, or Will the Real Lesbian Please Stand Up?" in *coming out stories*, 210. Quoted in Ann Snitow, Christine Stansell, and Sharon Thompson, "Introduction," in Snitow, Stansell, and Thompson, 25.

266 For more on Radicalesbians, see: Radicalesbians (New York City), "Leaving the Gay Men Behind," in Jay and Young, 290–93.

266–7 Development of the gay-straight conflict in various groups: Abbott and Love, 116–17; Brown, 191; Martin and Lyon, 292. Connell, author's interview.

267–8 Millett described her experiences: Kate Millett, *Flying*, 14–17. Excerpted: Kate Millett, "The Pain of Public Scrutiny," *Ms*, June 1974, p. 76.

267 ". . . strength I had." Millett, *Flying*, 14–15.

267 ". . . into respectability." Millett, *Flying*, 17.

267 "remarkable": "Who's Come a Long Way, Baby?" *Time*, 31 August 1970, p. 16.

267 "articulate rage." "The Liberation of Kate Millett," *Time*, 31 August 1970, p. 19.

268 ". . . liberationists as lesbians." From "Women's Lib: A Second Look," *Time*, 14 December 1970, p. 50.

268 Feminist press conference: Abbott and Love, 123–25.

268 ". . . 'She's a lesbian.' " Connell, author's interview.

268 NOW's second purge: Abbott and Love, 126–27. NOW resolution supporting lesbians: Abbott and Love, 131, 134. See also Haney, 110–11.

269 Political lesbians: Freeman, 140–42.

269 ". . . child raising." Martha Shelley, "Notes of a Radical Lesbian," in Morgan, *Sisterhood Is Powerful*, 307.

269 "instant Lesbians," Martin and Lyon, 298–99.

269 ". . . a gimmick." Pat Shea, "Bloodroot: Four Views of One Woman's Business," *Heresies* #7 2, no. 3 (Spring 1979): 69. Quoted in Snitow, Stansell, and Thompson, "Introduction," 23.

269–70 ". . . pressures against men." Balser, author's interview.

270 Pressure to become lesbian had ended by about 1973: Freeman, 139.

270–1 Lesbian separatism: Charlotte Bunch, interview by author, New Brunswick, NJ, 9 January 1991. According to Bunch, in 1971 The Furies were in touch with other lesbian separatist groups in four or five cities. Her analysis of heterosexism: Bunch, *Passionate Politics*, 176–81, 196–202.

270 ". . . threatening to others." Charlotte Bunch, *Passionate*, 9.

270 ". . . male supremacy," Bunch, *Passionate*, 175.

270 ". . . queer for a week." Bunch, *Passionate*, 188.

270–1 See Adrienne Rich, "Compulsory Heterosexuality and Lesbian Existence," in Snitow, Stansell, and Thompson, 212–41.

271 ". . . erotic energies" and "bonding against male tyranny": Rich, "Compulsory," 217 and 227.

271 Lesbian counterculture: Lesbian journals included *Ain't I a Woman?*, *The Furies*, *Amazon Quarterly*, *Lesbian Tide*, *Sinister Wisdom*, and *Lesbian Connection*; Adam, 91. The ultimate difference feminists: See Donovan, 166.

271 ". . . much isolation." Bunch, author's interview.

271–2 Defeat of Dade County ordinance: Adam, 103–4.

272 Organizing for the Houston conference: See Caroline Bird et al., *What Women Want: From the Official Report to the President, the Congress and the People of the United States*, 47–53.

272 ". . . all over." Bunch, author's interview.

272–3 Attack on gay rights ordinances after Houston: See Sasha Gregory Lewis, *Sunday's Women: A Report on Lesbian Life Today* (Boston: Beacon, 1979), 6. Adam, 104. Most child molesters are heterosexual: Daniel Goleman, "Homophobia: Scientists Find Clues to Its Roots," *New York Times*, 10 July 1990, p. C1.

273 California referendum: Adam, 104–7.

273–4 AIDS crisis and its impact on the gay community and gay rights: See Adam, 156–60. Also "The Future of Gay America," *Newsweek*, 12 March 1990, p. 20. Falwell's response: Adam, 156–57. See also Thomas Morgan, "Amid AIDS, Gay Movement Grows but Shifts," *New York Times*, 10 October 1987, p. A1. James Barron, "Homosexuals See 2 Decades of Gains, but Fear Setbacks," *New York Times*, 25 June 1989, p. A1.

274 Lesbians becoming leaders of gay organizations: Bunch, author's interview. See also Katherine Bishop, "Lesbians Clear Hurdles to Gain Posts of Power," *New York Times*, 30 December 1990, p. 12.

274 More than thirty studies found no significant differences between the children of single heterosexual mothers and those of lesbians. Georgia Dullea, "Gay Couples' Wish to Adopt Grows, Along With Increasing Resistance," *New York Times*, 7 February 1988, p. 26. Also, "The Future of Gay America," *Newsweek*, 12 March 1990, p. 20.

274 Lesbians' baby boom reported: David Margolick, "Lesbian Child-Custody Cases Test Frontiers of Family Law," *New York Times*, 4 July 1990, p. 1.

274–5 The Kowalski case: See Karen Thompson and Julie Andrzejewski, *Why Can't Sharon Kowalski Come Home?* (San Francisco: Spinsters/Aunt Lute Book Co., 1988). Also "Sharon Kowalski Finally Begins Rehabilitation," *National NOW Times*, July/August/September 1989, p. 6; Nadine Brozan, "2 Sides Are Bypassed in Lesbian Case," *New York Times*, 26 April 1991, p. A12.

275–6 Domestic partnerships: See Katherine Bishop, "Not Quite a Wedding, but Quite a Day for Couples by the Bay," *New York Times*, 15 February 1991, p. A16. Also, "The Future of Gay America," *Newsweek*, 12 March 1990, p. 20. Using state registration laws: See Tamar Lewin, "California Lets Nontraditional Families Register," *New York Times*, 17 December 1990, p. A15. The states that permitted non-profit associations to register in 1990 were Michigan, New Jersey, Oregon, Virginia, West Virginia, and Wisconsin.

276n Ozzie-and-Harriet families now just 27 percent: Philip S. Gutis, "Family Redefines Itself and Now the Law Follows," *New York Times*, 28 May 1989, sec. 4, p. 6.

276 Examples of homophobia in the military: "Marines Are Said to Suspend Alleged Lesbians," *New York Times*, 23 February 1988, p. A23. Jane Gross, "Navy Is Urged to Root Out Lesbians Despite Abilities," *New York Times*, 2 September 1990, p. 245.

276 Sodomy laws: Though prosecutions for sodomy were exceedingly rare, the threat was always there. See Robb London, "Gay Groups Turn to State Courts to

Win Rights," *New York Times,* 21 December 1990, p. B6. The Supreme Court case was *Hardwick* v. *Bowers;* see "Arrest in Man's Home Began Test of Georgia Law," *New York Times,* 1 July 1986, p. A19; Stuart Taylor, Jr., "High Court, 5–4, Says States Have the Right to Outlaw Private Homosexual Acts," *New York Times,* 1 July 1986, p. A1.

276 Groups for gays: James Barron, "Homosexuals See 2 Decades of Gains, but Fear Setbacks," *New York Times,* 25 June 1989, p. A1.

277 Laws banning discriminating against gays in 1990 summarized: "The Future of Gay America," *Newsweek,* 12 March 1990, p. 20. See also "A Gay Rights Law Is Voted in Massachusetts," *New York Times,* 1 November 1989, p. A27.

277 ". . . for twenty years." Charlotte Bunch, presentation, "Celebration of Our Work" conference, Rutgers University, New Brunswick, NJ, 22 May 1990.

chapter 14: Feminists and Family Issues

278 Critics of the movement: See particularly Sylvia Ann Hewlett, *A Lesser Life: The Myth of Women's Liberation in America* (New York: Warner Books, 1987).

279 Catherine East has written one of the best analyses of feminist efforts on family issues: Catherine East, "Critical Comments on *A Lesser Life: The Myth of Women's Liberation in America,*" available from the National Women's Political Caucus, 1986.

280 Conservative mutterings about child care noted in: Margaret O'Brien Steinfels, *Who's Minding the Children? The History and Politics of Day Care in America,* 205. On the risks of mother substitutes: Selma Fraiberg, *Every Child's Birthright: In Defense of Mothering* (New York: Basic Books, 1977), 82, 84. Day care's association with poverty: Sheila M. Rothman, *Woman's Proper Place: A History of Changing Ideals and Practices, 1870 to the Present,* 272. Why the term "child care" replaced "day care": Florence Falk-Dickler, interview by author, New York City, 11 August 1987.

280–1 FAP described in Steinfels, 17. For the story of the NWRO and the Nixon plan, see Guida West, *The National Welfare Rights Movement. The Social Protest of Poor Women,* especially 3, 15, 22–30, 89–90, 310–11. Some say that the FAP was Nixon's response to NWRO protests: West, 310–11. Brief history of Head Start: Steinfels, 83–86. NOW's Bill of Rights: Friedan, *Changed,* 101–2.

281 ". . . with strangers." Florence Falk-Dickler, interview by author.

281 ". . . on rape. . . ." Eleanor Smeal, telephone interview by author, 18 March 1988.

281n Elizabeth Chittick's belief noted in Rupp and Taylor, 183.

281–2 Child-care coalition: Smeal, Falk-Dickler, author's interviews. For further information, see "Suffer the Little Children . . . The American Child-Care Disgrace," *Ms,* May 1974, p. 94. Rochelle Beck, "Beyond the Stalemate in Child Care Public Policy" in *Day Care: Scientific and Social Policy Issues,* Edward F. Zigler and Edmund W. Gordon, eds., 308, 326. Carole Joffe, "Why the United States Has No Child-Care Policy," in *Families, Politics, and Public Policy: A Feminist Dialogue on Women and the State,* Irene Diamond, ed., 171–72. Recent profile of Edelman: Katherine Bouton, "Marion Wright Edelman: If you're under 18, she's working for you on Capitol Hill," *Ms,* July/August 1987, p. 98; see also Rothman, 271.

282 ". . . divides their parents." Quoted in Rothman, 270–71.

282 Feminists' attitudes to child care: Smeal, Falk-Dickler, author's interviews. NOW's stand on child care summarized: "Why Feminists Want Child Care," position paper drafted by Florence Falk-Dickler, n.d., from Falk-Dickler's files.

282n Ratings in *Dictionary of Occupational Titles* reported in *Womanpower* 1, no. 2 (November 1971) 8.

282–3 Story of the 1971 child-care bill can be found in: Edward F. Zigler and Jody Goodman, "The Battle for Day Care in America: A View from the Trenches," in Zigler and Gordon, 343–45. Also: Beck, in Zigler and Gordon, 326; Steinfels, 187. Feminist reaction to the bill: Smeal, author's interview. Summary of right wing's position: Zigler and Goodman, "The Battle for Day Care," 344; Steinfels, 191–94, 203–5. Brademas' response to conservatives: *Congressional Quarterly Weekly Report,* 11 December 1971 (Washington, D.C.: Congressional Quarterly, 1971), 2534.

282 ". . . got something." Bouton, 100.

283 Women's organizations urged letters to Congress: For example, "National Women's Political Caucus Day Care Alert," dated 30 July 1971. Effort wasn't enough: See Virginia Kerr, "Keeping the Heat On," *Ms*, April 1974, p. 67. Conservative mail campaign and White House statement on it: *NOW Newsletter*, Central New Jersey chapter, December 1971, p. 6.

283 ". . . implications," ". . . family-centered approach," and ". . . first inculcated." Jack Rosenthal, "President Vetoes Child Care Plan as Irresponsible," *New York Times*, 10 December 1971, p. A1.

283 Critics of Nixon veto: For example, Carl M. Selinger, "Nixon's Social Philosophy," Letter to the Editor, *New York Times*, 1 January 1972, p. 19.

283 ". . . mass action. . . ."

283 Attempts to pass child-care legislation after 1971 summarized: Zigler and Goodman, "The Battle for Day Care," 345–46. Also Rothman, 278. African-American analysis of the problem: Evelyn Moore, "Day Care: A Black Perspective" in Zigler and Gordon, 413–44, especially 420. Right-wing reaction in 1979: See Catherine East, "Critical Comments," 8.

284 ". . . anyone in day care." Quoted in Nadine Brozan, "White House Conference on the Family: A Schism Develops," *New York Times*, 7 January 1980, p. 8. Cited in Mandel, *In the Running*, 242.

284 ". . . terribly on this issue," Smeal, author's interview.

284–5 Red-baiting as a right-wing strategy: See Amy Swerdlow, "Women's Activism Undercut: Red-Baiting Erases Historical Record," *New Directions for Women*, March/April 1989, pp. 12–13.

285 Cranston's reasons for withdrawing bill given in James A. Levine, "The Prospects and Dilemmas of Child Care Information and Referral," in Zigler and Gordon, 379.

285 The child-care tax deduction: See Gail Sheehy, "The Brave Crusade of Elizabeth Barrett," *Good Housekeeping*, February 1972, p. 71; also Freeman, *Politics*, 202–3; Winget, "The Dilemma of Affordable Child Care," in Zigler and Gordon, 351, 358. Why deduction didn't help poor: Moore, in Zigler and Gordon, 431–32.

285 Title XX grants: Orth, 94. Also Winget, in Zigler and Gordon, 359–61, 380. Most of the money went to the middle class: Beck, in Zigler and Gordon, 317.

285–6 For an analysis of failure of 1971 bill, see Beck, in Zigler and Gordon, 308–9; also East, "Critical Comments." East also explores political differences between the United States and Western Europe. Consequences when coalition groups fight among themselves: Beck, in Zigler and Gordon, 311.

286 The classic recent study of the impact of divorce on women is Lenore J. Weitzman, *The Divorce Revolution: The Unexpected Social and Economic Consequences for Women and Children in America*. Changes in living standards: Weitzman, xii. Other researchers reported a less dramatic difference, but the trends were the same: Financially, life improved for men after divorce even as it grew worse for ex-wives and children. One hundred thousand women with children became poor each year: Barbara Ehrenreich, "What Makes Women Poor?" *For Crying Out Loud: Women and Poverty in the United States*, Rochelle Lefkowitz and Ann Withorn, eds., 20. Women headed almost half of all poor families: Ruth Sidel, *Women and Children Last: The Plight of Poor Women in Affluent America*, xvi.

287 Men rebelled: Ehrenreich, 29–51. As an example of the male attack on marriage, she cites Philip Wylie, "The Abdicating Male . . . and How the Gray Flannel Mind Exploits Him Through His Women," *Playboy*, November 1956, p. 29.

287n After industrialization: See Ehrenreich, 4.

287 Rising divorce rate: Weitzman, xvii, footnote. Divorce/marriage rates in 1963 and 1975: U.S. Department of Commerce, Bureau of the Census, *Statistical Abstracts of the U.S.* (Washington, D.C.: United States Government Printing Office, 1980), 87.

287 U.S. divorce law before reform: See Weitzman, especially x, 7–14. Also Mary Ann Glendon, *Abortion and Divorce in Western Law*, 63–111; and Mary Ann Glendon, *State, Law and Family: Family Law in Transition in the United States and Western Europe*, 227–33.

287–8 California's no-fault law: Weitzman, x, 15–16, 28–32.

288 Wave of reform after California: Weitzman, x, 41–43.

288 Weitzman's case against no-fault laws: Weitzman, 10–14, 368. Men's campaign against alimony: Weitzman, 16–17; see also Joe Interrante, "Dancing Along the Precipice: The Men's Movement in the '80s," *Radical America* 15, no. 5 (September-October 1981): 53–71. "Alimony drones": Weitzman, 144.

288–9 Figures on alimony granted before 1970 and after 1980: Lynn Hecht Schafran, "Gender Bias in the Courts," in *Women as Single Parents: Confronting Institutional Barriers in the Courts, the Workplace, and the Housing Market*, 47. Changes in alimony after reform: Weitzman, 32–36, 164–67.

289 Marital property: Weitzman, 47–49, 60, 70–76, 104–9. See also Claire Safran, "Partnership and Prejudice: The Economics of Divorce," *Lear's*, May 1989, p. 32. New laws passed by Congress: Weitzman, 118.

289–90 Child support: Weitzman, 264–83. See also Tamar Lewin, "New Law Compels Sweeping Changes in Child Support," *New York Times*, 25 November 1988, p. A1. The default problem: Weitzman, 283–307; also, Schafran, "Gender Bias," 50–56.

290 Child-custody changes: Weitzman, 49–51, 215–61; Schafran, "Gender Bias," 56–59. Until the 1830s, fathers had an almost absolute right to custody of the children in a divorce; then the states began to pass laws awarding custody to mothers while the children were of "tender years." This was less an acknowledgment of women's rights than a mistrust of men's ability to care for the very young; see Kaminer, 50–51. In contested cases, fathers won custody more than half the time: Harriet Cohen, interview by author, New York City, 11 April 1989.

290 Judges' decisions on custody: Lynn Hecht Schafran, telephone interview by author, 1 May 1989. Also Weitzman, 240–42; Cohen, author's interview.

290 ". . . in parenting." Schafran, author's interview.

292n Older women less likely to remarry: Weitzman, 204. Lynn Hecht Schafran, "How Stereotypes About Women Influence Judges," *Judges' Journal* 24, no. 1 (Winter 1985): 52.

290–1 Child custody given to wife-beaters: Schafran, author's interview.

291 Switch to best-interests standard and women's problems caused by joint custody: Cohen, author's interview; Weitzman, 231–35, 245–56, 310–12, 361; Schafran, "Gender Bias," 59. See also Nancy D. Polikoff, "Gender and Child-Custody Determinations: Exploding the Myths," in *Families, Politics, and Public Policy: A Feminist Dialogue on Women and the State*, Irene Diamond, ed. (New York: Longman, 1983), 192–93.

291 ". . . losing their children." Cohen, author's interview.

291 Hazards of mediation: Cohen, author's interview. Joanne Schulman, telephone interview by author, 23 April 1989.

291–2 The primary caretaker rule: Weitzman, 244–45; Glendon, *Abortion and Divorce*, 102.

292 Divorce, European style: See Glendon, *Abortion and Divorce*, 57, 74, 80–81, 104–111, 132–42. Schafran, author's interview. Also Weitzman, 94, 201.

292 "mythology of self-reliance" and "politics of compassion," Glendon, *Abortion and Divorce*, 132.

293 Glendon on American reluctance to pay for safety net: Betty Sue Flowers, ed., *Bill Moyers, A World of Ideas: Conversations with Thoughtful Men and Women about American Life Today and the Ideas Shaping Our Future* (New York: Doubleday, 1989), pp. 480–81.

293 Women's coalitions in fifty states: Cohen, author's interview. Feminist mistakes: Schulman, author's interview; see Weitzman, 248–49.

293 Roberts conceived idea of educating judges: Lynn Hecht Schafran, "Educating the Judiciary About Gender Bias," *Women's Rights Law Reporter* 9, no. 2 (Spring 1986): 111–12.

293 ". . . program *was* needed." Schafran, author's interview.

293–4 Need for data on divorce: Schafran and East (1985), author's interviews; also Weitzman, 362–63. Some women tried to sound the alarm: Also Schafran, East interviews. Some examples: The Citizen's Advisory Council on the Status of Women (CACSW) in its 1971 report noted that judges rarely awarded alimony and when they did, they took into account the wife's ability to support herself—this, at a time when the rush to no-fault had barely begun. In 1972, NOW–New York drafted model legislation that included compulsory payroll deductions for child support; see "NOW Announces Model Divorce Reform Bill," *The Spokeswoman* 2, no. 9 (1 March 1972): 4. The CACSW 1973 report recommended that the divorce laws explicitly recognize the homemaker's contribution to the marriage. The media ignored press releases on the CACSW position papers. See East, "Critical Comments," 10, 14.

294 How divorce became a national issue: Schafran, author's interview. Weitzman's book led to changes: Schafran, Schulman, author's interviews. Efforts by women's organizations: See Schafran, "Gender Bias," 68.

294 How tougher laws were passed: Schafran, author's interview. See Tamar Lewin, "New Law Compels Sweeping Changes in Child Support," *New York Times*, 25 November 1988, p. A1; also Schafran, "Gender Bias," 50. States must act or lose federal welfare money: Elizabeth Kolbert, "Child Support Standards Worked Out in Albany," *New York Times*, 23 June 1989, p. B3.

295 ". . . chief reason," Cohen, author's interview.

295 Few women or feminists on the bench: Schafran, "Gender Bias," 66.

295–6 NJEP: From Schafran, author's interview. See Lynn Hecht Schafran, "Documenting gender bias in the courts: the task force approach," *Judicature* 70, no. 5 (February–March 1987): 280–90; Norma J. Wikler, "Water on Stone: A Perspective on the Movement to Eliminate Gender Bias in the Courts," *Court Review* 26, no. 3 (Fall 1989): 6–13.

295 ". . . give you equality.' " Schafran, author's interview.

296 Controversy among feminists over New York divorce reform: Schafran and Cohen, author's interviews.

296 ". . . rock the boat," Schafran, author's interview.

296 Drawbacks of gender-neutral divorce laws: Weitzman, 35, 365–66; Schulman, author's interview.

297 ". . . primary caretaking" and ". . . treatment to men." Schulman, author's interview.

297 The 1979 Supreme Court alimony decision was *Orr* v. *Orr:* Weitzman, 45; Goldstein, 233–39; Schafran, author's interview.

297 Weitzman's suggestions: Weitzman, 378–95. Allowing judges less discretion: Schafran, author's interview. See also Schafran, "Gender Bias," 70.

297–8 ". . . life experience. . . ." Schafran, "Gender Bias," 70.

298 Family leave situation in United States and elsewhere in the West in 1980s: See "New-Parent Leave: U.S. Lag Assailed," *New York Times*, 18 September 1985, p. C6; "A New Family Issue," *Newsweek*, 26 January 1987, p. 22. Also Schroeder, 44–56. A major study: Sheila B. Kamerman and Alfred J. Kahn, "Company Maternity Leave Policies," *Working Woman*, February 1984, p. 79.

298 A few states mandate maternity leave: "Politics of Child Care," *New York Times*, 5 September 1988, p. 10.

299 Problems of pregnant employees before the 1970s: Peg Simpson, "A Victory for Women," *Civil Rights Digest*, Spring 1979, p. 13; "Sex Bias: Punishing Pregnancy," *Civil Liberties*, March 1974, p. 6; Goldstein, 471; Schroeder, 48; East, "Critical Comments." Legal challenges to school systems that automatically discharged pregnant teachers: Story told in Fishel and Pottker, *National Politics*, 23–45. Pregnancy as a "voluntary" disability: Fischel and Pottker, 38; Simpson, 17.

299n General Electric's disability policy: Goldstein, 476.

299 Feminist strategy on disability and reasons for it described: Citizens' Advisory Council on the Status of Women, press release on "Job-Related Maternity Benefits," November 1970; CACSW's position was reported in "Maternity Leave: A Study, a Recommendation, and the Costs," *Womanpower* 1, no. 3, (December 1971): 4. The Citizen's Advisory Council stated that "no additional or different benefits or restrictions should be applied to disability because of pregnancy or childbirth, and no pregnant woman employee should be in a better position . . . than an employee . . . suffering from other disability."

299 The Supreme Court decision: *General Electric Co.* v. *Gilbert.* See Goldstein, 469–480; Schroeder, 47–48; Simpson, 16.

299n ". . . for elderly men." Wolfe, author's interview, 1986.

300 Congress passes PDA: See Simpson; Anne L. Radigan, *Concept & Compromise: The Evolution of Family Leave Legislation in the U.S. Congress*, 5. For a 1984 survey of maternity leave policies: Kamerman and Kahn. Also Georgia Dullea, "Conference Discusses Parental Job Leave," *New York Times*, 11 March 1985, p. C11.

300 ". . . political environment." East, "Critical Comments," 6.

300 California's maternity leave law: Radigan, 5; Goldstein, 469–80. See also Stuart Taylor Jr., "Job Rights Backed in Pregnancy Case," *New York Times*, 14 January 1987, p. A1.

300 Controversy in women's movement over California law: Schafran, author's interview. Schafran also made her case in: Lynn Hecht Schafran, "Coming of Age: The New Pluralism in the Women's Movement," speech before the National Jewish Community Relations Advisory Council plenary session, Fort Lauderdale, Florida, 16 February 1987, pp. 3–7. For a news report on the controversy, see Tamar Lewin, "Debate Over Pregnancy Leave," *New York Times*, 3 February 1986, p. D1. Also East, "Critical Comments," 7.

300 ". . . terrible law." Schafran, author's interview.

300–1 Supreme Court ruling on California law: Radigan, 14, 23. Also Stuart Taylor Jr., "Justices Hear Debate Over Pregnancy Leave," *New York Times*, 9 October 1986, p. A30; Stuart Taylor Jr., "Job Rights Backed in Pregnancy Case," *New York Times*, 14 January 1987, p. A1.

301 Drafting of federal family leave law: Radigan provides a behind-the-scenes account: Radigan, 9–13; East, "Critical Comments," 6. Opposition to it: Radigan, 20.

301–3 Study of European leaves systems: Susanne A. Stoiber, *Parental Leave and "Woman's Place": The Implications and Impact of Three European Approaches to Family Leave Policy.*

303 ". . . opportunities for women." Stoiber, 60.

303 European Parliament proposal: Stoiber, 6–7.

303 Veto kills family leave bill: See Steven A. Holmes, "House Backs Bush Veto of Family Leave Bill," *New York Times*, 26 July 1990, p. A16; also Tamar Lewin, "Battle for Family Leave Will Be Fought in States," *New York Times*, 27 July 1990", p. A8.

304 The article that touched off the controversy over "Mommy tracks": Felice N. Schwartz, "Management Women and the New Facts of Life," *Harvard Business Review*, January–February 1989, p. 65. See also Tamar Lewin, " 'Mommy Career Track' Sets Off a Furor," *New York Times*, 8 March 1989, p. A18; "Letters" column, *New York Times*, 2 April 1989, sec. 4, p. 30.

304 ". . . and weekends." Schwartz, 70.

304 *Times* story on Mommy track in law firms: Jennifer A. Kingson, "Women in the Law Say Path Is Limited by 'Mommy Track,' " *New York Times*, 8 August 1988, p. 1.

304–5 Schafran on "parent tracks," hopes of male lawyers as women entered the profession: Lynn Hecht Schafran, "Lawyers' Lives, Clients' Lives: Can Women Liberate the Profession?" the Donald A. Gianella Memorial Lecture, delivered at Villanova University School of Law, Philadelphia, PA, 13 April 1989.

304 ". . . priority." Schafran, "Lawyers' Lives," 6.

305–6 Difference feminists' arguments are set forth, for example, in Elizabeth H. Wolgast, *Equality and the Righis of Women* (Ithaca: Cornell University Press, 1980); Sylvia A. Law, "Rethinking Sex and the Constitution," *University of Pennsylvania Law Review* 132 (1984): 955–1039.

306 For equality feminists' arguments, see Wendy W. Williams, "Equality's Riddle: Pregnancy and the Equal Treatment/Special Treatment Debate," *New York University Review of Law and Social Change* 13, no. 2 (1984–5): 325–80; Ruth Bader Ginsburg, "Some Thoughts on the 1980s Debate over Special Versus Equal Treatment for Women," *Law & Inequality: A Journal of Theory and Practice* 4, no. 1 (May 1986): 143–151; Kaminer, *Fearful Freedom.* Mechanical equality versus realistic equality: Schafran, personal communication.

306 Building on the successes of the civil rights movement: For example, Title VII (chapter 2).

306–7 Women need to have it both ways: Snitow, 216–17. Cott writes of feminism's "characteristic doubleness": Cott, 49.

307 ". . . we'll get it." Susanne A. Stoiber, during question period after panel on family leave, National Women's Research Council conference, Washington, D.C., 13 June 1989.

chapter 15: Violence Against Women

308 Statistics on sexual abuse and date rape: Susanna Downie, principal author and editor, *Decade of Achievement, 1977–1987: A Report on a Survey Based on the National Plan of Action for Women*, 60. One sociologist estimated that, out of every ten girls who were twelve years old in 1980, two or three would be sexually assaulted at some time in their lives. That meant a woman's chance of being raped was about the same as her chance of being divorced. See Allan Griswold Johnson, "On the Prevalence of Rape in the United States," *Signs* (Autumn 1980): 136–46.

308 Sexual harassment: Alliance Against Sexual Coercion, *Fighting Sexual Harassment: An Advocacy Handbook* (Boston: Alyson Publications and the Alliance Against Sexual Coercion, 1981), 79.

308 Statistic on battered women: Murray Straus, telephone interview by author, 7 March 1989. See Richard J. Gelles and Murray A. Straus, *Intimate Violence: The Causes and Consequences of Abuse in the American Family* (New York: Simon & Schuster, 1988). The figures on abuse given in this book are minimum estimates; Straus believes that the true figures are twice as high.

309 Rape among the ancient Hebrews: Susan Brownmiller, *Against Our Will: Men, Women and Rape*, 9–15. Rape in early English law: Brownmiller, 15–22.

309–10 History of laws against wife-beating in United States: See Del Martin, *Battered Wives*, 32; Susan Schechter, *Women and Male Violence: The Visions and Struggles of the Battered Women's Movement*, 217.

310 ". . . had been raped." Brownmiller, author's interview.

310 ". . . had been raped," Connell, author's interview.

310 Small percentage of rape victims went to the police: Brownmiller, 190.

310–11 Speakout on rape described: Gail Sheehy, "Nice Girls Don't Get Into Trouble," *New York*, 15 February 1971, p. 26; Brownmiller, 387–420. Also Noreen Connell and Cassandra Wilson, eds., *Rape: The First Sourcebook for Women*, 34.

310 ". . . like a precious egg," Sheehy, 26.

311 The NYRF rape conference generated a book: Connell and Wilson (see above). Rape in New York: See Edith Barnett, "Legal Aspects of Rape in New York State" in Connell and Wilson, 147–49.

311 New York City statistics: Brownmiller, 417.

311–2 How various states handled corroboration: Noreen Connell, "Introduction," 125–33, and Edith Barnett, "Legal Aspects of Rape in New York State," 134–36, both in Connell and Wilson.

312 ". . . guilt of the defendant." Quoted in Brownmiller, 419.

312 Study of rape juries described in Pamela Lakes Wood, "The Victim in a Forcible Rape Case: A Feminist View," in Connell and Wilson, 160–64.

312 Male fear of false rape accusations: Brownmiller, 13–14.

312 ". . . never so innocent." Quoted in Brownmiller, 413.

312 It was standard procedure to read the "Lord Hale Instruction": Lynn Hecht Schafran, "Eve, Mary, Superwoman: How Stereotypes About Women Influence Judges," *The Judges' Journal* 24, no. 1 (Winter 1985): 48.

312–3 Other rape myths: Brownmiller, 346–50.

313 The history of rape as an assault on black women: See Bell Hooks, *Ain't I a Woman: Black Women and Feminism*, especially chapters one and two. Also, Jacquelyn Dowd Hall, " 'The Mind That Burns in Each Body': Women, Rape, and Racial Violence," in Snitow, Stansell, and Thompson, 339–60. And Noreen Connell and Cassandra Wilson, "Interview with Essie Green Williams," in Connell and Wilson, 256–63.

313 ". . . sexual lust." Hooks, *Ain't I a Woman*, 33.

313 ". . . emasculate black men." Hooks, *Ain't I a Woman*, 34.

313 ". . . the prostitute." Hooks, *Ain't I a Woman*, 52–53.

313 Black men falsely accused of rape: Connell and Wilson, "Interview with Essie Green Williams," 260.

314 ". . . in a state of fear." Brownmiller, 5.

314 Rape crisis centers: See Cassandra Wilson, "Rape Groups," in Connell and Wilson, 194–207, and "Rape Crisis Centers," in Connell and Wilson, 189–92.

314 States rewrite rape laws: A spot check of twenty-five states in the mid-1970s found that fifteen had reformed their rape laws within the previous year as a result of efforts by women's groups. See "Women's Movement in the U.S. 1960–1975," a briefing paper prepared by the International Women's Year Secretariat staff, June 1975, p. 18. Gender-neutral rape laws: See Susan Estrich, *Real Rape: How the Legal System Victimizes Women Who Say No*, 81.

314 " '. . . rape for ya, Charlie.' " Quoted in Connell and Wilson, 169.

314–5 Problems that came with federal funding for antirape projects: Schechter, 39, 41–42, 185–86. Rape projects in 1976: Schechter, 39.

315 Date rapes ("simple" rapes): See Estrich, especially 4–7, 12, 20, 25. Also Laura Mansnerus, "Sketchy Statistics: The Rape Laws Change Faster Than Perceptions," *New York Times*, 19 February 1989, p. 20; Nadine Brozan, "Jurors in Rape Trials Studied," *New York Times*, 17 June 1985, p. C13.

315 Problems with laws requiring proof that assailant used force: Estrich, 20–22, 58–59, 62, 64–65, 71.

315–6 Rape on college campuses: William Celis 3d, "Growing Talk of Date Rape Separates Sex From Assault," *New York Times*, 2 January 1991, p. A1. One 1979 study found that 43 percent of males of high school and college age believed it was "acceptable" for a man to force sex on a woman by the fifth date, while 39 percent said it was "acceptable" if the man had simply spent a lot of money on her; see Daniel Goleman, "When the Rapist Is Not a Stranger: Studies Seek New Understanding," *New York Times*, 29 August 1989, p. C1.

316 For a feminist analysis of wife rape: Diana E. H. Russell, *Rape in Marriage*. Legal history of marital rape: "To Have and to Hold: The Marital Rape Exemption and the Fourteenth Amendment," *Harvard Law Review* 99 (1986): 1255–73. By 1980, only New Jersey, Oregon, and Nebraska had completely abolished the marital exemption for rape, though several other states had partially abolished it—wife rape was treated as a less serious form of rape in California, for example; see Russell, 21.

316 ". . . the perpetrator." Quoted in Russell, 17.

316 ". . . who can you rape?" Quoted in Russell, 18.

316n Wives may be raped but not battered: Russell, 145.

316–7 The Rideout case: Russell, 19–20. Wife rape worse than date rape: Russell, 191–92.

317 Changes in laws on wife rape: Laura X, telephone interview by author, 8 April 1991. The rape exemption for cohabiters in 1980: Russell, 21–22. Improvement by 1991: Laura X, author's interview.

317 Liabilities of gender-neutral phrase, "spousal rape": Russell, 9.

317–8 Trauma of incest: Judith Lewis Herman, M.D., "Violence in the Lives of Women: Treatment and Recovery," talk given at Harvard Medical School conference, "Women: Connections, Disconnections and Violations," Boston, 10 June 1989. See also Christina Robb, "A Theory of Empathy: The Quiet Revolution in Psychiatry," *Boston Globe Magazine*, 16 October 1988, p. 18.

318 Justice system fails to protect children from sexual abuse: See Lynn Hecht Schafran, "Gender Bias," 58.

318 The Elizabeth Morgan case can be tracked through reports in the press: Felicity Barringer, "Prison Releases a Defiant Mother," *New York Times*, 26 September 1989, p. A18; "Who Will Listen to Hilary?" *National NOW Times*, October/November/December 1988, p. 4; Felicity Barringer, "Girl in Custody Case Emerges in New Zealand," *New York Times*, 24 February 1990, p. 9; "Ruling on Custody Ends Bitter Case," *New York Times*, 1 December 1990, p. 11.

318–9 The underground railroad: "Secret Network Helps Children Flee Sex Abuse," *New York Times*, 20 June 1988, p. A16.

319 Plight of battered women before movement was organized: Schechter, 5, 11, 55, 162; Martin, 94–95, 102–4, 131.

319n Washington, D.C. statistics: Schechter, 54.

319–20 Why women stay with their abusers: Barbara Hart, interview by author, Reading, PA, 13 February 1989. See Barbara J. Hart, *Confronting Domestic Violence: Effective Police Response* (Harrisburg, Pennsylvania: Pennsylvania Coalition Against Domestic Violence, 1990), 9–10; Schechter, 16–20.

320 ". . . a process," Hart, author's interview.

320–1 Growth of a battered women's movement: Martin, 198–99, 207–25; Schechter, 56, 49–50, 79; Kathleen J. Tierney, "The Battered Women Movement and the Creation of the Wife Beating Problem," *Social Problems* 29, no. 3 (February 1982): 207–20.

321 Founding of NCADV: Carol Schmidt and Janet Nudleman of NCADV, telephone interviews by author, 7 March 1989.

321–2 Problems that came with funding: Lois Ahrens, "Battered Women's Refuges: Feminist Cooperatives vs. Social Service Institutions," *Aegis: Magazine on Ending Violence Against Women*, Summer/Autumn 1980, p. 41.

321 ". . . relationships with men." Quoted in Schechter, 48.

322 Defeat of domestic violence bill: Martin, 262; Schechter, 146, 185–95.

322 ". . . at a standstill," Susan Kelly-Dreiss, telephone interview by author, 6 March 1989.

322 Passage of 1984 bill establishing victims' fund: Janet Nudleman, author's interview.

322–3 How Reagan administration helped: Barbara Hart, author's interview.

323 Situation for battered women in 1991: NCADV, by telephone, April 1991. Women won suits against police: Crystal Nix, "For Police, Domestic Violence Is No Longer Low-Priority," *New York Times*, 31 December 1986, p. B1.

323 Negative side of the picture: Janet Nudleman, author's interview. See Cynthia Diehm and Margo Ross, "Battered Women," in *American Woman 1988–89*, Rix, ed., 292–302; Downie, 18; Eric Schmitt, "Turnabout in Aiding Victims of Family Abuse Is Lacking," *New York Times*, 17 January 1989, p. B1.

323–4 Danger of bringing charges against the batterer even when victim is unwilling: Hart, author's interview; Schechter, 175.

324 Origin of the term, "domestic violence": Kelly-Dreiss, author's interview.

324 Russell on battered husbands: Russell, 102–9. 95 percent of batterers are male: Diehm and Ross, 292.

324–5 Counseling programs for batterers: Hart, author's interview.

324 Certainty of jail deters battering: In 1984, a study done in Minneapolis found that when batterers were promptly arrested, they were only half as likely to commit another assault. Many police departments were finally convinced that tough tactics were worthwhile; by 1986, 46 percent of big-city police departments had instituted a prompt-arrest policy. See Andrew H. Malcolm, "Major Study of Domestic Violence Fails to Detect a Path to Killings," *New York Times*, 5 February 1990, p. B9.

325 ". . . intentional killers," ". . . nonviolent control," and ". . . never free." Hart, author's interview.

325n Drinking doesn't necessarily cause battering: Hart, author's interview; Russell, 156–57.

325–6 Battered women sentenced for murder: Hart, author's interview. See Jane Roberts Chapman, "Women in Prison," in *American Woman 1988–89*, Rix, ed., 303–309; Schechter, 171. Battered-woman syndrome: Hart, author's interview. See also Lenore Walker, *Terrifying Love: Why Battered Women Kill and How Society Responds* (New York: Harper & Row, 1990).

326–7 NYRF conference on prostitution: Brownmiller, author's interview. For a contemporary report on it, see "Prostitution Conference: Aftermath," *Majority Report*, no. 8 (January 1972): 11.

326–7 ". . . to sell your mind." Brownmiller, author's interview.

327 Many prostitutes are victims of childhood sexual abuse: See Jennifer James and Jane Meyerding, "Early Sexual Experience as a Factor in Prostitution," *Archives of Sexual Behavior* 7, no. 1 (1977), cited in Russell, 260. Barry's recommendations: Kathleen Barry, "UNESCO Report Studies Prostitution," *Whisper* 1, no. 3 (Winter 1986–87): 1. See also Bunch, *Passionate Politics*, 309.

327–8 The 1988 conference: "Trafficking in Women Internationally," New York City, 22 October 1988. Speaker from South Korea: Mi Kung Lee. From the Philippines: Aurora Javate de Dios. From Japan: Yayori Matsui. From Norway: Trine Thoen.

328 ". . . rape the practice," Robin Morgan, *Going Too Far*, 169.

328 "domino theory of sexuality." Alice Echols, "The New Feminism of Yin and Yang," in Snitow, Stansell, and Thompson, 70.

328 For a brief summary of the feminist porn controversy that describes the birth of the antiporn movement, see Eisenstein, 116–24; also Morgan, *Going Too Far*, 167. The antipornography point of view: Laura Lederer, ed., *Take Back the Night: Women on Pornography* (New York: William Morrow, 1980); Susan Griffin, *Pornography and Silence: Culture's Revenge Against Nature* (New York: Harper & Row, 1981); Andrea Dworkin, *Pornography: Men Possessing Women* (New York: Perigee/G.P. Putnam's, 1981).

328–9 The Dworkin-MacKinnon antiporn strategy: MacKinnon, 176–91. See also "Minneapolis Asked to Attack Pornography as Rights Issue," *New York Times*, 18 December 1983, p. 44; E. R. Shipp, "Civil Rights Law Against Pornography Is Challenged," *New York Times*, 15 May 1984, p. A14.

328 Psychological research: Edward I. Donnerstein and Daniel G. Linz, "The Question of Pornography: It Is Not Sex, but Violence, That Is an Obscenity in Our Society," *Psychology Today*, December 1986, p. 56.

329 ". . . in pictures or in words." "Minneapolis Asked to Attack Pornography as Rights Issue," *New York Times*, 18 December 1983, p. 44.

329 Antiporn feminists opposed by FACT: MacKinnon, 236. Lynn Hecht Schafran, "Coming of Age: The New Pluralism in the Women's Movement," speech before the National Jewish Community Relations Advisory Council plenary session, Fort Lauderdale, Florida, 16 February 1987, 7–12. For the argument against the antiporn ordinance, see Lisa Duggan, Nan D. Hunter, and Carole S. Vance, "False Promises: Feminist Antipornography Legislation," in *Caught Looking: Feminism, Pornography & Censorship* (New York: Caught Looking Inc., 1986), 72–85; Kaminer, 200–3.

330 Rape the theme of one out of eight films: See "The Killing Numbers," *Ms*, September/October 1990, p. 45. Danger of violence in the mass media: Donnerstein and Linz.

330 Opposing both the ordinance and violent porn: Schafran, "Coming of Age," 7–12.

330–1 Battered lesbians: Ellen Bell, "Women Abusing Women," reprinted in *Connexions*, no. 34 (1990): 28–30; originally published as "With Our Own Hands," in the British feminist quarterly, *Trouble and Strife*, no. 16, Summer 1989. See also "Lesbian Battery," *Ms*, September/October 1990, p. 48.

331 Campus seminars on rape: William Celis 3d, "Growing Talk of Date Rape Separates Sex From Assault," *New York Times*, 2 January 1991, p. A1. Clemency for battered women: Tamar Lewin, "More States Study Clemency for Women Who Killed Abusers," *New York Times*, 21 February 1991, p. A19.

331 Increase in violence against women: See Jane Caputi and Diana E. H. Russell, " 'Femicide': Speaking the Unspeakable," *Ms*, September/October 1990, pp. 34–37. United States imprisons high percentage of citizens: "U.S. Leads World in Imprisonment," *New York Times*, 7 January 1991, p. A14.

chapter 16: *Equal Pay and the Pauperization of Women*

332 Pearce's article: Diana Pearce, "The Feminization of Poverty: Women, Work, and Welfare," *Urban and Social Change Review* 11, no. 1 (February 1978): 28–36. Reprinted in Rochelle Lefkowitz and Ann Withorn, *For Crying Out Loud: Women and Poverty in the United States*, 29–46.

332–3 For a critique of the feminist reaction to the poverty issue, see Lefkowitz and Withorn, particularly the following chapters: Rochelle Lefkowitz and Ann Withorn, "Introduction," 4; Linda Burnham, "Has Poverty Been Feminized in Black America?" 69–83; Pamela Sparr, "Reevaluating Feminist Economics: 'Feminization of Poverty' Ignores Key Issues," 61–67.

333 Explanation of poverty threshold: See Robert D. Hershey Jr., "The Hand That Shaped America's Poverty Line as the Realistic Index," *New York Times*, 4 August 1989, p. A11. The *projected* poverty threshold for a family of three in 1991 was $11,092. See Jason DeParle, "Working Poor Gain Under Tax Accord," *New York Times*, 31 October 1990, p. A20.

333–4 Poverty threshold, as estimated, is unrealistic: Hershey, "The Hand That Shaped"; also Sara M. Evans and Barbara J. Nelson, *Wage Justice: Comparable Worth and the Paradox of Technocratic Reform*, 10.

334n Gallup poll: "Poverty Is Perceived as Increasing and State of the Poor Unimproved," *New York Times*, 23 August 1989, p. A14.

334 For the "culture of poverty" theory, see Oscar Lewis, *La Vida* (New York: Random House, 1966). A more recent version: Kenneth Auletta, *The Underclass*, (New York: Random House, 1982).

334 For a brief account of the findings of the University of Michigan study (called the PSID—the Panel Study of Income Dynamics), see Mary Corcoran, Greg J. Duncan, and Martha S. Hill, "The Economic Fortunes of Women and Children: Lessons from the Panel Study of Income Dynamics," *Signs* 10, no. 2 (Winter 1984): 232–48.

334 Changes in American poverty from 1960s to 1990s: See Sparr, in Lefkowitz and Withorn, 65; Deborah K. Zinn and Rosemary C. Sarri, "Turning Back the Clock on Public Welfare," *Signs* 10, no. 2 (Winter 1984): 369–70; Leonard Silk, "Poverty Strikes the Children Hardest: Now, to Figure Why the Poor Get Poorer," *New York Times*, 18 December 1988, sec. 4, p. 1; Peter Passell, "Forces in Society, and Reaganism, Helped Dig Deeper Hole for Poor," *New York Times*, 16 July 1989, p. 1. By 1988, 13.1 percent of Americans below poverty line: Felicity Barringer, "Number of Nation's Poor Remains at 32 Million for a Second Year," *New York Times*, 19 October 1989, p. A24.

334–5n James Lardner, "Rich, Richer: Poor, Poorer," *New York Times*, 19 April 1989, p. A27

334–5 Changes in profile of the poor: Passell, "Forces"; Silk, "Poverty Strikes." Children poor in 1969: Children's Defense Fund, by telephone, 7 June 1991.

335 Poverty among people of color: "Report Finds Poverty Among Children Is Up," *New York Times*, 2 February 1989, p. C13; Ruth Sidel, *Women and Children Last: The Plight of Poor Women in Affluent America*, 12.

335 Increase in women's poverty since 1959: Sparr, in Lefkowitz and Withorn, 65.

335 Poverty and single mothers: See Heather McLeod, "The Radcliffe Conferences: Women in the 21st Century: Defining the Challenge," *Radcliffe Quarterly*, March 1989, pp. 2–6; Aida Hurtado, "Relating to Privilege: Seduction and Rejection in the Subordination of White Women and Women of Color," *Signs* 14, no. 4 (Summer 1989): 833–55; Silk, "Poverty Strikes."

335 Racism causes poverty: Burnham in Lefkowitz and Withorn, 69–83. Black male unemployment in 1990: National Urban League African-American Adolescent Male Development Center, New York City, by telephone, 7 June 1991. See Burnham, 81; also Sidel, 109. Black women, divorce and remarriage: Burnham, 81.

335 Decline of heavy industry, rise of service sector: Evans and Nelson, 32–33; West, *The National Welfare Rights Movement*, 262.

336 Inadequate welfare benefits: Guida West, interview by author, New Brunswick, NJ, 17 August 1989. See Sidel, 87–99.

336n Welfare benefits in 1989: Michael de Courcy Hinds, "Pulling Families Out of Welfare Is Proving to Be an Elusive Goal," *New York Times*, 2 April 1990, p. A1. Poverty threshold: U.S. Census Bureau, author's telephone call, 26 April 1991.

336 The laws that banned sex discrimination in employment were the Equal Pay Act, Title VII, Title IX, and Title VIII of the Public Health Service Act.

336 Comparison of antidiscrimination laws in the United States and Western Europe: Joyce Gelb, *Feminism and Politics*, 107–14, 164–71. The AT&T settlement: Harvey D. Shapiro, "Women on the Line, Men at the Switchboard" *New York Times Magazine*, 20 May 1973, p. 26. The original settlement was estimated at $38 million, but the total eventually reached $50 million; see Paul Delaney, "Action Reviewed on Bias Charges," *New York Times*, 12 February 1974, p. 36.

336–7 Discrimination went underground: See Ralph E. Winter, *Wall Street Journal*,

"Changing Bias: All Applying Are Equal but Some Are More So at Many Companies," 6 June 1973, p. 1.

337 Problems with enforcement: Marcia Greenberger, interview by author, Washington, D.C., 13 January 1988.

337 ". . . before she left." Greenberger, author's interview.

337 ". . . on the merits." Greenberger, author's interview.

338 ". . . and more." Eleanor Holmes Norton, lecture, Princeton University, Princeton, NJ, 28 September 1989.

338 Progress and lack of progress for women: Sidel, 61, 67. From the end of World War II until the 1980s, women's pay remained less than 60 percent of men's: Evans and Nelson, 29.

338 How *Dictionary of Occupational Titles* is used: Ronnie Steinberg and Lois Haignere, "Separate but Equivalent: Equal Pay for Work of Comparable Worth," in *Gender at Work: Perspectives on Occupational Segregation and Comparable Worth*, 18–19. See U.S. Department of Labor, Employment and Training Administration, *Dictionary of Occupational Titles*, 4th ed., 1977, and 1986 supplement (Washington, D.C.: United States Department of Labor, 1977, 1986).

338 Feminist case for pay equity: Steinberg and Haignere, 19.

338–9 Arguments for and against pay equity summarized: Evans and Nelson, 24–25, 42, 165; Steinberg and Haignere, 18–20; Feldberg, 321; Teresa Ammott and Julie Matthaei, "Comparable Worth, Incomparable Pay," in Lefkowitz and Withorn, 320–325.

338n Figures for Minnesota from: Sociologists for Women in Society, "Facts about Pay Equity," April 1986. Studies around the country: Steinberg and Haignere, 17.

339–40 The Sears case is documented in *Signs* 11, no. 4 (Summer 1986). In that issue, see: Sandi E. Cooper, "Introduction to the Documents," 753–56; "Offer of Proof Concerning the Testimony of Dr. Rosalind Rosenberg," 757–66; "Written Testimony of Alice Kessler-Harris," 767–79. For a discussion of the traps inherent in the equality-difference debate, as illustrated by the Sears case, see Joan Wallach Scott, *Gender and the Politics of History* (New York: Columbia University Press, 1988), 167–77.

340 Campaign for pay equity in the state of Washington: Evans and Nelson, 32–41; also Steinberg and Haignere, 18. For an account of how Minnesota's pay equity bills were passed, see Evans and Nelson, 69–91; Steinberg and Haignere, 21.

341 ". . . since Looney Tunes." See "Business and the Law: States Leading on Pay Equity," *New York Times*, 22 June 1987, p. D2.

341 ". . . can be paid more," Quoted in Evans, 40.

341 Switch from lawsuits to legislation and labor negotiations: Tamar Lewin, "Pay Equity for Women's Jobs Finds Success Outside Courts," *New York Times*, 7 October 1989, p. A1. Figures for 1991: Lisa Hubbard, National Committee on Pay Equity, telephone interview by author, 22 February 1991. See National Committee on Pay Equity, *Pay Equity Activity in the Public Sector 1979–1989* (Washington, D.C.: National Committee on Pay Equity, 1989), especially 4–6.

341 Frances Hutner, personal communication, 5 October 1989.

341 Minnesota's experience with pay equity summarized: Evans and Nelson, 98. Though most of the Minnesota pay equity beneficiaries were women, 10 percent were men who worked in predominantly female jobs.

341–42 Advantages and disadvantages of pay equity as a strategy: Evans and Nelson, 11–14, 57–58, 111–12, 123–24, 162–73.

342–3 Tish Sommers's story is told in Laurie Shields, *Displaced Homemakers: Organizing for a New Life*, xi, 25–26.

343 Founding of Alliance for Displaced Homemakers: Shields, 25–28, 46–48. See also Kathleen Kautzer, "Growing Numbers, Growing Force: Older Women Organize," in Lefkowitz and Withorn, 159.

343 ". . . for both sexes. . . ." Shields, xiv.

343 Pilot program: Shields, 50, 52, 71.

343 ". . . friends, and relatives" Shields, 52.

343 ". . . all that alimony." Shields, 55.

343 First center established; Shields's tour and growth of network: Shields, 61, 63, 76–89.

343–4 Opposition by Schlafly: Shields, 130. Situation in 1979: Shields, xiii. Survival during the Reagan years, situation in 1990: Communication from National Displaced Homemakers Network, 6 June 1990.

344 Founding of OWLEF: Shields, 176–77; Kautzer, 158–63. Founding of OWL: Margaret Mann, Director of Field Services, OWL, by telephone, 7 June 1991. See Judy Klemesrud, " 'If Your Face Isn't Young': Women Confront Problems of Aging," *New York Times*, 10 October 1980, p. A24.

344–5 Women's problems with pensions: Mary L. Heen, "Sex Discrimination in Pensions and Retirement Annuity Plans After *Arizona Governing Committee v. Norris*: Recognizing and Remedying Employer Non-Compliance," *Women's Rights Law Reporter* 8, no. 3 (Summer 1985): 155–76, especially 158. Also Margaret W. Newton, "Women and Pension Coverage," in *American Woman 1988–89*, Rix, ed., 264–70; Don McLeod, "Retirement Far from a Golden Pond for Women in Pension Crunch," *AARP Bulletin* 31, no. 7 (August 1990): 1; Sidel, 162; Shields, 205.

345 Pension reform laws affecting Foreign Service, military: Anne Moss, "Women's Pension Reform: Congress Inches Toward Equity," *University of Michigan Journal of Law Reform* 19, no. 1 (Fall 1985): 165–68. Congress passes REA: Sidel, 161. Poverty among older women in the late 1980s: McLeod, "Retirement"; Tamar Lewin, "Change in Social Security for Women Is Urged," *New York Times*, 10 May 1990, p. A27.

345–6 Reforming social security: Tish Sommers, "Epilogue," in Shields, 202–5. For more on how the system developed, see Sidel, 82–83. Most women collect social security as their husband's dependent: "Heading for Hardship: Retirement Income for American Women in the Next Century," report from the Older Women's League, Washington, D.C., May 1990. Yearly earnings are recorded and then averaged, after first eliminating the five years during which the individual earned the least. Thus, a woman who stayed home for fifteen years to raise children accumulated ten years of zero income to bring down her average. 1979 change in the law: Hilda Kahne, "Economic Security of Older Women: Too Little for Late in Life," Working Paper 102, Wellesley College Center for Research on Women, Wellesley, MA, 1981, pp. 12–16.

346 Health insurance: Shields, 207. Law passed in 1986: Lawrence M. Fisher, "Message From Older Women," *New York Times*, 29 September 1986, p. B13.

346–7 Older women's economic problems in the 1990s: "Heading for Hardship."

347–53 History of the National Welfare Rights Organization: Guida West, *The National Welfare Rights Movement. The Social Protest of Poor Women*. Also Guida West, author's interview. See also Frances Fox Piven and Richard A. Cloward, *Poor People's Movements: Why They Succeed, How They Fail*, 264–361.

347 History of welfare system: West, 17–19. In 1972, welfare rights activist Johnnie Tillmon noted that "on the average, another baby means another $35 a month— barely enough for food and clothing. Having babies for profit is a lie that only men could make up, and only men could believe." Johnnie Tillmon, "Welfare Is a Women's Issue," *Ms*, Spring, 1972, pp. 111–16.

347–8 Keeping the welfare rolls down before the 1960s: West, 18, 46, 293; West, author's interview. See also Piven and Cloward, 264–68.

348 Situation changed in late 1960s: West, 1, 238–39; Piven and Cloward, 265, 273.

348 Tillmon's initial organizing: See Tillmon, "Welfare"; West, xiii.

348 Wiley founds NWRO: West, 24–25. Piven and Cloward describe their involvement: Piven and Cloward, 275.

349 NWRO's founding conference and structure: West, 30, 53, 55, 57; Piven and Cloward, 288, 293.

349 How local WROs operated: West, author's interview. See West, 40, 98–99, 251; Piven and Cloward, 297.

349 Mass of contradictions: West, author's interview. See West, 3, 15.

349 ". . . people there are." Quoted in West, 246.

349 How to change the system: Piven and Cloward's view given in Piven and Cloward, 276. Wiley's position: West, author's interview.

350 NWRO's achievements and growth: West, author's interview. See West, 6, 229–30, 295; Piven and Cloward, 295, 309, 325.
350 ". . . happen to anybody. . . . " Johnnie Tillmon, "Welfare Is a Women's Issue," *Ms*, Spring 1972, p. 111.
350 ". . . away from welfare." Tillmon made this statement at a NOW meeting in the late 1960s. Quoted in West, 47.
350 Nixon's Family Assistance Plan and the backlash against welfare rights groups: West, author's interview. See West, 300, 310–12; Piven and Cloward, 305, 333.
350 Decline in NWRO's membership: Piven and Cloward, 326–30, 335.
351 ". . . was gradually lost." Piven and Cloward, 330.
351 Conflicts within NWRO: West, 38, 81, 86, 94
351 ". . . national protest movement." West, 94.
351 Transformation of NWRO: Piven & Cloward, 349–51; West, 116, 119–20.
351 ". . . strictly a women's organization." Quoted in West, 122.
351 The end of NWRO: West, 35, 123.
351 ". . . and deference," Frances Fox Piven and Richard A. Cloward, "Foreword," in West, viii.
351–2n The iron law of oligarchy was proposed by Robert Michels in a classic work on European socialist parties. See Frederick D. Miller, "The End of SDS and the Emergence of Weathermen: Demise Through Success," in Freeman, *Social Movements*, 281.
352–3 NWRO's relations with white liberals: West, 248. With black women's groups: West, 237–40, 250. With white feminist organizations: West, 247, 251–61. The dependency issue: West, 89, 244–45. Cross fertilization: West, 4, 15, 122, 254–261.
353 ". . . in the movement." West, author's interview.
353 Second wave of welfare rights activism: Sidel, 86–88, 97. The inadequacy of the female-headed family: Ken Auletta, *The Underclass*; Martin Anderson, *Welfare* (Stanford, CA: Hoover Institution Press, 1978). For a response to the right wing's argument, see Sara McLanahan, "Family Structure and the Reproduction of Poverty," *American Journal of Sociology* 90, no. 4 (1985): 873–98.
353–4 The University of Michigan study: Corcoran, Duncan, and Hill, "Economic Fortunes," 243–46. Also Greg J. Duncan, Martha S. Hill, and Saul D. Hoffman, "Welfare Dependence Within and Across Generations," *Science* 239, (29 January 1988): 267–471; Sidel, 97–99.
354 The Family Support Act of 1988: Martin Tolchin, "Congress Leaders and White House Agree on Welfare," *New York Times*, 27 September 1988, p. A1; "Real Welfare Reform, at Last," *New York Times*, editorial, 1 October 1988, p. 26.
354 ". . . revolving door." West, author's interview.
354 Revived welfare rights movement and problems it faced: West, author's interview.
355 Welfare situation in the 1990s: Theresa Funiciello, "The Poverty Industry: Do Government and Charities Create the Poor?" *Ms*, November/December 1990, p. 33.
355 Feminist strategies for changing the welfare system: West, author's interview; Funiciello, "The Poverty Industry."
355 "Enabling rights" suggested by Kaminer, *A Fearful Freedom*, 16–18. In the 1970 *Dandridge* case, which delivered a body blow to the welfare rights movement, the Supreme Court explicitly stated that although the welfare laws addressed the most basic economic needs of the poor, those needs weren't fundamental rights like the right to free speech.

chapter 17: Diversity: From the Melting Pot to the Salad Bowl

357 NWPC's steering committee: See "'Goals Set by Women's Political Caucus,'" *New York Times*, 13 July 1971, p. 37.
357 Harris didn't see herself as a token: LaDonna Harris, telephone interview by author, 19 June 1990.
358 ". . . few were interested." Faust, author's interview.

358 White feminists' assumptions about women of color: For example, Jane Chapman, who attended meetings of the Leadership Conference on Civil Rights in Washington in 1970–71 as a NOW representative, recalled that the black women at the meetings made it clear that they didn't want to be considered part of "this feminist craziness." Chapman, author's interview.

358 Why women of color were reluctant to join white feminist groups: From discussion during a panel on integrating NOW, annual conference, Cincinnati, Ohio, 21–23 July 1989.

358 Mistake to downplay differences between women: Echols, 15; Eisenstein, "Introduction," in Eisenstein and Jardine, xv–xxiv. Also Spelman, 12–15.

358 ". . . fusing way." Quoted in Echols, 89–90.

359 Shared viewpoint an achievement: Elizabeth V. Spelman, *Inessential Woman*, 13. On invisibility, 153.

359 ". . . recognize themselves in it" and ". . . nugget of womanness," Spelman, 159.

359 Racism to assume: Spelman, 124.

359–60 Wolfe's story: author's interview, 1986.

360 ". . . important to them." Leslie Wolfe, telephone interview by author, 28 May 1990.

360–1 For more on the Houston conference, see Caroline Bird, *What Women Want*, 16, 59–60; Sarah Harder, "Flourishing in the Mainstream: The U.S. Women's Movement Today," in *American Woman 1990–91*, Rix, ed., 275; *The Spirit of Houston: The First National Women's Conference*, Official Report, 156–57.

361–2 Founding of NIWC: Sharon Parker, telephone interview by author, 22 June 1990. See Sharon Parker, "Why 'Women of Color,' " *Network News*, Fall 1988, p. 1; "NIWC Background and Accomplishments" from NIWC. Overview of women-of-color organizations in 1990: Parker, author's interview; Wolfe, author's interview, 1990.

362 ". . . feminist, but . . ." Parker, author's interview.

363 ". . . In charge. *Serious*. . . ." Alice Walker, *In Search of Our Mothers' Gardens* (New York: Harcourt Brace, 1983), xi.

363 1972 poll: Giddings, 345. In 1985, African-American women were still more in favor of feminism than white women were—78 percent to 72 percent. For more on various surveys, see Ethel Klein, "The Diffusion of Consciousness in the United States and Western Europe," in Mary Fainsod Katzenstein and Carol McClurg Mueller, ed., *The Women's Movements of the United States and Western Europe: Consciousness, Political Opportunity, and Public Policy*, 27.

363 Fear that employers would favor white women: Bell Hooks, *Feminist Theory: From Margin to Center*, 97–98 (hereafter called *Margin to Center*). For an account of government-encouraged competition between "minorities"—redefined to include women—see Dirk Johnson, "Women and Minorities Compete for Share of Highway Contracts," *New York Times*, 5 March 1988, p. A1.

363 ". . . serious flaw." Toni Morrison, "What the Black Woman Thinks About Women's Lib," *New York Times Magazine*, 22 August 1971, p. 15.

364 ". . . another planet." Giddings, 299.

364 Family their bulwark: Hooks, *Margin to Center*, 37.

364 ". . . the Voting Rights Act." Quoted in Charlayne Hunter, "Many Blacks Wary of 'Women's Liberation' Movement," *New York Times*, 17 November 1970, p. 47; also in Giddings, 308.

364 ". . . really responsible." Quoted in Echols, 75.

364 ". . . Negro Family." Quoted in Giddings, 325. See also Lee Rainwater and William L. Yancey, *The Moynihan Report and the Politics of Controversy* (Cambridge, MA: M.I.T. Press, 1967), 24.

364 " . . . is to strut." Giddings, 326.

364 Female dominance—the problem and the solution: Rainwater and Yancey, 29; Giddings, 328.

365 For an analysis of "black matriarchy" and the influence of the Moynihan report, see Patricia Hill Collins, "A Comparison of Two Works on Black Family Life," *Signs*

14, no. 4 (Summer 1989): 875–84. Giddings discusses masculine power and the report: 314–35. Many believed black men's chauvinism stemmed from frustration: Bell Hooks, "Feminism: A Movement to End Sexist Oppression," in Phillips, 63.

365 ". . . important person." Carolyn Bird, "Woman Power," *New York*, March 1969, p. 38. Quoted in Giddings, 329.

365 ". . . guerilla warfare" and ". . . be a man.' " Michele Wallace, "A Black Feminist's Search for Sisterhood," in *All the Women Are White, All the Blacks Are Men, but Some of Us Are Brave: Black Women's Studies*, Gloria T. Hull, Patricia Bell Scott, and Barbara Smith, eds., 9.

365 Reality of employment for black women: See Hooks, *Ain't I a Woman*, 145–46.

365–6 Gays and homophobia in the black community: Jewelle L. Gomez and Barbara Smith, "Taking the Home out of Homophobia: Black Lesbian Health," in *The Black Women's Health Book*, Evelyn C. White, ed., 198–213. The rape issue: Giddings, 310, 322–23.

366 The need to broaden the feminist view of reproductive rights: Sharon Parker, author's interview. See also E. J. Dionne Jr., "Tepid Black Support Worries Advocates of Abortion Rights," *New York Times*, 16 April 1989, p. A1.

366 Feminist theories that offended black women: Giddings, 304; Hooks, *Margin to Center*, 50–54.

366 ". . . gay men are Black." Audre Lorde, "There Is No Hierarchy of Oppressions," *Interracial Books for Children Bulletin* 14, nos. 3–4 (September 1983): 9.

366 Racism not just an add-on to sexism: Spelman, 14, 77.

366 The feminism of Kathleen Cleaver: Giddings, 311, 316.

367 For more on NBFO, see Jones, 277–78, 319; Giddings, 344; Wallace, 11. Also Barbara Campbell, "Black Feminists Form Group Here," *New York Times*, 16 August 1973, p. 36.

367n Jones on black feminism: Jacqueline Jones, *Labor of Love, Labor of Sorrow*, 277–278.

367 The Combahee River Collective: Combahee River Collective, "A Black Feminist Statement," in Hull, Scott, and Smith, 13–22. Also Giddings, 344.

367 The National Coalition of 100 Black Women was founded in 1981 and by the end of the decade had thirty chapters in twenty states and the District of Columbia. Giddings, 352.

367 Founding of African-American Women for Reproductive Freedom: Wolfe, author's interview, 1990, and Parker, author's interview.

367–8 For a 1990 status report on Hispanic Americans, see Gloria Bonilla- Santiago, "A Portrait of Hispanic Women in the United States," in *The American Woman 1990–91*, Rix, ed., 249–57. Also Lawrence K. Altman, "Many Hispanic Americans Reported in Ill Health and Lacking Insurance," *New York Times*, 9 January 1991, p. A16.

368 ". . . long history." Veronica Collazo, telephone interview by author, 16 December 1990.

368 In 1990, the major organizations for Latinas included MANA, the Mexican-American Women's National Association; the Comision Feminil Mexicana Nacional, headquartered in California; NACOPRA, the National Conference of Puerto Rican Women; the National Association of Cuban-American Women and Men, which started out as the National Association of Cuban-American Women and was still predominantly female; the National Network of Hispanic Women, for professional women; and the Hispanic Women's Council. Collazo, author's interview.

368–70 History of MANA: Elvira Valenzuela Crocker, phone interview by author, 11 January 1991.

368 ". . . Hispanic spectrum" and ". . . Chicana and a feminist," Crocker, author's interview.

369 ". . . option for women." Crocker, author's interview.

369 ". . . family focus," Crocker, author's interview.

369 Statistics on education: Crocker, author's interview; Bonilla-Santiago, 252.

369 ". . . expectations of me." Crocker, author's interview.

370 History of Pan Asia and other API groups: Irene Lee, telephone interview by author, 21 June 1990. See "Pan Asia and Public Policy," in *Pan Asian Women: A Vital*

Force (Washington, D.C.: Organization of Pan Asian American Women, 1985), 10–17; and Juanita Tamayo Lott, "Asian and Pacific American Women as Vital Forces Across the Nation," also in *Pan Asian Women*, 18–22. Also Juanita Tamayo Lott, "A Portrait of Asian and Pacific American Women," in *American Women 1990–91*, Rix, ed., 258–64.

370–1 In 1980, 27 percent of APA women over the age of twenty-five had had four or more years of college, compared to 21 percent of white men and 13 percent of white women; Lott, "A Portrait," 260. Comparison to what white men earn is between median annual incomes; also Lott, "A Portrait," 261.

371 ". . . little English." Lee, author's interview.

372 Background on Native Americans: Based partly on author's interview with LaDonna Harris. See Matthew Snipp, "A Portrait of American Indian Women and Their Labor Force Experiences," in *American Woman 1990–1991*, Rix, ed., 265–72; Daniel Golden, "The Most Desolate Place," *Boston Globe Magazine*, 19 November 1989, p. 18; Daniel Golden, "The Legacy of Wounded Knee," *Boston Globe Magazine*, 26 November 1989, p. 20.

372–3 Why Native American women were less likely to form groups separate from men: LaDonna Harris, author's interview. See Paula Gunn Allen, *The Sacred Hoop: Recovering the Feminine in American Indian Traditions* (Boston: Beacon Press, 1986), 2–3, 30–37.

373 Organizing around women's concerns on reservations: Snipp; Golden, "The Most Desolate Place."

373 ". . . relative who is not." Golden, "The Most Desolate Place," 74.

373 Organizing against domestic violence: Loretta Webster, telephone interview by author, 22 June 1990.

373–4 ". . . our heritage" and ". . . the Indian community." Webster, author's interview.

374 Ada Deer's struggle described: Jane B. Katz, "Introduction," in *I Am the Fire of Time: The Voices of Native American Women*, Jane B. Katz, ed. (New York: Dutton, 1977), xviii.

374–5 History of AIO: LaDonna Harris, author's interview.

374 ". . . see fit." LaDonna Harris, author's interview.

375 Disability rights activists challenge women's movement: Patrisha Wright, telephone interview by author, 12 December 1990; Judy Heumann, telephone interview by author, 19 December 1990.

375–6 History of the disability rights movement: Wright, Heumann, author's interviews. The law that contained Section 504 was the Vocational Rehabilitation Act. Passage of the law and the 1977 demonstrations described: Roberta Ann Johnson, "Mobilizing the Disabled," in Freeman, *Social Movements*, 82–100.

376 Increase in the number of disabled Americans: Simi Litvak, Hale Zukas, and Judith E. Heumann, *Attending to America: Personal Assistance for Independent Living*, 2–19. One out of six Americans: Wright, author's interview.

376 Overview of the disability rights movement: Wright, author's interview.

376 ". . . pass a bill." Wright, author's interview.

376 Groups headed by women: Heumann, author's interview.

377 Amending the Fair Housing Act, passage of the ADA: Wright, author's interview. See Steven A. Holmes, "House Approves Bill Establishing Broad Rights for Disabled People," *New York Times*, 23 May 1990, p. A1; Robert Pear, "U.S. Proposes Rules to Bar Obstacles for the Disabled," *New York Times*, 22 January 1991, p. A1.

377 ". . . inaccessible . . ." Judy Heumann, author's interview.

377 ". . . cost-neutral. . . ." and ". . . making contributions." Judith Heumann, "How Women with Disabilities Can Advance into the Mainstream of Society," paper prepared for Seminar on Disabled Women, Vienna, Austria, 20–24 August 1990, pp. 15, 16.

377–8 Importance of personal attendants: Heumann, author's interview. The impact of public policy on disabled people was made poignantly clear when Larry McAfee, a man paralyzed in a motorcycle accident, successfully petitioned the courts to have his respirator removed so that he could die. The state was willing to pay for McAfee's care in a nursing home but not for care in the community, and he couldn't face the future. Pressured by disability groups, health officials finally agreed to place McAfee in a group home where he shared personal attendants with several other quadriplegics. He found a job and changed his mind about committing suicide. See Steven A. Holmes, "Disabled People Say Home Care Is Needed to Use New Rights," *New York Times,* 14 October 1990, p. 22.

378 Push for federal personal-assistance law, situation in the states: Wright, Heumann, author's interviews. See Litvak, Zukas, and Heumann, *Attending to America,* 7; Holmes, "Disabled People."

378–9 Heumann's point that personal assistance is a women's issue, and her concerns about abortion and the goals of genetic research: Heumann, author's interview. See Judy Heumann, "How Women with Disabilities Can Advance," 6.

378n Unequal pay for the disabled: Wright, author's interview.

379 ". . . as equals" and ". . . not perfect." Heumann, author's interview.

379n Problems getting health insurance: Sandra Blakeslee, "Ethicists See Omens of an Era of Genetic Bias," *New York Times,* 27 December 1990, p. B9.

379–80 Conference for women in their twenties: Rebecca Davis, interview by author, Princeton, NJ, 5 December 1989; Leslie Wolfe, author's interview, 1990. See Rebecca Davis, "Young Women Fight Movement Racism," *New Directions for Women,* January/February 1990, p. 5.

380 Hooks' comment: Hooks, *Margin to Center,* 53.

380 ". . . across the gulf." Wolfe, author's interview, 1990.

380–1 YWCA a model: Alice Levine, telephone interview by author, 6 June 1990. AAUW undertook a serious struggle: Parker, author's interview.

381 Founding and first year of Dallas Rainbow NOW were described by Karen Ashmore, panelist, NOW annual conference, San Francisco, CA, 30 June 1990.

381 ". . . I've ever done." Karen Ashmore, NOW conference.

381–2 History of NYWAR: Danette Wilson, telephone interview by author, 16 May 1990.

382 ". . . challenged the organization." Wilson, author's interview.

382 Action taken by McIntosh: Emily Jane Style, personal communication. McIntosh, of the Wellesley College Center for Research on Women, was also co-director with Style of the S.E.E.D. (Seeking Education Equity and Diversity) Project on Inclusive Curriculum.

382 West's decision: Author's interview.

382 A long way to go: Asetoyer, author's interviews; Wolfe, author's interview 1990.

382 ". . . our needs." Luz Alvarez Martinez, author's interview.

383 ". . . name a few. . . ." Hooks, *Ain't I a Woman,* 194.

383 Nothing would change: Hooks, *Margin to Center,* 15.

383 ". . . we must rescue. . . ." Hooks, *Talking Back: Thinking Feminist, Thinking Black,* 21.

383 What women must attack: Hooks, *Margin to Center,* 117–31.

383 Bunch on domination: Bunch, *Passionate Politics,* 150–51, 337.

383–4 Projections of future American demographics: See Marian Wright Edelman, "Fighting for the Rights of Children: Each of Us Can Be a Flea," *Radcliffe Quarterly,* September 1989, pp. 18–19; Tom Wicker, "A Needed Revolution," *New York Times,* 15 January 1990, p. A17; William A. Henry III, "Beyond the Melting Pot," *Time,* 9 April 1990, p. 28.

384 Not melting pot but salad bowl: Emily Jane Style, comment at Seminar on Perspectives, Rutgers University, 25 January 1989.

384 ". . . value of our diversity." Lucinda M. Finley, "Transcending Equality Theory: A Way Out of the Maternity and the Workplace Debate," *Columbia Law Review* 86, no. 6 (October 1986): 1153.

384 ". . . that I'm Black. . . ." Pat Parker, *Movement in Black: Collected Poetry of Pat Parker 1961–1978* (Oakland, CA: Diana Press, 1978); Foreword by Audre Lorde; Introduction by Judy Grahn.

chapter 18: Why the ERA Lost

385 Jane Mansbridge discusses the ERA as a movement: Mansbridge, *ERA*, 121, 178–86, 303.

386 The "blanket amendment": See Amelia R. Fry, "Alice Paul and the ERA," in *Rights of Passage: The Past and Future of the ERA*, Joan Hoff-Wilson, ed., 11–12.

386 The *Yale Law Journal* article was written by several young feminist legal scholars and Thomas Emerson, an authority on constitutional law; Griffiths distributed the article to all members of the House and Bayh inserted it into the Congressional Record. See Barbara A. Brown, Thomas I. Emerson, Gail Falk, and Ann E. Freedman, "The Equal Rights Amendment: A Constitutional Basis of Equal Rights for Women," *Yale Law Journal* 80 (1971): 955–62.

386 63 percent of public supported ERA: Mary Frances Berry, *Why ERA Failed*, 78.

386–7 Early ratifications: Mansbridge, *ERA*, 12–13.

387 Founding of ERA Ratification Council: Marguerite Rawalt, author's interview. See Mason, 825–27; Elizabeth Pleck, "Failed Strategies; Renewed Hope," in Hoff-Wilson, 106–19.

387 ". . . in state politics." Sandler, author's interview.

387 Schlafly's initial attack on the ERA: "The Right to Be a Woman," *Phyllis Schlafly Report* 6, no. 4 (November 1972). Readers' response noted: Mansbridge, *ERA*, 110–112, 283.

387 Schlafly's background: See, for example, Ehrenreich, 152–61; Mansbridge, *ERA*, 174.

387–8 ". . . is political." Mansbridge, author's interview.

388 ERA would have passed in 1973: Pleck, "Failed Strategies," 109. See also Eileen Shanahan, "Opposition Rises to Amendment on Equal Rights," *New York Times*, 15 January 1973, p. 1. Feminist response to opponents: Mansbridge, *ERA*, 74–76; also Shanahan, "Opposition Rises."

388 Labor admits defeat: "Women's Rights Boosted. AFL-CIO Switch Backs ERA Effort," *Trenton Times*, 19 October 1973, n.p. Ratification loses momentum: Mansbridge, *ERA*, 13. ERA Ratification Council still on a shoestring: Pleck, "Failed Strategies," 108–9.

388 Efforts to rescind vote to ratify: See Eileen Shanahan, "Stiff Fight Looms Over Ratification of Equal Rights Amendment," *New York Times*, 29 January 1974, p. 15; "Tennessee Sets Back Vote on Amendment," *New York Times*, 20 March 1974, p. 24; Susan Fog, "Amendment Needs 5 More States' Approval," *Sunday Star Ledger* (Newark), 20 October 1974, p. 6. Article V of the Constitution, which deals with the ratification process, says nothing about rescinding. The U.S. Supreme Court decided only one case where a state rescinded ratification, and it sidestepped by ruling that only Congress could decide questions of rescission. Twice, Congress did decide and rejected states' attempts to rescind. See Berry, 72; "ERA," in *do it NOW* 7, no. 6 (June 1974): 12.

338–9 Initial assumptions about ERA: Mansbridge, *ERA*, 6. Fundamentalists involved: Mansbridge, *ERA*, 174–75. ERA would do more for homemakers: Griffiths, author's interview.

389n Impact of state ERAs on divorce settlements: See Schafran, "Coming of Age."

389n Gender difference in support for ERA: Nadine Brozan, "58% in Gallup Poll Favor Equal Rights," *New York Times*, 10 April 1975, p. 45.

389 Antifeminist arguments against ERA and feminist responses: Mansbridge, *ERA*, 92–93, 110–11; Catherine East, "The First Stage," 10; Edith Mayo and Jerry K. Frye, "The ERA: Postmortem of a Failure in Political Communication," in Hoff-Wilson, 85–89; Shanahan, "Opposition Rises"; *The Spirit of Houston*, 57; East, "Critical Comments," 17.

389–90 Antifeminist predictions: Mansbridge, *ERA*, 128–29; Catherine East, author's interview, 1985; Jane Dehart-Mathews and Donald Mathews, "The Cultural Politics of the ERA's Defeat," in Hoff-Wilson, 44–53.

390 "Potty politics": See Mayo and Frye, 85; Mansbridge, *ERA*, 91, 111, 114, 284–285 (note 62).

390 ". . . she was doing." Catherine East, author's interview, 1985. See also Mansbridge, *ERA*, 144.

390–1 Analysis of ERA press coverage: See Catherine East, "The Legal Impact of the Equal Rights Amendment," 17–20; also "New Directions for News," 2–5; and Catherine East and Dorothy Jurney, "Summary: How Did Newspapers Report Issues of Importance to Women?" 6; all are in *A Newspaper Study . . . New Directions for News*, sponsored by the Women Studies Program and Policy Center of The George Washington University, Washington, D.C., September 1983.

391 ERA stalls: Mansbridge, *ERA*, 13–14, 177; Mason, 1000.

391 Women's movement grows: Berry, 67; Mason, 894, 904–8, 940–44; Smeal, 25.

391 ERA extension campaign: Mansbridge, *ERA*, 13; Berry, 70; Paterson, 236–37; Mason, 1006–7.

392 Betrayal in Florida: Mason, 1000. Insurance industry: Smeal, 33–37; Berry, 78.

392n Cost to women of gender-based insurance rates: See "Sex and the Insurance Policy," *Business Week*, 7 February 1983, p. 83; Nick Ravo, "Hartford Weighs Insurance Curbs," *New York Times*, 28 February 1988, p. 33.

392 Conflict between NOW and other organizations: Mansbridge, *ERA*, 131.

392 Close calls: Mansbridge, *ERA*, 184. Carter's draft plan and the legal challenge to male-only draft registration: Major General Jeanne Holm, *Women in the Military: An Unfinished Revolution* (Novato, California: Presidio Press, 1982), 347–62. Feminist reaction: Mansbridge, *ERA*, 71–76.

393 Combat issue and what the polls showed: Mansbridge, *ERA*, 85–86 and 60–66.

393 Schlafly took credit for Reagan's election: Jerome L. Himmelstein, "The New Right," in Robert C. Liebman and Robert Wuthnow, The New Christian Right: Mobilization and Legitimation, 27.

393 The gender gap and the way NOW used it: Kathy Bonk, "The Selling of the 'Gender Gap': The Role of Organized Feminism," in *The Politics of the Gender Gap: The Social Construction of Political Influence*, Carol M. Mueller, ed., 82–101.

393 Supreme Court decision on the draft: Mansbridge, *ERA*, 74–89; Holm, 363–78. The case was *Rostker* v. *Goldberg*, 453 U.S. 57. See also Goldstein, 249–66.

393 Feminists believed insurance industry was funding anti-ERA groups: East, author's interview, 1985; Pleck, in Hoff-Wilson, 115. NOW's finances: Berry, 78, 80; Pleck, in Hoff-Wilson, 115.

393–4 New activists: East, author's interview, 1988. College missionaries: Hazel Staats-Westover, personal communication. Older women on sabbaticals: For example, in 1982 NOW sent 52 "equality riders" to the unratified states; eight planned to stay until the end of the ratification drive; NOW-New York Board of Directors Meeting, minutes, 3 May 1982, p. 2, in NOW-New York archives at Tamiment Library, New York University. More than 450 organizations: Janet K. Boles, "The Equal Rights Amendment as a Non-Zero-Sum Game," in Hoff-Wilson, 58. Polls: Elizabeth Pleck, "Notes on the Defeat of the ERA," Working Paper No. 103, Wellesley College Center for Research on Women, Wellesley, MA, 1983, p. 2. Opposition stronger: Mansbridge, *ERA*, 2, 18.

394 Pro-ERA fast in Illinois: Berenice Carroll, "Direct Action and Constitutional Rights: The case of the ERA," in Hoff-Wilson, 63–75; also Mansbridge, *ERA*, 153–154, 291. Nathaniel Sheppard, Jr., "Women Say They'll End Fast but Not Rights Fight," *New York Times*, 24 June 1982, p. A16.

394 Grass Roots Group of Second Class Citizens: Berry, 81; Mansbridge, *ERA*, 166.

394 ERA fails in Illinois: Berry, 81.

394 ". . . wise God," and ". . . washing the dishes." Quoted in Berry, 82.

395 East's statement, author's interview, 1988; see East, "Critical Comments," 16. A switch in a couple of votes: Jane Mansbridge, lecture, Princeton, NJ, 27 March 1986. Needed more women legislators: Mansbridge, *ERA*, 150–51.

395 Difficulty of amending the Constitution: Mansbridge, *ERA*, 29; Berry, 64; Arthur S. Line, "Foreword," viii, and Hoff-Wilson, "Introduction," 41, both in Hoff-Wilson.

395–6 Conflict of interests between feminists and traditional homemakers: Mansbridge, *ERA*, 98–110.

396 ". . . all of them?" Ehrenreich, 146, 151.

396 Homemaker's fears: Jane DeHart Matthews, presentation at "Women and Tradition" conference, Rutgers University, New Brunswick, NJ, 21 May 1985. Schlafly on duty and romance: Phyllis Schlafly, *The Power of the Positive Woman* (New Rochelle, NY: Arlington House, 1977), 76; cited in Kaminer, 58, 222.

396 ". . . trusting them too well." Ehrenreich, 152.

397 ERA wouldn't mean courts ordered women into front lines, wouldn't expand abortion rights: See Mansbridge, *ERA*, 3, 86–89, 120–28, 129–33, 178–86.

397 Mansbridge on social-movement dynamics and NOW's assumptions: *ERA*, 68–89.

397 ". . . and premises." Mansbridge, *ERA*, 81.

397 ". . . do the job." Sandler, author's interview.

397 ". . . to defend them." Mansbridge, *ERA*, 68–69.

397–8 ". . . darn kids.' " Griffiths, author's interview.

398n Military women in the Middle East: Jane Gross, "New Home Front Develops as Women Hear Call to Arms," *New York Times*, 18 September 1990, p. A1.

398n Pentagon took in more women because so many black men were applying: Cynthia Enloe, *Does Khaki Become You? The Militarization of Women's Lives* (Boston: South End Press, 1983), 136–37.

398 Feminists' needed to be consistent: Mansbridge, *ERA*, 71–74, 76. Ban on women in combat-related jobs: Mansbridge, *ERA*, 72–74.

398 Female upper-body strength: Mansbridge, *ERA*, 68. Women in police and fire departments: Mansbridge, Princeton lecture. Women tested on combat skills: Mansbridge, *ERA*, 70–71. Survey of opinion on women in the military: Mansbridge, *ERA*, 69–70.

399 ". . . for a bad one." Mansbridge, *ERA*, 89.

399 Why both sides focused on combat issue: Mansbridge, *ERA*, 47.

399–400 The abortion issue: Mansbridge, *ERA*, 122–28.

399 Hames's opinion: Personal communication, April 1991.

400 Homophobia: Lesbian visibility sometimes caused controversy: Mansbridge, 130–31. Gay rights resolution at Houston conference: *The Spirit of Houston*, 119, 166; Catherine East, author's interview, 1985.

400 ". . . ERA through first,' " Griffiths, author's interview.

400 ". . . prolesbian people they are," *The Spirit of Houston*, 119.

400 ". . . who are lesbians." Quoted in *The Spirit of Houston*, 166.

400–1 Changes achieved even without an ERA: Mansbridge, *ERA*, 56–59, 90–98. Why an ERA was still necessary: Mansbridge, *ERA*, 59, 60. For a discussion of the ERA's probable impact as of 1977, see *The Spirit of Houston*, 49–51, 57.

401–2 For explanations of the Supreme Court's interpretation of the fourteenth amendment, see Goldstein, 88–90; Ruth Bader Ginsburg, "The Burger Court's Grapplings with Sex Discrimination," in *The Burger Court: The Counter Revolution That Wasn't*, Vincent Blasi, ed., Foreword by Anthony Lewis (New Haven: Yale University Press, 1983), 132–56, especially 133.

402 ". . . decision-makers to change." Ruth Bader Ginsburg, interview by author, Washington, D.C., 22 June 1989. Ginsburg became a United States Circuit Judge for the U.S. Court of Appeals, District of Columbia Circuit.

403 ". . . right place to go" and ". . . complaining about." Ginsburg, author's interview.

403 ". . . giant step." Ginsburg, author's interview.

403–4 Account of the *Reed* case: Ginsburg, author's interview. See Goldstein, 112–114. Court watchers agreed: Mansbridge, *ERA*, 49. The Reed brief was written by Ginsburg and Mel Wulf, then Legal Director of the ACLU; Sally Reed's Idaho lawyer argued the case before the Supreme Court.

403 The tender years doctrine: See Weitzman, 216.

403 ". . . Richard's estate." Ginsburg, author's interview.

404–5 The *Frontiero* case: Ginsburg, author's interview. See Ruth Bader Ginsburg, Address at Symposium on "Feminism in the Law: Theory, Practice and Criticism," University of Chicago Law School, 14 October 1988 (hereafter Ginsburg, Chicago Symposium); Goldstein, 115–26. See also Bob Woodward and Scott Armstrong, *The Brethren: Inside the Supreme Court* (New York: Avon, 1979), 301–3.

404 ". . . basis as *Reed*," Ginsburg, author's interview.

405 Court wavers: See Ruth Bader Ginsburg, "Sexual Equality under the Fourteenth and Equal Rights Amendments," *Washington University Law Quarterly* 1979, no. 1 (Winter): 161–78.

405 *Craig* v. *Boren:* Ginsburg, author's interview. See Ginsburg, in Blasi, 140–41; Goldstein, 165–78; Mansbridge, *ERA*, 141, 246, note 15. Powell's separate opinion: Goldstein, 170–71.

405–6 The alimony case was *Orr* v. *Orr*, 440 U.S. 268 (1979); Goldstein, 232–39. The statutory rape case was *Michael M* v. *Superior Court*, 450 U.S. 464 (1981): See Ginsburg in Blasi, 153–54; Goldstein, 268–82.

406 Feminist critiques of the statutory rape decision and the Court's mind-set: Sylvia A. Law, "Rethinking Sex and the Constitution," *University of Pennsylvania Law Review* 132, no. 5 (June 1984): 955–1040, especially 998–1002; Ann E. Freedman, "Sex Equality, Sex Differences, and the Supreme Court," *Yale Law Journal* 92, no. 6 (May 1983): 913–68, especially 956–57.

407 Supreme Court's 1977 decision on disparate impact: Ginsburg, author's interview. See Goldstein, 504–12; Freedman, 944–49. The case was *Dothard* v. *Rawlinson*, 433 U.S. 321 (1977).

407 The *Feeney* case: Goldstein, 240–49; Ginsburg in Blasi, 146–47.

407n Veterans' preference laws in other states: Goldstein, 240–49; Ginsburg in Blasi, 146–47.

408 Attempt to revive ERA in 1983. See Berry, 101–8; feminists expected the House to pass the amendment, but believed the Republican-controlled Senate would reject it or would pass it with crippling amendments attached.

408 Feminists hammer out positions: East, author's interview, 1985. Those positions were presented during congressional hearings. See U.S. Congress, Senate, Subcommittee on the Constitution of the Committee on the Judiciary, *The Impact of the Equal Rights Amendment: Hearing on S.J. 10*, 98th Cong., 2nd sess., 24 January 1984, pp. 437–544 (hereafter called *Impact*).

408–9 Freedman's testimony and opponents' responses: *Impact*, 437–532.

409 ". . . really means," *Impact*, 26 May 1983, p. 94.

409 ". . . the advantage?" *Impact*, 1 November 1983, p. 342.

409 Congress rejects ERA in 1983: Berry, 101–7; Mansbridge, *ERA*, 187; William E. Farrell, "U.S. Amendment on Equal Rights Beaten in House," *New York Times*, 16 November 1983, p. A1. Feminist strategy after the defeat: Berry, 118.

410 Release of energy after ERA's defeat: Mansbridge, *ERA*, 195.

410 Lawyers from difference side of the divide: See Sylvia A. Law, "Rethinking Sex and the Constitution," *University of Pennsylvania Law Review* 132, no. 5 (June 1984): 955–1040. See also Mansbridge, *ERA*, 196. Ginsburg summarized the issues involved: Ginsburg, Chicago Symposium. Williams's argument: Wendy Williams, "Equality's Riddle: Pregnancy and the Equal Treatment/Special Treatment Debate," *New York University Review of Law and Social Change* 13, no. 2 (1984–85): 325–80.

410 ". . . sell equality short." Williams, 380.

410–1 What the ratification campaign achieved: State laws changed: Mansbridge, *ERA*, 189–90, 307. Public opinion shifted: Boles in Hoff-Wilson, 57. Antifeminist movement created: Mansbridge, author's interview. Feminist organizations grew: Mansbridge, Princeton lecture. Other women's groups also benefited; NWPC activists went door-to-door in the unratified states, getting petitions signed and collecting money, and came away with lists of sympathizers that they could use at election time: Catherine East, author's interview, 1985.

411 Campaigners went into politics or lobbied: East, author's interview, 1985. NOW's triumph in Florida: Smeal, 13; NOW PAC/NOW Equality PAC, "Woman Elect 1990," mailing, March 1990, p. 2.

411 ". . . and paid." Nancy Stultz, author's interview, Princeton, NJ, 18 December 1987.

411 Ironic benefit: Ginsburg, author's interview. See Hoff-Wilson, "Introduction," in Hoff-Wilson, xvi.

chapter 19: *The Eclipse of the Gender Gap*

415 ". . . we can do *anything*." Geraldine A. Ferraro with Linda Bird Francke, *Ferraro: My Story*, 21.

415–6 Gender gap discredited: See Maureen Dowd, "Reassessing Women's Political. Role: The Lasting Impact of Geraldine Ferraro," *New York Times Magazine*, 30 December 1984, p. 18. Also "Portrait of the Electorate," *New York Times*, 8 November 1984, p. A19.

416–7 History of the "woman vote" after suffrage: Cott, 99–114; Carol M. Mueller, "The Empowerment of Women: Polling and the Women's Voting Bloc," in *The Politics of the Gender Gap: The Social Construction of Political Influence*, Carol M. Mueller, ed., 19–20. Also Chafe, 27–31. Most suffrage leaders were actually quite cautious about predicting how women would vote: Cott, 111.

417 New laws repealed; feminists lost credibility: Chafe, 28–30.

417 Congress passed more women's bills in the 1970s: Freeman, *Politics*, 202.

417 Gender gaps during the 1970s and in 1980: Mildred Jeffrey, author's interview. See Mueller, "Empowerment," in Mueller, 27; also Carol M. Mueller, "Continuity and Change in Women's Political Agenda," in Mueller, 293.

418 Theories explaining the gender gap: Kathy Bonk, "The Selling of the 'Gender Gap': The Role of Organized Feminism," in Mueller, 88; Smeal, 19–21; Mueller, "Empowerment," in Mueller, 26–28; Abzug, 126–28.

418 NOW's campaign to exploit the gender gap: Recounted in Bonk, in Mueller, 82–101, and in Mueller, "Empowerment," also in Mueller, 18, 25–28. See also Smeal, 12–13. Gender gap in 1982: Mueller, "Empowerment," 31, and Mueller, "Continuity," 295, both in Mueller. Feminist fears and what press reported: Bonk, in Mueller, 87, 93–94.

418 ". . . politically expendable." Smeal, 13.

418 Conclusions feminists drew from loss of ERA: Susan Carroll, interview by author, 9 May 1988. See Smeal, 12–13.

418–9 Surveys show gender differences in attitudes: Arthur Miller, "Gender and the Vote: 1984," in Mueller, 279–80. For results of various polls, see also "The Gender Gap," fact sheet from the Center for the American Woman and Politics, July 1987.

419 Gap was related more to issues than a tendency to vote for a woman: Mueller, "Empowerment," in Mueller, 29–30.

419 ". . . Republicans in 1984." Quoted in Ferraro, 61.

419 Reagan administration's symbolic gestures: Mueller, "Empowerment," in Mueller, 30–31.

419 ". . . concern for women." Quoted in Mueller, "Empowerment," in Mueller, 31.

419 Gender gap in 1983: Howell Raines, "President Is Assailed by Women's Leader; 2d Term Is Opposed," *New York Times*, 10 July 1983, p. 1.

419–20 Bills passed thanks partly to gender gap: See Bonk, in Mueller, 97; Smeal, 61; Mueller, "Empowerment," in Mueller, 32. For more on pension reform: Marian Lief Palley, "The Women's Movement in Recent American Politics," in *The American Woman 1987–88*, Rix, ed., 171; Gelb and Palley, 187–95.

420 Fewer candidates shy away from women's issues: Susan Carroll, author's interview.

420 Reagan policies threaten women on welfare and those working for social agencies: Steven P. Erie and Martin Rein, "Women and the Welfare State," in Mueller, 173–91.

420 Feminists discuss running a woman for President: The key group that picked Ferraro as the best candidate called themselves "Team A." Members were Nanette Falkenberg, head of NARAL, Mildred Jeffrey, congressional staffers Eleanor Lewis and Joan McLean, and Joanne Howes, director of the Women's Vote Project; Joanne Symons, political director of the American Nurses Association, and Ranny Cooper, director of Ted Kennedy's Fund for a Democratic Majority, joined the team at a later stage: Ferraro, 71–72. Other feminists were also holding similar discussions—see Abzug, 194–95.

420 NWPC's 1983 convention: Ferraro, 24–26; Mary Houghton, "Ferraro Victory: NWPC played Key Role," *Women's Political Times* 9, no. 5 (August- September 1984): 1; "quantum leap," quoted in Houghton, 1. See also Ferraro, 23–25; Howell Raines, "Democrats Line Up on Feminist Issues," *New York Times*, 11 July 1983, p. A1.

421 ". . . a dangerous man." Quoted in Mary Houghton, "Caucus Power in San Antonio," *Women's Political Times* 8, no. 4 (July-August 1983): 1.

421 ". . . Republican Party." Quoted in Howell Raines, "Democrats Line Up."

421 Feminists agree to seek vice-presidency: Abzug, 195; Ferraro, 24–25. Male candidates willing to consider woman on ticket: Houghton, "Ferraro Victory."

421 ". . . she's a woman . . . ." Friedan's remarks in Jane Perlez, "Women, Power and Politics," *New York Times Magazine*, 24 June 1984, p. 27.

421 Shift from one symbolic goal to another: Mueller, "Empowerment," in Mueller, 26.

421 Jackson committed to woman running mate: Phil Gailey, "Will a Woman Be a Vice-Presidential Candidate," *New York Times*, 12 November 1983, p. 10. NOW endorses Mondale: Bernard Weinraub, "Women's Endorsement Seems a 2-Way Race," *New York Times*, 2 December 1983, p. A24; Bernard Weinraub, "NOW, in First Endorsement, Backs Mondale," *New York Times*, 11 December 1983, p. 1.

421–2 Controversy over NOW's endorsement described, fact that Mondale's campaign neglected women's issues noted: Perlez, 28.

422 Gender gap takes on a different meaning: Julio Borquez, Edie N. Goldenberg, and Kim Fridkin Kahn, "Press Portrayals of the Gender Gap," in Mueller, 124–47.

422 ". . . be reelected." Jeffrey, author's interview.

422 NWPC presents memo to Mondale: Ferraro, 90; Houghton, "Ferraro Victory," 4. NWPC's whip system: Houghton, "Ferraro Victory," 1; Perlez, p. 23.

422 Rumors about Reilly's attitude: Howell Raines, "Mondale's Tough Choice: His Aides Try to Alleviate 'Super Pressure' to Pick a Woman, and Feminists Are Split," *New York Times*, 3 July 1984, p. 1. NOW resolution: Sandra Salmans, "NOW Resolution Meeting Opposition of Feminists," *New York Times*, 4 July 1984, p. A10. The NOW resolution actually demanded a woman or a member of a minority group on the ticket, but the press focused on the demand for a woman: See Gloria Steinem, "Election Roundup: What No One Else Would Tell You About the Ferraro Campaign," *Ms*, December 1984, p. 53.

422 Other feminists denounced the resolution: Millie Jeffrey recalled that "after that, we thought we were done for with Walter Mondale." Jeffrey, author's interview.

422 ". . . at this point." Quoted in Salmans.

422 Twenty-three women reassure Mondale: Salmans; Ferraro, 106. His response to feminist pressure: Ferraro, 96.

423 ". . . to make history," Quoted in Ferraro, 96.

423 NWPC survey of delegates: Mary Houghton, "Ferraro victory." Mondale interviews candidates: Howell Raines, "Mondale's Tough Choice." Mondale's choice and reasons for it: Bernard Weinraub, "Ideas for His Speech Led Mondale to Mrs. Ferraro," *New York Times*, 15 July 1984, p. 1.

423 Male Democrats question choice: David E. Rosenbaum, "Democrats Praise Selection; Many Feminists Are Elated," *New York Times*, 13 July 1984, p. A8; Howell Raines, "Mondale Decision: Praise Ignores Risks," *New York Times*, 13 July 1984, p. A1.

423–4 Black feminists disillusioned: Mary Frances Berry, *Why ERA Failed*, 116; Sharron Hannon, Susan Lindsay, and Ginny Montes, "Chisholm will continue to lead black women's political group," *Southern Feminist*, July–August 1985, p. 3; Ferraro, 152–53.

424 Republican efforts to win women's vote: Perlez, 31. Feminist reaction: Demetra Lambros, "GOP snubs women's rights," *Women's Political Times* 9, no. 5 (August/ September 1984): 1. Full text of Kathy Wilson's statement: "The plight of the Republican feminist," *Women's Political Times*, same issue, p. 2. Caucus endorses Mondale: Mary Houghton, "NWPC Endorses Mondale and Ferraro," *Women's Political Times* 9, no. 6 (October 1984): 1.

424 Phone lines jammed but Mondale's staff fails to follow through: Houghton,

"Ferraro victory." Friedan's remark: Maureen Dowd, "Reassessing Women's Political Role."
424 Story of the Ferraro campaign from her book.
424–5 ". . . best Vice President." Ferraro, 136.
425 ". . . senator from Texas." Ferraro, 151.
425 ". . . the controversy." Ferraro, 273.
425–6 The controversy over Ferraro's financial affairs: Ferraro, 143–44, 156–82.
426 Anti-abortion demonstrators and story linking them to Reagan campaign: Ferraro, 236–37.
426 ". . . favoring abortion." Quoted in Ferraro, 222.
426 ". . . actually have one." Ferraro, 222.
426 Ferraro begins to stress women's issues: Ferraro, 282.
427 Republican strategy for winning the women's vote: Bill Peterson, "Reagan Did Understand Women," *Washington Post*, 3 March 1985, p. C5. Also Mueller, "Empowerment," in Mueller, 31–32.
427–8 Election results, 1984: See Maureen Dowd, "Reassessing Women's Political Role"; Peterson, "Reagan Did Understand Women"; "Portrait of the Electorate," *New York Times*, 8 November 1984, p. A19; Bella Abzug and Mim Kelber, "Despite the Reagan Sweep, a Gender Gap Remains," *New York Times*, 23 November 1984, p. A35.
428 CBS estimate: Michelle Kahan, "Was There a Gender Gap in 1984?," *News & Notes about Women Public Officials* 3, no. 2 (February/March 1985): 2; from the Center for the American Woman and Politics (CAWP), Rutgers University, New Brunswick, NJ.
428 ". . . more very soon." Quoted in Maureen Dowd, "Women Reject Blame for Mondale Loss," *New York Times*, 14 November 1984, p. A22.
428 ". . . no appeal to males." In Maureen Dowd, "Reassessing Women's Political Role," p. 18.
428 Male boss's reactions to Ferraro's defeat: Dowd, "Reassessing Women's Political Role"; Bill Peterson, "Reagan Did Understand Women." Real gender gap said to be Democratic party's problem with men: Borquez, Goldenberg, and Kahn, in Mueller, 146. Women's issues not taken as seriously: Catherine East, author's interview, 1985. Probably an excuse: Mildred Jeffrey, author's interview.
428 Feminist responses to criticism. Voters go by top of ticket: Ferraro, 313. Gap decided some races: Michelle Kahan; also Maureen Dowd, "Reassessing Women's Political Role." Mondale's staff blew their chance: Maureen Dowd, "Reassessing Women's Political Role"; Ferraro, 194. Registered 1.8 million women: "Women's Vote Effort Lauded," *New York Times*, 17 February 1985, p. 26. Women voted at higher rate than men: Bill Peterson, "Reagan Did Understand Women"; "Sex Differences in Voter Turnout," CAWP Fact Sheet, July 1987.
429 Campaign for white male vote: Maureen Dowd, "Reassessing Women's Political Role."
429 ". . . the women's vote." Quoted in Bill Peterson, "Reagan Did Understand Women."
429 ". . . the national level." Ferraro, 213.
429 ". . . choose Dianne [Feinstein]?' " Ferraro, 174.
429 ". . . for American women." Mueller, "Empowerment," in Mueller, 34.
429 ". . . Americans don't share." Gloria Steinem, "Election Roundup," 53.
429–30 Post-election Gallup poll and exit polls: Ferraro, 311. Mildred Jeffrey's comment: author's interview.
430 Press treatment of the gender gap after 1984: Bonk, in Mueller, 101.
430 How gender gap affected 1986 election: See "The Gender Gap," CAWP Fact Sheet, July 1987, p. 2.
430–1 The 1988 presidential campaign: Mildred Jeffrey, author's interview. Both candidates middle-of-the-road: See, for example, Robin Toner, "Dukakis Asserts He Is a 'Liberal' but in Old Tradition of His Party," *New York Times*, 31 October 1988, p. A1; R. W. Apple Jr., "Bush's Growing Appeal Fails to Include Women," *New York Times*, 27 October 1988, p. 15.
431 Feminist strategy in 1988: Smeal described it during a workshop at the annual

NOW convention, Buffalo, NY, 25 June 1988. Also Mildred Jeffrey, author's interview. See Nadine Brozan, "Smeal, President of NOW, to Step Down and Seek Women to Run for Public Office," *New York Times*, 3 July 1987, p. A8.

430–2 NOW explores possibility of a third party, sets up Commission: "NOW Names Commission for Responsive Democracy," p. 1, and "NOW Commission to Evaluate Political Climate," p. 2, both in *National NOW Times*, Summer 1990. Also: Ellie Smeal, "Why I Support a New Party," *Ms.* January/February 1991, p. 72. Public cynicism hits new high: Michael Oreskes, "America's Politics Loses Way As Its Vision Changes World," *New York Times*, 18 March 1990, p. A1. Few voted in 1990: Philip Shenon, "Voter Turnout Still Poor, with 3 Exceptions," *New York Times*, 11 November 1990, p. 27.

432n More women oppose war in Persian Gulf: Louis Harris, "The Gender Gulf," *New York Times*, 7 December 1990, p. A35.

432 Gender gap in 1990: See "Gender Gap a Factor in a Majority of Races in 1990," *CAWP News & Notes*, Winter 1991, 4.

432 Why U.S. had gender gap and Western Europe didn't: See Pippa Norris, "The Gender Gap: A Cross-National Trend?" in Mueller, 217–34.

chapter 20: The New Right and the War on Feminism

433 ". . . unit of government" and ". . . from her husband." Judy Mann, "Listening In on Speech by 'Pro-Family' Orator," *Washington Post*, 31 October 1980, p. B1.

434 Gilder's book was recommended reading: See Edwin McDowell, "How the Imprimatur of a President Can Benefit Authors and Their Books," *New York Times*, 16 May 1981, p. 13. For a feminist commentary on Gilder's ideas, see Smeal, 69.

434n George F. Gilder, *Sexual Suicide* (New York: Quadrangle, 1973); George F. Gilder, *The Naked Nomads: Unmarried Men in America* (New York: Quadrangle, 1974).

434–5 The formative years of the New Right are described in Sidney Blumenthal, *The Rise of the Counter-Establishment: From Conservative Ideology to Political Power*. See also Rebecca E. Klatch, *Women of the New Right*.

434–5 Anti-Communists join forces with free-marketers: Blumenthal, 14–31. Right-wingers felt marginalized: Blumenthal, 241.

435 Conservative goal was to create a counterestablishment: Blumenthal, 4–11.

435 Goldwater's defeat: At the time, there were only two major right-wing organizations, Young Americans for Freedom and the extremist John Birch Society; see John B. Judis, "Conservatism and the Price of Success," in *The Reagan Legacy*, Sidney Blumenthal and Thomas Byrne Edsall, eds., 136–37.

435 Rise of Reagan: Blumenthal, 31, 36, 40–41, 55–68.

435–6 Anti-abortion Catholics organize: Connie Paige, *The Right to Lifers: Who They Are, How They Operate, Where They Get Their Money*, 51, 57–58, 71–74.

436 Right-wing Protestants are politicized. Religious revival during the 1970s: See Phillip E. Hammond, "Another Great Awakening?" 207; Robert C. Liebman, "The Making of the New Christian Right," 228; and Donald Heinz, "The Struggle to Define America," 138; all are in Robert C. Liebman and Robert Wuthnow, *The New Christian Right: Mobilization and Legitimation*. See also Sidney Blumenthal, "Reaganism and the Neokitsch Aesthetic" in Blumenthal and Edsall, 285; Paige, 154–78.

436 Sinful to focus on social reform: James L. Guth, "The New Christian Right," in Liebman and Wuthnow, 41. Issues that disturbed conservative Christians: Liebman, in Liebman and Wuthnow, 227–28, 235–36; John H. Simpson, "Moral Issues and Status Politics," in Liebman and Wuthnow, 201–2.

436 Viguerie sees ways to build a movement: Paige, 126–36.

436–7 Reagan's advisors build an alliance: Paige, 154–78.

437 Feminist suspicions: Paige, 156. Religious conservatives themselves wondered: See, for example, E. J. Dionne Jr., "A Conservative Call for Compassion," *New York Times*, 30 November 1987, p. B12. Right-wingers held contradictory beliefs: Himmelstein, in Liebman and Wuthnow, 22.

437 Reagan campaign broke new ground: See Paige, 195–99; Guth, in Liebman and Wuthnow, 37–39; Jonathan Alter, "Death of a Conservative," *Newsweek*, 1 December 1987, p. 23.

437-8 Campaign issues: Judis, in Blumenthal and Edsall, 148; Paige, 198–99. Reagan elected by 26 percent of population: Paige, 180. Why conservative Christians in South voted for Reagan: Guth, in Liebman and Wuthnow, 37–38.

438 Poverty rate tops 15 percent: See Michael Harrington, *The Next Left: The History of a Future* (New York: Holt, 1986), 102.

438 How Reagan budget predictions went awry: Blumenthal, 230–39. Also David Stockman, *The Triumph of Politics: The Inside Story of the Reagan Revolution,* especially 104–8, 292–96; William Greider, *The Education of David Stockman and Other Americans,* especially 14–20, 35–39, 47–48, 59. Worst recession since the Great Depression: Judis, in Blumenthal and Edsall, 153.

438 For more on supply-side economics, see Greider, 7–8, 47–48, 74; also Blumenthal, 87–121.

438-9 Administration cuts social programs; feminists and liberals save some: Schroeder, 120–23; Ferraro, 134–36; Smeal, 46–50. Cuts in housing development funds: Robert Kuttner, "Reaganism, Liberalism, and the Democrats," in Blumenthal and Edsall, 126. Disabled ruled ineligible for benefits: Two thirds were later reinstated—indicating that most should never have lost their benefits in the first place; see Gregory Spears, "Study cites improper cutoffs from Social Security," *Boston Sunday Globe,* 3 December 1989, p. 9.

439n WIC saves money: See "For Children: A Fair Chance," *New York Times,* editorial, 6 September 1987, p. 14. Also, "What Happens When Mothers Get Food," *New York Times,* editorial, 3 February 1986, p. A24.

439 Record deficit: See Greider, 67; Stockman, 405. Belief that administration deliberately created deficit to force reduction in social spending: See Tom Wicker, "A Deliberate Deficit," *New York Times,* 19 July 1985, p. A27; Blumenthal, 236. David Stockman wrote that, "a drastic shrinking of the welfare state was not [Reagan's] conception of the Reagan Revolution. It was mine." Stockman, 299. Deficit tied Democrats' hands: William Schneider, "The Political Legacy of the Reagan Years," in Blumenthal and Edsall, 54.

439 Economy began to recover: Stockman, 405.

439-40 Gap between rich and poor widens: Schneider, in Blumenthal and Edsall, 54–55; Schroeder, 142–45; Kuttner, in Blumenthal and Edsall, 126–27; James Lardner, "Rich, Richer; Poor, Poorer," *New York Times,* 19 April 1989, p. A27. Growing numbers of women and children among the homeless: Mitchel Levitas, "Homeless in America," *New York Times Magazine,* 10 June 1990, p. 44; see especially p. 88.

440 New Right claims "reverse discrimination": Smeal, 71–72. Stockman on why equality is unjust: Blumenthal, 220.

440 ". . . called them that." Wilma Scott Heide, "Revolution: Tomorrow Is NOW!" Speech at NOW conference, February 1973; published in *Vital Speeches of the Day, 1973* (Southold, NY: City News Publishing Co., 1973), 403–8.

440 Liberal defense of affirmative action: Smeal, 71–77; Don Edwards, "Keep Affirmative Action," *New York Times,* 13 February 1986, p. A31.

440 Why many businesses backed affirmative action: See Stuart Taylor Jr., "3 Bias Cases Before Supreme Court Could Reshape Law on Racial Goals," *New York Times,* 23 February 1986, p. 28; Kenneth B. Noble, "U.S. Action Against Bias Seen as Already Weak," *New York Times,* 2 September 1985, p. 11; "Firing the Hiring Scorekeeper," *New York Times,* editorial, 23 September 1985, p. A18.

440-1 Reagan administration undermines Executive Order: See Smeal, 74; Abzug, 147–48; Robert Pear, "U.S. Plans to Ease Rules for Hiring Women and Blacks," *New York Times,* 3 April 1983, p. A1; Stephen Engelberg, "Attack on Quotas Opposed by Cities," *New York Times,* 4 May 1985, p. A1.

441 Justice Department switches to case-by-case approach; enforcement agencies' budgets slashed: Smeal, 71–77. Civil Rights Commission a travesty: "Face Facts About Civil Rights," *New York Times,* editorial, 8 October 1986, p. A35.

441 Justice Department attacks Title IX: See Project on Equal Education Rights, et al., *Injustice Under the Law: The Impact of the Grove City College Decision on Civil Rights in America* (Washington, D.C.: PEER, 1985).

441-2 History of the Civil Rights Restoration Act: See "Civil Rights Restoration Act Introduced," *Campaign Report* 2, no. 12 (6 March 1987) (published by The 80%

Majority Campaign): 1. Anti-abortion amendment: Catherine East, letter to women's organizations, dated 15 April 1987; "Return to Basic Civil Rights Focuses on Abortion," *NARAL News* 19, no. 1 (May 1987): 4; "Despite Setback, Push Still On for Civil Rights Bill," *Congressional Quarterly*, 6 February 1988, pp. 254–55.

442 Feminists outraged: Irvin Molotsky, "House Passes Bill to Upset a Limit on U.S. Rights Law," *New York Times*, 3 March 1988, p. A1. Coalition caved in: "Civil Rights without Abortion Rights—Passage of S557," *Campaign Report* 3, no. 3 (21 March 1988): 1. Congress overrode veto: Julie Johnson, "Civil Rights Bill's Foes Mount 11th-Hour Drive," *New York Times*, 22 March 1988, p. A22.

442 New Supreme Court decisions undercutting antidiscrimination laws: For a summary, see Tom Wicker, "No Place for Lucas," *New York Times*, 4 July 1989, p. 29; also Susan Rasky, "Rights Groups Work on Measure to Reverse Court's Bias Rulings," *New York Times*, 30 December 1989, p. 11.

The Supreme Court's 1989 decisions that undermined antidiscrimination litigation were: *Richmond* v. *Croson* (struck down a city ordinance that set aside 30 percent of public works contracts for minority companies; policies that favor minorities must meet the same strict-scrutiny test as policies that favor whites); *Wards Cove* v. *Atonio* (ruled that it's up to employees to prove that a job requirement that screens out women, or men of color, is *not* a business necessity—previously, the burden of proof had been on the employer); *Patterson* v. *McLean Credit Union* (declared that a much-used racial discrimination law applied only to hiring, not to racially biased treatment on the job); *Martin* v. *Wilks* (court-approved affirmative action settlements can be challenged years later by white workers—such settlements are not final); *Lorrance* v. *A.T.&T.* (a discriminatory seniority system must be challenged soon after it's adopted).

442 Fate of the Civil Rights Act of 1990: Steven A. Holmes, "On Job Rights Bill, a Vow to Try Again in January," *New York Times*, 26 October 1990, p. A25.

442–3 Attempts to undermine WEEA: Leslie Wolfe, interview by author, 17 November 1986, Washington, D.C. See Theresa Cusick, "A Clash of Ideologies: The Reagan Administration Versus the Women's Educational Equity Act" (Washington, D.C.: PEER, the Project on Equal Education Rights, Summer 1983); Leslie R. Wolfe, "The New Women's Educational Equity Act: Still Alive and Making a Difference," in *Resources for Educational Equity* (Washington, D.C.: PEER, the Project on Equal Education Rights, Spring 1985).

442 ". . . education budget." Wolfe, author's interview, 1986.

442 ". . . feminist groups." Quoted in Cusick, 2.

442 ". . . like to preserve." Wolfe, author's interview, 1986.

443 Eagle Forum: Mansbridge, *ERA*, 174.

443 Right-wingers take over NACWEP: Joy Simonson, interview by author, 18 November 1986, Washington, D.C. See Cusick.

443n Simonson helped draft WEEA: Mary Ann Millsap, "Sex Equity in Education," in *Women in Washington*, Tinker, ed., 96.

443 ". . . house that night," and ". . . voting me out." Simonson, author's interview.

444 ". . . meeting with us." Sandler, author's interview.

444 Right-wingers burrow into the bureaucracy: Blumenthal, 33–34; Judis, in Blumenthal and Edsall, 139; Smeal, 7.

444 Reagan fills federal bench with conservatives: See Judis, in Blumenthal and Edsall, 140; Schneider, in Blumenthal and Edsall, 55. ABA rates Reagan judges less qualified: Lincoln Caplan, "The Reagan Challenge to the Rule of Law," in Blumenthal and Edsall, 233–34. Conservative judges more often pro-prosecution, etc.: See "Judging the Judges," *Newsweek*, 14 October 1985, p. 73. The irony of appointing idealogues: Noted in "Judging the Judges." Bush continued to appoint right-wingers: Neil A. Lewis, "Bush Travels Reagan's Course in Naming Judges," *New York Times*, 10 April 1990, p. A1.

445 O'Connor may owe selection partly to gender gap: Ferraro, 61. Conservatives lobbied against her: Paige, 223–24; Guth, in Liebman and Wuthnow, 39. Dubious evidence of prochoice sympathies: Andrew H. Merton, *Enemies of Choice: The Right-to-Life Movement and Its Threat to Abortion*, 170.

445 Reagan's Court appointments in 1986: Stuart Taylor, "More Vigor for the Right: Court Would Ease Toward Conservatism Without Abruptly Changing Its Direction," *New York Times,* 18 June 1986, p. A1. Feminists oppose Rehnquist: Stuart Taylor Jr., "Rehnquist Called Rights 'Extremist,' " *New York Times,* 29 July 1986, p. A14. NARAL opposed both Rehnquist and Scalia; see "Strategies for Confirmation Debate on Rehnquist and Scalia," *Campaign Report* 2, no. 1 (21 July 1986): 1.

445 Justice Powell resigns: Stuart Taylor Jr., "Powell Leaves High Court; Took Key Role on Abortion and on Affirmative Action," *New York Times,* 27 June 1987, p. A1. Bork's reputation: See "Robert Bork's Views on a Wide Range of Legal Issues, in His Own Words," *New York Times,* 13 September 1987, p. 36; Stuart Taylor Jr., "Of Bork and Tactics," *New York Times,* 21 October 1987, p. A23.

445 Bork nomination a crusade for both sides: Kenneth B. Noble, "Bork Backers Flood Senate With Mail," *New York Times,* 3 September 1987, p. A16. Bork opposition largest coalition ever: Stuart Taylor Jr., "Bork Tells Panel He Is Not Liberal, Not Conservative," *New York Times,* 14 September 1987, p. A1. Hearings televised and polls show growing opposition to Bork: Taylor, "Of Bork and Tactics." Bork nomination defeated: Linda Greenhouse, "What Went Wrong: Reagan's Popularity Was Not Enough to End Fears of Shift on Social Issues," *New York Times,* 7 October 1987, p. B10.

445–6 Reagan urged voters to elect Republicans to help him replace liberal judges: Taylor, "Of Bork and Tactics."

446 Ginsburg nomination: "Nominee to Court Says Judges Should Avoid Making Policy," *New York Times,* 2 December 1987, p. A26. Far right not happy about choice of Kennedy: At one point, Senator Jesse Helms threatened a filibuster if Kennedy was the nominee; see Tom Wicker, "Opting for a Fight," *New York Times,* 5 November 1987, p. A35. NARAL and ACLU undecided: Linda Greenhouse, "Apres Bork, the Liberals' Silence in Regard to Kennedy Is Deafening," *New York Times,* 4 December 1987, p. A32.

446 ". . . defeat him." East, author's interview, 13 January 1988.

446 NOW opposed Kennedy: Greenhouse, "Apres Bork." Senate confirms Kennedy: Linda Greenhouse, "Senate, 97 to 0, Confirms Kennedy to High Court," *New York Times,* 4 February 1988, p. A18. Questioned about the right to privacy during his Senate confirmation hearing, Anthony Kennedy replied that the Constitution's due process clause "is quite expansive, quite sufficient, to protect the values of privacy that Americans legitimately think are part of their constitutional heritage." Many senators apparently heard in this nonanswer whatever they wanted to hear —hence, Kennedy's unanimous confirmation. See Linda Greenhouse, "Opponents Find Judge Souter Is a Hard Choice to Oppose," *New York Times,* 9 September 1990, p. 4.

446 Kennedy's record proves Bork defeat a hollow victory: Linda Greenhouse, "The Year the Court Turned to the Right," *New York Times,* 7 July 1989, p. A1.

446 Top courts cite state constitution to expand rights and Brennan's comment on this development: Robert Pear, "State Courts Surpass U.S. Bench in Cases on Rights of Individuals," *New York Times,* 4 May 1986, p. A1.

446 Feminists tried for bipartisan support: East, author's interview, 4 December 1988.

446–7 Feminist lobbyists now professionals: Gelb and Palley, 2–3, 54–55, 209. Development of women's caucus in Congress: See Patricia Schroeder and the Hon. Olympia Snowe, "Preface," in *American Woman 1987–88,* Rix, ed., 19–23. Also Ferraro, 47; Schroeder, 108–14.

447 After 1980 election, feminists and civil rights groups lost their clout: Thomas Byrne Edsall, "The Reagan Legacy," in Blumenthal and Edsall, 15. Gender gap in 1982 helped women's issues: See Bonk, in Mueller, 97; Smeal, 61; Mueller, "Empowerment," in Mueller, 32. Ninety-eighth Congress passed record number of laws for women: Anne L. Radigan, "Federal Policy-Making and Family Issues," in *Women as Single Parents: Confronting Institutional Barriers in the Courts, the Workplace, and the Housing Market,* Elizabeth M. Mulroy, ed. (Dover, MA: Auburn House, 1988), 214.

447n Conservative opposition to the domestic violence law: Schroeder, 158–59.
447 Gender gap discredited in 1984 but it cost Republicans control of the Senate in 1986: See chapter 19; also Schneider, in Blumenthal and Edsall, 90–91. Insider trading: Patricia Blau Reuss, "Congressional 'Insider Trading' Limited Public Policy Gains for Women," *WEAL Washington Report* 17, no. 4–6 (Winter 1988–89), 3.
447 Rhetoric of Bush administration less hostile to feminism: East, personal communication, April 1991.
448–9 History of the family leave bill: Anne L. Radigan, *Concept & Compromise: The Evolution of Family Leave Legislation in the U.S. Congress*, Schroeder, 44–56. Bill's defeat and campaigns for similar laws in states: Steven A. Holmes, "House Backs Bush Veto of Family Leave Bill," *New York Times*, 26 July 1990, p. A16; Tamar Lewin, "Battle for Family Leave Will Be Fought in States," *New York Times*, 27 July 1990, p. A8.
449 Leaves bill was watered down: Radigan, 17, 21–22, 24–25. Also Steven A. Holmes, "Senate Sends Parental Leave Bill to White House, *New York Times*, 15 June 1990, p. A13. State leave laws: Women's Legal Defense Fund, by telephone, 7 June 1991.
449 1984 child-care bill: Schroeder, 80.
449 Multiple child-care bills in 1988: Linda Greenhouse, "Despite Support, a Child Care Bill Fails to Emerge," *New York Times*, 6 June 1988, p. A14.
449–50 History of the ABC bill: Schroeder, 56–86; see also "Mr. Bush and the ABCs of Child Care," *New York Times*, editorial, 26 July 1988, p. A20; Linda Greenhouse, "Church-State Debate Blocks Day Care Bill," *New York Times*, 8 September 1988, p. B9; Steven A. Holmes, "Congress Agrees on Tentative Plan on Child Care for Low-Income Families," *New York Times*, 27 October 1990, 9.
450 Support for working parents in Western Europe: See Hillary Rodham Clinton, "In France, Day Care Is Every Child's Right," *New York Times*, 7 April 1990, p. A25; Schroeder, 172. Child-care advocates criticize Bush administration: Karen De Witt, "U.S. Plan on Child Care Is Reported to Be Stalled," *New York Times*, 27 January 1991, p. 18.
450 Cycles of change and backlash: East, author's interview, 1985. Freeman, "Preface," *Social Movements of the Sixties and Seventies*, xv.
450 Reagan policies produced speculative boom: Judis, in Blumenthal and Edsall, 154–55. Conservatives claimed credit for ruining Soviet economy: Christopher Lasch, "The Costs of Our Cold War Victory," *New York Times*, 13 July 1990, p. A27. What arms race did to US economy: Patricia Schroeder, lecture, Rutgers University, New Brunswick, NJ, 10 April 1989. Soviets and United States destroyed one another: Lasch, "The Costs of Our Cold War Victory."
451 To religious conservatives, free-marketers seemed materialistic: E. J. Dionne Jr., "A Conservative Call for Compassion," *New York Times*, 30 November 1987, p. B12.
451 ". . . one more Mercedes." Stockman, 54.
451–2 NCPAC had lost support and power: Judis, in Blumenthal and Edsall, 161. Viguerie's financial problems: Judis, 161; Edsall, 38—both in Blumenthal and Edsall. Moral Majority out of business: Wayne King, "Falwell Quits as Moral Majority Head," *New York Times*, 4 November 1987, p. A14; Peter Steinfels, "Moral Majority to Dissolve; Says Mission Accomplished," *New York Times*, 12 June 1989, p. A14. United States most religious industrialized nation: Liebman, "The Making of the New Christian Right," in Liebman and Wuthnow, 234. Churches shouldn't get into politics: Anson Shupe and William Stacey, "Moral Majority Constituency," in Liebman and Wuthnow, 109. Falwell's audience declined: Liebman, "The Making," in Liebman and Wuthnow, 232.
452 Phillips's 1990 forecast: Kevin Phillips, *The Politics of Rich and Poor: Wealth and the American Electorate in the Reagan Aftermath* (New York: Random House, 1990). Lower and middle income Americans disillusioned: Michael Oreskes, "Alienation From Government Grows, Poll Finds, ' *New York Times*, 19 September 1990, p. A26.
452 Reagan legacy. For more on the deficit, impact on labor unions, see Edsall, in Blumenthal and Edsall, 3–4, 33–34. Impact on tax system: Edsall, in Blumenthal

and Edsall, 41–44. Even the Democrats moved to the right: "Introduction," in Blumenthal and Edsall, x–xi.

452 New Right's infrastructure: Judis, in Blumenthal and Edsall, 137–46. See also Fox Butterfield, "The Right Breeds a College Press Network," *New York Times*, 24 October 1990, p. A1.

452 ". . . marched backwards." Patricia Schroeder, lecture, Rutgers University, New Brunswick, NJ, 10 April 1989.

chapter 21: *The Unending Struggle over Abortion*

453–4 ". . . to conceive. . . . " George Gilder, *Sexual Suicide* (New York: Quadrangle, 1973), 134.

454 U.S. women have more unwanted pregnancies and abortions: Gina Kolata, "U.S. Experts Applaud Growth in Options for Contraception," *New York Times*, 9 June 1988, p. B17; statistics are from surveys of patients at abortion clinics, hospitals, and doctors' offices. Abortion rate compared to the Netherlands, fact that U.S. women have fewer contraceptive choices: "Abortion as a Contraceptive," *Newsweek*, 13 June 1988, p. 71.

454n Research on birth control dried up: Philip J. Hilts, "U.S. Is Decades Behind Europe in Contraceptives, Experts Report," *New York Times*, 15 February 1990, p. A1:5.

455 Contraceptive failure and abortion: Hilts, "U.S. Is Decades Behind." Ninety percent of abortions done in first trimester: "Abortion: Are Medicine and Law on a Collision Course?" *Medical World News*, 8 July 1985, p. 66.

455 For a spectrum of feminist opinions on abortion, see, for example: Judy D. Simmons, "Abortion: A Matter of Choice," in *The Black Women's Health Book*, Evelyn C. White, ed., 120–27; Barbara Ehrenreich, "The Woman Behind the Fetus," *New York Times*, 28 April 1989, p. A39; Patricia Schroeder, "A Common Ground in the Abortion Issue," *New York Times*, Letter to the Editor, 15 May 1990, p. A24; Frances Kissling, "The Challenge of Prochoice Politics: Shaping the Moral Questions," *Conscience: A Newsjournal of Prochoice Catholic Opinion* 10, no. 1 (January/February 1989): 16; Brooke, RFOC Flyer, 9 April 1989, reprinted in *Feminism Lives* (Durham, NC: Radical Feminist Organizing Committee, 1989), 145.

455 Abortion polls: See Tamar Lewin, "Views on Abortion Are Sharply Split 16 Years After Supreme Court Ruling," *New York Times*, 22 January 1989, p. 21. Also "Translating Public Opinion Polls into Political Clout," *Campaign Report* 3, no. 4 (25 April 1988): 1; published by The 80% Majority Campaign.

455–6 1979 meeting of pro- and anti-abortion groups: Paige, 106–9.

455–6 ". . . killed by abortion." Paige, 107.

456 ". . . condition of dependency." Quoted in Merton, 1.

456 Competing amendments and the issues behind them: The combination pill suppressed ovulation, but it could also change the uterine lining so that it wouldn't support implantation. Because in any particular woman at any given time, there was no way to tell whether that had happened, it could easily be argued that the combination pill was an abortifacient. See "Supreme Court Is Briefed on Contraceptives as Abortifacients," *Campaign Report* 1, no. 15 (4 November 1985): 3.

456 IUD, morning-after pill, combination pill, considered murder: "HLA/HLB Threatens Birth Control," excerpts from statements by anti-abortion leaders, assembled by NOW, dated 10 February 1982. See also "Supreme Court Is Briefed," *Campaign Report*.

456–7 Conflicts in religious right over constitutional amendments: Merton, 102–4; Paige, 114–15, 119–21, 227–30. Fact that 57 percent of conservatives opposed any amendment: Paige, 221–22.

457 Conflicts over contraception: Joseph Berger, "Catholic Dissent on Church Rules Found," *New York Times*, 25 November 1985, p. A7. NRLC behind-the-scenes opposition to contraceptives: "The Unnoticed Crusade Against Contraception," *Campaign Report* 4, no. 7 (6 April 1990): 1.

457 ". . . sexually permissive." Brown made this comment on ABC television,

"20/20," 15 August 1985. Quoted in Planned Parenthood pamphlet, "The Far Right: What They Say About Your Rights."

457 ". . . for pleasure." Quoted in Linda Witt, "Man with a Mission," *Sunday Magazine*, supplement to *Chicago Tribune*, 11 August 1985, n.p. Cited in "The Far Right: What They Say About Your Rights."

457 Feminists slow to see the danger: Ann Baker, telephone interview by author, 20 November 1990. See Paige, 115–16.

457 Feminist campaign against HLA: Merton, 219–23.

457 ". . . female would not?" Patricia Bailey, "We must give up nothing," *Women's Political Times* 8, no. 4 (July–August 1983): 5. Quoted in Abzug, 28–29.

457–8 Feminists point out inconsistency in approving abortion only for rape: Kaminer, 175.

458 Funding cut off for most vulnerable: Schroeder, 35. See also CARASA, Susan E. Davis, ed. *Women Under Attack*, 55; Paige, 109–12; "Federal Funding Bill Introduced in House," *NARAL News* 20, no. 2 (Spring 1988): 4. In polls, most Americans said government shouldn't pay for abortions: See "The Battle Over Abortion," *Time*, 17 July 1989, p. 62. This story reports a shift in public opinion: for almost the first time a majority—57 percent—opposed state laws that prohibited Medicaid from paying for abortions.

458 Family planning clinics lost funding: See Spencer Rich, "Abortion Fight Batters Family Planning Effort," *Washington Post*, 3 September 1987, A21. Title X, created in 1970, funded family planning clinics so that they could provide birth control and infertility services for low-income and other women.

458 ". . . pills for our kids." See Lionel Barber, "Conservative to Head Family Planning Office," *Washington Post*, 22 August 1985, p. A21. Cited in Planned Parenthood pamphlet, "The Far Right: What They Say About Your Rights."

458 Mexico City announcement: James Kim, "A War on the U.S. War on Abortion," *New York Times*, 9 October 1988, sec. 4, p. 7. U.S. drops support for Planned Parenthood: CARASA, 62; Neil A. Lewis, "White House and Pro-Choice Groups Wage Battle Over Abortions Abroad," *New York Times*, 1 June 1987, p. A12. Abortions and women's mortality rates both increase: Jodi L. Jacobson, "Anti-Abortion Policy Leads to . . . More Abortions," *World Watch*, May–June 1988, p. 9ff, cited in Judith Wagner DeCew, "Threatening Constitutional Protection for Abortion," *Radcliffe Quarterly*, December 1989, 6; also Kim, "A War on the U.S. War on Abortion."

458–9 For a summary of restrictive state laws and Supreme Court decisions on them, see "The Court's Major Abortion Decisions Since Roe v. Wade," *New York Times*, 26 June 1990, p. A20.

459 Parental notification and consent laws: See Linda Greenhouse, "Battle on Abortion Turns to Rights of Teen-Agers," 16 July 1989, 1; "The Tragedy of Parental Involvement Laws," *National NOW Times*, January/February 1990, p. 5. Seventeen states had parental laws: Alan Guttmacher Institute, by telephone, 10 June 1991.

459 Conservative and feminist positions on parental notification summarized: "The Tragedy of Parental Involvement Laws"; see also Ann E. Levine, "The Law Has Failed," *New York Times*, Letter to the Editor, 27 November 1989, p. A18. Polls showed majority favored restricting teenagers: Tamar Lewin, "Abortion Ruling Likely to Spur Judicial Hearings," *New York Times*, 27 June 1990, p. A14.

459–60 Idaho girl shot: "No Common Ground," *Newsweek*, 2 July 1990, p. 53–54. Becky Bell's story: Rochelle Sharpe, "She Died Because of a Law," *Ms*, July/August 1990, p. 80; see also "The Tragedy of Parental Involvement Laws," *National NOW Times*. In 1990, the Bells were instrumental in the defeat of a parental consent/notification referendum in Oregon: Ann Baker, author's interview.

460 Supreme Court decisions on parental notification and consent, and husband's consent: Paige, 109–12; also "The Court's Major Abortion Decisions Since Roe v. Wade," *New York Times*, 26 June 1990, p. A20. The *Akron* decision triggered violence in anti-abortion movement: Noted by Faye Ginsburg in her presentation, "Nurturing Female Power: Contradictions in Gender Identity among Mid-Western Women Activists," at 8th Berkshire Conference on the History of Women, Douglass College, New Brunswick, NJ, 8 June 1990.

460 Senator Frank's strategy: Smeal, 83–84.

460 Attacks on clinics: See "Anti-Abortion Militants Hold Secret Conference," *Campaign Report* 2, no. 16 (12 June 1987): 2; Adele Simmons, "Reagan's Silence on Abortion Terror," *New York Times*, 29 July 1985, p. A15. There were 3 attacks in 1983; 24 in 1984; 12 in 1985; 18 in 1986. Patients intimidated in Everett: See Dudley Clendinen, "Abortion Clinics Report Anxieties," *New York Times*, 20 January 1985, p. 24. Also "Court Watch," *Campaign Report* 1, no. 2 (29 April 1985): 5.

460–1 Anti-abortion activists' defense of militancy: See, for example, "Update on Clinic Bombings—Indianapolis, Cincinnati, New York," *Campaign Report* 2, no. 12 (6 March 1987), especially p. 7. Oregon letter bombs: "An Abortion Clinic Is Site of Bombing; No One Is Injured," *New York Times*, 11 December 1985, p. B8. Manhattan bombing: "Bomb Explodes at Abortion Clinic in Midtown, Injuring 2 Passers-By," *New York Times*, 30 October 1986, p. B7. Attempted bombing of Planned Parenthood: Samuel G. Freedman, "Abortion Bombings Suspect: A Portrait of Piety and Rage," *New York Times*, 7 May 1987, p. B1.

461 Clinic blockades: Baker, author's interview. See "Anti-Abortion Militants Hold Secret Conference," *Campaign Report* 2, no. 16 (12 June 1987): 2; "Anti-Abortion Militants Hold Women Hostage in Several Cities," *Campaign Report* 3, no. 8 (15 August 1988): 1; Ronald Smothers, "Atlanta Protests Prove Magnet for Abortion Foes," *New York Times*, 13 August 1988, p. 6. 2000 account for most of 9500 arrests: "Good News From All Over," *Campaign Report* 3, no. 13 (5 December 1988): 4. Scheidler was linked to anti-abortion Catholics, Terry to anti-abortion Protestant fundamentalists: Ann Baker, author's interview.

461 Abortion clinics hard hit: Baker, author's interview. Private doctors stop doing abortions: "Rebuffed by Courts, Anti-Abortion Chief Regroups," *New York Times*, 5 March 1990, p. B2.

461–2 Feminist escort services: "Pro-Choice Organizations Respond to Operation Rescue," *Campaign Report* 3, no. 10 (29 August 1988): 2. Feminist attorneys went to court: "Anti-Abortion Militants Hold Women Hostage in Several Cities." Injunctions often ineffective: "Groundbreaking Federal Suit Filed Against Clinic Terrorists," *Campaign Report* 1, no. 11 (12 September 1985): 5. Suits under RICO law: See "Groundbreaking Federal Suit." Also John Herbers, "NOW Seeks to Curb Anti-Abortionists," *New York Times*, 11 June 1986, p. A21.

462 Terry announces end of Operation Rescue, Baker suspects a ruse: "Does Operation Bully Have a Future?" *Campaign Report* 4, no. 2 (26 January 1990): 1.

462 Recruiting falters as jail becomes real deterrent: "Wait 'Til Next Year—Anti-Abortion Crusade Challenges," *Campaign Report* 4, no. 6 (26 March 1990): 1. Few abortions prevented, but patients still intimidated: Baker, author's interview.

462 Missouri law that led to the *Webster* decision: Judith Wagner DeCew, "Threatening Constitutional Protection for Abortion," *Radcliffe Quarterly*, December 1989, p. 6; also Kaminer, 169–70, 233, note 23, and 234, note 26.

462n For more on viability, see "Abortion: Are Medicine and the Law on a Collision Course?" *Medical World News*, 8 July 1985, p. 66; Gina Kolata, "Survival of the Fetus: A Barrier Is Reached," *New York Times*, 18 April 1989, p. C1.

462–3 Supreme Court's decision in *Webster* and controversy over the law's preamble: Judith Wagner DeCew, "Threatening Constitutional Protection." See also "Excerpts from Court Decision on the Regulation of Abortion," *New York Times*, 4 July 1989, p. 12.

463 Justice O'Connor's opinion: "A Woman's Right, Barely Viable," *New York Times*, editorial, 4 July 1989, p. 28; Linda Greenhouse, "The Year the Court Turned to the Right," *New York Times*, 7 July 1989, p. A1.

463 End of *Roe* predicted: Bruce Fein, "The Court Is Ready to Overturn 'Roe,' " *New York Times*, 5 July 1989, p. A21.

463 NRLC's model bill: Timothy Egan, "Idaho Governor Vetoes Measure Intended to Test Abortion Ruling," *New York Times*, 31 March 1990, p. A1. Outlawing abortion for birth control: Kate Michelman, "Making the '90s the Decade of Choice," *NARAL News* 22, no. 1 (Spring 1990): 1.

463–4 More than forty states considered laws: Kate Michelman, "Political Action for a Pro-Choice America," *NARAL News* 22, no. 2 (Summer 1990): 1. Louisiana outlaws almost all abortions: Roberto Suro, "Louisiana Lawmakers Adopt Toughest Anti-Abortion Law in U.S.," *New York Times*, 27 June 1990, p. A14. The Louisiana bill was unclear about what was to be done to a woman who had an abortion, but some believed that, the way it was worded, she—like the abortionist—could get ten years at hard labor and a $100,000 fine. See Frances Frank Marcus, "Louisiana Senate Sustains Roemer's Veto of Anti-Abortion Bill," *New York Times*, 8 July 1990, p. 10. Idaho bill: Egan, "Idaho Governor Vetoes Measure."

464 ". . . emotional strain. Always." and ". . . found them there." Quoted in Merton, 176.

464 Pennsylvania anti-abortion law: See Michael deCourcy Hinds, "Stringent Curbs on Abortion Gain in Pennsylvania, *New York Times*, 25 October 1989, p. A1; Michael DeCourcy Hinds, "Pennsylvania Passes Anti-Abortion Measure, *New York Times*, 15 November 1989, p. A19; Tamar Lewin, "States Testing the Limits on Abortion," *New York Times*, 2 April 1990, p. A14; Tamar Lewin, "Quiet Trial Could Lead to Major Abortion Ruling," *New York Times*, 5 August 1990, p. A4.

464–5 Guam bans abortion: Jane Gross, "Stiffest Restrictions on Abortion in U.S. Are Voted in Guam," *New York Times*, 16 March 1990, p. A1; "Law Restricts Abortion in Guam," *New York Times*, 20 March 1990, p. A14.

465 Benshoof challenges Guam law: Tamar Lewin, "A.C.L.U. Lawyer Runs Afoul of Guam's New Abortion Act," *New York Times*, 21 March 1990, p. A24; Neil A. Lewis, "Judge in Guam Rejects Strict Law on Abortion," *New York Times*, 24 August 1990, p. A12.

465 South Carolina's parental consent bill: "Curbs on Abortion for Young Gain in Michigan and South Carolina," 15 February 1990, p. B18. New Supreme Court decisions summarized: "More Threats to a Woman's Liberty," *New York Times*, editorial, 26 June 1990, p. A22. Souter's views on abortion: Neil A. Lewis, "Souter Deflects Senators' Queries on Abortion Views," *New York Times*, 14 September 1990, p. A1.

465 The sixteen states originally expected to pass anti-abortion laws after *Webster* were Alabama, Florida, Georgia, Idaho, Indiana, Kentucky, Louisiana, Minnesota, Mississippi, Missouri, Nebraska, Oklahoma, Pennsylvania, South Carolina, Utah, and Wyoming. Political observers believed that three other states—Arkansas, Montana, and Texas—probably would have passed such laws but they weren't in session in 1990. See "Wait 'Til Next Year—Anti-Abortion Crusade Challenges," *Campaign Report* 4, no. 6 (26 March 1990): 1. Situation report, summer of 1990: *NARAL News* 22, no. 2 (Summer 1990): 1.

465–6 Prochoice march in Washington, April 1989: Robin Toner, "Right to Abortion Draws Thousands to Capital Rally," *New York Times*, 10 April 1989, p. A1. O'Dell's comments were made in a speech at a NOW-New Jersey conference on reproductive rights, Haslet, NJ, 17 September 1989. Polls found most Americans believed abortion could never be outlawed: "The Threat to Roe," *NARAL News* 18, no. 2 (August 1986): 2. Increase in NOW's membership reported: "NOW Members Are Told to Seek New Allies in Fight on Abortion," *New York Times*, 23 July 1989, p. 25. Other feminist groups inundated with volunteers: author's telephone calls to ACLU, NARAL, Planned Parenthood, and the Fund for the Feminist Majority, May 1991. See E. J. Dionne Jr., "Abortion Ruling Shakes Up Races for Legislatures," *New York Times*, 10 July 1989, p. B8.

466 Media notes changed climate: R. W. Apple Jr., "An Altered Political Climate Suddenly Surrounds Abortion," *New York Times*, 13 October 1989, p. A1. Right-to-lifers assumed to be single-issue voters: Paige, 234–37. That assumption was based on scant evidence: Ann Baker, panel, NOW-New Jersey conference, 17 September 1989, Haslet, NJ. A 1982 poll found that 32 percent of prochoice voters were willing to base their vote on the single issue of abortion, compared to 30 percent of anti-abortion voters: Smeal, 31.

466 House approves Medicaid abortions for rape or incest: R. W. Apple Jr., "An Altered Political Climate." The final tally revealed that twenty-nine legislators had switched sides—twenty-seven of them had become prochoice; see "29 Reversed Votes on Easing Abortion Curbs," *New York Times*, 15 October 1989, p. 29. Bush's veto: Robin Toner, "Veto on Abortion Is Upheld in House," *New York Times*, 26 October 1989, p. A20. Anti-abortion bills defeated in Florida: Jeffrey Schmalz, "Abortion Access Stands in Florida," *New York Times*, 12 October 1989, p. A23; Richard L. Berke, "The Abortion-Rights Movement Has Its Day," *New York Times*, 15 October 1989, sec. 4, p. 1.

466n Role women lawmakers played in Florida: NOW PAC/NOW Equality PAC, "Woman Elect 1990," mailing, March 1990, p. 2. NOW helped elect more women to Florida legislature: See chapter 18.

466–7 1989 election tests the prochoice vote: E. J. Dionne Jr., "Abortion Ruling Shakes Up Races for Legislatures," *New York Times*, 10 July 1989, p. B8. Feminist organizations campaign: See "Campaign '89, *NARAL News* 21, no. 4 (Winter 1989): 4; "Abortion Rights Candidates Win Big with NOW's Support," *National NOW Times*, October/November/December 1989, p. 3. Prochoice candidates elected, and exit polls show abortion was a major concern: R. W. Apple Jr., "Backlash at the Polls," *New York Times*, 9 November 1989, p. B14.

467 Catholic bishops and priests take punitive action: "Wait 'Til Next Year—Anti-Abortion Crusade Challenges," *Campaign Report* 4, no. 6 (26 March 1990): 1; also, Peter Steinfels, "Bishops Warn Politicians on Abortion," *New York Times*, 8 November 1989, p. A18. Killea, barred from receiving communion, wins election: Ari L. Goldman, "Legislator Barred From Catholic Rite," *New York Times*, 17 November 1989, p. A18; "Democrat Penalized by Church in Abortion Stand Wins Election," *New York Times*, 7 December 1989, p. B25. Killea's campaign manager was interviewed on "The McNeil/Lehrer News Hour," 8 December 1989.

467 Abortion less an issue in 1990: Robin Toner, " 'Silver Bullet' of '90 Races? Not Abortion," *New York Times*, 21 October 1990, p. 1. But see also Peggy Simpson, "Election 1990: A Mixed Bag," *Ms*, January/February 1991, p. 88.

467 Feminists had high hopes for RU 486: "RU 486," *NARAL News* 22, no. 2 (Summer 1990): 4. Development of the drug and religious right's attempt to block it: See Steven Greenhouse, "Drug Maker Stops All Distribution of Abortion Pill," 27 October 1988, p. A1; Steven Greenhouse, "France Ordering Company to Sell Its Abortion Drug," *New York Times*, 29 October 1988, p. A1. Also, Mark Dowie, "Reluctant Crusader: Etienne-Emile Baulieu," *American Health*, March 1990, p. 81.

468 One third of French women having abortions chose RU 486: Gina Kolata, "After Large Study of Abortion Pill, French Maker Considers Wider Sale," 8 March 1990, p. B10. RU-486 shows promise as treatment for several conditions: Dowie, "Reluctant Crusader"; Deborah Franklin, "Brave New Pill," *Hippocrates*, May/June 1987, p. 22. Anti-abortion groups wanted total ban: Gina Kolata, "Influence of Abortion Critics Barring Sale of Drug in U.S.," *New York Times*, 22 February 1988, p. A1. Right-to-life groups also threatened to boycott companies that were producing other drugs with proven medical value that were known to cause abortions: See Gina Kolata, "U.S. May Allow Anti-Ulcer Drug Tied to Abortion," *New York Times*, 29 October 1988, p. 1.

468 In 1989, FDA banned bringing RU 486 into country; French company reluctant to export it: See Philip J. Hilts, "F.D.A. Says It Allows Study of Abortion Drug," *New York Times*, 20 November 1990, p. C9.

468 ". . . safety for women." Eleanor Smeal, The Feminist Majority Foundation, undated letter to potential contributors, mailed in 1989.

468 RU 486 might cause birth defects: Franklin, "Brave New Pill."

469 Update on state abortion laws in 1991: Alan Guttmacher Institute, by telephone, 10 June 1991. See *State Reproductive Health Monitor*, published by the Alan Guttmacher Institute, Washington, D.C., December 1989, December 1990, and May 1991.

469 Baker's belief: Ann Baker, author's interview.

469 Feminist plans for action if *Roe* were overturned: Shireen Miles of the Federation of Feminist Women's Health Centers, author's interview.

470 Court decides Pennsylvania case: Linda Greenhouse, "High Court, 5–4, Affirms Right to Abortion But Allows Most of Pennsylvania's Limits," *New York Times*, 30 June 1992, p. A1.

470 Both sides condemned the decision: Gina Kolata, "Ruling Inspires Groups to Fight Harder," *New York Times,* 30 June 1992, p. A17.

470 Some welcomed *Roe's* reaffirmation: Anna Quindlen, "One Vote," *New York Times,* 1 July 1992, p. A23.

chapter 22: *The Women's Movement in the 1980s*

471 ". . . didn't work." Nancy Chodorow, Deirdre English, Arlie Hochschild, Karen Paige, Lillian Rubin, Ann Swidler, and Norma Wikler, "Feminist 1984: Taking Stock on the Brink of an Uncertain Future," *Ms,* January 1984, p. 102.

471 ". . . movement left. . . . " Ann Taylor Fleming, "The American Wife," *New York Times Magazine,* 26 October 1986, p. 39.

472 Feminist organizations had to lay off employees: Catherine East, author's interview, 1985. NOW in debt: Phil Gailey, "NOW Chief Describes Plans to Fight 'Fascists and Bigots,' " *New York Times,* 6 September 1985, p. A18. NOW's membership down: Cathy Trost, "Smeal Plans to Take Tough Line to Resuscitate Women's Issues, Boost NOW Membership, Funds," *Wall Street Journal,* 5 September 1985, p. 64. Government funding had dried up, foundations had other priorities: East, author's interview, 1985.

472–3 The young saw themselves as postfeminist: Susan Bolotin, "Voices from the Post-Feminist Generation," *New York Times Magazine,* 17 October 1982, p. 28. Smeal's comments: Author's interview. Comments by Crumpacker: Author's interview, 25 January 1989.

473 Women who had seen the light: Anita Shreve, "Careers and the Lure of Motherhood," *New York Times Magazine,* 21 November 1982, p. 38. Judy Klemesrud, "Mothers Who Shift Back From Jobs to Homemaking," *New York Times,* 19 January 1983, p. C1.

473–4 Sex bias in newsrooms: Linda Cunningham, speech to New Jersey Presswomen, Princeton, NJ, 22 June 1985. In 1989, women held only 6 percent of top management jobs in the news media and 25 percent of middle-management jobs: Susan F. Rasky, "Study Finds Sex Bias in News Companies," *New York Times,* 11 April 1989, p. C22.

474 Study on women who postpone marriage: William R. Greer, "Marriage Research Puts 3 in Spotlight," *New York Times,* 19 July 1986, p. 52; Felicity Barringer, "Marriage Study That Caused Furor Is Revised to Omit Impact of Career," *New York Times,* 11 November 1989, p. 10. "Too Late for Prince Charming?" *Newsweek,* 2 June 1986, p. 54.

474 An example of 1980s feminist-bashing: Sylvia Ann Hewlett, *A Lesser Life: The Myth of Women's Liberation in America* (New York: Warner Books, 1987).

474 For a critique of Betty Friedan's *The Second Stage,* see Eisenstein, 137–38. Lenore Weitzman's study was published as *The Divorce Revolution*—see chapter 14.

474 ". . . male competitive model." Hewlett, 33.

474 "stuck midway." Quoted in "Feminism's Identity Crisis," *Newsweek,* 31 March 1986, p. 58.

475 ". . . be like this!" Laudie Porter, personal communication.

475 The need to destroy female stereotype: Traits considered unhealthy in males were thought to be normal in females—women were expected to be submissive, unadventurous, and highly emotional, among other things. See Phyllis Chesler, *Women and Madness* (New York: Doubleday, 1972), especially 68–69.

475 ". . . or life style." Quoted in Eisenstein, 61.

475–6 The drawbacks of androgyny: See Eisenstein, 58–68.

476 Miller's theories, in Jean Baker Miller, *Toward a New Psychology of Women,* especially 25–38. See also Eisenstein, 58–68.

476 Daly's theories: See, for example, Mary Daly, *Gyn/Ecology: The Metaethics of Radical Feminism.* Critics of difference feminism: Eisenstein, 107–15; Linda K. Kerber, et al. "On *In a Different Voice:* An Interdisciplinary Forum: Viewpoint," *Signs* 11, no. 2 (Winter 1986): 304–33.

477 ". . . reproductive biology. . . ." Firestone, *Dialectic,* 206.

477 Feminist reevaluation of motherhood: See Alice S. Rossi, "A Biosocial Perspective on Parenting," *Daedalus* 106 (1977): 1–31; Adrienne Rich, *Of Woman Born;* Dorothy Dinnerstein, *The Mermaid and the Minotaur: Sexual Arrangements and Human Malaise;* Nancy Chodorow, *The Reproduction of Mothering;* Sara Ruddick, *Maternal Thinking: Toward a Politics of Peace.*

477 A woman can never "father" a child: Chodorow, 11. Statistics on how women's lives had changed: Ray Marshall, "Work & Women in the 1980s," (Washington, D.C.: Women's Research and Education Institute, 1983), 7–8.

477n Changes in life expectancy: See Philip J. Hilts, "Life Expectancy for Blacks in U.S. Shows Sharp Drop," *New York Times,* 29 November 1990, p. A1.

478 1990 conference speech: Ann Snitow, "Sex, the Doctor, the Feminist, and the Baby: Current Problems in the Discussion of the New Reproductive Technologies," presentation at 8th Berkshire Conference on the History of Women, Douglass College, New Brunswick, NJ, 10 June 1990. See Ann Snitow, "Motherhood—Reclaiming the Demon Texts," *Ms,* May/June 1991, p. 34.

478–9 ". . . seems gone. . . . " Snitow, "Motherhood," p. 34. ". . . embraced nurturance" and ". . . . process of change." Snitow, "Motherhood," 37.

479 Threatened by equality: Kaminer, 1, 10, 205–16. Female chauvinism: Kaminer, 5.

479 ". . . goes with it." Kaminer, 4.

479 Special protection implies women are victims: See, for example, Lisa Duggan, Nan D. Hunter, and Carole S. Vance, "False Promises: Feminist Antipornography Legislation," in *Caught Looking: Feminism, Pornography & Censorship,* Kate Ellis et al., eds. (New York: Caught Looking Inc., 1986), 72–85.

479–80 A difference feminist's defense of women's roles and values: Jean Bethke Elshtain, "Antigone's Daughters: Reflections on Female Identity and the State," in Diamond, 300–11.

480 For a brief discussion of the way the American ethic of individualism affected the women's movement, see Irene Diamond, "Introduction," *Families, Politics, and Public Policy,* Irene Diamond, ed., 1–14, especially 11–12.

480–1 Karst's article: Kenneth L. Karst, "Woman's Constitution," *Duke Law Journal* 1984, no. 3 (June 1984): 447–508.

480n Gilligan on hierarchies and networks: See Carol Gilligan, *In a Different Voice,* 62 and 173.

480n For more about CLS, see Reginia Gagnier, "Feminist Postmodernism: The End of Feminism or the Ends of Theory?" in Rhode, 21–30.

481 ". . . jurisprudence of rights." Karst, 480.

481 Constitution based on women's values: Carrie Menkel-Meadow, "Portia in a Different Voice: Speculations on a Women's Lawyering Process," *Berkeley Women's Law Journal* 1, no. 1 (Fall 1985): 39–63.

481 Need to strike a balance between needs of individual and community and comparison to Western Europe: see Lucinda M. Finley, "Transcending Equality Theory: A Way Out of the Maternity and the Workplace Debate," *Columbia Law Review* 86, no. 6 (October 1986): 1118–82.

481–2 Problems with the principle that likes must be treated alike: Finley, 1142.

482 Equal opportunity versus equal results: Finley suggested that the controversy over whether women needed equal or special treatment was essentially a debate between "two strands of liberal equality theory—formal versus substantive equality, or equal opportunity versus equal outcomes." Formal equality treats likes alike: Finley, 1144.

483 Absence of "female" values is dangerous: See, for example, Sara Ruddick, *Maternal Thinking.*

483 Fused goals: Author's observation. Also, see Carol Mueller, "Women's Movement Success and the Success of Social Movement Theory," Working Paper no. 110, Wellesley College Center for Research on Women, 1983, p. 6.

483–4 For more on ecofeminism, see Lindsy Van Gelder, "It's Not Nice to Mess with Mother Nature," *Ms,* January/February 1989, p. 60.

484 Continuing feminist commitment to radical equality: Author's observations.

For more on women's leadership style: Marilyn Loden, *Feminine Leadership, or How to Succeed in Business Without Being One of the Boys* (New York: Times Books, 1985), especially 48–49.

484–5 Women's spirituality movement: See Lindsy Van Gelder, "It's Not Nice"; Mary Jo Weaver, "Who Is the Goddess and Where Does She Get Us?" *Journal of Feminist Studies in Religion* 5, no. 1 (Spring 1989): 49–64. Religion panels extremely popular: Hazel Staats-Westover, personal communication. Urge to reclaim religion found in every generation of feminists: In the late nineteenth century, first-wave pioneer Elizabeth Cady Stanton published *The Woman's Bible*, a revisionist text so radical that afterward she was virtually read out of the women's movement; see Elisabeth Griffith, 210–13.

485 ". . . myth of origins" and ". . . real future." Weaver, 63, 64.

485–6 The Mexico City conference: Rosalind Harris, interview by author, New York, NY, 5 February 1986.

486 ". . . world's property." Original source is the International Labor Organization (ILO). Cited in Kristin Helmore, "The Neglected Resource: Women in the Developing World," *Christian Science Monitor*, 17 December 1985, n.p. (for a reprint: International Women's Tribune Center, New York).

486 Women everywhere carry double burden: See Robin Morgan, *Sisterhood Is Global*, 3. Women support one third of households, head two thirds of world's poorest families: Marvine Howe, "U.N. Fund Helps Women Help Themselves," *New York Times*, 3 November 1988, p. A6.

486 At Copenhagen, delegates avoided women's issues: Bunch, 296–97. Conference paralyzed: Elaine Sciolino, "As Their 'Decade' Ends, Women Take Stock," *New York Times*, 10 July 1985, p. A1.

486 Account of Forum at Copenhagen: Rosalind Harris, author's interview.

486 ". . . I can imagine." Rosalind Harris, author's interview.

486–7 For reports of official conference at Nairobi, see: Elaine Sciolino, "As Their 'Decade' Ends"; "U.N. Women's Conference Drops Reference to Zionism as Racism," *New York Times*, 27 July 1985, p. 1; Elaine Sciolino, "In Nairobi, Consensus," *New York Times*, 29 July 1985, p. A6. Size and scope of Forum: Rosalind Harris, author's interview. For reports on the Forum, see: Judith Zinsser, "Nairobi Confab Ends on High Note," *New Directions for Women* 14, no. 5 (September/October 1985): 1. Elaine Sciolino, "Political Wars in the 'Peace Tent' in Kenya," *New York Times*, 13 July 1985, p. 44.

487 Number of female delegates increased: Zinsser; Bunch, 346–52. Helped create climate for compromise: Bunch, 347. Forum becomes primary for many: Rosalind Harris, author's interview.

487 Changes over the decade in attitudes toward lesbians: Bunch, 346–52.

488 For more on DAWN, see: Gita Sen, Caren Grown, and the DAWN group, "Introduction," in *Development, Crises, and Alternative Visions: Third World Women's Perspectives* (New York: Monthly Review Press, 1987), 15–22; Bunch, 322; Marvine Howe; Kristin Helmore; Morgan, *Sisterhood Is Global*, 2–3.

488 Increase in concern about older women's problems: Rosalind Harris, author's interview.

488 Changes in attitude to feminism: Rosalind Harris, author's interview; Bunch, 346–52.

488–9 Nairobi workshops on religion: Elaine Sciolino, "In Nairobi, Consensus." Women everywhere faced with rising fundamentalism: Rosalind Harris, author's interview.

489 What the Decade accomplished: See Bunch, 323.

489 Meetings in Brussels, at Wellesley, other international feminist conferences: Charlotte Bunch, Seminar on Perspectives, Rutgers University, 1 February 1989.

489 International Feminist Network Against Female Sexual Slavery: Judy Klemesrud, "A Personal Crusade Against Prostitution," *New York Times*, 24 June 1985, p. C16.

489 Feminist responses to prostitution, sex tourism: See chapter 15; also Bunch, 335–36.

489–90 Dalkon Shield sold in Third World: Sybil Shainwald, author's interview.

Reagan hurts family planning efforts worldwide: See chapter 21. Boys-only schools for Afghan rebels: Bunch, 352. RU-486 held back by manufacturer: See chapter 21.
490 Foundations interested in international projects: Kay Klotzburger, personal communication. Global Center: Bunch, author's interview.

chapter 23: *The Future of Feminism: The 1990s and Beyond*

491 Marches on Washington were held in April 1989 and April 1992. See "Over 750,000 Vow 'We Won't Go Back!'" *National NOW Times* 24, no. 4 (April 1992): 1. Medical research ignores women: Barbara J. Culliton, "NIH Push for Women's Health," 383.
491 For Anita Hill's story, see Rosemary L. Bray, "Taking Sides Against Ourselves," *New York Times Magazine,* 17 November 1991, p. 56. EMILY's List: Personal communication from Stephanie Cohen. Women's reaction to the hearings: R. W. Apple Jr., "Sisterhood Is Political," *New York Times,* 24 May 1992, Sec. 4, p. 1.
492 Energy dissipated: Elizabeth Cavendish, legal director of NARAL, interview by author, 7 August 1998. Family and Medical Leave Act signed: Patricia Schroeder, *24 Years of House Work . . . and the Place Is Still a Mess,* 80. Clinton's appointments: Tobi Walker and Rochelle McPherson, "Executive Power: Top Women Officials in the Clinton Administration," *CAWP News & Notes* 9, no. 2 (October 1993): 23.
492 "Revenge of the white male": Diane Minor, "'94 Election Results: Nightmare on Helms Street," *National NOW Times* 27, no. 2 (January 1995): 1. Resembled the 1980s: Susan Faludi's best-seller *Backlash: The Undeclared War Against American Women* provides an in-depth account of the backlash of the 1980s. Together with Gloria Steinem's *Revolution from Within: A Book of Self-Esteem,* also a 1992 best-seller, Faludi's book helped propel the movement forward in the early nineties.
492 Clinton demolished obstacles: Beth Corbin, "Clinton 100 Day Report Card Falls Short of Honor Roll," *National NOW Times* 25, no. 4 (June 1993): 3. Organizations such as the National Right to Life Committee and Americans United for Life drafted antichoice bills and offered them to state legislators: Ann Baker, interview by author, 6 August 1998. NARAL tracks state actions on abortion and publishes an annual report: National Abortion and Reproductive Rights Action League, *Who Decides? A State-by-State Review of Abortion and Reproductive Rights.* Congressional abortion restrictions: Lisa Bennett-Haigney, "March to Stop Right's Anti-Abortion Legislation, Lies," *National NOW Times* 28, no. 2 (March 1996): 2.
492 "Partial birth" abortion bans: For a feminist discussion of the controversy, see Angela Bonavoglia, "Late-Term Abortion: Separating Fact from Fiction," *Ms,* May/June 1997, p. 54.
492 Method is one of several: Deborah Sontag, "'Partial Birth' Just One Way, Physicians Say," *New York Times,* 3 March 1997, p. A1. Would force riskier procedure: "Bans on Abortion Procedures Would Be Detrimental to Women's Health," *Reproductive Rights Update,* April 1997, p. 2. For the prochoice position, see "Answers to Tough Questions in the Controversy About Bans on So-Called 'Partial-Birth' Abortions," ACLU Reproductive Freedom Project, April 1997.
492n Rosenfield.
492–3 Late-term reality: Frank Rich, "Partial-Truth Abortion," *New York Times,* 9 March 1997, p. 15. Bills were broadly drafted: Allan Rosenfield, M.D., F.A.C.O.G., Dean, Columbia School of Public Health, Statement on "H.R. 1833 'Partial Birth Abortion Ban Act,'" *Reproductive Rights Update,* April 1997, p. 10.
493 ". . . crafty manner." Cavendish, author's interview.
493 No exception for women's health: Jerry Gray, "Senators Pass Ban on Form of Abortion," *New York Times,* 8 December 1995, p. B14.
493 Courts overturn ban: Cavendish, author's interview.
493 ". . . legislatures so far." Cavendish, author's interview.
493 Why harassment of abortion providers lessened: Baker, author's interview.
493–4 Killing of Dr. Gunn: Mary Lou Greenberg, "Clinics Under the Gun: Blockades, Firebombs, Murder," *On the Issues,* Fall 1993, p. 36. Operation Rescue split: Timothy Egan, "Is Abortion Violence a Plot? Conspiracy Is Not Confirmed," *New York Times,* 18 June 1995, p. 1. About FACE: "The ACLU's Role in Stopping Clinic Violence," *Reproductive Rights Update,* June 1995, p. 2.

494 Committed six murders: Rick Bragg, "Bomb Kills Guard at an Alabama Abortion Clinic," *New York Times,* 30 January 1998, p. A1. Hill's appearance on *Nightline:* See Laura Flanders, *Real Majority, Media Minority,* 63. Trosch on *Geraldo:* Diane Minor, "2 Murdered, 5 Injured in Latest Clinic Violence," *National NOW Times* 27, no. 3 (March 1995): 1.

494 ". . . moral question." Ted Koppel, quoted in Flanders, 63.

494 Take the heat off clinics: "RU-486," *NARAL News* 22, no. 2 (Summer 1990): 4. History of RU-486 in the United States: Ellie Smeal, interview by author, 11 August 1998. Status in 1998: Katharine Q. Seelye, "House Votes to Block F.D.A. On Approval of Abortion Pill," *New York Times,* 25 June 1998, p. A20.

494 Methotrexate abortions: Cavendish, author's interview.

494 NOW's civil suit: Kim Gandy, "Jury Finds Scheidler, Operation Rescue Guilty," *National NOW Times* 30, no. 3 (Summer 1998): 1.

495 ". . . illusion of reality." Rehnquist opinion quoted in "A More Detailed Look at the Casey Decision," *Reproductive Rights Update,* 1 August 1992, p. 8.

495 Shrinking number of providers: Medical Students for Choice (MSFC), "The Problem Is Provider Shortage," Berkeley, CA, 26 March 1998, http://www.ms4c.org. Prolife lecture and waiting period: Carey Goldberg with Janet Elder, "Public Still Backs Abortion, but Wants Limits, Poll Says," *New York Times,* 16 January 1998, p. A1. Other restrictions summarized: Mira Weinstein, "On 25th Anniversary of *Roe v. Wade,* NOW Asks 'Who Still Has a Choice?'" *National NOW Times* 30, no. 1 (January 1998): 1.

495 ". . . where we are right now." Cavendish, author's interview.

495 Prochoicers complacent: Debra Dodson, interview by author, 29 July 1998.

495 ". . . reversing *Roe* completely." Baker, author's interview.

495n Polls on abortion: Goldberg with Elder, "Public Still Backs Abortion."

495–6 Women ran for Congress in record numbers: Irwin N. Gertzog and Ruth B. Mandel, "'Year of the Woman': A Note of Caution," *CAWP News & Notes* 8, no. 3 (Fall 1992): 1. Women ready to move up: Patricia Ireland, president of NOW, interview by author, 23 July 1998. For details on the 1992 election, see "Women in Elective Office 1993," CAWP Fact Sheet, November 1993.

496 Christian Coalition targeted feminists: Minor, "'94 Election Results," 12. Who voted in 1994: John Stoltenberg, "Male Virgins, Blood Covenants and Family Values," *On the Issues,* Spring 1995, p. 25. Feminists lost their seats: Minor, "'94 Election Results," 3, 12. Defunding the Congressional Caucus for Women's Issues: Dodson, author's interview.

496 1996 women's vote drive: "Women's Groups Launch Voter Outreach Campaign," *CAWP News & Notes* 10, no. 3 (Winter 1996): 12.

496 ". . . resonate with women." Dodson, author's interview.

496 For more on the 1996 election: See Debra Dodson, "Women Voters and the Gender Gap," *CAWP News & Notes* 11, no. 2 (Spring 1997): 27.

496 Women elected to Congress in 1996: See Diane Minor, "New Year, New Congress: Political Clashes Imminent," *National NOW Times* 29, no. 1 (January 1997): 1. Also "Women in the U.S. Congress 1998," CAWP Fact Sheet, n.d.

496 Political women cared about women's issues: "The Impact of Women in Public Office: An Overview," CAWP Report, 1991. Feminists questioned: For example, Leslie Wolfe, president of CWPS, said she was not willing to vote for candidates "just because they have ovaries" unless they supported a progressive, feminist agenda. Leslie Wolfe, interview by author, 6 July 1998. Women more supportive of feminist issues: Dodson, author's interview.

496n NOW's estimate on parity in Congress: Jill Hofmans, "'94 Campaign Challenge: Re-elect, Reinforce Feminist Friends," *National NOW Times* 26, no. 5 (September 1994): 1.

496–7 *Time* article: Ginia Bellafante, "Feminism: It's All About Me!" *Time,* 29 June 1998, p. 54. For a feminist critique of the article: Carolyn Waldron, "'Is Feminism Dead?' Is Not the Question: Reframing Mainstream Media's Debate on the Women's Movement," *Extra!* 11, no. 5 (September/October 1998): 14.

497 ". . . and self-obsession." Bellafante, "Feminism," 57.

497 McBeal: Bellafante, "Feminism," 58.

497 Attack was a yawn: Ireland, author's interview. For more on right-wing women and the media, see Flanders, 152–56. Critique of Christina Hoff Sommers: Flanders, 140–47.

497 ". . . the beautiful girls." Quoted in Flanders, 144.

497 Sommers's right-wing support: Flanders, 145.

497 NOW's activities in the 1990s are reported in the *National NOW Times*. Membership ups and downs: Ireland, author's interview. 1998 membership: Ireland, author's interview. For more on the Native American chapter, see AnitaMarie Murano, "The People of the Seneca Nation Speak Out," *National NOW Times* 30, no. 2 (March 1998): 13.

497 ". . . in adversity." Ireland, author's interview.

497n NOW's estimate: Ireland, author's interview.

497–8 NOW opposed welfare bill: Ireland, author's interview. See Loretta A. Kane, "Activists Go 'Hungry for Justice' in Welfare Fight," *National NOW Times* 28, no. 4 (October 1996): 1.

498 "'. . . taking my taxes.'" Ireland, author's interview.

498 Less than 1 percent of the budget: Gayle Kirshenbaum, "Why All but One Woman Senator Voted Against Welfare," *Ms*, March/April 1996, p. 16. Stereotyping: Flanders, 14–23.

498 CWPS efforts on behalf of women on welfare: Wolfe, author's interview. See "Policy Update: Senator Wellstone, Center Press Case for Postsecondary Education for Women on Welfare," *Affiliates Quarterly Report*, Summer 1998, p. 5; CWPS Report, *Getting Smart About Welfare*, 1998.

498 ". . . makes a difference." Wolfe, author's interview.

498 Toughest campaign: Smeal, author's interview.

498 ". . . orchestrated lies." Smeal, author's interview.

498 For more on the right-wing assault on affirmative action, see Holcomb B. Noble, "Struggling to Bolster Minorities in Medicine," *New York Times*, 29 September 1998, p. F7.

498–9 The Feminist Majority's college program: Smeal, author's interview.

499 The graying of the women's movement: See page 472.

499 Young women's organizations in the early nineties: Bonnie Pfister, "Communiques from the Front," *On the Issues*, Summer 1993, p. 23.

499 Third Wave: Vivien Labaton, interview by author, 4 September 1998.

499 ". . . their own organizations." Aileen Hernandez, interview by author, 8 July 1998.

499 Background on NCNW: Dorothy Height, interview by author, 25 September 1998.

500 NCNW in the 1990s: Height, author's interview.

500 ". . . being lost." Height, author's interview.

500 NCNW in Africa: Height, author's interview.

500 MANA's activities in the 1990s: Elisa Sanchez, interview by author, 21 July 1998; also Wilma Espinoza, interview by author, 10 July 1998.

500 ". . . become elected officials." Sanchez, author's interview.

500 ". . . scared people." Espinoza, author's interview.

500–1 AWU's projects in the 1990s: Elaine Kim, interview by author, 14 August 1998.

500 ". . . do something on them." Kim, author's interview.

501 By 1998 there were more than 700 undergraduate programs in women's studies, about two dozen master's degree programs, and five Ph.D. programs, plus a number of others that offered a combined Ph.D.—in women's studies and psychology, for example, or women's studies and literature. Bonnie Zimmerman, interview by author, 10 September 1998.

501 ". . . is gone." Zimmerman, author's interview.

501 Women's studies more inclusive: Zimmerman, author's interview.

501 Gender studies vs. women's studies: Zimmerman, author's interview.

501 ". . . out of women's studies." Zimmerman, author's interview.

501 Challenges from conservatives: Zimmerman, author's interview.

501 ". . . experiences of men." Martha C. Nussbaum, *Cultivating Humanity: A Classical Defense of Reform in Liberal Education*, 194.

501 Studies of classroom sex discrimination: For example, American Association of University Women, *How Schools Shortchange Girls: The AAUW Report*. See also Sue V. Rosser, "Warming Up the Classroom Climate for Women," 31–44. Take Our Daughters to Work Day: Kristen Golden, "Take Our Daughters to Work Day Takes a Hit," *Ms*, July/August 1995, p. 92.

501–2 More girls played high school sports: "Good News! 1997" *Ms*, January/February 1998, p. 19. Women in the Olympics and new basketball leagues: See Linda Joplin, "Twenty-Five Years After Title IX: Women Gain in Steps, Not Leaps," *National NOW Times* 29, no. 3 (May 1997): 11.

502 Students not feminists: Zimmerman, author's interview.

502 ". . . sense to them." Zimmerman, author's interview.

502 For a brief summary of VAWA's provisions, see "VAWA: An Act of Courage," *Ms*, January/February 1995, p. 53. For a history of VAWA: David Frazee, "Gender-Justice Breakthrough," *On the Issues*, Fall 1995, p. 42.

502 ". . . a better job." Rita Smith, interview by author, 27 July 1998.

502 Rewarded the states: Catherine S. Manegold, "Quiet Winners in House Fight on Crime: Women," *New York Times*, 25 August 1994, p. A19. Problems with mandatory arrest: Smith, author's interview; also Sue Osthoff, interview by author, 15 July 1998.

502–3 Undocumented aliens: Osthoff, author's interview. Ayuda and the predicament of immigrant women: Leslye E. Orloff, "Addressing the Needs of Battered Immigrant Women," *Network News*, March/April 1995, p. 3.

503 Sixty percent on welfare have been battered: "New Studies: Violence Locks Women Into Poverty," *National NOW Times* 28, no. 2 (March 1996): 6. Why they couldn't keep jobs: Smith, author's interview. Welfare option for battered women: Lynn Hecht Schafran, interview by author, 1 September 1998.

503 Child custody problems: Smith, author's interview.

503 ". . . cannot provide." Osthoff, author's interview.

503 Fewer batterers killed: Osthoff, author's interview.

503 Feminist lawyers went to court: Schafran, author's interview.

503–4 Half of all women sexually harassed: Martha F. Davis, "Economic Justice," NOW LDEF, n.d., http://www.nowldef.org. The job-side decision was in *Harris v. Forklift Systems*: see "Sexually Harassed, but Promoted: Do You Have a Legal Claim?" NOW LDEF, 16 April 1998, http://www.nowldef.org. For more on the school case: "Case Summary: *Gebser v. Lago Vista Independent School District*, NOW LDEF, n.d., http://www.nowldef.org.

503 ". . . the school side." Schafran, author's interview.

504 ". . . by a faculty member." Schafran, author's interview.

504 Most satisfactory news and decision: Schafran, author's interview. See Linda Greenhouse, "Military College Can't Bar Women, High Court Rules," *New York Times*, 27 June 1996, p. A1. Jeffrey Rosen, "The New Look of Liberalism on the Court," *New York Times Magazine*, 5 October 1997, p. 60.

504 Three-state strategy: "Congressional Research Service Analyzes Three-State Strategy," *The Woman Activist*, February 1998, p. 2.

504 Federal women's rights bill: Ireland, author's interview.

504 ". . . toward a new ERA." Ireland, author's interview.

505 Birth of breast cancer movement: Cynthia Pearson, interview by author, 13 August 1998. Dr. Love tells the story of breast cancer activism in the second edition of her book: Susan M. Love, M.D., with Karen Lindsey, *Dr. Susan Love's Breast Book*, 515–26.

505 ". . . the White House." Love, 518.

505 Successes of the National Breast Cancer Coalition: Pearson, author's interview; also Love, 515–26. Since the 1970s, the women's health movement had been demanding a seat at the policy-making table, and the National Breast Cancer Coalition set out to get one: Pearson, author's interview.

505 Research on women's health neglected: For an excellent discussion of this issue, see Judith H. LaRosa, Ph.D., and Vivian W. Pinn, M.D., "Gender Bias in Biomedical Research," *Journal of the American Medical Women's Association*, September/October 1993, p. 145–151. Also Culliton, 383.

505 ". . . rats were male." Schroeder, 78.

505 ". . . lasting changes." Pearson, author's interview.

505 What the press conference accomplished: Pearson, author's interview.

505–6 Health reform bill and relations with Congress after 1994: Pearson, author's interview.

506 Problems with long-acting contraceptives: Pearson, author's interview. See Lisa Cox and Aleah Nesteby, "Network Hosts Meeting on Informed Consent and Long-Acting Contraception," *Network News,* May/June 1998, p. 3. Also: "Is Depo Provera Safe?" *Ms,* January/February 1993, p. 72.

506 AIDS activism: Leslie R. Wolfe, "Envisioning the Millennium: Feminism and Globalization," lecture, Hood College, 3 June 1998.

506 Women of color organizations grew: Pearson, author's interview.

506 National Black Women's Health Project: Julia Scott, interview by author, 21 August 1998.

506 ". . . so alarming." Scott, author's interview.

506–7 National Latina Health Organization: Luz Alvarez Martinez, interview by author, 18 September 1998. For more about Latina adolescents, see report by Luz Alvarez Martinez, "Latinas and Reproductive Health," National Latina Health Organization, Oakland, CA, 1998.

507 ". . . still developing?" Martinez, author's interview.

507 Native American Women's Health Education Research Center: Charon Asetoyer, interview by author, 17 August 1998. See Native American Women's Health Education Resource Center, "Native American Women Uncover Norplant Abuses," *Ms,* September/October 1993, p. 69.

507 National Asian Women's Health Organization: Mary Chung, interview by author, 22 September 1998.

508 Gay rights laws and the Colorado amendment: Rebecca Isaacs, interview by author, 4 September 1998. Piecemeal strategy: "Maine Repeals Civil Rights Law," National Gay and Lesbian Task Force, Washington, D.C., 10 February 1998, http://www.ngltf.org.

508 Same-sex marriage: Isaacs, author's interview. See Kimberlee Ward, "NOW Plans Day of Action for Same-Sex Marriage," *National NOW Times* 29, no. 1 (January 1997): 1. Also Barbara Hays, "Lesbian Rights a Hot Issue in State Legislatures," *National NOW Times* 30, no. 3 (Summer 1998): 3.

508 Ban on gays in the military: Isaacs, author's interview. See Jennifer Egan, "Uniforms in the Closet," *New York Times Magazine,* 28 June 1998, p. 26.

508 ". . . day and age." Isaacs, author's interview.

508–9 Religious right attack on gays and lesbians: Isaacs, author's interview. Trent Lott: "The History Behind Trent Lott," editorial, *New York Times,* 10 July 1998, p. A14. Ad campaign: Laurie Goodstein, "The Architect of the 'Gay Conversion' Campaign," *New York Times,* 13 August 1998, p. A10.

509 ". . . gentler bigotry." Isaacs, author's interview.

509 Public attitudes: Alan S. Yang, "From Wrongs to Rights: Public Opinion on Gay and Lesbian Americans Moves Toward Equality," report from the NGLTF Policy Institute, New York, NY, 1998. Gay voters: Dr. Robert Bailey, with Introduction by Rich Tafel, "Out & Voting: The Gay, Lesbian and Bisexual Vote in Congressional House Elections, 1990–1996," National Gay and Lesbian Task Force Policy Institute, New York, NY, 16 September 1998, http://www.ngltf.org.

509 Growth of global women's movement: Charlotte Bunch, interview by author, 27 July 1998.

509 Women's human rights: Bunch, author's interview. See Charlotte Bunch, Samantha Frost, and Niamh Reilly, "Making the Global Local: International Networking for Women's Human Rights." Also Jennifer Tierney, "America: The World's Cop Is a Cop-Out," *On the Issues,* Fall 1998, p. 20.

509–10 A European Community investigation concluded that impregnation was a deliberate Serbian strategy: See Jean Bethke Elshtain, "Let's Finally Right the Wrongs: Rape *Is* a War Crime," *On the Issues,* Summer 1993, p. 36. New policies in granting asylum: Bunch, author's interview. See Celia W. Dugger, "U.S. Grants Asylum to Woman Fleeing Female Genital Mutilation Rite," *New York Times,* 14 June 1996, p. A1.

509 ". . . really means." Bunch, author's interview.

510 Population conference: Bunch, author's interview. See Sonia Correa and Rosalind Petchesky, "Exposing the Numbers Game," *Ms,* September/October 1994, p. 10. Also

Jane Zones, "Network Board Members Go to Cairo," *Network News,* March/April 1995, p. 2.

510 Final document, Cairo conference: Correa and Petchesky, "Exposing the Numbers Game." Also Wolfe, "Envisioning the Millennium."

510 Beijing conference: Bunch, author's interview. See Charlotte Bunch, Mallika Dutt, and Susana Fried, "Beijing '95: A Global Referendum on the Human Rights of Women," 7–12. Also Robin Morgan, "Dispatch From Beijing," *Ms,* January/February 1996, p. 1?

510 ". . . easily suppressed." Ireland, author's interview.

510–11 Conditions for women in the 1960s: Some items on the list were suggested by Lynn Hecht Schafran, "Coming of Age: The New Pluralism in the Women's Movement," speech before the National Jewish Community Relations Advisory Council plenary session, Fort Lauderdale, FL, 16 February 1987, pp. 13–14.

511 Seneca Falls anniversary and NOW conference: Ellen Eardley and Rebecca Farmer, "NOW Honors History and Forms Feminist Vision at 1998 Women's Rights Convention and Vision Summit," *National NOW Times* 30, no. 4 (Fall 1998): 2.

511–12 Lauren Penoyer's amendment: Ireland, author's interview.

512 ". . . results or not." Ireland, author's interview.

512 ". . . and fighting back." "1998 Declaration of Sentiments," *National NOW Times* 30, no. 4 (Fall 1998): 4.

Bibliography

Abbott, Sidney, and Love, Barbara. *Sappho Was a Right-on Woman: A Liberated View of Lesbianism*. New York: Stein & Day, 1972.

Abzug, Bella, with Kelber, Mim. *Gender Gap: Bella Abzug's Guide to Political Power for American Women*. Boston: Houghton Mifflin, 1984.

Adam, Barry D. *The Rise of a Gay and Lesbian Movement*. Boston: G. K. Hall, 1987.

Atkinson, Ti-Grace. *Amazon Odyssey*. New York: Links, 1974.

Barnard, Thomas H. "The Conflict between State Protective Legislation and Federal Laws Prohibiting Sex Discrimination: Is It Resolved?" *Wayne Law Review* 17 (1971): 25–65.

Beasley, Maurine, and Gibbons, Sheila, eds. *Women in Media: A Documentary Source Book*. Washington, D.C.: Women's Institute for Freedom of the Press, 1977.

Berry, Mary Frances. *Why ERA Failed: Politics, Women's Rights and the Amending Process of the Constitution*. Bloomington: Indiana University Press, 1986.

Bird, Caroline. *Born Female: The High Cost of Keeping Women Down*, rev. ed. New York: Pocket Books, 1968.

Bird, Caroline, et al., with an introductory statement by Gloria Steinem. *What Women Want: From the Official Report to the President, the Congress and the People of the United States*. New York: Simon & Schuster, 1979.

Blumenthal, Sidney. *The Rise of the Counter-Establishment: From Conservative Ideology to Political Power*. New York: Times Books, 1986.

Blumenthal, Sidney, and Edsall, Thomas Byrne, eds. *The Reagan Legacy*. New York: Pantheon, 1988.

Boston Women's Health Book Collective. *The New Our Bodies, Ourselves. A Book By and For Women*. New York: Simon & Schuster, 1984.

Bouchier, David. "The Deradicalisation of Feminism: Ideology and Utopia in Action." *Sociology* 13, no. 3 (September 1979): 387–402.

Brauer, Carl M. "Women Activists, Southern Conservatives, and the Prohibition of Sex Discrimination in Title VII of the 1964 Civil Rights Act." *Journal of Southern History* 49, no. 1 (February 1983): 37–56.

Brownmiller, Susan. *Against Our Will: Men, Women and Rape.* New York: Bantam, 1975.

Bunch, Charlotte. *Passionate Politics: Feminist Theory in Action.* New York: St. Martin's Press, 1987.

Cassell, Joan. *A Group Called Women: Sisterhood & Symbolism in the Feminist Movement.* New York: David McKay, 1977.

Chafe, William H. *The American Woman: Her Changing Social, Economic, and Political Roles, 1920–1970.* London: Oxford University Press, 1972.

Chapman, Jane Roberts. "Policy Centers: An Essential Resource." In *Women in Washington: Advocates for Public Policy,* edited by Irene Tinker. Beverly Hills, CA: Sage, 1983, 177–91.

Chisholm, Shirley. *The Good Fight.* New York: Harper & Row, 1973.

Chodorow, Nancy. *The Reproduction of Mothering: Psychoanalysis and the Sociology of Gender.* Berkeley: University of California Press, 1978.

Committee for Abortion Rights and Against Sterilization Abuse (CARASA), Susan E. Davis, ed. *Women Under Attack: Victories, Backlash and the Fight for Reproductive Freedom.* Boston: South End Press, 1988.

Congressional Quarterly. *National Party Conventions 1831–1984.* Washington, D.C.: Congressional Quarterly, 1987.

Connell, Noreen, and Wilson, Cassandra, eds. *Rape: The First Sourcebook for Women.* New York: New American Library, 1974.

Corea, Gena.*The Hidden Malpractice: How American Medicine Treats Women as Patients and Professionals.* New York: William Morrow, 1977.

———. *The Mother Machine: Reproductive Technologies from Artificial Insemination to Artificial Wombs.* New York: Harper & Row, 1985.

Corea, Gena, et al., ed. *Man-Made Women: How New Reproductive Technologies Affect Women.* Bloomington: Indiana University Press, 1987.

Cott, Nancy. *The Grounding of Modern Feminism.* New Haven, CT: Yale University Press, 1987.

Daly, Mary. *Gyn/Ecology: The Metaethics of Radical Feminism.* Boston: Beacon Press, 1979.

Diamond, Irene, ed. *Families, Politics, and Public Policy: A Feminist Dialogue on Women and the State.* New York: Longman, 1983.

Dinnerstein, Dorothy. *The Mermaid and the Minotaur: Sexual Arrangements and Human Malaise.* New York: Harper & Row, 1977.

Donner, Frank J. *The Age of Surveillance: The Aims and Methods of America's Political Intelligence System.* New York: Knopf, 1980.

Donovan, Josephine. *Feminist Theory: The Intellectual Traditions of American Feminism.* New York: Frederick Ungar, 1985.

Downie, Susanna, principal author and editor, and many other subauthors, including Dr. Irene Frieze, research consultant. *Decade of Achievement: 1977–1987. A Report on a Survey Based on the National Plan of Action for Women.* Beaver Dam, WI: National Women's Conference Center, 1988.

Dreifus, Claudia, ed. *Seizing Our Bodies. The Politics of Women's Health.* New York: Vintage, 1977.

East, Catherine. "Critical Comments on *A Lesser Life. The Myth of Women's Liberation in America.*" The National Women's Political Caucus, Washington, DC, 1986.

———. "The First Stage. ERA in Washington, 1961–1972." *Women's Political Times,* September 1982, p. 7–10.

———. "Newer Commissions." In *Women in Washington: Advocates for Public Policy,* edited by Irene Tinker. Beverly Hills, CA: Sage, 1983, 35–44.

Echols, Alice. Foreword by Ellen Willis. *Daring to Be Bad: Radical Feminism in America 1967–1974.* Minneapolis: University of Minnesota Press, 1989.

Ehrenreich, Barbara. *The Hearts of Men: American Dreams and the Flight from Commitment.* Garden City, NY: Anchor, 1983.

Eisenstein, Hester. *Contemporary Feminist Thought.* Boston: G. K. Hall, 1983.

Eisenstein, Hester, and Jardine, Alice, ed. *The Future of Difference*. New Brunswick, NJ: Rutgers University Press, 1985.

Ellickson, Katherine Pollak. "The President's Commission on the Status of Women," 1976. Copies available from Walter P. Reuther Library, Wayne State University, Detroit, MI 48202.

Estrich, Susan. *Real Rape: How the Legal System Victimizes Women Who Say No*. Cambridge, MA: Harvard University Press, 1987.

Evans, Sara. *Personal Politics: The Roots of Women's Liberation in the Civil Rights Movement & the New Left*. New York: Vintage Books, 1979.

Ferraro, Geraldine A., with Francke, Linda Bird. *Ferraro: My Story*. New York: Bantam Books, 1985.

Ferree, Myra Marx, and Hess, Beth B. *Controversy and Coalition: The New Feminist Movement*. Boston: Twayne, 1985.

Firestone, Shulamith. *The Dialectic of Sex: The Case for Feminist Revolution*. New York: Bantam Books, 1970.

Firestone, Shulamith, and Koedt, Anne, eds. *Notes From the Second Year: Women's Liberation—the Major Writings of the Radical Feminists*. New York: New York Radical Women, Self-published, 1970.

Fishel, Andrew, and Pottker, Janice. *National Politics and Sex Discrimination in Education*. Lexington, MA: Lexington Books, 1977.

Flexner, Eleanor. *Century of Struggle: The Woman's Rights Movement in the United States*, rev. ed. Cambridge, MA: Belknap Press of Harvard University Press, 1975.

Forman, James. *The Making of Black Revolutionaries*. Washington, D.C.: Open Hand, 1985.

Freeman, Jo. *The Politics of Women's Liberation*. New York: Longman, 1975.

———. "The Tyranny of Structurelessness." In *Radical Feminism*, edited by Anne Koedt, Ellen Levine, and Anita Rapone. New York: Quadrangle, 1973, 285–99.

Freeman, Jo, ed. *Social Movements of the Sixties and Seventies*. New York: Longman, 1983.

Friedan, Betty. *The Feminine Mystique*, with new introduction and epilogue. New York: Dell (A Laurel Book), 1974.

———. *It Changed My Life: Writings on the Women's Movement*, with new introduction. New York: Norton, 1985.

———. *The Second Stage*, rev. ed. New York: Summit Books, 1986.

Gardner, Gerald H. F. "Want-ads Tomorrow: Neutral with Respect to Sex." In *NOW vs. The Pittsburgh Press. Revolution in Microcosm*. Pittsburgh: Know Inc., March 1971.

Gelb, Joyce. *Feminism and Politics: A Comparative Perspective*. Berkeley: University of California Press, 1989.

Gelb, Joyce, and Palley, Marian Lief. *Women and Public Policies*, rev. expanded. Princeton, NJ: Princeton University Press, 1987.

Giddings, Paula. *When and Where I Enter: The Impact of Black Women on Race and Sex in America*. New York: Bantam Books, 1984.

Gilligan, Carol. *In a Different Voice. Psychological Theory and Women's Development*. Cambridge, MA: Harvard University Press, 1982.

Gitlin, Todd. *The Sixties: Years of Hope, Days of Rage*. Toronto: Bantam Books, 1987.

———. *The Whole World Is Watching: Mass Media in the Making and Unmaking of the New Left*. Berkeley: University of California Press, 1980.

Glendon, Mary Ann. *Abortion and Divorce in Western Law*. Cambridge, MA: Harvard University Press, 1987.

———. *State, Law and Family: Family Law in Transition in the United States and Western Europe*. New York: North-Holland Publishing Co., 1977.

Goldstein, Leslie Friedman. *The Constitutional Rights of Women: Cases in Law and Social Change*, rev. 2d ed. Madison: University of Wisconsin Press, 1988.

Gordon, Linda. *Birth Control in America: Woman's Body, Woman's Right*. New York: Penguin, 1976.

Greer, Germaine. *The Female Eunuch*. New York: McGraw-Hill, 1970.

Greider, William. *The Education of David Stockman and Other Americans*. New York: New American Library, 1986.

Griffith, Elisabeth. *In Her Own Right: The Life of Elizabeth Cady Stanton*. New York: Oxford University Press, 1984.

Griffiths, Martha. Unpublished article. Included in microfilm with Ingersoll interview.

Haire, Doris B. *The Cultural Warping of Childbirth*. Seattle, WA: International Childbirth Education Association, 1972.

Haney, Eleanor Humes. *A Feminist Legacy: The Ethics of Wilma Scott Heide and Company*. "Foreword" by Elizabeth Duncan Koontz. Buffalo, NY: Margaretdaughters, Inc., 1985.

Harrison, Cynthia E. "A 'New Frontier' for Women: The Public Policy of the Kennedy Administration." *Journal of American History* 67, no. 3 (December 1980): 630–646.

———. *On Account of Sex: The Politics of Women's Issues 1945–1968*. Berkeley: University of California Press, 1988.

Hernandez, Aileen C. "E.E.O.C. and the Women's Movement 1965–1975." Paper presented at Symposium on the Tenth Anniversary of the Equal Employment Opportunity Commission. Rutgers University Law School, 28–29 November 1975.

Hershey, Lenore. *Between the Covers: The Lady's Own Journal*. New York: Coward-McCann, 1983.

Hoff-Wilson, Joan, ed. *Rights of Passage: The Past and Future of the ERA*. Bloomington: Indiana University Press, 1986.

Hole, Judith, and Levine, Ellen. *Rebirth of Feminism*. New York: Quadrangle/New York Times Book Co., 1971.

Hooks, Bell. *Ain't I a Woman: Black Women and Feminism*. Boston: South End Press, 1981.

———. *Feminist Theory: From Margin to Center*. Boston: South End Press, 1984.

———. *Talking Back: Thinking Feminist, Thinking Black*. Boston: South End Press, 1989.

Hull, Gloria T.; Scott, Patricia Bell; and Smith, Barbara. *All the Women Are White, All the Blacks Are Men, but Some of Us Are Brave: Black Women's Studies*. New York: The Feminist Press, 1982.

Ingersoll, Fern S. "Former Congresswomen Look Back." In *Women in Washington: Advocates for Public Policy*, edited by Irene Tinker. Beverly Hills, CA: Sage, 1983, 191–207.

———. Interview with Martha W. Griffiths for Former Members of Congress, Session 6, 29 October 1979, 73–5. Available through many public libraries from New York Times Microfilming Corporation of America.

Jaggar, Alison M. *Feminist Politics and Human Nature*. Totowa, NJ: Rowman & Allanheld, 1983.

Jay, Karla, and Young, Allen, ed. *Out of the Closets: Voices of Gay Liberation*. New York: Douglas, 1972.

Jones, Beverly, and Brown, Judith. "Toward a Female Liberation Movement," 1968. (Can be ordered from Redstockings, 1960s Women's Liberation Archives for Action, 290 Ninth Ave., #2G, New York, NY 10001 (include stamped, self-addressed envelope with requests for information).

Jones, Jacqueline. *Labor of Love, Labor of Sorrow: Black Women, Work and the Family, from Slavery to the Present*. New York: Vintage, 1985.

Jones, Rochelle, and Woll, Peter. *The Private World of Congress*. New York: The Free Press, 1979.

Kaminer, Wendy. *A Fearful Freedom: Women's Flight from Equality*. Reading, MA: Addison-Wesley, 1990.

Katzenstein, Mary Fainsod, and Mueller, Carol McClurg, eds. *The Women's Movements of the United States and Western Europe: Consciousness, Political Opportunity, and Public Policy*. Philadelphia: Temple University Press, 1987.

Keefe, William J. *Parties, Politics, and Public Policy in America*, 5th ed. Washington, D.C.: Congressional Quarterly Press, 1988.

Kelly, Joan. *Women, History, and Theory. The Essays of Joan Kelly*. Chicago: The University of Chicago Press, 1984.

King, Mary. *Freedom Song: A Personal Story of the 1960's Civil Rights Movement*. New York: Morrow, 1987.

Klatch, Rebecca E. *Women of the New Right*. Philadelphia: Temple University Press, 1987.

Klein, Ethel. *Gender Politics: From Consciousness to Mass Politics*. Cambridge, MA: Harvard University Press, 1984.

Koedt, Anne. "The Myth of the Vaginal Orgasm." In *Notes From the Second Year*, edited by Shulamith Firestone and Anne Koedt. New York: New York Radical Women, Self-published, 1970, 37–41.

Koedt, Anne; Levine, Ellen; and Rapone, Anita. *Radical Feminism*. New York: Quadrangle Books, 1973.

Lader, Lawrence. *Abortion II: Making the Revolution*. Boston: Beacon Press, 1973.

Lefkowitz, Rochelle, and Withorn, Ann, eds. *For Crying Out Loud: Women and Poverty in the United States*. New York: Pilgrim Press, 1986.

Liebman, Robert C., and Wuthnow, Robert. *The New Christian Right: Mobilization and Legitimation*. New York: Aldine, 1983.

Lindenfeld, Frank, and Whitt, Joyce Rothschild, eds. *Workplace Democracy and Social Change*. Boston: Porter-Sargent, 1981.

Litvak, Simi; Zukas, Hale; and Heumann, Judith E. *Attending to America: Personal Assistance for Independent Living*. Berkeley, CA: World Institute on Disability, 1987.

Loden, Marilyn. *Feminine Leadership or How to Succeed in Business Without Being One of the Boys*. New York: Times Books, 1985.

Luker, Kristin. *Abortion and the Politics of Motherhood*. Berkeley: University of California Press, 1984.

MacKinnon, Catherine. *Feminism Unmodified: Discourses on Life and Law*. Cambridge, MA: Harvard University Press, 1987.

Mandel, Ruth B. *In the Running: The New Woman Candidate*. Boston: Beacon Press, 1981.

———. "The Political Woman." In *The American Woman 1988–89*, edited by Sara E. Rix. New York: Norton, 1988, 78–122.

Mansbridge, Jane J. *Beyond Adversary Democracy*, rev. preface. Chicago: University of Chicago Press, 1980.

———. *Why We Lost the ERA*. Chicago: University of Chicago Press, 1986.

Martin, Del. *Battered Wives*. New York: Pocket Books, 1976.

Martin, Del, and Lyon, Phyllis. *Lesbian/Woman*. New York: Bantam Books, 1972.

Martindale, David. "Flight Attendants: Who Are They, and What Do They Want from Us?" *Frequent Flyer*, August 1985, 65–74.

Mason, John T., Jr., interviewer. "The Reminiscences of Marguerite Rawalt." 1983. Oral History Research Office, Columbia University, New York City.

McAdam, Doug. *Freedom Summer*. New York: Oxford University Press, 1988.

———. *Political Process and the Development of Black Insurgency 1930–1970*. Chicago: University of Chicago Press, 1982.

Merton, Andrew H. *Enemies of Choice: The Right-to-Life Movement and Its Threat to Abortion*. Boston: Beacon Press, 1981.

Milbauer, Barbara, with Obrentz, Bert N. *The Law Giveth: Legal Aspects of the Abortion Controversy*. New York: Atheneum, 1983.

Miller, Jean Baker. *Toward a New Psychology of Women*. Boston: Beacon Press, 1976.

Millett, Kate. *Flying*. New York: Alfred A. Knopf, 1974.

———. *Sexual Politics* 1970. New York: Avon Books, 1971.

Millsap, Mary Ann. "Equity in Education." In *Women in Washington: Advocates for Public Policy*, edited by Irene Tinker. Beverly Hills, CA: Sage, 1983, 91–119.

Mohr, James C. *Abortion in America. The Origins and Evolution of National Policy*. Oxford, England: Oxford University Press, 1978.

Morgan, Robin. *Going Too Far: The Personal Chronicle of a Feminist*. New York: Vintage, 1968.

Morgan, Robin, ed. *Sisterhood Is Global: The International Women's Movement Anthology*. Garden City, NY: Anchor, 1984.

———, ed. *Sisterhood Is Powerful: An Anthology of Writings from the Women's Liberation Movement*. New York: Vintage, 1970.

Mueller, Carol M., ed. *The Politics of the Gender Gap: The Social Construction of Political*

Influence. Vol. 12, Sage Yearbooks in Women's Policy Studies. Newbury Park, CA: Sage, 1988.

National Advisory Council on Women's Educational Programs. "Title IX: The Half Full, Half Empty Glass." Washington, D.C.: NACWEP, 1981.

National Women's Health Network. *Abortion Then and Now: Creative Responses to Restricted Access*. Washington, D.C.: National Women's Health Network, 1989.

New York Radical Women. *Notes from the First Year*, June 1968. (Can be ordered from Redstockings, 1960s Women's Liberation Archives for Action, 290 Ninth Ave., #2G, New York, NY 10001 (include stamped, self-addressed envelope with requests for information).

Nielsen, Georgia Panter. *From Sky Girl to Flight Attendant. Women and the Making of a Union*. Ithaca, NY: ILR Press, 1982.

Paige, Connie. *The Right to Lifers: Who They Are, How They Operate, Where They Get Their Money*. New York: Summit Books, 1983.

Paterson, Judith. *Be Somebody: A Biography of Marguerite Rawalt*. Austin, TX: Eakin Press, 1986.

Payne, Charles. "Ella Baker and Models of Social Change." *Signs* 14, no. 4 (Summer 1989): 885–99.

Perry, Susan, and Dawson, Jim. *Nightmare: Women and the Dalkon Shield*. New York: Macmillan, 1985.

Petchesky, Rosalind Pollack. *Abortion and Woman's Choice: The State, Sexuality, and Reproductive Freedom*. The Northeastern Series in Feminist Theory. Boston: Northeastern University Press, 1984.

Peterson, Esther. "The Kennedy Commission." In *Women in Washington: Advocates for Public Policy*, edited by Irene Tinker. Beverly Hills, CA: Sage, 1983, 21–34.

Phillips, Anne, ed. *Feminism and Equality*. New York: New York University Press, 1987.

Piven, Frances Fox, and Cloward, Richard A. *Poor People's Movements: Why They Succeed, How They Fail*. New York: Pantheon, 1977.

President's Commission on the Status of Women. *American Women: Report of the President's Commission on the Status of Women*, 1963.

Project on Equal Education Rights. "Stalled at the Start: Government Action on Sex Bias in the Schools." Washington, D.C.: PEER and NOW Legal Defense and Education Fund, 1978.

Radigan, Anne L. *Concept & Compromise: The Evolution of Family Leave Legislation in the U.S. Congress*. Washington, D.C.: Women's Research and Education Institute, 1988.

Rawalt, Marguerite. "The Equal Rights Amendment." In *Women in Washington: Advocates for Public Policy*, edited by Irene Tinker. Beverly Hills, CA: Sage, 1983, 49–78.

Redstockings. *Feminist Revolution*, abridged ed. with additional writings. New York: Random House, 1978. (Can be ordered from Redstockings, 1960s Women's Liberation Archives for Action, 290 Ninth Ave., #2G, New York, NY 10001. Include stamped, self-addressed envelope with requests for information.)

Rhode, Deborah L., ed. *Theoretical Perspectives on Sexual Difference*. New Haven, CT: Yale University Press, 1990.

Rich, Adrienne. *Of Woman Born: Motherhood as Experience and Institution*. New York: Bantam Books, 1976.

Rix, Sara E., ed. *The American Woman 1987–88: A Report in Depth*. New York: Norton, 1987.

———. *The American Woman 1988–89: A Status Report*. New York: Norton, 1988.

———. *The American Woman 1990–91: A Status Report*. New York: Norton, 1990.

Robinson, D.A. "Two Movements in Pursuit of Equal Employment Opportunity." *Signs* 4 (Spring 1979): 413-33.

Rossi, Alice S., and Calderwood, Ann, eds. *Academic Women on the Move*. New York: Russell Sage Foundation, 1973.

Rothman, Barbara Katz. *Recreating Motherhood. Ideology and Technology in a Patriarchal Society*. New York: Norton, 1989.

Rothman, Sheila M. *Woman's Proper Place: A History of Changing Ideals and Practices, 1870 to the Present.* New York: Basic Books, 1978.

Ruddick, Sara. *Maternal Thinking: Toward a Politics of Peace.* New York: Ballantine, 1989.

Rupp, Leila J., and Taylor, Verta. *Survival in the Doldrums: The American Women's Rights Movement, 1945 to the 1960s.* New York: Oxford University Press, 1987.

Russell, Diana E. H. *Rape in Marriage.* New York: Macmillan, 1982.

Ruzek, Sheryl Burt. *The Women's Health Movement: Feminist Alternatives to Medical Control.* New York: Praeger, 1978.

Sandler, Bernice. "A Little Help from Our Government: WEAL and Contract Compliance." In *Academic Women on the Move,* edited by Alice S. Rossi and Ann Calderwood. New York: Russell Sage Foundation, 1973, 439–55.

Sayres, Sohnya, et al. *The 60s Without Apology.* Minneapolis: University of Minnesota Press, 1984.

Schafran, Lynn Hecht. "Gender Bias in the Courts." In *Women as Single Parents: Confronting Institutional Barriers in the Courts, the Workplace, and the Housing Market,* edited by Elizabeth A. Mulroy. Dover, MA: Auburn House, 1988, 39–72.

Schechter, Susan. *Women and Male Violence: The Visions and Struggles of the Battered Women's Movement.* Boston: South End Press, 1982.

Schroeder, Congresswoman Pat, with Camp, Andrea, and Lipner, Robyn. *Champion of the Great American Family.* New York: Random House, 1989.

Seaman, Barbara. *The Doctors' Case Against the Pill.* New York: Avon, 1970.

Shalev, Carmel. *Birth Power: The Case for Surrogacy.* New Haven, CT: Yale University Press, 1989.

Shields, Laurie. *Displaced Homemakers: Organizing for a New Life.* Epilogue by Tish Sommers. New York: McGraw-Hill, 1981.

Sidel, Ruth. *Women and Children Last: The Plight of Poor Women in Affluent America.* New York: Penguin Books, 1987.

Sitkoff, Harvard. *The Struggle for Black Equality, 1954–1980.* New York: Hill & Wang, 1981.

Smeal, Eleanor. *Why and How Women Will Elect the Next President.* New York: Harper & Row, 1984.

Snitow, Ann. "Pages from a Gender Diary: Basic Divisions in Feminism." *Dissent* (Spring 1989): 205-224.

Snitow, Ann; Stansell, Christine; and Thompson, Sharon. *Desire: The Politics of Sexuality.* London: Virago Press, 1983.

Spelman, Elizabeth V. *Inessential Woman: Problems of Exclusion in Feminist Thought.* Boston: Beacon Press, 1988.

The Spirit of Houston: The First National Women's Conference. Official Report. Washington, D.C.: National Commission on the Observance of International Women's Year, 1978.

Steinfels, Margaret O'Brien. *Who's Minding the Children? The History and Politics of Day Care in America.* New York: Simon & Schuster, 1973.

Stimpson, Catharine R., with Cobb, Nina Kressner. *Women's Studies in the United States.* New York: Ford Foundation, 1986.

Stockman, David. *The Triumph of Politics: The Inside Story of the Reagan Revolution.* New York: Avon, 1986.

Stoiber, Susanne A. *Parental Leave and "Woman's Place": The Implications and Impact of Three European Approaches to Family Leave Policy.* Washington, D.C.: Women's Research and Education Institute, 1989.

Stoper, Emily. "The Student Non-Violent Coordinating Committee: Rise and Fall of a Redemptive Organization." In *Social Movements of the Sixties and Seventies,* edited by Jo Freeman. New York: Longman, 1983, 320–34.

Swerdlow, Amy. "Women's Activism Undercut: Red-Baiting Erases Historical Record." *New Directions for Women,* March/April 1989, 12–13.

Tinker, Irene. "The Federal Government Considers the Status of Women." In *Women in Washington: Advocates for Public Policy,* edited by Irene Tinker. Beverly Hills, CA: Sage, 1983, 17–20.

Tinker, Irene, ed. *Women in Washington: Advocates for Public Policy.* Beverly Hills, CA: Sage, 1983.

Tuchman, Gaye. "Introduction: The Symbolic Annihilation of Women by the Mass Media." In *Hearth & Home: Images of Women in the Mass Media,* edited by Gaye Tuchman, Arlene Kaplan Daniels, and James Benet. New York: Oxford University Press, 1978, 3–38.

———. *Making News. A Study in the Construction of Reality.* New York: Free Press, 1978.

U.S. Congress. House of Representatives. Congresswoman Martha Griffiths speaking about the EEOC. *Congressional Record,* 89th Congress, 2nd session, 20 June 1966. 112:13689–94.

———. Debate on Sex Amendment to Title VII. *Congressional Record,* 88th Congress, 2nd session, 8 February 1964, 110, pt. 2: 2577–84.

U.S. Congress. Senate. Subcommittee on the Constitution of the Committee on the Judiciary. *The Impact of the Equal Rights Amendment: Hearing on S.J. 10,* 98th Congress, 2nd session, 24 January 1984, 437–532.

Warrior, Betsy. *Battered Women's Directory,* 8th edition. Boston: Betsy Warrior, 1982.

Weitzman, Lenore J. *The Divorce Revolution: The Unexpected Social and Economic Consequences for Women and Children in America.* New York: The Free Press, 1985.

West, Guida. *The National Welfare Rights Movement. The Social Protest of Poor Women.* New York: Praeger, 1981.

White, Evelyn C., ed. *The Black Women's Health Book: Speaking for Ourselves.* Seattle, WA: Seal Press, 1990.

Wistrant, Birgitta. Edited and translated by Jeanne Rosen. *Swedish Women on the Move.* Stockholm: The Swedish Institute, 1981.

Women's Research and Education Institute. *Gender at Work: Perspectives on Occupational Segregation and Comparable Worth.* Washington, D.C.: Women's Research and Education Institute, 1984.

Woodward, Bob, and Armstrong, Scott. *The Brethren: Inside the Supreme Court.* New York: Simon & Schuster, 1979.

Zigler, Edward F., and Gordon, Edmund W. *Day Care: Scientific and Social Policy Issues.* Boston: Auburn House, 1982.

Updated Bibliography for the 1999 Edition

American Association of University Women. *How Schools Shortchange Girls: The AAUW Report.* Washington, D.C.: American Association of University Women Educational Foundation; National Education Association, 1992.

Bunch, Charlotte; Dutt, Mallika; and Fried, Susana. "Beijing '95: A Global Referendum on the Human Rights of Women." *Canadian Women's Studies* 16, no. 3 (Summer 1996): 7–12.

Bunch, Charlotte; Frost, Samantha; and Reilly, Niamh. "Making the Global Local: International Networking for Women's Human Rights." In *Women's International Human Rights: A Reference Guide,* edited by Kelly D. Askin and Dorean Koenig. Ardsley, NY: Transnational Publications, forthcoming.

Culliton, Barbara J. "NIH Push for Women's Health." *Nature* 353 (3 October 1992): 383.

Faludi, Susan. *Backlash: The Undeclared War Against American Women.* New York: Crown, 1991.

Flanders, Laura. *Real Majority, Media Minority: The Cost of Sidelining Women in Reporting.* Monroe, ME: Common Courage Press, 1997.

La Rosa, Judith H., Ph.D., and Pinn, Vivian W., M.D. "Gender Bias in Biomedical Research." *Journal of the American Medical Women's Association,* September/October 1993: 145–51.

Love, Susan M., M.D., with Lindsey, Karen. *Dr. Susan Love's Breast Book,* 2d ed. Reading, MA: Addison-Wesley, 1995.

National Abortion and Reproductive Rights Action League. *Who Decides? A State-by-State Review of Abortion and Reproductive Rights.* Washington, D.C.: NARAL Foundation and NARAL, 1998.

Nussbaum, Martha C. *Cultivating Humanity: A Classical Defense of Reform in Liberal Education.* Cambridge, MA: Harvard University Press, 1997.

Rosser, Sue V. "Warming Up the Classroom Climate for Women." In *The Feminist Teacher Anthology: Pedagogies and Classroom Strategies,* edited by Gail E. Cohee et al. New York: Teachers College Press, 1998, 31–44.

Schroeder, Patricia. *24 Years of House Work . . . and the Place Is Still a Mess: My Life in Politics.* Kansas City: Andrews McMeel, 1998.

Steinem, Gloria. *Revolution From Within: A Book of Self-Esteem.* Boston: Little, Brown, 1992.

Index

National Center on Women and Family
    Law, 293
National Clearinghouse on Marital and
    Date Rape, 317
National Coalition Against Domestic
    Violence (NCADV), 321, 447n
National Coalition for Women and Girls
    in Education (NCWGE), 206, 214,
    226
National Coalition of 100 Black Women,
    367
National Collegiate Athletic Association
    (NCAA), 215
National Commission on Consumer
    Finance, 148
National Conference for a New Politics
    (NCNP), 77, 78
National Conference of Catholic Bishops
    (NCCB), 436
National Conservative Political Action
    Committee (NCPAC), 200, 437, 451
National Council of Negro Women, 29,
    364
National Federation of Business and
    Professional Women's Clubs
    (BPW), 34, 35, 38, 53, 125–26, 129,
    131, 147, 391, 392
National Federation of Republican
    Women, 387, 419
National Institute for Women of Color,
    (NIWC), 356, 361
National Judicial Education Program to
    Promote Equality for Women and
    Men in the Courts (NJEP), 295

National Organization for Women
    (NOW), 23, 60–66, 187, 228, 261,
    266, 267, 352, 358, 361, 421, 423,
    440
  abortion rights supported by, 49, 66,
    67, 68, 165, 431, 466
  C-R scorned by, 87, 88, 262
  ERA supported by, 49, 66–68, 122–23,
    129, 134, 391, 392, 397, 399, 418, 457
  founding of, 23, 49, 52–55, 56, 66, 77,
    123, 186, 348
  leadership of, 23, 53, 57, 96–97, 115,
    147
  lesbian purges at, 263–64, 268
  local chapters of, 58–59, 144, 149, 150,
    281, 321, 362, 381, 466
  media and, 107, 111, 113, 118
  membership of, 23, 53, 56–57, 58, 97,
    108, 115, 144, 147, 392, 411, 466,
    472
  protective laws fought by, 56, 61–64,
    66, 107
  recruits to, 58–59, 70, 358, 431

in specialized alliances, 138, 144, 148,
    210, 211, 293, 295, 298, 345, 392, 448
National Plan of Action, 272
National Political Congress of Black
    Women, 424
National Rifle Association, 199
National Right to Life Committee
    (NRLC), 435–36, 457, 463, 464, 468
National S.E.E.D. Project on Inclusive
    Curriculum, 223
National Welfare Rights Organization
    (NWRO), 80, 280, 281, 347–53, 354
  demise of, 350–52
  membership of, 348, 349, 350
  race, class, and gender in, 349, 351,
    357
  successes of, 350, 351
National Women's Conference, 272, 400
National Women's Health Network
    (NWHN), 228, 237, 240, 241, 245,
    246, 247, 251, 258, 381
National Women's Law Center, 217, 337
National Woman's Party (NWP), 28, 29,
    31, 33, 34, 36, 39, 44, 53, 67, 129
National Women's Political Caucus
    (NWPC), 185, 187–88, 190, 357, 358,
    420–21, 422–23, 424
National Women's Studies Association
    (NWSA), 223
Native American women, 247–48, 250,
    357, 360, 361, 371, 458
  families of, 373–74
  in leadership positions, 372–73, 374–
    375
  on reservations, 372, 373
  see also women of color
Native American Women's Health and
    Education Resource Center, 247–
    248
NBC, 111
Nelson, Barbara, 342
New England Free Press, 101
New Left, 15, 71, 83, 99, 109, 141, 144,
    358
  women's liberation movement and,
    70–77, 78, 82, 84, 88
New Right, 15–16, 34, 55, 158, 416, 433–
    452, 482
  civil rights under, 440–44
  Congress and, 438, 441–42, 443, 444,
    445, 446–50
  ERA and, 387–91, 393, 394, 411
  future of, 450–52
  presidency won by, 437–46
  reactionary cast of, 433–37
  religious groups in, 435–37, 438, 451–
    452
  Supreme Court and, 441, 442, 444–46
  think tanks of, 435, 452

Rodriguez-Trias, Helen, 250
Roe v. *Wade*, 158, 168, 170, 172–81, 235,
    251, 367, 399, 411, 445
  challenges to, 454, 456–58, 462–65,
    469
Roosevelt, Eleanor, 35
Rosenberg, Rosalind, 339–40
Rosenthal, Kris, 85, 86
Rothman, Barbara Katz, 254
Rothman, Lorraine, 232–33, 234
rubella, 163
RU-486, 467–68, 470, 490
Russell, Diana, 324
Rutgers University, 186, 490

Sanders, Beulah, 357
Sandler, Bernice "Bunny," 208–11, 213,
    214, 225, 387, 397, 444
Sanger, Margaret, 228
Sarachild, Kathie, 78, 82, 87–89, 119
Scalia, Antonin, 445
Schafran, Lynn Hecht, 290, 293, 294,
    295, 296, 297, 300, 304–5, 306, 330
Scheidler, Joe, 457, 461
Scheuer, James H., 21
Schlafly, Phyllis, 272, 323, 343, 387–91,
    393, 394, 396, 397, 400, 443
Schneider, Claudine, 201
schools:
  athletic programs in, 206, 207, 215–16
  biased classrooms in, 225–26
  climate of discouragement in, 218–19,
    491
  hiring practices in, 207, 338
  math and science classes in, 206, 218–
    219
  prayer in, 128, 436
  see also education; universities and
    colleges
Schroeder, Patricia, 452
Schulman, Joanne, 293, 296–97
Schwartz, Felice N., 304
Seaman, Barbara, 237
Sears, 339–40
Second Stage, The (Friedan), 474
second-wave feminism:
  consciousness transformed in, 52, 55,
    59, 109, 142, 331, 406, 432, 492–93
  deradicalizing of, 106, 118–20, 146–
    147
  diversity in, 93, 356–84, 471, 482
  gathering of, 47–48, 49, 375
  liberal wing of, *see* liberal feminism
  political opportunities offered to, 10–
    11, 32, 55–56
  radical wing of, *see* women's
    liberation movement
  timing of, 55–56
Section 504, 375, 376, 377

self-defense, 79, 83, 84, 85, 87, 139, 314
self-help groups, 228, 231–35, 245, 294,
    314
Senate, U.S., 150, 198, 214, 322
  ERA in, 33, 124, 127–29, 130–34, 386
  Judiciary Committee of, 127–128, 130,
    131, 223
  Title VII in, 43–44, 46
  see also Congress, U.S.
"sex antagonism," 27
sex discrimination, 16–25, 52, 200, 344,
    361, 434, 476
  abortion and, 175
  complacency and, 19, 45, 47, 337
  definition of, 45–47
  economics of, 19, 20, 147–52
  in education, 58, 59, 68, 147, 205, 208–
    226, 270, 296, 441, 472
  fourteenth amendment and, 35–36
  heterosexism vs., 260, 266, 268, 270–
    271
  institutionalization of, 77, 270
  intended, 407
  in medical system, 227, 241, 244–45,
    257
  pervasiveness of, 19, 59, 77, 411
  porn and, 328–29
  racial discrimination vs., 42–43, 73,
    77, 79–80, 91, 359, 364, 366, 401–3
  in workplace, 16–25, 31–32, 35–36,
    37–47, 48, 52, 58, 59–64, 68, 110–11,
    136, 147, 182, 188, 244–45, 270, 289,
    296, 300, 308, 333, 336–38, 339–40,
    365, 407, 472
sex education, 394, 436
sexes:
  differences between, 29, 30, 48, 92,
    146–47, 182, 221, 385–86, 410, 483
  legal classification of, 402, 404–6
sex-roles theory, 91
sex stereotypes:
  dismantling of, 68, 146, 282, 303, 403,
    404, 405–6
  durability of, 197
  employment decisions based on, 46,
    59, 63
  of familial roles, 30, 90, 389, 395, 427,
    433
  in media, 58, 92, 107, 110, 111–14
  oppression internalized through, 88
  reinforcement of, 265, 266, 476–77

  in textbooks, 58, 205, 206, 213, 219,
    227, 394, 442
sex tours, 327–28, 489
sexual activity, 434
  abstaining from, 160, 182, 267
  deviation in, 133, 136
  double standard in, 74, 406